More File Formats for Popular PC Software

A PROGRAMMER'S REFERENCE

Related Titles of Interest from John Wiley & Sons, Inc.

C Programming Language: An Applied Perspective, Miller & Quilici

C Wizard's Programming Reference, Schwaderer

File Formats for Popular PC Software: A Programmer's Reference, Walden

Local Area Networks: The Second Generation, Madron

PC DOS, 2nd Edition, Ashley & Fernandez

JCL for IBM VSE Systems: A Self-teaching Guide, Ashley, Fernandez & Beamesderfer

The 80286 Architecture, Morse & Albert

The 80386 Architecture, Morse, Isaacson & Albert

An Introduction to Assembly Language Programming for the 8086 Family, Skinner

COBOL: A Wiley Programmer's Reference, Ashley & Fernandez

IBM PC Assembly Language, Tabler

IBM Personal System/2: A Business Perspective, Hoskins

Modems and Communications on the IBM PC's, Schwaderer

More File Formats for Popular PC Software

A PROGRAMMER'S REFERENCE

Jeff Walden

John Wiley & Sons, Inc.
New York • Chichester • Brisbane • Toronto • Singapore

Publisher: Stephen Kippur
Editor: Therese A. Zak
Managing Editor: Ruth Greif
Electronic Production Services: Publishers Network

This publication is designed to provide accurate and authoritative information in regard to the subject
matter covered. It is sold with the understanding that the publisher is not engaged in rendering legal,
accounting, or other professional service. If legal advice or other expert assistance is required, the
services of a competent professional person should be sought. FROM A DECLARATION OF PRIN-
CIPLES JOINTLY ADOPTED BY A COMMITTEE OF THE AMERICAN BAR ASSOCIATION AND A
COMMITTEE OF PUBLISHERS.

Library of Congress Cataloging-in-Publication Data

Walden, Jeff, 1951-
        More file formats for popular PC software: a programmer's reference / Jeff Walden.
                p.   cm.
ISBN 0-471-85077-2
        1. File management (Computer science) 2. Microcomputers-Programming.
 I. Title
QA76.9.f5W35 1987
005.74'068—dc19   87-20294
                                                                                    CIP

Printed in the United States of America
87 88 10 9 8 7 6 5 4 3 2

Foreword

More File Formats for Popular PC Software should be a standard reference for programmers, students of PC software design, and advanced users willing to do a little programming to shift their data from place to place.

When Jeff Walden first mentioned to me that he was writing a book providing the detailed file format specifications for today's most popular PC programs, I admired his initiative and wished him good luck. I believed he had an uphill battle ahead of him, for it used to be common thinking that file formats were somehow "proprietary" and to be guarded from the public.

Nothing could be further from the truth! File formats information should be open to the public—users have a right to freely access and share their data, even if not through the original program that wrote it out to disk.

Experience had shown that the commercial success of a program is often linked to the program's "open-ness." All PC data is stored in one file format or another; for users to get the most out of personal computers, there must exist "free trade" between the file formats of PC programs. Detailed documentation of their file formats is the key to such free trade.

The strong success of the original *File Formats for Popular PC Software* is a good sign the PC using public does indeed desire to move their information in and out a variety of file formats.

The new *More File Formats* will add to the ability of the PC public to truly be the owners of their information. Through these books, PC software is finally achieving an open architecture that matches that of the original IBM PC's open hardware design.

It may seem a little contradictory, but I have a dream that by making more people aware of the file formats for their software, we can perhaps remove the need for people to be concerned with them.

In a world in which no program understands the files produced by any other program, all users are very aware of the formats that keep data in separate, closed worlds. As more programs learn to read and write foreign file formats, users can begin to forget that those separate worlds exist. They can focus on their data and information, not "I must write in the XYZ format, because that's the only one my typesetter can accept."

More File Formats, and the original *File Formats,* are timely because there are more PC programmers who need access to the data on their PCs than ever before. More and more powerful programming languages are becoming available that empower end users to do their own programming. Fast and interactive language interpreters and compilers have sold by the hundreds of thousands. Many of the programmers using these tools now need access to the data they've captured using popular PC software. This book is the key to unlocking that data.

By Robert Carr
Chief Scientist, Ashton-Tate

Acknowledgments

This book would not have been possible without the wholehearted cooperation of the manufacturers whose works are represented here. Nothing—or few things, at any rate—is as tough as following the meagre spoor that a program leaves behind on disk.

Specifically, and in no order of importance, I'd especially like to thank the following people:

- **Ashton–Tate:**
  Steve Aubrey
  Robert Carr
  Chris Kirkpatrick
  David McLaughlin

- **Borland International:**
  Nan Borreson
  Kathleen Doler

- **Computer Associates:**
  Susan D'Elia
  Tim Gustavson
  Diana Wilson

- **Lifetree Software:**
  Vicki Boddie
  Ann Tse

- **Microsoft Corporation:**
  Greg Slyngstad
  Marty Taucher

- **WordPerfect/SSI:**
  Jeff Acerson

I'd also like to thank Connie Kellner of Publisher's Network, Morrisville, PA for her design and production from an electronic manuscript; and Teri Zak, my editor at Wiley, for her patience.

If I've goofed anywhere in this book, it's not because these people weren't willing to help. Now, for my next trick...

Introduction

What's Better than More of a Good Thing?

More File Formats for Popular PC Software picks up where the original *File Formats* book left off. You can't cover every important and useful software product in one volume. *More File Formats* contains just that—the "inside information" on how popular PC programs store their files on disk.

More File Formats is for programmers, data processing professionals, software authors or anyone who needs to know how to decipher all those happy faces, hearts, clubs, Greek letters, and strangely accented characters that appear on the screen when you enter TYPE.

Why are documented file formats important? They are important for connectivity, data sharing, and for producing corporate programs that read—and write—the data formats of widely used software programs. There are hundreds of reasons to want to know what comes out of a program in its native file format. When you know, you can read that data and all its formatting.

Just as important, when you know a program's file format, is the fact that you can externally prepare files for use with these programs. For example, you can extract mainframe data for analysis with SuperCalc4, and prepare the entire spreadsheet matrix *on the host* for downloading or other types of distribution.

What's in the Book?

More File Formats for Popular PC Software contains extensive documentation on six popular PC programs and one important data exchange format. They are:

- **Framework:** Ashton-Tate's word processor cum spreadsheet cum applications environment.
- **Reflex:** Borland's inexpensive and popular data base.
- **Rich Text Format:** Microsoft's text exchange format for Windows 2.0 Word, and beyond.
- **Super Project Plus:** Computer Associates' project management package.

- **SuperCalc4:** SuperCalc, the *other* standard spreadsheet.
- **Volkswriter 3:** Lifetree's entry-level word processing package with many advanced features.
- **WordPerfect:** WordPerfect is one of the favorite word processors in the corporate world.

More File Formats also contains extensive appendices: an expanded section of fully glossed sample files (files actually produced by the programs in the book and commented for you, byte by byte), and the Fileprint utility in Turbo Pascal that lets you print out short files in the appendix's "music staff" style.

This book contains no source code for any of the programs whose files are included. It's a programmer's book and is very condensed. Although each file format is provided courtesy of its respective manufacturer, none of the manufacturers whose file formats are documented here can accept support calls based on this information.

Contents

Chapter 2 Reflex Versions 1.0 and 1.1   **64**

Tables:

Chapter 3 Rich Text Format   78

Tables:

Chapter 6 Volkswriter 3 Volkswriter 3 v 1.0
(and Volkswriter Deluxe) 135

Chapter 7 WordPerfect Version 4.1 144

Tables:

Appendix A   171

Appendix B   175

Appendix C   361

## CHAPTER 1

Framework II

Versions 1.0 and 1.1

Ashton-Tate
20101 Hamilton Avenue
Torrance, CA 90502

Type of Product: Integrated, multiple-application package. Framework includes spreadsheet, data base, word processing, outlining, graphics, and telecommunications in one product.

Files Produced: Mixed ASCII and binary.

Points of Interest:
Framework has one commanding data structure: the frame. It employs the frame with a constancy and thoroughness that is awe-inspiring. Almost every bit of data in the file structure appears in the frame format, from the file header, to a top level "master" frame, down through any included frames, and to each cell of a spreadsheet. Understanding the frame structure is understanding Framework.

Conversion Information:
Framework II can import files from:
    ASCII text format
    IBM® DCA/Displaywrite™
    Wordstar®
    Multimate™
    dBase II®or dBase III™
    Lotus 1-2-3®
    DIF™ (Data Interchange Format)

Framework II can export files to:
    ASCII text format
    IBM® DCA/Displaywrite™
    Wordstar®
    Multimate™
    dBase II ™ Delimited
    Lotus 1-2-3®

Framework II File Format

Framework II produces variable-length files that remain easy to understand and trace because of the concept of the frame. Each frame has a header and contents. Contents can be text, numbers, formulas, graphs, or an array of indices to other frames, for example. Each frame has a frame ID number (FID) that Framework assigns internally. A frame can use the FID as a pointer to a parent frame or child frame. FIDs are not, strictly speaking, pointers. They neither point to a fixed memory address nor to a fixed location in the file. A FID is the internal "name" of a frame.

Assigning FIDs

When you create a Framework application within the program, Framework assigns FIDs. When you create a Framework application externally to Framework, you must assign your own FIDs. A FID is an even, two-byte integer in the range 0 to 32,000 (00h to 7Dh). Even the Framework desktop has a FID. Framework generally assigns 22 (16h) as the FID of the desktop, but not always. When creating a Framework file, it's safest to assign 00 as the desktop FID.

Important　　　　　　You **must** be consistent when creating your own FIDs. Every FID must be unique. Parent and child FIDs must refer to each other properly. Framework stores the FID of the largest frame as part of the file header. The program checks for that FID on loading and makes sure that it is indeed the largest. Any descrepancy will abort the load.

Types of Frames

There are 20 types of frames that Framework II recognizes, five of them reserved types. Table 1-1 lists the frame types and their identifying numbers.

Organizational Overview

The contents of the different frames vary from type to type, but they remain fairly consistent in organization. After a while, the pattern of a Framework file becomes readily apparent. For example, all frames begin on paragraph boundaries, and the FID for the frame is always the third and fourth byte. A paragraph is 16 bytes. If a frame does not fill a paragraph, Framework usually pads to the end with nulls. Occasionally, as do all programs, it pads with garbage—but that's easy to recognize.

The organization of a Framework file is much like an outline. The order of the frames as stored by the program is derived from its outline mode. In actual practice, the order of the frames in the file does not matter as long as the FIDs are correct and consistent.

Figure 1-1 illustrates the organization of a typical spreadsheet. Framework stores its frames starting at the desktop (and from left to right, top to bottom for contending frames on the desktop).

Table 1-1	Frame types and contents	
Code	**Type**	**Contents**
0	Text	word processing
1	Simple Glossary	empty library frame
2	Text Graph	graphics done with text
3	Graph	graphics done in a graphics mode
4	Edit	stores formulas, frame names
5	Reserved	
6	Simple Buffer	used internally (shouldn't appear)
7	Label	a spreadsheet cell containing text
8	Cell	a spreadsheet cell containing a value
9	Reserved	
10	Freefloat	frame containing other frames (drag on)
11	Composite Buffer	frame containing data base frames
12	Column	frame containing other frames (drag off)
13	SS Row	a single spreadsheet row
14	Spreadsheet	global spreadsheet information
15	Reserved	
16	EXE	frame containing a DOS file
17	Reserved	
18	Reserved	
19	Glossary	library frame with data

```
Spreadsheet frame
    Name frame for spreadsheet frame
    Any formula frame for spreadsheet frame
    Column Vector frame
        Row 1 frame
            Cell A1 frame
                Formula for Cell A1 frame
            Cell B1 frame
                Formula for Cell B1 frame
        Row 2 frame
            Cell A2 frame
                Formula for Cell A2 frame
            Cell B2 frame
                Formula for Cell B2 frame
```

Figure 1-1
Organization of part
of a typical spread-
sheet

Important   Because Framework can store its frames in many different orders, this chapter describes each frame type as offset from Byte 0, where 0 is the first byte of the frame. Frames always begin on paragraph boundaries.

The File Header

In Framework II, the file header is 48 bytes long.

Byte 0–1   **Header Size**   length: 2 bytes
Size of the header in paragraphs (16-byte units) counted from 1,
not 0. In Framework II, the header is three paragraphs (48 bytes).

Byte 2—3   **Header FID**   length: 2 bytes
Even the file header has its own frame ID. If you're creating a
framework file externally, the FID of the desktop is 00; the header
would logically be 02.

Byte 4   **Status Flags**   length: 1 byte
One-byte status flags. See "Status Flags" section.

Byte 5   **Frame Type ID**   length: 1 byte
This byte indicates the type of frame; in the case of the header, 00
for text.

Byte 6–7   **File ID**   length: 2 bytes
These bytes must hold the following values:
Byte 6: EDh
Byte 7: FBh

Byte 8–11   **Unused**   length: 4 bytes
Initialize to nulls (00h).

Byte 12–13   **Version Number**   length: 2 bytes
This integer must be >= 120 to be a valid Framework II file.

Byte 14–15   **Reserved**   length: 2 bytes
Initialize to nulls (00h).

Byte 16–17   **Checksum**   length: 2 bytes
The checksum is calculated as the sum of all the bytes in the file,
including all bytes in the header, modulo 16. Count the checksum
bytes as 00 during the calculation. An incorrect checksum will abort
the load.

Checksum is one of five file integrity checks that Framework
performs during the loading procedure. The others are Seek Count,
Maximum Frame Size, Next Frame Size, and Largest FID. If any of
the values stored in those locations don't agree with what Framework derives from the file, it will abort the load.

If the checksum itself is set to 00h, you can force Framework to
load the file whatever its condition or the state of the other integrity
checks—but you may crash the program.

Byte 18–19	**Number of Paragraphs (low)**	length: 2 bytes

This word contains the number of paragraphs in the file. It is actually the low word of a two-word field. The high word is at Bytes 30 and 31.

Byte 20–21	**Maximum Frame Size**	length: 2 bytes

This is the size, in paragraphs, of the largest frame in this file. It need not be the largest frame size that Framework can support.

Byte 22–23	**Next Frame Size**	length: 2 bytes

This is the size, in paragraphs, of the second largest frame in the file.

Byte 24–25	**Seek Count**	length: 2 bytes

Seek Count stores the total number of frames in the file. Remember that the file header, frame names, spreadsheet cells, and formulas are all frames. The maximum valid number here is 32,000 (7Dh). If the Seek Count doesn't agree with Framework's calculation during the loading process, it aborts the load.

Byte 26–27	**Largest FID**	length: 2 bytes

While FIDs are strictly the names of frames, this integer stores the largest FID as a value. Don't confuse this with the size of the largest frame.

Byte 28–29	**Reserved**	length: 2 bytes

Initialize these bytes to nulls (00h).

Byte 30–31	**Number of Paragraphs (high)**	length: 2 bytes

This is the high word of a two–word field. The low word is at Bytes 18 and 19. In all but extremely large (over one megabyte) files, this will be 0.

Byte 32–47	**Reserved**	length: 16 bytes

Initialize these bytes to nulls (00h).

General Frame Format

Every frame begins with this standard header.

Byte 0–1	**Frame Size**	length: 2 bytes

This integer holds the number of paragraphs in the frame.

Byte 2-3	**FID**	length: 2 bytes

This word uniquely identifies each frame in the file. IDs change as Framework reads the file into memory; the number has no other meaning than as a name by which one frame can reference another. When creating a Framework file externally to the program, you may use your own reference scheme, as long as it is consistent. (See "Assigning FIDs," earlier in this chapter.)

Byte 4 **Status Flags** length: 1 byte
One-byte status flags. See "Status Flags" section.

Byte 5 **Frame Type ID** length: 1 byte
This byte indicates the type of frame. See Table 1-1 for valid ID type numbers.

Byte 6–7 **Number of Elements** length: 2 bytes
This integer holds the number of elements in the contents area of the frame. Each frame can hold a variable number of elements (up to 64K). An element may be a byte, a character, a 16-bit word, a FID, or a frame. The Number of Elements will help you distinguish the garbage data that sometimes pads to the end of a paragraph boundary.

Byte 8–11 **Varies** length: 4 bytes
The contents of these bytes vary from frame type to frame type. See the offset values for the specific frame type.

Byte 12–13 **Formula Frame ID** length: 2 bytes
This word holds the FID of any formula that may be attached to this frame. If there is no formula, the value is 0.

Byte 14–16 **Formatting** length: 3 bytes
These three bytes hold formatting information for the frame. See the "Formats" section.

Byte 17 **Internal Value Type** length: 1 byte
See the "Value Structures" section.

Byte 18–27 **Value Structures** length: 10 bytes
This section may not be present on all frames, notably text frames. See the "Value Structures" section.

Byte 28–29 **Name Frame ID** length: 2 bytes
This word holds the FID of another frame containing the name of this frame. This section may not be present on all frames, notably spreadsheet components (rows, cells) that the user does not name.

Byte 30–31 **Status Flags** length: 2 bytes
See the "Status Flags" section.

Content Offsets

Because the exact organization of the header varies slightly with frame type, the contents of the frame are also offset differently from Byte 0 of the frame. Table 1-2 lists the content offsets for each type of frame.

| Important | Framework's offsets do not always adhere to the offsets shown here. Generally speaking, these hold. |

Table 1-2 Frame types and offsets

Code	Type	Offset
0	Text	80
1	Simple Glossary	80
2	Text Graph	80
3	Graph	80
4	Edit	10
5	Reserved	
6	Simple Buffer	8
7	Label	18
8	Cell	28
9	Reserved	
10	Freefloat	80
11	Composite Buffer	80
12	Column	80
13	SS Row	10
14	Spreadsheet	80
15	Reserved	
16	EXE	16
17	Reserved	
18	Reserved	
19	Glossary	80

Outline Frame Organization

An outline frame is one of three frame types that can contain other frames.

Byte 0–1 **Frame Size** length: 2 bytes
This integer holds the number of paragraphs in the frame.

Byte 2–3 **FID (Frame ID)** length: 2 bytes
This word uniquely identifies each frame in the file.

Byte 4 **Status Flags** length: 1 byte
One-byte status flags. See "Status Flags" section.

Byte 5 **Frame Type ID** length: 1 byte
This byte indicates the type of frame. An outline frame will be type 10 or 12.

Byte 6–7

Number of Elements   length: 2 bytes
This integer holds the number of FIDs (two bytes each) in the contents area of the frame.

Byte 8–9

Parent FID   length: 2 bytes
This word holds the frame ID of the parent of this frame. This word should be 00h if it has no parent and should appear on the desktop.

Byte 10–11

EXE FID   length: 2 bytes
This word will typically be 0. It holds the FID of the frame containing a DOS file.

Byte 12–13

Formula Frame ID   length: 2 bytes
This word holds the FID of any formula that may be attached to this frame. If there is no formula, the value is 0.

Byte 14–16

Formatting   length: 3 bytes
These three bytes hold formatting information for the frame. See the "Formats" section.

Byte 17

Internal Value Type   length: 1 byte
See the "Value Structures" section.

Byte 18–27

Value Structures   length: 10 bytes
See the "Value Structures" section.

Byte 28–29

Name Frame ID   length: 2 bytes
This word holds the FID of another frame containing the name of this frame.

Byte 30–31

Status Flags   length: 2 bytes
See the "Status Flags" section.

Byte 32–33

TLX   length: 2 bytes
This word holds the top left X coordinate of the contents of the frame, excluding the frame border, relative to its parent frame's absolute TLX (ABSTLX). It is 0 based. If this frame has no parent frame, it is "on the desktop," and TLX is relative to the desktop. A typical value for TLX is 1.

Byte 34–35

TLY   length: 2 bytes
This word holds the top left Y coordinate of the contents of this frame, excluding the frame border, relative to its parent's absolute TLY (ABSTLY). It is 0 based. If this frame has no parent frame, it is "on the desktop," and TLY is then relative to the desktop. A typical value for TLY is 3.

Byte 36–37

BRX   length: 2 bytes
This word holds the bottom right X coordinate of the contents of the frame, excluding the frame border, relative to its parent frame's absolute TLX (ABSTLX). It is 0 based. If this frame has no parent

frame, it is "on the desktop," and BRX is relative to the desktop. A typical value for BRX is 72.

Byte 38–39 **BRY** length: 2 bytes

This word holds the bottom right Y coordinate of the contents of this frame, excluding the frame border, relative to its parent's absolute TLY (ABSTLY). It is 0 based. If this frame has no parent frame, it is "on the desktop," and BRY is then relative to the desktop. A typical value for BRY is 13.

Byte 40–41 **Clipping TLX** length: 2 bytes

This word holds the 0-based, absolute, screen X coordinate of the first character position of the frame's clipping rectangle. Typically, this value is the same as TLX.

Byte 42–43 **Clipping TLY** length: 2 bytes

This word holds the 0-based, absolute, screen Y coordinate of the topmost visible row of the frame's clipping rectangle. A typical value is 4.

Byte 44–45 **Clipping BRX** length: 2 bytes

This word holds the 0-based, absolute, screen X coordinate of the rightmost character position of the frame's clipping rectangle. Typically, this value is 72.

Byte 46–47 **Clipping BRY** length: 2 bytes

This word holds the 0-based, absolute, screen Y coordinate of the bottommost row of the frame's clipping rectangle. A typical value is 14.

Byte 48–49 **Zoom ABSTLX** length: 2 bytes

This word holds the 0-based, absolute, screen X coordinate of the first character position of the frame. Typically, this value is the same as the Clipping TLX.

Byte 50–51 **Zoom ABSTLY** length: 2 bytes

This word holds the 0-based, absolute, screen Y coordinate of the topmost row of the frame. A typical value is the same as the Clipping TLY.

Byte 52–53 **Reserved** length: 2 bytes

Initialize these bytes to nulls.

Byte 54–55 **Reserved** length: 2 bytes

Initialize these bytes to nulls.

Byte 56–57 **First Visible Child** length: 2 bytes

Initialize these bytes to 1.

Byte 58–59 **Reserved** length: 2 bytes

Initialize these bytes to nulls.

Byte 60–61   **Style FID**   length: 2 bytes
This word contains the FID of a style frame. These bytes are typically 00h.

Byte 62–63   **Internal Page Number**   length: 2 bytes
Framework uses these bytes internally. Set them to nulls (00h).

Byte 64–65   **First Selected Element**   length: 2 bytes
These bytes contain a 1-based number designating which element in the frame's contents is the first selected element. A typical value is 1.

Byte 66–67   **Last Selected Element**   length: 2 bytes
These bytes contain a 1-based number equal to the last element + 1. It designates which element in the frame's contents is the last selected element. A typical value is 2.

Byte 68–73   **Unused**   length: 6 bytes
Initialize these bytes to nulls (00h).

Byte 74—79   **Escape Sequence**   length: 6 bytes
These six bytes comprise an escape sequence typical of those that begin paragraphs in Framework's text frames (an outline frame is a kind of text frame). The sequence typically contains the six bytes shown in Table 1-3. See also the section on text formatting.

Table 1-3	Typical escape sequence	
Byte Number	**Name**	**Typical Value**
74	Pad Begin	00h
75	Pad Ext	81h
76	Left Margin	01h
77	Right Margin	41h
78	First Paragraph Format	81h
79	Pad End Ext	00h

Byte 80–n   **Frame Contents**   length: n bytes
An outline frame contains an array of the FIDs of its child outline frames. Each FID is a two-byte word. The Number of Elements bytes contain the number of FIDs in the Frame Contents section.

Byte n + 1   **Frame Terminator**   length: 1 byte
The Frame Terminator character is the carriage return (0Dh, 13 ASC). Because Framework always begins a new frame on a new paragraph, the program generally pads to the end of the preceding paragraph with nulls (and sometimes with garbage). The carriage return denotes the end of the frame; any further characters are spurious.

Word Frame Organization

Word frames are where Framework stores running text. Other text—FRED formulas, names of frames, and so forth—appear in formula or edit frames.

Byte 0–1   **Frame Size**   length: 2 bytes
This integer holds the number of paragraphs in the frame.

Byte 2–3   **FID (Frame ID)**   length: 2 bytes
This word uniquely identifies each frame in the file.

Byte 4   **Status Flags**   length: 1 byte
One-byte status flags. See "Status Flags" section.

Byte 5   **Frame Type ID**   length: 1 byte
This byte indicates the type of frame. A word frame is type 0.

Byte 6–7   **Number of Elements**   length: 2 bytes
This integer holds the number of characters and escape code bytes in the content portion of the frame.

Byte 8–9   **Parent FID**   length: 2 bytes
This word holds the frame ID of the parent of this frame. This word should be 00h if the frame has no parent and should appear on the desktop.

Byte 10–11   **EXE FID**   length: 2 bytes
This word will typically be 0. It holds the FID of the frame containing a DOS file.

Byte 12–13   **Formula Frame ID**   length: 2 bytes
This word holds the FID of any formula that may be attached to this frame. If there is no formula, the value is 0.

Byte 14–16   **Formatting**   length: 3 bytes
These three bytes hold formatting information for the frame. See the "Formats" section.

Byte 17   **Internal Value Type**   length: 1 byte
See the "Value Structures" section.

Byte 18–27 **Value Structures** length: 10 bytes
See the "Value Structures" section.

Byte 28–29 **Name Frame ID** length: 2 bytes
This word holds the FID of another frame containing the name of this frame.

Byte 30–31 **Status Flags** length: 2 bytes
See the "Status Flags" section.

Byte 32–33 **TLX** length: 2 bytes
This word holds the top left X coordinate of the contents of the frame, excluding the frame border, relative to its parent frame's absolute TLX (ABSTLX). It is 0 based. If this frame has no parent frame, it is "on the desktop," and TLX is relative to the desktop. A typical value for TLX is 1.

Byte 34–35 **TLY** length: 2 bytes
This word holds the top left Y coordinate of the contents of this frame, excluding the frame border, relative to its parent's absolute TLY (ABSTLY). It is 0 based. If this frame has no parent frame, it is "on the desktop," and TLY is then relative to the desktop. A typical value for TLY is 3.

Byte 36–37 **BRX** length: 2 bytes
This word holds the bottom right X coordinate of the contents of the frame, excluding the frame border, relative to its parent frame's absolute *TLX* (ABSTLX). It is 0 based. If this frame has no parent frame, it is "on the desktop," and BRX is relative to the desktop. A typical value for BRX is 72.

Byte 38–39 **BRY** length: 2 bytes
This word holds the bottom right Y coordinate of the contents of this frame, excluding the frame border, relative to its parent's absolute *TLY* (ABSTLY). It is 0 based. If this frame has no parent frame, it is "on the desktop," and BRY is then relative to the desktop. A typical value for BRY is 13.

Byte 40–41 **Clipping TLX** length: 2 bytes
This word holds the 0-based, absolute-screen, X coordinate of the first character position of the frame's clipping rectangle. Typically, this value is the same as TLX.

Byte 42–43 **Clipping TLY** length: 2 bytes
This word holds the 0–based, absolute, screen Y coordinate of the topmost visible row of the frame's clipping rectangle. A typical value is 4.

Byte 44–45   **Clipping BRX**   length: 2 bytes
This word holds the 0-based, absolute, screen X coordinate of the rightmost character position of the frame's clipping rectangle. Typically, this value is 72.

Byte 46–47   **Clipping BRY**   length: 2 bytes
This word holds the 0-based, absolute, screen Y coordinate of the bottommost row of the frame's clipping rectangle. A typical value is 14.

Byte 48–49   **ABSTLX**   length: 2 bytes
This word holds the 0-based, absolute, screen X coordinate of the first character position of the frame. Typically, this value is the same as the Clipping TLX.

Byte 50–51   **ABSTLY**   length: 2 bytes
This word holds the 0-based, absolute, screen Y coordinate of the topmost row of the frame. A typical value is the same as the Clipping TLY.

Byte 52–53   **Scroll X**   length: 2 bytes
This word holds a zero or negative value that describes the portion of the contents of the frame visible in the horizontal direction. This value is typically 00h.

Byte 54–55   **Scroll Y**   length: 2 bytes
This word holds a zero or negative value that describes the portion of the contents of the frame visible in the vertical direction. This value is typically 00h.

Byte 56–57   **Reserved**   length: 2 bytes
Initialize these bytes to nulls.

Byte 58–59   **Reserved**   length: 2 bytes
Initialize these bytes to nulls.

Byte 60–61   **Style FID**   length: 2 bytes
This word contains the FID of a style frame. These bytes are typically 00h.

Byte 62–63   **Internal Page Number**   length: 2 bytes
Framework uses these bytes internally. Set them to nulls (00h).

Byte 64–65   **First Selected Element**   length: 2 bytes
These bytes contain a 1-based number designating which element in the frame's contents is the first selected element relative to the Ith line (offset 72). An element is any displayable character. A typical value is 1.

Byte 66–67   **Last Selected Element**   length: 2 bytes
These bytes contain a 1-based number equal to the last element selected + 1 relative to the Ith line (offset 72). A typical value is 2.

Byte 68–70   **Reserved**   length: 3 bytes
Initialize these bytes to nulls (00h).

Byte 71   **Tab Size**   length: 1 byte
Number of spaces for each tab stop on a line (counting from 1). A typical value is 8.

Byte 72–73   **Ith Line**   length: 2 bytes
This word contains a value that describes which line within the contents of the frame contains the current selection. The First Selected Element (offset 64), Last Selected Element (offset 66), and the Ith Line describe the selection. A typical value is 0.

Byte 74–79   **Escape Sequence**   length: 6 bytes
These six bytes comprise an escape sequence introducing the first paragraph in the text frame. The sequence typically contains the six bytes shown in Table 1-4. See also the section on text formatting.

Table 1-4   Escape sequence

Byte Number	Name	Typical Value
74	Pad Begin	00h
75	Pad Ext	81h
76	Left Margin	01h
77	Right Margin	41h
78	First Paragraph Format	81h
79	Pad End Ext	00h

Byte 80–n   **Frame Contents**   length: n bytes
A text frame contains text characters, escape sequences, hard and soft end-of-line characters, and other formatting information. See the section "Text Representation."

Byte n + 1   **Frame Terminator**   length: 1 byte
The Frame Terminator character is the carriage return (0Dh, 13 ASC). Because Framework always begins a new frame on a new paragraph, the program generally pads to the end of the preceding paragraph with nulls (and sometimes with garbage). The carriage return denotes the end of the frame; any further characters are spurious.

Spreadsheet Frame Organization

A spreadsheet frame (type 14) is really the master frame of a mini–Framework all by itself. It contains the FID of the column vector frame (edit type 04). Its own contents section is an array of FIDs for each row of the spreadsheet. Each row frame contains FIDs to each cell, and each cell contains the FID of its formula frame.

Below the level of the spreadsheet frame, column vector, row, cell, and formula frames have no names.

Byte 0–1   **Frame Size**   length: 2 bytes
This integer holds the number of paragraphs in the frame.

Byte 2–3   **FID (Frame ID)**   length: 2 bytes
This word uniquely identifies each frame in the file.

Byte 4   **Status Flags**   length: 1 byte
One-byte status flags. See "Status Flags" section.

Byte 5   **Frame Type ID**   length: 1 byte
This byte indicates the type of frame. A spreadsheet frame is type 14.

Byte 6–7   **Number of Elements**   length: 2 bytes
This integer holds the number of FIDs (two bytes each) in the content portion of the frame.

Byte 8–9   **Parent FID**   length: 2 bytes
This word holds the frame ID of the parent of this frame. This word should be 00h if the frame has no parent and should appear on the desktop.

Byte 10–11   **Column Vector FID**   length: 2 bytes
This word contains the FID of the frame containing the individual column width information.

Byte 12–13   **Formula Frame ID**   length: 2 bytes
This word holds the FID of any formula that may be attached to this frame. If there is no formula, the value is 0.

Byte 14–16   **Formatting**   length: 3 bytes
These three bytes hold formatting information for the frame. See the "Formats" section.

Byte 17   **Internal Value Type**   length: 1 byte
See the "Value Structures" section.

Byte 18–27   **Value Structures**   length: 10 bytes
See the "Value Structures" section.

Byte 28–29   **Name Frame ID**   length: 2 bytes
This word holds the FID of another frame containing the name of this frame.

Byte 30–31   **Status Flags**   length: 2 bytes
See the "Status Flags" section.

Byte 32–33   **TLX**   length: 2 bytes
This word holds the top left X coordinate of the contents of the frame, excluding the frame border, relative to its parent frame's absolute TLX (ABSTLX). It is 0 based. If this frame has no parent frame, it is "on the desktop," and TLX is relative to the desktop. A typical value for TLX is 1.

Byte 34–35   **TLY**   length: 2 bytes
This word holds the top left Y coordinate of the contents of this frame, excluding the frame border, relative to its parent's absolute TLY (ABSTLY). It is 0 based. If this frame has no parent frame, it is "on the desktop," and TLY is then relative to the desktop. A typical value for TLY is 3.

Byte 36–37   **BRX**   length: 2 bytes
This word holds the bottom right X coordinate of the contents of the frame, excluding the frame border, relative to its parent frame's absolute *TLX* (ABSTLX). It is 0 based. If this frame has no parent frame, it is "on the desktop," and BRX is relative to the desktop. A typical value for BRX is 72.

Byte 38–39   **BRY**   length: 2 bytes
This word holds the bottom right Y coordinate of the contents of this frame, excluding the frame border, relative to its parent's absolute *TLY* (ABSTLY). It is 0 based. If this frame has no parent frame, it is "on the desktop," and BRY is then relative to the desktop. A typical value for BRY is 13.

Byte 40–41   **Clipping TLX**   length: 2 bytes
This word holds the 0-based, absolute, screen X coordinate of the first character position beyond the row numbers. Except when a column is locked, this value is the leftmost character position within column A. A typical value is 5.

Calculate a clipping TLX of 5 by allowing one character position for the spreadsheet frame border and four character positions for the row numbers. This places the spreadsheet left frame border at X coordinate 0, the row numbers at X coordinate 1, and the first X coordinate for the first column at 5.

If the spreadsheet column is locked, then add the width of column A to the these values. For example, if column A is 9 characters wide, then the clipping TLX must be 14.

Byte 42–43　　**Clipping TLY**　　　　　　　　length: 2 bytes
This word holds the 0–based, absolute, screen Y coordinate of the topmost visible row, usually row 1. A typical value is 5.

Calculate a clipping TLY value by allowing one row for the frame border and one row for the column labels (A, B, C, etc.). This places the spreadsheet top frame border at Y coordinate 3, the column labels at Y coordinate 4, and the first row at Y coordinate 5.

If the spreadsheet is locked, then add 1 to the clipping TLY value to make it 6 in the previous example.

Byte 44–45　　**Clipping BRX**　　　　　　　　length: 2 bytes
This word holds the 0-based, absolute, screen X coordinate of the rightmost character position of the frame's clipping rectangle. Typically, this value is 72.

Byte 46–47　　**Clipping BRY**　　　　　　　　length: 2 bytes
This word holds the 0-based, absolute, screen Y coordinate of the bottommost row of the frame's clipping rectangle. A typical value is 14.

Byte 48–49　　**ABSTLX**　　　　　　　　length: 2 bytes
This word holds the 0-based, absolute, screen X coordinate of the first character position beyond the row numbers. Typically, this value is the leftmost character position within column A, and the same as the Clipping TLX.

Byte 50–51　　**ABSTLY**　　　　　　　　length: 2 bytes
This word holds the 0-based, absolute, screen Y coordinate of the topmost visible row—usually row 1. A typical value is the same as the Clipping TLY.

Byte 52–53　　**First Visible Column**　　　　　　length: 2 bytes
The word contains a 1-based column number of the first visible column in the current screen display. A typical value is 01h.

Byte 54–55　　**Last Visible Column**　　　　　　length: 2 bytes
This word holds a 1-based column number of the last visible column in the current screen display. You should initialize this word to 01h.

Byte 56–57　　**Last Visible Row**　　　　　　length: 2 bytes
This word holds a 1-based row number of the last visible row in the screen display. Set the Last Visible Row to 01h.

Byte 58–59 **First Visible Row** length: 2 bytes
This word holds the 1-based row number of the first visible row in the screen display. A typical value is 01h.

Byte 60–61 **Style FID** length: 2 bytes
This word contains the FID of a style frame. These bytes are typically 00h.

Byte 62–63 **Internal Page Number** length: 2 bytes
Framework uses these bytes internally. Set them to nulls (00h).

Byte 64–65 **First Selected Row** length: 2 bytes
These bytes contain a 1-based number designating the first selected row. A typical value is 1.

Byte 66–67 **Last Selected Row** length: 2 bytes
These bytes contain a 1-based number equal to the last row selected + 1. A typical value is 2.

Byte 68–69 **First Selected Column** length: 2 bytes
These bytes hold a 1-based column number of the first column selected. A typical value is 1.

Byte 70–71 **Last Selected Column** length: 2 bytes
This is a 1-based column number designating the last column selected + 1. A typical value is 2.

Byte 72–73 **Window Last Column** length: 2 bytes
This word contains the number of columns declared for this spreadsheet. The default value is 50.

Byte 74 **Delta First Visible Column** length: 1 byte
This byte contains the number of character positions that are clipped and not visible on the spreadsheet's left edge for the first visible column. The default value is 0.

Byte 75 **SS Bits** length: 1 byte
This byte contains a set of spreadsheet status flags. See "Status Flags."

Byte 76–77 **Window Last Row** length: 2 bytes
The number of rows declared for this spreadsheet. The default number is 100.

Byte 78–79 **Reserved** length: 2 bytes
Initialize these bytes to nulls (00h).

Byte 80–n **Frame Contents** length: n bytes
The contents of a spreadsheet frame contain an array of two–byte FIDs to the number contained in the Number of Elements word. Each entry is the FID of a row frame, ordered from top to bottom of

the spreadsheet and counted from 1. An FID of 00h indicates a completely empty row. The number of FIDs may be less than the number of rows declared for the spreadsheet; after the list of Number of Elements FIDs, the remaining rows are assumed to be empty.

Byte n + 1	**Frame Terminator**	length: 1 byte

The Frame Terminator character is the carriage return (0Dh, 13 ASC). Because Framework always begins a new frame on a new paragraph, the program generally pads to the end of the preceding paragraph with nulls (and sometimes with garbage). The carriage return denotes the end of the frame; any further characters are spurious.

Column Vector

The Column Vector frame is a variation on the Edit frame (type 4). It holds two important pieces of information: whether the data is part of a data base or spreadsheet, and the widths of each column.

Byte 0–1	**Paragraph Count**	length: 2 bytes

This word contains the 1-based count of the number of paragraphs in the frame.

Byte 2–3	**Frame ID**	length: 2 bytes

The Frame ID uniquely identifies every frame in the file.

Byte 4	**Frame Status**	length: 1 byte

See the section "Status Flags."

Byte 5	**Type ID**	length: 1 byte

This byte contains the type ID of the Column Vector frame. Column Vector is an edit frame (type 04h).

Byte 6–7	**Number of Elements**	length: 2 bytes

This word contains the 1-based number of entries in the contents section. In a Column Vector frame, the elements are two-byte FIDs, one for each of the "live" columns in the spreadsheet.

Byte 8–9	**DB Forms Frame ID**	length: 2 bytes

This word contains data to tell Framework whether it's dealing with a spreadsheet or a data base in this frame. The internal structure of a data base frame is very much like the structure of a spreadsheet frame. If the Column Vector frame is part of a spreadsheet frame, the DB Forms Frame ID is 00h. If the Column Vector frame is part of a data base frame, then this word contains the FID of the DB Forms frame.

Byte 10–n   **Column Widths**   length: n bytes
A separate two-byte word describes each column width. The
values of each width are calculated from 1. Each width corresponds in order to a column on the spreadsheet, from left to
right. If there are fewer width words than there are columns
defined for the spreadsheet, it means that the remaining columns all use the default width as set in FWSETUP.

Row Frame

There is a row frame for every row in the spreadsheet in which any cell contains data, a
formula, or a cell format. Rows generally appear in the file in order from top to bottom
starting with row 1. After each row frame come frames describing each cell and cell formula
(in column order).

Note	There is no absolute frame order in Framework; as

long as you apply FIDs consistently and completely, frames can appear in any
order.

Byte 0–1   **Paragraph Count**   length: 2 bytes
This word contains the 1-based count of the number of paragraphs
in the frame.

Byte 2–3   **Frame ID**   length: 2 bytes
The Frame ID uniquely identifies every frame in the file.

Byte 4   **Frame Status**   length: 1 byte
See the section "Status Flags."

Byte 5   **Type ID**   length: 1 byte
This byte contains the Type ID of the row. The Type ID of a row is
13 (0Dh).

Byte 6–7   **Number of Elements**   length: 2 bytes
This word contains the 1-based number of FIDs (each two bytes)
contained in the contents portion of the frame. Each is the ID of a
particular cell frame in the row described by this frame.

Byte 8–9   **Parent FID**   length: 2 bytes
This word contains the FID of the frame to which this frame belongs.
It tells from which spreadsheet frame this row comes.

Byte 10–n   **Array of Cells**   length: n bytes
The content portion of this frame is an array of two-byte words. Each
word corresponds to a cell in the row, in column order (A, B, C, etc.).
If a word is even, it is the FID of a cell in the row. If a word is odd,
it contains format information for the otherwise empty cell. Fewer
words in the content portion of the row frame indicate that the

remainder of the cells in that row are empty and default to the global spreadsheet format.

Value Cell

Value cells and text cells are the two types of cell frames in Framework II. Both can refer to formula frames.

Byte 0–1	**Paragraph Count**	length: 2 bytes

This word contains the 1-based count of the number of paragraphs in the frame.

Byte 2–3	**Frame ID**	length: 2 bytes

The Frame ID uniquely identifies every frame in the file.

Byte 4	**Frame Status**	length: 1 byte

See the section "Status Flags."

Byte 5	**Type ID**	length: 1 byte

This byte contains the type ID of the cell. A value cell has a Type ID of 08h.

Byte 6–7	**Number of Elements**	length: 2 bytes

This word contains the 1-based number of bytes (characters) in the content portion of the frame.

Byte 8–9	**Parent FID**	length: 2 bytes

This word contains the FID of the frame to which this frame belongs. It tells from which row frame this cell comes.

Byte 10–11	**Recalc**	length: 2 bytes

Framework sets these bytes to 01h when it has freshly recalculated the value of a cell. A value of 00h forces Framework to recalculate the cell value. You should generally set the value of this cell to 01h.

Byte 12–13	**Formula FID**	length: 2 bytes

This word holds the FID of the formula attached to this cell. The value is 00h if there is no formula.

Byte 14–16	**Frame Format**	length: 3 bytes

See "Formats" section.

Byte 17	**Internal Value Type**	length: 1 byte

See "Value Structures" section.

Byte 18–27	**Value Structure**	length: 10 bytes

See "Value Structures" section.

Byte 28–n	**Frame Contents**	length: n bytes

The content portion of a value cell contains the characters exactly as displayed by the cell—including all currency characters, thousands delimiters, decimal characters, and percent signs. In Framework II, a null follows a character string.

Byte n + 1	**Frame Terminator**	length: 1 byte

After the trailing null of the Frame Contents comes the Terminator character, a carriage return (ASCII 13, 0Dh). All other characters from the Terminator the the paragraph boundary should be disregarded.

Text Cell

Text cells hold the spreadsheet labels that the user types in.

Byte 0–1 **Paragraph Count** length: 2 bytes
This word contains the 1-based count of the number of paragraphs in the frame.

Byte 2–3 **Frame ID** length: 2 bytes
The Frame ID uniquely identifies every frame in the file.

Byte 4 **Frame Status** length: 1 byte
See the section "Status Flags."

Byte 5 **Type ID** length: 1 byte
This byte contains the type ID of the cell. A text cell has a Type ID of 07h.

Byte 6–7 **Number of Elements** length: 2 bytes
This word contains the 1-based number of bytes (characters) in the content portion of the frame.

Byte 8–9 **Parent FID** length: 2 bytes
This word contains the FID of the frame to which this frame belongs. It tells from which row frame this cell comes.

Byte 10–11 **Recalc** length: 2 bytes
Framework sets these bytes to 01h when it has freshly recalculated the value of a cell. A value of 00h forces Framework to recalculate the cell value. You should generally set the value of this cell to 01h.

Byte 12–13 **Formula FID** length: 2 bytes
This word holds the FID of the formula attached to this cell. The value is 00h if there is no formula.

Byte 14–16 **Frame Format** length: 3 bytes
See "Formats" section.

Byte 17 **Internal Value Type** length: 1 byte
See "Value Structures" section.

Byte 18–n **Frame Contents** length: n bytes
The Frame Contents hold the text label that the user has typed into the spreadsheet cell. In Framework II, text cells can "overlap" neighboring cells to their right (at least until those cells also contain data). A text cell can contain and display more text than the width of its column.

Data Base Frame Organization

A Framework II data base structure is very similar to a spreadsheet. The two structures vary in three important ways:

1. Bit #3 in SS Bits (Byte 75) in the data base frame contains a 1. This indicates that the frame is a data base frame. See the "Status Flags" section.
2. The DB Forms Frame ID (Byte 8) of the Column Vector frame contains the FID of the DB Forms Frame. The DB Forms Frame contains the data base's dBase view and Forms view information.
3. The DB Forms Frame contains two FIDs in its contents section: the FID of the frame containing the dBase view information and the FID of the frame containing the Forms view information.

Byte 0–1 **Frame Size** length: 2 bytes
This integer holds the number of paragraphs in the frame.

Byte 2–3 **FID (Frame ID)** length: 2 bytes
This word uniquely identifies each frame in the file.

Byte 4 **Status Flags** length: 1 byte
One-byte status flags. See "Status Flags" section.

Byte 5 **Frame Type ID** length: 1 byte
This byte indicates the type of frame. A data base frame is type 14 (as is the spreadsheet frame).

Byte 6–7 **Number of Elements** length: 2 bytes
This integer holds the number of FIDs (two bytes each) in the content portion of the frame.

Byte 8–9 **Parent FID** length: 2 bytes
This word holds the frame ID of the parent of this frame. This word should be 00h if the frame has no parent and should appear on the desktop.

Byte 10–11 **Column Vector FID** length: 2 bytes
This word contains the FID of the frame containing individual column width (field width, for data bases) information.

Byte 12–13   **Formula Frame ID**   length: 2 bytes
This word holds the FID of any formula that may be attached to this
frame. If there is no formula, the value is 0.

Byte 14–16   **Formatting**   length: 3 bytes
These three bytes hold formatting information for the frame. See
the "Formats" section.

Byte 17   **Internal Value Type**   length: 1 byte
See the "Value Structures" section.

Byte 18–27   **Value Structures**   length: 10 bytes
See the "Value Structures" section.

Byte 28–29   **Name Frame ID**   length: 2 bytes
This word holds the FID of another frame containing the name of
this frame.

Byte 30–31   **Status Flags**   length: 2 bytes
See the "Status Flags" section.

Byte 32–33   **TLX**   length: 2 bytes
This word holds the top left X coordinate of the contents of the
frame, excluding the frame border, relative to its parent frame's
absolute TLX (ABSTLX). It is 0 based. If this frame has no parent
frame, it is "on the desktop," and TLX is relative to the desktop. A
typical value for TLX is 1.

Byte 34–35   **TLY**   length: 2 bytes
This word holds the top left Y coordinate of the contents of this
frame, excluding the frame border, relative to its parent's absolute
TLY (ABSTLY). It is 0 based. If this frame has no parent frame, it is
"on the desktop," and TLY is then relative to the desktop. A typical
value for TLY is 3.

Byte 36–37   **BRX**   length: 2 bytes
This word holds the bottom right X coordinate of the contents of the
frame, excluding the frame border, relative to its parent frame's
absolute *TLX* (ABSTLX). It is 0 based. If this frame has no parent
frame, it is "on the desktop," and BRX is relative to the desktop. A
typical value for BRX is 72.

Byte 38–39   **BRY**   length: 2 bytes
This word holds the bottom right Y coordinate of the contents of this
frame, excluding the frame border, relative to its parent's absolute
TLY (ABSTLY). It is 0 based. If this frame has no parent frame, it is
"on the desktop," and BRY is then relative to the desktop. A typical
value for BRY is 13.

Byte 40–41

Clipping TLX   length: 2 bytes
This word holds the 0-based, absolute, screen X coordinate of the first character position beyond the row numbers. Except when a column is locked, this value is the leftmost character position within the first field. A typical value is 5. See "Clipping TLX" for the Spreadsheet Frame.

Byte 42–43

Clipping TLY   length: 2 bytes
This word holds the 0-based, absolute, screen Y coordinate of the topmost visible row, usually row 1. A typical value is 5. See "Clipping TLY" for the Spreadsheet Frame.

Byte 44–45

Clipping BRX   length: 2 bytes
This word holds the 0-based, absolute, screen X coordinate of the rightmost character position of the frame's clipping rectangle. Typically, this value is 72.

Byte 46–47

Clipping BRY   length: 2 bytes
This word holds the 0-based, absolute, screen Y coordinate of the bottommost row of the frame's clipping rectangle. A typical value is 14.

Byte 48–49

ABSTLX   length: 2 bytes
This word holds the 0-based, absolute, screen X coordinate of the first character position beyond the row numbers. Typically, this value is the leftmost character position within column A and the same as the Clipping TLX.

Byte 50–51

ABSTLY   length: 2 bytes
This word holds the 0 based, absolute, screen Y coordinate of the topmost visible row—usually row 1. A typical value is the same as the Clipping TLY.

Byte 52–53

First Visible Column   length: 2 bytes
The word contains a 1-based column number of the first visible column in the current screen display. A typical value is 01h.

Byte 54–55

Last Visible Column   length: 2 bytes
This word holds a 1-based column number of the last visible column in the current screen display. You should initialize this word to 01h.

Byte 56–57

Last Visible Row   length: 2 bytes
This word holds a 1-based row number of the last visible row in the screen display. Set the Last Visible Row to 01h.

Byte 58–59

First Visible Row   length: 2 bytes
This word holds the 1-based row number of the first visible row in the screen display. A typical value is 01h.

Byte 60–61   **Style FID**   length: 2 bytes
This word contains the FID of a style frame. These bytes are
typically 00h.

Byte 62–63   **Internal Page Number**   length: 2 bytes
Framework uses these bytes internally. Set them to nulls (00h).

Byte 64–65   **First Selected Row**   length: 2 bytes
These bytes contain a 1-based number designating the first selected row. A typical value is 1.

Byte 66–67   **Last Selected Row**   length: 2 bytes
These bytes contain a 1-based number equal to the last row
selected + 1. A typical value is 2.

Byte 68–69   **First Selected Column**   length: 2 bytes
These bytes hold a 1-based column number of the first column
selected. A typical value is 1.

Byte 70–71   **Last Selected Column**   length: 2 bytes
This is a 1-based column number designating the last column
selected + 1. A typical value is 2.

Byte 72–73   **Window Last Column**   length: 2 bytes
This word contains the number of columns declared for this data
base. The default value is 50.

Byte 74   **Delta First Visible Column**   length: 1 byte
This byte contains the number of character positions that are
clipped and not visible on the data base frame's left edge for the first
visible column. The default value is 0.

Byte 75   **SS Bits**   length: 1 byte
This byte contains a set of status flags. You must set bit #3 to 1,
indicating that this frame is a data base frame rather than a spreadsheet frame. See "Status Flags."

Byte 76–77   **Window Last Row**   length: 2 bytes
The number of rows declared for this data base. The default number
is 100.

Byte 78–79   **Reserved**   length: 2 bytes
Initialize these bytes to nulls (00h).

Byte 80–n   **Frame Contents**   length: n bytes
The contents of a data base frame contain an array of two-byte FIDs
to the number contained in the Number of Elements word. Each
entry is the FID of a row frame (a date base record), ordered from
top to bottom of the data base, and counted from 1. A FID of 00h indicates a completely empty record. The number of FIDs may be
less than the number of rows declared for the data base; after the

list of Number of Elements FIDs, the remaining rows are assumed to be empty.

Byte n + 1 **Frame Terminator** length: 1 byte
The Frame Terminator character is the carriage return (0Dh, 13 ASC). Because Framework always begins a new frame on a new paragraph, the program generally pads to the end of the preceding paragraph with nulls (and sometimes with garbage). The carriage return denotes the end of the frame; any further characters are spurious.

DB Forms Frame

Byte 0–1 **Frame Size** length: 2 bytes
This integer holds the number of paragraphs in the frame.

Byte 2–3 **FID (Frame ID)** length: 2 bytes
This word uniquely identifies each frame in the file.

Byte 4 **Status Flags** length: 1 byte
One-byte status flags. See "Status Flags" section.

Byte 5 **Frame Type ID** length: 1 byte
This byte indicates the type of frame. A data base forms frame is type11 (0Bh).

Byte 6–7 **Number of Elements** length: 2 bytes
This integer holds the number of FIDs (two bytes each) in the content portion of the frame. There are two FIDs only in the content portion of a DB Forms frame.

Byte 8–29 **Reserved** length: 22 bytes
All these bytes are reserved in the DB Forms Frame. Set them to nulls (00h).

Byte 30–31 **Status Flags** length: 2 bytes
See the "Status Flags" section.

Byte 32–33 **TLX** length: 2 bytes
This word holds the top left X coordinate of the contents of the frame, excluding the frame border, relative to its parent frame's absolute TLX (ABSTLX). It is 0 based. If this frame has no parent frame, it is "on the desktop," and TLX is relative to the desktop. A typical value for TLX is 1.

Byte 34–35   **TLY**   length: 2 bytes
This word holds the top left Y coordinate of the contents of this frame, excluding the frame border, relative to its parent's absolute TLY (ABSTLY). It is 0 based. If this frame has no parent frame, it is "on the desktop," and TLY is then relative to the desktop. A typical value for TLY is 3.

Byte 36–37   **BRX**   length: 2 bytes
This word holds the bottom right X coordinate of the contents of the frame, excluding the frame border, relative to its parent frame's absolute *TLX* (ABSTLX). It is 0 based. If this frame has no parent frame, it is "on the desktop," and BRX is relative to the desktop. A typical value for BRX is 72.

Byte 38–39   **BRY**   length: 2 bytes
This word holds the bottom right Y coordinate of the contents of this frame, excluding the frame border, relative to its parent's absolute *TLY* (ABSTLY). It is 0 based. If this frame has no parent frame, it is "on the desktop," and BRY is then relative to the desktop. A typical value for BRY is 13.

Byte 40–41   **Clipping TLX**   length: 2 bytes
This word holds the 0-based, absolute, screen X coordinate of the first character position beyond the row numbers. Except when a column is locked, this value is the leftmost character position within the first field. A typical value is 5. See "Clipping TLX" for the Spreadsheet Frame

Byte 42–43   **Clipping TLY**   length: 2 bytes
This word holds the 0-based, absolute, screen Y coordinate of the topmost visible row, usually row 1. A typical value is 5. See "Clipping TLY" for the Spreadsheet Frame.

Byte 44–45   **Clipping BRX**   length: 2 bytes
This word holds the 0-based, absolute, screen X coordinate of the rightmost character position of the frame's clipping rectangle. Typically, this value is 72.

Byte 46–47   **Clipping BRY**   length: 2 bytes
This word holds the 0-based, absolute, screen Y coordinate of the bottommost row of the frame's clipping rectangle. A typical value is 14.

Byte 48–49   **ABSTLX**   length: 2 bytes
This word holds the 0-based, absolute, screen X coordinate of the first character position beyond the row numbers. Typically, this value is the leftmost character position within column A, and the same as the Clipping TLX.

Byte 50–51 **ABSTLY**   length: 2 bytes
This word holds the 0-based, absolute,screenY coordinate of the topmost visible row—usually row 1. A typical value is the same as the Clipping TLY.

Byte 52–53 **Reserved**   length: 2 bytes
Initialize these bytes to nulls (00h).

Byte 54–55 **Number of Open Records** length: 2 bytes
Typically, the Number of Open Records value is the same as the Windows Last Row value (Byte 76) of the data base frame.

Byte 56–63 **Reserved**   length: 8 bytes
Initialize these bytes to nulls (00h).

Byte 64–65 **Data Base View Indicator** length: 2 bytes
This word defines the view that the frame displays:
0: Table view
1: Forms view
2: dBase view

Byte 66–67 **Data Base View Indicator + 1** length: 2 bytes

Byte 68–79 **Reserved**   length: 12 bytes
Set these bytes to nulls (00h).

Byte 80–83 **Frame Contents**   length: n bytes
The DB Form frame contains two, 2-byte FIDs. The first entry is the FID of the Forms View frame. The second is the FID of the dBase View frame.

Byte 84 **Frame Terminator**   length: 1 byte
The Frame Terminator character is the carriage return (0Dh, 13 ASC). Because Framework always begins a new frame on a new paragraph, the program generally pads to the end of the preceding paragraph with nulls (and sometimes with garbage). The carriage return denotes the end of the frame; any further characters are spurious.

Forms View Frame

The Forms View frame contains one FID for every field in the data base. Each FID points to a Forms View Field Frame.

Byte 0–1 **Paragraph Count**   length: 2 bytes
The number of paragraphs in the current frame.

Byte 2–3	**Frame ID**	length: 2 bytes
	This frame's FID.	
Byte 4	**Status Flags**	length: 1 byte
	See the "Status Flags" section.	
Byte 5	**Frame Type ID**	length: 1 byte
	The frame type ID of a Forms View Frame is 11.	
Byte 6–7	**Number of Elements**	length: 2 bytes
	This word holds the number of words in the contents portion of the frame. The number should be 2.	
Byte 8–9	**Parent FID**	length: 2 bytes
	This word contains the FID of the frame that is the parent of the Forms View Frame.	
Byte 10–11	**EXE FID**	length: 2 bytes
	This is the frame ID of a frame holding an externally compiled and linked program. Typically, the EXE FID is null (00h).	
Byte 12–13	**Formula FID**	length: 2 bytes
	This is the FID of a frame that contains the formula for this frame (contents are nulls if there is no formula).	
Byte 14–16	**Formatting**	length: 3 bytes
	These three bytes hold formatting information for the frame. See the "Formats" section.	
Byte 17	**Internal Value Type**	length: 1 byte
	See the "Value Structures" section.	
Byte 18–27	**Value Structure**	length: 10 bytes
	See the "Value Structures" section.	
Byte 28–29	**Name FID**	length: 2 bytes
	The FID of the frame holding the name of this frame.	
Byte 30–31	**Frame Status Flags**	length: 2 bytes
	See the "Status Flags" section.	
Byte 32–79	**Reserved**	length: 47 bytes
	Framework uses these bytes internally. When constructing a Framework file outside of the Framework program, set these bytes to nulls (00h).	
Byte 80–n	**Frame Contents**	length: n bytes
	The Contents portion of a Forms View frame contains one FID for every field in the data base.	

Byte n + 1   **Frame Terminator**   length: 1 byte
The frame terminator character is the carriage return (0Dh, ASCII 13). Because Framework begins each new frame on a paragraph boundary, pad to the last byte of the terminator's paragrah with nulls (00h).

Forms View Field Frame

There is one Forms View Field frame for every field in the data base. These frames describe the screen position of the field. It is a good idea (although not strictly mandatory) for each Forms View Field to have a different TLX and TLY, so that all fields are visible.

Byte 0–1   **Frame Size**   length: 2 bytes
This integer holds the number of paragraphs in the frame.

Byte 2–3   **FID (Frame ID)**   length: 2 bytes
This word uniquely identifies each frame in the file.

Byte 4   **Status Flags**   length: 1 byte
One-byte status flags. See "Status Flags" section.

Byte 5   **Frame Type ID**   length: 1 byte
This byte indicates the type of frame. A Forms View Field frame is type 0 (text).

Byte 6–7   **Number of Elements**   length: 2 bytes
This integer holds the number of bytes (characters and escape codes) in the content portion of this frame. When creating an empty Framework data base outside of the Framework program, set these bytes to nulls because the contents portion of the frame is initially empty (no data in the field).

Byte 8–9   **Parent FID**   length: 2 bytes
This word holds the frame ID of the parent of this frame. The parent of the Forms View Field frame is the Data Base Frame.

Byte 10–11   **EXE FID** length: 2 bytes
This word contains the FID of a frame containing an externally compiled and linked program. Typically, it's null.

Byte 12–13   **Formula Frame ID**   length: 2 bytes
This word holds the FID of any formula that may be attached to this frame. If there is no formula, the value is 0.

Byte 14–16   **Formatting**   length: 3 bytes
These three bytes hold formatting information for the frame. See the "Formats" section.

Byte 17   **Internal Value Type**   length: 1 byte
See the "Value Structures" section.

Byte 18–27   **Value Structures**   length: 10 bytes
See the "Value Structures" section.

Byte 28–29   **Name Frame ID**   length: 2 bytes
This word holds the FID of another frame containing the name of this frame.

Byte 30–31   **Status Flags**   length: 2 bytes
See the "Status Flags" section.

Byte 32–33   **TLX**   length: 2 bytes
This word holds the top left X coordinate of the contents of the frame, excluding the frame border, relative to its parent frame's absolute TLX (ABSTLX). It is 0 based. If this frame has no parent frame, it is "on the desktop," and TLX is relative to the desktop. A typical value for TLX is 1.

Byte 34–35   **TLY**   length: 2 bytes
This word holds the top left Y coordinate of the contents of this frame, excluding the frame border, relative to its parent's absolute TLY (ABSTLY). It is 0 based. If this frame has no parent frame, it is "on the desktop," and TLY is then relative to the desktop. A typical value for TLY is 3.

Byte 36–37   **BRX**   length: 2 bytes
This word holds the bottom right X coordinate of the contents of the frame, excluding the frame border, relative to its parent frame's absolute *TLX* (ABSTLX). It is 0 based. If this frame has no parent frame, it is "on the desktop," and BRX is relative to the desktop. A typical value for BRX is 72.

Byte 38–39   **BRY**   length: 2 bytes
This word holds the bottom right Y coordinate of the contents of this frame, excluding the frame border, relative to its parent's absolute *TLY* (ABSTLY). It is 0 based. If this frame has no parent frame, it is "on the desktop," and BRY is then relative to the desktop. A typical value for BRY is 13.

Byte 40–41   **Clipping TLX**   length: 2 bytes
This word holds the 0-based, absolute, screen X coordinate of the first character position beyond the row numbers. Except when a column is locked, this value is the leftmost character position within the first field. A typical value is 5. See "Clipping TLX" for the Spreadsheet Frame.

Byte 42–43   **Clipping TLY**   length: 2 bytes
This word holds the 0-based, absolute, screen Y coordinate of the topmost visible row, usually row 1. A typical value is 5. See "Clipping TLY" for the Spreadsheet Frame.

Byte 44–45　　　**Clipping BRX**　　　　　　　length: 2 bytes
This word holds the 0-based, absolute, screen X coordinate of the rightmost character position of the frame's clipping rectangle. Typically, this value is 72.

Byte 46–47　　　**Clipping BRY**　　　　　　　length: 2 bytes
This word holds the 0-based, absolute, screen Y coordinate of the bottommost row of the frame's clipping rectangle. A typical value is 14.

Byte 48–49　　　**ABSTLX**　　　　　　　　length: 2 bytes
This word holds the 0-based, absolute, screen X coordinate of the first character position beyond the row numbers. Typically, this value is the leftmost character position within column A, and the same as the Clipping TLX.

Byte 50–51　　　**ABSTLY**　　　　　　　　length: 2 bytes
This word holds the 0-based, absolute, screen Y coordinate of the topmost visible row—usually row 1. A typical value is the same as the Clipping TLY.

Byte 52–53　　　**Scroll X**　　　　　　　　length: 2 bytes
This word is a 0 or negative value, and describes the portion of the contents of the frame in the horizontal direction that is visible. Its value is typically 0.

Byte 54–55　　　**Scroll y**　　　　　　　　length: 2 bytes
This word is a 0 or negative value, and describes the portion of the contents of the frame in the vertical direction that is visible. Its value is typically 0.

Byte 56–59　　　**Reserved**　　　　　　　　length: 4 bytes
These words are reserved by Framework. Set them to nulls (00h).

Byte 60–61　　　**Style FID**　　　　　　　　length: 2 bytes
This word contains the FID of a style frame. These bytes are typically 00h.

Byte 62–63　　　**Internal Page Number**　　　　length: 2 bytes
Framework uses these bytes internally. Set them to nulls (00h).

Byte 64–65　　　**First Selected Element**　　　length: 2 bytes
These bytes contain a 1-based number designating the first selected element relative to the lth line (Byte 72). An element is any displayable character. A typical value is 1.

Byte 66–67　　　**Last Selected Element**　　　length: 2 bytes
These bytes contain a 1-based number equal to the last element selected + 1, relative to the lth line (Byte 72). A typical value is 2.

Byte 68–70   **Reserved**   length: 3 bytes
These bytes are reserved. Set them to nulls (00h).

Byte 71   **Tab Size**   length: 1 byte
This byte contains the number of spaces for a Tab stop. Typically between 5 and 8.

Byte 72–73   **Ith Line**   length: 2 bytes
This word tells which line within the contents of the frame contains the current selection. The First Selected Element (Byte 64), Last Selected Element (Byte 66), and Ith Line describe the current selection. Typically 0.

Byte 74   **Reserved**   length: 1 byte
Set this reserved byte to a null.

Byte 75   **Margins**   length: 1 byte
This byte is typically set to C1h (ASCII 193). This indicates a left and right margin of zero. See the section "Text Representation."

Byte 76   **First Paragraph Left Margin**   length: 1 byte
This is the left margin value for the first paragraph. Framework ignores this value if the value of Byte 75 is C1h.

Byte 77   **First Paragraph Right Margin**   length: 1 byte
This is the right margin value for the first paragraph. Framework ignores this value if the value of Byte 75 is C1h.

Byte 78   **First Paragraph Format**   length: 1 byte
This is the code for the text format of the first paragraph. See the section "Text Representation."

Byte 79   **Reserved**   length: 1 byte
Set this byte equal to 00h.

Byte 80–n   **Frame Contents**   length: n bytes
The contents of this frame is the text of the field contents. If you're creating an empty data base, this section should initially be empty.

Byte n + 1   **Frame Terminator**   length: 1 byte
The Frame Terminator character is the carriage return (0Dh, 13 ASC). Because Framework always begins a new frame on a new paragraph, the program generally pads to the end of the preceding paragraph with nulls (and sometimes with garbage). The carriage return denotes the end of the frame; any further characters are spurious.

dBase View Frame

The dBase View frame contains one FID for every field in the data base. Each FID points to a dBase View Field frame.

Byte 0–1   **Frame Size**   length: 2 bytes
This integer holds the number of paragraphs in the frame.

Byte 2–3   **FID (Frame ID)**   length: 2 bytes
This word uniquely identifies each frame in the file.

Byte 4   **Status Flags**   length: 1 byte
One-byte status flags. See "Status Flags" section.

Byte 5   **Frame Type ID**   length: 1 byte
This byte indicates the type of frame. A dBase View frame type is 11.

Byte 6–7   **Number of Elements**   length: 2 bytes
This integer holds the number of FIDs in the content portion of the frame. There will be one FID for every field in the data base.

Byte 8–9   **Parent FID**   length: 2 bytes
This word holds the frame ID of the parent of this frame.

Byte 10–11 **EXE FID**   length: 2 bytes
This word contains the FID of a frame containing an externally compiled and linked program. Typically, it's null.

Byte 12–13 **Formula Frame ID**   length: 2 bytes
This word holds the FID of any formula that may be attached to this frame. If there is no formula, the value is 0.

Byte 14–16 **Formatting**   length: 3 bytes
These three bytes hold formatting information for the frame. See the "Formats" section.

Byte 17   **Internal Value Type**   length: 1 byte
See the "Value Structures" section.

Byte 18–27 **Value Structures**   length: 10 bytes
See the "Value Structures" section.

Byte 28–29 **Name Frame ID**   length: 2 bytes
This word holds the FID of another frame containing the name of this frame.

Byte 30–31 **Status Flags**   length: 2 bytes
See the "Status Flags" section.

Byte 32–79 **Reserved**   length: 2 bytes
Framework uses these bytes internally. Set these bytes to nulls (00h).

Byte 80–n   **Frame Contents**   length: n bytes
This frame contains one FID for every field in the data base.

Byte n + 1   **Frame Terminator**   length: 1 byte
The Frame Terminator character is the carriage return (0Dh, 13 ASC). Because Framework always begins a new frame on a new paragraph, the program generally pads to the end of the preceding paragraph with nulls.

dBase View Field Frame

There is one dBase View Field frame for every field in the data base. These frames describe the screen position of the field. It is a good idea for every dBase View Field to have a different TLX and TLY, so that all fields are visible.

Byte 0–1   **Frame Size**   length: 2 bytes
This integer holds the number of paragraphs in the frame.

Byte 2–3   **FID (Frame ID)**   length: 2 bytes
This word uniquely identifies each frame in the file.

Byte 4   **Status Flags**   length: 1 byte
One-byte status flags. See "Status Flags" section.

Byte 5   **Frame Type ID**   length: 1 byte
This byte indicates the type of frame. A dBase View Field frame is type 0 (text).

Byte 6–7   **Number of Elements**   length: 2 bytes
This integer holds the number of bytes (characters and escape codes) in the content portion of this frame. When creating an empty Framework data base outside of the Framework program, set these bytes to nulls because the contents portion of the frame is initially empty (no data in the field).

Byte 8–9   **Parent FID**   length: 2 bytes
This word holds the frame ID of the parent of this frame. The parent of the Forms View Field frame is the Data Base Frame.

Byte 10–11   **EXE FID**   length: 2 bytes
This word contains the FID of a frame containing an externally compiled and linked program. Typically, it's null.

Byte 12–13   **Formula Frame ID**   length: 2 bytes
This word holds the FID of any formula that may be attached to this frame. If there is no formula, the value is 0.

Byte 14–16   **Formatting**   length: 3 bytes
These three bytes hold formatting information for the frame. See the "Formats" section.

Byte 17   **Internal Value Type**   length: 1 byte
See the "Value Structures" section.

Byte 18–27   **Value Structures**   length: 10 bytes
See the "Value Structures" section.

Byte 28–29   **Name Frame ID**   length: 2 bytes
This word holds the FID of another frame containing the name of this frame.

Byte 30–31   **Status Flags**   length: 2 bytes
See the "Status Flags" section.

Byte 32–33   **TLX**   length: 2 bytes
This word holds the top left X coordinate of the contents of the frame, excluding the frame border, relative to its parent frame's absolute TLX (ABSTLX). It is 0 based. If this frame has no parent frame, it is "on the desktop," and TLX is relative to the desktop. A typical value for TLX is 1.

Byte 34–35   **TLY**   length: 2 bytes
This word holds the top left Y coordinate of the contents of this frame, excluding the frame border, relative to its parent's absolute TLY (ABSTLY). It is 0 based. If this frame has no parent frame, it is "on the desktop," and TLY is then relative to the desktop. A typical value for TLY is 3.

Byte 36–37   **BRX**   length: 2 bytes
This word holds the bottom right X coordinate of the contents of the frame, excluding the frame border, relative to its parent frame's absolute *TLX* (ABSTLX). It is 0 based. If this frame has no parent frame, it is "on the desktop," and BRX is relative to the desktop. A typical value for BRX is 72.

Byte 38–39   **BRY**   length: 2 bytes
This word holds the bottom right Y coordinate of the contents of this frame, excluding the frame border, relative to its parent's absolute *TLY* (ABSTLY). It is 0 based. If this frame has no parent frame, it is "on the desktop," and BRY is then relative to the desktop. A typical value for BRY is 13.

Byte 40–41   **Clipping TLX**   length: 2 bytes
This word holds the 0-based, absolute, screen X coordinate of the first character position beyond the row numbers. Except when a column is locked, this value is the leftmost character position within the first field. A typical value is 5. See "Clipping TLX" for the Spreadsheet Frame.

Byte 42–43   **Clipping TLY**   length: 2 bytes
This word holds the 0-based, absolute, screen Y coordinate of the topmost visible row, usually row 1. A typical value is 5. See "Clipping TLY" for the Spreadsheet Frame.

Byte 44–45   **Clipping BRX**   length: 2 bytes
This word holds the 0-based, absolute, screen X coordinate of the rightmost character position of the frame's clipping rectangle. Typically, this value is 72.

Byte 46–47   **Clipping BRY**   length: 2 bytes
This word holds the 0-based, absolute, screen Y coordinate of the bottommost row of the frame's clipping rectangle. A typical value is 14.

Byte 48–49   **ABSTLX**   length: 2 bytes
This word holds the 0-based, absolute, screen X coordinate of the first character position beyond the row numbers. Typically, this value is the leftmost character position within column A, and the same as the Clipping TLX.

Byte 50–51   **ABSTLY**   length: 2 bytes
This word holds the 0-based, absolute, screen Y coordinate of the topmost visible row—usually row 1. A typical value is the same as the Clipping TLY.

Byte 52–53   **Scroll X**   length: 2 bytes
This word is a 0 or negative value and describes the portion of the contents of the frame in the horizontal direction that is visible. Its value is typically 0.

Byte 54–55   **Scroll y**   length: 2 bytes
This word is a 0 or negative value and describes the portion of the contents of the frame in the vertical direction that is visible. Its value is typically 0.

Byte 56–59   **Reserved**   length: 4 bytes
These words are reserved by Framework. Set them to nulls (00h).

Byte 60–61   **Style FID**   length: 2 bytes
This word contains the FID of a style frame. These bytes are typically 00h.

Byte 62–63   **Internal Page Number**   length: 2 bytes
Framework uses these bytes internally. Set them to nulls (00h).

Byte 64–65   **First Selected Element**   length: 2 bytes
These bytes contain a 1-based number designating the first selected element relative to the lth line (Byte 72). An element is any displayable character. A typical value is 1.

Byte 66–67   **Last Selected Element**   length: 2 bytes
These bytes contain a 1-based number equal to the last element selected + 1, relative to the lth line (Byte 72). A typical value is 2.

Byte 68–70 **Reserved** length: 3 bytes
These bytes are reserved. Set them to nulls (00h).

Byte 71 **Tab Size** length: 1 byte
This byte contains the number of spaces for a Tab stop. Typically between 5 and 8.

Byte 72–73 **Ith Line** length: 2 bytes
This word tells which line within the contents of the frame contains the current selection. The First Selected Element (Byte 64), Last Selected Element (Byte 66), and Ith Line describe the current selection. Typically 0.

Byte 74 **Reserved** length: 1 byte
Set this reserved byte to a null.

Byte 75 **Margins** length: 1 byte
This byte is typically set to C1h (ASCII 193). This indicates a left and right margin of zero. See the section "Text Representation."

Byte 76 **First Paragraph Left Margin** length: 1 byte
This is the left margin value for the first paragraph. Framework ignores this value if the value of Byte 75 is C1h.

Byte 77 **First Paragraph Right Margin** length: 1 byte
This is the right margin value for the first paragraph. Framework ignores this value if the value of Byte 75 is C1h.

Byte 78 **First Paragraph Format** length: 1 byte
This is the code for the text format of the first paragraph. See the section "Text Representation."

Byte 79 **Reserved** length: 1 byte
Set this byte equal to 00h.

Byte 80–n **Frame Contents** length: n bytes
The contents of this frame is the text of the field contents. If you're creating an empty data base, this section should initially be empty.

Byte n + 1 **Frame Terminator** length: 1 byte
The Frame Terminator character is the carriage return (0Dh, 13 ASC). Because Framework always begins a new frame on a new paragraph, the program generally pads to the end of the preceding paragraph with nulls (and sometimes with garbage). The carriage return denotes the end of the frame; any further characters are spurious.

Composite Frame Organization

The composite frame is very close to the outline frame in organization.

Byte 0–1   **Frame Size**   length: 2 bytes
This integer holds the number of paragraphs in the frame.

Byte 2–3   **FID (Frame ID)**   length: 2 bytes
This word uniquely identifies each frame in the file.

Byte 4   **Status Flags**   length: 1 byte
One-byte status flags. See "Status Flags" section.

Byte 5   **Frame Type ID**   length: 1 byte
This byte indicates the type of frame. A composite frame will be type
10 or 12.

Byte 6–7   **Number of Elements**   length: 2 bytes
This integer holds the number of FIDs (two bytes each) in the
contents area of the frame.

Byte 8–9   **Parent FID**   length: 2 bytes
This word holds the frame ID of the parent of this frame. This word
should be 00h if the frame has no parent and should appear on the
desktop.

Byte 10–11   **EXE FID**   length: 2 bytes
This word will typically be 0. It holds the FID of the frame containing
a DOS file.

Byte 12–13   **Formula Frame ID**   length: 2 bytes
This word holds the FID of any formula that may be attached to this
frame. If there is no formula, the value is 0.

Byte 14–16   **Formatting**   length: 3 bytes
These three bytes hold formatting information for the frame. See
the "Formats" section.

Byte 17   **Internal Value Type**   length: 1 byte
See the "Value Structures" section.

Byte 18–27   **Value Structures**   length: 10 bytes
See the "Value Structures" section.

Byte 28–29   **Name Frame ID**   length: 2 bytes
This word holds the FID of another frame containing the name of
this frame.

Byte 30–31   **Status Flags**   length: 2 bytes
See the "Status Flags" section.

Byte 32–33   **TLX**   length: 2 bytes
This word holds the top left X coordinate of the contents of the

frame, excluding the frame border, relative to its parent frame's absolute TLX (ABSTLX). It is 0 based. If this frame has no parent frame, it is "on the desktop," and TLX is relative to the desktop. A typical value for TLX is 1.

Byte 34–35 **TLY** length: 2 bytes
This word holds the top left Y coordinate of the contents of this frame, excluding the frame border, relative to its parent's absolute TLY (ABSTLY). It is 0 based. If this frame has no parent frame, it is "on the desktop," and TLY is then relative to the desktop. A typical value for TLY is 3.

Byte 36–37 **BRX** length: 2 bytes
This word holds the bottom right X coordinate of the contents of the frame, excluding the frame border, relative to its parent frame's absolute *TLX* (ABSTLX). It is 0 based. If this frame has no parent frame, it is "on the desktop," and BRX is relative to the desktop. A typical value for BRX is 72.

Byte 38–39 **BRY** length: 2 bytes
This word holds the bottom right Y coordinate of the contents of this frame, excluding the frame border, relative to its parent's absolute *TLY* (ABSTLY). It is 0 based. If this frame has no parent frame, it is "on the desktop," and BRY is then relative to the desktop. A typical value for BRY is 13.

Byte 40–41 **Clipping TLX** length: 2 bytes
This word holds the 0-based, absolute, screen X coordinate of the first character position of the frame's clipping rectangle. Typically, this value is the same as TLX.

Byte 42–43 **Clipping TLY** length: 2 bytes
This word holds the 0-based, absolute, screen Y coordinate of the topmost visible row of the frame's clipping rectangle. A typical value is 4.

Byte 44–45 **Clipping BRX** length: 2 bytes
This word holds the 0-based, absolute, screen X coordinate of the rightmost character position of the frame's clipping rectangle. Typically, this value is 72.

Byte 46–47 **Clipping BRY** length: 2 bytes
This word holds the 0-based, absolute, screen Y coordinate of the bottommost row of the frame's clipping rectangle. A typical value is 14.

Byte 48–49 **Zoom ABSTLX** length: 2 bytes
This word holds the 0-based, absolute, screen X coordinate of the first character position of the frame. Typically, this value is the same as the Clipping TLX.

Byte 50–51 **Zoom ABSTLY** length: 2 bytes
This word holds the 0-based, absolute, screen Y coordinate of the topmost row of the frame. A typical value is the same as the Clipping TLY.

Byte 52–53 **Reserved** length: 2 bytes
Initialize these bytes to nulls.

Byte 54–55 **Reserved** length: 2 bytes
Initialize these bytes to nulls.

Byte 56–57 **Last Visible Child** length: 2 bytes
Initialize these bytes to 1.

Byte 58–59 **First Visible Child** length: 2 bytes
Initialize these bytes to nulls.

Byte 60–61 **Style FID** length: 2 bytes
This word contains the FID of a style frame. These bytes are typically 00h.

Byte 62–63 **Internal Page Number** length: 2 bytes
Framework uses these bytes internally. Set them to nulls (00h).

Byte 64–65 **First Selected Element** length: 2 bytes
These bytes contain a 1-based number designating which element in the frame's contents is the first selected element. A typical value is 1.

Byte 66–67 **Last Selected Element** length: 2 bytes
These bytes contain a 1-based number equal to the last element + 1. It designates which element in the frame's contents is the last selected element. A typical value is 2.

Byte 68–73 **Unused** length: 6 bytes
Initialize these bytes to nulls (00h).

Byte 74–79 **Escape Sequence** length: 6 bytes
These six bytes comprise an escape sequence typical of those that begin paragraphs in Framework's text frames (an outline frame is a kind of text frame). The sequence typically contains the six bytes shown in Table 1-5. See also the section on text formatting.

Byte 80–n **Frame Contents** length: n bytes
An outline frame contains an array of the FIDs of its child outline frames. Each FID is a two-byte word. The Number of Elements bytes contain the number of FIDs in the Frame Contents section, counting from 1.

Byte n + 1 **Frame Terminator** length: 1 byte
The Frame Terminator character is the carriage return (0Dh, 13

ASC). Because Framework always begins a new frame on a new paragraph, the program generally pads to the end of the preceding paragraph with nulls (and sometimes with garbage). The carriage return denotes the end of the frame; any further characters are spurious.

Table 1-5	Typical escape sequence	
Byte Number	**Name**	**Typical Value**
74	Pad Begin	00h
75	Pad Ext	81h
76	Left Margin	01h
77	Right Margin	41h
78	First Paragraph Format	81h
79	Pad End Ext	00h

Graph Frame Organization

The contents section of a Framework II graph frame is an extremely device-dependent bit map of the graph. Rather than try to reproduce such a bit map externally, the best way to create a graph frame is to make use of Framework's automatic recalculation capabilities and have Framework create the bit map for you when you load the frame.

To have Framework create the graph for you, you must do three things.

1. You create a formula frame containing a valid Framework graph formula. A graph frame without a formula will not work. Bytes 12 and 13, the Formula FID, must be non-zero and must be the valid FID of a formula frame.

2. You must use an special "undefined" code for the Picture Device Identifier (Bytes 20 and 21). The Picture Device Identifier is the code that tells Framework how to display the bit map in its contents section. Framework supports over 20 display adapters, each with its own bit map. By using the "formally undefined" code of 99 as PDI, you force Framework to recalculate the graph using the adapter specified in FWSETUP and the graph formula in the formula frame.

3. You must leave the contents portion of the frame blank (pad with nulls to the paragraph boundary). Framework will recalculate the graph and create its bit map automatically.

Byte 0–1   **Frame Size**   length: 2 bytes
This integer holds the number of paragraphs in the frame.

Byte 2–3   **FID (Frame ID)**   length: 2 bytes
This word uniquely identifies each frame in the file.

Byte 4 **Status Flags** length: 1 byte
One-byte status flags. See "Status Flags" section.

Byte 5 **Frame Type ID** length: 1 byte
This byte indicates the type of frame. A graph frame will be type 03.

Byte 6–7 **Number of Elements** length: 2 bytes
This integer holds the number of FIDs (two bytes each) in the contents area of the frame.

Byte 8–9 **Parent FID** length: 2 bytes
This word holds the frame ID of the parent of this frame. This word should be 00h if the frame has no parent and should appear on the desktop.

Byte 10–11 **EXE FID** length: 2 bytes
This word will typically be 0. It holds the FID of the frame containing a DOS program.

Byte 12–13 **Formula Frame ID** length: 2 bytes
This word holds the FID of any formula that may be attached to this frame. There must be a Framework graph formula.

Byte 14–16 **Formatting** length: 3 bytes
These three bytes hold formatting information for the frame. See the "Formats" section.

Byte 17 **Internal Value Type** length: 1 byte
See the "Value Structures" section. Framework accepts a null at this location until it actually draws the graph; then the internal value type is 7.

Byte 18–19 **Primitive List FID** length: 2 bytes
This word contains the FID of the graph's primitive list information. Framework creates its own list of graphic primitives and places it in a frame when it draws the graph. When you're creating a Framework file externally to Framework, you may specify a null for this FID. Framework will fill in the correct FID after it draws the graph.

Byte 20–21 **Picture Device Identifier** length: 2 bytes
This word holds the code of the display adapter, which works with the bit map contents of the frame. Set this word to 99 (63h) for "undefined." A null will also work at this location until Framework draws the graph. After the program draws the graph, this location will have the code for the graphic adapter specified in the FWSETUP file.

Byte 22–27 **Reserved** length: 6 bytes
Initialize these bytes to nulls (00h).

Byte 28–29 **Name Frame ID** length: 2 bytes
This word holds the FID of another frame containing the name of this frame.

Byte 30–31　　　**Status Flags**　　　　　　　　　length: 2 bytes
　　　　　　　　　　See the "Status Flags" section.

Byte 32–33　　　**TLX**　　　　　　　　　　　　length: 2 bytes
　　　　　　　　　　This word holds the top left X coordinate of the contents of the frame, excluding the frame border, relative to its parent frame's absolute TLX (ABSTLX). It is 0 based. If this frame has no parent frame, it is "on the desktop," and TLX is relative to the desktop. A typical value for TLX is 1.

Byte 34–35　　　**TLY**　　　　　　　　　　　　length: 2 bytes
　　　　　　　　　　This word holds the top left Y coordinate of the contents of this frame, excluding the frame border, relative to its parent's absolute TLY (ABSTLY). It is 0 based. If this frame has no parent frame, it is "on the desktop," and TLY is then relative to the desktop. A typical value for TLY is 3.

Byte 36–37　　　**BRX**　　　　　　　　　　　　length: 2 bytes
　　　　　　　　　　This word holds the bottom right X coordinate of the contents of the frame, excluding the frame border, relative to its parent frame's absolute *TLX* (ABSTLX). It is 0 based. If this frame has no parent frame, it is "on the desktop," and BRX is relative to the desktop. A typical value for BRX is 72.

Byte 38–39　　　**BRY**　　　　　　　　　　　　length: 2 bytes
　　　　　　　　　　This word holds the bottom right Y coordinate of the contents of this frame, excluding the frame border, relative to its parent's absolute *TLY* (ABSTLY). It is 0 based. If this frame has no parent frame, it is "on the desktop," and BRY is then relative to the desktop. A typical value for BRY is 13.

Byte 40–41　　　**Clipping TLX**　　　　　　　　length: 2 bytes
　　　　　　　　　　This word holds the 0-based, absolute, screen X coordinate of the first character position of the frame's clipping rectangle. Typically, this value is the same as TLX.

Byte 42–43　　　**Clipping TLY**　　　　　　　　length: 2 bytes
　　　　　　　　　　This word holds the 0-based, absolute, screen Y coordinate of the topmost visible row of the frame's clipping rectangle. A typical value is 4.

Byte 44–45　　　**Clipping BRX**　　　　　　　　length: 2 bytes
　　　　　　　　　　This word holds the 0-based, absolute, screen X coordinate of the rightmost character position of the frame's clipping rectangle. Typically, this value is 72.

Byte 46–47　　　**Clipping BRY**　　　　　　　　length: 2 bytes
　　　　　　　　　　This word holds the 0-based, absolute, screen Y coordinate of the bottommost row of the frame's clipping rectangle. A typical value is 14.

Byte 48–49   **Zoom ABSTLX**   length: 2 bytes
This word holds the 0-based, absolute, screen X coordinate of the first character position of the frame. Typically, this value is the same as the Clipping TLX.

Byte 50–51   **Zoom ABSTLY**   length: 2 bytes
This word holds the 0-based, absolute, screen Y coordinate of the topmost row of the frame. A typical value is the same as the Clipping TLY.

Byte 52–53   **ScrollX**   length: 2 bytes
Initialize these bytes to nulls.

Byte 54–55   **ScrollY**   length: 2 bytes
Initialize these bytes to nulls.

Byte 56–57   **Last Visible Child**   length: 2 bytes
Initialize these bytes to 00h.

Byte 58–59   **First Visible Child**   length: 2 bytes
Initialize these bytes to nulls (00h).

Byte 60–61   **Style FID**   length: 2 bytes
This word contains the FID of a style frame. These bytes are typically 00h.

Byte 62–63   **Internal Page Number**   length: 2 bytes
Framework uses these bytes internally. Set them to nulls (00h).

Byte 64–65   **First Selected Element**   length: 2 bytes
These bytes contain a 1-based number designating which element in the frame's contents is the first selected element. A typical value is 1.

Byte 66–67   **Last Selected Element**   length: 2 bytes
These bytes contain a 1-based number equal to the last element + 1. It designates which element in the frame's contents is the last selected element. A typical value is 2.

Byte 68–73   **Unused**   length: 6 bytes
Initialize these bytes to nulls (00h).

Byte 74–79   **Escape Sequence**   length: 6 bytes
These six bytes comprise an escape sequence typical of those that begin paragraphs in Framework's text frames (an outline frame is a kind of text frame). The sequence typically contains the six bytes shown in Table 1-5. See also the section on text formatting.

Byte 80–n   **Frame Contents**   length: n bytes
The contents of the graph frame is a bit map dependent on the type of display adapter installed at the time the graph frame was created.

To get around having to create a bit map (or worse, many different bit maps) the frame contents of a graph frame should be nulls.

Byte n + 1 **Frame Terminator** length: 1 byte
The Frame Terminator character is the carriage return (0Dh, 13 ASC). Pad to the end of the paragraph with nulls.

EXE Frame Organization

The capabilities of the EXE frame are particularly powerful—and not documented in the Framework user's guide.

You can use the EXE frame to contain assembly language programs (or programs externally compiled and linked down to assembly language). The ability to run assembly routines from inside Framework II gives a programmer enormous control and speed. For example, routines can insert or extract characters from Framework frames, invoke other assembly routines, create a custom desktop, and perform many other tasks.

The general procedure for using assembly routines with Framework is to create a frame with a FRED program in it. The FRED program uses the undocumented command @EXEC. Its parameters are the assembly program's name and entry point. Then load the assembly program from disk to the desktop as you would any Framework file. Framework loads the assembly program into the EXE frame format described here.

For more information on working with assembly language routines, see *Framework II Developer's Toolkit*, from Ashton-Tate.

Byte 0–1 **Frame Size** length: 2 bytes
This integer holds the number of paragraphs in the frame.

Byte 2–3 **FID (Frame ID)** length: 2 bytes
This word uniquely identifies each frame in the file.

Byte 4 **Status Flags** length: 1 byte
One-byte status flags. See "Status Flags" section.

Byte 5 **Frame Type ID** length: 1 byte
This byte indicates the type of frame. An EXE frame is type 16 (0Fh).

Byte 6–7 **Number of Elements** length: 2 bytes
This integer holds the number of bytes in the contents area of the frame.

Byte 8–9 **Stack Segment Paragraph Bias** length: 2 bytes

Byte 10–11 **Stack Pointer Initialize Value** length: 2 bytes

Byte 12–13 **Code Segment Paragraph Bias** length: 2 bytes

Byte 14–15 **Instruction Pointer Initialize Value** length: 2 bytes

Byte 16–n   **Frame Contents**   length: n bytes
The contents of an EXE frame is an assembly language program
(or a program in a higher-level language compiled and linked to assembly language).

It must be executable code.

It cannot have any segment fixups.

The first four bytes must be nulls. Framework "plugs in" the address
of its service routine transfer vector.

For more detailed information see *Framework II Developer's
Toolkit*, from Ashton-Tate.

Formula Frame Organization

A formula frame holds a formula for a spreadsheet cell or a FRED program.

Byte 0–1   **Frame Size**   length: 2 bytes
This integer holds the number of paragraphs in the frame.

Byte 2–3   **FID (Frame ID)**   length: 2 bytes
This word uniquely identifies each frame in the file.

Byte 4   **Status Flags**   length: 1 byte
One-byte status flags. See "Status Flags" section.

Byte 5   **Frame Type ID**   length: 1 byte
This byte indicates the type of frame. A formula frame is type 04h.

Byte 6–7   **Number of Elements**   length: 2 bytes
This integer holds the number of bytes in the contents area of the
frame.

Byte 8–9   **Reserved**   length: 2 bytes
Initialize these bytes to nulls (00h).

Byte 10–n   **Frame Contents**   length: n bytes
The content portion of this frame contains text. That text is a
formula.

Byte n + 1   **Frame Terminator**   length: 1 byte
A carriage return character terminates the frame.

Buffer Frame Organization

Byte 0–1 | **Frame Size** | length: 2 bytes
This integer holds the number of paragraphs in the frame.

Byte 2–3 | **FID (Frame ID)** | length: 2 bytes
This word uniquely identifies each frame in the file.

Byte 4 | **Status Flags** | length: 1 byte
One-byte status flags. See "Status Flags" section.

Byte 5 | **Frame Type ID** | length: 1 byte
This byte indicates the type of frame. A buffer frame is type 06h.

Byte 6–7 | **Number of Elements** | length: 2 bytes
This integer holds the number of bytes in the contents area of the frame.

Byte 8–n | **Frame Contents** | length: n bytes
The content portion of this frame contains text. That text is a formula.

Byte n + 1 | **Frame Terminator** | length: 1 byte
A carriage return character terminates the frame.

Label/Edit Frame Organization

Framework II uses the label/edit frame (type 04h) for several purposes such as holding the name of another frame. It's primarily a simplified text frame; simplified, because other frames use it—it never appears on screen.

Byte 0–1 | **Frame Size** | length: 2 bytes
This integer holds the number of paragraphs in the frame.

Byte 2–3 | **FID (Frame ID)** | length: 2 bytes
This word uniquely identifies each frame in the file.

Byte 4 | **Status Flags** | length: 1 byte
One byte status flags. See "Status Flags" section.

Byte 5 | **Frame Type ID** | length: 1 byte
This byte indicates the type of frame. A label/edit frame is type 04h.

Byte 6–7 | **Number of Elements** | length: 2 bytes
This integer holds the number of bytes in the contents area of the frame.

Byte 8–9 **Parent FID** length: 2 bytes
This word holds the FID of the parent of the label/edit frame. This frame should not appear on the desktop; there should be a legal FID here.

Byte 10–n **Frame Contents** length: n bytes
The content portion of this frame contains text. That text may be a formula that is attached to another frame, or the name of another frame.

Byte n + 1 **Frame Terminator** length: 1 byte

A carriage return character terminates the frame.

Text Representation in Framework

Many of Framework II's frames store text. Even a spreadsheet cell frame stores as text the value each cell displays. In Framework, wherever text goes, formatting for that text can follow.

Terms and Definitions

Framework II stores all text characters, other than **extended characters,** as ASCII values in single bytes. Extended characters comprise multiple bytes and include hard ends-of-lines, text attribute escape strings, page breaks, soft hyphens, and so forth.

Table 1-6 shows how Framework organizes the escape sequence for an extended character.

Table 1-6	Order of an extended character
Byte	**Contents**
0	leading zero byte (null)
1	type-information byte (non-zero)
2–n	variable-length information bytes (non-zero)
n+1	trailing zero byte (null)

Zero (null) can occur in text *only* at the beginning and at the end of an extended character. It always delimits such an extended character.

Important No routine that places text in a frame should insert a zero (null) character or the hex characters FE or FF in running text. These are characters of special significance in Framework.

The type-information byte contains the type number of the extended character and uses its upper two bits to describe the contents of the character. When set, these upper two bits indicate that the first or second byte of the word should really be zero. Framework uses this approach because zero is a special value.

Even though these bits override whatever non-zero value is stored in the extended character, the actual bytes must still be present and must still be non-zero, for some routines used by Framework assume a fixed length for a given type of extended character. When scanning a Framework file, though, it's a good idea to scan for the extended character rather than to assume a fixed length. Ashton-Tate advises that some items, such as page breaks, may change in the future.

Table 1-7 shows the type-information byte.

Table 1-7	The type-information byte
Bit	**Meaning**
7	first byte following the type byte is really a zero
6	second byte following the type byte is really a zero
0–5	type number (1 to 63)

Table 1-8 lists the extended character type numbers that are defined.

Table 1-8	Extended character type number
Value	**Meaning**
01	hard EOL with paragraph attributes
02	hard EOL with no attribute*
03	hard page break with page number
04	soft page break with page number
05	attribute change—short (1 byte)
06	attribute change—long(2 bytes)*
07	soft hyphen
08	text marker (1 byte marker number)

*Framework II does not currently use these codes.

Hard End-of-Line (EOL)

A hard EOL (end-of-line) with paragraph attributes always *precedes* every new paragraph containing text. (Framework II uses the hard EOL with no attributes for line spacing between paragraphs. It carries no attributes because there is no text in the paragraph it's defining.)

The first paragraph in a text frame has a hard EOL as part of the frame header. Framework's own service routines (Words menu) can't access the attributes of this "built-in" hard EOL.

Table 1-9 describes the six bytes of a hard EOL with paragraph attributes.

Table 1-9	Hard EOL with paragraph attributes
Byte	**Values**
first	leading 0 (the zero byte)
second	hard EOL type (01)
third	left margin (0 encoded with bit 7 of type byte)
fourth	right margin (0 encoded with bit 6 of type byte)
fifth	lower two bits: paragraph type
	0: flush right
	1: align left
	2: justified
	3: centered
	upper six bits: signed paragraph indent (+30 to −30)
	(0 encoded as −0 or 80h)
sixth	trailing zero byte

Table 1-10 describes a hard EOL with no paragraph attributes. Blank paragraphs use this type of EOL.

Table 1-10	Hard EOL with no paragraph attributes
Byte	**Values**
first	leading 0 (the zero byte)
second	hard EOL type (02)
third	trailing zero byte

Changing Attributes

Framework II uses an escape sequence to indicate a change in attribute. An attribute change can occur anywhere in text. When a zero occurs within an attribute, the bits of the type-byte must encode it so that it becomes non-zero.

Framework assumes that a normal text attribute follows any hard EOL at the beginning of a frame. If many paragraphs have a non-normal attribute, each paragraph must have an attribute escape string following the hard EOL.

> **Note**   The definition of normal, nonattributed text is the
absence of any set attribute bit.

Table 1-11 describes Framework's short attribute.

Table 1-11	Short attribute

Byte	Values
first	0 (leading zero)
second	short attribute type 05 (85 if next byte is 00 and 7th bit set)
third	attribute byte
	bit 0: bold if 1
	bit 1: italics if 1
	bit 2: underlined if 1
	bit 3: inverted if 1
	bit 4: reserved
	bit 5: reserved
	bit 6: reserved
	bit 7: reserved
fourth	0 (trailing zero)

Framework also defines a long attribute string that includes color information. Framework II does not use the long attribute.

Table 1-12	Long attribute

Byte	Values
first	0 (leading zero)
second	short attribute type 05 (85 if next byte is 00 and 7th bit set)
third	attribute byte
	bit 0: bold if 1
	bit 1: italics if 1
	bit 2: underlined if 1
	bit 3: inverted if 1
	bit 4: reserved
	bit 5: reserved
	bit 6: reserved
	bit 7: reserved
fourth	color information
fifth	0 (trailing zero)

Soft Hyphens

Framework II skips over an embedded soft hyphen except when it occurs as the last character in a line *and* is preceded by an alphanumeric character. In that case, Framework displays and prints the soft hyphen as a normal hyphen character (-). Text-wrapping code recognizes the soft hyphen as a legal word delimiter and will wrap a word fraction that contains a soft hyphen.

Spaces

Framework considers spaces entered into text by the user to be **hard spaces.** The character code for a hard space is the ASCII space code, 20h. Occasionally, the word-wrapping code for Framework will add a **soft space.** The code for a soft space is FFh.

The third type of space Framework supports is the **non-breaking space.** Framework displays and prints a non-breaking space as a normal space character, but the program code sees it as a nonspace character.

Framework uses nonbreaking space characters to separate different parts of dates, first and last names, or any other place that the user would like to keep two words from being broken to two different lines by the word-wrapping code. The nonbreaking space is ASCII 254 (FEh).

Delimiters

Text display and formatting follows these rules:

- End-of-line delimiters are soft EOL, hard EOL, soft page break, hard page break, and end of frame.
- End-of-paragraph delimiters are hard EOL, hard page break, and end of frame.
- End of page delimiters are soft and hard page breaks.

Framework always displays a hard page break as a separate line. It displays a soft page break as a separate line only if the Frame:View Pagination option is *on* for the frame. Page breaks are *not* counted as separate lines for printing purposes.

Illegal Characters

Table 1-13 shows a list of characters that Framework II cannot display in the IBM character set.

Table 1-13	Illegal display characters	
Hex	**Name**	**Use**
0Dh	CR	soft EOL
09h	Tab	tab
00h	ASCII null	text item escape character
FEh		nonbreaking space
FF		soft space

Note Routines that write Framework files should not casually insert 00h, FEh, or FFh into a frame.

Page Breaks

The page break information that Framework saves in the frame reflects the state of the document the last time that it performed the Frames:View Pagination command. The saved frame does not show the pagination changes that any subsequent editing of the document produces until Frames:View Pagination calculates the pagination again.

The user can select hard and soft page breaks in order to copy them. Thus, a document may appear to have missing or duplicate page numbers unless Framework performs a Frames:View Pagination immediately before it analyzes the text.

A hard page break (one that the user has entered via the Edit:Begin New Page command) comprises the five bytes in Table 1-14.

Table 1-14	Extended character for hard page break
Byte	**Values**
first	leading 0 (the zero byte)
second	hard page break (type 03)
third	low byte of page number (type byte encodes a page 0)
fourth	high byte of page number
fifth	trailing 0

Note A page number of zero indicates that Framework has not calculated page numbers since the user created this hard page break.

Table 1-15 shows the five bytes that describe a soft page break (generated by the Frames:View Pagination command).

Table 1-15	Extended character for soft page break
Byte	**Values**
first	leading 0 (the zero byte)
second	soft page break (type 04)
third	low byte of page number (type byte encodes a page 0)
fourth	high byte of page number
fifth	trailing 0

Status Flags

These tables provide bit maps for three status locations. Table 1-16 is the content status byte (usually at Byte 4 in a frame). Table 1-17 is the frame status word at Bytes 30 and 31. Table 1-18 is the SS Bits status byte used for spreadsheets.

Table 1-16	Content status (Byte 4)
Bit	**Description**
0	internal flag (set to 0)
1	internal flag (set to 0)
2	internal flag (set to 0)
3	internal flag (set to 0)
4	internal flag (set to 0)
5	frame editing protection (1 if frame is protected)
6	formula constant (1 if formula for frame is a constant)
7	not used

Table 1-17	Frame status (Bytes 30 and 31)
Bit	**Description**
0	visible border (1 if frame border is visible)
1	internal flag (set to 0)
2	visible frame nametabs (1 if nametabs visible)
3	frame nametabs (1 if nametabs displayed on left, 0 if on right)
4	not used
5	not used

(Table Continued)

Table 1-17 (Continued)

Bit	Description
6	show frame type on nametab (1 to show type—G, E, W, C, D...)
7	not used
8	outline mode page numbers (1 if page numbers show)
9	internal flag (set to 0)
10	not used
11	not used
12	Roman numerals if numbering on (1 for Roman numerals)
13	number frames (1 to number the frames)
14	outline mode (1 if the frame is in outline mode)
15	internal flag (set to 0)

Table 1-18	SS Bits (Byte 75)

Bit	Description
0	recalc order (0 row-wise, 1 natural)
1	recalc type (0 automatic, 1 manual)
2	title lock (0 off, 1 on)
3	DB flag (0 spreadsheet, 1 data base)
4	reserved
5	reserved
6	reserved
7	reserved

Format Words

These tables describe the format words used by the spreadsheet and data base frames. Table 1-19 is the first two bytes of the three-byte format field. Table 1-20 is the third byte.

Table 1-19	Format word, global for spreadsheet, local for cell (Bytes 14 and 15)

Bit	Description
0	1 is global (spreadsheet level)
1–6	number of decimal places user sets in numbers menu
7	protection (0 off, 1 on)
8–10	number format
	0: general
	1: decimal
	2: currency

(Table Continued)

Table 1-19 (Continued)

Bit	Description
	3: business
	4: scientific
	5: percent
	6: integer
	7: not used
11	local alignment set
	1: local alignment is set
	0: local alignment not set
12	local numeric format (applies to cell frames only)
	1: local numeric format set
	0: local numeric format not set
13	local number of decimal places
	1: local number of decimal places set
	0: local number of decimal places not set
14–15	alignment
	0: general
	1: left
	2: center
	3: right

Table 1-20	Third byte of 3-byte frame format information

Bit	Description
0–3	number of decimal places that the user has typed in;
	example: user types 1.0000; four decimal places stored
4	cell underline (used only in cell frames)
	0: cell not underlined
	1: cell underlined
5–7	simple constant format specification;
	example: user types in 1.0000; 1 is stored;
	user types in 1E12 and 4 is stored

Value Structures

Word, outline, composite, and value cell frames incorporate a 10-byte value structure preceded by a single-byte internal value type ID. The internal value type ID and the value structure represent the kind of value stored in the contents section of the frame.

The values of different value type IDs take up different amounts of the 10-byte structure. Table 1-21 lists the type of value, its type ID, and the number of bytes it uses in the value structure.

Table 1-21	Internal value types		
Name		**Type ID**	**#Bytes Used**
string		0	0
Framework constant		1	2
date		2	8
integer		3	2
BCD number		5	10
graph		7	

String Values

String values do not fill in any part of the value structure except the type. The actual string is in the content portion of the frame. The number of bytes in the string (including attributes) is in the Number of Elements field at bytes 6 and 7.

Framework Constant

Framework uses 14 different constants. The first word (two bytes) of the 10-byte value structure contains the numerical equivalent of the constant. Table 1-22 lists the constants and their equivalents.

Table 1-22	Framework constants and their equivalents		
Constant	**Equivalent**	**Constant**	**Equivalent**
NA_ERR	0	TBD_ERR	7
VALUE_ERR	1	FALSE_VAL	8
DIV0_ERR	2	NO_VAL	9
NUM_ERR	3	TRUE_VAL	10
REF_ERR	4	YES_VAL	11
NAME_ERR	5	OFF_VAL	26
NULL_ERR	6	ON_VAL	27

Integer Values

When the internal value type ID is 3 (integer) the first 2 bytes of the 10-byte value structure contain a two's complement representation of a numeric value between −32768 and +32767—a standard 8086 integer.

Binary-Coded Decimal Number Value

Framework uses all five words of the value structure for a BCD number. The program stores it as an IEEE standard (8087) Packed Decimal number—with one difference. Framework uses the unused 7 bits in the sign byte as an exponent (with a +64 bias). The decimal place is assumed as being to the right of the least significant digit.

Framework makes no attempt to keep the value normalized to any representation. This implies that comparisons must normalize on the exponent values before performing the actual comparison. Table 1-23 shows the organization of the BCD over the 10 bits of the value structure.

Table 1-23	Organization of BCD number over the 10 bits of the value structure		
Byte	**Contents**	**Byte**	**Contents**
0	d1|d0	5	d11|d10
1	d3|d2	6	d13|d12
2	d5|d4	7	d15|d14
3	d7|d6	8	d17|d16
4	d9|d8	9	s|x

where:

d# represents the 18-digit floating-point number
s is the sign bit
x is a 7-bit exponent.

Note   The "x" field is not used by the 8087. In the specifications, it is defined as 0.

Date Values

Framework uses the first eight bytes of the value structure to store a date value. Table 1-24 lists the bytes and their contents.

Table 1-24	Organization of Framework date structure		
Byte	**Contents**	**Byte**	**Contents**
0–1	year	5	minute
2	month	6	second
3	day	7	1/100 seconds
4	hour		

Note	Framework stores the number of the year low byte/high byte. For example, it would store the year 1986:

byte. For example, it would store the year 1986:

Byte 0: C2h
Byte 1: 07h

Full Frame Structures

Table 1-25 provides a comparative chart of Framework's major frame types. Variant types are listed in Tables 1-26 and 1-27.

Table 1-25	Framework's major frames				
Offset	**Spreadsheet**	**Word**	**Outline**	**Graph**	**DB Forms**
00	paragraph cnt	paragraph cnt	paragraph cnt	paragraph cnt	paragraph cnt
02	FID	FID	FID	FID	FID
04	frame status	frame status	frame status	frame status	frame status
05	frame type (14)	frame type (00)	frame type (11)	frame type (03)	frame type (11)
06	# elements	# elements	# elements	# elements	# elements
08	parent FID	parent FID	parent FID	parent FID	parent FID
0A	col vector FID	EXE FID	EXE FID	EXE FID	reserved
0C	formula FID	formula FID	formula FID	formula FID	reserved
0E	2-byte format	2-byte format	2-byte format	2-byte format	reserved
10	1-byte format	1-byte format	1-byte format	1-byte format	reserved
11	int.value type	int.value type	int.value type	int.value type (7)	reserved
12	internal values	internal values	internal values	primitives FID	reserved
14				picture device	reserved
16				reserved	reserved
18				reserved	reserved
1A			reserved	reserved	
1C	name FID	name FID	name FID	name FID	reserved
1E	status flags	status flags	status flags	status flags	status flags
20	TLX	TLX	TLX	TLX	TLX
22	TLY	TLY	TLY	TLY	TLY
24	BRX	BRX	BRX	BRX	BRX
26	BRY	BRY	BRY	BRY	BRY
28	clip TLX	clip TLX	clip TLX	clip TLX	clip TLX
2A	clip TLY	clip TLY	clip TLY	clip TLY	clip TLY
2C	clip BRX	clip BRX	clip BRX	clip BRX	clip BRX
2E	clip BRY	clip BRY	clip BRY	clip BRY	clip BRY
30	ABS TLX	ABS TLX	ABS TLX	ABS TLX	ABS TLX
32	ABS TLY	ABS TLY	ABS TLY	ABS TLY	ABS TLY
34	1st vis col	scroll x	reserved	scroll x	reserved
36	last vis col	scroll y	reserved	scroll y	reserved

(Table Continued)

Table 1-25 (Continued)

Offset	Spreadsheet	Word	Outline	Graph	DB Forms
38	last vis row	reserved	1st vis child	1st vis child	num open recs
3A	1st vis row	reserved	reserved	last vis child	reserved
3C	style FID	style FID	style FID	style FID	reserved
3E	pagenum	pagenum	pagenum	pagenum	reserved
40	1st sel row	1st sel elem	1 sel elem	reserved	1st sel elem
42	last sel row	last sel elem	last sel elem	reserved	last sel elem
44	1st sel col	reserved	reserved	reserved	0
45		reserved	reserved	reserved	
46	last sel col	reserved	reserved	reserved	0
47		tab	reserved	reserved	
48	wind last col	lth line	reserved	reserved	reserved
4A	delta 1st vis col	pad begin	pag begin	reserved	reserved
4B	ss bits	pad type	pad type	reserved	reserved
4C	wind last row	1st para lm	1st para lm	reserved	reserved
4D		1st para rm	1st para rm	reserved	reserved
4E	reserved	1st para fmt	1st para fmt	reserved	reserved
4F	reserved	pad end	pad end	reserved	reserved
50	contents	contents	contents	contents	contents

Table 1-26	Variant frame structures			

Offset	Value Cell	Label Cell	EXE	Column Vector
00	paragraph cnt	paragraph cnt	paragraph cnt	paragraph cnt
02	FID	FID	FID	FID
04	frame status	frame status	frame status	frame status
05	frame type (8	frame type (7)	frame type (16)	frame type (4)
06	# elements	# elements	# elements	# elements
08	parent FID	parent FID	ss para bias	db forms FID
0A	0	0	sp init	contents
0C	formula FID	formula FID	cs para bias	
0E	2-byte format	2-byte format	ip init	
10	1-byte format	1-byte format	exe map	
11	int.value type	int.value type		
12	internal values	label map		
14				
16				
18				
1A				
1C	cell map			

Table 1-27	Variant frame structures			
Offset	**Row**	**Label/Edit**	**Formula**	**Buffer**
00	paragraph cnt	paragraph cnt	paragraph cnt	paragraph cnt
02	FID	FID	FID	FID
04	frame status	frame status	frame status	frame status
05	frame type (3)	frame type (4)	frame type (4)	frame type (6)
06	# elements	# elements	# elements	# elements
08	parent FID	parent FID	reserved	parent FID
0A	row map	edit map	edit map	contents

## CHAPTER 2

Reflex

Versions 1.0 and 1.1

Borland International
4585 Scotts Valley Dr.
Scotts Valley, CA 95066

Type of Product: Data base management.

Files Produced: Mixed binary and ASCII strings.

Points of Interest:

A Reflex file generated by the program can have several more parts than you need to create if you're writing a Reflex-formatted file externally to the program.

Figuring offset values in Reflex can be tricky because they are inconsistently calculated. Most often they begin with 0, occasionally with 1. They vary, however, in the byte from which they are calculated, sometimes including the offset index itself, sometimes not. The file format text calls out these variations where they were discovered.

Reflex Data Base Structure

Reflex is a RAM-based data base manager which produces a single DOS data file with the extension **.RXD**. The program may create other files with other filename extensions to hold report and graph definitions, for example.

The .RXD file contains a fixed-length, 512-byte header block, followed by a variable number of variable-length data sections. Borland advises that the order of sections is unimportant and may not remain the same in future versions.

Important
See the sample PEOPLE.RXD file in the Appendix B "Sample File Contents" for a glossed, byte-by-byte explanation of one of the files supplied by Borland with the Reflex data base manager.

The File Header

Because the file header is of fixed length, each element of the header is at a particular offset location from the start of the file (byte 0). Figure 2-1 shows the C-language definition of a Reflex file header.

```
typedef struct {
/* data file section descriptor */
      int   dfType;              /* section type code */
      long  dfAddr;              /* start address in file (bytes) */
      long  dfLen;               /* length (bytes) */
      } DFDESC;

typedef struct {
/* header structure */
      int   hdrsize;             /* headersize = 512 */
      char  stamp[12];           /* ID string */
      int   dirty;               /* >0 means corrupt file */
      int   verViews;            /* view info version */
      int   verModels;           /* model info version */
      int   verData;             /* raw data version */
      int   rRecalc              /* >0 means must recalc */
      char  screenType;          /* screen type at creation */
      char  checkSum;            /* file checksum */
      char  reserved[38];        /* reserved = 0 (nulls) */
      int   sectionCt;           /* number of sections */
      DFDESC  dfSection[];       /* section descriptors */
      } DFHDR;
```

Figure 2-1 C-language definition of a Reflex file header.

Note   Reflex uses these standard C definitions in its structures:

- **char:** 8-bit word (one byte)
- **int:** signed 16-bit word (two bytes, lsb first)
- **unsigned:** unsigned 16-bit word (two bytes, lsb first)
- **long:** signed 32-bit double word (four bytes)
- **HANDLE:** 32-bit long pointer (offset, segment pair)

Header Contents

Byte 0–1   **Header Size**   length: 2 bytes
This location holds the constant 512 (200h).

Byte 2–13   **ID String**   length: 12 bytes
The ID string is a constant that lets you identify different versions of Reflex. A null terminates each of the strings. The characters *[S]* denote the space character (ASCII 32, 20h), and the characters *[null]* denote a null (ASCII 0, 00h).

Version	ID String
1.0, 1.1	3Q.!&*[S]*$!&&*[null]*
1.14	3Q.!&@#$!&&*[null]*

Byte 14–15   **Dirty File**   length:2 bytes
A non-zero value implies a corrupted file.

Note   The next three integers—view info version level, modeling system version level, and raw data version level—provide a cascading level of precedence for detecting file corruption. If the raw data version level is incorrect, you can assume that the modeling system and view info version levels are also corrupted. If modeling changes, you can assume that view info is corrupted.

Byte 16–17   **View Info Version Level**   length: 2 bytes
For Reflex version 1.0, 1.1, and 1.14, contents must be 7 (07 00h).

Byte 18–19   **Modeling System Version Level**   length: 2 bytes
For Reflex version 1.0, 1.1, and 1.14 contents must be 4 (04 00h).

Byte 20–21   **Raw Data Version Level**   length: 2 bytes
For Reflex version 1.0 contents must be 3 (03 00h).

For Reflex version 1.1 and 1.14, with up to and including 128 fields per record, the contents must be 3 (03 00h).

For Reflex version 1.1 and 1.14, with 129 or more fields per record, the contents must be 4 (04 00h).

Byte 22–23   **Forced Recalc**   length: 2 bytes
Normally, this integer contains two nulls. Any non-zero value forces Reflex to do a total recalculation when it loads the file. When the merge facility creates the file, this value is automatically set to nulls.

Byte 24   **Screen Type**   length: 1 byte
This location shows the screen type that was active when the file was last written. The value affects only view information. Table 2-1 lists the screen types and their codes.

Reflex 1.0 supports IBM CGA and Hercules Monochrome Graphics only; releases 1.1 and 1.14 support additional graphics devices and set the appropriate type automatically.

Table 2-1	Screen type display codes

Code	Display
0	IBM Color Graphics Adapter (640x200)
1	Hercules Monochrome Graphics
2	IBM 3270 PC APA
3	IBM Enhanced Graphics Adapter (640x350)
4	IBM Professional Graphics Adapter
5	AT&T 6300, 6300 Plus (640x400)
6	Sigma 400
7	STB SuperRes 400

Byte 25   **Checksum**   length: 1 byte
Reflex sets the checksum value to make the byte checksum of the entire file equal to 107 (6Bh).

Byte 26–63   **Reserved**   length: 38 bytes
The reserved bytes must be nulls (00h).

Byte 64–65   **Section Count**   length: 2 bytes
The section count holds the number of data sections in the file. The count begins with 1, not 0.

Data Sections

Data sections provide Reflex with a map of the .RXD file. They tell the type of section, its starting position in the file, and its length. Data section descriptions begin immediately after the section count. There is one description for each data section.

Each data section description has three parts:

- Type code—a two-byte integer
- Start position (byte number in the file)—a long pointer
- Length of section—a long pointer

There can be as many as 12 sections. Reflex requires the three basic data sections; the others are optional. The order of the data section descriptions is "unimportant" according to Borland (although the program produces them in the order listed here).

Table 2-2 lists the 12 section types and their codes.

Table 2-2	Section types				
Code	**Section Type**		**Code**	**Section Type**	
Basic Data Types			View Types		
2	Field Directory		5	View Manager State	
9	Data Base Master Record		24	View Manager Scaling	
1	Data Records		12	Form View	
			13	List View	
Modeling Types			14	Crosstab View	
17	Global Filter				
11	Global Models				
21	Global Model Override Vectors				

Twelve data section descriptors start at Byte 66 of the header and extend up to and include Byte 185.

Note Reflex treats a section with length 0 as though it did not exist.

Unused Header Area

Reflex maintains an unused area of the header from the end of the data section descriptors through and including Byte 511. The unused bytes must be nulls (00h).

The Field Directory

The field directory contains four elements: a global sort specification, a map to a pool of field name labels, the pool itself, and a set of information on each field's data type, format, and sort order. Because of the variable number of fields a data base may have and the variably sized labels that identify each field, it's not possible to supply absolute byte offsets for the remaining information in the Reflex file.

Reflex numbers fields from 0 through 249. This is the field ID. The first field has an ID of 0. The maximum FID is 127 for Reflex release 1.0, and 249 for release 1.1 and 1.14.

Global Sort Specification

The first 12 bytes of the field directory section make up the global sort specification. A sort specification is an array of up to five sort-field specs and a sort-spec terminator. The terminator is the value 255 (FFh). Figure 2-2 shows the C declaration for the Global sort spec.

```
typedef struct {                              /* field sort spec */
        unsigned  isAscending     : 1;        /* TRUE if ascending */
        unsigned  fldType         : 7;        /* used internally */
        char  fieldID;                        /* field ID number */
```

Figure 2-2 Global sort declarations

The fieldID is a number between 0 and 249 that Reflex uses as an index to the field directory table (see below). FieldIDs greater than 249 are reserved.

Field Directory Table

Immediately following the global sort specification is the field directory table. Its total length depends on the number of fields in the data base. The field directory table includes four members in the following order:

- **An integer index** to the first byte of the field name pool calculated from the byte *following* the two index bytes, and beginning its count with 1 (not 0). If the index integer to the first byte of the pool were at Bytes 524 and 525, and if its value were 12 (0C 00h), the first byte of the field name pool would begin at Byte 538. The first byte of the field name pool is part of an integer containing the length of the pool.
- **An array of integers**, one per field name. Each integer is an offset index to the position in the field name pool where its field begins. The integer value is calculated from the first byte of the actual name pool, starting its count at

0. The integer indices are arranged in *alphabetical order* (ignoring ASCII upper- and lower-case differences) based on the field names to which they refer.

- **An integer** giving the length of the field name pool in bytes. The first byte of this value is the target of the first integer index in this list. The length of the field name pool is calculated from 0 and begins at the first byte of this length integer. For example, if the length integer were 44 (2C 00h) and were located at Bytes 538 and 539, the end of the field name string pool would be located at Byte 583.

- **The field name pool.** The pool is an array of null-terminated ASCII strings. The strings are otherwise undelimited. Reflex orders the names according to field ID number—the order in which the fields appear on screen. The maximum length for a field name is 73 characters, plus the terminating null.

Field Descriptor Table

The field descriptor table immediately follows the field name pool. It is an array of field descriptor structures; Figure 2-3 shows the C definition of a field descriptor.

```
typedef struct {                        /* field descriptor */
        unsigned  nameOffset;           /* field offset */
        char      dataType;             /* field type */
        unsigned  precision : 5;        /* decimal precision */
        unsigned  format : 3;           /* field format */
        unsigned  fldOffset;            /* offset in record */
        ETREC     etr;                  /* repeating text */
        unsigned  isDescend : 1;        /* global sort */
        unsigned  sortPos : 7;          /* pos in sort spec */
        char      reserved;             /* must = 0 (nulls) */
        } FLDDESC;

typedef struct {                        /* enumerated text */
        HANDLE    index;                /* long ptr to index */
        HANDLE    pcol;                 /* long ptr to text */
        } ETREC;
```

Figure 2-3 Field descriptor structures in C

There is one field descriptor structure in the file for each field in the record. Each field descriptor occurs in the file in field ID order, and it refers to its particular field name through an offset index calculated from the first byte of the preceding name pool (this time, *not* including its initial length integer).

Each field descriptor is 16 bytes long. It consists of the following:

Byte 0–1   **Field name offset**   length: 2 bytes
An integer that holds an index into the field name pool for this field's field name. The maximum allowable length for a field name is 73 characters (plus the terminating null).

Byte 2   **Data type**   length: 1 byte
Data type tells Reflex the kind of data stored in the field. Table 2-3 lists the Reflex field types and their codes for the Data type byte.

Table 2-3	Reflex field types
Type	**Comment**
0 Untyped	No field type determined yet
1 Text	Stored in record
2 Repeating Text	Offset into Enumerated Text pool
3 Date	16-bit Julian
4 Numeric	64-bit IEEE floating point
5 Integer	16-bit signed integer

Byte 3   **Precision and Format**   length: 1 byte
Precision makes up the first five bits of this byte; the format value makes up the other three. Reflex ignores format information for text and repeating text types.

Table 2-4 shows formatting values for Date types. Table 2-5 shows formatting for numeric and integer types.

Table 2-4	Formatting for date types		
Code	**Format**	**Code**	**Format**
0	Use default MM/DD/YY	3	Display as DD–Mon–YY
1	Display as MM/DD/YY	4	Display as Mon–YY
2	Display as MM/YY	5	Display as Month DD, YYYY

Table 2-5	Formatting for numeric and integer types	
Code		**Format**
0	None	Use default General
1	Fixed	Display as –XXX.YY
2	Scientific	Display as –X.XXe+ZZ
3	General	Display as Fixed or Scientific for minimum width
4	Currency	Display as ($X,XXX.YY)
5	Financial	Display as (X,XXX.YY)

For all numeric formats except General, Reflex uses the precision member to determine the number of digits following the decimal point. Legal values are 0 through 15.

Byte 4–5   **Field Offset**   length: 2 bytes
Field offset (fldOffset) holds the offset within the record of the particular data corresponding to this descriptor. It is the byte offset of the field from the beginning of the record. You can calculate this value as 4 plus the sum of the size of all previous fields. Field sizes are shown in Table 2-6.

Table 2-6	Field sizes for calculating offsets		
Type	**Offset**	**Type**	**Offset**
Untyped	0 bytes	Date	2 bytes
Text	2 bytes	Numeric	8 bytes
Repeating text	2 bytes	Integer	2 bytes

Byte 6–13   **Enumerated Text Record(ETREC)**   length: 8 bytes
The ETREC consists of two 32-bit longs; a pointer to the enumerated text pool for the data base, and an index into the pool. If present, the pool occurs between the end of the field directory and the start of the master record.

Byte 14   **Sort Position**   length: 1 byte
The sort position byte comprises the one-bit *isDescend* flag and the seven-bit *sortPos* members. Both are normally zero. If Reflex references the field in the global sort specification, it sets these two members to reflect the field's position (counting from one) within the sort spec and the ascending/descending status.

Byte 15   **Reserved**   length: 1 byte
This byte must be null (00h).

Default Display Formats

Immediately following the last field descriptor structure are three words that represent the global default display formats. For Reflex versions 1.14 and earlier, these words must be 19, 1, and 0. (The bytes as they appear are: 13 00 01 00 00 00h).

Enumerated Text Tables

Between the default display formats and the master record fall the enumerated text tables for all fields with repeating-text data types. If there are no such fields in the data base, the enumerated text tables do not appear.

Each repeating-text field has a pair of variable-length structures. Each structure is a word containing the size of the structure in bytes, followed by the number of bytes of actual data. The first structure of each pair contains an index into the text pool; the second is the text pool.

Reflex stores the enumerated text tables in reverse field ID order. For example, if there were two repeating-text type fields, with field IDs 2 and 5, the structures would occur in the following order:

Structure 1:	Index for FID 5
Structure 2:	Text pool for FID 5
Structure 3:	Index for FID 2
Structure 4:	Text pool for FID 2

The enumerated text index is an array of words representing the byte offset of each unique text string in the enumerated text pool. Reflex maintains the index in ascending ASCII order. The text pool contains the actual text values, reference counts for each value, and a list of free blocks within the pool.

To read a pool, use an offset from the index or from a data record to locate the beginning of the ASCII text string. The word preceding the first byte of the string is a count of the number of records referencing the string. When a reference count drops to zero, Reflex deletes the string.

Reflex keeps a free list of deleted strings and compacts them periodically.

Important   Borland states that non-Reflex programs need not concern themselves with the free list; but they must initialize an empty free list when writing a file with repeating-text type fields.

You can write an empty free list by making the first three bytes of the enumerated text pool nulls (00h).

The Master Record

The master record appears immediately after the enumerated text table (or after the end of the field directory, if there is no enumerated text table). It consists of two integers (two bytes each).

1. The total number of records stored in the file. The maximum number of records you may store in a Reflex file is 65,520 (FFF0h).
2. The number of records stored that passed the most recently applied global filter.

How Reflex Stores Its Data

Reflex stores its data in the data records section (section type 1) whose offset location appears in the section descriptions in the file header.

The first word of the data records section is the record number of the current record, counting 0 as the first record. The current record is the active record selection in the Form, List, or Graph view.

Note	If the value of the current record word is equal to

or greater than FFF0h (the 65,520-record maximum for Reflex), a blank record was the current selection when the file was last written.

After the first word of the data records section, Reflex stores each record in record ID order. A data record consists of a record header, an array of integer indices (one for each field in the record) into the text pool of data, and the text pool itself.

Record Header

A record header is fixed in length. Because the number of fields in a record varies with the data base, the index array is of variable length. The text pool also varies in length, but the maximum size of the data in any one field is 254 plus the final null byte. Figure 2-4 provides the C definition of a record header.

```
typedef struct{
     unsigned isInvis : 1;
     unsigned reserved : 7;
     unsigned recID;
     char   ctFlds;
} RECHDR;
```

Figure 2-4 C definition of a record header

Reflex organizes each record structure as follows:

Byte 0–1   **Record Size**   length: 2 bytes
This integer stores the size of the following data record in bytes calculated from 0 and from Byte 0 of the record (the first byte of the Record Size integer).

Byte 2   **Invisible/reserved**   length: 1 byte
The first bit of this byte serves as a flag to tell Reflex that the record did not pass the most recent global filter application. A value of 1 denotes that the record did not pass the filter and is invisible. The reserved area is used internally by Reflex. Set it to 0 when creating a Reflex file externally.

Byte 3–4   **Record ID**   length: 2 bytes
Reflex uses this value internally. Borland advises that the value stored in this location on disk is "meaningless." Set it to null when creating a Reflex file externally.

Byte 5 **Field Count** length: 1 byte

Field count contains the number of fields containing data in a particular record. Its value is between 0 and the number of fields defined in the field directory. It is always one *greater* than the highest field ID containing data. All fields with field IDs higher than the field count contain null data for that record.

Fixed-Length Data Section

After the header is Reflex's "fixed-length data section." This section contains numeric and date data, or an offset into the text pool.

Reflex stores each field's data sequentially, in field ID order. There is one variably sized structure for each data type. Reflex lists the data type of each field in the field descriptors found earlier in the file.

All fields have special values that represent *null* and *error*. Reflex displays *null* values as blank cells and treats them as zeros when referencing them in formulas. Error values display as ERROR in Reflex and always produce an *error* value when a formula references them.

Table 2-7 shows how Reflex represents different field types in the fixed length data section.

Table 2-7	Representation of different field types
Field Type	**Representation**
Untyped	No data stored
Integer	16-bit signed integer
	null: −32768
	error: −32767
Numeric	64-bit IEEE floating-point real
	Most significant word (MSW) determines special values
	null: MSW = 0x7FFF (plus infinity, !0 mantissa)
	error: MSW = 0x7FF0 (plus infinity)
Date	16-bit unsigned integer representing the number of days since December 31, 1899
	null: 0 (December 31, 1899)
	error: 65535 (0xFFFF—June 5, 2079)
Text	16-bit unsigned integer representing the offset into the variable-length text pool following the fixed length data section. The offset is calculated from 0

(Table Continued)

Table 2-7 (Continued)

File	Extension
	starting from the byte following the Record Size byte (starting with Byte 2 of the record).
	null: offset = 0 or string = ""
	error: offset = 1 or string = "ERROR"
Repeating Text	16–bit unsigned integer representing the offset into the enumerated text pool of the field in the field directory. The value is offset from the beginning of the text pool to the first byte of the ASCII string.
	null: offset = 0 or string = ""
	error: offset = 1 or string = "ERROR"

Variable-Length Text Pool

The variable-length text pool for the record appears immediately after the fixed-length data section. An ASCII null (00h) terminates each text string; there is no other delimiter. No gaps exist between the terminator of one string and the first byte of the next string.

The strings may be in any order, as long as they correspond to the offset information in the fixed-length data section. Each field may reference one string only.

View and Modeling Information

The remaining nine sections of the file contain internal information only. Borland advises that when writing a Reflex file externally, you can safely omit these sections.

Reflex Parameters and Limits

Table 2-8	Files Reflex produces and their extensions

File	Extension
Data Base	.RXD
Crosstab Specification	.RXC
Graph Picture File	.RXP
Report Specification	.RXR
Translate Specification	.RXT
Configuration File	.RX
Driver File	.RX
Print to Disk File	.PRN

Table 2-9	Reflex limits and capacities
Item	**Maximum**
Records on disk	65,520
Records in memory	32,500 (memory–limited)
Fields in record	250 (0 through 249)
Bytes in record	16,000
Characters in field	254
Field name	73 characters
Size of form	500 characters wide
	500 lines long
Significance	15 digits
Smallest number	1.7E –308 (approximate)
Largest number	1.79E +308 (approximate)
Earliest date	1/01/00 (Jan. 01, 1900)
Latest date	6/04/2079 (June 04, 2079)

## CHAPTER 3

Rich Text Format

Microsoft Corporation
16011 NE 36th Way
PO Box 97017
Redmond, WA 98073-9717

Type of Product: Data exchange format for text and documents.

Files Produced: ASCII text.

Points of Interest:

Rich Text Format (RTF) aspires to be for personal computer documents what DIF or SYLK are to spreadsheets. RTF is the clipboard format for Microsoft Windows 2.0 and allows Windows applications to trade document text *and its formatting*. Additionally, Microsoft advises that both Microsoft Word 3.X and above for the Macintosh and Microsoft Word 4.X and above for PC/MS-DOS can save and read documents in Rich Text Format.

More information is available for DIF and SYLK in *File Formats for Popular PC Software*.

Rich Text Format

Rich Text Format (RTF) uses the printable ASCII characters to encode text formatting properties, document structures, and document properties. RTF can encode special characters to keep them within the printable set, although it can use character codes outside of the printable set.

Control Words

RTF uses "control words" and "control symbols" to encode the text and properties. This makes the format extendible over time (much like SYLK—as long as two programs agree on the convention, you can extend RTF).

A *control word* takes the form:

\lettersequence<delimiter>

where <delimiter> is:

> A space (the space is part of the control word, and delimits it)

> A digit or -. This means that a parameter follows. A space or any other non-letter or -digit delimits the following sequence.

> Any other non-letter or -digit. This terminates the control word, but is not part of the control word.

Important A "letter" is only an ASCII upper-or-lower case letter character.

A *control symbol* consists of a \ (backslash) character followed by a single non-letter. They require no further delimiting.

Because control symbols are relatively few in number, Microsoft encourages the use of control words. In control symbols, the symbol implies the parameter. A program that does not understand a control symbol can ignore the corresponding parameter as well.

In addition to control words and symbols, there are braces:

> {   = group start
>
> }   = group end

RTF uses grouping to format and delineate document structure, such as footnotes, headers, titles, and so forth.

Control words, symbols, and braces constitute control information; all other characters are "plain text."

> **Note** To express the \, {, and } characters in their non-control meanings, use \\, \{, and \}, respectively. Some control words control properties that have only two states (bold, italic, keep together, etc.). When one of these words occurs in text with no parameter or with any non-zero parameter, it turns on the property. When it has a zero parameter, it turns off the property.

What to Do with RTF Text

Microsoft makes several suggestions on how to read and take action about RTF text.

Reading an RTF Text Stream

Your concerns when programmatically reading an RTF text stream are:

- Separating control information from plain text.
- Acting on control information.
- Collecting and disposing of "plain text" information as directed by the current group state.

Some control information contributes special characters to the text stream. Other information changes the "program state" (which includes properties of the document as a *whole*) and a stack of "group states" (which apply to *parts* of the document).

When the reading program encounters the { character, it should save the group state. Encountering the } character, it should restore the group state. The current group state specifies:

1. The "destination" (the part of the document that the plain text is building up).
2. The character formatting properties, such as bold or italic.
3. The paragraph formatting properties, such as justified.
4. The section formatting properties, such as the number of columns.

What an RTF Reader Must Do

Microsoft advises that a program to read RTF text procede as follows:

1. Read the "next character."
2. If the next character = { , then stack the current state. The current state does not change. Continue.
3. If the next character = }, then unstack the current state. This changes the state in general.
4. If the next character = \, then collect the control word or symbol parameter, if any. Look up the word in the symbol table and act accordingly.

   The action leaves the parameter available for use by the action. Leave a read pointer before or after the delimiter, as appropriate. After the action, continue.

5. If the next character is "plain text," write it to the current destination using the current formatting properties.

Symbol Table Actions

For a given symbol table entry, the possible actions are:

Change destination: change the destination to the one described in the entry. Desintation changes are legal only immediately after a { character. Other restrictions may also apply—for example, you may not nest footnotes.

Change formatting property: the symbol table describes the property and whether it requires the parameter.

Special character: the symbol table entry describes the character code.

End of paragraph: you may view this as another special character.

End of section: you may view this as another special character.

Ignore

Special Characters

If a reading program does not recognize a special character, it should simply ignore it. This is the method by which two programs can transfer specialized information between them and still work with other programs. Microsoft also advises that the RTF specification may be changed and extended in the future.

Table 3-1 lists special characters and their meanings.

Table 3-1	Special characters and their meanings
Character	**Meaning**
\chpgn	current page number (as in headers)
\chftn	auto-numbered footnote reference (footnote to follow in a group)
\chdate	current date (as in headers)
\chtime	current time (as in headers)
|	formula character
\~	nonbreaking space
\-	nonrequired hyphen
_	nonbreaking hyphen
\'hh	any hex value (identifies 8-bit values)
\page	required page break
\line	required line break (no paragraph break)
\par	end of paragraph
\sect	end of section and end of paragraph
\tab	same as ASCII 9

RTF accepts the ASCII code 9 as \tab. It accepts either \10 or \13 as \par. RTF ignores ASCII 10 and ASCII 13; you may use them to include carriage returns for easier readability, but which will have no effect on the interpretation as long as they do not occur within a control word. Microsoft suggests that you insert carriage returns at least every 255 characters for easier transportability via electronic text mail systems.

Destinations

Changing destinations resets all properties to default. Changes are legal only at the beginning of a group (text and controls enclosed by braces).

\rtf<*param*>   **Document**

The destination for the \rtf control word is the document. The parameter is the version of the writing program. When the { precedes the command, it marks the beginning of an RTF document. The } character marks the end. The ending brace is legal only once after the starting brace.

Small-scale RTF interchange, where other methods for marking the end of the string are available (as in a string constant) need not include this identification but will start with the document destination as the default.

Before any text in the file, you may declare the character set:

\ansi   The text is the ANSI character set that Windows uses (the default case).

\mac   The text is the Macintosh character set.

\pc   The text is the IBM PC character set.

\colortbl   **Color Table**

The destination is the color table. The color table defines the red, green, and blue indices for color numbers, starting with 0. Semicolons delimit each set of color definitions and define the next sequential color number. The indices are the same as those used in Windows.

\red000   red index

\green000 green index

\blue000   blue index

The following example defines colors 0 and 2. Note that the example omits color 1 by using two contiguous semicolons:

{\colortbl\red128\green0\blue64;;\red64\green128\blue0;}

\fonttbl   **Font Table**

The destination is the font table. The font table assigns the font name and family to the font numbers used.

The text is the font name delimited by semicolons. The font "default" specifies that the writing program assigned no font and the reading program should use whatever font is the default for the particular output device being used. If the control word designates no font, default is assumed.

The font table (if it exists) must occur before the style-sheet definition and any text in the file. Possible families are:

\fnil

Don't know the family (use the default font).

\froman

Roman family; proportionally spaced, serif (examples: Times Roman, Century Schoolbook, Garamond, etc.)

\fswiss

Swiss family; proportionally spaced, sans serif (examples: Helvetica, Swiss, etc.)

\fmodern

Fixed pitch, serif or sans serif (Pica, Elite, Courier, etc.)

\fscript

Script family (Cursive, etc.)

\fdecor

Decorative fonts (Old English, etc.)

Example:

{\fonttbl\f0\froman Tms Rmn;\f1\fswiss Helv;\f2\fnil Default;}

\stylesheet **Style Sheet**

This destination is the style sheet for the document. The reading program should interpret text between semicolons as style names that stand for the formatting properties in effect. For example, the commands:

{\stylesheet{\s0\f3\fs20\qj Normal;}{\s1\f3\fs24\b\qc Heading Level 3;}}

Define style 0 with the name "Normal" to use the 10-point size of font 3 (font 3 is defined in the font table below) and justify it. Style 1 is defined with the name "Heading Level 3" and uses the 12-point size of font 3, bold and centered. These fields may be present if the destination is \stylesheet:

\sbasedon000

Defines the style number on which the current style is based. If the control word \sbasedon is omitted, the style is not based on any style.

\snext000

Defines the next style associated with the current style. If this control word is omitted, the next style is itself.

\pict   **Picture**

The destination is a picture. The plain text describes the picture as a hex dump (string of characters 0, 1...9, a...e, f). The following parameters may also exist if the destination is a picture, but they are optional. If they are not present, the default frame size equals the picture size.

\pich000

Defines the picture-frame height in pixels. The picture frame is the area set aside for the image. The picture itself does not necessarily fill the frame.

\picw000

Defines the picture-frame width in pixels.

\picscaled

Scales the picture up or down to fit within the specified size of the frame.

\wmetafile

Identifies the picture as being a windows meta file.

\macpict

Identifies the picture as being in the Macintosh Quick Draw format.

\bin000

This is a special field that includes binary information within the file (in lieu of hex). The parameter defines the number of bytes of binary information that follows.

\footnote   **Footnote**

The destination is a footnote text. The group must immediately follow the footnote reference character(s).

\header   **Header**

The destination is the header text for the current section. The group must precede the first plain text character in the section.

\hearderl   **Left-hand header**

Same as header, but for left-hand (even) pages.

\headerr   **Right-hand header**

Same as header, but for right-hand (odd) pages.

\headerf	First page header
	Same as header, but for first page only.
\footer	Footer
	The destination is the footer text for the current section. The group must precede the first plain text character in the section.
\footerl	Left-hand footer
	Same as footer, but for left-hand (even) pages.
\footerr	Right-hand footer
	Same as footer, but for right-hand (odd) pages.
\footerf	First page footer
	Same as footer, but for first page only.
\ftnsep	Footnote separator
	The destination is the separator of a footnote.
\ftnsepc	Continued footnote separator
	The destination is the separator of a continued footnote.
\ftncn	Continued footnote notice
\info	Information block
	This text is the information block for the document. Parts of the text are further classified by the "properties" of the text (Table 3-2), such as "title." These are not formatting properties, but a device to delimit and identify parts of the information from one text in the group.
\comment	Comment text
	The text of comments should be ignored.

Document Formatting Properties

Table 3-2 lists the formatting properties and defaults for a document as a whole (000 stands for a number which may be signed).

Table 3-2	Document formatting properties	

Command	Default	Meaning
\paperw000	12240	paper width in twips
\paperh000	15840	paper height
\margl000	1800	left margin
\margr000	1800	right margin
\margt000	1440	top margin
\margb000	1440	bottom margin
\facingp		facing pages (enables gutters and odd/even headers); a 0 parameter disables
\gutter000		gutter width (inside of facing pages)
\ogutter000		outside gutter width
\deftab000	720	default tab width
\widowctrl		enable wido control (0 disables)
\endnotes		footnotes at end of section
\ftnbj		footnotes at bottom of page (default)
\ftntj		footnotes beneath text (top justified)
\ftnstart000	1	starting footnote number
\ftnrestart		restart footnotes each page (0 disables)
\pgnstart000	1	starting page number
\linestart000	1	starting line number
\landscape		printed in landscape format (0 disables)

Note	A twip is 1/20th of a point or 1/1440th of an inch.

Section Formatting Properties

Table 3-3 lists the formatting properties that apply to sections of a document.

Table 3-3	Section formatting properties	

Command	Default	Meaning
\sectd		reset to default section properties
\sbknone		section break continuous (no break)
\sbkcol		section break starts new column
\sbkpage		section break starts new page (default)
\sbkeven		section break starts even page
\sbkodd		section break starts odd page
\pgnrestart		restart page numbers at 1 (0 disables)

(Table Continued)

Table 3-3 (Continued)

Command	Default	Meaning
\pgndec		page number format decimals
\pgnucrm		page number format upper-case roman
\pgnlcrm		page number format lower-case roman
\pgnucltr		page number format upper- case letter
\pgnlcltr		page number format lower-case letter
\pgnx000	720	auto page number X position
\pgny000	720	auto page number Y position
\linemod000		line number modulus
\linex000	360	line number text distance
\linerestart		line number restart at 1 (default)
\lineppage		line number restart on each page
\linecont		line number continued from previous section
\headery000	720	header Y position from top of page
\footery000	720	footer Y position from bottom of page
\vertalt		vertically align starting at top of page (default)
\vertalc		vertically align in the center of page
\vertalj		vertically justify to top and bottom margins
\vertalb		vertically align, starting at the bottom
\cols000	1	number of columns (snaking)
\colsx000	720	space between columns
\endnhere		include endnotes in this section (0 disables)
\titlepg		title page is special (0 disables)

Paragraph formatting properties

Table 3-4 lists the formatting properties that belong to paragraphs.

Table 3-4	Paragraph formatting Properties	
Command	**Default**	**Meaning**
\pard		reset to default paragraph properties
\s000		style (see Note1)
\q1		quad left (default)
\qr		right
\qj		justified
\qc		centered
\fi000	0	first line indent
\li000	0	left indent
\ri000	0	right indent
\sb000	0	space before
\sa000	0	space after

(Table Continued)

Command	Default	Meaning
\sl000	1 line (12 pts)	space between lines (see Note2)
\keep		keep this paragraph together (0 disables)
\keepn		keep with next paragraph (0 disables)
\sbys		side by side (0 disables)
\pagebb		page break before (0 disables)
\noline		no line numbering (0 disables)
\brdrt		border top
\brdrb		border bottom
\brdrl		border left
\brdrr		border right
\box		border all around
\brdrs		single thickness
\brdrth		thick border
\brdrsh		shadow
\brdrdb		double
\tqr		right flush tab (apply to next specified position)
\tqc		centered tab
\tqdec		decimal aligned tab
\tldot		tab leader dots
\tlhyph		tab leader hyphens
\tlul		tab leader underline
\tlth		tab leader thick line
\tx000		tab position
\tb000		bar tab position (see Note3)

Note 1   If a style is specified, you must still specify the paragraph formatting implied by that style with the paragraph.

Note 2   If the text fails to specify any \sl (space between lines) value, the default value is 12 points (one line). If \sl000 is specified, this means that the document should use auto line spacing where the tallest font on the line determines the line spacing.

Note 3   Bar tab position places a vertical bar at the specified position for the height of the entire current paragraph.

Character Formatting Properties

Table 3-5 lists the formatting properties that apply to the characters of the plain text.

Table 3-5	Character formatting properties	
Command	Default	Meaning
\plain		reset to default text properties
\b		bold (0 disables)
\i		italic (0 disables)
\strike		strikethrough (0 disables)
\outl		outline (0 disables)
\shad		shadow (0 disables)
\scaps		small caps (0 disables)
\caps		all caps (0 disables)
\v		invisible text (0 disables)
\f000		font number n
\fs000	24	font size in half points
\expnd000	0	(see Note1)
\ul		underline (0 disables)
\ulw		word underline
\uld		dotted underline
\uldb		double underline
\up000		superscript in half points
\dn000		subscript in half points
\cf000		foreground color (index into color table)
\cb000		background color

Note 1   Expansion/compression of the space between characters, expressed in quarter points. A negative value implies compression.

Information Block Commands

Tables 3-6 lists the commands of the information block. The plain text of the group specifies various fields. Think of the current field as a particular setting of the "sub-destination" property of the text.

You can use these information block commands to create document headers that list details such as the computer operator, the time of the document's creation, retrieval keywords, and so forth.

Table 3-6	Information block commands	
Command	**Default**	**Meaning**
\title		the title follows in plain text
\subject		the subject follows in plain text
\operator		
\author		
\keywords		
\doccomm		document comments (not \comment)
\version		
\nextfile		the name of the "next" file follows

Table 3-7 lists other properties that assign their parameters directly to the information block.

Table 3-7	Commands that assign properties to the information block	
Command	**Default**	**Meaning**
\verno000		internal version number
\creatim		creation time follows
\yr000		year assigned to a time field
\mo000		
\dy000		
\hr000		
\min000		
\sec000		
\revtim		revision time follows
\printtim		last print time follows
\buptim		backup time follows
\edmins000		editing minutes
\nofpages000		
\nofwords000		
\nofchars000		
\id000		internal ID number

Sample RTF File

This text is an example of how RTF text appears in a file.

{\rtf0\pc{\fonttbl\f1\froman Times;} {\stylesheet {\s0 Normal;}
{\s1\i\qj\snext2\f1 Question;} {\s2\qj\f1 Answer;}}
{\s0\f1\b\qc Questions and Answers\par }
{\s1 \i\qj 1. What is the left margin of this document?\par}
{\s2\qj\li720\f1 Since no document parameters were specified, the
default of 1800 twips (1.25") is used.\par}}

## CHAPTER 4

SuperCalc4
Versions 1.0 and 1.1

Computer Associates International, Inc.
2195 Fortune Dr.
San Jose, CA 95131-1820

Type of Product: Spreadsheet with graphics and data management.

Files Produced Binary.

Points of Interest:
SuperCalc has gone through several iterations since its introduction on the PC. Much of its file format, however, has remained the same. This chapter covers SuperCalc4, but you may also use it to decipher files produced by SuperCalcs 1, 2, and 3. Computer Associates' Super Data Interchange format (now called XDIF) is available in *File Formats for Popular PC Software.*

Conversion Information:
SuperCalc4 can import:
- 1-2-3 (.WKS and .WK1 files)
- VisiCalc (.VC files)
- DIF and XDIF (Super Data Interchange format)
- CSV (comma-separated values—mail merge)
- Numbers and Text

SuperCalc4 can export:
- 1-2-3 (.WKS, .WK1, and .PIC files)
- DIF and XDIF
- CSV
- SuperCalc3 files (SuperCalc4 can read them automatically)

SuperCalc4 File Format

SuperCalc is primarily a spreadsheet, and one that has grown over time. Its latest incarnation, SuperCalc4, supports a matrix of 255 columns and 9,999 rows. The columns are lettered on screen (A-IU). Internally, numbers represent the columns and rows. The column numeric range is 0 through 254; the row numeric range is 0 through 9998. The representation of cell A1 is (0,0).

The file is a succession of header sections, a cell contents section of variable length, a graph "footer," and a list of named areas in the matrix.

Note Probably because the program maintains such a high level of compatibility with files produced by its earlier versions, the header section is organized in a confusing fashion. The Sample Spreadsheet file for SuperCalc4 (see Appendix B) reveals an entirely undocumented header section apparently dealing with dates beginning around Byte 2000.

Cells

SuperCalc uses three bytes to refer to cells; one byte (0–254) for the column reference, and a two-byte (integer) word (0–9998) for the row reference. In many of the cell references in the file, the column comes first. In others, the row comes first.

The section titled "Internal Cell Formatting" discusses cell contents in detail. Briefly, however, cells appear in multiples of eight bytes, called Cell Allocation Units (CAU). The maximum cell length is 240 bytes (30 CAU). There is a maximum of 227 bytes available for contents.

Each cell requires three prefix bytes (holding the row and column numbers), three formatting bytes, and ten bytes for a BCD (binary coded decimal) value. Discounting only the prefix bytes and counting the formatting and BCD bytes, together with the 227 bytes for contents, makes the maximum of 240.

There are five types of BCD values, all determined by the last byte of the ten-byte BCD component. Table 4-1 lists these five types. Not all cells have BCD components. If bit 5 of the first format byte is set, the cell is a constant and will not have a BCD value.

Table 4-1	The five BCD types
Value of Final Byte	**Meaning**
0	standard 8-byte floating point (8 bytes, a null, 10th byte)
2	calendar function (9 bytes: days since 1 March 1900)
4	text (9 bytes treated as a numeric constant)
8	ERROR code (the 9-byte string: 0 0 ERROR 0 0)
16	N/A code (the 9-byte string: 0 0 N/A 0 0 0 0)

Warning Earlier versions of SuperCalc did not force Byte 10 of the BCD component to zero. Worksheet files prepared with those earlier versions therefore may have random values in that byte. Earlier versions did, however, set to zero the region of the header where the Valid flag is now. SuperCalc4 checks the Valid flag whenever it loads a file. If the Valid flag is 0, SuperCalc4 forces all BCD component byte 10s to zero during the load. As a result, SuperCalc4 treats all such values in earlier files as floating point.

SuperCalc limits text cells to 227 characters plus the three header bytes. There is no 10-byte BCD component to a text cell.

The first content character of a text cell is either a single quote (') or double quote ("). The double quote denotes a text cell; the single quote denotes a repeating text cell (the cell contents expand to fill the width of the cell for drawing a line across a spreadsheet, for example). SuperCalc4 will repeat text only if the Text Left format is set for the original cell and all the cells over which the repeating text will extend.

Cell, Column, and Row Formatting

In SuperCalc4, formatting is hierarchical. With number one as the most powerful formatting, precedence runs:

1. cell formatting
2. row formatting
3. column formatting
4. global formatting

A spreadsheet always has at least global formatting defined.

Column Format Table

The column format table contains a two-byte entry for each of the spreadsheet's 255 columns. The first byte of the pair holds the column width, and the second byte holds the formatting information. A column width or format byte containing nulls (00h) assumes the default format.

The column format table appears in the header.

Row Format Table

The row format table holds a one-byte formatting entry for each of the first 254 rows of the spreadsheet matrix and a single formatting byte for the remaining rows 255–9999.

File Header

The SuperCalc4 header runs to 1538 bytes. After that comes variable-length information.
    This section provides offset information into the header starting from Byte 0, the first byte of the file.

Byte 0–19   **Program and version**   length: 20 bytes
This field consists of the string
SuperCalc<spc>ver.<spc><spc>1.10
where <spc> represents the space character (20h).

Byte 20–21   **Newline**   length: 2 bytes
This field contains a carriage return (0Dh) and a line feed (0Ah) in that order.

Byte 22–102   **Worksheet title vector**   length: 80 bytes
This field picks up the text from cell A1 as a title for the worksheet. It terminates with a Control-Z (1Ah).

Byte 103–105   **Column and row display formatting tables** length: 3 bytes
The first two bytes of this field are an integer, set to nulls. The third byte is reserved and is also null.

User–Defined Format Table

Byte 106–121   **User-defined formats**   length: 16 bytes
This field consists of eight two-byte fields. The first byte of each field represents a column format. See Column format table (Byte 547 et seq.). The second represents a row format. See Row format table (Byte 1057 et seq.).

Byte 122–130   **GRADEF (graph definition)**   length: 9 bytes

Byte 131   **Far right column**   length: 1 byte
This byte holds the column number of the column farthest right that still contains data; essentially, the rightmost limit of the active spreadsheet matrix.

Byte 132–133   **Bottom row**   length: 2 bytes
This integer holds the row number of the bottom row (highest-numbered row) on the matrix that still contains data.

Byte 134   **Current chart number**   length: 1 byte
The number of the currently displayed graph. SuperCalc4 can define nine graphs in any one file.

Chart Descriptor

Byte 135–136   **Data block start row**   length: 2 bytes
The row number of the starting data block for the current chart.

Byte 137   **Data block start column**   length: 1 byte
The starting column of the data block.

Byte 138–139   **Data block end row**   length: 2 bytes
The ending row for the data block.

Byte 140   **Data block end column**   length: 1 byte
The ending column for the data block.

Byte 141–200   **Series definitions**   length: 60 bytes
This area consists of ten six-byte fields.

Byte 201–202   **Point label start row**   length: 2 bytes
The row number of the starting point labels cell for the current chart.

Byte 203   **Point label start column**   length: 1 byte
The starting column of the point labels cell.

Byte 204–205   **Point label end row**   length: 2 bytes
The ending row for the point labels cell.

Byte 206   **Point label end column**   length: 1 byte
The ending column for the point labels cell.

Byte 207–266   **Point label definitions**   length: 60 bytes
This area consists of ten six-byte fields.

Byte 267–273   **Label definitions**   length: 6 bytes
You should initialize this field to nulls.

Byte 274–278   **Label range information**   length: 6 bytes
The six bytes are the row (two bytes) and column (one byte) cell locations of the starting cell and ending cell of the column or row holding the graph labels. Cells must be in either the same column or the same row. When preparing a SuperCalc4 spreadsheet externally to the program, you should initialize this field to nulls.

Byte 279–338   **Label definitions**   length: 60 bytes
This area consists of ten six-byte fields.

Byte 339–350   **Title block**   length: 12 bytes
This area consists of four three-byte fields. Each field is a row (two bytes) and column (one byte) cell location. The four fields specify:
1. cell location of main graph title
2. cell location of graph subtitle
3. cell location of X-axis title
4. cell location of Y-axis title

Byte 351–356

X-axis scaling block   length: 6 bytes
This area consists of two three-byte fields. The first field is the row and column location of the minimum X-axis value in the series being graphed. The second field is the location maximum X-axis value in the series being graphed.

Byte 357–362

Y-axis scaling block   length: 6 bytes
This area consists of two three-byte fields. The first field is the row and column location of the minimum Y-axis value in the series being graphed. The second field is the location maximum Y-axis value in the series being graphed.

Byte 363–364

VCMPAR   length: 2 bytes
The *second* byte of VCMPAR defines the graph type:
01 = pie chart
02 = clustered bar
03 = stacked bar
04 = line
05 = XY
06 = area
07 = hi-lo
The first byte is undefined.

Byte 365

Resolution   length: 1 byte
This byte tells SuperCalc4 how to display the graph.
0 = medium resolution
1 = high resolution
2 = monochrome adapter and display

Byte 366

Pie chart legends   length: 1 byte
This byte tells SuperCalc4 how to display the legends of a pie chart.
0 = block legends
1 = radial legends

Byte 367

Plot direction   length: 1 byte
This byte controls where the program plots the graph.
0 = screen
1 = plotter

Byte 368–382

Graph formats buffer   length: 15 bytes
This area consists of five three-byte fields. Each three-byte field is the row (two bytes) and column (one byte) location of a cell. The fields are:
1.   axis label formats
2.   time label formats
3.   variable label formats
4.   data label formats
5.   percent format

Byte 383–384   **Default scaling**   length: 2 bytes
This word consists of two bytes. The first byte contains the default X-axis scaling. The second byte contains the default Y-axis scaling.

Byte 385–386   **Manual scaling**   length: 2 bytes
This word consists of two bytes. The first byte contains the number of divisions for manual X-axis scaling. The second byte contains the number of divisions for manual Y-axis scaling.

Byte 387   **Pie flag**   length: 1 byte
A non-zero value in this byte tells the program to draw the pie chart with all segments exploded.

Byte 388   **Pie segment flag**   length: 1 byte
If bit zero of this byte is set on, it tells the program to explode only segment 1 of the pie.

Byte 389   **Pie var/time**   length: 1 byte
0 = var wise
1 = time wise

Byte 390   **Pie val**   length: 1 byte

Byte 391–396   **Data management input range**   length: 6 bytes
This area consists of two three-byte fields. Each field contains the row (two bytes) and column (one byte) location of a cell in the following order:
1. input range starting row
2. input range starting column
3. input range ending row
4. input range ending column

Byte 397–402   **Data management criteria range**   length: 6 bytes
This area consists of two three-byte fields. Each field contains the row (two bytes) and column (one byte) location of a cell in the following order:
1. criteria range starting row
2. criteria range starting column
3. criteria range ending row
4. criteria range ending column

Byte 403–408   **Data management output range**   length: 6 bytes
This area consists of two three-byte fields. Each field contains the row (two bytes) and column (one byte) location of a cell in the following order:
1. output range starting row
2. output range starting column
3. output range ending row
4. output range ending column

Worksheet Window Toggles for Window 1

Byte 409–411   **Toggle1**   length: 3 bytes
This field consists of three bytes.
1. expression display toggle:
    0 = display value
    1 = display formula
2. window-dependent toggle flags:
    bit 0 (Tab over empty/protect); 0 = no, 1 = yes
    bit 1 (Auto advance); 0 = no, 1 = yes
    The other bits are currently unused.
3. Video border toggle:
    0 = display the border
    1 = suppress the border

Video Window Vectors

Byte 412   **Sync**   length: 1 byte
This byte controls the synchronization between windows.
0 = no sync
1 = sync

Byte 413   **Split screen**   length: 1 byte
This byte controls whether and how the screen is split. A zero in the most significant bit signifies a horizontal split; a one in the most significant bit signifies a vertical split.
0 = no split
1 = screen split horizontally and window one active (01h)
2 = screen split horizontally and window two active (02h)
129 = screen split vertically and window one active (81h)
130 = screen split vertically and window two active (82h)

Logical and Physical Window Storage Vectors

Byte 414–444   **Window1**   length: 30 bytes
This area is the control vector for the left or upper window (window 1). See Window Control Vectors.

Byte 445–475   **Window2**   length: 30 bytes
This area is the control vector for the right or lower window (window 2). See Window Control Vectors.

Byte 476–478	**Toggle2**	length: 3 bytes

This field consists of three bytes.
1. expression display toggle:
       0 = display value
       1 = display formula
2. window-dependent toggle flags:
       bit 0 (Tab over empty/protect); 0 = no, 1 = yes
       bit 1 (Auto advance); 0 = no, 1 = yes
       The other bits are currently unused.
3. video border toggle:
       0 = display the border
       1 = suppress the border

Byte 479	**Cursor direction**	length: 1 byte

This byte stores the direction the cursor was last going.
1 = left
2 = right
3 = down
4 = up

New Global Worksheet Commands

Byte 480	**Computation flag**	length: 1 byte

This byte is the natural order computation flag.
0 = ignore the natural order of computation
1 = follow the natural order of computation

Byte 481	**Quote flag**	length: 1 byte

This byte controls whether SuperCalc4 requires a quotation mark to precede text entries.
0 = " not needed
1 = " is needed

Byte 482	**Natural-order computation counter** length: 1 byte

Counts the number of computations; the range is from 0 to 99.

Byte 483	**Auto-solve**	length: 1 byte

This byte controls whether SuperCalc4 will automatically solve natural order computations. Any non-zero value sets Auto-solve to True.

Byte 484–489	**Solve convergence range**	length: 6 bytes

This area consists of two three-byte fields. Each field is a row (two bytes) and column (one byte) cell location. The first cell location is the start of the convergence range and the second location is the end of the convergence range.

Byte 490

Delta flag length: 1 byte
Any non-zero value in this field means to use the value in the Delta cell; a zero means to converge the series to .01.

Byte 491

Delta cell length: 3 bytes
These three bytes hold the location of the cell to use as the convergence Delta.

Byte 494–544

Spacer length: 50 bytes
This area is a null-filled spacer.

Byte 545

Worksheet format version number length: 1 byte
This byte contains a value that tells which version of SuperCalc created the worksheet.

0 = SuperCalc1 version 1.06 or earlier generated this worksheet. This versio used 16-byte cell allocation units (CAU).

1 = SuperCalc1 version 1.07 or later generated this worksheet with 8-byte CAUs; *or* this worksheet was generated by SuperCalc2 or SuperCalc3 *without* using the hide or user-defined formats.

2 = SuperCalc2 or SuperCalc3 generated this worksheet and *does* use the hide or user defined formats.

3 = SuperCalc3 generated this worksheet using SuperCalc3-specific features.

4 = SuperCalc4 generated this worksheet.

Byte 546

Valid field length: 1 byte
This field tells whether Byte 10 of the BCD number is meaningful.

0 = If SuperCalc2 or a later version generated the file, this means that Byte 10 of the BCD value is meaningful.

1 = If SuperCalc1 generated the file, all BCD-value tenth bytes will be set to zero when loaded into a SuperCalc2, 3, or 4.

Byte 547–1056

Column width formats length: 510 bytes
This area consists of 255 two-byte fields, one field for each column on the spreadsheet, occupied or not. A width-byte value from 1 to 127 (01h to 7Fh) indicates the width of the column. A column width of 255 (FFh) indicates a zero-width column; a 0 width indicates that the column should use the global column width (see Video Window Control Vector Definitions, Byte 21). Table 4-2 describes the format byte.

Table 4-2	Format byte in column formatting table	

Bit	Value	Meaning
		Value formats:
0–2	000	use global format definition
	001	use dollars and cents ($)
	010	integer
	011	exponential (E)
	100	general format
	101	graphic (histogram) format
	110	hide
	111	reserved
		Text formats:
3–4	00	use global justification
	01	left justify text
	10	right justify text
	11	reserved
		User defined:
5	0	interpret bits 0–2 as above
	1	use user-defined column formats (Note1) and interpret bits 0-2 as index values 1 to 8 (000 = 1, 001 = 2, 010 = 3, etc.) into the user-defined column area.
		Value formats:
6–7	00	use global justification definition
	01	right justify values
	10	left justify values
	11	reserved

Note 1   Bit 5 was set to zero in SuperCalc1. See Byte 106 et seq. for user-defined column formats.

Byte 1057–1311   **Row format table**   length: 255 bytes
This area consists of 255 one-byte fields. Each of the first 254 bytes carries the row formatting information for the first 254 rows in order, starting at row 0; the 255th byte carries the formatting for all the remaining 9745 rows. Table 4-3 describes the row formatting byte.

Bit	Value	Meaning
		Value formats:
0–2	000	use column/global format definition
	001	use dollars and cents ($)
	010	integer
	011	exponential (E)
	100	general format
	101	graphic (histogram *) format
	110	hide
	111	reserved
		Text formats:
3–4	00	use column/global justification
	01	left justify text
	10	right justify text
	11	reserved
		User defined:
5	0	interpret bits 0–2 as above
	1	use user–defined row formats (note1) and interpret bits 0–2 as index values 1 to 8 (000 = 1, 001 =2, 010 = 3, etc.) into the user-defined row area.
		Value formats:
6–7	00	use global justification definition
	01	right justify values
	10	left justfity values
	11	reserved

Table 4-3 Format byte in row formatting table

Note 1 Bit 5 was set to zero in SuperCalc1. See Byte 106 *et seq.* for user-defined row formats.

Global Worksheet Toggles

Byte 1312   **Computation order flag**   length: 1 byte
A 0 value means to compute along columns; a 1 means to compute along rows.

Byte 1313   **Auto/manual toggle**   length: 1 byte
A 0 value means to recalculate when ordered (manually); a 1 means to use automatic recalculation.

Byte 1314–1407   **Spacers**   length: 94 bytes
This field consists of 94 null bytes.

New SuperCalc4 Header Information

Byte 1408–1409 **Header2 length** length: 2 bytes
The length of this second header section, new for SuperCalc4. The length figure includes the length word in its count.

Byte 1410–1411 **Header2 version number** length: 2 bytes
This two-byte field holds an ASCII H (48h) in its first byte and a hex 2 (02h) in its second.

Printer Information

Byte 1412–1413 **Printer header length** length: 2 bytes
This integer holds the length of the header's printer information only. In the Sample Spreadsheet, this figure was 115 bytes (73h).

Byte 1414 **Printer default flags** length: 1 byte

Byte 1415 **Printer margin default** length: 1 byte

Byte 1416 **Reserved** length: 1 byte

Byte 1417 **Start keep** length: 1 byte
Start of copy of printer variables from SCEX.

Byte 1418 **Length to keep** length: 1 byte
Length of the printer variables that are kept with KEEP.

Byte 1419 **Set-up length** length: 1 byte
This is the length byte for the printer set-up string.

Byte 1420–1479 **Set-up string** length: 60 bytes
This field is the printer set-up string. Fill unused bytes with nulls.

Byte 1480 **End of string** length: 1 byte
A null string terminating character.

Byte 1481 **Border character** length: 1 byte
ASCII code of character to use for spreadsheet border.

Byte 1482 **Border toggle** length: 1 byte
0 = don't use borders
1 = use borders

Byte 1483 **Printer mode** length: 1 byte
Bit 1 = Auto form feed off/on
Bit 2 = DS
Bit 3 = End line feed
The other bits are unused.

Byte 1484	**Paper wait flag**	length: 1 byte
	0 = don't wait for paper	
	1 = wait for paper	

| Byte 1485–1486 | **Page length** | length: 2 bytes |

The first byte of this two-byte field contains the page length in an integer number of lines (usually 66). The second byte is reserved.

| Byte 1487–1488 | **Page width** | length: 2 bytes |

The first byte of this two-byte field contains the page width in an integer number of characters (default is 80). The second byte is reserved.

Byte 1489–1490	**Top margin**	length: 2 bytes
Byte 1491–1492	**Bottom margin**	length: 2 bytes
Byte 1493–1494	**Left margin**	length: 2 bytes
Byte 1495	**Send to printer flag**	length: 1 byte

SuperCalc can send either its display or cell contents to a printer. If this byte contains a 1 value, SuperCalc sends values as displayed on the screen. If this byte contains a zero value, Super-Calc sends the cell contents.

| Byte 1496 | **Formatting flag** | length: 1 byte |

When SuperCalc sends to the printer, a 0 in this byte means to print formatted output; a 1 means to print unformatted.

| Byte 1497 | **Number of copies** | length: 1 byte |
| Byte 1498–1501 | **Reserved** | length: 4 bytes |

These bytes should contain nulls.

Start of Non-Kept Printer Values

Byte 1502	**Number of headers active**	length: 1 byte
Byte 1503	**Number of footers active**	length: 1 byte
Byte 1504	**Titles flag (output)**	length: 1 byte
	0 = none	
	1 = automatic	
	2 = manual	

| Byte 1505 | **Reserved** | length: 1 byte |
| | Set to null. | |

| Byte 1506–1512 | **Print range** | length: 7 bytes |

Null-terminated, six-byte field.

Byte 1513–1519	**Horizontal title range**	length: 7 bytes
	Null-terminated, six-byte field.	
Byte 1520–1527	**Vertical title range**	length: 7 bytes
	Null-terminated, six-byte field.	

"Other Values" Area

Byte 1528–1529	**Length of "other values"**	length: 2 bytes
Byte 1530–1532	**Start learn range**	length: 3 bytes
	This field is a cell location: row (two bytes) and column (one byte).	
Byte 1533–1535	**End learn range**	length: 3 bytes
	This field is a cell location: row (two bytes) and column (one byte).	
Byte 1536–1537	**Global labels flag**	length: 2 bytes
	The first byte of this word is the global labels flag. The second is reserved.	

Variable Part of File

Starting at byte 1538 is the variable length area for header and footer strings (if any). Then, in order, come:

1. Cell data, followed by at least one Control-Z (1Ah), padded to the next end of sector boundary by more Control-Zs, if necessary
2. Graph footer
3. Names list for named areas

Video Window Control Vector Definitions

This section is a detail of the 31-byte window vectors that appear at Bytes 414 and 445 in the header. Both vectors are the same. For convenience, the offsets appear from byte 0 of the vector, not the header.

Window Dimensions

Window dimensions reflect the limits of the configured video terminal that SuperCalc is installed to use.

Byte 0–3   **Physical window dimensions**   length: 4 bytes
These four bytes hold, in order:
1. upper left line of terminal or screen
2. upper left column of terminal or screen
3. lower right line of terminal or screen
4. lower right column of terminal or screen

Byte 4–13   **Logical window dimensions**   length: 10 bytes
This ten-byte area contains four fields, in this order and size:
1. upper left cell of video window (column first, then row; three bytes)
2. lower right cell of video window (column first, then row; three bytes)
3. last column scrollable on right (one byte)
4. cell of current cursor location (column first, then row; three bytes)

Title Locking Variables

Byte 14   **Hlock flag**   length: 1 byte
Horizontal locked row flag.
0 = inactive
1 = active

Byte 15–20   **Upper left/lower right**   length: 6 bytes
This area contains two three-byte fields. Each field is a cell location (row first, cell last). The first location is the upper left cell location of the horizontal locking area, and the second location is the lower right cell location of the horizontal locking area.

Byte 21   **Vlock flag**   length: 1 byte
Vertical locked row flag.
0 = inactive
1 = active

Byte 22–27   **Upper left/lower right**   length: 6 bytes
This area contains two three-byte fields. Each field is a cell location (row first, cell last). The first location is the upper left cell location of the vertical locking area, and the second location is the lower right cell location of the vertical locking area.

Global Formatting Constants

| Byte 28 | **Global column width** | length: 1 byte |
| Byte 29–30 | **Global display format** | length: 2 bytes |

The first byte of this word controls global text formatting. The second byte controls global numeric formatting. Table 4-4 describes byte 1, and Table 4-5 describes byte 2.

Table 4-4	Global formatting constants, Byte 1

Bit	Value	Meaning
0–1	01	text left justified
	10	text right justified
	11	reserved

Table 4-5	Global formatting constants, Byte 2

Bit	Value	Meaning
		Value formats:
0–2	000	use column/global format definition
	001	use dollars and cents ($)
	010	integer
	011	exponential (E)
	100	general format
	101	graphic (histogram) format
	110	hide
	111	reserved
3–4		not used
		User defined:
5	0	interpret bits 0–2 as above
	1	use user-defined global formats (Note1) and interpret bits 0–2 as index values 1 to 8 (000 = 1, 001 = 2, 010 = 3, etc.) into the user-defined formats area.
		Value formats:
6–7	00	not used
	01	right justify values
	10	left justify values
	11	reserved

Note 1	Bit 5 was set to zero in SuperCalc1. See Byte 106 et seq. for user-defined formats.

Internal Cell Definitions

Each cell area begins with its cell location as a three-byte prefix. The cell location contains a two-byte row location and a one-byte column location, in that order. After the cell prefix comes cell formatting and contents. For convenience, offsets in this chapter are from the beginning of cell contents, ignoring the three-byte cell location prefix.

Byte 0   **Cell type byte**   length: 1 byte
                        Table 4-6 describes the cell type byte.

Table 4-6	Cell type byte	
Bit	**Value**	**Meaning**
0–3		unused
4	0	not a constant
	1	data field constant; no BCD component
5	0	field unprotected
	1	field protected
6–7	00	text data in cell
	01	value or expression in cell
	10	expression with cell references in cell
	11	reserved

Byte 1   **Cell format byte**   length: 1 byte
                        Table 4-7 describes the contents of the cell format byte.

Table 4-7	Cell formatting byte	
Bit	**Value**	**Meaning**
		Value formats:
0–2	000	use row/column/global format definition
	001	use dollars and cents ($)
	010	integer
	011	exponential (E)
	100	general format
	101	graphic (histogram) format
	110	hide
	111	reserved
		Text formats:
3–4	00	use row/column/global justification
	01	left justified
	10	right justified
	11	reserved

(Table Continued)

Table 4-7 (Continued)

Bit	Value	Meaning
		User defined:
5	0	interpret bits 0–2 as above
	1	use user-defined global formats (Note1) and interpret bits 0–2 as index values 1 to 8 (000 = 1, 001 = 2, 010 = 3, etc.) into the user-defined formats area.
		Value formats:
6–7	00	use row/column/global justification
	01	right justify
	10	left justify
	11	reserved

Note 1   Bit 5 was set to zero in SuperCalc1. See Byte 106 et seq. for user-defined formats.

Byte 2   **Cell length byte**   length: 1 byte
This byte holds the number of cell allocation units (eight bytes each in SuperCalc4) for the cell.

Text Cells

Byte 3–240   **Text cell contents**   length: 238 bytes
Text cells contain ASCII-coded text terminated with an end-of-string null (00h). SuperCalc4 allocates 240 bytes because 240 is the nearest multiple of the eight-byte CAU.

Value, Formula, and Reference Cells

Byte 3–12   **BCD expression value**   length: 10 bytes
See Table 4-1 and the introductory information about the BCD component.

Byte 13–240   **Expression**   length: 228 bytes
Expression text string in ASCII terminated with an end-of-string null.

Graph Footer

SuperCalc can define a maximum of nine graphic charts. Each chart has a graphic descriptor associated with it. The current chart's graphic descriptor is located in the Graphic Section Header. If you have defined more than one graph, then all defined graphs will have a graphic descriptor in the Graphic Descriptors section. The current graph appears twice (once in the header, and once among the descriptors).

The size of the Graphic Section varies depending on the number of graphs. Its format is:

1. Graphic Section Header—256 bytes.

2. Graphic Descriptors—one for each graph (1–9); 256 bytes for each descriptor.

3. Graph Title Headers—nine consecutive Graph Title Headers. 64 bytes for each header.

4. End of File—128 bytes of 1Ah (Control-Z).

Graphic Section Header

The GS Header indicates the beginning of the graphic section and tells which chart is active. Only the first 13 bytes are significant; the remaining bytes are all nulls (13 bytes of data followed by 243 nulls). Table 4-8 describes its format:

Table 4-8	Graphic section header

Byte	Meaning
0–2	must be 1Ah (Control-Z)
3	must be DAh
4–12	nine bytes, each byte associated with a graphic descriptor in the order Byte 4 = descriptor 1, Byte 5 = descriptor 2, etc.
13–255	Nulls

If the content of bytes 4–12 is null (00h), it indicates that the corresponding graph is not defined. Otherwise, the graph is defined in the Graphic Descriptor.

Graphic Descriptor

After the section header is up to nine graphic descriptors. SuperCalc4 allocates each one 256 bytes. Each descriptor has the same format.

Note	Rows and columns are numbered from 1, not 0.

Byte offsets are from the 0 byte of each descriptor.

Byte 0–1 **Data block start row** length: 2 bytes
The row number of the starting data block for the current chart.

Byte 2 **Data block start column** length: 1 byte
The starting column of the data block.

Byte 3–4 **Data block end row** length: 2 bytes
The ending row for the data block.

Byte 5

Data block end column length: 1 byte
The ending column for the data block.

Byte 6–65

Series definitions length: 60 bytes
This area consists of ten six-byte fields. The fields are each two cell locations, one field for each of ten variables.

Byte 67–68

Point label start row length: 2 bytes
The row number of the starting point labels cell for the current chart.

Byte 69

Point label start column length: 1 byte
The starting column of the point labels cell.

Byte 70–71

Point label end row length: 2 bytes
The ending row for the point labels cell.

Byte 72

Point label end column length: 1 byte
The ending column for the point labels cell.

Byte 73–132

Point label definitions length: 60 bytes
This area consists of ten six-byte fields.

Byte 133–138

Label definitions length: 6 bytes
You should initialize this field to nulls.

Byte 139–144

Label range information length: 6 bytes
The six bytes are the row (two bytes) and column (one byte) cell locations of the starting cell and ending cell of the column or row holding the graph labels. Cells must be in either the same column or the same row. When preparing a SuperCalc4 spreadsheet externally to the program, you should initialize this field to nulls.

Byte 145–204

Label definitions length: 60 bytes
This area consists of ten six-byte fields. The fields are each two cell locations, one field for each of ten variables.

Byte 205–216

Title block length: 12 bytes
This area consists of four three-byte fields. Each field is a row (two bytes) and column (one byte) cell location. The four fields specify:
1. cell location of main graph title
2. cell location of graph subtitle
3. cell location of X-axis title
4. cell location of Y-axis title

Byte 217–222

X-axis scaling block length: 6 bytes
This area consists of two three-byte fields. The first field is the row and column location of the minimum X-axis value in the series being graphed. The second field is the location maximum X-axis value in the series being graphed.

Byte 223–228   **Y-axis scaling block**   length: 6 bytes
This area consists of two three-byte fields. The first field is the row
and column location of the minimum Y-axis value in the series being
graphed. The second field is the location of the maximum Y-axis
value in the series being graphed.

Byte 229–230   **VCMPAR**   length: 2 bytes
The *second* byte of VCMPAR defines the graph type:
01 = pie chart
02 = clustered bar
03 = stacked bar
04 = line
05 = XY
06 = area
07 = hi-lo
The first byte is undefined.

Byte 231   **Resolution**   length: 1 byte
This byte tells SuperCalc4 how to display the graph.
0 = medium resolution
1 = high resolution
2 = monochrome adapter and display

Byte 232   **Pie chart legends**   length: 1 byte
This byte tells SuperCalc4 how to display the legends of a pie chart.
0 = block legends
1 = radial legends

Byte 233   **Plot direction**   length: 1 byte
This byte controls where the program plots the graph.
0 = screen
1 = plotter

Byte 234–248   **Graph formats buffer**   length: 15 bytes
This area consists of five three-byte fields. Each three-byte field is
the row (two bytes) and column (one byte) location of a cell. The
fields are:
1. axis label formats
2. time label formats
3. variable label formats
4. data label formats
5. percent format

Byte 249–250   **Default scaling**   length: 2 bytes
This word consists of two bytes. The first byte contains the default
X-axis scaling. The second byte contains the default Y-axis scaling.

Byte 251–252   **Manual scaling**   length: 2 bytes
This word consists of two bytes. The first byte contains the number
of divisions for manual X-axis scaling. The second byte contains the
number of divisions for manual Y-axis scaling.

Byte 253   **Pie flag**   length: 1 byte
A non–zero value in this byte tells the program to draw the pie chart
with all segments exploded.

Byte 254   **Pie segment flag**   length: 1 byte
If bit zero of this byte is set on, it tell the program to explode only
segment 1 of the pie.

Byte 255   **Pie var/time**   length: 1 byte
0 = var wise
1 = time wise

Byte 3256   **Pie val**   length: 1 byte

Graphic Title Header

This area holds the nine title headers, one for each graph. Each title header occupies 64
bytes. The first 40 bytes contain the main title of the associated graph, and the 51st byte
contains the graph type as duplicated in the second byte of VCMPAR. The remaining
bytes are nulls.

End of Graph Header

This section consists of 128 bytes of 1Ah to indicate the end of the graph header.

Names List

The names list follows the graph header in the file if there are named areas in the
spreadsheet to list. If there is no graph header, there will be a sector (128 bytes) of 1Ah
(Control-Z) separating the names list from the end of cell data.
    The names list defines a series of named ranges for the file. It consists of a series of
variable-length records with the following format:

Byte 0   **Length**   length: 1 byte
Length of name in characters (max 31).

Byte 1   **Name**   length: n bytes
Name of length n characters (n = maximum of 31).

Byte 1 + n   **Range**   length: 6 bytes
This area consists of two three-byte fields. Each field consists of a
row (two bytes) and a column (one byte) cell location. The first

location is the range beginning, and the second location is the range end.

Byte 1 + n + 6   **Synonym list header flag**   length: 1 byte
  0 = if not at top of synonym list
FFh = at top of synonym list

At least one Control-Z (1Ah) follows the names list. The file is padded with Control-Zs to the nearest 128-byte boundary.

## CHAPTER 5

Super Project Plus

Version 2.0

Computer Associates International, Inc.
2195 Fortune Drive
San Jose, CA 95131–1820

Type of Product: Project management software

Files Produced: Binary

Conversion Information:
Version 2.0 of Super Project Plus does not import or export data.

Super Project File Format

Super Project Plus is a project management package that performs pert charting, gantt charting, critical path analysis, resource management, and so forth.

Its files consist of a series of variably sized records. Several of the records may appear many times. If there is no data for a record (for example, no defined holidays), the record will not appear at all.

Records must appear in a particular order:

1. Header records
2. Project records
3. Task records
4. Resource records
5. Resource assignment records
6. Link records
7. Holiday records
8. Select records
9. Select criteria records
10. Public project record

Four bytes (two integers) precede each and every record, including the header record. The first integer is the record type and the second is the length of the record. For clarity in listing offsets, this chapter includes those four bytes in each record description.

Table 5-1 summarizes the record types.

Table 5-1	Record type IDs		
Byte 0	**Byte1**	**Dec**	**Meaning**
FF	81	32279	end-of-file record
A1	81	33185	link record
A2	81	33186	project record
A3	81	33187	holiday record
A4	81	33188	task record
A6	81	33190	resource record
A7	81	33191	preference record
A8	81	33192	resource assignment record
AA	81	33194	file header record
AB	81	33195	select header record
AC	81	33196	select criteria record
AD	81	33197	public project record
AE	81	33198	print driver record
00	00	0	any type of record

Notes on Field and Record Contents

Coordinate 0,0 of the pert chart is at the center of the available area. Figure 5-1 illustrates the coordinate system.

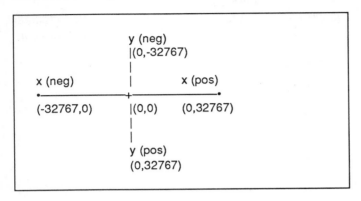

Figure 5-1 Pert chart coordinate system

Date fields contain a 1-based number representing the days relative to 1 January 1951. There is no 0 date.

Hour fields contain a number between 0 and 23 signifying the hour of the day. 0 is the first hour (12 p.m. to 1 a.m.), 1 is the second (1 a.m. to 2 a.m.) and so forth.

Each record header provides the length of the record, and the next record begins at the following byte. However, Super Project Plus does not always fill with data the entire record size it reserves. Sometimes, the tail of the record consists of nulls, spaces, or "garbage."

> **Note** Although there is an absolute record order in the file, there is no absolute offset information for the file as a whole because the file consists of a variable number of records. Other records may not appear at all because they're not needed for a given model. This chapter therefore provides offset information for each individual record.

Header Record

The first record to appear in a Super Project file is always the header record.

Byte 0–1   **Record Type**   length: 2 bytes
The record type of a file header record is 33194 (81 AAh). See Table 5-1 for a listing of record types.

Byte 2–3   **Record Length**   length: 2 bytes
The length of the *contents* portion of the record, in bytes, as measured starting with Byte 4. The record length does not include the first four bytes of the record. A header record is usually 80 bytes in length.

Byte 4–33 **Copyright Notice** length: 30 bytes
The copyright string is:
(C) 1985 Computer Associates
plus two trailing space characters.

Byte 34–35 **Spaces** length: 2 bytes
Two more space characters (20h).

Byte 36–43 **Creation Date** length: 8 bytes
Date on which the project model was first created. The format is
mm-dd-yy.

Byte 44 **Space** length: 1 byte
One space character.

Byte 45–55 **Time** length: 11 bytes
Time at which the project model was first created. The format is
hh:mm:ss:hh, where the second hh signifies a two-digit, hun-
dredths-of-a-second figure.

Byte 56–58 **Spaces** length: 3 bytes
Three space characters.

Byte 59–67 **Version and Release** length: 9 bytes
For version 2.00, the version and release information is:
VER: 2.00
There are no trailing spaces in this field.

Byte 68–80 **Spaces** length: 13 bytes
A string of 13 space characters (20h).

Byte 81 **End of File Character** length: 1 byte
This byte is a single Control–Z (ASCII 26, 1Ah).

Byte 82–131 **Unused** length: 50 bytes
You should initialize this unused area to nulls (00h).

Project Record

There is one project record per project file. It immediately follows the header record.

Byte 0–1 **Record Type** length: 2 bytes
The record type of a project record is 33186 (81 A2h). See Table 5-
1 for a listing of record types.

Byte 2–3 **Record Length** length: 2 bytes
The length of the *contents* portion of the record, in bytes, as
measured starting with Byte 4. The record length does not include
the first four bytes of the record.

Byte 4–59   **Reserved**   length: 56 bytes
This section comprises 14 four-byte units that Super Project uses internally. A Super Project file will contain data here; a file prepared externally to the program should initialize these bytes to nulls.

Byte 60–61   **Project Flags**   length: 2 bytes
This 16-bit word contains a set of flag bits. Table 5-2 lists the bits and their meanings.

Table 5-2	Project record flag bits (1 = yes)

Bit	Meaning
0	Is this project selected?
1	Has project been modified since last checkpoint?
2	Is this project locked?
3	Is this project a sub-project?
4	Is this project a super-project?
5	If memory is needed, do not roll project out?
6	Begin calculation with (1 = start, 0 = finish)
7	Recalculate this project?
8	Is default duration in hours?
9	Is default resource allocation in percent?
10	Have the holidays been optimized?
11	Is the task filter active?
12	Is the resource filter active?
13	Is the resource assignment filter active?
14	Undefined
15	Unused

Byte 62–65   **Undefined**   length: 4 bytes
Initialize this four-byte sequence to nulls when preparing a file externally to the program.

Byte 66–67   **Displacement of Starting Task**   length: 2 bytes

Byte 68–69   **Displacement of Starting Resource Assignment** length: 2 bytes

Byte 70–71   **Project ID Number**   length: 2 bytes
Super Project assigns the project ID number internally starting from 1.

Byte 72–73   **Next Task ID Number Available**   length: 2 bytes
The number of the next task to be assigned when the file was last saved.

Byte 74–75   **Next Resource ID Number Available**   length: 2 bytes
The number of the next resource to be assigned when the file was last saved.

Byte 76–77 **Number of Tasks in the Project** length: 2 bytes

Byte 78–79 **Number of Resources in the Project** length: 2 bytes

Byte 80–81 **Critical Path Duration in Days** length: 2 bytes
The length of the critical path in whole days.

Byte 82–83 **Critical Path Duration in Remaining Hours** length: 2 bytes
If the critical path length does not end on a day boundary, this word holds the number of additional hours.

Byte 84–85 **Project Revision Number** length: 2 bytes
If the project has not been revised, this word is a null.

Byte 86–87 **Undefined** length: 2 bytes
Set to nulls.

Byte 88–95 **Project Total Variable Costs** length: 8 bytes
This field is a double-precision floating-point number.

Byte 96–103 **Project Total Fixed Costs** length: 8 bytes
This field is a double-precision floating-point number.

Byte 104–111 **Project Total Actual Costs** length: 8 bytes
This field is a double-precision floating-point number.

Byte 112–115 **Project Total Actual Hours** length: 4 bytes

Byte 116–119 **Project Total Resource Assignment Hours** length: 4 bytes

Byte 120–123 **Resource Assignment Overscheduled** length: 4 bytes

Byte 124–125 **Project Start Date** length: 2 bytes

Byte 126–127 **Project Finish Date** length: 2 bytes

Byte 128 **Project Start Hour** length: 1 byte

Byte 129 **Project Finish Hour** length: 1 byte

Byte 130–131 **Original Creation** length: 2 bytes
This is the date that the project was originally created.

Byte 132–133 **Last Written to Disk** length: 2 bytes
This is the date that the project was last written to disk.

Byte 134–137 **Time Last Written to Disk** length: 4 bytes
This is a four-byte long integer representing the time that the project was last written to disk.

Byte 138–139 **Project Lock Combination** length: 2 bytes
This is a word interpreted by the program as 16 bits.

Byte 140–143 **Default Resource Assignment Rate** length: 4 bytes
This is a four-byte floating-point number.

Byte 144–147   **Default Fixed Amount**   length: 2 bytes
This is a four-byte floating-point number.

Byte 148–163   **Project Work Week**   length: 16 bytes
Super Project organizes the 16 bytes of the work week field into seven two-byte integers, one each for Sunday through Saturday, and two nulls. Each integer contains the number of hours in that particular work day.

Byte 164–184   **Bit Mask for Work Hours**   length: 21 bytes
Super Project organizes the 21-byte bit mask field into seven three-byte fields, each representing a day of the week from Sunday through Saturday.

Byte 185–186   **Default Project Task Duration**   length: 2 bytes

Byte 187–188   **Default Project Resource Assignment Priority**   length: 2 bytes

Byte 189–190   **Default Project Overscheduled Priority**   length: 2 bytes

Byte 191–192   **Default Resource Assignment Allocation Type**   length: 2 bytes

Byte 193–194   **Default Allocation Hours per Day**   length: 2 bytes

Byte 195–196   **Default Resource Assignment Work Hours**   length: 2 bytes

Byte 197–200   **Default Resource Assignment Overtime Rate**   length: 4 bytes
This field is a four-byte floating-point number.

Byte 201–202   **Days per Symbol/Task Gantt Chart**   length: 2 bytes

Byte 203–204   **Days per Symbol/Resource Gantt Chart**   length: 2 bytes

Byte 205–208   **Project ID Code**   length: 4 bytes

Byte 209–223   **Connected Project Filespec**   length: 15 bytes
The path and file name of any connected project.

Byte 223–238   **Project Filespec**   length: 15 bytes
The path and file name of the project.

Byte 239–255   **Project Author**   length: 17 bytes

Byte 256–272   **Project Leader**   length: 17 bytes

Byte 273–329   **Project Description**   length: 57 bytes

Byte 330–331   **ULX**   length: 2 bytes
Upper left X coordinate (column) of the pert chart.

Byte 332–333   **ULY**   length: 2 bytes
Upper left Y coordinate (row) of the pert chart.

Byte 334–415   **Directory of Project File**   length: 81 bytes

Byte 416–436 **Unused** length: 21 bytes
The remainder of the record is padded with nulls.

Task Record

Task records for each task in the project follow the project record. A task record may have two sizes, depending on whether a subproject connects to it.

Byte 0–1 **Record Type** length: 2 bytes
The record type of a task record is 33188 (81 A4h). See Table 5-1 for a listing of record types.

Byte 2–3 **Record Length** length: 2 bytes
The length of the *contents* portion of the record, in bytes, as measured starting with Byte 4. The record length does not include the first four bytes of the record.

Byte 4–35 **Reserved** length: 32 bytes
This section comprises eight four-byte units that Super Project uses internally. A Super Project file will contain data here; a file prepared externally to the program should initialize these bytes to nulls.

Byte 36–37 **Task Flags** length: 2 bytes
This 16-bit word contains a set of flag bits. Table 5-3 lists the bits and their meaning.

Table 5-3	Task record flag bits (1 = yes)

Bit	Meaning
0	Is this task selected?
1	Is this task connected to a subproject?
2	Is this task on a critical path?
3	Is this task in conflict?
4	Is this task delay in hours or days? (1 = hours, 0 = days)
5	undefined
6	undefined
7	undefined
8	undefined
9	undefined
10	undefined
11	undefined
12	undefined
13	Was a "must start date" entered?
14	Was a "must finish date" entered?
15	Are durations in hours or days for task? (1 = hours, 0 = days)

Byte 38–39	**Undefined**	length: 2 bytes

Initialize this two-byte sequence to nulls when preparing a file externally to the program.

Byte 40–41	**Y Coordinate Pert Task Box Center** length: 2 bytes	
Byte 42–43	**X Coordinate Pert Task Box Center** length: 2 bytes	
Byte 44–45	**Task ID Number Displayed**	length: 2 bytes

This is the task ID number that this task displays on screen.

Byte 46–47	**Undefined**	length: 2 bytes

Initialize this two-byte sequence to nulls when preparing a file externally to the program.

Byte 48–49	**First Hook**	length: 2 bytes

This is the first hook to show on task details.

Byte 50–51	**Early Start Date**	length: 2 bytes
Byte 52–53	**Late Start Date**	length: 2 bytes
Byte 54–55	**Early Finish Date**	length: 2 bytes
Byte 56–57	**Late Finish Date**	length: 2 bytes
Byte 58–59	**Must Start Date**	length: 2 bytes
Byte 60–61	**Must Finish Date**	length: 2 bytes
Byte 62–63	**Actual Start Date**	length: 2 bytes
Byte 64–65	**Actual Finish Date**	length: 2 bytes
Byte 66–67	**Scheduled Start Date**	length: 2 bytes
Byte 68–69	**Scheduled Finish Date**	length: 2 bytes
Byte 70–71	**Planned Start Date**	length: 2 bytes
Byte 72–73	**Planned Finish Date**	length: 2 bytes
Byte 74	**Early Start Hour**	length: 1 byte
Byte 75	**Late Start Hour**	length: 1 byte
Byte 76	**Early Finish Hour**	length: 1 byte
Byte 77	**Late Finish Hour**	length: 1 byte
Byte 78	**Must Start Hour**	length: 1 byte
Byte 79	**Must Finish Hour**	length: 1 byte
Byte 80	**Actual Start Hour**	length: 1 byte
Byte 81	**Actual Finish Hour**	length: 1 byte
Byte 82	**Scheduled Start Hour**	length: 1 byte

Byte 83	Scheduled Finish Hour	length: 1 byte
Byte 84	Planned Start Hour	length: 1 byte
Byte 85	Planned Finish Hour	length: 1 byte
Byte 86–87	Task Duration	length: 2 bytes

This value can hold either hours or days, depending on the flag bits.

Byte 88–89	Task Actual Duration	length: 2 bytes

This value can also hold either hours or days.

Byte 90–91	Total Float	length: 2 bytes
Byte 92–93	Free Float	length: 2 bytes
Byte 94–95	Task Delay	length: 2 bytes
Byte 96–97	Task Finish Delay	length: 2 bytes
Byte 98–114	Task Name	length: 17 bytes
Byte 115–171	Task Description	length: 57 bytes
Byte 172-188	Word Breakdown Structure	length: 17 bytes
Byte 189–193	Undefined	length: 5 bytes

Initialize these five bytes to nulls when preparing a file externally to the program.

Connected Task Record Addenda

If a task is connected to a subproject, there are an additional seven fields appended to the end of the task record.

Byte 194–201	Variable Cost of Connected Project	length: 8 bytes

This field is an eight-byte double-precision real.

Byte 202–209	Fixed Cost of Connected Project	length: 8 bytes

This field is an eight-byte double-precision real.

Byte 210–217	Actual Cost of Connected Project	length: 8 bytes

This field is an eight-byte double-precision real.

Byte 218–221	Actual Hours of Connected Project	length: 4 bytes

This field is four bytes long.

Byte 222–225	Hours of Connected Project	length: 4 bytes

This field is four bytes long.

Byte 226–229	Overscheduled Hours of Connected Project	length: 4 bytes

This field is four bytes long.

Byte 230–244	Connected Project Filename	length: 15 bytes

Resource Record

After all the task records, Super Project Plus writes all the resource records.

Byte 0–1 **Record Type** length: 2 bytes
The record type of a resource record is 33190 (81 A6h). See Table 5-1 for a listing of record types.

Byte 2–3 **Record Length** length: 2 bytes
The length of the *contents* portion of the record, in bytes, as measured starting with Byte 4. The record length does not include the first four bytes of the record.

Byte 4–39 **Reserved** length: 36 bytes
This section comprises nine four-byte units that Super Project uses internally. A Super Project file will contain data here; a file prepared externally to the program should initialize these bytes to nulls.

Byte 40–41 **Resource Flags** length: 2 bytes
This 16-bit word contains a set of flag bits. Table 5-4 lists the bits and their meaning.

Table 5-4	Resource record flag bits (1 = yes)		
Bit	**Meaning**	**Bit**	**Meaning**
0	undefined	8	undefined
1	undefined	9	undefined
2	undefined	10	unused
3	Is default allocation in percent?	11	unused
4	Is resource hidden on the gantt chart?	12	unused
5	undefined	13	unused
6	Is resource selected?	14	unused
7	Are the holidays optimized?	15	unused

Byte 42–43 **First Hook** length: 2 bytes
This is the first resource hook to show.

Byte 44–45 **Internal Resource ID Number** length: 2 bytes

Byte 46–61 **Work Hours for Each Day of the Week** length: 16 bytes
Super Project divides these 16 bytes into eight words. Each of the first seven words represent a day of the week, Sunday through Saturday. The last word is set to nulls.

Byte 62–63 **Default Resource Assignment Priority** length: 2 bytes

Byte 64–65 **Undefined** length: 2 bytes
Used internally by Super Project.

| Byte 66–67 | **Cost Accrual Method** | length: 2 bytes |

0 = accrue at the beginning
1 = prorate the accrual
2 = accrue at the end

| Byte 68–69 | **Number of Resource Units** | length: 2 bytes |

| Byte 70–73 | **Number of Hours Resource is Overscheduled** | length: 4 bytes |

This field is a four-byte long integer.

| Byte 74–77 | **Number of Calendar Overtime Hours** | length: 4 bytes |

This field is a four-byte long integer.

| Byte 78–81 | **Default Resource Assignment Allocation Type** | length: 4 bytes |

| Byte 82–83 | **Default Resource Assignment Allocation Hours** | length: 2 bytes |

| Byte 84–85 | **Default Resource Assignment Hours** | length: 2 bytes |

| Byte 86–89 | **Default Resource Assignment Rate** | length: 4 bytes |

| Byte 90–91 | **Default Fixed Cost** | length: 2 bytes |

| Byte 92–95 | **Default Resource Assignment Overtime Rate** | length: 4 bytes |

| Byte 96–106 | **Resource Name** | length: 11 bytes |

| Byte 107–163 | **Resource Description** | length: 57 bytes |

| Byte 164–170 | **Work Code** | length: 7 bytes |

| Byte 170–173 | **Undefined** | length: 3 bytes |

Resource Assignment Record

The resource assignment records follow all the resource records.

| Byte 0–1 | **Record Type** | length: 2 bytes |

The record type of a resource assignment record is 33192 (81 A8h). See Table 5-1 for a listing of record types.

| Byte 2–3 | **Record Length** | length: 2 bytes |

The length of the *contents* portion of the record, in bytes, as measured starting with Byte 4. The record length does not include the first four bytes of the record.

| Byte 4–5 | **Resource Assignment Task ID** | length: 2 bytes |

| Byte 6–7 | **Resource Assignment Resource ID** | length: 2 bytes |

Byte 8–43   **Undefined**   length: 36 bytes
These 36 bytes are a series of eight four-byte fields that Super Project uses internally. Initialize this sequence to nulls when preparing a file externally to the program.

Byte 36–37   **Resource Assignment Flags**   length: 2 bytes
This 16-bit word contains a set of flag bits. Table 5-5 lists the bits and their meanings.

Table 5-5	Resource assignment record flag bits (1 = yes)			
Bit	**Meaning**		**Bit**	**Meaning**
0	undefined		8	unused
1	Is resource assignment the lead assignment?		9	unused
2	Is resource assignment in conflict?		10	unused
3	Is resource assignment of a linked project?		11	unused
4	Is resource assignment allocation in percent?		12	unused
5	Is resource assignment selected?		13	unused
6	unused		14	unused
7	unused		15	unused

Byte 46–47   **Scheduled Start Date**   length: 2 bytes

Byte 48–49   **Scheduled Finish Date**   length: 2 bytes

Byte 50–51   **Late Start Date**   length: 2 bytes

Byte 52–53   **Late Finish Date**   length: 2 bytes

Byte 54   **Scheduled Start Hour**   length: 1 byte

Byte 55   **Scheduled Finish Hour**   length: 1 byte

Byte 56   **Late Start Hour**   length: 1 byte

Byte 57   **Late Finish Hour**   length: 1 byte

Byte 58–59   **Total Float**   length: 2 bytes

Byte 60–61   **Delay From Task Scheduled Start** length: 2 bytes

Byte 62–63   **Priority**   length: 2 bytes

Byte 64–65   **Hours to Work on this Task**   length: 2 bytes

Byte 66–67   **Overscheduled Hours on this Task** length: 2 bytes

Byte 68–69   **Actual Hours on this Task**   length: 2 bytes

Byte 70–73   **Resource Assign Allocation Type** length: 4 bytes

Byte 74–75   **Allocation Hours**   length: 2 bytes

Byte 76–79	Actual Cost	length: 4 bytes
Byte 80–83	Assignment Rate	length: 4 bytes
Byte 84–87	Assignment Fixed Cost	length: 4 bytes
Byte 88–89	Number of Units Resource Assignment	length: 2 bytes
Byte 90–91	Undefined	length: 2 bytes

Byte 92–93   **First Day**   length: 2 bytes
Allocation on first day of resource assignment.

Byte 94–95   **Last Day**   length: 2 bytes
Allocation on last day of resource assignment.

Byte 96–99	Undefined	length: 4 bytes
Byte 100–101	Resource Assignment Finish Delay	length: 2 bytes
Byte 102–107	Undefined	length: 6 bytes

Link Record

Link records follow the last of the resource assignment records.

Byte 0–1   **Record Type**   length: 2 bytes
The record type of a link record is 33185 (81 A1h). See Table 5–1 for a listing of record types.

Byte 2–3   **Record Length**   length: 2 bytes
The length of the *contents* portion of the record, in bytes, as measured starting with Byte 4. The record length does not include the first four bytes of the record.

Byte 4–5   **Link from Task ID**   length: 2 bytes

Byte 6–7   **Link to Task ID**   length: 2 bytes

Byte 8–31   **Undefined**   length: 24 bytes
These 24 bytes are a series of six four–byte fields that Super Project uses internally. Initialize this sequence to nulls when preparing a file externally to the program.

Byte 32–33   **Link Flags**   length: 2 bytes
This 16-bit word contains a set of flag bits. Table 5–6 lists the bits and their meanings.

Table 5-6	Link record flag bits (1 = yes)		
Bit	**Meaning**	**Bit**	**Meaning**
0	Is this link selected?	7	unused
1	Is this link a critical link?	8	unused
2	undefined	9	unused
3	Is lead lag in hours or days?	10	unused
	(1 = hours, 0 = days)	11	unused
4	unused	12	unused
5	unused	13	unused
6	unused	14	unused
		15	unused

Byte 34–35   **Link Lead/Lag Duration**   length: 2 bytes

Byte 36   **Link Type**   length: 1 byte
FS = 0
SS = 1
FF = 2

Holiday Record

Holdiday records follow the last link record. A holiday is an exception to the regular working hours per day. Holidays may be either project or resource holidays. Super Project first writes its resource holidays, then the project holidays.

Byte 0–1   **Record Type**   length: 2 bytes
The record type of a holiday record is 33187 (81 A3h). See Table 5–1 for a listing of record types.

Byte 2–3   **Record Length**   length: 2 bytes
The length of the *contents* portion of the record, in bytes, as measured starting with Byte 4. The record length does not include the first four bytes of the record.

Byte 4–5   **Resource ID Number**   length: 2 bytes
This word holds nulls if the holiday is a project holiday.

Byte 6–13   **Undefined**   length: 8 bytes
These are two four-byte fields that Super Project uses internally. Initialize this sequence to nulls when preparing a file externally to the program.

Byte 14–15   **Holiday Date**   length: 2 bytes

Byte 16–25   **Holiday Name**   length: 10 bytes

Byte 26–27   **Hours**   length: 2 bytes
                   Hours to work on the holiday.

Byte 28–29   **Holiday Flags**   length: 2 bytes
                   This 16-bit word contains a set of flag bits. Table 5-7 lists the bits
                   and their meaning.

Table 5-7	Holiday record flag bits (1 = yes)		
Bit	**Meaning**	**Bit**	**Meaning**
0	Is holiday a project holiday?	8	unused
1	Does holiday define hours to work that day?	9	unused
2	unused	10	unused
3	unused	11	unused
4	unused	12	unused
5	unused	13	unused
6	unused	14	unused
7	unused	15	unused

Select Header Record

After any holiday records, Super Project writes select information. Each select criteria set consists of a select header record followed by a set of select criteria records.

Byte 0–1   **Record Type**   length: 2 bytes
                   The record type of a select header record is 33195 (81 ABh). See
                   Table 5-1 for a listing of record types.

Byte 2–3   **Record Length**   length: 2 bytes
                   The length of the *contents* portion of the record, in bytes, as
                   measured starting with Byte 4. The record length does not include
                   the first four bytes of the record.

Byte 4–15   **Undefined**   length: 12 bytes
                   Super Project divides this field into three four-byte fields. The
                   program uses these fields internally; initialize them to nulls when
                   creating a project externally to the program.

Byte 16–17   **Screen**   length: 2 bytes
                   The screen display that the select criteria is set for:
                   Resource gantt = 125 (7Dh)
                   Task details and task gantt = 124 (7Ch)
                   Resource details = 126 (7Eh)

Byte 18–19   **Undefined**   length: 2 bytes

Byte 20–36   **Name of the Select Criteria**   length: 17 bytes

Byte 37–40   **Bit Flags**   length: 4 bytes

These four bytes are 32-bit flags that correspond to fields in order on each of the different select screens, and determine whether to show the field on a report. Super Project does not use all bit flags.

Byte 41–42   **Sort Key One Criteria ID**   length: 2 bytes

Byte 43–44   **Sort Key Two Criteria ID**   length: 2 bytes

Byte 45–46   **Sort Key Three Criteria ID**   length: 2 bytes

Byte 47–48   **Undefined**   length: 2 bytes

Select Criteria Record

After a select criteria header, Super Project writes all the select criteria records that belong to that header.

Byte 0–1   **Record Type**   length: 2 bytes

The record type of a select criteria record is 33196 (81 ACh). See Table 5-1 for a listing of record types.

Byte 2–3   **Record Length**   length: 2 bytes

The length of the *contents* portion of the record, in bytes, as measured starting with Byte 4. The record length does not include the first four bytes of the record.

Byte 4–7   **Undefined**   length: 4 bytes

This is a single four-byte field. The program uses this field internally; initialize them to nulls when creating a project externally to the program.

Byte 8   **Select Criteria Field**   length: 1 byte

Comments

Byte 9   **Lower or Upper**   length: 1 byte

If this is a lower select criteria, the value of this field is 0; if an upper, the value of the field is 1.

Byte 10   **Select Criteria Data Type**   length: 1 byte

This value must correspond to the type of field.

Byte 11   **Extra Length**   length: 1 byte

This field holds the extra length of the field value that follows.

Byte 12–13   **Value**   length: 2 byte

Byte 14–n   **Field Value**   length: variable bytes

This field is a variable number of bytes. It holds the field value. The "Extra Length" field holds this field's length.

ID Tables for Select Criteria

Tables 5-8, 5-9, and 5-10 list IDs, values, and data types for use with the select criteria records.

Table 5-8	ID list for task details and task gantt screens		
ID	**Meaning**	**Value**	**Type**
NDID	ID	01	integer
NDNAME	name	28	string
NDWBS		31	string
NDDUR	duration	22	integer
NDSDELAY	delay	26	integer
NDACTDUR	actual duration	23	integer
NDFLOAT	float	24	integer
NDTSTA	start	06	date
NDTFIN	finish	07	date
NDSSTA	scheduled start	10	date
NDSFIN	scheduled finish	11	date
NDASTA	actual start	08	date
NDAFIN	actual finish	09	date
NDTOTAL		36	double precision
NDTOTACT	total actual duration	35	dourble precision
NDTOTHRS	total hours	37	long
NDTOTAHR	total actual hours	38	long
NDDESC	description	29	string

Table 5-9	ID list for resource detail screen		
ID	**Meaning**	**Value**	**Type**
RSNAME	name	96	string
RSWORKTY	work hours	98	string
RSOVRHRS	hours overscheduled	99	long
RSOVRATE	resource rate	100	double precision
RSOVRTIM	overtime rate	101	long
RSUNITS	resource units	110	integer
RSTOTVAR	total variable cost	102	double precision
RSTOTFIX	total fixed cost	103	double precision
RSTOTAL	total cost	104	double precision
RSTOTACT	total actual cost	105	double precision
RSTOTHRS	total hours	106	long
RSTOTAHR	total actual hours	107	long
RSDESC	resource description	97	string

Table 5-10	ID list for resource gantt screen		
ID	**Meaning**	**Value**	**Type**
HKRSRC	resource	53	string
HKNODE		52	string
HKPRI	priority	61	integer
HKHOUR		62	integer
HKUNITS	resource units	70	integer
HKALLOCHR	allocated hours	66	integer
HKALLOC	allocation type	65	string
HKOVER		63	integer
HKACTUAL		64	integer
HKSTA	start	54	date
HKFIN	finish	55	date
HKRATE		68	double precision
HKVAR	variable cost	72	double precision
HKFIX	fixed cost	69	double precision
HKTOTAL		74	double precision
HKCOST		67	double precision

Public Project Record

Public project records make up the last group of records in the Super Project file. Each contains the name of a project to which the current project links.

Byte 0–1   **Record Type**   length: 2 bytes
The record type of a public project record is 33197 (81 ADh). See Table 5-1 for a listing of record types.

Byte 2–3   **Record Length**   length: 2 bytes
The length of the *contents* portion of the record, in bytes, as measured starting with Byte 4. The record length does not include the first four bytes of the record.

Byte 4–15   **Undefined**   length: 12 bytes
This is a field consisting of three four-byte fields. The program uses these fields internally; initialize them to nulls when creating a project externally to the program.

Byte 16–97   **Linked Project File Name**   length: 82 bytes

Byte 98–99   **Undefined**   length: 2 bytes

## CHAPTER 6

Volkswriter 3

Volkswriter 3 v 1.0
(and Volkswriter Deluxe)

Lifetree Software Inc.
411 Pacific Street
Monterey, CA 93940

Type of Product: Word processing software

Files Produced: Extended ASCII (00h–FFh)

Points of Interest:

Volkswriter 3 supports a 250-character-wide ruler line. The program automatically wraps files with line lengths longer than 250 characters (or with no delimited line length).

Conversion Information:

Volkswriter 3 can convert both ways between DCA (revisable text format), Wordstar, and ASCII text files.

Volkswriter 3 File Format

Volkswriter creates ASCII files that can contain the IBM extended ASCII character set (00 to 255). Each file consists of a text section and a layout "footer" at the end of the file. The main difference between files that Volkswriter 3 produces and files that the earlier Volkswriter Deluxe version produces is that Volkswriter 3 incorporates the footer into the document file; Volkswriter Deluxe produces a separate file with the footer information in it.

The footer holds ruler and other formatting information. According to the manufacturer, after loading the size file specified in the DOS directory, Volkswriter scans it *backwards*, looking for the first non-Control-Z character. The footer arrangement thus makes sense.

Volkswriter pads its files with Control-Z characters (ASCII 26, 1Ah) to the sector boundary.

There are no absolute offsets in the text portion of a Volkswriter file because the program places its formatting commands within running text. In the footer section, however, the formatting and rulers fall in a particular order.

Types of File Commands

Volkswriter places two kinds of commands in the running text of the document. These are single-character *control commands* and *embedded text commands*. Control commands are always characters of ASCII code 32 or less. Embedded commands are text—often several characters long—beginning with two period characters (ASCII 46, 2Eh). Embedded text commands always start in column 1 of any line.

Table 6-1 lists the control commands.

Table 6-1	Volkswriter control commands		
ASCII	**Command**	**ASCII**	**Command**
00	forced space	17	end block
01	reserved	18	boldface
02	reserved	19	reserved
03	font 1 (default)	20	end of paragraph
04	font 2	21	reserved
05	font 3	22	soft hyphen
06	font 4	23	reserved
07	center	24	superscript
08	reserved	25	subscript
09	reserved	26	Ctrl-Z end of file
10	linfeed (w. CR)	27	reserved
11	reserved	28	strike-through
12	reserved	29	shadow print
13	return (w LF)	30	reserved
14	reserved	31	underlining
15	reserved	32	reserved
16	begin block		

The begin block and end block codes are "transient": Volkswriter saves them only if it saves the file with the block action uncompleted. (For example, highlighting a section of text and then saving the file before applying any other command to the text.)

Volkswriter uses some of the reserved codes internally (begin and end column, for example), but does not save them with the file. When the program exports a file, it strips all control commands.

A combined carriage return/line feed (in that order) is Volkswriter's newline character. It marks where the program wrapped the line when it last saved the file. Volkswriter ends a paragraph (or a line that does not wrap) with ASCII 20 (14h).

Embedded Text Commands

Volkswriter's embedded text commands appear in the running text. Each has a double-dot prefix (..). Text commands have six guidelines:

1. Text commands must begin in column 1 of the line they appear in.
2. The two prefix characters must be periods (ASCII 46, 2Eh).
3. You can fit 250 embedded text commands in one document on a 256K computer. For each additional 64K of memory above that, you can add 1,000 additional commands to the document. These numbers hold regardless of document size.
4. A layout change counts as a double-dot text command.
5. Text commands do not work with Textmerge list files.
6. There may be no spaces in an embedded text command other than those specified.

The legal embedded text commands for Volkswriter 3 and Volkswriter Deluxe are:

..text   **Comment**
A comment is a line of text that is placed in a file and displays on screen but will not print. The Comment command is good for one line. The characters text can be any text up to the line length you have set.

..CMDtext   **Printer command**
The ..CMD sends text directly to the printer. Use ..CMD to send printer escape codes.

..END   **Halt printing**
The ..END command stops printing as though the program had reached the end of the document. Use ..END to place nonprinting information at the bottom of the document.

..FILE   **Textmerge file**
Specifies the file of data to use with the Textmerge capabilities of Volkswriter.

..FOOTnnxxtext   **Footer**

This command sets the footer for a document where:

nn   must be a two-digit number (03 or 35, for example). The number specifies the absolute line number on the page (starting at the top) where Volkswriter places the footer. The line number must be greater than the line number of the last line of text in the body of the page. If the line number is less than or equal to the line number of the last line of text, Volkswriter ignores the header.

xx   must be two text header control characters as specified in Table 6-2.

text   is the text of the footer. Two number signs (##) together will place a page number in the footer.

Table 6-2	Footer control characters		
1st X	**Meaning**	**2nd X**	**Meaning**
O	odd pages	L	flush left footer
E	even pages	R	flush right footer
		C	centered footer
		A	alternating fl/fr on odd and even pages

..HEADnnxxtext   **Header**

This command sets the header for a document where

nn   must be a two-digit number (03 or 35, for example). The number specifies the absolute line number on the page (starting at the top) where Volkswriter places the header. The line number must be less than the line number of the first line of text in the body of the page. If the line number is greater than or equal to the line number of the first line of text, Volkswriter ignores the header.

xx   must be two text header control characters as specified in Table 6-3.

text   the text of the header. Two number signs (##) together will place a page number in the header.

Table 6-3	Header control characters		
1st X	**Meaning**	**2nd X**	**Meaning**
O	odd pages	L	flush left header
E	even pages	R	flush right header
		C	centered header
		A	alternating fl/fr on odd and even pages

..Layout nnn

Layout change

The ..Layout nnn command changes the layout (margins, tab settings, etc.) to the nth layout in the file VWSTYLE.LYT. There may be as many as 400 layouts in the VWSTYLE.LYT file; however, you may include a maximum of 15 of them in any one document—and switch among those 15 as often as you like within that document. The command LAYOUT 000 signals the beginning of the format footer.

..NORM

Normal interpretation

The ..NORM command toggles Volkswriter to its normal mode of interpreting embedded and control commands before sending text to the printer. See also "..VERB."

..PAGE

Forced page break

The ..Page command forces a page to end and a new page to begin.

..PAUSEtext

Pause and prompt

During printing, when Volkswriter encounters a ..PAUSE command, it temporarily halts printing and displays text on the status line. The program waits for the user to press any key before continuing. You can use this command to pass a message to the user at print time ("remove letterhead"). If you supply no text string, Volkswriter uses the default message , "Press any key to continue."

..PGNOxxxxx

Page number

You can reset the current page number with the ..PGNO command. Follow the command with one to five digits (0–99999). If you use the 0, Volkswriter prompts the user at print time to enter the page number.

..PRINTfilespec

Print another file

The ..PRINT command suspends printing of the current document and starts printing the document specified by filespec. When Volkswriter reaches the end of the filespec document , it resumes printing the original document, where it left off.

There must be no blanks between the word "..PRINT" and the name of the document to be printed..The document specified by filespec must not itself include any ..PRINT commands.

..VERB

Verbatim

This command Toggles Volkswriter so that it no longer interprets embedded commands or control commands before sending its text to the printer. It sends the text "verbatim." See also "..NORM."

Volkswriter File Footer

The Volkswriter file footer appears at the end of the document.
   Preceding the footer are:
   1.   The final end of paragraph marker for the text of the document (ASCII 20, 14h).
   2.   The two-byte newline character made up of a carriage return and a line feed(ASCII 13ASCII 10, 0D 0Ah).
   3.   Two Control-Z characters (ASCII 25, 1Ah).
   4.   The string:
       LAYOUT 000
   5.   Another two-byte newline character (carriage return/line feed).
   6.   Enough Control-Z characters to pad to the end of the sector.

A sector is 128 bytes. The footer starts at the beginning of the next sector following the text unless 0D 0Ah (newline) are the last two bytes of the text sector (thus the two Control-Zs; LAYOUT string, newline, and Control-Z pads won't fit). In that case there is a full sector of Control-Z end-of-file characters before the footer.

Footer Records

There may be from 1 to 15 layout records in the footer. Each layout record takes the same form, with the exception of the first three bytes of the first layout record. Those three bytes are present only for the first record.
   There must be one record for each ..LAYOUT nnn command embedded in the text. They appear in numerical order.
   Additionally, there are some fields in the layout records other than the first that Volkswriter simply ignores. For example, the first layout record establishes the form length. Later layout records may have a value in this field, but Volkswriter ignores it.
   If you are preparing a Volkswriter file externally to Volkswriter, you may safely set any reserved fields to nulls.

Important   Volkswriter "DOS file mode" files do not contain any layout information. Volkswriter pads the end of a DOS file mode file to the end of a sector with end-of-file characters (ASCII 26, 1Ah).

Footer Record Fields and Offsets

The offsets for these footer record fields start at Byte 0 as the first byte of the first footer record. Subsequent footer records lack Bytes 0–2. As a result, decrease the offsets for later records by three.

Byte 0–1 **Record Length** length: 2 bytes
This integer is the length of all layout records in the footer taken together. Volkswriter creates this field only once, in the first layout record.

Byte 2 **Version Number** length: 1 byte

Byte 3 **Number of Layouts** length: 1 byte
This byte holds the number of layouts in the footer, counting from 1. After the first record, Volkswriter ignores the contents of this byte.

Byte 4 **Unused** length: 1 byte
Volkswriter does not use this byte, nor is it reserved. Volkswriter ignores the contents of this byte.

Byte 5–7 **Reserved** length: 3 bytes
Set these bytes to nulls when creating a Volkswriter file externally to the program.

Byte 8 **Printer Code** length: 1 byte
This byte holds the number of the printer driver. A null in this byte works with "any" printer. After the first record, Volkswriter ignores the contents of this byte.

Byte 9 **Form Length** length: 1 byte
This byte holds the number of lines per page on the form. After the first record, Volkswriter ignores the contents of this byte.

Byte 10 **Lines per Inch** length: 1 byte
This byte holds the number of lines per inch that the document will print. A typical figure is 6.

Byte 11 **Spacing** length: 1 byte
This byte holds the spacing code for the lines of text in the document.
0 = single spacing
1 = double spacing
2 = triple spacing, and so forth
The maximum value for this field appears to be 255 (FFh).

Byte 12 **Characters per Line, Inch, or Unit** length: 1 byte
A value of 6 in this field signifies six lines per inch.

Byte 13–14 **Reserved** length: 2 bytes
Both of these bytes must be nulls (00h).

Byte 15 **Odd Page/Left Border Margin** length: 1 byte
The left-hand margin for the odd numbered pages in the document. This setting permits an offset to allow for binding. Volkswriter ignores the content of this field after the first record.

Byte 16–21   **Reserved**   length: 6 bytes
The content of these six bytes should be nulls.

Byte 22   **Pagination on Flag**   length: 1 byte
A nonzero value in this field turns on pagination while this layout is in force.

Byte 23   **Printer Reset Flag**   length: 1 byte
A nonzero value in this field resets the printer. Volkswriter ignores this field after the first record.

Byte 24   **Reformat on Flag**   length: 1 byte
A nonzero value in this field turns on automatic text reformatting while this layout is in force.

Byte 25   **Reserved**   length: 1 byte
The contents of this field should be null (00h).

Byte 26   **Continuous Forms**   length: 1 byte
A nonzero value in this field means that the printer uses continuous form paper. Volkswriter ignores this field after the first record.

Byte 27   **Top Margin**   length: 1 byte
This field holds the number of lines in the top margin of the page. Volkswriter ignores this field after the first record.

Byte 28–33   **Reserved**   length: 6 bytes
These bytes should be set to nulls.

Byte 34   **Justification Flag**   length: 1 byte
A nonzero value in this field means that Volkswriter justifies the text while the layout is in force.

Byte 35   **Proportional Spacing Flag**   length: 1 byte
A nonzero value in this field means that Volkswriter proportionally spaces the text while the layout is in force.

Byte 36–41   **Reserved**   length: 6 bytes
These bytes should be set to nulls.

Byte 42–43   **Margin Line Length**   length: 2 bytes
The length of the following margin or ruler line. Volkswriter currently supports a 250-character ruler and stores a 250-character ruler in the footer record, regardless of the margin settings. Consequently, the margin line length field should be set to 250.

Byte 44–294   **Margin Line**   length: 250 bytes
The Volkswriter margin line is a 250-character string. The characters of the string have special meaning. Table 6-4 lists the characters of the Margin Line and their special meanings.

Table 6-4	Margin line characters
Character	**Meaning**
—	nonsignificant character
+	tab
.	decimal tab (user may specify any nonruler character)
\	left margin
#	first line of paragraph (indent/outdent)
/	right margin
@	start of hyphenation zone

Byte 295   **Top Margin (First Page)** length: 1 byte
The top margin for the first page of the document (as opposed to every page). Volkswriter ignores the contents of this field after the first record.

Byte 296   **Even Page/Right Border Margin** length: 1 byte
The right border margin for even numbered pages. See Odd/Left Border Margin. Volkswriter ignores the contents of this field after the first record.

Byte 297–316 **Reserved**   length: 20 bytes
Set the value of these bytes to null (00h).

## CHAPTER 7

WordPerfect
Version 4.1

**WordPerfect Software
323 North State Street
Orem, UT 84057**

Type of Product   Word processor

Files Produced: ASCII text

Points of Interest:
WordPerfect files do not use Control-Z as an end-of-file character. The program can also do columnar math.

Conversion Information:
WordPerfect comes with a conversion program that converts in both directions between several formats. The conversion program does not always preserve formatting information. The supported formats are:

> WordPerfect
> DCA Revisable format
> Navy DIF
> WordStar
> MultiMate
> Seven-Bit telecommunications (strips high-bit formatting codes)
> Mail Merge
> WordPerfect Secondary Merge
> Spreadsheet DIF

WordPerfect File Format

WordPerfect produces ASCII files with embedded formatting (function) codes. There is no file header or footer. The embedded codes carry all formatting—text, paragraph, or document information, any modes (such as calculations), and setup (printer information). As a result, there is no byte offset information required.

The table portion of this chapter provides two lengthy lists of the formatting codes in numerical order (divided into single- and multi-byte codes) and five other tables of those same codes divided into these arbitrary categories:

- **Text Codes:** These are codes that effect the running text without having a side effect on the paragraph or the document as a whole. Example: boldface text.

- **Paragraph Codes:** These codes control the formatting of the paragraph without controlling the document. Example: justification.

- **Document Codes:** These codes control the overall appearance of the document. Example: form length.

- **Calculation Codes:** These codes refer to the column math capabilities of WordPerfect.

- **Setup Codes/Miscellaneous:** These codes are a catchall for items that don't fall into the other categories. Example: reverse video command.

Cautions   WordPerfect Software advises that WordPerfect files do not use a Control-Z as an end-of-file character. If you're creating a WordPerfect file externally to the program, you may place a Control-Z at the end-of-the file. If you do, you *must* pad to the end of the paragraph (16-byte boundary) with ASCII nulls (00h). Padding with garbage may cause WordPerfect to crash.

Initial margin settings are 10 and 74. It's best to keep line length under 59 characters unless you specifically change the margins. You should not pad to the margin with spaces (ASCII 32, 20h).

When writing spelling or grammar checking routines that read WordPerfect files, WordPerfect Software advises to allow for hyphenations (codes A9h to AEh).

Single- and Multi-Byte Codes

About half the WordPerfect codes are single byte, and half multi-byte. Multi-byte codes are those above ASCII 192 (C0h). The code number of the multi-byte codes generally appear twice, bracketing the contents of the code string itself.

For clarity, this chapter uses angle brackets to textually separate the bytes of a multi-byte code.

For example:

<C6><old position><new position><C6>

is the code for setting a new page number position. C6 is the hexadecimal number of the code; old position and new position are codes that describe where the number should go, and the trailing C6 is the second appearance of the page number code.

SSI advises that where a multi-byte code expects an "old position," you can safely insert a null (00h); WordPerfect will take care of the updating.

Secondary Merge Files

WordPerfect secondary merge files have no beginning-of-field or beginning-of-record code. The-end -of-field separator is Control-R followed by a hard return (line feed), and the-end-of record separator is a Control-E followed by a hard return.

Function Code Tables

Table 7-1 is a list of single-byte function codes in numerical order. Table 7-2 is the list of multi-byte function codes in numerical order. Tables 7-3, 7-4, 7-5, 7-6, and 7-7 are, respectively, the codes pertaining to text, paragraph, document, calculation, and setup/miscellaneous formatting.

Table 7-1	Single-byte function codes (All codes are one byte in length.)		
Octal	**Hex**	**Decimal**	**Meaning**
011	09	009	tab
012	0A	010	hard new line
013	0B	011	soft new page
014	0C	012	hard new page
015	0D	013	soft new line
200	80	128	no-op (always deleted)
201	81	129	right justification on
202	82	130	right justification off
203	83	131	end of centered text
204	84	132	end of aligned or flushed text
205	85	133	temporary starting point for math calculations
206	86	134	center page from top to bottom
207	87	135	begin column mode
210	88	136	end column mode
211	89	137	tab after the right margin

(Table Continued)

Table 7-1 (Continued)

Octal	Hex	Decimal	Meaning
212	8A	138	widow/orphan control on
213	8B	139	widow/orphan control off
214	8C	140	hard end of line and soft end of page
215	8D	141	footnote number (appears only inside of footnotes)
216	8E	142	Reserved
217	8F	143	Reserved
220	90	144	red line on
221	91	145	red line off
222	92	146	strike out on
223	93	147	strike out off
224	94	148	underline on
225	95	149	underline off
226	96	150	reverse video on (reserved)
227	97	151	reverse video off (reserved)
230	98	152	table of contents placeholder
231	99	153	overstrike
232	9A	154	cancel hyphenation of following word
233	9B	155	end of generated text
234	9C	156	bold off
235	9D	157	bold on
236	9E	158	hyphenation off
237	9F	159	hyphenation on
240	A0	160	hard space
241	A1	161	do subtotal
242	A2	162	subtotal entry
243	A3	163	do total
244	A4	164	total entry
245	A5	165	do grand total
246	A6	166	math calculation column
247	A7	167	begin math mode
250	A8	168	end math mode
251	A9	169	hard hyphen in line
252	AA	170	hard hyphen at end of line
253	AB	171	hard hyphen at end of page
254	AC	172	soft hyphen
255	AD	173	soft hyphen at end of line

(Table Continued)

Table 7-1 (Continued)

Octal	Hex	Decimal	Meaning
256	AE	174	soft hyphen at end of page
257	AF	175	end of text columns and end of line
260	B0	176	end of text columns and end of page
274	BC	188	superscript
275	BD	189	subscript
276	BE	190	advance printer 1/2 line up
277	BF	191	advance printer 1/2 line down

Table 7-2	Multi-byte formatting codes

Each code comprises several bytes; some are variable in length. The length figures are in bytes.

Octal	Hex	Decimal	Length	Meaning
300	C0	192	6	**margin reset** <C0><old left><old right><new left><new right><C0>
301	C1	193	4	**spacing reset** uses half-line values <C1><old spacing><new spacing><C1>
302	C2	194	3	**left margin release** <C2><# spaces to go left><C2>
303	C3	195	5	**center following text** <C3><type><center col #> < start col #><C3><text><83> type = 0 for centering between margins type = 1 for centering around current column <83> is the code for ending centered text.
304	C4	196	5	**align or flush right** <C4><align char><align col#> <start col#><C4><text><84> If align char = 12 (new line), this is a flush right command and the align col# is the

(Table Continued)

Table 7-2 (Continued)

Octal	Hex	Decimal	Length	Meaning
				right margin; otherwise, the align col# is the next tab stop. If the high bit of the align char is set, then this is a dot leader align or dot leader flush right. <84> is the code for ending aligned or flushed right text.
305	C5	197	6	**reset hyphenation zone ("hotzone")** <C5><old left><old right><new left> <new right><C5>
306	C6	198	4	**set page number position** <C6><old pos code> <new pos code><C6> Code: 0 = none 1 = top left 2 = top center 3 = top right 4 = top L&R 5 = bot left 6 = bot center 7 = bot right 8 = bot L&R
307	C7	199	6	**set page number** <C7><old# high order> <old# low ord><new# hi ord> <old# low ord><C7> Only the low-order 15 bits determine the page number. If the high order bit is set, the numbers are Roman numerals; if not, Arabic numbers.
310	C8	200	8	**set page number column positions** <C8><old left><old center><old right> <new left><new center><new right><C8>
311	C9	201	42	**set tabs** <C9><old tab table (20 bytes)> <new tab table (20 bytes)><C9> Each bit represents one character position counting from bit 0 to bit 159. There are a maximum of 160 characters allowed in a WordPerfect line.

(Table Continued)

Table 7-2 (Continued)

Octal	Hex	Decimal	Length	Meaning
312	CA	202	3	**conditional end of page** <CA><number of single-spaced lines not to be broken><CA>
313	CB	203	6	**set pitch and/or font** <CB><old pitch><old font> <new pitch><new font><CB> If the pitch is a negative value, then the font is proportional.
314	CC	204	4	**set temporary margin** (indent) <CC><old tempmargin> <new tempmargin><CC>
315	CD	205	3	**old end of temporary margin** (no longer used) <CD><tempmargin><CD>
316	CE	206	4	**set top margin** <CE><old top margin> <new top margin><CE>
317	CF	207	3	**suppress page characteristics** <CF><suppress codes><CF> Codes: (any or all bits may be inclusive or'd together) 1 = all suppressed 2 = page numbers suppressed 4 = page numbers moved to bottom 10 = all headers suppressed 20 = header *a* suppressed 40 = header *b* suppressed 100 = footer *a* suppressed 200 = footer *b* suppressed
320	D0	208	6	**set form length** <D0><old form len><old # text lines> <new form len><new # text lines><D0>
321	D1	209	var	**header/footer** <D1><old def byte><# half-lines used by old header/footer><FF> <FF><lmargin><rmargin><text>

(Table Continued)

Table 7-2 (Continued)

Octal	Hex	Decimal	Length	Meaning
				<FF><#half lines used by new header/footer><new def byte><D1> Def Byte contents are type (two low-order bits) and occurrence (six high bits). The low-order 2 bits of the Def byte *must* be correct. **Type** **Occurrence** 0 = header *a* 0 = never 1 = header *b* 1 = all pages 2 = footer *a* 2 = odd pages 3 = footer *b* 4 = even pages
322	D2	210	var	**footnote** (not used in version 4.0 and above; see 342/E4) <D2><fn#><# half lines><FF><lmargin><rmargin><text><D2>
323	D3	211	4	**set footnote number** (not used in version 4.0 and above; see 344/E4) <D3><old line #><new line #><D3
324	D4	212	4	**advance to half line #** (stored in half-line units) <D4><old line #> <advance to half line #><D4>
325	D5	213	4	**set lines per inch** (6 or 8 lpi are the only valid values) <D5><old lpi code><new lpi code><D5>
326	D6	214	6	**set extended tabs** <D6><old start><old increment><new start><new increment><D6>
327	D7	215	var	**define math columns** <D7><old column def (24 bytes)>[<old calc 0>]<0>[<old calc 1>]<0> [<old calc 2>]<0>[<old calc3>] <0><D7><new column def (24 bytes)> [<new calc0>]<0>[<new calc 1>]<0> [<new calc 2>]<0>[<new calc 3>] <0><D7>

(Table Continued)

Table 7-2 (Continued)

Octal	Hex	Decimal	Length	Meaning
				See "define columns" (code DDh) for the 24-byte column definition.
330	D8	216	4	**set alignment character** <D8><old char><new char><D8>
331	D9	217	4	**set left margin release** (# of columns to go left) <D9><old #><new #><D9> (not used in version 4.0 and above)
332	DA	218	4	**set underline mode** <DA><old mode><new mode><DA> 0 = normal underlining (breaks at word spaces) 1 = double underlining (breaks) 2 = single underlining (continuous) 3 = double underlining (continuous)
333	DB	219	4	**sheet feeder bin number** <DB><old #><new #><DB> WordPerfect stores the number as one less than the bin number (bin #1 = 0)
334	DC	220	var	**end of page function** (inserted by WordPerfect) <DC><# of half lines at end of page, low 7 bits><high 7 bits> <# of half lines used for footnotes> <# pages used for footnotes> <# footnotes on this page> <ceop flag><suppress code><DC> If end of page is for the last column on the page, then after the suppress code and before the final function code there are five more bytes: <# of half lines for col 1> <# half lines for col 2> <# of half lines for col 3> <# half lines for col 4> <line # of column on (0 if none on this page)>

(Table Continued)

Table 7-2 (Continued)

Octal	Hex	Decimal	Length	Meaning
335	DD	221	24	**define columns** <DD><old # cols><l1><r1><l2> <r2><l3><r3><l4><r4><l5><r5> <new # cols><l1><r1><l2> <r2><l3><r3><l4><r4><l5><r5> <DD> # cols:low-order 7 bits = the number high-order 1 bit = 1 if parallel columns
336	DE	222	4	**end of temporary margin** <DE><old left temp margin> <old right temp margin><DE>
337	DF	223	var	**invisible characters** <DF><text in 7-bit characters><DF> If a character has an ASCII code >= 6Fh (ASCII 191), the text portion of this function represents it as <6F><(char − 6F)>. For example, the character ASCII 232 (E8h) would appear as: <6F><(E8 − 6F)> or: <6F><79h>.
340	E0	224	4	**left/right temporary margin** pre-4.0 format: <E0> <new rt temp margin> <new lt temp margin><E0> 4.0 and later format: <E0><0> <difference between old and new left margin<E0>
341	E1	225	3	**extended character** <E1><character><E1>
342	E2	226	var	**new footnote/endnote** <E2><def><a><b><c><d> <old ftnote line><# lines page 1> <# lines page 2><# lines page n> <# pages><FF> <l margin><r margin><text><E2> where: def: bit 0: 0 = use numbers, 1 = use characters bit1: 0 = footnote, 1 = endnote

(Table Continued)

Table 7-2 (Continued)

Octal	Hex	Decimal	Length	Meaning
				a,b: if def bit 0 is a 0, then a,b are foot note and endnote numbers if def bit 0 is a 1, then a = # of characters and b = a character c,d: number of lines in footnote/ endnote
				Note: a,b and c,d are 14-bit numbers split into two 7-bit bytes, high-order byte first. For endnotes, there is only a null between \<d\> and \<FF\>.
343	E3	227	150	**footnote information (options) function** \<E3\>\<old values 74 bytes\> \<new values 74 bytes\>\<E3\> **Byte Meaning** 1 spacing in footnotes 2 spacing between footnotes 3 number of lines to keep together 4 flag byte (bits: b ln en ft n) n: 1 if numbering starts on each page en, ft: 0 = use numbers 1 = use characters 2 = use letters ln: 0 = no line separator 1 = 2 inch line 2 = line from left to right margin b: 0 = footnotes after text 1 = footnotes at bottom of page 5 # of characters used in place of footnote numbers 6–10 "numbering" characters (null terminated if < 5) 11 # of displayable chars in string for footnote (text) 12–26 string for footnote (text) 27 # of displayable chars in string for endnote (text) 28–42 string for endnote (text)

(Table Continued)

Table 7-2 (Continued)

Octal	Hex	Decimal	Length	Meaning
				43 # of displayable characters in string for footnote (note)
				44–58 string for footnote (note)
				59 # of displayable characters in string for endnote (note)
				60–74 string for endnote (note)
344	E4	228	6	**new set footnote #** <E4><olde # high><old # low> <new # high><new # low><E4> Footnote numbers are 14-bit numbers split into two 7-bit bytes, high-order byte first.
345	E5	229	23	**paragraph number definition** <E5><old 7 level numbers> <old 7 def bytes><new 7 def bytes><E5> A def byte is two nibbles:

style (low nibble)

0 = caps Roman

1 = lower-case Roman number

2 = caps letter number

3 = lower-case letter

4 = Arabic

5 = Arabic with previous levels separated by ".". (Ex: 3.4.1)

punctuation (high nibble)

0 = nothing

1 = "." after

2 = ")" after

3 = "(" before, ")" after

Octal	Hex	Decimal	Length	Meaning
346	E6	230	11	**paragraph number** <E6><new level #><def byte> <old 7 numbers><E6> Level number is 0 for first level, 1 for second, and so forth.
347	E7	231	3	**begin marked text** <E7><def, info><E7><text><E8> <def, info><E8> The def, info byte is two nibbles:

(Table Continued)

Table 7-2 (Continued)

Octal	Hex	Decimal	Length	Meaning
				definition **information**
				(high nibble) **(low nibble)**
				0 = table of contents level (0–6)
				2 = list list # (0–4)
350	E8	232	3	**end marked text**
				<E8><def, info><E8>
				The def, info byte is the same as E7.
351	E9	233	8	**define marked text**
				<E9><def, info><5-byte definition><E9>
				The def, info byte is the same as for mark and end mark, except that the low nibble is significant only for lists.
				For the table of contents, the five definition bytes represent five levels.
				For index and lists only, the first definition byte is significant.
				Definition bytes:
				0 = no page numbers
				1 = page # after text, preceded by two spaces
				2 = page # after text, in parentheses, preceded by one space
				3 = page # flush right
				4 = page # flush right with dot leader
352	EA	234	var	**define index mark**
				<EA><30-byte, null-terminated format string><EA>
353	EB	235	32	**date/time function**
				<EB><30-byte, null-terminated format string><EB>
354	EC	236	4	**block protect**
				<EC><def><# of half lines in block><EC>
				Def: 0 for block protect on
				1 for block protect off

Function Codes by Type

The following tables are lists of the WordPerfect function codes arbitrarily divided into groups based on what they refer to: text, paragraphs, the document as a whole, math calculations, and setup/miscellaneous.

Table 7-3		Function codes relating to text		
Octal	**Hex**	**Decimal**	**Length**	**Meaning**
011	09	009	1	tab
203	83	131	1	end of centered text
204	84	132	1	end of aligned or flushed text
222	92	146	1	strike out on
223	93	147	1	strike out off
224	94	148	1	underline on
225	95	149	1	underline off
231	99	153	1	overstrike
234	9C	156	1	bold off
235	9D	157	1	bold on
240	A0	160	1	hard space
251	A9	169	1	hard hyphen in line
252	AA	170	1	hard hyphen at end of line
253	AB	171	1	hard hyphen at end of page
274	BC	188	1	superscript
275	BD	189	1	subscript
276	BE	190	1	advance printer 1/2 line up
277	BF	191	1	advance printer 1/2 line down
303	C3	195	5	**center following text** <C3><type><center col #><start col #><C3><text><83> type = 0 for centering between margins type = 1 for centering around current column <83> is the code for ending centered text.
332	DA	218	4	**set underline mode** <DA><old mode><new mode><DA>

(Table Continued)

Table 7-3 (Continued)

Octal	Hex	Decimal	Length	Meaning
				0 = normal underlining (breaks at word spaces) 1 = double underlining (breaks) 2 = single underlining (continuous) 3 = double underlining (continuous)
337	DF	223	var	**invisible characters** <DF><text in 7-bit characters><DF> If a character has an ASCII code >= 6Fh (ASCII 191), the text portion of this function represents it as <6F><(char − 6F)>. For example, the character ASCII 232 (E8h) would appear as: <6F><(E8 − 6F)> or: <6F><79h>.
341	E1	225	3	**extended character** <E1><character><E1>
347	E7	231	3	**begin marked text** <E7><def, info><E7><text><E8> <def, info><E8> The def, info byte is two nibbles: **definition** **information** **(high nibble)** **(low nibble)** 0 = table of contents level (0–6) 2 = list list # (0–4)
350	E8	232	3	**end marked text** <E8><def, info><E8> The def, info byte is the same as E7.
351	E9	233	8	**define marked text** <E9><def, info><5–byte definition><E9> The def, info byte is the same as for mark and end mark, except that the low nibble is significant only for lists. For the table of contents, the five definition bytes represent five levels.

(Table Continued)

Table 7-3 (Continued)

Octal	Hex	Decimal	Length	Meaning
				For index and lists only, the first definition byte is significant.
				Definition bytes:
				0 = no page numbers
				1 = page # after text, preceded by two spaces
				2 = page # after text, in parentheses, preceded by one space
				3 = page # flush right
				4 = page # flush right with dot leader

Table 7-4 — Function codes relating to paragraphs

Octal	Hex	Decimal	Length	Meaning
012	0A	010	1	hard new line
015	0D	013	1	soft new line
201	81	129	1	right justification on
202	82	130	1	right justification off
203	83	131	1	end of centered text
204	84	132	1	end of aligned or flushed text
211	89	137	1	tab after the right margin
212	8A	138	1	widow/orphan control on
213	8B	139	1	widow/orphan control off
220	90	144	1	red line on
221	91	145	1	red line off
232	9A	154	1	cancel hyphenation of following word
236	9E	158	1	hyphenation off
237	9F	159	1	hyphenation on
252	AA	170	1	hard hyphen at end of line
254	AC	172	1	soft hyphen
255	AD	173	1	soft hyphen at end of line
300	C0	192	6	**margin reset** <C0><old left><old right><new left> <new right><C0>

(Table Continued)

Table 7-4 (Continued)

Octal	Hex	Decimal	Length	Meaning
301	C1	193	4	**spacing reset—uses half-line values** <C1><old spacing><new spacing><C1>
302	C2	194	3	**left margin release** <C2><# spaces to go left><C2>
304	C4	196	5	**align or flush right** <C4><align char><align col#> <start col#><C4><text><84> If align char = 12 (new line), this is a flush right command and the align col# is the right margin; otherwise, the align col# is the next tab stop. If the high bit of the align char is set, then this is a dot leader align or dot leader flush right. <84> is the code for ending aligned or flushed right text.
305	C5	197	6	**reset hyphenation zone ("hotzone")** <C5><old left><old right><new left> <new right><C5>
311	C9	201	42	**set tabs** <C9><old tab table (20 bytes)><new tab table (20 bytes)><C9> Each bit represents one character position counting from bit 0 to bit 159. There are a maximum of 160 characters allowed in a WordPerfect line.
314	CC	204	4	**set temporary margin (indent)** <CC><old tempmargin><new tempmargin><CC>
315	CD	205	3	**old end of temporary margin (no longer used)** <CD><tempmargin><CD>
324	D4	212	4	**advance to half line #** **(stored in half-line units)** <D4><old line #><advance to half line #><D4>

(Table Continued)

Table 7-4 (Continued)

Octal	Hex	Decimal	Length	Meaning
326	D6	214	6	**set extended tabs** <D6><old start><old increment> <new start><new increment><D6>
330	D8	216	4	**set alignment character** <D8><old char><new char><D8>
331	D9	217	4	**set left margin release** **(# of columns to go left)** <D9><old #><new #><D9> (not used in version 4.0 and above)
336	DE	222	4	**end of temporary margin** <DE><old left temp margin> <old right temp margin><DE>
345	E5	229	23	**paragraph number definition** <E5><old 7 level numbers><old 7 def bytes><new 7 def bytes><E5> A def byte is two nibbles: **style** / **punctuation** **(low nibble)** / **(high nibble)** 0 = caps Roman / 0 = nothing 1 = lower-case Roman / 1 = "." after number 2 = caps letter / 2 = ")" after number 3 = lower-case letter / 3 = "(" before, ")" after 4 = Arabic 5 = Arabic with previous levels separated by "." (Ex: 3.4.1)
346	E6	230	11	**paragraph number** <E6><new level #><def byte> <old 7 numbers><E6> Level number is 0 for first level, 1 for second, and so forth.

Table 7-5			Function codes relating to the entire document and its format	

Octal	Hex	Decimal	Length	Meaning
013	0B	011	1	soft new page
014	0C	012	1	hard new page
206	86	134	1	center page from top to bottom
207	87	135	1	begin column mode
210	88	136	1	end column mode
211	89	137	1	tab after the right margin
212	8A	138	1	widow/orphan control on
213	8B	139	1	widow/orphan control off
214	8C	140	1	hard end of line and soft end of page
230	98	152	1	table of contents placeholder
233	9B	155	1	end of generated text
253	AB	171	1	hard hyphen at end of page
256	AE	174	1	soft hyphen at end of page
306	C6	198	4	**set page number position** <C6><old pos code><new pos code><C6> Code: 0 = none 1 = top left 2 = top center 3 = top right 4 = top L&R 5 = bot left 6 = bot center 7 = bot right 8 = bot L&R
307	C7	199	6	**set page number** <C7><old# high order> <old# low ord><new# hi ord> <old# lo ord><C7> only the low-order 15 bits determine the page number. If the high-order bit is set, the numbers are Roman numerals; if not, Arabic numbers.

(Table Continued)

Table 7-5 (Continued)

Octal	Hex	Decimal	Length	Meaning
310	C8	200	8	**set page number column positions** <C8><old left><old center><old right> <new left><new center><new right><C8>
312	CA	202	3	**conditional end of page** <CA><number of single-spaced lines not to be broken><CA>
313	CB	203	6	**set pitch and/or font** <CB><old pitch><old font> <new pitch><new font><CB> If the pitch is a negative value, then the font is proportional.
316	CE	206	4	**set top margin** <CE><old top margin> <new top margin><CE>
317	CF	207	3	**suppress page characteristics** <CF><suppress codes><CF> Codes: (any or all bits may be inclusive or'd together) 1 = all suppressed 2 = page numbers suppressed 4 = page numbers moved to bottom 10 = all headers suppressed 20 = header a suppressed 40 = header b suppressed 100 = footer a suppressed 200 = footer b suppressed
320	D0	208	6	**set form length** <D0><old form len><old # text lines> <new form len><new # text lines><D0>

(Table Continued)

Table 7-5 (Continued)

Octal	Hex	Decimal	Length	Meaning
321	D1	209	var	**header/footer**
				<D1><old def byte><# half-lines used by old header/footer><FF>
				<FF><lmargin><rmargin><text>
				<FF><#half lines used by new header/footer><new def byte><D1>
				Def Byte contents are type (two low-order bits) and occurrence (six high bits). The low-order two bits of the Def byte *must* be correct.

Type	Occurrence
0 = header a	0 = never
1 = header b	1 = all pages
2 = footer a	2 = odd pages
3 = footer b	4 = even pages

Octal	Hex	Decimal	Length	Meaning
322	D2	210	var	**footnote**
				(not used in version 4.0 and above; see 342/E4)
				<D2><fn#><# half lines><FF>
				<lmargin><rmargin><text><D2>
323	D3	211	4	**set footnote number**
				(not used in version 4.0 and above; see 344/E4)
				<D3><old line #><new line #><D3
325	D5	213	4	**set lines per inch**
				(6 or 8 lpi are the only valid values)
				<D5><old lpi code><new lpi code><D5>
333	DB	219	4	**sheet feeder bin number**
				<DB><old #><new #><DB>
				WordPerfect stores the number as one less than the bin number (bin #1 = 0)
334	DC	220	var	**end-of-page function**
				(inserted by WordPerfect)

(Table Continued)

Table 7-5 (Continued)

Octal	Hex	Decimal	Length	Meaning
				<DC><# of half lines at end of page, low 7 bits><high 7 bits>
				<# of half lines used for footnotes>
				<# pages used for footnotes>
				<# footnotes on this page><ceop flag><suppress code><DC>
				If end of page is for the last column on the page, then after the suppress code and before the final function code there are five more bytes:
				<# of half lines for col 1><# half lines for col 2>
				<# of half lines for col 3><# half lines for col 4>
				<line # of column on (0 if none on this page)>
335	DD	221	24	**define columns**
				<DD><old # cols><l1><r1><l2><r2><l3> <r3><l4><r4><l5><r5>
				<new # cols><l1><r1><l2><r2><l3> <r3><l4><r4><l5><r5><DD>
				# cols: low order 7 bits = the number high order 1 bit = 1 if parallel columns
342	E2	226	var	**new footnote/endnote**
				<E2><def><a><b><c><d><old ftnote line>
				<# lines page 1><# lines page 2>
				<# lines page n><# pages><FF>
				<l margin><r margin><text><E2>
				where:
				def: bit 0: 0 = use numbers, 1 = use characters
				bit 1: 0 = footnote, 1 = endnote
				a,b: if def bit 0 is a 0, then a,b are footnote and endnote numbers

(Table Continued)

Table 7-5 (Continued)

Octal	Hex	Decimal	Length	Meaning
				if def bit 0 is a 1, then a = # of characters and b = a character c,d: number of lines in footnote/endnote
				Note: a,b and c,d are 14-bit numbers split into two 7-bit bytes, high-order byte first. For endnotes, there is only a null between \<d\> and \<FF\>.
343	E3	227	150	**footnote information (options) function** \<E3\>\<old values 74 bytes\> \<new values 74 bytes\>\<E3\>

Byte	Meaning
1	spacing in footnotes
2	spacing between footnotes
3	number of lines to keep together
4	flag byte (bits: b ln en ft n)
	n: 1 if numbering starts on each page
	en, ft: 0 = use numbers
	1 = use characters
	2 = use letters
	ln: 0 = no line separator
	1 = 2 inch line
	2 = line from left to right margin
	b: 0 = footnotes after text
	1 = footnotes at bottom of page
5	# of characters used in place of footnote numbers
6–10	"numbering" characters (null terminated if < 5)
11	# of displayable chars in string for footnote (text)
12–26	string for footnote (text)
27	# of displayable chars in string for endnote (text)

(Table Continued)

Table 7-5 (Continued)

Octal	Hex	Decimal	Length	Meaning
				28–42 string for endnote (text)
				43 # of displayable characters in string for footnote (note)
				44–58 string for footnote (note)
				59 # of displayable characters in string for endnote (note)
				60–74 string for endnote (note)
344	E4	228	6	**new set footnote #** <E4><old # high><old # low> <new # high><new # low><E4> Footnote numbers are 14-bit numbers split into two 7-bit bytes, high-order byte first.
345	E5	229	23	**paragraph number definition** <E5><old 7 level numbers> <old 7 def bytes><new 7 def bytes><E5> A def byte is two nibbles:

style (low nibble)

0 = caps Roman
1 = lower-case Roman
2 = caps letter
3 = lower-case letter

4 = Arabic
5 = Arabic with previous
   levels separated by "."
   (Ex: 3.4.1)

punctuation (high nibble)

0 = nothing
1 = "." after number
2 = ")" after number
3 = "(" before, ")" after

Octal	Hex	Decimal	Length	Meaning
346	E6	230	11	**paragraph number** <E6><new level #><def byte> <old 7 numbers><E6> Level number is 0 for first level, 1 for second, and so forth.

(Table Continued)

Table 7-5 (Continued)

Octal	Hex	Decimal	Length	Meaning
351	E9	233	8	**define marked text**
				<E9><def, info><5-byte definition><E9>
				The def, info byte is the same as for mark and end mark, except that the low nibble is significant only for lists.
				For the table of contents, the five definition bytes represent five levels.
				For index and lists only, the first definition byte is significant.
				Definition bytes:
				0 = no page numbers
				1 = page # after text, preceded by two spaces
				2 = page # after text, in parentheses, preceded by one space
				3 = page # flush right
				4 = page # flush right with dot leader
352	EA	234	var	**define index mark**
				<EA><30-byte, null-terminated format string><EA>
353	EB	235	32	**date/time function**
				<EB><30-byte, null-terminated format string><EB>
354	EC	236	4	**block protect**
				<EC><def><# of half lines in block><EC>
				Def: 0 for block protect on
				1 for block protect off

Table 7-6		Function codes relating to math		

Octal	Hex	Decimal	Length	Meaning
205	85	133	1	temporary starting point for math calculations
241	A1	161	1	do subtotal
242	A2	162	1	subtotal entry
243	A3	163	1	do total
244	A4	164	1	total entry
245	A5	165	1	do grand total
246	A6	166	1	math calculation column
247	A7	167	1	begin math mode
250	A8	168	1	end math mode
327	D7	215	var	**define math columns** <D7><old column def (24 bytes)> [<old calc 0>]<0>[<old calc 1>]<0> [<old calc 2>]<0>[<old calc 3>]<0><D7> <new column def (24 bytes)> [<new calc 0>]<0>[<new calc 1>]<0> [<new calc 2>]<0>[<new calc 3>]<0><D7> See "define columns" (code DDh) for the 24-byte column definition.

Table 7-7		Function codes relating to setup or miscellaneous		

Octal	Hex	Decimal	Length	Meaning
200	80	128	1	no-op (always deleted)
216	8E	142	1	reserved
217	8F	143	1	reserved
226	96	150	1	reverse video on (reserved)
227	97	151	1	reverse video off (reserved)
257	AF	175	1	end-of-text columns and end of line
260	B0	176	1	end-of-text columns and end of page

A number of the programs covered in this Reference Guide have particularly complex file formats. While the byte offset documentation may be enough for most programmers, it can help to look at selected printouts from time to time.

As a spreadsheet sample, a fairly simple principal and interest calculation is used (see Sample 1). As a word-processing sample, most of the first two paragraphs of the Gettysburg Address was used (see Sample 2). As a control procedure, each sample was formatted the same way.

```
              1           2           3           4           5              6              7            8

                                              PAYMENT ANALYSIS WORKSHEET
                                              =========================

  3  LOAN AMT   $4,800.00
  4  INTEREST      18.50%
  5  MO PMT      $174.73
  6  PERIODS         36
  7
  8  ----------------------------------------------------------------------------------------------------
  9  PMT NO     INT PD     PRC PD     REMAIN BAL  INT TO DATE   PRC TO DATE   PAID TO DATE
 10  ----------------------------------------------------------------------------------------------------
 11     1        $74.00    $100.73    $4,699.27      $74.00       $100.73        $174.73
 12     2        $72.45    $102.28    $4,596.99     $146.45       $203.01        $349.46
 13     3        $70.87    $103.86    $4,493.13     $217.32       $306.87        $524.19
```

Sample 1 Simple principal and interest calculation used as a control for spreadsheet programs.

The Gettysburg Address

Fourscore and seven years ago our fathers brought forth on this
continent, a new nation, conceived in <u>Liberty</u>, and dedicated to
the proposition that all men are created equal.

Now we are engaged in a great civil war, testing whether that
nation or any nation so conceived and so dedicated can long
endure. We are met on a great battlefield of that war. We have
come to dedicate a portion of that field, as a final resting
place for those who here gave their lives that that nation might
live. It is altogether fitting and proper that we do this.

Sample 2 A portion of the Gettysburg address used as a control for word-processing
programs.

Sample Spreadsheet Files

Framework II Sample File
Reflex Sample File
Super Project Sample File
SuperCalc4 Sample File
Volkswriter 3 Sample File
WordPerfect Sample File

Framework II Sample File

BYTE	0	1	2	3	4	5	6	7	8	9	10	11	12	13	14	15
HEX	03	00	2A	03	02	00	ED	FB	00	00	00	00	8C	00	00	00
DEC	3	0	42	3	2	0	237	251	0	0	0	0	140	0	0	0
ASC	^C	^@		^C	^B	^@	237	251	^@	^@	^@	^@	140	^@	^@	^@
ALT	ETX	NUL		ETX	STX	NUL	237	251	NUL	NUL	NUL	NUL	140	NUL	NUL	NUL
SYM			*													

# Paragraphs in Header	FID	Status Flag	Type ID	File ID	Unused	Version #	Reserved
←———— Header ————→							

BYTE	16	17	18	19	20	21	22	23	24	25	26	27	28	29	30	31
HEX	4E	6E	68	01	2C	00	08	00	82	00	54	0C	00	00	00	00
DEC	78	110	104	1	44	0	8	0	130	0	84	12	0	0	0	0
ASC				^A		^@	^H	^@	130	^@		^L	^@	^@	^@	^@
ALT				SOH		NUL	BS	NUL	130	NUL		FF	NUL	NUL	NUL	NUL
SYM	N	n	b		,						T					

Checksum	# Paragraphs (Low Part)	Largest Frame	2nd Largest Frame	# Frames In File	Largest FID	Reserved	# Paragraphs (High Part)

BYTE	32	33	34	35	36	37	38	39	40	41	42	43	44	45	46	47
HEX	00	00	00	00	00	00	00	00	00	00	00	00	00	00	00	00
DEC	0	0	0	0	0	0	0	0	0	0	0	0	0	0	0	0
ASC	^@	^@	^@	^@	^@	^@	^@	^@	^@	^@	^@	^@	^@	^@	^@	^@
ALT	NUL	NUL	NUL	NUL	NUL	NUL	NUL	NUL	NUL	NUL	NUL	NUL	NUL	NUL	NUL	NUL
SYM																

←——————————————— Reserved ———————————————→

End of Header ————→

BYTE	48	49	50	51	52	53	54	55	56	57	58	59	60	61	62	63
HEX	06	00	66	02	03	0A	03	00	16	00	00	00	00	00	04	00
DEC	6	0	102	2	3	10	3	0	22	0	0	0	0	0	4	0
ASC	^F	^@		^B	^C	^J	^C	^@	^V	^@	^@	^@	^@	^@	^D	^@
ALT	ACK	NUL		STX	ETX	LF	ETX	NUL	SYN	NUL	NUL	NUL	NUL	NUL	EOT	NUL
SYM			f													

# Paragraphs This Frame	FID	Status Flag	Type ID	# Elements	Parent FID	EXE FID	Formula FID	Format Info

BYTE	64	65	66	67	68	69	70	71	72	73	74	75	76	77	78	79
HEX	00	00	00	00	00	00	00	00	00	00	00	00	68	02	05	00
DEC	0	0	0	0	0	0	0	0	0	0	0	0	104	2	5	0
ASC	^@	^@	^@	^@	^@	^@	^@	^@	^@	^@	^@	^@		^B	^E	^@
ALT	NUL	NUL	NUL	NUL	NUL	NUL	NUL	NUL	NUL	NUL	NUL	NUL		STX	ENQ	NUL
SYM													b			

Format	Internal Value Type	Value Structure	Name FID	Status Flags

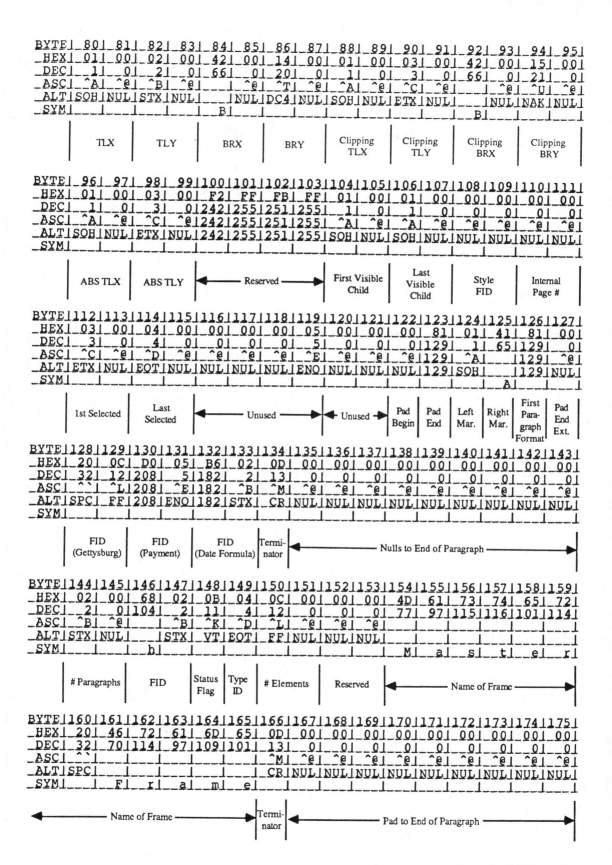

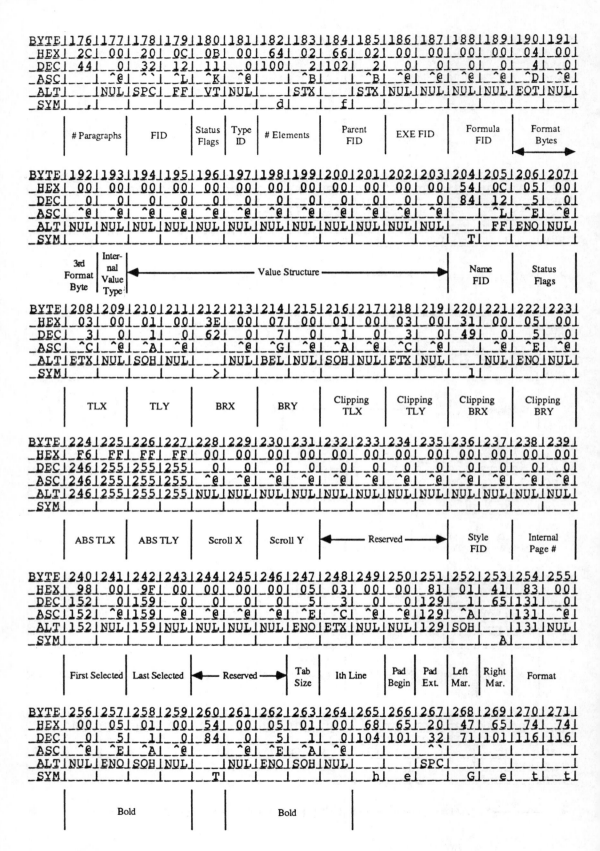

```
BYTE|272|273|274|275|276|277|278|279|280|281|282|283|284|285|286|287|
HEX | 79| 73| 62| 75| 72| 67| 20| 41| 64| 64| 72| 65| 73| 73| 00| 85|
DEC |121|115| 98|117|114|103| 32| 65|100|100|114|101|115|115| 00|133|
ASC |   |   |   |   |   |   |^` |   |   |   |   |   |   |   |   |^@|133|
ALT |   |   |   |   |   |   |SPC|   |   |   |   |   |   |   |   |NUL|133|
SYM | y | s | b | u | r | g |   | A | d | d | r | e | s | s |   |   |
```

Formatting →

```
BYTE|288|289|290|291|292|293|294|295|296|297|298|299|300|301|302|303|
HEX | 01| 00| 00| 81| 01| 41| 81| 00| 00| 81| 01| 41| 81| 00| 46| 6F|
DEC |  1|  0|  0|129|  1| 65|129|  0|  0|129|  1| 65|129|  0| 70|111|
ASC |^A |^@ |^@ |129|^A |   |129|^@ |^@ |129|^A |   |129|^@ |   |   |
ALT |SOH|NUL|NUL|129|SOH|   |129|NUL|NUL|129|SOH|   |129|NUL|   |   |
SYM |   |   |   |   |   |   | A |   |   |   |   |   |   | A |   | F | o |
```

|←——————— Empty Paragraph ———————→|←—— Paragraph Escape Sequence ——→|

```
BYTE|304|305|306|307|308|309|310|311|312|313|314|315|316|317|318|319|
HEX | 75| 72| 73| 63| 6F| 72| 65| 20| 61| 6E| 64| 20| 73| 65| 76| 65|
DEC |117|114|115| 99|111|114|101| 32| 97|110|100| 32|115|101|118|101|
ASC |   |   |   |   |   |   |   |^` |   |   |   |^` |   |   |   |   |
ALT |   |   |   |   |   |   |   |SPC|   |   |   |SPC|   |   |   |   |
SYM | u | r | s | c | o | r | e |   | a | n | d |   | s | e | v | e |
```

```
BYTE|320|321|322|323|324|325|326|327|328|329|330|331|332|333|334|335|
HEX | 6E| 20| 79| 65| 61| 72| 73| 20| 61| 67| 6F| 20| 6F| 75| 72| 20|
DEC |110| 32|121|101| 97|114|115| 32| 97|103|111| 32|111|117|114| 32|
ASC |   |^` |   |   |   |   |   |^` |   |   |   |^` |   |   |   |^` |
ALT |   |SPC|   |   |   |   |   |SPC|   |   |   |SPC|   |   |   |SPC|
SYM | n |   | y | e | a | r | s |   | a | g | o |   | o | u | r |   |
```

```
BYTE|336|337|338|339|340|341|342|343|344|345|346|347|348|349|350|351|
HEX | 66| 61| 74| 68| 65| 72| 73| 20| 62| 72| 6F| 75| 67| 68| 74| 20|
DEC |102| 97|116|104|101|114|115| 32| 98|114|111|117|103|104|116| 32|
ASC |   |   |   |   |   |   |   |^` |   |   |   |   |   |   |   |^` |
ALT |   |   |   |   |   |   |   |SPC|   |   |   |   |   |   |   |SPC|
SYM | f | a | t | h | e | r | s |   | b | r | o | u | g | h | t |   |
```

```
BYTE|352|353|354|355|356|357|358|359|360|361|362|363|364|365|366|367|
HEX | 66| 6F| 72| 74| 68| 20| 6F| 6E| 20| 74| 68| 69| 73| 0D| 63| 6F|
DEC |102|111|114|116|104| 32|111|110| 32|116|104|105|115| 13| 99|111|
ASC |   |   |   |   |   |^` |   |   |^` |   |   |   |   |^M |   |   |
ALT |   |   |   |   |   |SPC|   |   |SPC|   |   |   |   |CR |   |   |
SYM | f | o | r | t | h |   | o | n |   | t | h | i | s |   | c | o |
```

```
BYTE|368|369|370|371|372|373|374|375|376|377|378|379|380|381|382|383|
HEX | 6E| 74| 69| 6E| 65| 6E| 74| 20| 61| 20| 6E| 65| 77| 20| 6E| 61|
DEC |110|116|105|110|101|110|116| 32| 97| 32|110|101|119| 32|110| 97|
ASC |   |   |   |   |   |   |   | ^`|   |   | ^`|   |   |   | ^`|   |
ALT |   |   |   |   |   |   |   |SPC|   |SPC|   |   |   |SPC|   |   |
SYM | n | t | i | n | e | n | t |   | a |   | n | e | w |   | n | a |


BYTE|384|385|386|387|388|389|390|391|392|393|394|395|396|397|398|399|
HEX | 74| 69| 6F| 6E| 2C| 20| 63| 6F| 6E| 63| 65| 69| 76| 65| 64| 20|
DEC |116|105|111|110| 44| 32| 99|111|110| 99|101|105|118|101|100| 32|
ASC |   |   |   |   | ^`|   |   |   |   |   |   |   |   |   |   | ^`|
ALT |   |   |   |   |SPC|   |   |   |   |   |   |   |   |   |   |SPC|
SYM | t | i | o | n | , |   | c | o | n | c | e | i | v | e | d |   |


BYTE|400|401|402|403|404|405|406|407|408|409|410|411|412|413|414|415|
HEX | 69| 6E| 20| 00| 05| 04| 00| 4C| 69| 62| 65| 72| 74| 79| 00| 85|
DEC |105|110| 32| 01|  5|  4|  0| 76|105| 98|101|114|116|121|  0|133|
ASC |   |   | ^`| ^@| ^E| ^D| ^@|   |   |   |   |   |   |   | ^@|133|
ALT |   |   |SPC|NUL|ENQ|EOT|NUL|   |   |   |   |   |   |   |NUL|133|
SYM | i | n |   |   |   |   |   | L | i | b | e | r | t | y |   |   |
```

	Underline Escape Sequence		Underline Off

```
BYTE|416|417|418|419|420|421|422|423|424|425|426|427|428|429|430|431|
HEX | 01| 00| 2C| 20| 61| 6E| 64| 20| 64| 65| 64| 69| 63| 61| 74| 65|
DEC |  1|  0| 44| 32| 97|110|100| 32|100|101|100|105| 99| 97|116|101|
ASC | ^A| ^@|   | ^`|   |   |   | ^`|   |   |   |   |   |   |   |   |
ALT |SOH|NUL|   |SPC|   |   |   |SPC|   |   |   |   |   |   |   |   |
SYM |   |   | , |   | a | n | d |   | d | e | d | i | c | a | t | e |
```

Underline Off

```
BYTE|432|433|434|435|436|437|438|439|440|441|442|443|444|445|446|447|
HEX | 64| 20| 74| 6F| 0D| 74| 68| 65| 20| 70| 72| 6F| 70| 6F| 73| 69|
DEC |100| 32|116|111| 13|116|104|101| 32|112|114|111|112|111|115|105|
ASC |   | ^`|   |   | ^M|   |   |   | ^`|   |   |   |   |   |   |   |
ALT |   |SPC|   |   | CR|   |   |   |SPC|   |   |   |   |   |   |   |
SYM | d |   | t | o |   | t | h | e |   | p | r | o | p | o | s | i |
```

Word Wrap

```
BYTE|448|449|450|451|452|453|454|455|456|457|458|459|460|461|462|463|
HEX | 74| 69| 6F| 6E| 20| 74| 68| 61| 74| 20| 61| 6C| 6C| 20| 6D| 65|
DEC |116|105|111|110| 32|116|104| 97|116| 32| 97|108|108| 32|109|101|
ASC |   |   |   |   | ^`|   |   |   |   | ^`|   |   |   | ^`|   |   |
ALT |   |   |   |   |SPC|   |   |   |   |SPC|   |   |   |SPC|   |   |
SYM | t | i | o | n |   | t | h | a | t |   | a | l | l |   | m | e |
```

BYTE	464	465	466	467	468	469	470	471	472	473	474	475	476	477	478	479
HEX	6E	20	61	72	65	20	63	72	65	61	74	65	64	20	65	71
DEC	110	32	97	114	101	32	99	114	101	97	116	101	100	32	101	113
ASC						^^								^^		
ALT		SPC				SPC								SPC		
SYM	n		a	r	e		c	r	e	a	t	e	d		e	q

BYTE	480	481	482	483	484	485	486	487	488	489	490	491	492	493	494	495
HEX	75	61	6C	2E	00	81	01	41	81	00	00	81	01	41	81	00
DEC	117	97	108	46	0	129	1	65	129	0	0	129	1	65	129	0
ASC					^@	129	^A		129	^@	^@	129	^A		129	^@
ALT					NUL	129	SOH		129	NUL	NUL	129	SOH		129	NUL
SYM	u	a	l	.				A						A		

BYTE	496	497	498	499	500	501	502	503	504	505	506	507	508	509	510	511
HEX	4E	6F	77	20	77	65	20	61	72	65	20	65	6E	67	61	67
DEC	78	111	119	32	119	101	32	97	114	101	32	101	110	103	97	103
ASC				^^		^^					^^					
ALT				SPC		SPC					SPC					
SYM	N	o	w		w	e		a	r	e		e	n	g	a	g

BYTE	512	513	514	515	516	517	518	519	520	521	522	523	524	525	526	527
HEX	65	64	20	69	6E	20	61	20	67	72	65	61	74	20	63	69
DEC	101	100	32	105	110	32	97	32	103	114	101	97	116	32	99	105
ASC			^^			^^		^^						^^		
ALT			SPC			SPC		SPC						SPC		
SYM	e	d		i	n		a		g	r	e	a	t		c	i

BYTE	528	529	530	531	532	533	534	535	536	537	538	539	540	541	542	543
HEX	76	69	6C	20	77	61	72	2C	20	74	65	73	74	69	6E	67
DEC	118	105	108	32	119	97	114	44	32	116	101	115	116	105	110	103
ASC				^^					^^							
ALT				SPC					SPC							
SYM	v	i	l		w	a	r	,		t	e	s	t	i	n	g

BYTE	544	545	546	547	548	549	550	551	552	553	554	555	556	557	558	559
HEX	20	77	68	65	74	68	65	72	20	74	68	61	74	0D	6E	61
DEC	32	119	104	101	116	104	101	114	32	116	104	97	116	13	110	97
ASC	^^								^^					^M		
ALT	SPC								SPC					CR		
SYM		w	h	e	t	h	e	r		t	h	a	t		n	a

BYTE	560	561	562	563	564	565	566	567	568	569	570	571	572	573	574	575
HEX	74	69	6F	6E	20	6F	72	20	61	6E	79	20	6E	61	74	69
DEC	116	105	111	110	32	111	114	32	97	110	121	32	110	97	116	105
ASC					^`			^`				^`				
ALT					SPC			SPC				SPC				
SYM	t	i	o	n		o	r		a	n	y		n	a	t	i

BYTE	576	577	578	579	580	581	582	583	584	585	586	587	588	589	590	591
HEX	6F	6E	20	73	6F	20	63	6F	6E	63	65	69	76	65	64	20
DEC	111	110	32	115	111	32	99	111	110	99	101	105	118	101	100	32
ASC			^`			^`										^`
ALT			SPC			SPC										SPC
SYM	o	n		s	o		c	o	n	c	e	i	v	e	d	

BYTE	592	593	594	595	596	597	598	599	600	601	602	603	604	605	606	607
HEX	61	6E	64	20	73	6F	20	64	65	64	69	63	61	74	65	64
DEC	97	110	100	32	115	111	32	100	101	100	105	99	97	116	101	100
ASC				^`			^`									
ALT				SPC			SPC									
SYM	a	n	d		s	o		d	e	d	i	c	a	t	e	d

BYTE	608	609	610	611	612	613	614	615	616	617	618	619	620	621	622	623
HEX	20	63	61	6E	20	6C	6F	6E	67	0D	65	6E	64	75	72	65
DEC	32	99	97	110	32	108	111	110	103	13	101	110	100	117	114	101
ASC	^`				^`					^M						
ALT	SPC				SPC					CR						
SYM		c	a	n		l	o	n	g		e	n	d	u	r	e

BYTE	624	625	626	627	628	629	630	631	632	633	634	635	636	637	638	639
HEX	2E	20	20	57	65	20	61	72	65	20	6D	65	74	20	6F	6E
DEC	46	32	32	87	101	32	97	114	101	32	109	101	116	32	111	110
ASC		^`	^`			^`				^`				^`		
ALT		SPC	SPC			SPC				SPC				SPC		
SYM	.			W	e		a	r	e		m	e	t		o	n

BYTE	640	641	642	643	644	645	646	647	648	649	650	651	652	653	654	655
HEX	20	61	20	67	72	65	61	74	20	62	61	74	74	6C	65	66
DEC	32	97	32	103	114	101	97	116	32	98	97	116	116	108	101	102
ASC	^`		^`						^`							
ALT	SPC		SPC						SPC							
SYM		a		g	r	e	a	t		b	a	t	t	l	e	f

```
BYTE|656|657|658|659|660|661|662|663|664|665|666|667|668|669|670|671|
_HEX|_69|_65|_6C|_64|_20|_6F|_66|_20|_74|_68|_61|_74|_20|_77|_61|_72|
_DEC|105|101|108|100|_32|111|102|_32|116|104|_97|116|_32|119|_97|114|
_ASC|___|___|___|___|_^`|___|___|_^`|___|___|___|___|_^`|___|___|___|
_ALT|___|___|___|___|SPC|___|SPC|___|___|___|___|___|SPC|___|___|___|
_SYM|_i_|_e_|_l_|_d_|___|_o_|_f_|___|_t_|_h_|_a_|_t_|___|_w_|_a_|_r_|


BYTE|672|673|674|675|676|677|678|679|680|681|682|683|684|685|686|687|
_HEX|_2E|_20|_20|_57|_65|_20|_68|_61|_76|_65|_0D|_63|_6F|_6D|_65|_20|
_DEC|_46|_32|_32|_87|101|_32|104|_97|118|101|_13|_99|111|109|101|_32|
_ASC|___|_^`|_^`|___|___|_^`|___|___|___|___|_^M|___|___|___|___|_^`|
_ALT|___|SPC|SPC|___|SPC|___|___|___|___|___|CR_|___|___|___|___|SPC|
_SYM|_._|___|___|_W_|_e_|___|_h_|_a_|_v_|_e_|___|_c_|_o_|_m_|_e_|___|


BYTE|688|689|690|691|692|693|694|695|696|697|698|699|700|701|702|703|
_HEX|_74|_6F|_20|_64|_65|_64|_69|_63|_61|_74|_65|_20|_61|_20|_70|_6F|
_DEC|116|111|_32|100|101|100|105|_99|_97|116|101|_32|_97|_32|112|111|
_ASC|___|___|_^`|___|___|___|___|___|___|___|___|_^`|___|_^`|___|___|
_ALT|___|___|SPC|___|___|___|___|___|___|___|___|SPC|___|SPC|___|___|
_SYM|_t_|_o_|___|_d_|_e_|_d_|_i_|_c_|_a_|_t_|_e_|___|_a_|___|_p_|_o_|


BYTE|704|705|706|707|708|709|710|711|712|713|714|715|716|717|718|719|
_HEX|_72|_74|_69|_6F|_6E|_20|_6F|_66|_20|_74|_68|_61|_74|_20|_66|_69|
_DEC|114|116|105|111|110|_32|111|102|_32|116|104|_97|116|_32|102|105|
_ASC|___|___|___|___|___|_^`|___|___|_^`|___|___|___|___|_^`|___|___|
_ALT|___|___|___|___|___|SPC|___|SPC|___|___|___|___|___|SPC|___|___|
_SYM|_r_|_t_|_i_|_o_|_n_|___|_o_|_f_|___|_t_|_h_|_a_|_t_|___|_f_|_i_|


BYTE|720|721|722|723|724|725|726|727|728|729|730|731|732|733|734|735|
_HEX|_65|_6C|_64|_2C|_20|_61|_73|_20|_61|_20|_66|_69|_6E|_61|_6C|_20|
_DEC|101|108|100|_44|_32|_97|115|_32|_97|_32|102|105|110|_97|108|_32|
_ASC|___|___|___|___|_^`|___|_^`|___|_^`|___|___|___|___|___|___|_^`|
_ALT|___|___|___|___|SPC|___|SPC|___|SPC|___|___|___|___|___|___|SPC|
_SYM|_e_|_l_|_d_|_._|___|_a_|_s_|___|_a_|___|_f_|_i_|_n_|_a_|_l_|___|


BYTE|736|737|738|739|740|741|742|743|744|745|746|747|748|749|750|751|
_HEX|_72|_65|_73|_74|_69|_6E|_67|_0D|_70|_6C|_61|_63|_65|_20|_66|_6F|
_DEC|114|101|115|116|105|110|103|_13|112|108|_97|_99|101|_32|102|111|
_ASC|___|___|___|___|___|___|___|_^M|___|___|___|___|___|_^`|___|___|
_ALT|___|___|___|___|___|___|___|CR_|___|___|___|___|___|SPC|___|___|
_SYM|_r_|_e_|_s_|_t_|_i_|_n_|_g_|___|_p_|_l_|_a_|_c_|_e_|___|_f_|_o_|
```

```
BYTE|752|753|754|755|756|757|758|759|760|761|762|763|764|765|766|767|
HEX | 72| 20| 74| 68| 6F| 73| 65| 20| 77| 68| 6F| 20| 68| 65| 72| 65|
DEC |114| 32|116|104|111|115|101| 32|119|104|111| 32|104|101|114|101|
ASC |   | ^`|   |   |   |   |   | ^`|   |   |   | ^`|   |   |   |   |
ALT |   |SPC|   |   |   |   |   |SPC|   |   |   |SPC|   |   |   |   |
SYM | r |   | t | h | o | s | e |   | w | h | o |   | h | e | r | e |


BYTE|768|769|770|771|772|773|774|775|776|777|778|779|780|781|782|783|
HEX | 20| 67| 61| 76| 65| 20| 74| 68| 65| 69| 72| 20| 6C| 69| 76| 65|
DEC | 32|103| 97|118|101| 32|116|104|101|105|114| 32|108|105|118|101|
ASC | ^`|   |   |   |   | ^`|   |   |   |   |   | ^`|   |   |   |   |
ALT |SPC|   |   |   |   |SPC|   |   |   |   |   |SPC|   |   |   |   |
SYM |   | g | a | v | e |   | t | h | e | i | r |   | l | i | v | e |


BYTE|784|785|786|787|788|789|790|791|792|793|794|795|796|797|798|799|
HEX | 73| 20| 74| 68| 61| 74| 20| 74| 68| 61| 74| 20| 6E| 61| 74| 69|
DEC |115| 32|116|104| 97|116| 32|116|104| 97|116| 32|110| 97|116|105|
ASC |   | ^`|   |   |   |   | ^`|   |   |   |   | ^`|   |   |   |   |
ALT |   |SPC|   |   |   |   |SPC|   |   |   |   |SPC|   |   |   |   |
SYM | s |   | t | h | a | t |   | t | h | a | t |   | n | a | t | i |


BYTE|800|801|802|803|804|805|806|807|808|809|810|811|812|813|814|815|
HEX | 6F| 6E| 20| 6D| 69| 67| 68| 74| 0D| 6C| 69| 76| 65| 2E| 20| 20|
DEC |111|110| 32|109|105|103|104|116| 13|108|105|118|101| 46| 32| 32|
ASC |   |   | ^`|   |   |   |   |   | ^M|   |   |   |   |   | ^`| ^`|
ALT |   |   |SPC|   |   |   |   |   | CR|   |   |   |   |   |SPC|SPC|
SYM | o | n |   | m | i | g | h | t |   | l | i | v | e | . |   |   |


BYTE|816|817|818|819|820|821|822|823|824|825|826|827|828|829|830|831|
HEX | 49| 74| 20| 69| 73| 20| 61| 6C| 74| 6F| 67| 65| 74| 68| 65| 72|
DEC | 73|116| 32|105|115| 32| 97|108|116|111|103|101|116|104|101|114|
ASC |   |   | ^`|   |   | ^`|   |   |   |   |   |   |   |   |   |   |
ALT |   |   |SPC|   |   |SPC|   |   |   |   |   |   |   |   |   |   |
SYM | I | t |   | i | s |   | a | l | t | o | g | e | t | h | e | r |


BYTE|832|833|834|835|836|837|838|839|840|841|842|843|844|845|846|847|
HEX | 20| 66| 69| 74| 74| 69| 6E| 67| 20| 61| 6E| 64| 20| 70| 72| 6F|
DEC | 32|102|105|116|116|105|110|103| 32| 97|110|100| 32|112|114|111|
ASC | ^`|   |   |   |   |   |   |   | ^`|   |   |   | ^`|   |   |   |
ALT |SPC|   |   |   |   |   |   |   |SPC|   |   |   |SPC|   |   |   |
SYM |   | f | i | t | t | i | n | g |   | a | n | d |   | p | r | o |
```

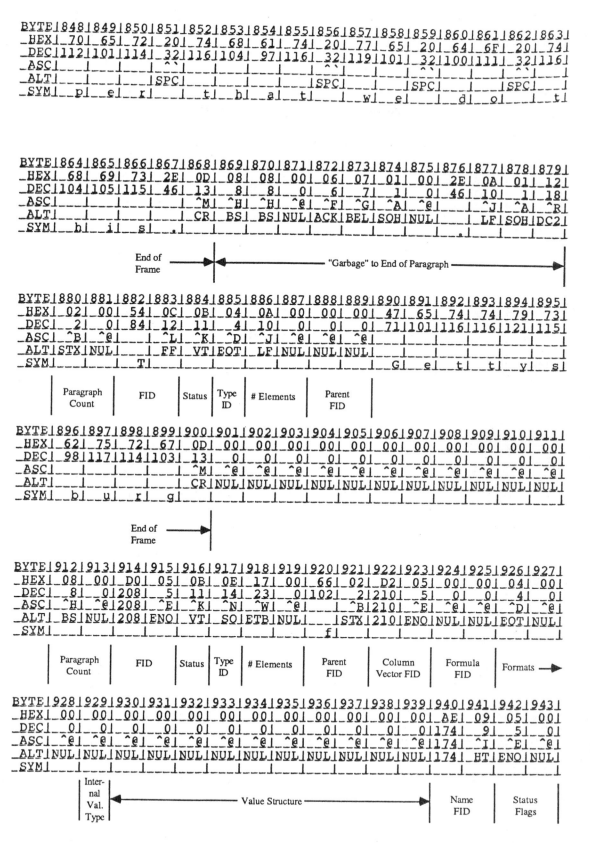

```
BYTE|944|945|946|947|948|949|950|951|952|953|954|955|956|957|958|959|
HEX | 02| 00| 0C| 00| 3E| 00| 16| 00| 05| 00| 0B| 00| 31| 00| 14| 00|
DEC |  2|  0| 12|  0| 62|  0| 22|  0|  5|  0| 11|  0| 49|  0| 20|  0|
ASC | ^B| ^@| ^L| ^@|  _| ^@| ^V| ^@| ^E| ^@| ^K| ^@|  _| ^@| ^T| ^@|
ALT |STX|NUL| FF|NUL|   |NUL|SYN|NUL|ENQ|NUL| VT|NUL|   |NUL|DC4|NUL|
SYM |   |   |   |   |  >|   |   |   |   |   |   |   |  1|   |   |   |
```

TLX	TLY	BRX	BRY	Clip TLX	Clip TLY	Clip BRX	Clip BRY

```
BYTE|960|961|962|963|964|965|966|967|968|969|970|971|972|973|974|975|
HEX | F9| FF| 0B| 00| 01| 00| 06| 00| 0A| 00| 01| 00| 00| 00| 00| 00|
DEC |249|255| 11|  0|  1|  0|  6|  0| 10|  0|  1|  0|  0|  0|  0|  0|
ASC |249|255| ^K| ^@| ^A| ^@| ^F| ^@| ^J| ^@| ^A| ^@| ^@| ^@| ^@| ^@|
ALT |249|255| VT|NUL|SOH|NUL|ACK|NUL| LF|NUL|SOH|NUL|NUL|NUL|NUL|NUL|
SYM |   |   |   |   |   |   |   |   |   |   |   |   |   |   |   |   |
```

ABS TLX	ABS TLY	First Visible Column	Last Visible Column	Last Visible Row	First Visible Row	Style FID	Internal Page #

```
BYTE|976|977|978|979|980|981|982|983|984|985|986|987|988|989|990|991|
HEX | 01| 00| 02| 00| 01| 00| 02| 00| 33| 00| 00| 81| 62| 00| 81| 00|
DEC |  1|  0|  2|  0|  1|  0|  2|  0| 51|  0|  0|129| 98|  0|129|  0|
ASC | ^A| ^@| ^B| ^@| ^A| ^@| ^B| ^@|   | ^@| ^@|129|   | ^@|129| ^@|
ALT |SOH|NUL|STX|NUL|SOH|NUL|STX|NUL|   |NUL|NUL|129|   |NUL|129|NUL|
SYM |   |   |   |   |   |   |   |   |  3|   |   |  b|   |   |   |   |
```

First Selected Row	Last Selected Row	First Selected Column	Last Selected Column	# Columns	Delta First Vis. Col.	Spread Sheet Status Flags	Window Last Row	Reserved

```
BYTE|992|993|994|995|996|997|998|999|  0|  1|  2|  3|  4|  5|  6|  7|
HEX | 40| 06| 00| 00| D4| 05| F8| 05| 18| 06| 2C| 06| 00| 00| CE| 06|
DEC | 64|  6|  0|  0|212|  5|248|  5| 24|  6| 44|  6|  0|  0|206|  6|
ASC |   | ^F| ^@| ^@|212| ^E|248| ^E| ^X| ^F|   | ^F| ^@| ^@|206| ^F|
ALT |   |ACK|NUL|NUL|212|ENQ|248|ENQ|CAN|ACK|   |ACK|NUL|NUL|206|ACK|
SYM | @ |   |   |   |   |   |   |   |   |   |   |   |   |   |   |   |
```

FID Row 1	Empty Row (2)	FID Row 3	FID Row 4	FID Row 5	FID Row 6	FID Row 7 (Empty)	FID Row 8

```
BYTE|  8|  9| 10| 11| 12| 13| 14| 15| 16| 17| 18| 19| 20| 21| 22| 23|
HEX | D4| 06| F6| 06| FC| 06| 06| 07| 10| 07| AE| 07| B8| 07| C2| 07|
DEC |212|  6|246|  6|252|  6|  6|  7| 16|  7|174|  7|184|  7|194|  7|
ASC |212| ^F|246| ^F|252| ^F| ^F| ^G| ^P| ^G|174| ^G|184| ^G|194| ^G|
ALT |212|ACK|246|ACK|252|ACK|ACK|BEL|DLE|BEL|174|BEL|184|BEL|194|BEL|
SYM |   |   |   |   |   |   |   |   |   |   |   |   |   |   |   |   |
```

FID Row 9	FID Row 10	FID Row 11	FID Row 12	FID Row 13	FID Row 14	FID Row 15	FID Row 16

```
BYTE| 24| 25| 26| 27| 28| 29| 30| 31| 32| 33| 34| 35| 36| 37| 38| 39|
HEX | CC| 07| D6| 07| E0| 07| EA| 07| F4| 07| FE| 07| 90| 08| 0D| 00|
DEC |204|  7|214|  7|224|  7|234|  7|244|  7|254|  7|144|  8| 13|  0|
ASC |204| ^G|214| ^G|224| ^G|234| ^G|244| ^G|254| ^G|144| ^H| ^M| ^@|
ALT |204|BEL|214|BEL|224|BEL|234|BEL|244|BEL|254|BEL|144| BS| CR|NUL|
SYM |   |   |   |   |   |   |   |   |   |   |   |   |   |   |   |   |
```

FID Row 17	FID Row 18	FID Row 19	FID Row 20	FID Row 21	FID Row 22	FID Row 23	End of Frame

BYTE	40	41	42	43	44	45	46	47	48	49	50	51	52	53	54	55
HEX	02	00	D2	05	03	04	09	00	00	00	09	00	0D	00	0A	00
DEC	2	0	210	5	3	4	9	0	0	0	9	0	13	0	10	0
ASC	^B	^@	210	^E	^C	^D	^I	^@	^@	^@	^I	^@	^M	^@	^J	^@
ALT	STX	NUL	210	ENQ	ETX	EOT	HT	NUL	NUL	NUL	HT	NUL	CR	NUL	LF	NUL
SYM																

# Paragraphs	FID	Flags	Type ID	# Elements	DB Forms FID	Column 1	Column 2	Column 3

BYTE	56	57	58	59	60	61	62	63	64	65	66	67	68	69	70	71
HEX	0C	00	09	00	0A	00	0A	00	09	00	09	00	00	00	04	00
DEC	12	0	9	0	10	0	10	0	9	0	9	0	0	0	4	0
ASC	^L	^@	^I	^@	^J	^@	^J	^@	^I	^@	^I	^@	^@	^@	^D	^@
ALT	FF	NUL	HT	NUL	LF	NUL	LF	NUL	HT	NUL	HT	NUL	NUL	NUL	EOT	NUL
SYM																

Column 4	Column 5	Column 6	Column 7	Column 8	Column 9	Defaults	End of Frame

BYTE	72	73	74	75	76	77	78	79	80	81	82	83	84	85	86	87
HEX	02	00	AE	09	0B	04	08	00	00	00	50	61	79	6D	65	6E
DEC	2	0	174	9	11	4	8	0	0	0	80	97	121	109	101	110
ASC	^B	^@	174	^I	^K	^D	^H	^@	^@	^@	80	97	121	109	101	110
ALT	STX	NUL	174	HT	VT	EOT	BS	NUL	NUL	NUL						
SYM											P	a	y	m	e	n

Paragraph Count	FID	Frame Status	Type ID	# Elements	Parent FID	Name

BYTE	88	89	90	91	92	93	94	95	96	97	98	99	100	101	102	103
HEX	74	73	0D	00	00	00	00	00	00	00	00	00	00	00	00	00
DEC	116	115	13	0	0	0	0	0	0	0	0	0	0	0	0	0
ASC			^M	^@	^@	^@	^@	^@	^@	^@	^@	^@	^@	^@	^@	^@
ALT			CR	NUL	NUL	NUL	NUL	NUL	NUL	NUL	NUL	NUL	NUL	NUL	NUL	NUL
SYM	t	s														

End of Frame

BYTE	104	105	106	107	108	109	110	111	112	113	114	115	116	117	118	119
HEX	02	00	40	06	0B	0D	04	00	D0	05	01	00	01	00	01	00
DEC	2	0	64	6	11	13	4	0	208	5	1	0	1	0	1	0
ASC	^B	^@		^F	^K	^M	^D	^@	208	^E	^A	^@	^A	^@	^A	^@
ALT	STX	NUL		ACK	VT	CR	EOT	NUL	208	ENQ	SOH	NUL	SOH	NUL	SOH	NUL
SYM			@													

Paragraph Count (Row 1)	FID	Status	Type	# Elements	Parent FID	Format A1	Format B1	Format C1

BYTE	120	121	122	123	124	125	126	127	128	129	130	131	132	133	134	135
HEX	44	06	0D	00	0F	0A	07	00	12	00	00	00	00	00	04	00
DEC	68	6	13	0	15	10	7	0	18	0	0	0	0	0	4	0
ASC		^F	^M	^@	^O	^J	^G	^@	^R	^@	^@	^@	^@	^@	^D	^@
ALT		ACK	CR	NUL	SI	LF	BEL	NUL	DC2	NUL	NUL	NUL	NUL	NUL	EOT	NUL
SYM	D															

FID Cell D1	End of Frame

BYTE	136	137	138	139	140	141	142	143	144	145	146	147	148	149	150	151
HEX	04	00	44	06	0B	07	1E	00	40	06	01	00	00	00	01	00
DEC	4	0	68	6	11	7	30	0	64	6	1	0	0	0	1	0
ASC	^D	^@			^F	^K	^G	^^	^@			^F	^A	^@	^@	^@	^A	^@
ALT	EOT	NUL			ACK	VT	BEL	RS	NUL			ACK	SOH	NUL	NUL	NUL	SOH	NUL
SYM			D								@							

Paragraph Count	FID (Cell D1)	Status	Type	# Elements	Parent FID	Reserved (0 is OK)	Formula FID	Format →

BYTE	152	153	154	155	156	157	158	159	160	161	162	163	164	165	166	167
HEX	10	00	00	05	04	00	50	61	79	6D	65	6E	74	20	41	6E
DEC	16	0	0	5	4	0	80	97	121	109	101	110	116	32	65	110
ASC	^P	^@	^@	^E	^D	^@									^^	^`			
ALT	DLE	NUL	NUL	ENQ	EOT	NUL								SPC		
SYM							P	a	y	m	e	n	t		A	n

Format	Internal Value Type	← Escape Sequence →	Label →

BYTE	168	169	170	171	172	173	174	175	176	177	178	179	180	181	182	183
HEX	61	6C	79	73	69	73	20	57	6F	72	6B	73	68	65	65	74
DEC	97	108	121	115	105	115	32	87	111	114	107	115	104	101	101	116
ASC								^^	^`								
ALT							SPC									
SYM	a	l	y	s	i	s		W	o	r	k	s	h	e	e	t

← Label Text →

BYTE	184	185	186	187	188	189	190	191	192	193	194	195	196	197	198	199
HEX	0D	00	00	00	00	00	00	00	00	00	00	00	00	00	00	00
DEC	13	0	0	0	0	0	0	0	0	0	0	0	0	0	0	0
ASC	^M	^@	^@	^@	^@	^@	^@	^@	^@	^@	^@	^@	^@	^@	^@	^@
ALT	CR	NUL	NUL	NUL	NUL	NUL	NUL	NUL	NUL	NUL	NUL	NUL	NUL	NUL	NUL	NUL
SYM																

End of Frame

BYTE	200	201	202	203	204	205	206	207	208	209	210	211	212	213	214	215
HEX	01	00	D4	05	0B	0D	02	00	D0	05	D8	05	DA	05	0D	00
DEC	1	0	212	5	11	13	2	0	208	5	218	5	218	5	13	0
ASC	^A	^@	212	^E	^K	^M	^B	^@	208	^E	216	^E	218	^E	^M	^@
ALT	SOH	NUL	212	ENQ	VT	CR	STX	NUL	208	ENQ	216	ENQ	218	ENQ	CR	NUL
SYM																

Paragraph Count	FID (Row 3)	Status	Type	# Elements	Parent FID	FID Cell A3	FID Cell B3	End of Frame

BYTE	216	217	218	219	220	221	222	223	224	225	226	227	228	229	230	231
HEX	02	00	D8	05	0B	07	08	00	D4	05	01	00	00	00	01	00
DEC	2	0	216	5	11	7	8	0	212	5	1	0	0	0	1	0
ASC	^B	^@	216	^E	^K	^G	^H	^@	212	^E	^A	^@	^@	^@	^A	^@
ALT	STX	NUL	216	ENQ	VT	BEL	BS	NUL	212	ENQ	SOH	NUL	NUL	NUL	SOH	NUL
SYM																

Paragraph Count	FID (Cell A3)	Status	Type	# Elements	Parent FID	Reserved 0 is OK	Formula FID	Formats

BYTE	232	233	234	235	236	237	238	239	240	241	242	243	244	245	246	247
HEX	00	00	4C	6F	61	6E	20	41	6D	74	0D	00	00	00	00	00
DEC	0	0	76	111	97	110	32	65	109	116	13	0	0	0	0	0
ASC	^@	^@					^^`					^M	^@	^@	^@	^@	^@
ALT	NUL	NUL					SPC				CR	NUL	NUL	NUL	NUL	NUL
SYM			L	o	a	n		A	m	t						

Field segmentation: Internal Value Type ← Contents of Cell → End of Frame

BYTE	248	249	250	251	252	253	254	255	256	257	258	259	260	261	262	263
HEX	03	00	DA	05	4B	08	0A	00	D4	05	01	00	00	00	01	12
DEC	3	0	218	5	75	8	10	0	212	5	1	0	0	0	1	18
ASC	^C	^@	218	^E		^H	^J	^@	212	^E	^A	^@	^@	^@	^A	^R
ALT	ETX	NUL	218	ENQ		BS	LF	NUL	212	ENQ	SOH	NUL	NUL	NUL	SOH	DC2
SYM					K											

Field segmentation: Paragraph Count | Cell FID | Status | Type | # Elements | Parent FID | Reserved | Formula FID | Formats

BYTE	264	265	266	267	268	269	270	271	272	273	274	275	276	277	278	279
HEX	00	03	C0	12	00	00	00	00	00	00	12	2E	24	34	2C	38
DEC	0	3	192	18	0	0	0	0	0	0	18	46	36	52	44	56
ASC	^@	^C	192	^R	^@	^@	^@	^@	^@	^@	^R					
ALT	NUL	ETX	192	DC2	NUL	NUL	NUL	NUL	NUL	NUL	DC2					
SYM												.	$	4	,	8

Field segmentation: I.V.T. ← Value Structure → Internal Value Displayed

BYTE	280	281	282	283	284	285	286	287	288	289	290	291	292	293	294	295
HEX	30	30	2E	30	30	20	0D	00	00	00	00	00	00	00	00	00
DEC	48	48	46	48	48	32	13	0	0	0	0	0	0	0	0	0
ASC						^^`	^M	^@	^@	^@	^@	^@	^@	^@	^@	^@
ALT						SPC	CR	NUL	NUL	NUL	NUL	NUL	NUL	NUL	NUL	NUL
SYM	0	0	.	0	0											

Field segmentation: ← Value Displayed → End of Frame

BYTE	296	297	298	299	300	301	302	303	304	305	306	307	308	309	310	311
HEX	01	00	F8	05	0B	0D	02	00	D0	05	FC	05	FE	05	0D	00
DEC	1	0	248	5	11	13	2	0	208	5	252	5	254	5	13	0
ASC	^A	^@	248	^E	^K	^M	^B	^@	208	^E	252	^E	254	^E	^M	^@
ALT	SOH	NUL	248	ENQ	VT	CR	STX	NUL	208	ENQ	252	ENQ	254	ENQ	CR	NUL
SYM																

Field segmentation: Paragraph Count | FID (Row 4) | Status | Type | # Elements | Parent FID | FID Cell A4 | FID Cell B4 | End of Frame

BYTE	312	313	314	315	316	317	318	319	320	321	322	323	324	325	326	327
HEX	02	00	FC	05	0B	07	08	00	F8	05	01	00	00	00	01	00
DEC	2	0	252	5	11	7	8	0	248	5	1	0	0	0	1	0
ASC	^B	^@	252	^E	^K	^G	^H	^@	248	^E	^A	^@	^@	^@	^A	^@
ALT	STX	NUL	252	ENQ	VT	BEL	BS	NUL	248	ENQ	SOH	NUL	NUL	NUL	SOH	NUL
SYM																

Field segmentation: Paragraph Count | FID Cell A4 | Status | Type | # Elements | Parent FID | Reserved | Formula FID | Formatting

```
BYTE| 328| 329| 330| 331| 332| 333| 334| 335| 336| 337| 338| 339| 340| 341| 342| 343|
HEX | 00 | 00 | 49 | 6E | 74 | 65 | 72 | 65 | 73 | 74 | 0D | 00 | 00 | 00 | 00 | 00 |
DEC |  0 |  0 | 73 |110 |116 |101 |114 |101 |115 |116 | 13 |  0 |  0 |  0 |  0 |  0 |
ASC | ^@ | ^@ |    |    |    |    |    |    |    |    | ^M | ^@ | ^@ | ^@ | ^@ | ^@ |
ALT |NUL |NUL |    |    |    |    |    |    |    |    | CR |NUL |NUL |NUL |NUL |NUL |
SYM |    |    |  I |  n |  t |  e |  r |  e |  s |  t |    |    |    |    |    |    |

     | I.V.T. |<------------- Contents ------------->| End of
                                                       Frame
```

```
BYTE| 344| 345| 346| 347| 348| 349| 350| 351| 352| 353| 354| 355| 356| 357| 358| 359|
HEX | 03 | 00 | FE | 05 | 4B | 08 | 06 | 00 | F8 | 05 | 01 | 00 | 00 | 00 | 01 | 15 |
DEC |  3 |  0 |254 |  5 | 75 |  8 |  6 |  0 |248 |  5 |  1 |  0 |  0 |  0 |  1 | 21 |
ASC | ^C | ^@ |254 | ^E |    | ^H | ^F | ^@ |248 | ^E | ^A | ^@ | ^@ | ^@ | ^A | ^U |
ALT |ETX |NUL |254 |ENQ |    | BS |ACK |NUL |248 |ENQ |SOH |NUL |NUL |NUL |SOH |NAK |
SYM |    |    |    |    |  K |    |    |    |    |    |    |    |    |    |    |    |

  | Paragraph | FID     | Status | Type | # Elements | Parent FID | Reserved | Formula FID | Formatting
  | Count     | Cell B4 |
```

```
BYTE| 360| 361| 362| 363| 364| 365| 366| 367| 368| 369| 370| 371| 372| 373| 374| 375|
HEX | 23 | 05 | 00 | 00 | 00 | 00 | 00 | 00 | 00 | 50 | 18 | 2E | 31 | 38 | 2E | 35 |
DEC | 35 |  5 |  0 |  0 |  0 |  0 |  0 |  0 |  0 | 80 | 24 | 46 | 49 | 56 | 46 | 53 |
ASC |    | ^E | ^@ | ^@ | ^@ | ^@ | ^@ | ^@ | ^@ |    | ^X |    |    |    |    |    |
ALT |    |ENO |NUL |NUL |NUL |NUL |NUL |NUL |NUL |    |CAN |    |    |    |    |    |
SYM |  # |    |    |    |    |    |    |    |    |  P |    |  . |  1 |  8 |  . |  5 |

  | I.V.T.|<------------- Value Structure ------------->|<----- Contents ----->
```

```
BYTE| 376| 377| 378| 379| 380| 381| 382| 383| 384| 385| 386| 387| 388| 389| 390| 391|
HEX | 30 | 25 | 0D | 0D | 0D | 25 | 0D | 00 | 00 | 00 | 00 | 00 | 00 | 00 | 00 | 00 |
DEC | 48 | 37 | 13 | 13 | 13 | 37 | 13 |  0 |  0 |  0 |  0 |  0 |  0 |  0 |  0 |  0 |
ASC |    |    | ^M | ^M | ^M |    | ^M | ^@ | ^@ | ^@ | ^@ | ^@ | ^@ | ^@ | ^@ | ^@ |
ALT |    |    | CR | CR | CR |    | CR |NUL |NUL |NUL |NUL |NUL |NUL |NUL |NUL |NUL |
SYM |  0 |  % |    |    |    |  % |    |    |    |    |    |    |    |    |    |    |

  <----- Contents ----->| End of
                          Frame
```

```
BYTE| 392| 393| 394| 395| 396| 397| 398| 399| 400| 401| 402| 403| 404| 405| 406| 407|
HEX | 01 | 00 | 18 | 06 | 0B | 0D | 02 | 00 | D0 | 05 | 1C | 06 | 1E | 06 | 0D | 00 |
DEC |  1 |  0 | 24 |  6 | 11 | 13 |  2 |  0 |208 |  5 | 28 |  6 | 30 |  6 | 13 |  0 |
ASC | ^A | ^@ | ^X | ^F | ^K | ^M | ^B | ^@ |208 | ^E | ^\ | ^F | ^^ | ^F | ^M | ^@ |
ALT |SOH |NUL |CAN |ACK | VT | CR |STX |NUL |208 |ENO | FS |ACK | RS |ACK | CR |NUL |
SYM |    |    |    |    |    |    |    |    |    |    |    |    |    |    |    |    |

  | Paragraph | FID     | Status | Type | # Elements | Parent FID | Cell FID | Cell FID | End of Frame
  | Count     | (Row 5) |
```

```
BYTE| 408| 409| 410| 411| 412| 413| 414| 415| 416| 417| 418| 419| 420| 421| 422| 423|
HEX | 02 | 00 | 1C | 06 | 0B | 07 | 06 | 00 | 18 | 06 | 01 | 00 | 00 | 00 | 01 | 00 |
DEC |  2 |  0 | 28 |  6 | 11 |  7 |  6 |  0 | 24 |  6 |  1 |  0 |  0 |  0 |  1 |  0 |
ASC | ^B | ^@ | ^\ | ^F | ^K | ^G | ^F | ^@ | ^X | ^F | ^A | ^@ | ^@ | ^@ | ^A | ^@ |
ALT |STX |NUL | FS |ACK | VT |BEL |ACK |NUL |CAN |ACK |SOH |NUL |NUL |NUL |SOH |NUL |
SYM |    |    |    |    |    |    |    |    |    |    |    |    |    |    |    |    |

  | Paragraph | Cell FID | Status | Type | # Elements | Parent FID | Reserved | Formula FID | Formatting
  | Count     |
```

BYTE	424	425	426	427	428	429	430	431	432	433	434	435	436	437	438	439
HEX	00	00	4D	6F	20	50	6D	74	0D	00	00	00	00	00	00	00
DEC	0	0	77	111	32	80	109	116	13	0	0	0	0	0	0	0
ASC	^@	^@			^^				^M	^@	^@	^@	^@	^@	^@	^@
ALT	NUL	NUL			SPC				CR	NUL	NUL	NUL	NUL	NUL	NUL	NUL
SYM			M	o		P	m	t								

I.V.T. ◄———— Contents ————► | End of Frame

BYTE	440	441	442	443	444	445	446	447	448	449	450	451	452	453	454	455
HEX	03	00	1E	06	4B	08	08	00	18	06	01	00	00	00	01	12
DEC	3	0	30	6	75	8	8	0	24	6	1	0	0	0	1	18
ASC	^C	^@	^^	^F		^H	^H	^@	^X	^F	^A	^@	^@	^@	^A	^R
ALT	ETX	NUL	RS	ACK		BS	BS	NUL	CAN	ACK	SOH	NUL	NUL	NUL	SOH	DC2
SYM					K											

Paragraph Count | FID | Status | Type | # Elements | Parent FID | Reserved | Formula FID | Formatting

BYTE	456	457	458	459	460	461	462	463	464	465	466	467	468	469	470	471
HEX	22	05	00	00	00	00	00	00	30	47	17	31	24	31	37	34
DEC	34	5	0	0	0	0	0	0	48	71	23	49	36	49	55	52
ASC		^E	^@	^@	^@	^@	^@	^@			^W					
ALT		ENQ	NUL	NUL	NUL	NUL	NUL	NUL			ETB					
SYM	"								0	G		1	$	1	7	4

I.V.T. ◄———— Value Structure ————►◄———— Contents ————►

BYTE	472	473	474	475	476	477	478	479	480	481	482	483	484	485	486	487
HEX	2E	37	33	20	0D	00	00	04	00	00	00	81	01	FF	81	00
DEC	46	55	51	32	13	0	0	4	0	0	0	129	1	255	129	0
ASC				^^	^M	^@	^@	^D	^@	^@	^@	129	^A	255	129	^@
ALT				SPC	CR	NUL	NUL	EOT	NUL	NUL	NUL	129	SOH	255	129	NUL
SYM	.	7	3													

◄———— Contents ————► | End of Frame

BYTE	488	489	490	491	492	493	494	495	496	497	498	499	500	501	502	503
HEX	01	00	2C	06	0B	0D	02	00	D0	05	30	06	32	06	0D	00
DEC	1	0	44	6	11	13	2	0	208	5	48	6	50	6	13	0
ASC	^A	^@		^F	^K	^M	^B	^@	208	^E		^F		^F	^M	^@
ALT	SOH	NUL		ACK	VT	CR	STX	NUL	208	ENO		ACK		ACK	CR	NUL
SYM			.								0		2			

Paragraph Count | FID (Row 6) | Status | Type | # Elements | Parent FID | Cell FID | Cell FID | End of Frame

BYTE	504	505	506	507	508	509	510	511	512	513	514	515	516	517	518	519
HEX	02	00	30	06	0B	07	07	00	2C	06	01	00	00	00	01	00
DEC	2	0	48	6	11	7	7	0	44	6	1	0	0	0	1	0
ASC	^B	^@		^F	^K	^G	^G	^@		^F	^A	^@	^@	^@	^A	^@
ALT	STX	NUL		ACK	VT	BEL	BEL	NUL		ACK	SOH	NUL	NUL	NUL	SOH	NUL
SYM			0						.							

Paragraph Count | FID | Status | Type | # Elements | Parent FID | Reserved | Formula FID | Formatting

Block 1 (Bytes 520–535)

BYTE	520	521	522	523	524	525	526	527	528	529	530	531	532	533	534	535
HEX	00	00	50	65	72	69	6F	64	73	0D	00	00	00	00	00	00
DEC	0	0	80	101	114	105	111	100	115	13	0	0	0	0	0	0
ASC	^@	^@								^M	^@	^@	^@	^@	^@	^@
ALT	NUL	NUL								CR	NUL	NUL	NUL	NUL	NUL	NUL
SYM			P	e	r	i	o	d	s							

I.V.T.	Contents	End of Frame

Block 2 (Bytes 536–551)

BYTE	536	537	538	539	540	541	542	543	544	545	546	547	548	549	550	551
HEX	02	00	32	06	4B	08	03	00	2C	06	01	00	00	00	01	00
DEC	2	0	50	6	75	8	3	0	44	6	1	0	0	0	1	0
ASC	^B	^@		^F		^H	^C	^@		^F	^A	^@	^@	^@	^A	^@
ALT	STX	NUL		ACK		BS	ETX	NUL		ACK	SOH	NUL	NUL	NUL	SOH	NUL
SYM			2		K				,							

Paragraph Count	FID	Status	Type	# Elements	Parent FID	Reserved	Formula FID	Format

Block 3 (Bytes 552–567)

BYTE	552	553	554	555	556	557	558	559	560	561	562	563	564	565	566	567
HEX	00	03	24	00	00	00	00	00	00	50	18	2E	33	36	20	0D
DEC	0	3	36	0	0	0	0	0	0	80	24	46	51	54	32	13
ASC	^@	^C		^@	^@	^@	^@	^@	^@		^X				^`	^M
ALT	NUL	ETX		NUL	NUL	NUL	NUL	NUL	NUL		CAN				SPC	CR
SYM			$							P		.	3	6		

I.V.T.	Value Structure	Contents	End of Frame

Block 4 (Bytes 568–583)

BYTE	568	569	570	571	572	573	574	575	576	577	578	579	580	581	582	583
HEX	02	00	CE	06	0B	0D	07	00	D0	05	D2	06	01	00	01	00
DEC	2	0	206	6	11	13	7	0	208	5	210	6	1	0	1	0
ASC	^B	^@	206	^F	^K	^M	^G	^@	208	^E	210	^F	^A	^@	^A	^@
ALT	STX	NUL	206	ACK	VT	CR	BEL	NUL	208	ENQ	210	ACK	SOH	NUL	SOH	NUL
SYM																

Paragraph Count	FID (Row 8)	Status	Type	# Elements	Parent FID	Cell FID	Formatting	Formatting

Block 5 (Bytes 584–599)

BYTE	584	585	586	587	588	589	590	591	592	593	594	595	596	597	598	599
HEX	01	00	01	00	01	00	AC	09	0D	00	00	00	00	00	00	00
DEC	1	0	1	0	1	0	172	9	13	0	0	0	0	0	0	0
ASC	^A	^@	^A	^@	^A	^@	172	^I	^M	^@	^@	^@	^@	^@	^@	^@
ALT	SOH	NUL	SOH	NUL	SOH	NUL	172	HT	CR	NUL	NUL	NUL	NUL	NUL	NUL	NUL
SYM																

Formatting	Formatting	Formatting	Cell FID	End of Frame

Block 6 (Bytes 600–615)

BYTE	600	601	602	603	604	605	606	607	608	609	610	611	612	613	614	615
HEX	06	00	D2	06	0B	07	4A	00	CE	06	01	00	00	00	01	00
DEC	6	0	210	6	11	7	74	0	206	6	1	0	0	0	1	0
ASC	^F	^@	210	^F	^K	^G		^@	206	^F	^A	^@	^@	^@	^A	^@
ALT	ACK	NUL	210	ACK	VT	BEL		NUL	206	ACK	SOH	NUL	NUL	NUL	SOH	NUL
SYM							J									

Paragraph Count	FID	Status	Type	# Elements	Parent FID	Reserved	Formula FID	Formatting

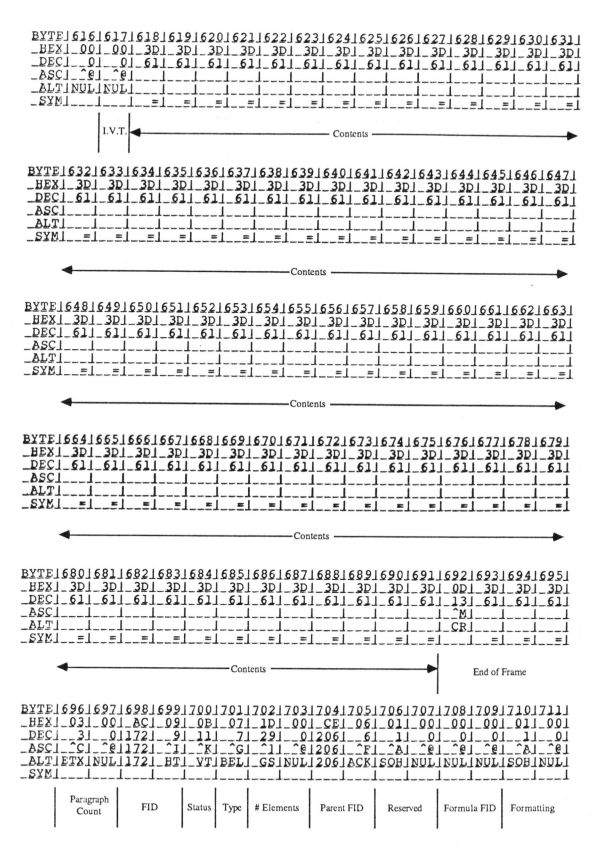

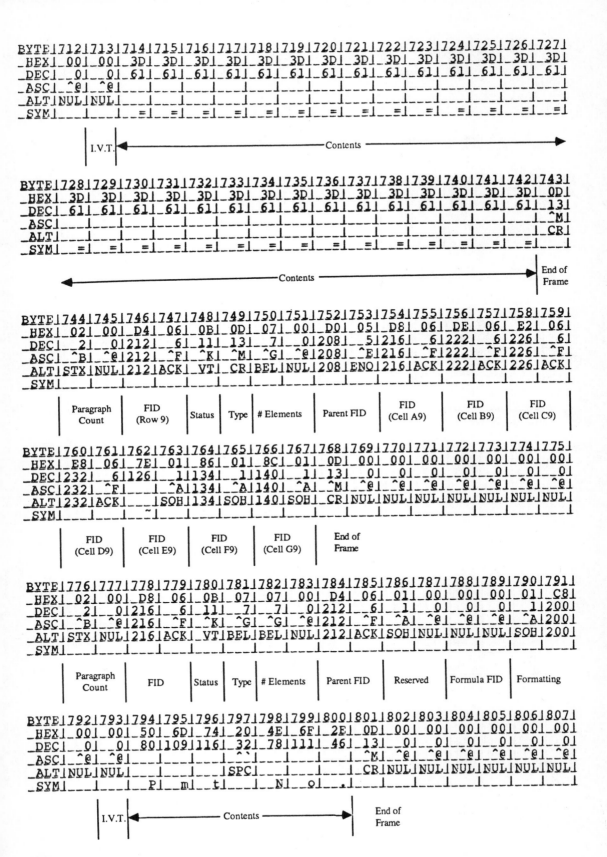

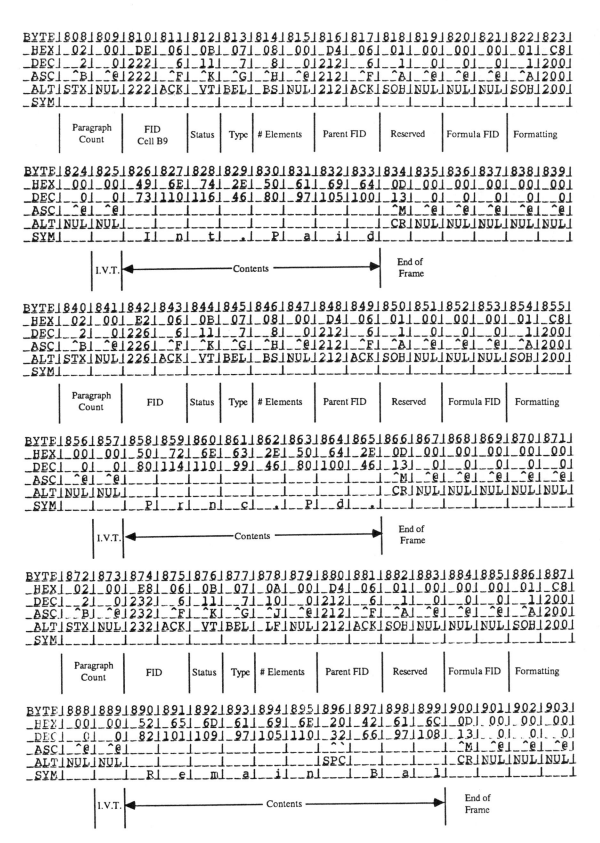

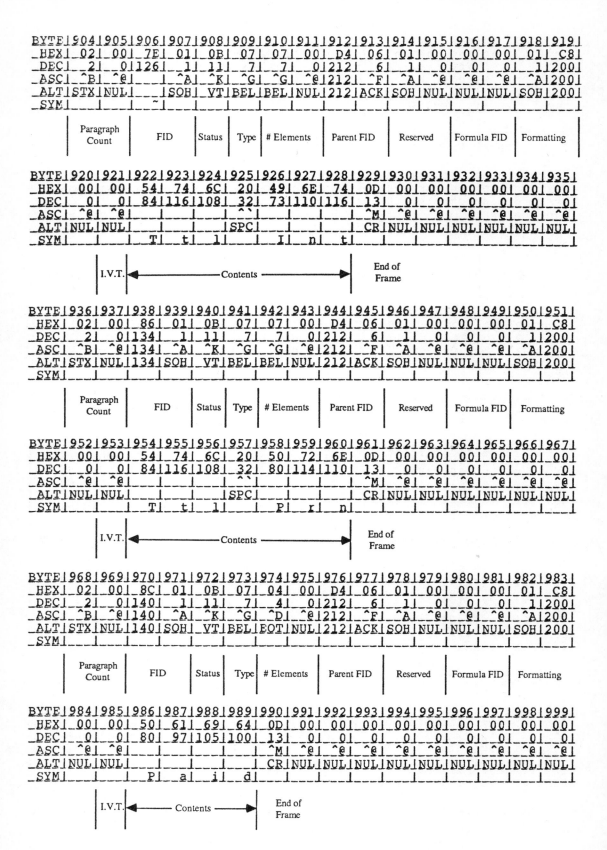

BYTE	0	1	2	3	4	5	6	7	8	9	10	11	12	13	14	15
HEX	02	00	F6	06	0B	0D	09	00	D0	05	FA	06	01	00	01	00
DEC	2	0	246	6	11	13	9	0	208	5	250	6	1	0	1	0
ASC	^B	^@	246	^F	^K	^M	^I	^@	208	^E	250	^F	^A	^@	^A	^@
ALT	STX	NUL	246	ACK	VT	CR	HT	NUL	208	ENQ	250	ACK	SOH	NUL	SOH	NUL
SYM																

Paragraph Count	FID	Status	Type	# Elements	Parent FID	FID A10	Format	Format

BYTE	16	17	18	19	20	21	22	23	24	25	26	27	28	29	30	31
HEX	01	00	01	00	01	00	A6	09	01	00	A4	09	0D	00	3D	0D
DEC	1	0	1	0	1	0	166	9	1	0	164	9	13	0	61	13
ASC	^A	^@	^A	^@	^A	^@	166	^I	^A	^@	164	^I	^M	^@		^M
ALT	SOH	NUL	SOH	NUL	SOH	NUL	166	HT	SOH	NUL	164	HT	CR	NUL		CR
SYM															=	

Format	Format	Format	FID G10	Format	FID I10	End of Frame

BYTE	32	33	34	35	36	37	38	39	40	41	42	43	44	45	46	47
HEX	06	00	FA	06	0B	07	4A	00	F6	06	01	00	00	00	01	00
DEC	6	0	250	6	11	7	74	0	246	6	1	0	0	0	1	0
ASC	^F	^@	250	^F	^K	^G		^@	246	^F	^A	^@	^@	^@	^A	^@
ALT	ACK	NUL	250	ACK	VT	BEL		NUL	246	ACK	SOH	NUL	NUL	NUL	SOH	NUL
SYM							J									

Paragraph Count	FID Cell A10	Status	Type	# Elements	Parent FID	Reserved	Formula Frame	Formatting

BYTE	48	49	50	51	52	53	54	55	56	57	58	59	60	61	62	63
HEX	00	00	3D	3D	3D	3D	3D	3D	3D	3D	3D	3D	3D	3D	3D	3D
DEC	0	0	61	61	61	61	61	61	61	61	61	61	61	61	61	61
ASC	^@	^@														
ALT	NUL	NUL														
SYM			=	=	=	=	=	=	=	=	=	=	=	=	=	=

I.V.T. ◄─────────────── Contents ───────────────►

BYTE	64	65	66	67	68	69	70	71	72	73	74	75	76	77	78	79
HEX	3D	3D	3D	3D	3D	3D	3D	3D	3D	3D	3D	3D	3D	3D	3D	3D
DEC	61	61	61	61	61	61	61	61	61	61	61	61	61	61	61	61
ASC																
ALT																
SYM	=	=	=	=	=	=	=	=	=	=	=	=	=	=	=	=

◄─────────────── Contents ───────────────►

BYTE	80	81	82	83	84	85	86	87	88	89	90	91	92	93	94	95
HEX	3D	3D	3D	3D	3D	3D	3D	3D	3D	3D	3D	3D	3D	3D	3D	3D
DEC	61	61	61	61	61	61	61	61	61	61	61	61	61	61	61	61
ASC																
ALT																
SYM	=	=	=	=	=	=	=	=	=	=	=	=	=	=	=	=

◄─────────────── Contents ───────────────►

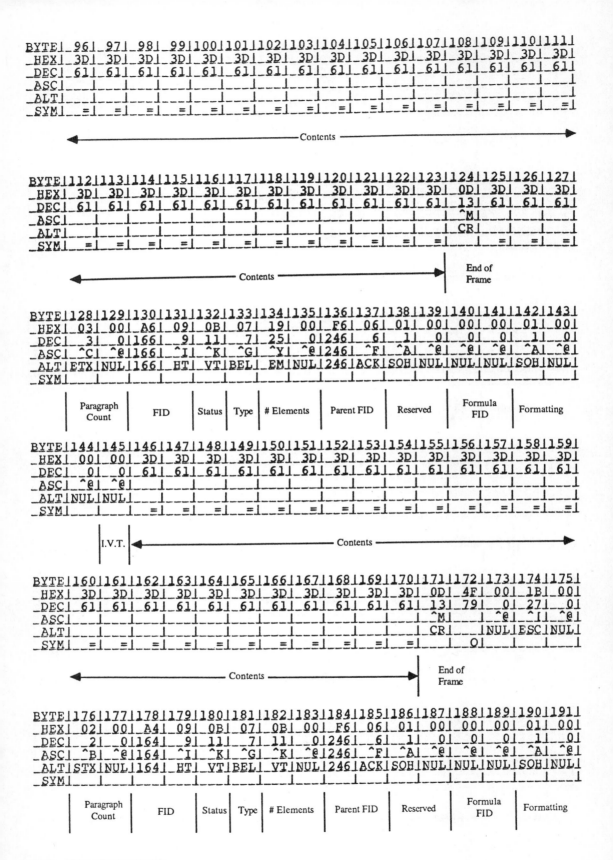

BYTE	192	193	194	195	196	197	198	199	200	201	202	203	204	205	206	207
HEX	00	00	3D	3D	3D	3D	3D	3D	3D	3D	3D	3D	3D	0D	00	00
DEC	01	01	61	61	61	61	61	61	61	61	61	61	61	13	01	01
ASC	^@	^@												^M	^@	^@
ALT	NUL	NUL												CR	NUL	NUL
SYM				=	=	=	=	=	=	=	=	=	=			

I.V.T.	◄──────── Contents ────────►	End of Frame

BYTE	208	209	210	211	212	213	214	215	216	217	218	219	220	221	222	223
HEX	02	00	FC	06	0B	0D	07	00	D0	05	FE	06	4C	08	5A	08
DEC	2	0	252	6	11	13	7	0	208	5	254	6	76	8	90	8
ASC	^B	^@	252	^F	^K	^M	^G	^@	208	^E	254	^F		^H		^H
ALT	STX	NUL	252	ACK	VT	CR	BEL	NUL	208	ENQ	254	ACK		BS		BS
SYM													L		Z	

Paragraph Count	FID	Status	Type	# Elements	Parent FID	FID A11	FID B11	FID C11

BYTE	224	225	226	227	228	229	230	231	232	233	234	235	236	237	238	239
HEX	66	08	A2	09	9E	09	9A	09	0D	00	00	00	00	00	04	00
DEC	102	8	162	9	158	9	154	9	13	0	0	0	0	0	4	0
ASC		^H	162	^I	158	^I	154	^I	^M	^@	^@	^@	^@	^@	^D	^@
ALT		BS	162	HT	158	HT	154	HT	CR	NUL	NUL	NUL	NUL	NUL	EOT	NUL
SYM	f															

FID D11	FID E11	FID F11	FID G11	End of Frame

BYTE	240	241	242	243	244	245	246	247	248	249	250	251	252	253	254	255
HEX	02	00	FE	06	4B	08	02	00	FC	06	01	00	00	00	01	00
DEC	2	0	254	6	75	8	2	0	252	6	1	0	0	0	1	0
ASC	^B	^@	254	^F		^H	^B	^@	252	^F	^A	^@	^@	^@	^A	^@
ALT	STX	NUL	254	ACK		BS	STX	NUL	252	ACK	SOH	NUL	NUL	NUL	SOH	NUL
SYM					K											

Paragraph Count	FID Cell A11	Status	Type	# Elements	Parent FID	Reserved	Formula FID	Formatting

BYTE	256	257	258	259	260	261	262	263	264	265	266	267	268	269	270	271
HEX	00	03	01	00	00	00	00	00	30	47	17	31	31	20	0D	00
DEC	0	3	1	0	0	0	0	0	48	71	23	49	49	32	13	0
ASC	^@	^C	^A	^@	^@	^@	^@	^@			^W				^M	^@
ALT	NUL	ETX	SOH	NUL	NUL	NUL	NUL	NUL			ETB			SPC	CR	NUL
SYM									0	G		1	1			

I.V.T.	◄──────── Value Structure ────────►	Contents	End of Frame

BYTE	272	273	274	275	276	277	278	279	280	281	282	283	284	285	286	287
HEX	03	00	4C	08	0B	08	07	00	FC	06	01	00	50	08	01	12
DEC	3	0	76	8	11	8	7	0	252	6	1	0	80	8	1	18
ASC	^C	^@		^H	^K	^H	^G	^@	252	^F	^A	^@		^H	^A	^R
ALT	ETX	NUL		BS	VT	BS	BEL	NUL	252	ACK	SOH	NUL		BS	SOH	DC2
SYM			L										P			

Paragraph Count	FID B11	Status	Type	# Elements	Parent FID	Reserved	Formula FID B11	Formatting

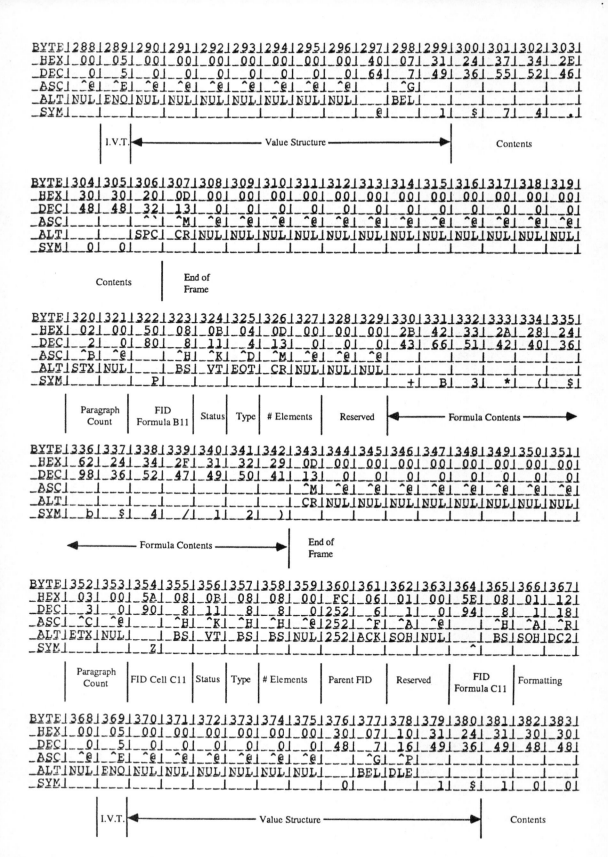

BYTE	288	289	290	291	292	293	294	295	296	297	298	299	300	301	302	303
HEX	00	05	00	00	00	00	00	00	00	40	07	31	24	37	34	2E
DEC	01	5	0	0	0	0	0	0	0	64	7	49	36	55	52	46
ASC	^@	^E	^@	^@	^@	^@	^@	^@	^@		^G					
ALT	NUL	ENO	NUL	NUL	NUL	NUL	NUL	NUL	NUL		BEL					
SYM										@		1	$	7	4	.

I.V.T. ◄──────────── Value Structure ────────────► Contents

BYTE	304	305	306	307	308	309	310	311	312	313	314	315	316	317	318	319
HEX	30	30	20	0D	00	00	00	00	00	00	00	00	00	00	00	00
DEC	48	48	32	13	0	0	0	0	0	0	0	0	0	0	0	0
ASC			^^	^M	^@	^@	^@	^@	^@	^@	^@	^@	^@	^@	^@	^@
ALT			SPC	CR	NUL	NUL	NUL	NUL	NUL	NUL	NUL	NUL	NUL	NUL	NUL	NUL
SYM	0	0														

Contents | End of Frame

BYTE	320	321	322	323	324	325	326	327	328	329	330	331	332	333	334	335
HEX	02	00	50	08	0B	04	0D	00	00	00	2B	42	33	2A	28	24
DEC	2	0	80	8	11	4	13	0	0	0	43	66	51	42	40	36
ASC	^B	^@		^H	^K	^D	^M	^@	^@	^@						
ALT	STX	NUL		BS	VT	EOT	CR	NUL	NUL	NUL						
SYM			P								+	B	3	*	(	$

Paragraph Count | FID Formula B11 | Status | Type | # Elements | Reserved | ◄──── Formula Contents ────►

BYTE	336	337	338	339	340	341	342	343	344	345	346	347	348	349	350	351
HEX	62	24	34	2F	31	32	29	0D	00	00	00	00	00	00	00	00
DEC	98	36	52	47	49	50	41	13	0	0	0	0	0	0	0	0
ASC								^M	^@	^@	^@	^@	^@	^@	^@	^@
ALT								CR	NUL	NUL	NUL	NUL	NUL	NUL	NUL	NUL
SYM	b	$	4	/	1	2	)									

◄──────── Formula Contents ────────► | End of Frame

BYTE	352	353	354	355	356	357	358	359	360	361	362	363	364	365	366	367
HEX	03	00	5A	08	0B	08	08	00	FC	06	01	00	5E	08	01	12
DEC	3	0	90	8	11	8	8	0	252	6	1	0	94	8	1	18
ASC	^C	^@		^H	^K	^H	^H	^@	252	^F	^A	^@		^H	^A	^R
ALT	ETX	NUL		BS	VT	BS	BS	NUL	252	ACK	SOH	NUL		BS	SOH	DC2
SYM			Z										^			

Paragraph Count | FID Cell C11 | Status | Type | # Elements | Parent FID | Reserved | FID Formula C11 | Formatting

BYTE	368	369	370	371	372	373	374	375	376	377	378	379	380	381	382	383
HEX	00	05	00	00	00	00	00	00	30	07	10	31	24	31	30	30
DEC	0	5	0	0	0	0	0	0	48	7	16	49	36	49	48	48
ASC	^@	^E	^@	^@	^@	^@	^@	^@		^G	^P					
ALT	NUL	ENO	NUL	NUL	NUL	NUL	NUL	NUL		BEL	DLE					
SYM									0			1	$	1	0	0

I.V.T. ◄──────────── Value Structure ────────────► Contents

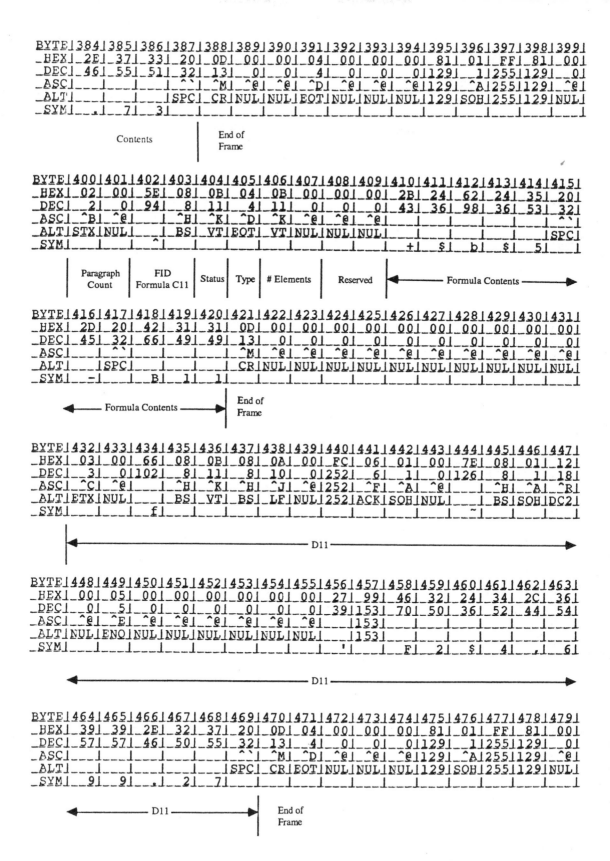

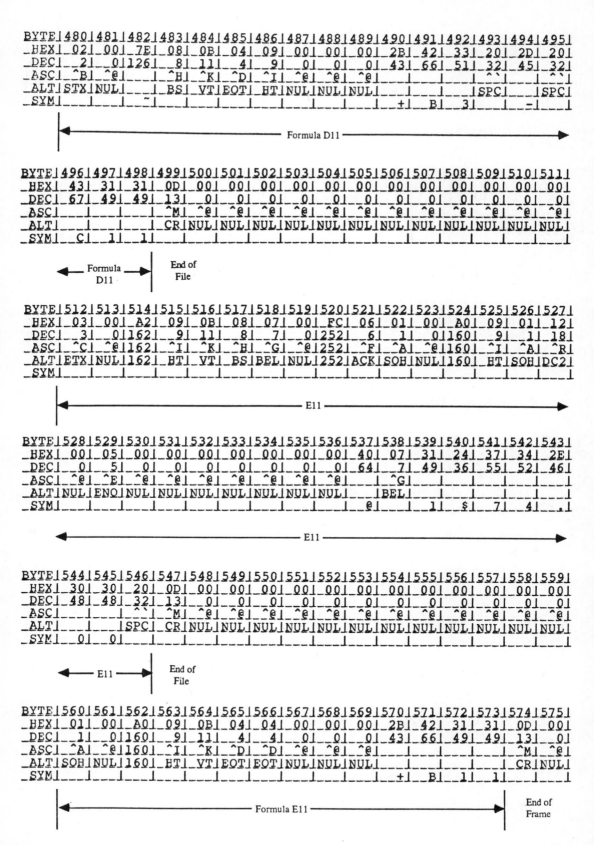

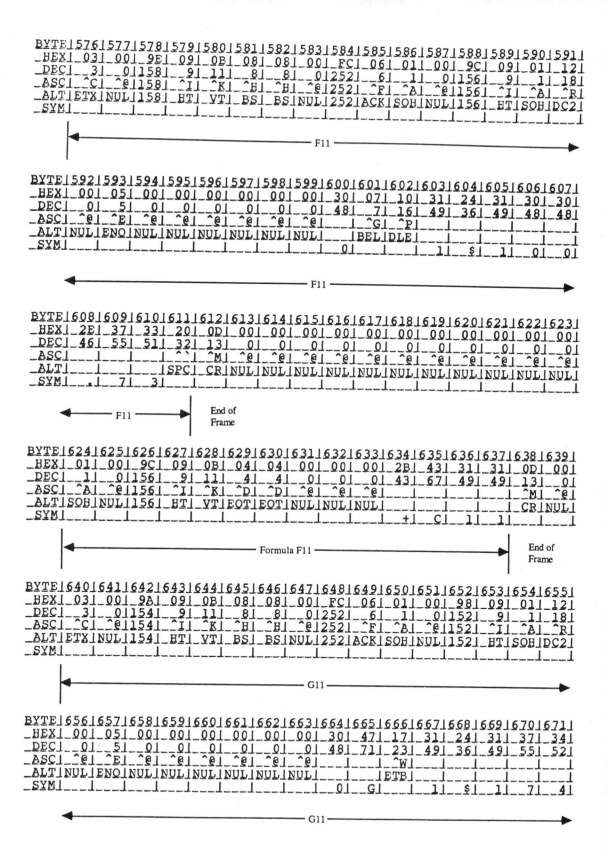

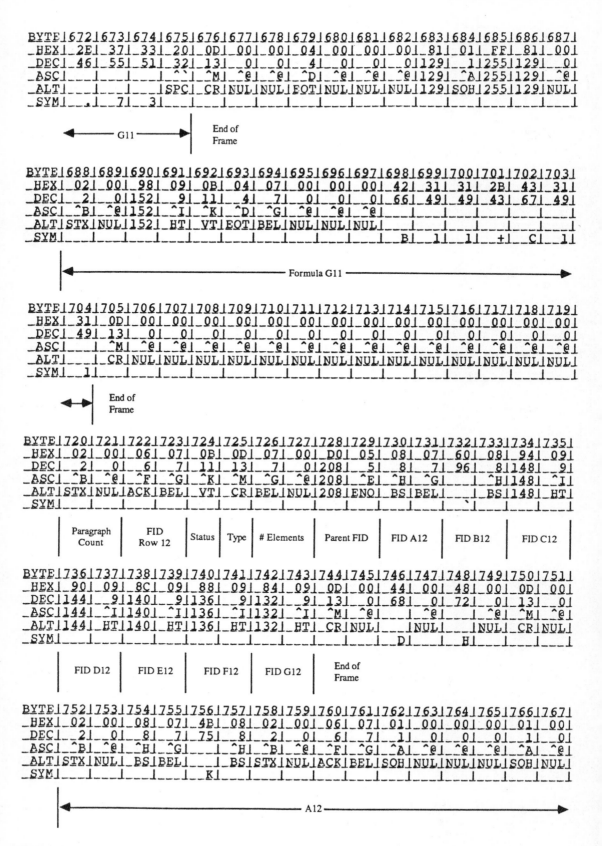

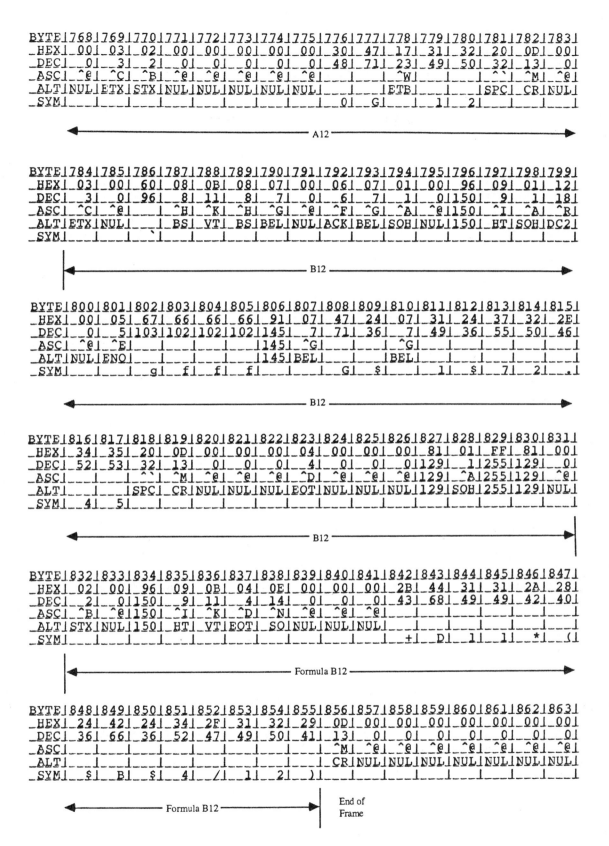

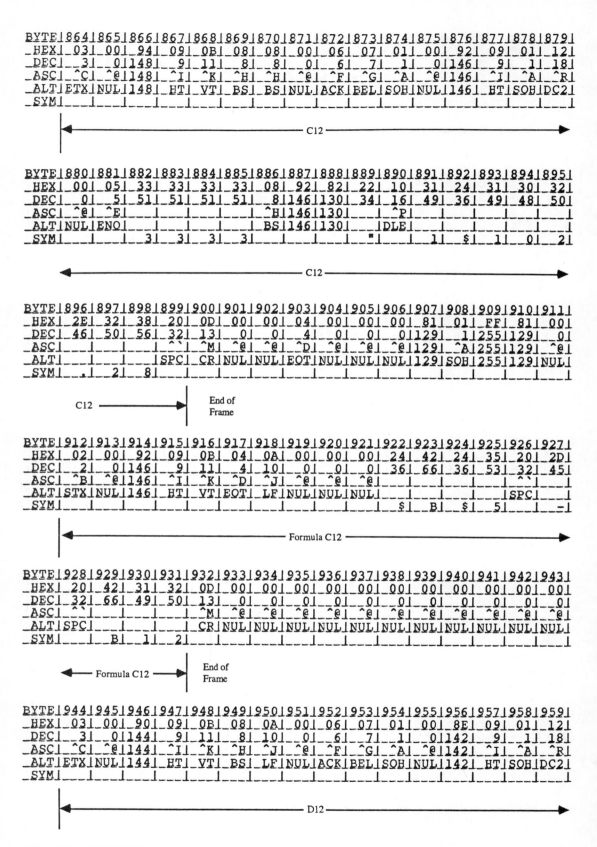

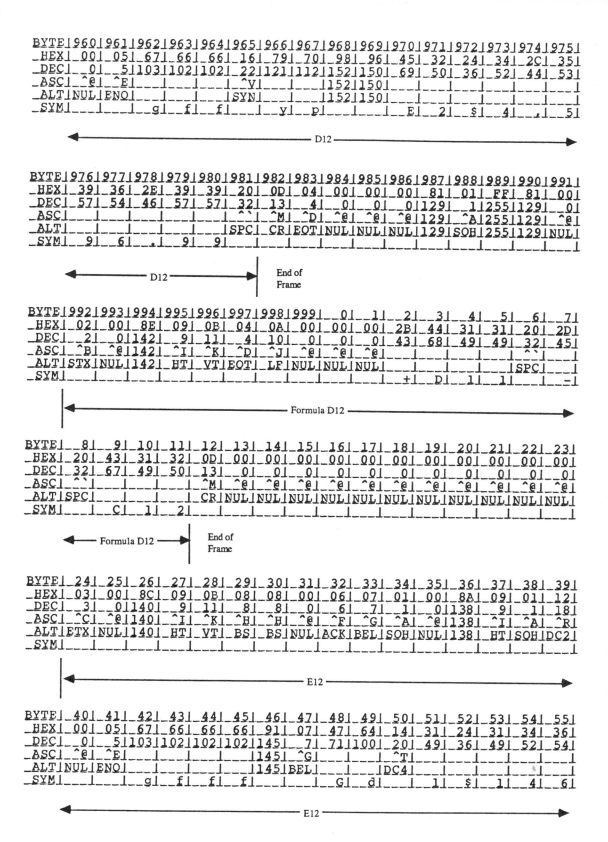

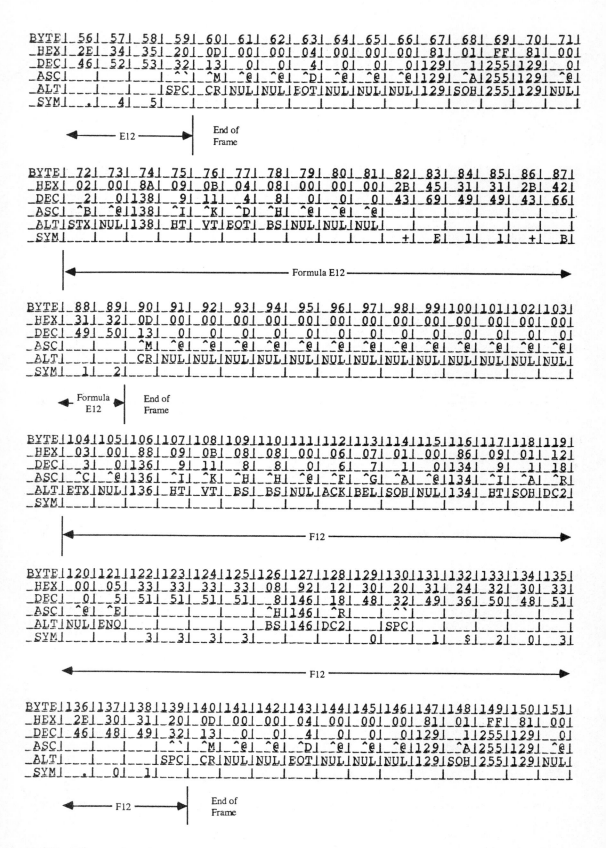

```
BYTE| 56| 57| 58| 59| 60| 61| 62| 63| 64| 65| 66| 67| 68| 69| 70| 71|
HEX| 2E| 34| 35| 20| 0D| 00| 00| 04| 00| 00| 00| 81| 01| FF| 81| 00|
DEC| 46| 52| 53| 32| 13| 0| 0| 4| 0| 0| 0|129| 1|255|129| 0|
ASC| | | | ^^| ^M| ^@| ^@| ^D| ^@| ^@| ^@|129| ^A|255|129| ^@|
ALT| | | | SPC| CR|NUL|NUL|EOT|NUL|NUL|NUL|129|SOH|255|129|NUL|
SYM| .| 4| 5| | | | | | | | | | | | | |

         <----- E12 ----->|  End of
                          |  Frame


BYTE| 72| 73| 74| 75| 76| 77| 78| 79| 80| 81| 82| 83| 84| 85| 86| 87|
HEX| 02| 00| 8A| 09| 0B| 04| 08| 00| 00| 00| 2B| 45| 31| 31| 2B| 42|
DEC| 2| 0|138| 9| 11| 4| 8| 0| 0| 0| 43| 69| 49| 49| 43| 66|
ASC| ^B| ^@|138| ^I| ^K| ^D| ^H| ^@| ^@| ^@| | | | | | |
ALT|STX|NUL|138| HT| VT|EOT| BS|NUL|NUL|NUL| | | | | | |
SYM| | | | | | | | | | | +| E| 1| 1| +| B|

         <------------------ Formula E12 ------------------>


BYTE| 88| 89| 90| 91| 92| 93| 94| 95| 96| 97| 98| 99|100|101|102|103|
HEX| 31| 32| 0D| 00| 00| 00| 00| 00| 00| 00| 00| 00| 00| 00| 00| 00|
DEC| 49| 50| 13| 0| 0| 0| 0| 0| 0| 0| 0| 0| 0| 0| 0| 0|
ASC| | | ^M| ^@| ^@| ^@| ^@| ^@| ^@| ^@| ^@| ^@| ^@| ^@| ^@| ^@|
ALT| | | CR|NUL|NUL|NUL|NUL|NUL|NUL|NUL|NUL|NUL|NUL|NUL|NUL|NUL|
SYM| 1| 2| | | | | | | | | | | | | | |

     <- Formula ->|  End of
        E12       |  Frame


BYTE|104|105|106|107|108|109|110|111|112|113|114|115|116|117|118|119|
HEX| 03| 00| 88| 09| 0B| 08| 08| 00| 06| 07| 01| 00| 86| 09| 01| 12|
DEC| 3| 0|136| 9| 11| 8| 8| 0| 6| 7| 1| 0|134| 9| 1| 18|
ASC| ^C| ^@|136| ^I| ^K| ^H| ^H| ^@| ^F| ^G| ^A| ^@|134| ^I| ^A| ^R|
ALT|ETX|NUL|136| HT| VT| BS| BS|NUL|ACK|BEL|SOH|NUL|134| HT|SOH|DC2|
SYM| | | | | | | | | | | | | | | | |

         <------------------------ F12 ------------------------>


BYTE|120|121|122|123|124|125|126|127|128|129|130|131|132|133|134|135|
HEX| 00| 05| 33| 33| 33| 33| 08| 92| 12| 30| 20| 31| 24| 32| 30| 33|
DEC| 0| 5| 51| 51| 51| 51| 8|146| 18| 48| 32| 49| 36| 50| 48| 51|
ASC| ^@| ^E| | | | | ^H|146| ^R| | ^^| | | | | |
ALT|NUL|ENQ| | | | | BS|146|DC2| |SPC| | | | | |
SYM| | | 3| 3| 3| 3| | | | 0| | 1| $| 2| 0| 3|

         <------------------------ F12 ------------------------>


BYTE|136|137|138|139|140|141|142|143|144|145|146|147|148|149|150|151|
HEX| 2E| 30| 31| 20| 0D| 00| 00| 04| 00| 00| 00| 81| 01| FF| 81| 00|
DEC| 46| 48| 49| 32| 13| 0| 0| 4| 0| 0| 0|129| 1|255|129| 0|
ASC| | | | ^^| ^M| ^@| ^@| ^D| ^@| ^@| ^@|129| ^A|255|129| ^@|
ALT| | | | SPC| CR|NUL|NUL|EOT|NUL|NUL|NUL|129|SOH|255|129|NUL|
SYM| .| 0| 1| | | | | | | | | | | | | |

         <----- F12 ----->|  End of
                          |  Frame
```

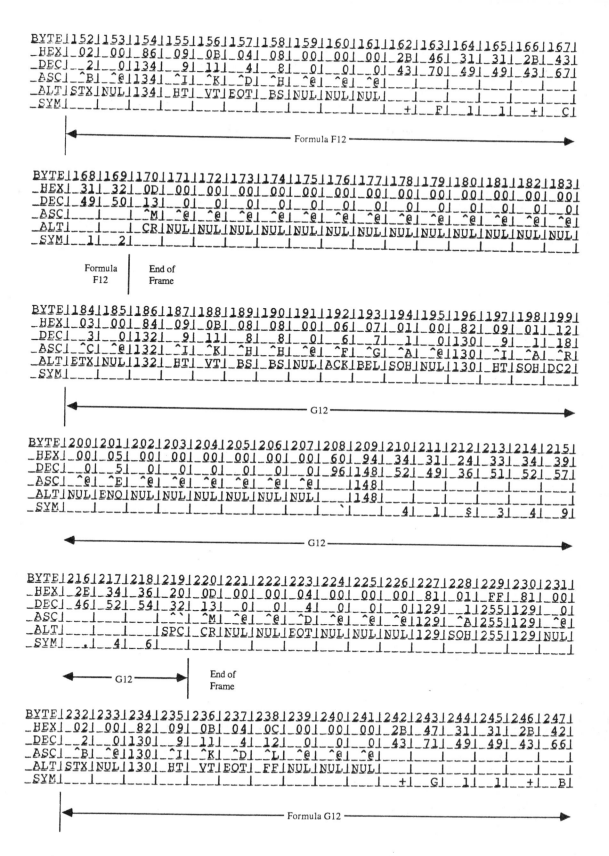

```
BYTE| 248| 249| 250| 251| 252| 253| 254| 255| 256| 257| 258| 259| 260| 261| 262| 263|
 HEX| 31| 32| 2B| 43| 31| 32| 0D| 00| 00| 00| 00| 00| 00| 00| 00| 00|
 DEC| 49| 50| 43| 67| 49| 50| 13| 0| 0| 0| 0| 0| 0| 0| 0| 0|
 ASC| _| _| _| _| _| _| ^M| ^@| ^@| ^@| ^@| ^@| ^@| ^@| ^@| ^@|
 ALT| _| _| _| _| _| _| CR| NUL| NUL| NUL| NUL| NUL| NUL| NUL| NUL| NUL|
 SYM| 1| 2| +| C| 1| 2| | | | | | | | | | |
```

```
|<------------- Formula G12 ------------->|   End of
                                              Frame
```

```
BYTE| 264| 265| 266| 267| 268| 269| 270| 271| 272| 273| 274| 275| 276| 277| 278| 279|
 HEX| 02| 00| 10| 07| 0B| 0D| 07| 00| D0| 05| 12| 07| 80| 09| 7C| 09|
 DEC| 2| 0| 16| 7| 11| 13| 7| 0| 208| 5| 18| 7| 128| 9| 124| 9|
 ASC| ^B| ^@| ^P| ^G| ^K| ^M| ^G| ^@| 208| ^E| ^R| ^G| 128| ^I| _| ^I|
 ALT| STX| NUL| DLE| BEL| VT| CR| BEL| NUL| 208| ENQ| DC2| BEL| 128| HT| _| HT|
 SYM| | | | | | | | | | | | | | | | |
```

| | Paragraph Count | FID Row 13 | Status | Type | # Elements | Parent FID | FID A13 | FID B13 | FID C13 |

```
BYTE| 280| 281| 282| 283| 284| 285| 286| 287| 288| 289| 290| 291| 292| 293| 294| 295|
 HEX| 78| 09| 74| 09| 70| 09| 6C| 09| 0D| 00| 00| 00| 00| 00| 21| 00|
 DEC| 120| 9| 116| 9| 112| 9| 108| 9| 13| 0| 0| 0| 0| 0| 33| 0|
 ASC| _| ^I| _| ^I| _| ^I| _| ^I| ^M| ^@| ^@| ^@| ^@| ^@| _| ^@|
 ALT| _| HT| _| HT| _| HT| _| HT| CR| NUL| NUL| NUL| NUL| NUL| _| NUL|
 SYM| x| | t| | p| | 1| | | | | | | | | |
```

| | FID D13 | FID E13 | FID F13 | FID G13 | End of Frame |

```
BYTE| 296| 297| 298| 299| 300| 301| 302| 303| 304| 305| 306| 307| 308| 309| 310| 311|
 HEX| 02| 00| 12| 07| 4B| 08| 02| 00| 10| 07| 01| 00| 00| 00| 01| 00|
 DEC| 2| 0| 18| 7| 75| 8| 2| 0| 16| 7| 1| 0| 0| 0| 1| 0|
 ASC| ^B| ^@| ^R| ^G| _| ^H| ^B| ^@| ^P| ^G| ^A| ^@| ^@| ^@| ^A| ^@|
 ALT| STX| NUL| DC2| BEL| _| BS| STX| NUL| DLE| BEL| SOH| NUL| NUL| NUL| SOH| NUL|
 SYM| | | | | K| | | | | | | | | | | |
```

| | Paragraph Count | FID A13 | Status | Type | # Elements | Parent FID | Reserved | Formula FID | Formatting |

```
BYTE| 312| 313| 314| 315| 316| 317| 318| 319| 320| 321| 322| 323| 324| 325| 326| 327|
 HEX| 00| 03| 03| 00| 00| 00| 00| 00| 30| 47| 17| 31| 33| 20| 0D| 00|
 DEC| 0| 3| 3| 0| 0| 0| 0| 0| 48| 71| 23| 49| 51| 32| 13| 0|
 ASC| ^@| ^C| ^C| ^@| ^@| ^@| ^@| ^@| _| ^W| _| _| _| _| ^M| ^@|
 ALT| NUL| ETX| ETX| NUL| NUL| NUL| NUL| NUL| _| ETB| _| _| SPC| CR| NUL|
 SYM| | | | | | | | | 0| G| | 1| 3| | | |
```

```
| I.V.T. |<------------- Value Structure ------------->| Contents | End of Frame
```

```
BYTE| 328| 329| 330| 331| 332| 333| 334| 335| 336| 337| 338| 339| 340| 341| 342| 343|
 HEX| 03| 00| 80| 09| 0B| 08| 07| 00| 10| 07| 01| 00| 7E| 09| 01| 12|
 DEC| 3| 0| 128| 9| 11| 8| 7| 0| 16| 7| 1| 0| 126| 9| 1| 18|
 ASC| ^C| ^@| 128| ^I| ^K| ^H| ^G| ^@| ^P| ^G| ^A| ^@| _| ^I| ^A| ^R|
 ALT| ETX| NUL| 128| HT| VT| BS| BEL| NUL| DLE| BEL| SOH| NUL| _| HT| SOH| DC2|
 SYM| | | | | | | | | | | | | ~| | | |
```

```
|<--------------------------------- B13 --------------------------------->|
```

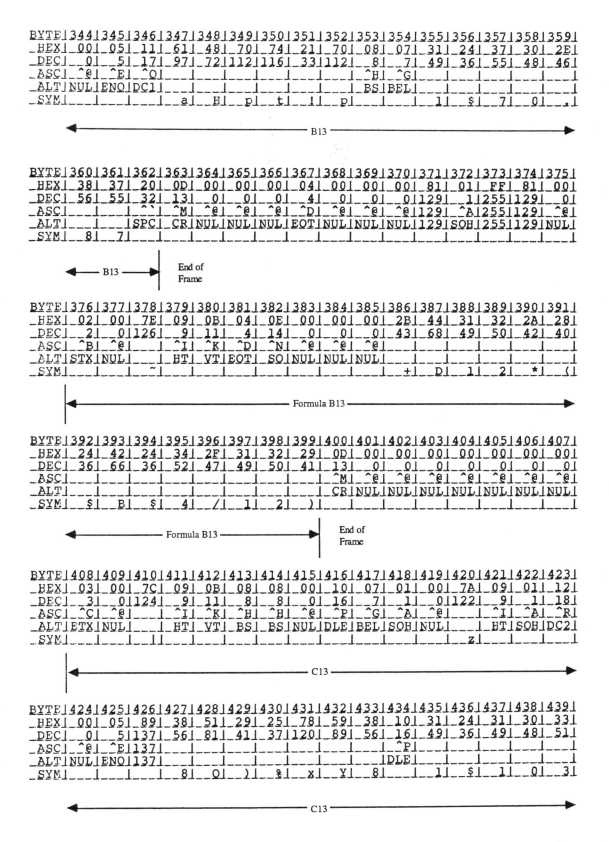

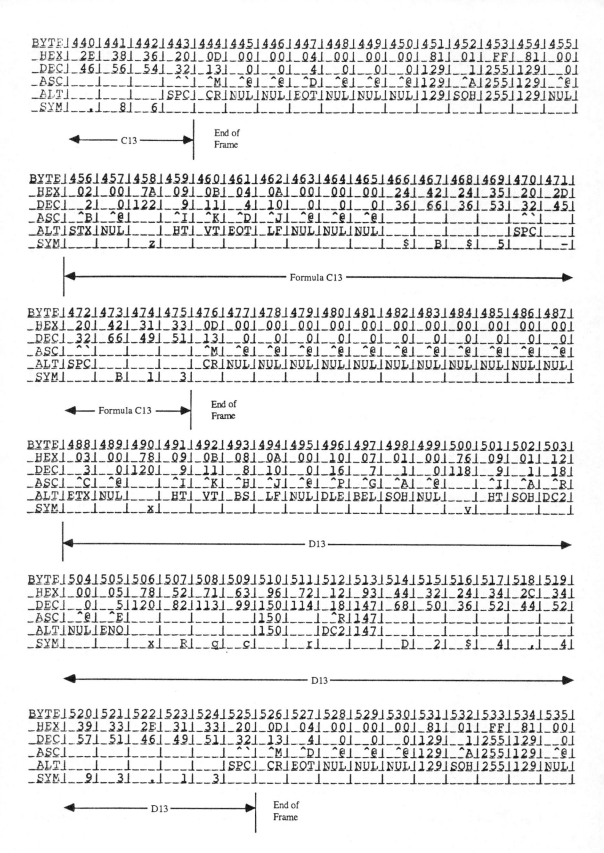

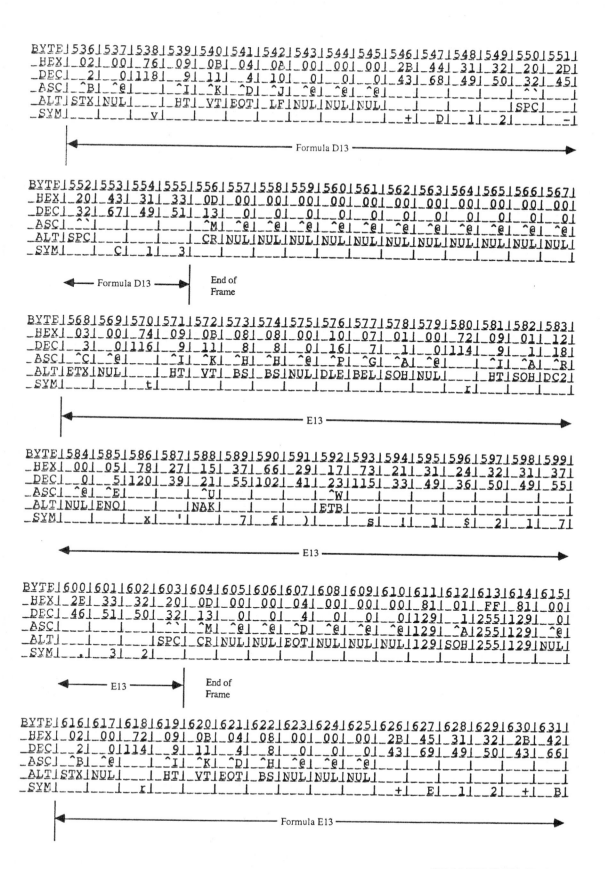

```
BYTE|632|633|634|635|636|637|638|639|640|641|642|643|644|645|646|647|
 HEX| 31| 33| 0D| 00| 00| 00| 00| 00| 00| 00| 00| 00| 00| 00| 00| 00|
 DEC| 49| 51| 13|  0|  0|  0|  0|  0|  0|  0|  0|  0|  0|  0|  0|  0|
 ASC|   |   | ^M| ^@| ^@| ^@| ^@| ^@| ^@| ^@| ^@| ^@| ^@| ^@| ^@| ^@|
 ALT|   |   | CR|NUL|NUL|NUL|NUL|NUL|NUL|NUL|NUL|NUL|NUL|NUL|NUL|NUL|
 SYM| 1|  3|   |   |   |   |   |   |   |   |   |   |   |   |   |   |
```

```
      Formula          End of
        E13            Frame
```

```
BYTE|648|649|650|651|652|653|654|655|656|657|658|659|660|661|662|663|
 HEX| 03| 00| 70| 09| 0B| 08| 08| 00| 10| 07| 01| 00| 6E| 09| 01| 12|
 DEC|  3|  0|112|  9| 11|  8|  8|  0| 16|  7|  1|  0|110|  9|  1| 18|
 ASC| ^C| ^@|   | ^I| ^K| ^H| ^H| ^@| ^P| ^G| ^A| ^@|   | ^I| ^A| ^R|
 ALT|ETX|NUL|   | HT| VT| BS| BS|NUL|DLE|BEL|SOH|NUL|   | HT|SOH|DC2|
 SYM|   |   |  p|   |   |   |   |   |   |   |   |   |  n|   |   |   |
```

```
|<---------------------------- F13 ---------------------------->|
```

```
BYTE|664|665|666|667|668|669|670|671|672|673|674|675|676|677|678|679|
 HEX| 00| 05| 22| 72| 84| 62| 33| 70| 72| 68| 30| 31| 24| 33| 30| 36|
 DEC|  0|  5| 34|114|132| 98| 51|112|114|104| 48| 49| 36| 51| 48| 54|
 ASC| ^@| ^E|   |   |132|   |   |   |   |   |   |   |   |   |   |   |
 ALT|NUL|ENQ|   |   |132|   |   |   |   |   |   |   |   |   |   |   |
 SYM|   |   |  "|  r|   |  b|  3|  p|  r|  h|  0|  1|  $|  3|  0|  6|
```

```
|<---------------------------- F13 ---------------------------->|
```

```
BYTE|680|681|682|683|684|685|686|687|688|689|690|691|692|693|694|695|
 HEX| 2E| 38| 37| 20| 0D| 00| 00| 04| 00| 00| 00| 81| 01| FF| 81| 00|
 DEC| 46| 56| 55| 32| 13|  0|  0|  4|  0|  0|  0|129|  1|255|129|  0|
 ASC|   |   |   | ^^| ^M| ^@| ^@| ^D| ^@| ^@| ^@|129| ^A|255|129| ^@|
 ALT|   |   |   |SPC| CR|NUL|NUL|EOT|NUL|NUL|NUL|129|SOH|255|129|NUL|
 SYM| .|  8|  7|   |   |   |   |   |   |   |   |   |   |   |   |   |
```

```
     |<--- F13 --->|   End of
                        frame
```

```
BYTE|696|697|698|699|700|701|702|703|704|705|706|707|708|709|710|711|
 HEX| 02| 00| 6E| 09| 0B| 04| 08| 00| 00| 00| 2B| 46| 31| 32| 2B| 43|
 DEC|  2|  0|110|  9| 11|  4|  8|  0|  0|  0| 43| 70| 49| 50| 43| 67|
 ASC| ^B| ^@|   | ^I| ^K| ^D| ^H| ^@| ^@| ^@|   |   |   |   |   |   |
 ALT|STX|NUL|   | HT| VT|EOT| BS|NUL|NUL|NUL|   |   |   |   |   |   |
 SYM|   |   |  n|   |   |   |   |   |   |   |  +|  F|  1|  2|  +|  C|
```

```
|<------------------------ Formula F13 ------------------------>|
```

```
BYTE|712|713|714|715|716|717|718|719|720|721|722|723|724|725|726|727|
 HEX| 31| 33| 0D| 00| 00| 00| 00| 00| 00| 00| 00| 00| 00| 00| 00| 00|
 DEC| 49| 51| 13|  0|  0|  0|  0|  0|  0|  0|  0|  0|  0|  0|  0|  0|
 ASC|   |   | ^M| ^@| ^@| ^@| ^@| ^@| ^@| ^@| ^@| ^@| ^@| ^@| ^@| ^@|
 ALT|   |   | CR|NUL|NUL|NUL|NUL|NUL|NUL|NUL|NUL|NUL|NUL|NUL|NUL|NUL|
 SYM| 1|  3|   |   |   |   |   |   |   |   |   |   |   |   |   |   |
```

```
      Formula          End of
        F13            Frame
```

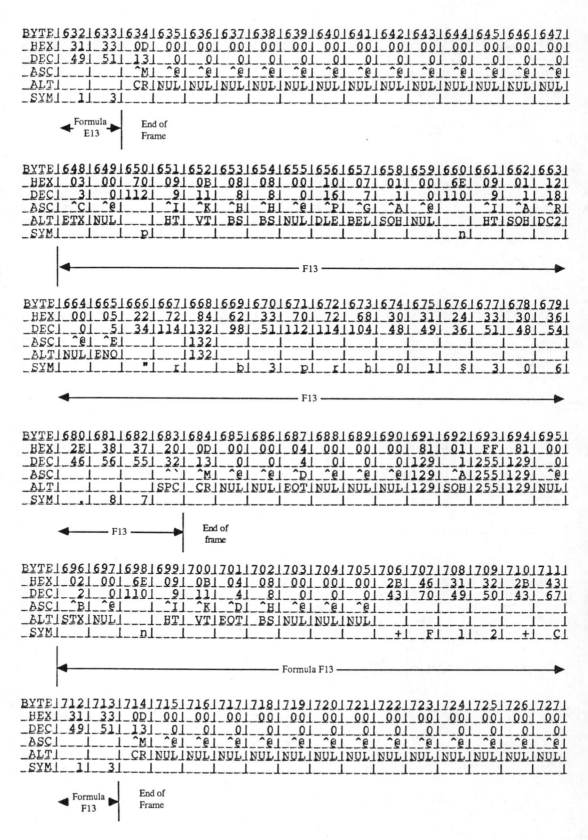

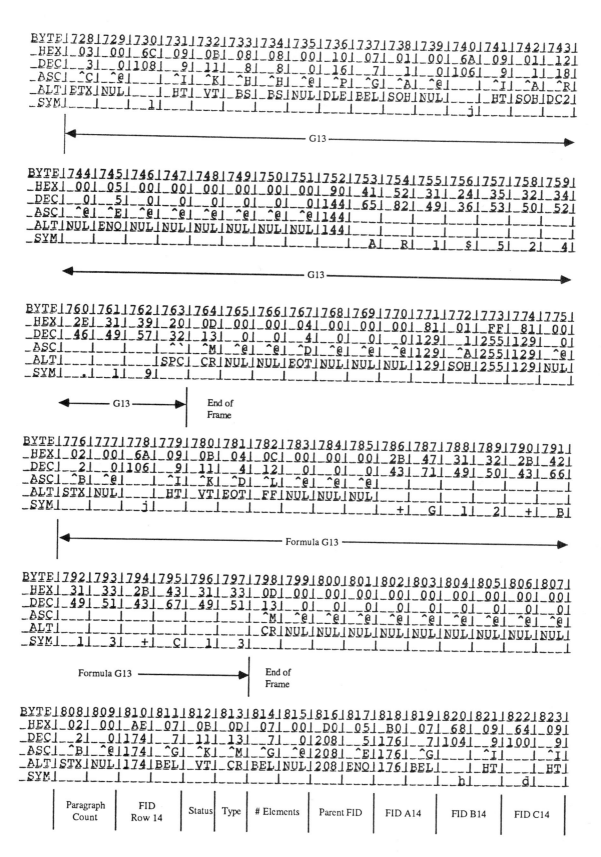

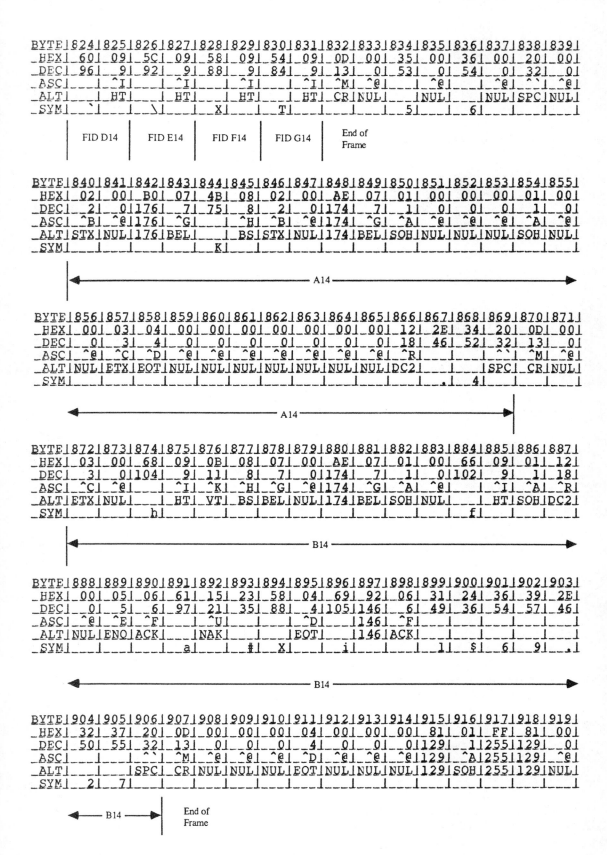

```
BYTE|824|825|826|827|828|829|830|831|832|833|834|835|836|837|838|839|
_HEX| 60| 09| 5C| 09| 58| 09| 54| 09| 0D| 00| 35| 00| 36| 00| 20| 00|
_DEC| 96|  9| 92|  9| 88|  9| 84|  9| 13|  0| 53|  0| 54|  0| 32|  0|
_ASC|___| ^I|___| ^I|___| ^I|___| ^I| ^M| ^@|___| ^@|___| ^@| ^^| ^@|
_ALT|___| HT|___| HT|___| HT|___| HT| CR|NUL|___|NUL|___|NUL|SPC|NUL|
_SYM| `_|___| \_|___| X_|___| T_|___|___|___| 5_|___| 6_|___|___|___|
```

| | FID D14 | FID E14 | FID F14 | FID G14 | End of Frame |

```
BYTE|840|841|842|843|844|845|846|847|848|849|850|851|852|853|854|855|
_HEX| 02| 00| B0| 07| 4B| 08| 02| 00| AE| 07| 01| 00| 00| 00| 01| 00|
_DEC|  2|  0|176|  7| 75|  8|  2|  0|174|  7|  1|  0|  0|  0|  1|  0|
_ASC| ^B| ^@|176| ^G|___| ^H| ^B| ^@|174| ^G| ^A| ^@| ^@| ^@| ^A| ^@|
_ALT|STX|NUL|176|BEL|___| BS|STX|NUL|174|BEL|SOH|NUL|NUL|NUL|SOH|NUL|
_SYM|___|___|___|___| K_|___|___|___|___|___|___|___|___|___|___|___|
```

←――――――――――――――――― A14 ―――――――――――――――――→

```
BYTE|856|857|858|859|860|861|862|863|864|865|866|867|868|869|870|871|
_HEX| 00| 03| 04| 00| 00| 00| 00| 00| 00| 00| 12| 2E| 34| 20| 0D| 00|
_DEC|  0|  3|  4|  0|  0|  0|  0|  0|  0|  0| 18| 46| 52| 32| 13|  0|
_ASC| ^@| ^C| ^D| ^@| ^@| ^@| ^@| ^@| ^@| ^@| ^R|___|___|___| ^M| ^@|
_ALT|NUL|ETX|EOT|NUL|NUL|NUL|NUL|NUL|NUL|NUL|DC2|___|___|SPC|_CR|NUL|
_SYM|___|___|___|___|___|___|___|___|___|___|___| ._| 4_|___|___|___|
```

←――――――――――――――――― A14 ―――――――――――――――――→

```
BYTE|872|873|874|875|876|877|878|879|880|881|882|883|884|885|886|887|
_HEX| 03| 00| 68| 09| 0B| 08| 07| 00| AE| 07| 01| 00| 66| 09| 01| 12|
_DEC|  3|  0|104|  9| 11|  8|  7|  0|174|  7|  1|  0|102|  9|  1| 18|
_ASC| ^C| ^@|___| ^I| ^K| ^H| ^G| ^@|174| ^G| ^A| ^@|___| ^I| ^A| ^R|
_ALT|ETX|NUL|___| HT| VT| BS|BEL|NUL|174|BEL|SOH|NUL|___| HT|SOH|DC2|
_SYM|___|___| h_|___|___|___|___|___|___|___|___|___| f_|___|___|___|
```

←――――――――――――――――― B14 ―――――――――――――――――→

```
BYTE|888|889|890|891|892|893|894|895|896|897|898|899|900|901|902|903|
_HEX| 00| 05| 06| 61| 15| 23| 58| 04| 69| 92| 06| 31| 24| 36| 39| 2E|
_DEC|  0|  5|  6| 97| 21| 35| 88|  4|105|146|  6| 49| 36| 54| 57| 46|
_ASC| ^@| ^E| ^F|___| ^U|___|___| ^D|___|146| ^F|___|___|___|___|___|
_ALT|NUL|ENO|ACK|___|NAK|___|___|EOT|___|146|ACK|___|___|___|___|___|
_SYM|___|___|___| a_|___| #_| X_|___| i_|___|___|___| 1_| $_| 6_| 9_| ._|
```

←――――――――――――――――― B14 ―――――――――――――――――→

```
BYTE|904|905|906|907|908|909|910|911|912|913|914|915|916|917|918|919|
_HEX| 32| 37| 20| 0D| 00| 00| 00| 04| 00| 00| 00| 81| 01| FF| 81| 00|
_DEC| 50| 55| 32| 13|  0|  0|  0|  4|  0|  0|  0|129|  1|255|129|  0|
_ASC|___|___| ^^| ^M| ^@| ^@| ^@| ^D| ^@| ^@| ^@|129| ^A|255|129| ^@|
_ALT|___|___|SPC| CR|NUL|NUL|NUL|EOT|NUL|NUL|NUL|129|SOH|255|129|NUL|
_SYM| 2_| 7_|___|___|___|___|___|___|___|___|___|___|___|___|___|___|
```

←― B14 ―→| End of Frame

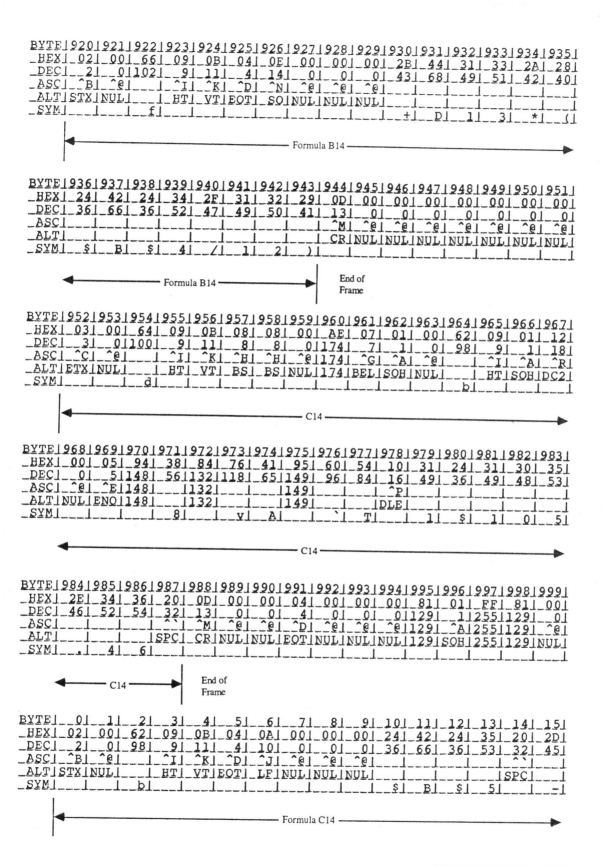

```
BYTE| 16| 17| 18| 19| 20| 21| 22| 23| 24| 25| 26| 27| 28| 29| 30| 31|
HEX| 20| 42| 31| 34| 0D| 00| 00| 00| 00| 00| 00| 00| 00| 00| 00| 00|
DEC| 32| 66| 49| 52| 13| 0| 0| 0| 0| 0| 0| 0| 0| 0| 0| 0|
ASC| ^^|   |   |   | ^M| ^@| ^@| ^@| ^@| ^@| ^@| ^@| ^@| ^@| ^@| ^@|
ALT|SPC|   |   |   | CR|NUL|NUL|NUL|NUL|NUL|NUL|NUL|NUL|NUL|NUL|NUL|
SYM|   | B| 1| 4|   |   |   |   |   |   |   |   |   |   |   |   |

    ◄── Formula C14 ──►|  End of
                          Frame


BYTE| 32| 33| 34| 35| 36| 37| 38| 39| 40| 41| 42| 43| 44| 45| 46| 47|
HEX| 03| 00| 60| 09| 0B| 08| 0A| 00| AE| 07| 01| 00| 5E| 09| 01| 12|
DEC| 3| 0| 96| 9| 11| 8| 10| 0| 174| 7| 1| 0| 94| 9| 1| 18|
ASC| ^C| ^@|   | ^I| ^K| ^H| ^J| ^@|174| ^G| ^A| ^@|   | ^I| ^A| ^R|
ALT|ETX|NUL|   | HT| VT| BS| LF|NUL|174|BEL|SOH|NUL|   | HT|SOH|DC2|
SYM|   |   | `|   |   |   |   |   |   |   |   |   | ^|   |   |   |

    |◄─────────────────────── D14 ───────────────────────►


BYTE| 48| 49| 50| 51| 52| 53| 54| 55| 56| 57| 58| 59| 60| 61| 62| 63|
HEX| 00| 05| 89| 08| 03| 46| 42| 63| 66| 87| 43| 32| 24| 34| 2C| 33|
DEC| 0| 5|137| 8| 3| 70| 66| 99|102|135| 67| 50| 36| 52| 44| 51|
ASC| ^@| ^E|137| ^H| ^C|   |   |   |   |135|   |   |   |   |   |   |
ALT|NUL|ENQ|137| BS|ETX|   |   |   |   |135|   |   |   |   |   |   |
SYM|   |   |   |   |   | F| B| c| f|   | C| 2| $| 4| ,| 3|

    ◄─────────────────────── D14 ───────────────────────►


BYTE| 64| 65| 66| 67| 68| 69| 70| 71| 72| 73| 74| 75| 76| 77| 78| 79|
HEX| 38| 37| 2E| 36| 37| 20| 0D| 04| 00| 00| 00| 81| 01| FF| 81| 00|
DEC| 56| 55| 46| 54| 55| 32| 13| 4| 0| 0| 0|129| 1|255|129| 0|
ASC|   |   |   |   |   | ^^| ^M| ^D| ^@| ^@| ^@|129| ^A|255|129| ^@|
ALT|   |   |   |   |   |SPC| CR|EOT|NUL|NUL|NUL|129|SOH|255|129|NUL|
SYM| 8| 7| .| 6| 7|   |   |   |   |   |   |   |   |   |   |   |

    ◄──── D14 ────►|  End of
                      Frame


BYTE| 80| 81| 82| 83| 84| 85| 86| 87| 88| 89| 90| 91| 92| 93| 94| 95|
HEX| 02| 00| 5E| 09| 0B| 04| 0A| 00| 00| 00| 2B| 44| 31| 33| 20| 2D|
DEC| 2| 0| 94| 9| 11| 4| 10| 0| 0| 0| 43| 68| 49| 51| 32| 45|
ASC| ^B| ^@|   | ^I| ^K| ^D| ^J| ^@| ^@| ^@|   |   |   |   | ^^|   |
ALT|STX|NUL|   | HT| VT|EOT| LF|NUL|NUL|NUL|   |   |   |   |SPC|   |
SYM|   |   | ^|   |   |   |   |   |   |   | +| D| 1| 3|   | -|

    ◄─────────────────────── Formula D14 ───────────────────────►


BYTE| 96| 97| 98| 99|100|101|102|103|104|105|106|107|108|109|110|111|
HEX| 20| 43| 31| 34| 0D| 00| 00| 00| 00| 00| 00| 00| 00| 00| 00| 00|
DEC| 32| 67| 49| 52| 13| 0| 0| 0| 0| 0| 0| 0| 0| 0| 0| 0|
ASC| ^^|   |   |   | ^M| ^@| ^@| ^@| ^@| ^@| ^@| ^@| ^@| ^@| ^@| ^@|
ALT|SPC|   |   |   | CR|NUL|NUL|NUL|NUL|NUL|NUL|NUL|NUL|NUL|NUL|NUL|
SYM|   | C| 1| 4|   |   |   |   |   |   |   |   |   |   |   |   |

    Formula D14 ──►|  End of
                      Frame
```

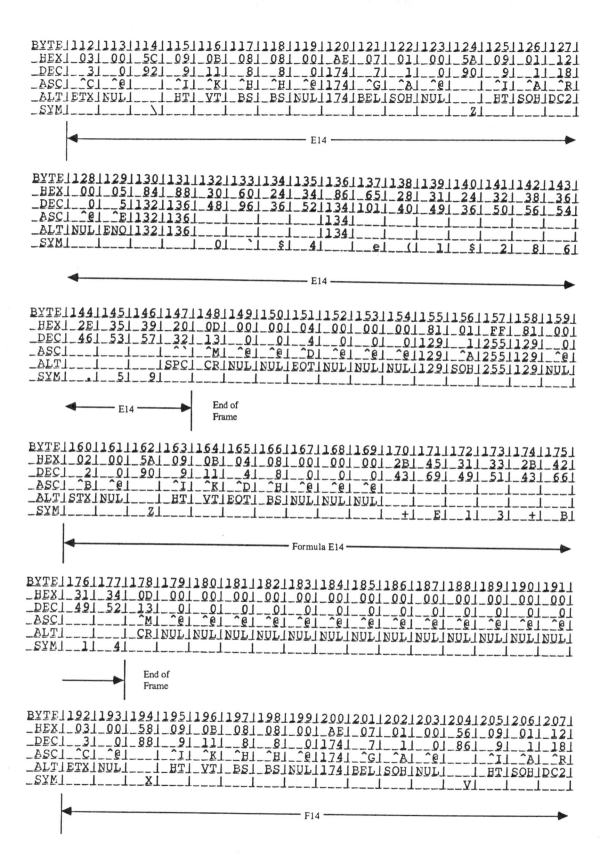

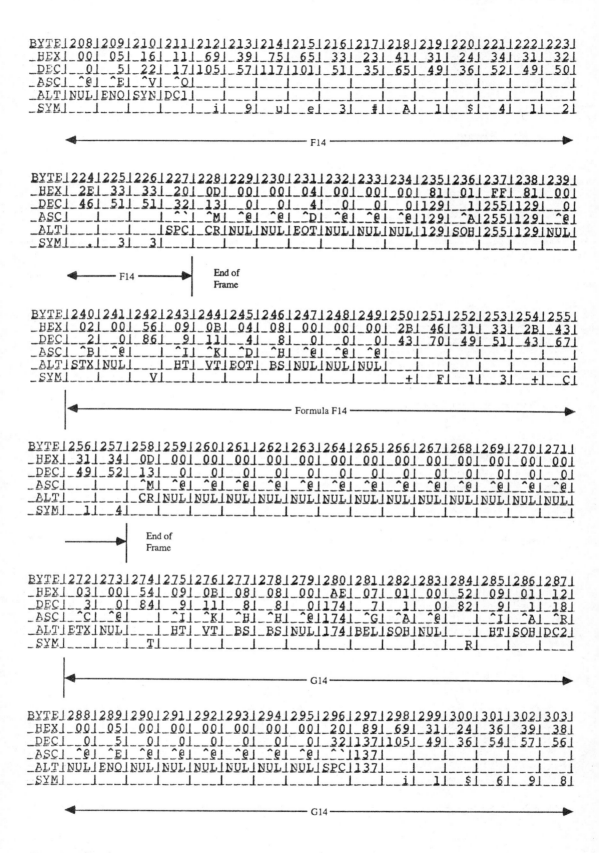

```
BYTE|208|209|210|211|212|213|214|215|216|217|218|219|220|221|222|223|
 HEX| 00| 05| 16| 11| 69| 39| 75| 65| 33| 23| 41| 31| 24| 34| 31| 32|
 DEC|  0|  5| 22| 17|105| 57|117|101| 51| 35| 65| 49| 36| 52| 49| 50|
 ASC| ^@| ^E| ^V| ^Q|   |   |   |   |   |   |   |   |   |   |   |   |
 ALT|NUL|ENQ|SYN|DC1|   |   |   |   |   |   |   |   |   |   |   |   |
 SYM|   |   |   |   |  i|  9|  u|  e|  3|  #|  A|  1|  $|  4|  1|  2|
```

◄─────────────────────────── F14 ───────────────────────────►

```
BYTE|224|225|226|227|228|229|230|231|232|233|234|235|236|237|238|239|
 HEX| 2E| 33| 33| 20| 0D| 00| 00| 04| 00| 00| 00| 81| 01| FF| 81| 00|
 DEC| 46| 51| 51| 32| 13|  0|  0|  4|  0|  0|  0|129|  1|255|129|  0|
 ASC|   |   |   | ^^| ^M| ^@| ^@| ^D| ^@| ^@| ^@|129| ^A|255|129| ^@|
 ALT|   |   |   |SPC| CR|NUL|NUL|EOT|NUL|NUL|NUL|129|SOH|255|129|NUL|
 SYM|  .|  3|  3|   |   |   |   |   |   |   |   |   |   |   |   |   |
```

◄─── F14 ───► │ End of
               │ Frame

```
BYTE|240|241|242|243|244|245|246|247|248|249|250|251|252|253|254|255|
 HEX| 02| 00| 56| 09| 0B| 04| 08| 00| 00| 00| 2B| 46| 31| 33| 2B| 43|
 DEC|  2|  0| 86|  9| 11|  4|  8|  0|  0|  0| 43| 70| 49| 51| 43| 67|
 ASC| ^B| ^@|   | ^I| ^K| ^D| ^H| ^@| ^@| ^@|   |   |   |   |   |   |
 ALT|STX|NUL|   | HT| VT|EOT| BS|NUL|NUL|NUL|   |   |   |   |   |   |
 SYM|   |   |  V|   |   |   |   |   |   |   |  +|  F|  1|  3|  +|  C|
```

◄─────────────────────────── Formula F14 ───────────────────────────►

```
BYTE|256|257|258|259|260|261|262|263|264|265|266|267|268|269|270|271|
 HEX| 31| 34| 0D| 00| 00| 00| 00| 00| 00| 00| 00| 00| 00| 00| 00| 00|
 DEC| 49| 52| 13|  0|  0|  0|  0|  0|  0|  0|  0|  0|  0|  0|  0|  0|
 ASC|   |   | ^M| ^@| ^@| ^@| ^@| ^@| ^@| ^@| ^@| ^@| ^@| ^@| ^@| ^@|
 ALT|   |   | CR|NUL|NUL|NUL|NUL|NUL|NUL|NUL|NUL|NUL|NUL|NUL|NUL|NUL|
 SYM|  1|  4|   |   |   |   |   |   |   |   |   |   |   |   |   |   |
```

│ End of
│ Frame

```
BYTE|272|273|274|275|276|277|278|279|280|281|282|283|284|285|286|287|
 HEX| 03| 00| 54| 09| 0B| 08| 08| 00| AE| 07| 01| 00| 52| 09| 01| 12|
 DEC|  3|  0| 84|  9| 11|  8|  8|  0|174|  7|  1|  0| 82|  9|  1| 18|
 ASC| ^C| ^@|   | ^I| ^K| ^H| ^H| ^@|174| ^G| ^A| ^@|   | ^I| ^A| ^R|
 ALT|ETX|NUL|   | HT| VT| BS| BS|NUL|174|BEL|SOH|NUL|   | HT|SOH|DC2|
 SYM|   |   |  T|   |   |   |   |   |   |   |   |   |  R|   |   |   |
```

◄─────────────────────────── G14 ───────────────────────────►

```
BYTE|288|289|290|291|292|293|294|295|296|297|298|299|300|301|302|303|
 HEX| 00| 05| 00| 00| 00| 00| 00| 00| 20| 89| 69| 31| 24| 36| 39| 38|
 DEC|  0|  5|  0|  0|  0|  0|  0|  0| 32|137|105| 49| 36| 54| 57| 56|
 ASC| ^@| ^E| ^@| ^@| ^@| ^@| ^@| ^@| ^^|137|   |   |   |   |   |   |
 ALT|NUL|ENQ|NUL|NUL|NUL|NUL|NUL|NUL|SPC|137|   |   |   |   |   |   |
 SYM|   |   |   |   |   |   |   |   |   |   |  i|  1|  $|  6|  9|  8|
```

◄─────────────────────────── G14 ───────────────────────────►

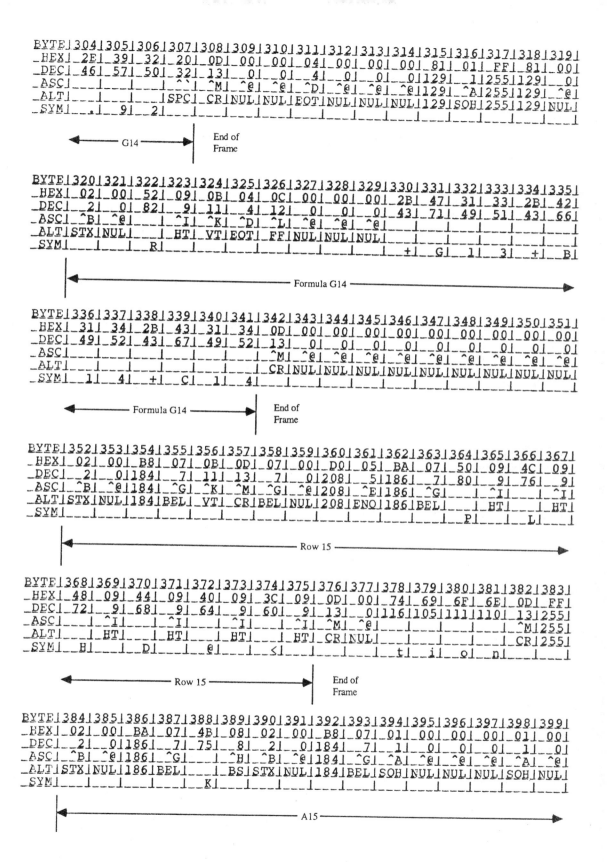

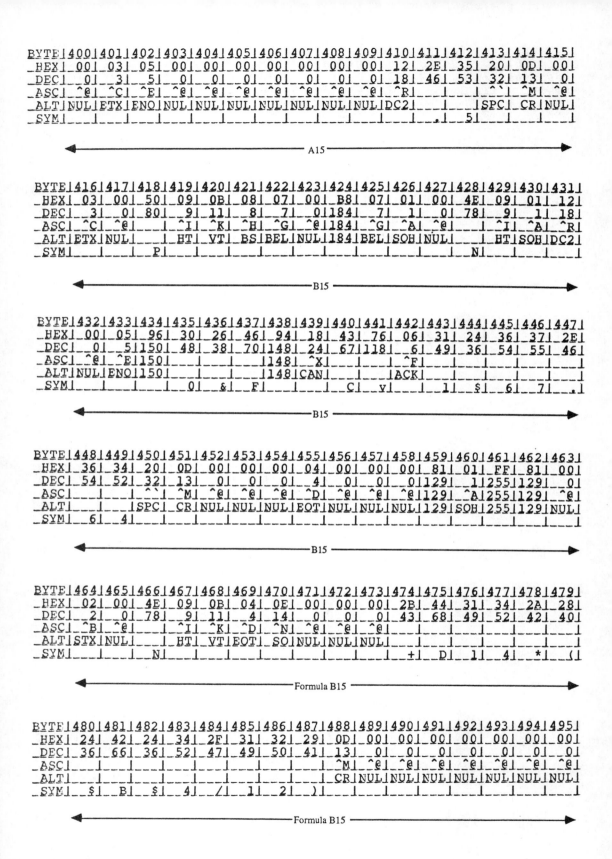

```
BYTE|400|401|402|403|404|405|406|407|408|409|410|411|412|413|414|415|
_HEX| 00| 03| 05| 00| 00| 00| 00| 00| 00| 00| 12| 2E| 35| 20| 0D| 00|
_DEC| 0| 3| 5| 0| 0| 0| 0| 0| 0| 0| 18| 46| 53| 32| 13| 0|
_ASC| ^@| ^C| ^E| ^@| ^@| ^@| ^@| ^@| ^@| ^@| ^R|   |   | ^^| ^M| ^@|
_ALT|NUL|ETX|ENQ|NUL|NUL|NUL|NUL|NUL|NUL|NUL|DC2|   |   |SPC| CR|NUL|
_SYM|   |   |   |   |   |   |   |   |   |   |   | .| 5|   |   |   |
```

◄─────────────────────────── A15 ───────────────────────────►

```
BYTE|416|417|418|419|420|421|422|423|424|425|426|427|428|429|430|431|
_HEX| 03| 00| 50| 09| 0B| 08| 07| 00| B8| 07| 01| 00| 4E| 09| 01| 12|
_DEC| 3| 0| 80| 9| 11| 8| 7| 0|184| 7| 1| 0| 78| 9| 1| 18|
_ASC| ^C| ^@|   | ^I| ^K| ^H| ^G| ^@|184| ^G| ^A| ^@|   | ^I| ^A| ^R|
_ALT|ETX|NUL|   | HT| VT| BS|BEL|NUL|184|BEL|SOH|NUL|   | HT|SOH|DC2|
_SYM|   |   | P|   |   |   |   |   |   |   |   |   | N|   |   |   |
```

◄─────────────────────────── B15 ───────────────────────────►

```
BYTE|432|433|434|435|436|437|438|439|440|441|442|443|444|445|446|447|
_HEX| 00| 05| 96| 30| 26| 46| 94| 18| 43| 76| 06| 31| 24| 36| 37| 2E|
_DEC| 0| 51|150| 48| 38| 70|148| 24| 67|118| 6| 49| 36| 54| 55| 46|
_ASC| ^@| ^E|150|   |   |   |148| ^X|   |   | ^F|   |   |   |   |   |
_ALT|NUL|ENQ|150|   |   |   |148|CAN|   |   |ACK|   |   |   |   |   |
_SYM|   |   |   | 0| &| F|   |   | C| v|   | 1| $| 6| 7| .|
```

◄─────────────────────────── B15 ───────────────────────────►

```
BYTE|448|449|450|451|452|453|454|455|456|457|458|459|460|461|462|463|
_HEX| 36| 34| 20| 0D| 00| 00| 00| 04| 00| 00| 00| 81| 01| FF| 81| 00|
_DEC| 54| 52| 32| 13| 0| 0| 0| 4| 0| 0| 0|129| 1|255|129| 0|
_ASC|   |   | ^^| ^M| ^@| ^@| ^@| ^D| ^@| ^@| ^@|129| ^A|255|129| ^@|
_ALT|   |   |SPC| CR|NUL|NUL|NUL|EOT|NUL|NUL|NUL|129|SOH|255|129|NUL|
_SYM| 6| 4|   |   |   |   |   |   |   |   |   |   |   |   |   |   |
```

◄─────────────────────────── B15 ───────────────────────────►

```
BYTE|464|465|466|467|468|469|470|471|472|473|474|475|476|477|478|479|
_HEX| 02| 00| 4E| 09| 0B| 04| 0E| 00| 00| 00| 2B| 44| 31| 34| 2A| 28|
_DEC| 2| 0| 78| 9| 11| 4| 14| 0| 0| 0| 43| 68| 49| 52| 42| 40|
_ASC| ^B| ^@|   | ^I| ^K| ^D| ^N| ^@| ^@| ^@|   |   |   |   |   |   |
_ALT|STX|NUL|   | HT| VT|EOT| SO|NUL|NUL|NUL|   |   |   |   |   |   |
_SYM|   |   | N|   |   |   |   |   |   |   | +| D| 1| 4| *| (|
```

◄─────────────────────────── Formula B15 ───────────────────────────►

```
BYTE|480|481|482|483|484|485|486|487|488|489|490|491|492|493|494|495|
_HEX| 24| 42| 24| 34| 2F| 31| 32| 29| 0D| 00| 00| 00| 00| 00| 00| 00|
_DEC| 36| 66| 36| 52| 47| 49| 50| 41| 13| 0| 0| 0| 0| 0| 0| 0|
_ASC|   |   |   |   |   |   |   |   | ^M| ^@| ^@| ^@| ^@| ^@| ^@| ^@|
_ALT|   |   |   |   |   |   |   |   | CR|NUL|NUL|NUL|NUL|NUL|NUL|NUL|
_SYM| $| B| $| 4| /| 1| 2| )|   |   |   |   |   |   |   |   |
```

◄─────────────────────────── Formula B15 ───────────────────────────►

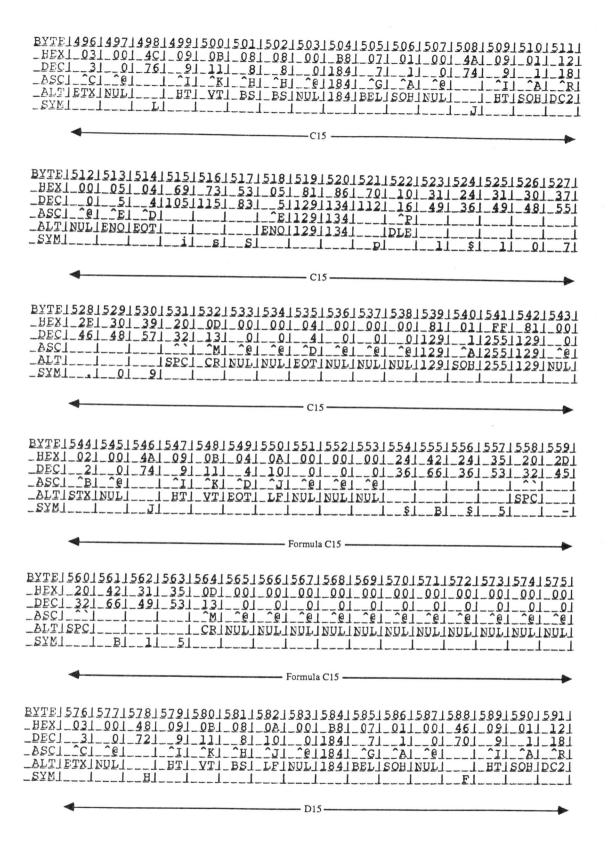

```
BYTE|592|593|594|595|596|597|598|599|600|601|602|603|604|605|606|607|
_HEX|_00|_05|_99|_71|_65|_90|_31|_95|_57|_80|_42|_32|_24|_34|_2C|_32|
_DEC|_0|__5|153|113|101|144|_49|149|_87|128|_66|_50|_36|_52|_44|_50|
_ASC|^@|_^E|153|___|___|144|___|149|_87|128|_66|_50|_36|_52|_44|_50|
_ALT|NUL|ENO|153|___|___|144|___|149|___|128|___|___|___|___|___|___|
_SYM|___|___|___|_q|__e|___|_1|___|_W|___|_B|__2|__$|__4|__,|__2|
```

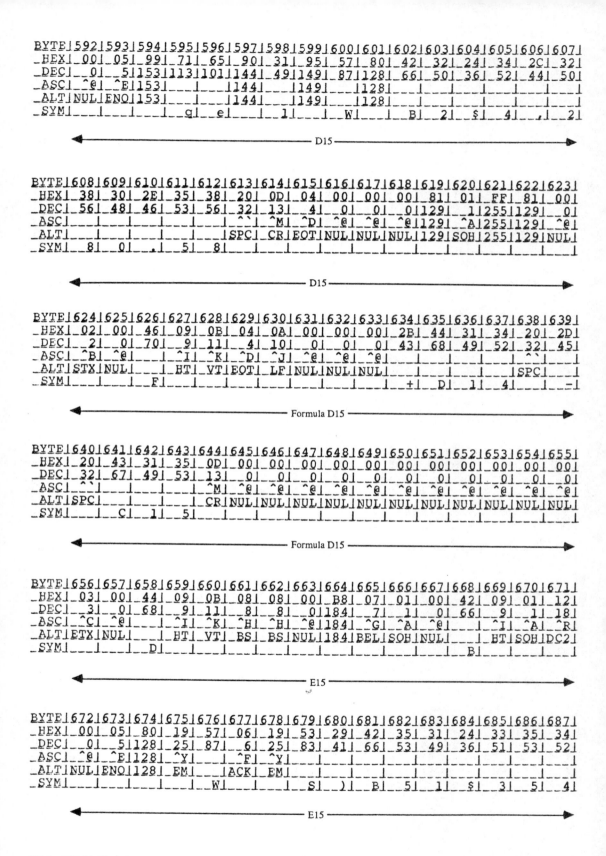

D15

```
BYTE|608|609|610|611|612|613|614|615|616|617|618|619|620|621|622|623|
_HEX|_38|_30|_2E|_35|_38|_20|_0D|_04|_00|_00|_00|_81|_01|_FF|_81|_00|
_DEC|_56|_48|_46|_53|_56|_32|_13|__4|__0|__0|__0|129|__1|255|129|__0|
_ASC|___|___|___|___|___|___|^^|_^M|_^D|_^@|_^@|_^@|129|_^A|255|129|_^@|
_ALT|___|___|___|___|___|SPC|_CR|EOT|NUL|NUL|NUL|129|SOH|255|129|NUL|
_SYM|__8|__0|__.|__5|__8|___|___|___|___|___|___|___|___|___|___|___|
```

D15

```
BYTE|624|625|626|627|628|629|630|631|632|633|634|635|636|637|638|639|
_HEX|_02|_00|_46|_09|_0B|_04|_0A|_00|_00|_00|_2B|_44|_31|_34|_20|_2D|
_DEC|__2|__0|_70|__9|_11|__4|_10|__0|__0|__0|_43|_68|_49|_52|_32|_45|
_ASC|^B|_^@|___|_^I|_^K|_^D|_^J|_^@|_^@|_^@|___|___|___|___|^^|___|
_ALT|STX|NUL|___|_HT|_VT|EOT|_LF|NUL|NUL|NUL|___|___|___|___|SPC|___|
_SYM|___|___|__F|___|___|___|___|___|___|___|__+|__D|__1|__4|___|__-|
```

Formula D15

```
BYTE|640|641|642|643|644|645|646|647|648|649|650|651|652|653|654|655|
_HEX|_20|_43|_31|_35|_0D|_00|_00|_00|_00|_00|_00|_00|_00|_00|_00|_00|
_DEC|_32|_67|_49|_53|_13|__0|__0|__0|__0|__0|__0|__0|__0|__0|__0|__0|
_ASC|^^|___|___|___|___|_^M|_^@|_^@|_^@|_^@|_^@|_^@|_^@|_^@|_^@|_^@|
_ALT|SPC|___|___|___|___|_CR|NUL|NUL|NUL|NUL|NUL|NUL|NUL|NUL|NUL|NUL|
_SYM|___|__C|__1|__5|___|___|___|___|___|___|___|___|___|___|___|___|
```

Formula D15

```
BYTE|656|657|658|659|660|661|662|663|664|665|666|667|668|669|670|671|
_HEX|_03|_00|_44|_09|_0B|_08|_08|_00|_B8|_07|_01|_00|_42|_09|_01|_12|
_DEC|__3|__0|_68|__9|_11|__8|__8|__0|184|__7|__1|__0|_66|__9|__1|_18|
_ASC|^C|_^@|___|_^I|_^K|_^H|_^H|_^@|184|_^G|_^A|_^@|___|_^I|_^A|_^R|
_ALT|ETX|NUL|___|_HT|_VT|_BS|_BS|NUL|184|BEL|SOH|NUL|___|_HT|SOH|DC2|
_SYM|___|___|__D|___|___|___|___|___|___|___|___|___|__B|___|___|___|
```

E15

```
BYTE|672|673|674|675|676|677|678|679|680|681|682|683|684|685|686|687|
_HEX|_00|_05|_80|_19|_57|_06|_19|_53|_29|_42|_35|_31|_24|_33|_35|_34|
_DEC|_0|__5|128|_25|_87|__6|_25|_83|_41|_66|_53|_49|_36|_51|_53|_52|
_ASC|^@|_^E|128|_^Y|___|_^F|_^Y|___|___|___|___|___|___|___|___|___|
_ALT|NUL|ENO|128|_EM|___|ACK|_EM|___|___|___|___|___|___|___|___|___|
_SYM|___|___|___|___|_W|___|___|_S|__)|__B|__5|__1|__$|__3|__5|__4|
```

E15
```
```

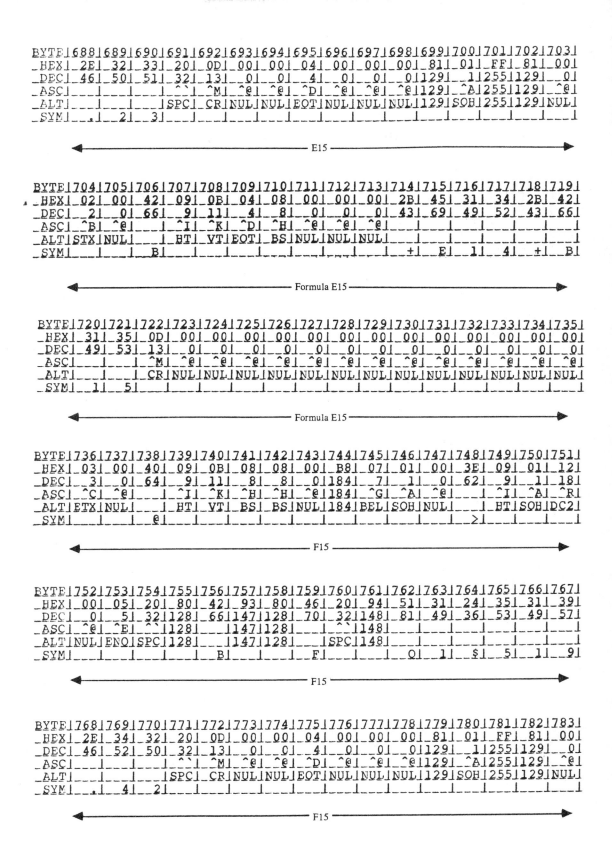

```
BYTE|688|689|690|691|692|693|694|695|696|697|698|699|700|701|702|703|
HEX | 2E| 32| 33| 20| 0D| 00| 00| 04| 00| 00| 00| 81| 01| FF| 81| 00|
DEC | 46| 50| 51| 32| 13|  0|  0|  4|  0|  0|  0|129|  1|255|129|  0|
ASC |   |   |   | ^`| ^M| ^@| ^@| ^D| ^@| ^@| ^@|129| ^A|255|129| ^@|
ALT |   |   |   |SPC| CR|NUL|NUL|EOT|NUL|NUL|NUL|129|SOH|255|129|NUL|
SYM | . | 2 | 3 |   |   |   |   |   |   |   |   |   |   |   |   |   |
```
◄─────────────────────── E15 ───────────────────────►

```
BYTE|704|705|706|707|708|709|710|711|712|713|714|715|716|717|718|719|
HEX | 02| 00| 42| 09| 0B| 04| 08| 00| 00| 00| 2B| 45| 31| 34| 2B| 42|
DEC |  2|  0| 66|  9| 11|  4|  8|  0|  0|  0| 43| 69| 49| 52| 43| 66|
ASC | ^B| ^@|   | ^I| ^K| ^D| ^H| ^@| ^@| ^@|   |   |   |   |   |   |
ALT |STX|NUL|   | HT| VT|EOT| BS|NUL|NUL|NUL|   |   |   |   |   |   |
SYM |   |   | B |   |   |   |   |   |   |   | + | E | 1 | 4 | + | B |
```
◄─────────────────────── Formula E15 ───────────────────────►

```
BYTE|720|721|722|723|724|725|726|727|728|729|730|731|732|733|734|735|
HEX | 31| 35| 0D| 00| 00| 00| 00| 00| 00| 00| 00| 00| 00| 00| 00| 00|
DEC | 49| 53| 13|  0|  0|  0|  0|  0|  0|  0|  0|  0|  0|  0|  0|  0|
ASC |   |   | ^M| ^@| ^@| ^@| ^@| ^@| ^@| ^@| ^@| ^@| ^@| ^@| ^@| ^@|
ALT |   |   | CR|NUL|NUL|NUL|NUL|NUL|NUL|NUL|NUL|NUL|NUL|NUL|NUL|NUL|
SYM | 1 | 5 |   |   |   |   |   |   |   |   |   |   |   |   |   |   |
```
◄─────────────────────── Formula E15 ───────────────────────►

```
BYTE|736|737|738|739|740|741|742|743|744|745|746|747|748|749|750|751|
HEX | 03| 00| 40| 09| 0B| 08| 08| 00| B8| 07| 01| 00| 3E| 09| 01| 12|
DEC |  3|  0| 64|  9| 11|  8|  8|  0|184|  7|  1|  0| 62|  9|  1| 18|
ASC | ^C| ^@|   | ^I| ^K| ^H| ^H| ^@|184| ^G| ^A| ^@|   | ^I| ^A| ^R|
ALT |ETX|NUL|   | HT| VT| BS| BS|NUL|184|BEL|SOH|NUL|   | HT|SOH|DC2|
SYM |   |   | @ |   |   |   |   |   |   |   |   |   | > |   |   |   |
```
◄─────────────────────── F15 ───────────────────────►

```
BYTE|752|753|754|755|756|757|758|759|760|761|762|763|764|765|766|767|
HEX | 00| 05| 20| 80| 42| 93| 80| 46| 20| 94| 51| 31| 24| 35| 31| 39|
DEC |  0|  5| 32|128| 66|147|128| 70| 32|148| 81| 49| 36| 53| 49| 57|
ASC | ^@| ^E| ^`|128|   |147|128|   | ^`|148|   |   |   |   |   |   |
ALT |NUL|ENQ|SPC|128|   |147|128|   |SPC|148|   |   |   |   |   |   |
SYM |   |   |   |   | B |   |   | F |   |   | O | 1 | $ | 5 | 1 | 9 |
```
◄─────────────────────── F15 ───────────────────────►

```
BYTE|768|769|770|771|772|773|774|775|776|777|778|779|780|781|782|783|
HEX | 2E| 34| 32| 20| 0D| 00| 00| 04| 00| 00| 00| 81| 01| FF| 81| 00|
DEC | 46| 52| 50| 32| 13|  0|  0|  4|  0|  0|  0|129|  1|255|129|  0|
ASC |   |   |   | ^`| ^M| ^@| ^@| ^D| ^@| ^@| ^@|129| ^A|255|129| ^@|
ALT |   |   |   |SPC| CR|NUL|NUL|EOT|NUL|NUL|NUL|129|SOH|255|129|NUL|
SYM | . | 4 | 2 |   |   |   |   |   |   |   |   |   |   |   |   |   |
```
◄─────────────────────── F15 ───────────────────────►

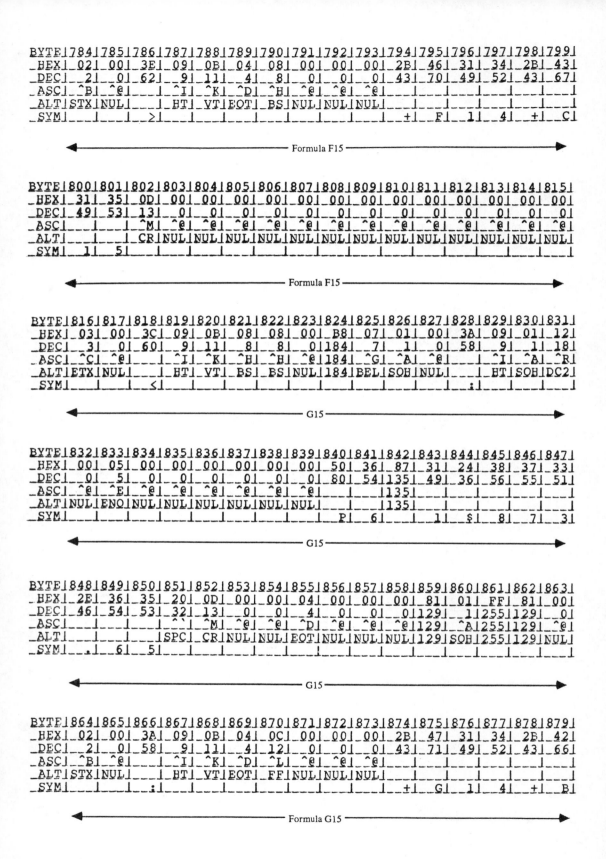

BYTE	784	785	786	787	788	789	790	791	792	793	794	795	796	797	798	799
HEX	02	00	3E	09	0B	04	08	00	00	00	2B	46	31	34	2B	43
DEC	2	0	62	9	11	4	8	0	0	0	43	70	49	52	43	67
ASC	^B	^@		^I	^K	^D	^H	^@	^@	^@						
ALT	STX	NUL		HT	VT	EOT	BS	NUL	NUL	NUL						
SYM			>								+	F	1	4	+	C

◄────────────── Formula F15 ──────────────►

BYTE	800	801	802	803	804	805	806	807	808	809	810	811	812	813	814	815
HEX	31	35	0D	00	00	00	00	00	00	00	00	00	00	00	00	00
DEC	49	53	13	0	0	0	0	0	0	0	0	0	0	0	0	0
ASC			^M	^@	^@	^@	^@	^@	^@	^@	^@	^@	^@	^@	^@	^@
ALT			CR	NUL	NUL	NUL	NUL	NUL	NUL	NUL	NUL	NUL	NUL	NUL	NUL	NUL
SYM	1	5														

◄────────────── Formula F15 ──────────────►

BYTE	816	817	818	819	820	821	822	823	824	825	826	827	828	829	830	831
HEX	03	00	3C	09	0B	08	08	00	B8	07	01	00	3A	09	01	12
DEC	3	0	60	9	11	8	8	0	184	7	1	0	58	9	1	18
ASC	^C	^@		^I	^K	^H	^H	^@	184	^G	^A	^@		^I	^A	^R
ALT	ETX	NUL		HT	VT	BS	BS	NUL	184	BEL	SOH	NUL		HT	SOH	DC2
SYM			<										:			

◄────────────── G15 ──────────────►

BYTE	832	833	834	835	836	837	838	839	840	841	842	843	844	845	846	847
HEX	00	05	00	00	00	00	00	00	50	36	87	31	24	38	37	33
DEC	0	5	0	0	0	0	0	0	80	54	135	49	36	56	55	51
ASC	^@	^E	^@	^@	^@	^@	^@	^@			135					
ALT	NUL	ENQ	NUL	NUL	NUL	NUL	NUL	NUL			135					
SYM									P	6		1	$	8	7	3

◄────────────── G15 ──────────────►

BYTE	848	849	850	851	852	853	854	855	856	857	858	859	860	861	862	863
HEX	2E	36	35	20	0D	00	00	04	00	00	00	81	01	FF	81	00
DEC	46	54	53	32	13	0	0	4	0	0	0	129	1	255	129	0
ASC				^`	^M	^@	^@	^D	^@	^@	^@	129	^A	255	129	^@
ALT				SPC	CR	NUL	NUL	EOT	NUL	NUL	NUL	129	SOH	255	129	NUL
SYM	.	6	5													

◄────────────── G15 ──────────────►

BYTE	864	865	866	867	868	869	870	871	872	873	874	875	876	877	878	879
HEX	02	00	3A	09	0B	04	0C	00	00	00	2B	47	31	34	2B	42
DEC	2	0	58	9	11	4	12	0	0	0	43	71	49	52	43	66
ASC	^B	^@		^I	^K	^D	^L	^@	^@	^@						
ALT	STX	NUL		HT	VT	EOT	FF	NUL	NUL	NUL						
SYM			:								+	G	1	4	+	B

◄────────────── Formula G15 ──────────────►

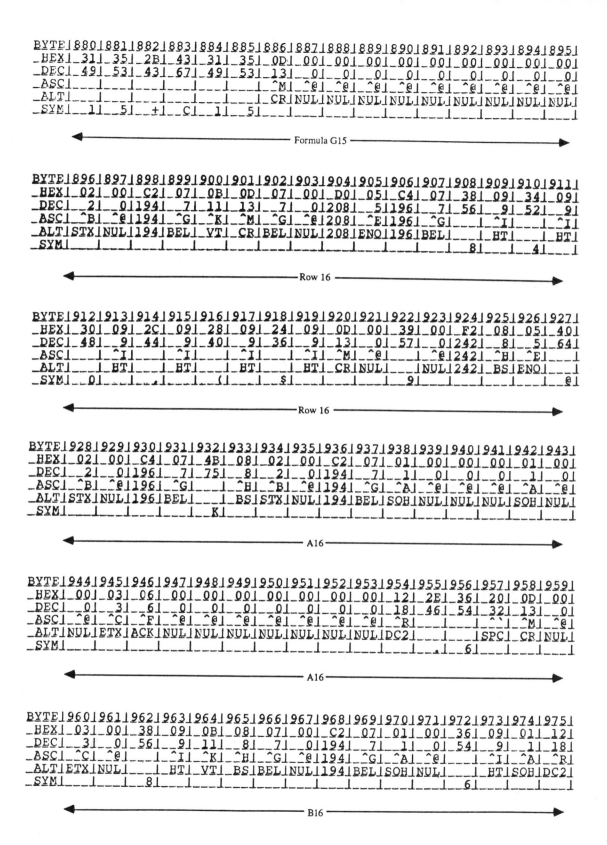

```
BYTE|880|881|882|883|884|885|886|887|888|889|890|891|892|893|894|895|
HEX | 31| 35| 2B| 43| 31| 35| 0D| 00| 00| 00| 00| 00| 00| 00| 00| 00|
DEC | 49| 53| 43| 67| 49| 53| 13|  0|  0|  0|  0|  0|  0|  0|  0|  0|
ASC |   |   |   |   |   |   | ^M| ^@| ^@| ^@| ^@| ^@| ^@| ^@| ^@| ^@|
ALT |   |   |   |   |   |   | CR|NUL|NUL|NUL|NUL|NUL|NUL|NUL|NUL|NUL|
SYM |  1|  5|  +|  C|  1|  5|   |   |   |   |   |   |   |   |   |   |
```

◄─────────────────── Formula G15 ───────────────────►

```
BYTE|896|897|898|899|900|901|902|903|904|905|906|907|908|909|910|911|
HEX | 02| 00| C2| 07| 0B| 0D| 07| 00| D0| 05| C4| 07| 38| 09| 34| 09|
DEC |  2|  0|194|  7| 11| 13|  7|  0|208|  5|196|  7| 56|  9| 52|  9|
ASC | ^B| ^@|194| ^G| ^K| ^M| ^G| ^@|208| ^E|196| ^G|   | ^I|   | ^I|
ALT |STX|NUL|194|BEL| VT| CR|BEL|NUL|208|ENQ|196|BEL|   | HT|   | HT|
SYM |   |   |   |   |   |   |   |   |   |   |   |   |  8|   |  4|   |
```

◄─────────────────── Row 16 ───────────────────►

```
BYTE|912|913|914|915|916|917|918|919|920|921|922|923|924|925|926|927|
HEX | 30| 09| 2C| 09| 28| 09| 24| 09| 0D| 00| 39| 00| F2| 08| 05| 40|
DEC | 48|  9| 44|  9| 40|  9| 36|  9| 13|  0| 57|  0|242|  8|  5| 64|
ASC |   | ^I|   | ^I|   | ^I|   | ^I| ^M| ^@|   | ^@|242| ^H| ^E|   |
ALT |   | HT|   | HT|   | HT|   | HT| CR|NUL|   |NUL|242| BS|ENQ|   |
SYM |  0|   |   |   |  (|   |  $|   |   |   |   |  9|   |   |   |  @|
```

◄─────────────────── Row 16 ───────────────────►

```
BYTE|928|929|930|931|932|933|934|935|936|937|938|939|940|941|942|943|
HEX | 02| 00| C4| 07| 4B| 08| 02| 00| C2| 07| 01| 00| 00| 00| 01| 00|
DEC |  2|  0|196|  7| 75|  8|  2|  0|194|  7|  1|  0|  0|  0|  1|  0|
ASC | ^B| ^@|196| ^G|   | ^H| ^B| ^@|194| ^G| ^A| ^@| ^@| ^@| ^A| ^@|
ALT |STX|NUL|196|BEL|   | BS|STX|NUL|194|BEL|SOH|NUL|NUL|NUL|SOH|NUL|
SYM |   |   |   |   |  K|   |   |   |   |   |   |   |   |   |   |   |
```

◄─────────────────── A16 ───────────────────►

```
BYTE|944|945|946|947|948|949|950|951|952|953|954|955|956|957|958|959|
HEX | 00| 03| 06| 00| 00| 00| 00| 00| 00| 00| 12| 2E| 36| 20| 0D| 00|
DEC |  0|  3|  6|  0|  0|  0|  0|  0|  0|  0| 18| 46| 54| 32| 13|  0|
ASC | ^@| ^C| ^F| ^@| ^@| ^@| ^@| ^@| ^@| ^@| ^R|   |   | ^^| ^M| ^@|
ALT |NUL|ETX|ACK|NUL|NUL|NUL|NUL|NUL|NUL|NUL|DC2|   |   |SPC| CR|NUL|
SYM |   |   |   |   |   |   |   |   |   |   |   |  .|  6|   |   |   |
```

◄─────────────────── A16 ───────────────────►

```
BYTE|960|961|962|963|964|965|966|967|968|969|970|971|972|973|974|975|
HEX | 03| 00| 38| 09| 0B| 08| 07| 00| C2| 07| 01| 00| 36| 09| 01| 12|
DEC |  3|  0| 56|  9| 11|  8|  7|  0|194|  7|  1|  0| 54|  9|  1| 18|
ASC | ^C| ^@|   | ^I| ^K| ^H| ^G| ^@|194| ^G| ^A| ^@|   | ^I| ^A| ^R|
ALT |ETX|NUL|   | HT| VT| BS|BEL|NUL|194|BEL|SOH|NUL|   | HT|SOH|DC2|
SYM |   |   |  8|   |   |   |   |   |   |   |   |   |  6|   |   |   |
```

◄─────────────────── B16 ───────────────────►

```
BYTE|976|977|978|979|980|981|982|983|984|985|986|987|988|989|990|991|
HEX| 00| 05| 52| 96| 55| 83| 77| 26| 92| 59| 06| 31| 24| 36| 35| 2E|
DEC|  0|  5| 82|150| 85|131|119| 38|146| 89|  6| 49| 36| 54| 53| 46|
ASC| ^@| ^E|   |150|   |131|   |   |146|   | ^F|   |   |   |   |   |
ALT|NUL|ENQ|   |150|   |131|   |   |146|   |ACK|   |   |   |   |   |
SYM|   |   |  R|   |  U|   |  w|  &|   |  Y|   |  1|  $|  6|  5|  .|
```
◄─────────────────────────────── B16 ───────────────────────────────►

```
BYTE|992|993|994|995|996|997|998|999|  0|  1|  2|  3|  4|  5|  6|  7|
HEX| 39| 39| 20| 0D| 00| 00| 00| 04| 00| 00| 00| 81| 01| FF| 81| 00|
DEC| 57| 57| 32| 13|  0|  0|  0|  4|  0|  0|  0|129|  1|255|129|  0|
ASC|   |   | ^^| ^M| ^@| ^@| ^@| ^D| ^@| ^@| ^@|129| ^A|255|129| ^@|
ALT|   |   |SPC| CR|NUL|NUL|NUL|EOT|NUL|NUL|NUL|129|SOH|255|129|NUL|
SYM|  9|  9|   |   |   |   |   |   |   |   |   |   |   |   |   |   |
```
◄─────────────────────────────── B16 ───────────────────────────────►

```
BYTE|  8|  9| 10| 11| 12| 13| 14| 15| 16| 17| 18| 19| 20| 21| 22| 23|
HEX| 02| 00| 36| 09| 0B| 04| 0E| 00| 00| 00| 2B| 44| 31| 35| 2A| 28|
DEC|  2|  0| 54|  9| 11|  4| 14|  0|  0|  0| 43| 68| 49| 53| 42| 40|
ASC| ^B| ^@|   | ^I| ^K| ^D| ^N| ^@| ^@| ^@|   |   |   |   |   |   |
ALT|STX|NUL|   | HT| VT|EOT| SO|NUL|NUL|NUL|   |   |   |   |   |   |
SYM|   |   |  6|   |   |   |   |   |   |   |  +|  D|  1|  5|  *|  (|
```
◄─────────────────────────── Formula B16 ───────────────────────────►

```
BYTE| 24| 25| 26| 27| 28| 29| 30| 31| 32| 33| 34| 35| 36| 37| 38| 39|
HEX| 24| 42| 24| 34| 2F| 31| 32| 29| 0D| 00| 00| 00| 00| 00| 00| 00|
DEC| 36| 66| 36| 52| 47| 49| 50| 41| 13|  0|  0|  0|  0|  0|  0|  0|
ASC|   |   |   |   |   |   |   |   | ^M| ^@| ^@| ^@| ^@| ^@| ^@| ^@|
ALT|   |   |   |   |   |   |   |   | CR|NUL|NUL|NUL|NUL|NUL|NUL|NUL|
SYM|  $|  B|  $|  4|  /|  1|  2|  )|   |   |   |   |   |   |   |   |
```
◄─────────────────────────── Formula B16 ───────────────────────────►

```
BYTE| 40| 41| 42| 43| 44| 45| 46| 47| 48| 49| 50| 51| 52| 53| 54| 55|
HEX| 03| 00| 34| 09| 0B| 08| 08| 00| C2| 07| 01| 00| 32| 09| 01| 12|
DEC|  3|  0| 52|  9| 11|  8|  8|  0|194|  7|  1|  0| 50|  9|  1| 18|
ASC| ^C| ^@|   | ^I| ^K| ^H| ^H| ^@|194| ^G| ^A| ^@|   | ^I| ^A| ^R|
ALT|ETX|NUL|   | HT| VT| BS| BS|NUL|194|BEL|SOH|NUL|   | HT|SOH|DC2|
SYM|   |   |  4|   |   |   |   |   |   |   |   |   |  2|   |   |   |
```
◄─────────────────────────────── C16 ───────────────────────────────►

```
BYTE| 56| 57| 58| 59| 60| 61| 62| 63| 64| 65| 66| 67| 68| 69| 70| 71|
HEX| 00| 05| 48| 03| 44| 16| 22| 73| 37| 87| 10| 31| 24| 31| 30| 38|
DEC|  0|  5| 72|  3| 68| 22| 34|115| 55|135| 16| 49| 36| 49| 48| 56|
ASC| ^@| ^E|   | ^C|   | ^V|   |   |   |135| ^P|   |   |   |   |   |
ALT|NUL|ENQ|   |ETX|   |SYN|   |   |   |135|DLE|   |   |   |   |   |
SYM|   |   |  H|   |  D|   |  "|  s|  7|   |   |  1|  $|  1|  0|  8|
```
◄─────────────────────────────── C16 ───────────────────────────────►

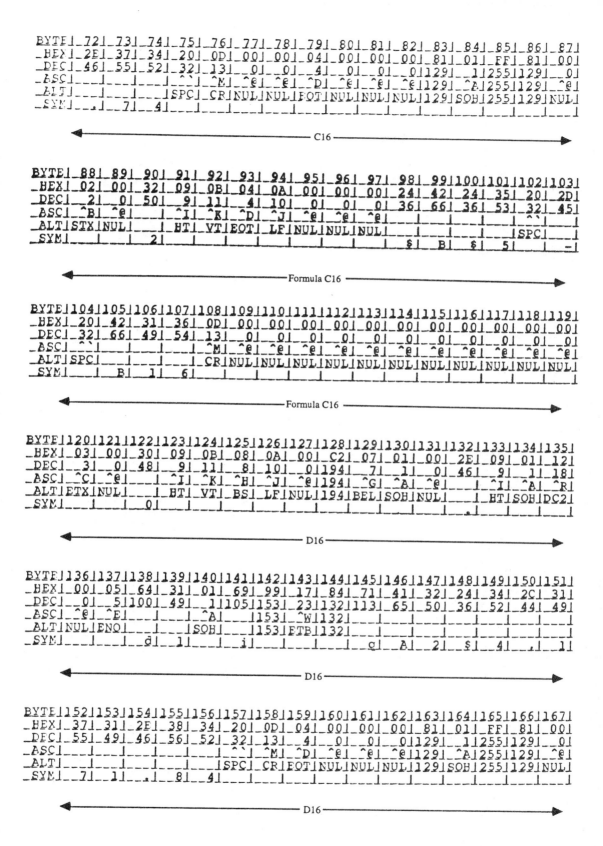

```
BYTE|168|169|170|171|172|173|174|175|176|177|178|179|180|181|182|183|
HEX | 02| 00| 2E| 09| 0B| 04| 0A| 00| 00| 00| 2B| 44| 31| 35| 20| 2D|
DEC |  2|  0| 46|  9| 11|  4| 10|  0|  0|  0| 43| 68| 49| 53| 32| 45|
ASC | ^B| ^@|   | ^I| ^K| ^D| ^J| ^@| ^@| ^@|   |   |   |   | ^^|   |
ALT |STX|NUL|   | HT| VT|EOT| LF|NUL|NUL|NUL|   |   |   |   |SPC|   |
SYM |   |   |  .|   |   |   |   |   |   |   |  +|  D|  1|  5|   |  -|

◄───────────────────────── Formula D16 ─────────────────────────►

BYTE|184|185|186|187|188|189|190|191|192|193|194|195|196|197|198|199|
HEX | 20| 43| 31| 36| 0D| 00| 00| 00| 00| 00| 00| 00| 00| 00| 00| 00|
DEC | 32| 67| 49| 54| 13|  0|  0|  0|  0|  0|  0|  0|  0|  0|  0|  0|
ASC | ^^|   |   |   | ^M| ^@| ^@| ^@| ^@| ^@| ^@| ^@| ^@| ^@| ^@| ^@|
ALT |SPC|   |   |   | CR|NUL|NUL|NUL|NUL|NUL|NUL|NUL|NUL|NUL|NUL|NUL|
SYM |   |  C|  1|  6|   |   |   |   |   |   |   |   |   |   |   |   |

◄───────────────────────── Formula D16 ─────────────────────────►

BYTE|200|201|202|203|204|205|206|207|208|209|210|211|212|213|214|215|
HEX | 03| 00| 2C| 09| 0B| 08| 08| 00| C2| 07| 01| 00| 2A| 09| 01| 12|
DEC |  3|  0| 44|  9| 11|  8|  8|  0|194|  7|  1|  0| 42|  9|  1| 18|
ASC | ^C| ^@|   | ^I| ^K| ^H| ^H| ^@|194| ^G| ^A| ^@|   | ^I| ^A| ^R|
ALT |ETX|NUL|   | HT| VT| BS| BS|NUL|194|BEL|SOH|NUL|   | HT|SOH|DC2|
SYM |   |   |  ,|   |   |   |   |   |   |   |   |   |  *|   |   |   |

◄──────────────────────────── E16 ───────────────────────────►

BYTE|216|217|218|219|220|221|222|223|224|225|226|227|228|229|230|231|
HEX | 00| 05| 32| 16| 13| 90| 96| 79| 21| 02| 42| 31| 24| 34| 32| 30|
DEC |  0|  5| 50| 22| 19|144|150|121| 33|  2| 66| 49| 36| 52| 50| 48|
ASC | ^@| ^E|   | ^V| ^S|144|150|   |   | ^B|   |   |   |   |   |   |
ALT |NUL|ENQ|   |SYN|DC3|144|150|   |   |STX|   |   |   |   |   |   |
SYM |   |   |  2|   |   |   |   |  y|  1|   |  B|  1|  $|  4|  2|  0|

◄──────────────────────────── E16 ───────────────────────────►

BYTE|232|233|234|235|236|237|238|239|240|241|242|243|244|245|246|247|
HEX | 2E| 32| 32| 20| 0D| 00| 00| 04| 00| 00| 00| 81| 01| FF| 81| 00|
DEC | 46| 50| 50| 32| 13|  0|  0|  4|  0|  0|  0|129|  1|255|129|  0|
ASC |   |   |   | ^^| ^M| ^@| ^@| ^D| ^@| ^@| ^@|129| ^A|255|129| ^@|
ALT |   |   |   |SPC| CR|NUL|NUL|EOT|NUL|NUL|NUL|129|SOH|255|129|NUL|
SYM |   |  .|  2|  2|   |   |   |   |   |   |   |   |   |   |   |   |

◄──────────────────────────── E16 ───────────────────────────►

BYTE|248|249|250|251|252|253|254|255|256|257|258|259|260|261|262|263|
HEX | 02| 00| 2A| 09| 0B| 04| 08| 00| 00| 00| 2B| 45| 31| 35| 2B| 42|
DEC |  2|  0| 42|  9| 11|  4|  8|  0|  0|  0| 43| 69| 49| 53| 43| 66|
ASC | ^B| ^@|   | ^I| ^K| ^D| ^H| ^@| ^@| ^@|   |   |   |   |   |   |
ALT |STX|NUL|   | HT| VT|EOT| BS|NUL|NUL|NUL|   |   |   |   |   |   |
SYM |   |   |  *|   |   |   |   |   |   |   |  +|  E|  1|  5|  +|  B|

◄───────────────────────── Formula E16 ─────────────────────────►
```

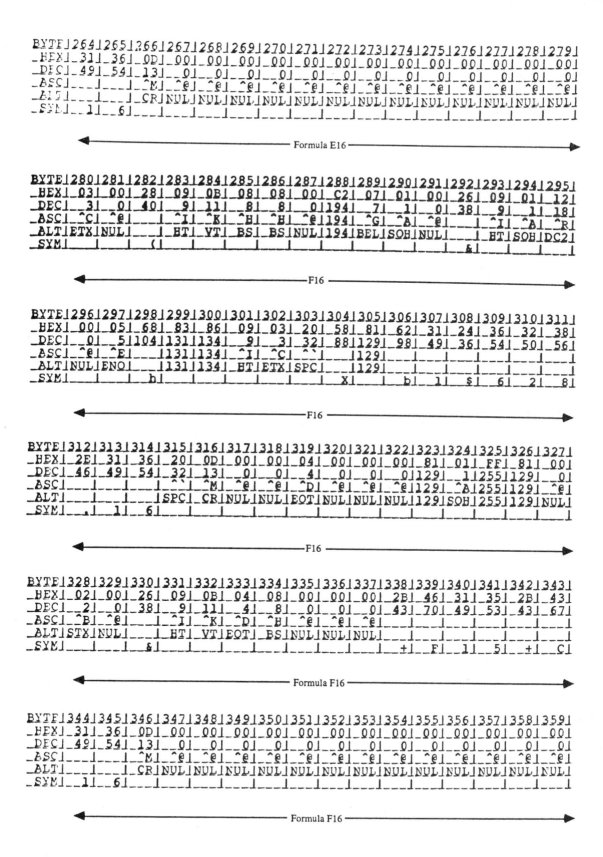

Formula E16

F16

F16

F16

Formula F16

Formula F16

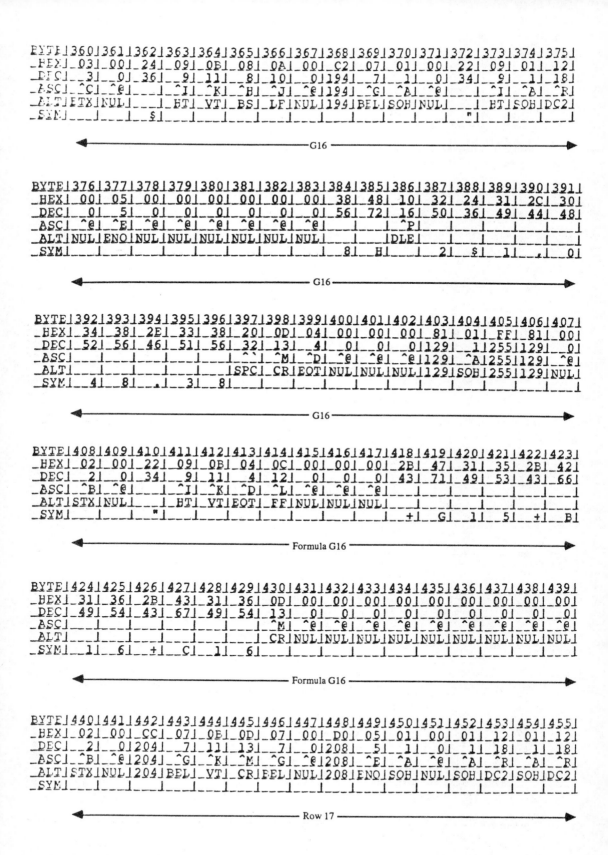

BYTE	360	361	362	363	364	365	366	367	368	369	370	371	372	373	374	375
HEX	03	00	24	09	0B	08	0A	00	C2	07	01	00	22	09	01	12
DEC	3	0	36	9	11	8	10	0	194	7	1	0	34	9	1	18
ASC	^C	^@		^I	^K	^H	^J	^@	194	^G	^A	^@		^I	^A	^R
ALT	ETX	NUL		BT	VT	BS	LF	NUL	194	BEL	SOH	NUL		BT	SOH	DC2
SYM			$										"			

← G16 →

BYTE	376	377	378	379	380	381	382	383	384	385	386	387	388	389	390	391
HEX	00	05	00	00	00	00	00	00	38	48	10	32	24	31	2C	30
DEC	0	5	0	0	0	0	0	0	56	72	16	50	36	49	44	48
ASC	^@	^E	^@	^@	^@	^@	^@	^@			^P					
ALT	NUL	ENO	NUL	NUL	NUL	NUL	NUL	NUL			DLE					
SYM									8	H		2	$	1	,	0

← G16 →

BYTE	392	393	394	395	396	397	398	399	400	401	402	403	404	405	406	407
HEX	34	38	2E	33	38	20	0D	04	00	00	00	81	01	FF	81	00
DEC	52	56	46	51	56	32	13	4	0	0	0	129	1	255	129	0
ASC							^^	^M	^D	^@	^@	^@	129	^A	255	129	^@
ALT						SPC	CR	EOT	NUL	NUL	NUL	129	SOH	255	129	NUL
SYM	4	8	.	3	8											

← G16 →

BYTE	408	409	410	411	412	413	414	415	416	417	418	419	420	421	422	423
HEX	02	00	22	09	0B	04	0C	00	00	00	2B	47	31	35	2B	42
DEC	2	0	34	9	11	4	12	0	0	0	43	71	49	53	43	66
ASC	^B	^@		^I	^K	^D	^L	^@	^@	^@						
ALT	STX	NUL		BT	VT	EOT	FF	NUL	NUL	NUL						
SYM			"									+	G	1	5	+	B

← Formula G16 →

BYTE	424	425	426	427	428	429	430	431	432	433	434	435	436	437	438	439
HEX	31	36	2B	43	31	36	0D	00	00	00	00	00	00	00	00	00
DEC	49	54	43	67	49	54	13	0	0	0	0	0	0	0	0	0
ASC							^M	^@	^@	^@	^@	^@	^@	^@	^@	^@
ALT							CR	NUL	NUL	NUL	NUL	NUL	NUL	NUL	NUL	NUL
SYM	1	6	+	C	1	6										

← Formula G16 →

BYTE	440	441	442	443	444	445	446	447	448	449	450	451	452	453	454	455
HEX	02	00	CC	07	0B	0D	07	00	D0	05	01	00	01	12	01	12
DEC	2	0	204	7	11	13	7	0	208	5	1	0	1	18	1	18
ASC	^B	^@	204	^G	^K	^M	^G	^@	208	^E	^A	^@	^A	^R	^A	^R
ALT	STX	NUL	204	BEL	VT	CR	BEL	NUL	208	ENO	SOH	NUL	SOH	DC2	SOH	DC2
SYM																

← Row 17 →

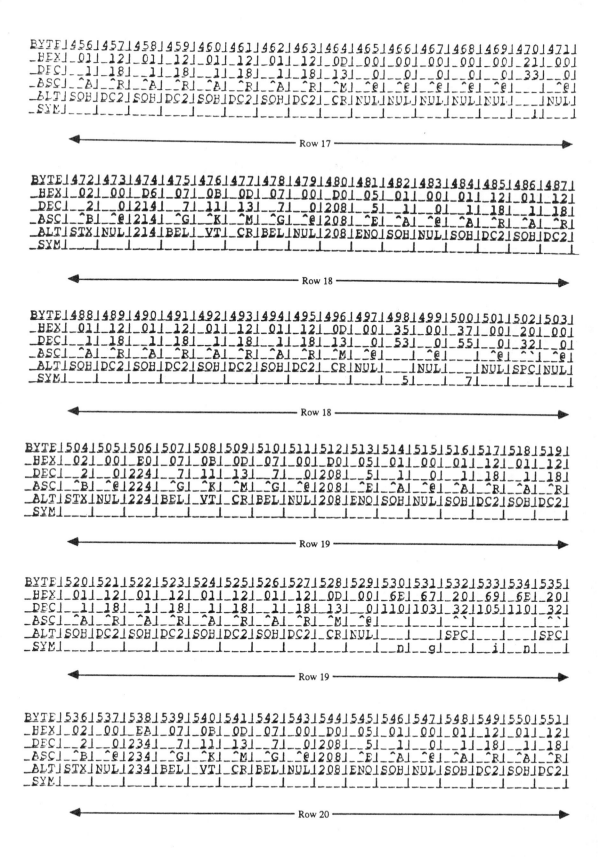

```
BYTE|456|457|458|459|460|461|462|463|464|465|466|467|468|469|470|471|
_HEX|_01|_12|_01|_12|_01|_12|_01|_12|_0D|_00|_00|_00|_00|_00|_21|_00|
_DEC|__1|_18|__1|_18|__1|_18|__1|_18|_13|__0|__0|__0|__0|__0|_33|__0|
_ASC|_^A|_^R|_^A|_^R|_^A|_^R|_^A|_^R|_^M|_^@|_^@|_^@|_^@|_^@|___|_^@|
_ALT|SOB|DC2|SOB|DC2|SOB|DC2|SOB|DC2|_CR|NUL|NUL|NUL|NUL|NUL|___|NUL|
_SYM|___|___|___|___|___|___|___|___|___|___|___|___|___|___|___|___|
```

◄────────────────────────── Row 17 ──────────────────────────►

```
BYTE|472|473|474|475|476|477|478|479|480|481|482|483|484|485|486|487|
_HEX|_02|_00|_D6|_07|_0B|_0D|_07|_00|_D0|_05|_01|_00|_01|_12|_01|_12|
_DEC|__2|__0|214|__7|_11|_13|__7|__0|208|__5|__1|__0|__1|_18|__1|_18|
_ASC|_^B|_^@|214|_^G|_^K|_^M|_^G|_^@|208|_^E|_^A|_^@|_^A|_^R|_^A|_^R|
_ALT|STX|NUL|214|BEL|_VT|_CR|BEL|NUL|208|ENQ|SOH|NUL|SOH|DC2|SOH|DC2|
_SYM|___|___|___|___|___|___|___|___|___|___|___|___|___|___|___|___|
```

◄────────────────────────── Row 18 ──────────────────────────►

```
BYTE|488|489|490|491|492|493|494|495|496|497|498|499|500|501|502|503|
_HEX|_01|_12|_01|_12|_01|_12|_01|_12|_0D|_00|_35|_00|_37|_00|_20|_00|
_DEC|__1|_18|__1|_18|__1|_18|__1|_18|_13|__0|_53|__0|_55|__0|_32|__0|
_ASC|_^A|_^R|_^A|_^R|_^A|_^R|_^A|_^R|_^M|_^@|___|_^@|___|_^@|_^^|_^@|
_ALT|SOB|DC2|SOB|DC2|SOB|DC2|SOB|DC2|_CR|NUL|___|NUL|___|NUL|SPC|NUL|
_SYM|___|___|___|___|___|___|___|___|___|___|_5_|___|_7_|___|___|___|
```

◄────────────────────────── Row 18 ──────────────────────────►

```
BYTE|504|505|506|507|508|509|510|511|512|513|514|515|516|517|518|519|
_HEX|_02|_00|_E0|_07|_0B|_0D|_07|_00|_D0|_05|_01|_00|_01|_12|_01|_12|
_DEC|__2|__0|224|__7|_11|_13|__7|__0|208|__5|__1|__0|__1|_18|__1|_18|
_ASC|_^B|_^@|224|_^G|_^K|_^M|_^G|_^@|208|_^E|_^A|_^@|_^A|_^R|_^A|_^R|
_ALT|STX|NUL|224|BEL|_VT|_CR|BEL|NUL|208|ENQ|SOH|NUL|SOH|DC2|SOH|DC2|
_SYM|___|___|___|___|___|___|___|___|___|___|___|___|___|___|___|___|
```

◄────────────────────────── Row 19 ──────────────────────────►

```
BYTE|520|521|522|523|524|525|526|527|528|529|530|531|532|533|534|535|
_HEX|_01|_12|_01|_12|_01|_12|_01|_12|_0D|_00|_6E|_67|_20|_69|_6E|_20|
_DEC|__1|_18|__1|_18|__1|_18|__1|_18|_13|__0|110|103|_32|105|110|_32|
_ASC|_^A|_^R|_^A|_^R|_^A|_^R|_^A|_^R|_^M|_^@|___|___|_^^|___|___|_^^|
_ALT|SOB|DC2|SOB|DC2|SOB|DC2|SOB|DC2|_CR|NUL|___|___|SPC|___|___|SPC|
_SYM|___|___|___|___|___|___|___|___|___|___|_n_|_g_|___|_i_|_n_|___|
```

◄────────────────────────── Row 19 ──────────────────────────►

```
BYTE|536|537|538|539|540|541|542|543|544|545|546|547|548|549|550|551|
_HEX|_02|_00|_EA|_07|_0B|_0D|_07|_00|_D0|_05|_01|_00|_01|_12|_01|_12|
_DEC|__2|__0|234|__7|_11|_13|__7|__0|208|__5|__1|__0|__1|_18|__1|_18|
_ASC|_^B|_^@|234|_^G|_^K|_^M|_^G|_^@|208|_^E|_^A|_^@|_^A|_^R|_^A|_^R|
_ALT|STX|NUL|234|BEL|_VT|_CR|BEL|NUL|208|ENQ|SOH|NUL|SOH|DC2|SOH|DC2|
_SYM|___|___|___|___|___|___|___|___|___|___|___|___|___|___|___|___|
```

◄────────────────────────── Row 20 ──────────────────────────►

FRAMEWORK II   233

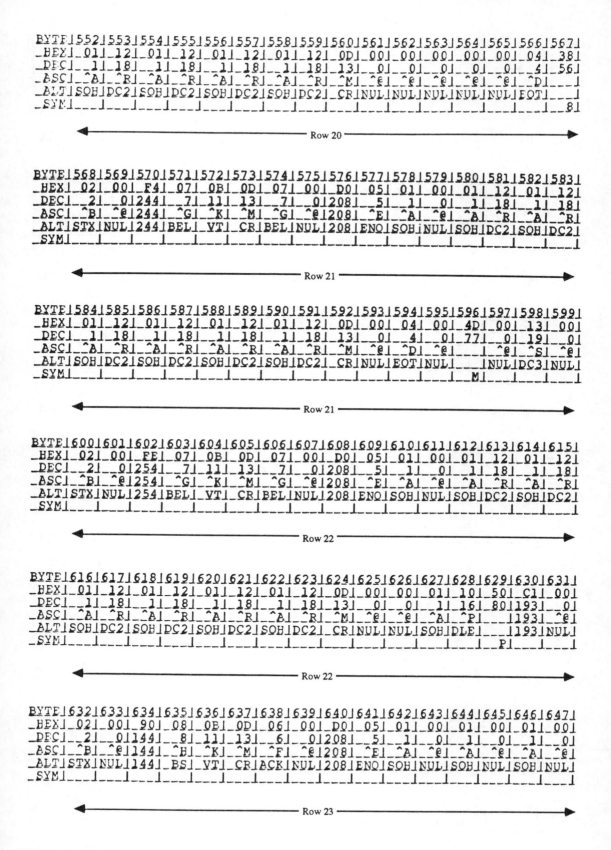

```
BYTE|552|553|554|555|556|557|558|559|560|561|562|563|564|565|566|567|
HEX | 01| 12| 01| 12| 01| 12| 01| 12| 0D| 00| 00| 00| 00| 00| 04| 38|
DEC |  1| 18|  1| 18|  1| 18|  1| 18| 13|  0|  0|  0|  0|  0|  4| 56|
ASC | ^A| ^R| ^A| ^R| ^A| ^R| ^A| ^R| ^M| ^@| ^@| ^@| ^@| ^@| ^D|   |
ALT |SOH|DC2|SOH|DC2|SOH|DC2|SOH|DC2| CR|NUL|NUL|NUL|NUL|NUL|EOT|   |
SYM |   |   |   |   |   |   |   |   |   |   |   |   |   |   |   |  8|
```

◄─────────────────────────── Row 20 ───────────────────────────►

```
BYTE|568|569|570|571|572|573|574|575|576|577|578|579|580|581|582|583|
HEX | 02| 00| F4| 07| 0B| 0D| 07| 00| D0| 05| 01| 00| 01| 12| 01| 12|
DEC |  2|  0|244|  7| 11| 13|  7|  0|208|  5|  1|  0|  1| 18|  1| 18|
ASC | ^B| ^@|244| ^G| ^K| ^M| ^G| ^@|208| ^E| ^A| ^@| ^A| ^R| ^A| ^R|
ALT |STX|NUL|244|BEL| VT| CR|BEL|NUL|208|ENQ|SOH|NUL|SOH|DC2|SOH|DC2|
SYM |   |   |   |   |   |   |   |   |   |   |   |   |   |   |   |   |
```

◄─────────────────────────── Row 21 ───────────────────────────►

```
BYTE|584|585|586|587|588|589|590|591|592|593|594|595|596|597|598|599|
HEX | 01| 12| 01| 12| 01| 12| 01| 12| 0D| 00| 04| 00| 4D| 00| 13| 00|
DEC |  1| 18|  1| 18|  1| 18|  1| 18| 13|  0|  4|  0| 77|  0| 19|  0|
ASC | ^A| ^R| ^A| ^R| ^A| ^R| ^A| ^R| ^M| ^@| ^D| ^@|   | ^@| ^S| ^@|
ALT |SOH|DC2|SOH|DC2|SOH|DC2|SOH|DC2| CR|NUL|EOT|NUL|   |NUL|DC3|NUL|
SYM |   |   |   |   |   |   |   |   |   |   |   |   |  M|   |   |   |
```

◄─────────────────────────── Row 21 ───────────────────────────►

```
BYTE|600|601|602|603|604|605|606|607|608|609|610|611|612|613|614|615|
HEX | 02| 00| FE| 07| 0B| 0D| 07| 00| D0| 05| 01| 00| 01| 12| 01| 12|
DEC |  2|  0|254|  7| 11| 13|  7|  0|208|  5|  1|  0|  1| 18|  1| 18|
ASC | ^B| ^@|254| ^G| ^K| ^M| ^G| ^@|208| ^E| ^A| ^@| ^A| ^R| ^A| ^R|
ALT |STX|NUL|254|BEL| VT| CR|BEL|NUL|208|ENQ|SOH|NUL|SOH|DC2|SOH|DC2|
SYM |   |   |   |   |   |   |   |   |   |   |   |   |   |   |   |   |
```

◄─────────────────────────── Row 22 ───────────────────────────►

```
BYTE|616|617|618|619|620|621|622|623|624|625|626|627|628|629|630|631|
HEX | 01| 12| 01| 12| 01| 12| 01| 12| 0D| 00| 00| 01| 10| 50| C1| 00|
DEC |  1| 18|  1| 18|  1| 18|  1| 18| 13|  0|  0|  1| 16| 80|193|  0|
ASC | ^A| ^R| ^A| ^R| ^A| ^R| ^A| ^R| ^M| ^@| ^@| ^A| ^P|   |193| ^@|
ALT |SOH|DC2|SOH|DC2|SOH|DC2|SOH|DC2| CR|NUL|NUL|SOH|DLE|   |193|NUL|
SYM |   |   |   |   |   |   |   |   |   |   |   |   |   |  P|   |   |
```

◄─────────────────────────── Row 22 ───────────────────────────►

```
BYTE|632|633|634|635|636|637|638|639|640|641|642|643|644|645|646|647|
HEX | 02| 00| 90| 08| 0B| 0D| 06| 00| D0| 05| 01| 00| 01| 00| 01| 00|
DEC |  2|  0|144|  8| 11| 13|  6|  0|208|  5|  1|  0|  1|  0|  1|  0|
ASC | ^B| ^@|144| ^H| ^K| ^M| ^F| ^@|208| ^E| ^A| ^@| ^A| ^@| ^A| ^@|
ALT |STX|NUL|144| BS| VT| CR|ACK|NUL|208|ENQ|SOH|NUL|SOH|NUL|SOH|NUL|
SYM |   |   |   |   |   |   |   |   |   |   |   |   |   |   |   |   |
```

◄─────────────────────────── Row 23 ───────────────────────────►

```
BYTE|648|649|650|651|652|653|654|655|656|657|658|659|660|661|662|663|
HEX | 01| 00| 01| 00| 01| 12| 0D| 00| 12| 00| 00| 00| 00| 00| 04| 00|
DEC |  1|  0|  1|  0|  1| 18| 13|  0| 18|  0|  0|  0|  0|  0|  4|  0|
ASC | ^A| ^@| ^A| ^@| ^A| ^R| ^M| ^@| ^R| ^@| ^@| ^@| ^@| ^@| ^D| ^@|
ALT |SOH|NUL|SOH|NUL|SOH|DC2| CR|NUL|DC2|NUL|NUL|NUL|NUL|NUL|EOT|NUL|
SYM |   |   |   |   |   |   |   |   |   |   |   |   |   |   |   |   |
```

◄──────────────────────────── Row 23 ────────────────────────────►

```
BYTE|664|665|666|667|668|669|670|671|672|673|674|675|676|677|678|679|
HEX | 06| 00| B6| 02| 0B| 00| 0F| 00| 66| 02| 00| 00| FE| 02| 04| 00|
DEC |  6|  0|182|  2| 11|  0| 15|  0|102|  2|  0|  0|254|  2|  4|  0|
ASC | ^F| ^@|182| ^B| ^K| ^@| ^O| ^@|   | ^B| ^@| ^@|254| ^B| ^D| ^@|
ALT |ACK|NUL|182|STX| VT|NUL| SI|NUL|   |STX|NUL|NUL|254|STX|EOT|NUL|
SYM |   |   |   |   |   |   |   | f1|   |   |   |   |   |   |   |   |
```

| Paragraph Count | FID | Status | Type | # Elements | Parent FID | EXE FID | Formula FID | Formatting |

```
BYTE|680|681|682|683|684|685|686|687|688|689|690|691|692|693|694|695|
HEX | 00| 00| 00| 00| 01| 00| 10| 00| 00| 00| 01| 00| B8| 02| 05| 00|
DEC |  0|  0|  0|  0|  1|  0| 16|  0|  0|  0|  1|  0|184|  2|  5|  0|
ASC | ^@| ^@| ^@| ^@| ^A| ^@| ^P| ^@| ^@| ^@| ^A| ^@|184| ^B| ^E| ^@|
ALT |NUL|NUL|NUL|NUL|SOH|NUL|DLE|NUL|NUL|NUL|SOH|NUL|184|STX|ENQ|NUL|
SYM |   |   |   |   |   |   |   |   |   |   |   |   |   |   |   |   |
```

| I.V.T. | Value Structure | Name FID | Frame Status Flags |

```
BYTE|696|697|698|699|700|701|702|703|704|705|706|707|708|709|710|711|
HEX | 43| 00| 0C| 00| 4E| 00| 0C| 00| 36| 00| 0A| 00| 41| 00| 0A| 00|
DEC | 67|  0| 12|  0| 78|  0| 12|  0| 54|  0| 10|  0| 65|  0| 10|  0|
ASC |   | ^@| ^L| ^@|   | ^@| ^L| ^@|   | ^@| ^J| ^@|   | ^@| ^J| ^@|
ALT |   |NUL| FF|NUL|   |NUL| FF|NUL|   |NUL| LF|NUL|   |NUL| LF|NUL|
SYM | C |   |   |   | N |   |   |   | 6 |   |   |   | A |   |   |   |
```

| TLX | TLY | BRX | BRY | Clipping TLX | Clipping TLY | Clipping BRX | Clipping BRY |

```
BYTE|712|713|714|715|716|717|718|719|720|721|722|723|724|725|726|727|
HEX | 36| 00| 0A| 00| 00| 00| 00| 00| 00| 00| 00| 00| 00| 00| 00| 00|
DEC | 54|  0| 10|  0|  0|  0|  0|  0|  0|  0|  0|  0|  0|  0|  0|  0|
ASC |   | ^@| ^J| ^@| ^@| ^@| ^@| ^@| ^@| ^@| ^@| ^@| ^@| ^@| ^@| ^@|
ALT |   |NUL| LF|NUL|NUL|NUL|NUL|NUL|NUL|NUL|NUL|NUL|NUL|NUL|NUL|NUL|
SYM | 6 |   |   |   |   |   |   |   |   |   |   |   |   |   |   |   |
```

| ABS TLX | ABS TLY | Scroll X | Scroll Y | Reserved | Reserved | Style FID | Internal Page # |

```
BYTE|728|729|730|731|732|733|734|735|736|737|738|739|740|741|742|743|
HEX | 05| 00| 06| 00| 00| 00| 00| 05| 00| 00| 00| 81| 01| 41| 81| 00|
DEC |  5|  0|  6|  0|  0|  0|  0|  5|  0|  0|  0|129|  1| 65|129|  0|
ASC | ^E| ^@| ^F| ^@| ^@| ^@| ^@| ^E| ^@| ^@| ^@|129| ^A|   |129| ^@|
ALT |ENQ|NUL|ACK|NUL|NUL|NUL|NUL|ENQ|NUL|NUL|NUL|129|SOH|   |129|NUL|
SYM |   |   |   |   |   |   |   |   |   |   |   |   | A |   |   |   |
```

| First Selected Element | Last Selected Element | Reserved | Tab Size | Ith Line | ◄─────── Escape Sequence ───────► |

```
BYTE|744|745|746|747|748|749|750|751|752|753|754|755|756|757|758|759|
_HEX| 00| 85| 01| 00| 4D| 61| 79| 20| 39| 2C| 20| 31| 39| 38| 37| 0D|
_DEC|  0|133|  1|  0| 77| 97|121| 32| 57| 44| 32| 49| 57| 56| 55| 13|
_ASC| ^@|133| ^A| ^@|   |   |   |  ^^|   |   |  ^^|   |   |   |   | ^M|
_ALT|NUL|133|SOH|NUL|   |   |   |SPC|   |   |SPC|   |   |   |   | CR|
_SYM|   |   |   |   |  M|  a|  y|   |  9|  ,|   |  1|  9|  8|  7|   |
```

◄───────────────────── Contents ─────────────────────►

```
BYTE|760|761|762|763|764|765|766|767|768|769|770|771|772|773|774|775|
_HEX| 02| 00| FE| 02| 0B| 04| 0D| 00| 00| 00| 40| 64| 61| 74| 65| 34|
_DEC|  2|  0|254|  2| 11|  4| 13|  0|  0|  0| 64|100| 97|116|101| 52|
_ASC| ^B| ^@|254| ^B| ^K| ^D| ^M| ^@| ^@| ^@|   |   |   |   |   |   |
_ALT|STX|NUL|254|STX| VT|EOT| CR|NUL|NUL|NUL|   |   |   |   |   |   |
_SYM|   |   |   |   |   |   |   |   |   |   |  @|  d|  a|  t|  e|  4|
```

Paragraph Count	FID	Status	Type	# Elements	Reserved	Contents

```
BYTE|776|777|778|779|780|781|782|783|784|785|786|787|788|789|790|791|
_HEX| 28| 40| 64| 61| 74| 65| 29| 0D| 00| 00| 00| 00| 00| 00| 00| 00|
_DEC| 40| 64|100| 97|116|101| 41| 13|  0|  0|  0|  0|  0|  0|  0|  0|
_ASC|   |   |   |   |   |   |   | ^M| ^@| ^@| ^@| ^@| ^@| ^@| ^@| ^@|
_ALT|   |   |   |   |   |   |   | CR|NUL|NUL|NUL|NUL|NUL|NUL|NUL|NUL|
_SYM|  (|  @|  d|  a|  t|  e|  )|   |   |   |   |   |   |   |   |   |
```

Contents | End of Frame

```
BYTE|792|793|794|795|796|797|798|799|800|801|802|803|804|805|806|807|
_HEX| 01| 00| B8| 02| 0B| 04| 05| 00| 00| 00| 54| 6F| 64| 61| 79| 0D|
_DEC|  1|  0|184|  2| 11|  4|  5|  0|  0|  0| 84|111|100| 97|121| 13|
_ASC| ^A| ^@|184| ^B| ^K| ^D| ^E| ^@| ^@| ^@|   |   |   |   |   | ^M|
_ALT|SOH|NUL|184|STX| VT|EOT|ENQ|NUL|NUL|NUL|   |   |   |   |   | CR|
_SYM|   |   |   |   |   |   |   |   |   |   |  T|  o|  d|  a|  y|   |
```

Paragraph Count	FID	Status	Type	# Elements	Reserved	Contents	End of Frame

```
BYTE|807|  0|  0|  0|  0|  0|  0|  0|  0|  0|  0|  0|  0|  0|  0|  0|
_HEX| 0D| XX| XX| XX| XX| XX| XX| XX| XX| XX| XX| XX| XX| XX| XX| XX|
_DEC| 13|  0|  0|  0|  0|  0|  0|  0|  0|  0|  0|  0|  0|  0|  0|  0|
_ASC| ^M|XXX|XXX|XXX|XXX|XXX|XXX|XXX|XXX|XXX|XXX|XXX|XXX|XXX|XXX|XXX|
_ALT| CR|XXX|XXX|XXX|XXX|XXX|XXX|XXX|XXX|XXX|XXX|XXX|XXX|XXX|XXX|XXX|
_SYM|   |   |   |   |   |   |   |   |   |   |   |   |   |   |   |   |
```

End of File

```
BYTE|  0|  0|  0|  0|  0|  0|  0|  0|  0|  0|  0|  0|  0|  0|  0|  0|
_HEX| XX| XX| XX| XX| XX| XX| XX| XX| XX| XX| XX| XX| XX| XX| XX| XX|
_DEC|  0|  0|  0|  0|  0|  0|  0|  0|  0|  0|  0|  0|  0|  0|  0|  0|
_ASC|XXX|XXX|XXX|XXX|XXX|XXX|XXX|XXX|XXX|XXX|XXX|XXX|XXX|XXX|XXX|XXX|
_ALT|XXX|XXX|XXX|XXX|XXX|XXX|XXX|XXX|XXX|XXX|XXX|XXX|XXX|XXX|XXX|XXX|
_SYM|   |   |   |   |   |   |   |   |   |   |   |   |   |   |   |   |
```

```
BYTE|  0|  0|  0|  0|  0|  0|  0|  0|  0|  0|  0|  0|  0|  0|  0|  0|
_HEX|_XX|_XX|_XX|_XX|_XX|_XX|_XX|_XX|_XX|_XX|_XX|_XX|_XX|_XX|_XX|_XX|
_DEC|__0|__0|__0|__0|__0|__0|__0|__0|__0|__0|__0|__0|__0|__0|__0|__0|
_ASC|XXX|XXX|XXX|XXX|XXX|XXX|XXX|XXX|XXX|XXX|XXX|XXX|XXX|XXX|XXX|XXX|
_ALT|XXX|XXX|XXX|XXX|XXX|XXX|XXX|XXX|XXX|XXX|XXX|XXX|XXX|XXX|XXX|XXX|
_SYM|___|___|___|___|___|___|___|___|___|___|___|___|___|___|___|___|
```

Reflex Sample File

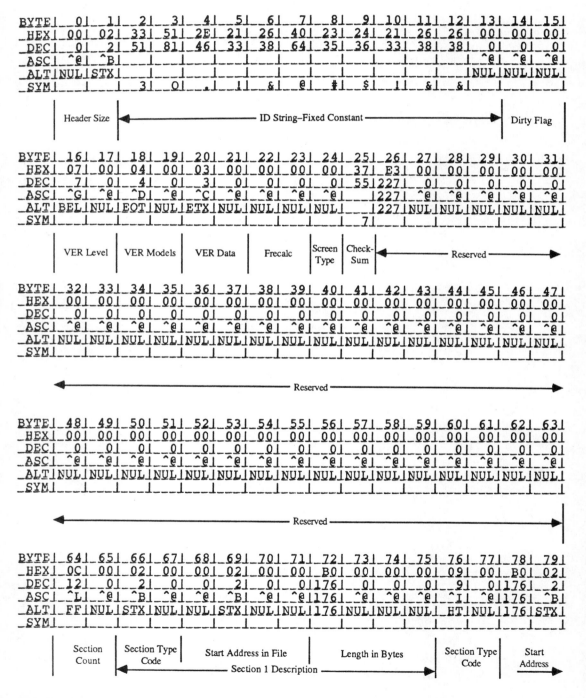

```
BYTE| 80| 81| 82| 83| 84| 85| 86| 87| 88| 89| 90| 91| 92| 93| 94| 95|
HEX | 00| 00| 04| 00| 00| 00| 01| 00| B4| 02| 00| 00| 11| 01| 00| 00|
DEC | 0 | 0 | 4 | 0 | 0 | 0 | 1 | 0 |180| 2 | 0 | 0 | 17| 1 | 0 | 0 |
ASC | ^@| ^@| ^D| ^@| ^@| ^@| ^A| ^@|180| ^B| ^@| ^@| ^Q| ^A| ^@| ^@|
ALT |NUL|NUL|EOT|NUL|NUL|NUL|SOH|NUL|180|STX|NUL|NUL|DC1|SOH|NUL|NUL|
SYM |   |   |   |   |   |   |   |   |   |   |   |   |   |   |   |   |
```

Start Address ← | Length in Bytes | Section Type Code ← | Start Address | Length in Bytes →

Section 3 Description →

```
BYTE| 96| 97| 98| 99|100|101|102|103|104|105|106|107|108|109|110|111|
HEX | 11| 00| C5| 03| 00| 00| 01| 00| 00| 00| 0B| 00| C6| 03| 00| 00|
DEC | 17| 0 |197| 3 | 0 | 0 | 1 | 0 | 0 | 0 | 11| 0 |198| 3 | 0 | 0 |
ASC | ^Q| ^@|197| ^C| ^@| ^@| ^A| ^@| ^@| ^@| ^K| ^@|198| ^C| ^@| ^@|
ALT |DC1|NUL|197|ETX|NUL|NUL|SOH|NUL|NUL|NUL| VT|NUL|198|ETX|NUL|NUL|
SYM |   |   |   |   |   |   |   |   |   |   |   |   |   |   |   |   |
```

Type Code | Start Address | Length | Type Code | Start

```
BYTE|112|113|114|115|116|117|118|119|120|121|122|123|124|125|126|127|
HEX | 08| 00| 00| 00| 15| 00| CE| 03| 00| 00| 12| 00| 00| 00| 05| 00|
DEC | 8 | 0 | 0 | 0 | 21| 0 |206| 3 | 0 | 0 | 18| 0 | 0 | 0 | 5 | 0 |
ASC | ^H| ^@| ^@| ^@| ^U| ^@|206| ^C| ^@| ^@| ^R| ^@| ^@| ^@| ^E| ^@|
ALT | BS|NUL|NUL|NUL|NAK|NUL|206|ETX|NUL|NUL|DC2|NUL|NUL|NUL|ENO|NUL|
SYM |   |   |   |   |   |   |   |   |   |   |   |   |   |   |   |   |
```

Length | Type Code | Start | Length | Type Code

```
BYTE|128|129|130|131|132|133|134|135|136|137|138|139|140|141|142|143|
HEX | E0| 03| 00| 00| E0| 00| 00| 00| 18| 00| C0| 04| 00| 00| 0A| 00|
DEC |224| 3 | 0 | 0 |224| 0 | 0 | 0 | 24| 0 |192| 4 | 0 | 0 | 10| 0 |
ASC |224| ^C| ^@| ^@|224| ^@| ^@| ^@| ^X| ^@|192| ^D| ^@| ^@| ^J| ^@|
ALT |224|ETX|NUL|NUL|224|NUL|NUL|NUL|CAN|NUL|192|EOT|NUL|NUL| LF|NUL|
SYM |   |   |   |   |   |   |   |   |   |   |   |   |   |   |   |   |
```

Start | Length | Type Code | Start | Length →

```
BYTE|144|145|146|147|148|149|150|151|152|153|154|155|156|157|158|159|
HEX | 00| 00| 0C| 00| CA| 04| 00| 00| 54| 00| 00| 00| 0D| 00| 1E| 05|
DEC | 0 | 0 | 12| 0 |202| 4 | 0 | 0 | 84| 0 | 0 | 0 | 13| 0 | 30| 5 |
ASC | ^@| ^@| ^L| ^@|202| ^D| ^@| ^@| T | ^@| ^@| ^@| ^M| ^@| ^^| ^E|
ALT |NUL|NUL| FF|NUL|202|EOT|NUL|NUL| T |NUL|NUL|NUL| CR|NUL| RS|ENO|
SYM |   |   |   |   |   |   |   |   |   |   |   |   |   |   |   |   |
```

Length | Type Code | Start | Length | Type Code | Start →

```
BYTE|160|161|162|163|164|165|166|167|168|169|170|171|172|173|174|175|
HEX | 00| 00| 0A| 01| 00| 00| 0E| 00| 28| 06| 00| 00| 00| 00| 00| 00|
DEC | 0 | 0 | 10| 1 | 0 | 0 | 14| 0 | 40| 6 | 0 | 0 | 0 | 0 | 0 | 0 |
ASC | ^@| ^@| ^J| ^A| ^@| ^@| ^N| ^@| ( | ^F| ^@| ^@| ^@| ^@| ^@| ^@|
ALT |NUL|NUL| LF|SOH|NUL|NUL| SO|NUL| ( |ACK|NUL|NUL|NUL|NUL|NUL|NUL|
SYM |   |   |   |   |   |   |   |   |   |   |   |   |   |   |   |   |
```

Start ← | Length | Type Code | Start | Length

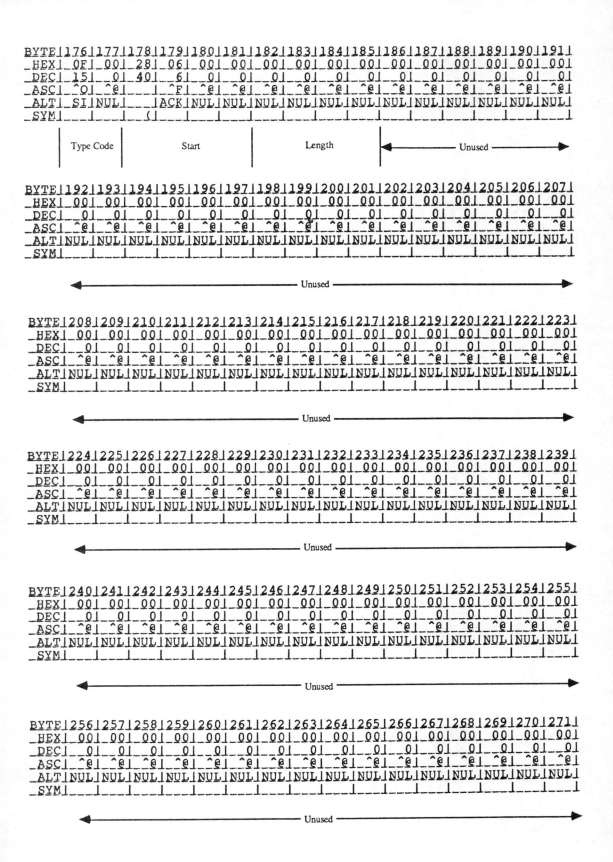

```
BYTE|176|177|178|179|180|181|182|183|184|185|186|187|188|189|190|191|
 HEX| 0F| 00| 28| 06| 00| 00| 00| 00| 00| 00| 00| 00| 00| 00| 00| 00|
 DEC| 15|  0| 40|  6|  0|  0|  0|  0|  0|  0|  0|  0|  0|  0|  0|  0|
 ASC| ^O| ^@|   | ^F| ^@| ^@| ^@| ^@| ^@| ^@| ^@| ^@| ^@| ^@| ^@| ^@|
 ALT| SI|NUL|   |ACK|NUL|NUL|NUL|NUL|NUL|NUL|NUL|NUL|NUL|NUL|NUL|NUL|
 SYM|   |   | ( |   |   |   |   |   |   |   |   |   |   |   |   |   |
```
| Type Code | Start | Length |◄——— Unused ———►|

```
BYTE|192|193|194|195|196|197|198|199|200|201|202|203|204|205|206|207|
 HEX| 00| 00| 00| 00| 00| 00| 00| 00| 00| 00| 00| 00| 00| 00| 00| 00|
 DEC|  0|  0|  0|  0|  0|  0|  0|  0|  0|  0|  0|  0|  0|  0|  0|  0|
 ASC| ^@| ^@| ^@| ^@| ^@| ^@| ^@| ^@| ^@| ^@| ^@| ^@| ^@| ^@| ^@| ^@|
 ALT|NUL|NUL|NUL|NUL|NUL|NUL|NUL|NUL|NUL|NUL|NUL|NUL|NUL|NUL|NUL|NUL|
 SYM|   |   |   |   |   |   |   |   |   |   |   |   |   |   |   |   |
```
◄————————————————————————— Unused —————————————————————————►

```
BYTE|208|209|210|211|212|213|214|215|216|217|218|219|220|221|222|223|
 HEX| 00| 00| 00| 00| 00| 00| 00| 00| 00| 00| 00| 00| 00| 00| 00| 00|
 DEC|  0|  0|  0|  0|  0|  0|  0|  0|  0|  0|  0|  0|  0|  0|  0|  0|
 ASC| ^@| ^@| ^@| ^@| ^@| ^@| ^@| ^@| ^@| ^@| ^@| ^@| ^@| ^@| ^@| ^@|
 ALT|NUL|NUL|NUL|NUL|NUL|NUL|NUL|NUL|NUL|NUL|NUL|NUL|NUL|NUL|NUL|NUL|
 SYM|   |   |   |   |   |   |   |   |   |   |   |   |   |   |   |   |
```
◄————————————————————————— Unused —————————————————————————►

```
BYTE|224|225|226|227|228|229|230|231|232|233|234|235|236|237|238|239|
 HEX| 00| 00| 00| 00| 00| 00| 00| 00| 00| 00| 00| 00| 00| 00| 00| 00|
 DEC|  0|  0|  0|  0|  0|  0|  0|  0|  0|  0|  0|  0|  0|  0|  0|  0|
 ASC| ^@| ^@| ^@| ^@| ^@| ^@| ^@| ^@| ^@| ^@| ^@| ^@| ^@| ^@| ^@| ^@|
 ALT|NUL|NUL|NUL|NUL|NUL|NUL|NUL|NUL|NUL|NUL|NUL|NUL|NUL|NUL|NUL|NUL|
 SYM|   |   |   |   |   |   |   |   |   |   |   |   |   |   |   |   |
```
◄————————————————————————— Unused —————————————————————————►

```
BYTE|240|241|242|243|244|245|246|247|248|249|250|251|252|253|254|255|
 HEX| 00| 00| 00| 00| 00| 00| 00| 00| 00| 00| 00| 00| 00| 00| 00| 00|
 DEC|  0|  0|  0|  0|  0|  0|  0|  0|  0|  0|  0|  0|  0|  0|  0|  0|
 ASC| ^@| ^@| ^@| ^@| ^@| ^@| ^@| ^@| ^@| ^@| ^@| ^@| ^@| ^@| ^@| ^@|
 ALT|NUL|NUL|NUL|NUL|NUL|NUL|NUL|NUL|NUL|NUL|NUL|NUL|NUL|NUL|NUL|NUL|
 SYM|   |   |   |   |   |   |   |   |   |   |   |   |   |   |   |   |
```
◄————————————————————————— Unused —————————————————————————►

```
BYTE|256|257|258|259|260|261|262|263|264|265|266|267|268|269|270|271|
 HEX| 00| 00| 00| 00| 00| 00| 00| 00| 00| 00| 00| 00| 00| 00| 00| 00|
 DEC|  0|  0|  0|  0|  0|  0|  0|  0|  0|  0|  0|  0|  0|  0|  0|  0|
 ASC| ^@| ^@| ^@| ^@| ^@| ^@| ^@| ^@| ^@| ^@| ^@| ^@| ^@| ^@| ^@| ^@|
 ALT|NUL|NUL|NUL|NUL|NUL|NUL|NUL|NUL|NUL|NUL|NUL|NUL|NUL|NUL|NUL|NUL|
 SYM|   |   |   |   |   |   |   |   |   |   |   |   |   |   |   |   |
```
◄————————————————————————— Unused —————————————————————————►

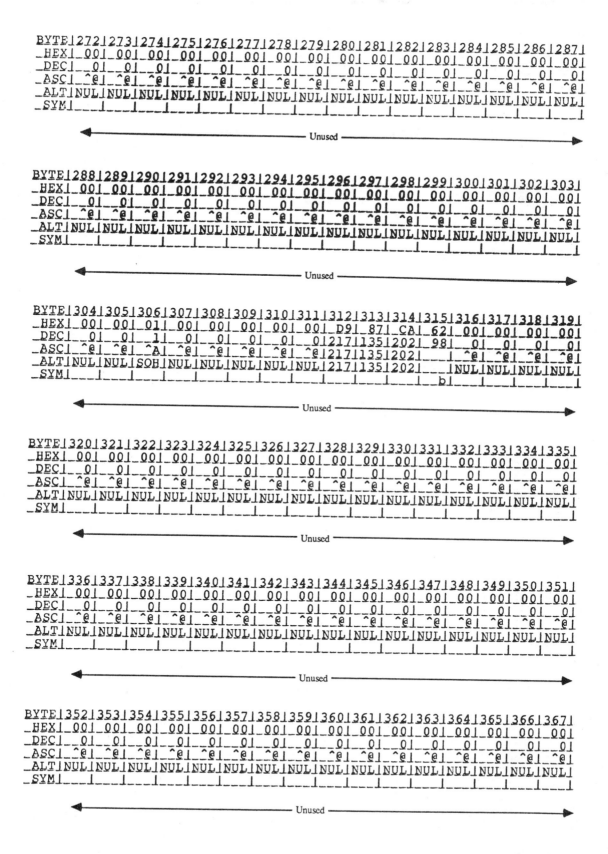

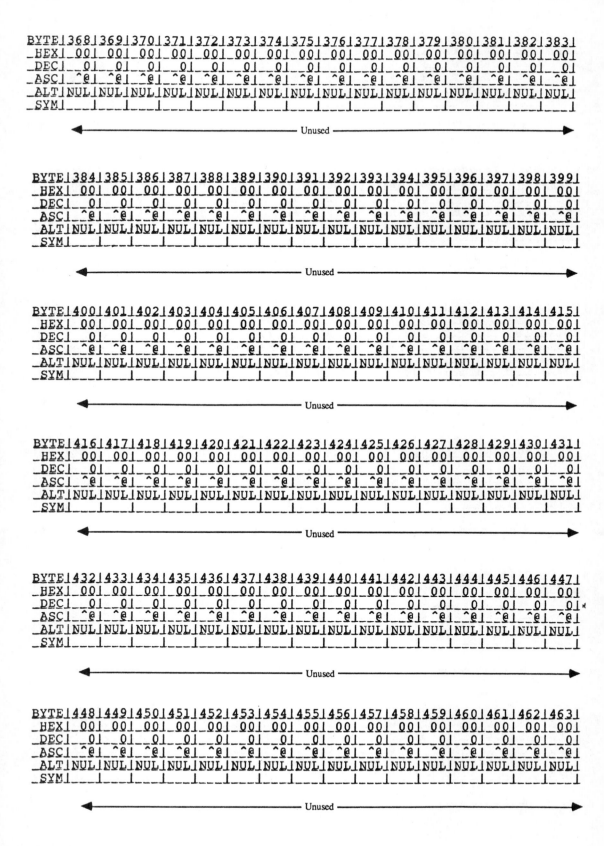

BYTE|368|369|370|371|372|373|374|375|376|377|378|379|380|381|382|383|
_HEX|_00|_00|_00|_00|_00|_00|_00|_00|_00|_00|_00|_00|_00|_00|_00|_00|
_DEC|__0|__0|__0|__0|__0|__0|__0|__0|__0|__0|__0|__0|__0|__0|__0|__0|
ASC|^@|_^@|_^@|_^@|_^@|_^@|_^@|_^@|_^@|_^@|_^@|_^@|_^@|_^@|_^@|_^@|
_ALT|NUL|NUL|NUL|NUL|NUL|NUL|NUL|NUL|NUL|NUL|NUL|NUL|NUL|NUL|NUL|
_SYM|___|___|___|___|___|___|___|___|___|___|___|___|___|___|___|___|

◄─────────────────────── Unused ───────────────────────►

BYTE|384|385|386|387|388|389|390|391|392|393|394|395|396|397|398|399|
_HEX|_00|_00|_00|_00|_00|_00|_00|_00|_00|_00|_00|_00|_00|_00|_00|_00|
_DEC|__0|__0|__0|__0|__0|__0|__0|__0|__0|__0|__0|__0|__0|__0|__0|__0|
ASC|^@|_^@|_^@|_^@|_^@|_^@|_^@|_^@|_^@|_^@|_^@|_^@|_^@|_^@|_^@|_^@|
_ALT|NUL|NUL|NUL|NUL|NUL|NUL|NUL|NUL|NUL|NUL|NUL|NUL|NUL|NUL|NUL|
_SYM|___|___|___|___|___|___|___|___|___|___|___|___|___|___|___|___|

◄─────────────────────── Unused ───────────────────────►

BYTE|400|401|402|403|404|405|406|407|408|409|410|411|412|413|414|415|
_HEX|_00|_00|_00|_00|_00|_00|_00|_00|_00|_00|_00|_00|_00|_00|_00|_00|
_DEC|__0|__0|__0|__0|__0|__0|__0|__0|__0|__0|__0|__0|__0|__0|__0|__0|
ASC|^@|_^@|_^@|_^@|_^@|_^@|_^@|_^@|_^@|_^@|_^@|_^@|_^@|_^@|_^@|_^@|
_ALT|NUL|NUL|NUL|NUL|NUL|NUL|NUL|NUL|NUL|NUL|NUL|NUL|NUL|NUL|NUL|
_SYM|___|___|___|___|___|___|___|___|___|___|___|___|___|___|___|___|

◄─────────────────────── Unused ───────────────────────►

BYTE|416|417|418|419|420|421|422|423|424|425|426|427|428|429|430|431|
_HEX|_00|_00|_00|_00|_00|_00|_00|_00|_00|_00|_00|_00|_00|_00|_00|_00|
_DEC|__0|__0|__0|__0|__0|__0|__0|__0|__0|__0|__0|__0|__0|__0|__0|__0|
ASC|^@|_^@|_^@|_^@|_^@|_^@|_^@|_^@|_^@|_^@|_^@|_^@|_^@|_^@|_^@|_^@|
_ALT|NUL|NUL|NUL|NUL|NUL|NUL|NUL|NUL|NUL|NUL|NUL|NUL|NUL|NUL|NUL|
_SYM|___|___|___|___|___|___|___|___|___|___|___|___|___|___|___|___|

◄─────────────────────── Unused ───────────────────────►

BYTE|432|433|434|435|436|437|438|439|440|441|442|443|444|445|446|447|
_HEX|_00|_00|_00|_00|_00|_00|_00|_00|_00|_00|_00|_00|_00|_00|_00|_00|
_DEC|__0|__0|__0|__0|__0|__0|__0|__0|__0|__0|__0|__0|__0|__0|__0|__0|×
ASC|^@|_^@|_^@|_^@|_^@|_^@|_^@|_^@|_^@|_^@|_^@|_^@|_^@|_^@|_^@|_^@|
_ALT|NUL|NUL|NUL|NUL|NUL|NUL|NUL|NUL|NUL|NUL|NUL|NUL|NUL|NUL|NUL|
_SYM|___|___|___|___|___|___|___|___|___|___|___|___|___|___|___|___|

◄─────────────────────── Unused ───────────────────────►

BYTE|448|449|450|451|452|453|454|455|456|457|458|459|460|461|462|463|
_HEX|_00|_00|_00|_00|_00|_00|_00|_00|_00|_00|_00|_00|_00|_00|_00|_00|
_DEC|__0|__0|__0|__0|__0|__0|__0|__0|__0|__0|__0|__0|__0|__0|__0|__0|
ASC|^@|_^@|_^@|_^@|_^@|_^@|_^@|_^@|_^@|_^@|_^@|_^@|_^@|_^@|_^@|_^@|
_ALT|NUL|NUL|NUL|NUL|NUL|NUL|NUL|NUL|NUL|NUL|NUL|NUL|NUL|NUL|NUL|
_SYM|___|___|___|___|___|___|___|___|___|___|___|___|___|___|___|___|

◄─────────────────────── Unused ───────────────────────►

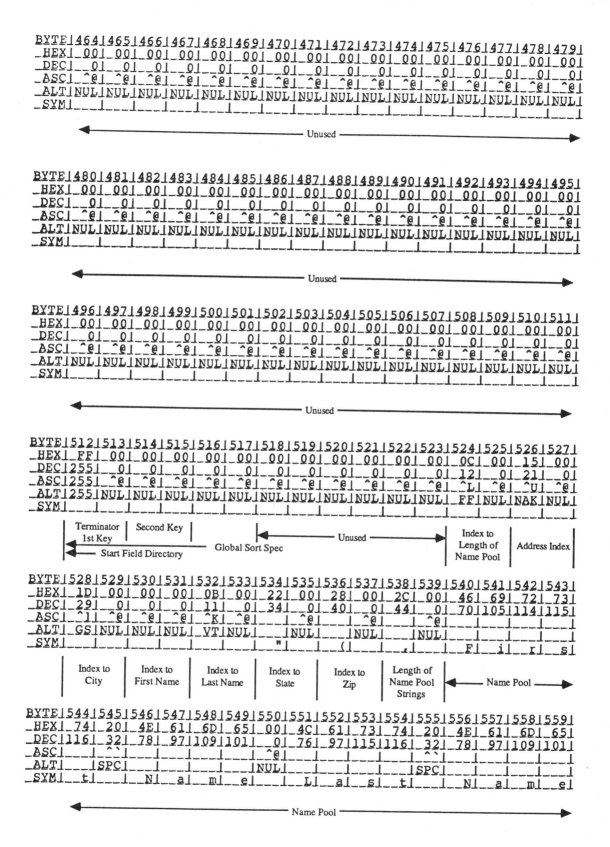

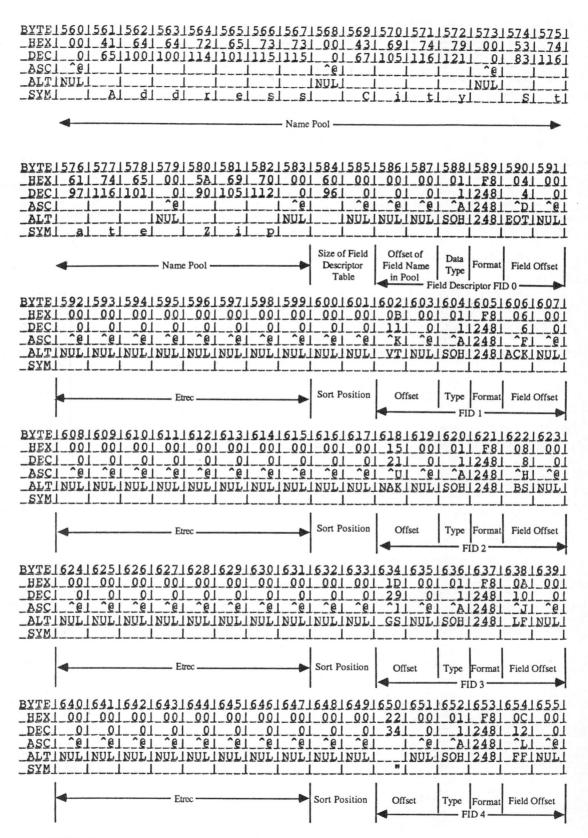

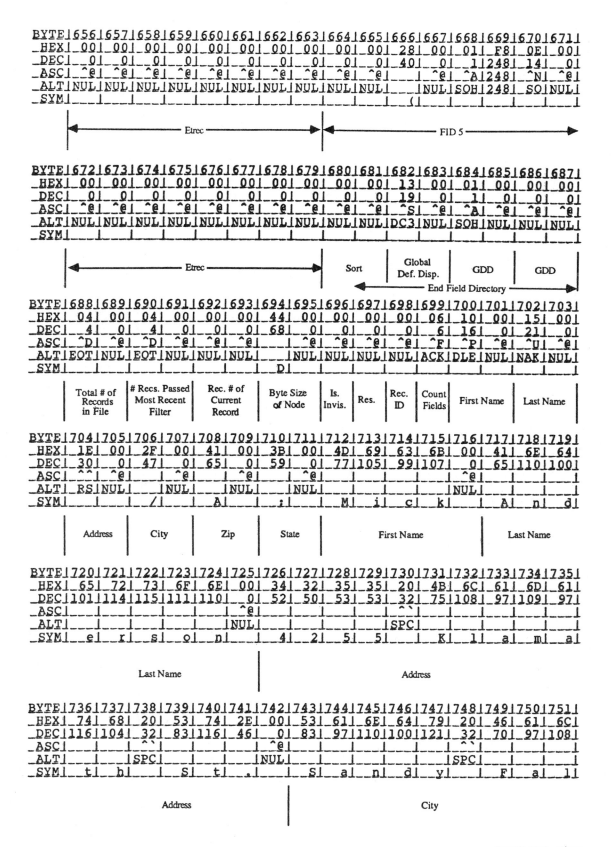

BYTE	656	657	658	659	660	661	662	663	664	665	666	667	668	669	670	671
HEX	00	00	00	00	00	00	00	00	00	00	28	00	01	F8	0E	00
DEC	0	0	0	0	0	0	0	0	0	0	40	0	1	248	14	0
ASC	^@	^@	^@	^@	^@	^@	^@	^@	^@	^@		^@	^A	248	^N	^@
ALT	NUL	NUL	NUL	NUL	NUL	NUL	NUL	NUL	NUL	NUL		NUL	SOH	248	SO	NUL
SYM											(					

← Etrec → | ← FID 5 →

BYTE	672	673	674	675	676	677	678	679	680	681	682	683	684	685	686	687
HEX	00	00	00	00	00	00	00	00	00	00	13	00	01	00	00	00
DEC	0	0	0	0	0	0	0	0	0	0	19	0	1	0	0	0
ASC	^@	^@	^@	^@	^@	^@	^@	^@	^@	^@	^S	^@	^A	^@	^@	^@
ALT	NUL	NUL	NUL	NUL	NUL	NUL	NUL	NUL	NUL	NUL	DC3	NUL	SOH	NUL	NUL	NUL
SYM																

← Etrec → | Sort | Global Def. Disp. | GDD | GDD
← End Field Directory →

BYTE	688	689	690	691	692	693	694	695	696	697	698	699	700	701	702	703
HEX	04	00	04	00	00	00	44	00	00	00	00	06	10	00	15	00
DEC	4	0	4	0	0	0	68	0	0	0	0	6	16	0	21	0
ASC	^D	^@	^D	^@	^@	^@		^@	^@	^@	^@	^F	^P	^@	^U	^@
ALT	EOT	NUL	EOT	NUL	NUL	NUL		NUL	NUL	NUL	NUL	ACK	DLE	NUL	NAK	NUL
SYM							D									

| Total # of Records in File | # Recs. Passed Most Recent Filter | Rec. # of Current Record | Byte Size of Node | Is. Invis. | Res. | Rec. ID | Count Fields | First Name | Last Name |

BYTE	704	705	706	707	708	709	710	711	712	713	714	715	716	717	718	719
HEX	1E	00	2F	00	41	00	3B	00	4D	69	63	6B	00	41	6E	64
DEC	30	0	47	0	65	0	59	0	77	105	99	107	0	65	110	100
ASC	^^	^@		^@		^@		^@					^@			
ALT	RS	NUL		NUL		NUL		NUL					NUL			
SYM			/		A		;		M	i	c	k		A	n	d

| Address | City | Zip | State | First Name | Last Name |

BYTE	720	721	722	723	724	725	726	727	728	729	730	731	732	733	734	735
HEX	65	72	73	6F	6E	00	34	32	35	35	20	4B	6C	61	6D	61
DEC	101	114	115	111	110	0	52	50	53	53	32	75	108	97	109	97
ASC						^@						^^				
ALT						NUL						SPC				
SYM	e	r	s	o	n		4	2	5	5		K	l	a	m	a

| Last Name | Address |

BYTE	736	737	738	739	740	741	742	743	744	745	746	747	748	749	750	751
HEX	74	68	20	53	74	2E	00	53	61	6E	64	79	20	46	61	6C
DEC	116	104	32	83	116	46	0	83	97	110	100	121	32	70	97	108
ASC			^^				^@						^^			
ALT			SPC				NUL						SPC			
SYM	t	h		S	t	.		S	a	n	d	y		F	a	l

| Address | City |

BYTE	752	753	754	755	756	757	758	759	760	761	762	763	764	765	766	767
HEX	6C	73	00	38	34	39	30	32	00	57	49	00	42	00	00	01
DEC	108	115	0	56	52	57	48	50	0	87	73	0	66	0	0	1
ASC			^@						^@			^@		^@	^@	^A
ALT			NUL						NUL			NUL		NUL	NUL	SOH
SYM	l	s		8	4	9	0	2		W	I		B			

Field labels: **Zip** — **State** — **Byte Size of Rec. 2** | **Is. Invis.** | **Rec. ID**

BYTE	768	769	770	771	772	773	774	775	776	777	778	779	780	781	782	783
HEX	00	06	10	00	17	00	21	00	2E	00	3F	00	39	00	53	61
DEC	0	6	16	0	23	0	33	0	46	0	63	0	57	0	83	97
ASC	^@	^F	^P	^@	^W	^@		^@		^@		^@		^@		
ALT	NUL	ACK	DLE	NUL	ETB	NUL		NUL		NUL		NUL		NUL		
SYM							1		.		?		9		S	a

Field labels: **Record ID** (←) | **Field Count** | **Offset FID 0** | **Offset FID 1** | **Offset FID 2** | **Offset FID 3** | **Offset FID 4** | **Offset FID 5**

BYTE	784	785	786	787	788	789	790	791	792	793	794	795	796	797	798	799
HEX	6D	75	65	6C	00	42	61	6C	64	72	69	64	67	65	00	36
DEC	109	117	101	108	0	66	97	108	100	114	105	100	103	101	0	54
ASC					^@										^@	
ALT					NUL										NUL	
SYM	m	u	e	l		B	a	l	d	r	i	d	g	e		6

BYTE	800	801	802	803	804	805	806	807	808	809	810	811	812	813	814	815
HEX	34	32	20	4D	61	69	6E	20	53	74	2E	00	42	72	69	64
DEC	52	50	32	77	97	105	110	32	83	116	46	0	66	114	105	100
ASC			^`					^`				^@				
ALT			SPC					SPC				NUL				
SYM	4	2		M	a	i	n		S	t	.		B	r	i	d

BYTE	816	817	818	819	820	821	822	823	824	825	826	827	828	829	830	831
HEX	67	65	70	6F	72	74	00	36	30	35	30	36	00	4E	45	00
DEC	103	101	112	111	114	116	0	54	48	53	48	54	0	78	69	0
ASC							^@						^@			^@
ALT							NUL						NUL			NUL
SYM	g	e	p	o	r	t		6	0	5	0	6		N	E	

End of Record 2 ────────►

BYTE	832	833	834	835	836	837	838	839	840	841	842	843	844	845	846	847
HEX	41	00	00	02	00	06	10	00	14	00	1B	00	2E	00	38	00
DEC	65	0	0	2	0	6	16	0	20	0	27	0	46	0	56	0
ASC		^@	^@	^B	^@	^F	^P	^@	^T	^@	^[	^@		^@		^@
ALT		NUL	NUL	STX	NUL	ACK	DLE	NUL	DC4	NUL	ESC	NUL		NUL		NUL
SYM	A												.		8	

```
BYTE|848|849|850|851|852|853|854|855|856|857|858|859|860|861|862|863|
HEX| 3B| 00| 41| 6E| 6E| 00| 43| 6F| 76| 69| 6E| 61| 00| 35| 34| 34|
DEC| 59|  0| 65|110|110|  0| 67|111|118|105|110| 97|  0| 35| 34| 34|
ASC|   |   |^@|   |   |   |^@|   |   |   |   |   |   |^@|   |   |
ALT|   |NUL|   |   |   |NUL|   |   |   |   |   |   |NUL|   |   |
SYM| ;|   |  A|  n|  n|   |  C|  o|  v|  i|  n|  a|   |  5|  4|  4|
```

```
BYTE|864|865|866|867|868|869|870|871|872|873|874|875|876|877|878|879|
HEX| 30| 20| 4B| 6E| 6F| 78| 76| 69| 6C| 6C| 65| 20| 52| 64| 2E| 00|
DEC| 48| 32| 75|110|111|120|118|105|108|108|101| 32| 82|100| 46|  0|
ASC|   |^^|   |   |   |   |   |   |   |   |   |   |^^|   |   |^@|
ALT|   |SPC|   | .|   |   |   |   |   |   |   |   |SPC|   |   |NUL|
SYM|  0|   |  K|  n|  o|  x|  v|  i|  l|  l|  e|   |  R|  d|  .|
```

```
BYTE|880|881|882|883|884|885|886|887|888|889|890|891|892|893|894|895|
HEX| 4B| 6E| 6F| 78| 76| 69| 6C| 6C| 65| 00| 54| 4E| 00| 34| 33| 39|
DEC| 75|110|111|120|118|105|108|108|101|  0| 84| 78|  0| 52| 51| 57|
ASC|   |   |   |   |   |   |   |   |   |^@|   |   |^@|   |   |
ALT|   |   |   |   |   |   |   |   |   |NUL|   |NUL|   |   |
SYM|  K|  n|  o|  x|  v|  i|  l|  l|  e|   |  T|  N|   |  4|  3|  9|
```

```
BYTE|896|897|898|899|900|901|902|903|904|905|906|907|908|909|910|911|
HEX| 30| 36| 00| 40| 00| 00| 03| 00| 06| 10| 00| 16| 00| 2A| 00| 1F|
DEC| 48| 54|  0| 64|  0|  0|  3|  0|  6| 16|  0| 22|  0| 42|  0| 31|
ASC|   |   |^@|   |^@|^@|^C|^@|^F|^P|^@|^V|^@|   |^@|^_|
ALT|   |NUL|   |NUL|NUL|ETX|NUL|ACK|DLE|NUL|SYN|NUL|   |NUL|US|
SYM|  0|  6|   |  @|   |   |   |   |   |   |   |   |   |  *|   |
```

```
BYTE|912|913|914|915|916|917|918|919|920|921|922|923|924|925|926|927|
HEX| 00| 27| 00| 3A| 00| 53| 61| 6C| 6C| 79| 00| 52| 61| 6E| 64| 6F|
DEC|  0| 39|  0| 58|  0| 83| 97|108|108|121|  0| 82| 97|110|100|111|
ASC|^@|   |^@|   |^@|   |   |   |   |   |^@|   |   |   |   |
ALT|NUL|   |NUL|   |NUL|   |   |   |   |   |NUL|   |   |   |   |
SYM|   | '|   | :|   |  S|  a|  l|  l|  y|   |  R|  a|  n|  d|  o|
```

```
BYTE|928|929|930|931|932|933|934|935|936|937|938|939|940|941|942|943|
HEX| 6C| 70| 68| 00| 48| 61| 6D| 70| 74| 6F| 6E| 00| 53| 43| 00| 31|
DEC|108|112|104|  0| 72| 97|109|112|116|111|110|  0| 83| 67|  0| 49|
ASC|   |   |   |^@|   |   |   |   |   |   |   |^@|   |   |^@|
ALT|   |   |NUL|   |   |   |   |   |   |   |NUL|   |NUL|   |
SYM|  l|  p|  h|   |  H|  a|  m|  p|  t|  o|  n|   |  S|  C|   |  1|
```

```
BYTE|944|945|946|947|948|949|950|951|952|953|954|955|956|957|958|959|
_HEX| 34| 36| 36| 38| 20| 47| 72| 61| 6E| 64| 20| 41| 76| 65| 00| 33|
_DEC| 52| 54| 54| 56| 32| 71|114| 97|110|100| 32| 65|118|101|  0| 51|
_ASC|___|___|___|___| ^^|___|___|___|___|___|___| ^`|___|___| ^@|___|
_ALT|___|___|___|SPC|___|___|___|___|___|SPC|___|___|___|NUL|___|___|
_SYM|  4|  6|  6|  8|___|  G|  r|  a|  n|  d|___|  A|  v|  e|___|  3|
```

```
BYTE|960|961|962|963|964|965|966|967|968|969|970|971|972|973|974|975|
_HEX| 39| 39| 31| 32| 00| 00| 00| 00| 00| 00| 00| 00| 00| 00| 01| 00|
_DEC| 57| 57| 49| 50|  0|  0|  0|  0|  0|  0|  0|  0|  0|  0|  1|  0|
_ASC|___|___|___|___| ^@| ^@| ^@| ^@| ^@| ^@| ^@| ^@| ^@| ^@| ^A| ^@|
_ALT|___|___|___|___|NUL|NUL|NUL|NUL|NUL|NUL|NUL|NUL|NUL|NUL|SOH|NUL|
_SYM|  9|  9|  1|  2|___|___|___|___|___|___|___|___|___|___|___|___|
```

End Data Records ───────────────► | Gl. Filter | ◄─── Global Models ────► | ◄───►

◄──────── Var. Cen. Text Pool (if any) Here

```
BYTE|976|977|978|979|980|981|982|983|984|985|986|987|988|989|990|991|
_HEX| 00| 00| 04| 00| 00| 00| 00| 00| 00| 00| 00| 00| 00| 00| 00| 00|
_DEC|  0|  0|  4|  0|  0|  0|  0|  0|  0|  0|  0|  0|  0|  0|  0|  0|
_ASC| ^@| ^@| ^D| ^@| ^@| ^@| ^@| ^@| ^@| ^@| ^@| ^@| ^@| ^@| ^@| ^@|
_ALT|NUL|NUL|EOT|NUL|NUL|NUL|NUL|NUL|NUL|NUL|NUL|NUL|NUL|NUL|NUL|NUL|
_SYM|___|___|___|___|___|___|___|___|___|___|___|___|___|___|___|___|
```

◄──────────── Global Model Override Vectors ────────────►

```
BYTE|992|993|994|995|996|997|998|999|  0|  1|  2|  3|  4|  5|  6|  7|
_HEX| 22| 00| 01| 00| 00| 00| 01| 00| 00| 00| FF| FF| 00| 00| 00| 00|
_DEC| 34|  0|  1|  0|  0|  0|  1|  0|  0|  0|255|255|  0|  0|  0|  0|
_ASC|___| ^@| ^A| ^@| ^@| ^@| ^A| ^@| ^@| ^@|255|255| ^@| ^@| ^@| ^@|
_ALT|___|NUL|SOH|NUL|NUL|NUL|SOH|NUL|NUL|NUL|255|255|NUL|NUL|NUL|NUL|
_SYM|  "|___|___|___|___|___|___|___|___|___|___|___|___|___|___|___|
```

◄──────────────── View Manager State ────────────────►

```
BYTE|  8|  9| 10| 11| 12| 13| 14| 15| 16| 17| 18| 19| 20| 21| 22| 23|
_HEX| 00| 00| 00| 00| 00| 00| 00| 00| 00| 00| 00| 00| 00| 00| 00| 00|
_DEC|  0|  0|  0|  0|  0|  0|  0|  0|  0|  0|  0|  0|  0|  0|  0|  0|
_ASC| ^@| ^@| ^@| ^@| ^@| ^@| ^@| ^@| ^@| ^@| ^@| ^@| ^@| ^@| ^@| ^@|
_ALT|NUL|NUL|NUL|NUL|NUL|NUL|NUL|NUL|NUL|NUL|NUL|NUL|NUL|NUL|NUL|NUL|
_SYM|___|___|___|___|___|___|___|___|___|___|___|___|___|___|___|___|
```

◄──────────────── View Manager State ────────────────►

```
BYTE| 24| 25| 26| 27| 28| 29| 30| 31| 32| 33| 34| 35| 36| 37| 38| 39|
_HEX| 00| 00| 00| 00| 90| 00| 00| 00| 01| 00| 00| 00| 15| 00| 80| 02|
_DEC|  0|  0|  0|  0|144|  0|  0|  0|  1|  0|  0|  0| 21|  0|128|  2|
_ASC| ^@| ^@| ^@| ^@|144| ^@| ^@| ^@| ^A| ^@| ^@| ^@| ^U| ^@|128| ^B|
_ALT|NUL|NUL|NUL|NUL|144|NUL|NUL|NUL|SOH|NUL|NUL|NUL|NAK|NUL|128|STX|
_SYM|___|___|___|___|___|___|___|___|___|___|___|___|___|___|___|___|
```

◄──────────────── View Manager State ────────────────►

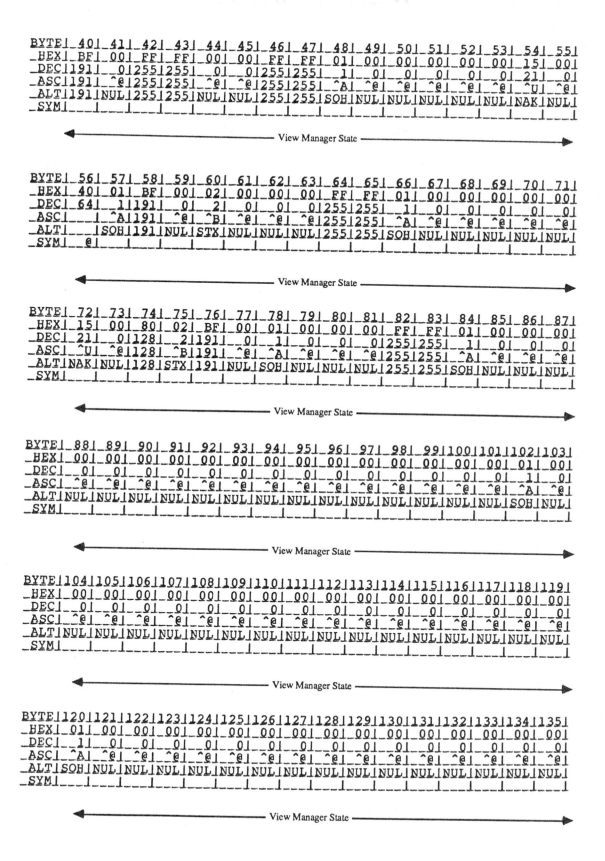

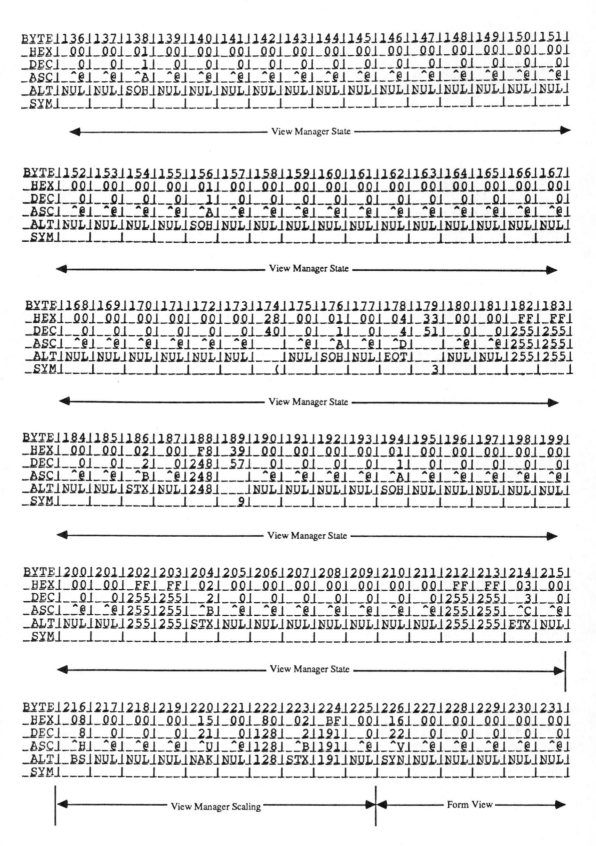

```
BYTE|136|137|138|139|140|141|142|143|144|145|146|147|148|149|150|151|
HEX | 00| 00| 01| 00| 00| 00| 00| 00| 00| 00| 00| 00| 00| 00| 00| 00|
DEC |  0|  0|  1|  0|  0|  0|  0|  0|  0|  0|  0|  0|  0|  0|  0|  0|
ASC | ^@| ^@| ^A| ^@| ^@| ^@| ^@| ^@| ^@| ^@| ^@| ^@| ^@| ^@| ^@| ^@|
ALT |NUL|NUL|SOH|NUL|NUL|NUL|NUL|NUL|NUL|NUL|NUL|NUL|NUL|NUL|NUL|NUL|
SYM |   |   |   |   |   |   |   |   |   |   |   |   |   |   |   |   |
```
← ─────────────── View Manager State ─────────────── →

```
BYTE|152|153|154|155|156|157|158|159|160|161|162|163|164|165|166|167|
HEX | 00| 00| 00| 00| 01| 00| 00| 00| 00| 00| 00| 00| 00| 00| 00| 00|
DEC |  0|  0|  0|  0|  1|  0|  0|  0|  0|  0|  0|  0|  0|  0|  0|  0|
ASC | ^@| ^@| ^@| ^@| ^A| ^@| ^@| ^@| ^@| ^@| ^@| ^@| ^@| ^@| ^@| ^@|
ALT |NUL|NUL|NUL|NUL|SOH|NUL|NUL|NUL|NUL|NUL|NUL|NUL|NUL|NUL|NUL|NUL|
SYM |   |   |   |   |   |   |   |   |   |   |   |   |   |   |   |   |
```
← ─────────────── View Manager State ─────────────── →

```
BYTE|168|169|170|171|172|173|174|175|176|177|178|179|180|181|182|183|
HEX | 00| 00| 00| 00| 00| 00| 28| 00| 01| 00| 04| 33| 00| 00| FF| FF|
DEC |  0|  0|  0|  0|  0|  0| 40|  0|  1|  0|  4| 51|  0|  0|255|255|
ASC | ^@| ^@| ^@| ^@| ^@| ^@|  (| ^@| ^A| ^@| ^D|  3| ^@| ^@|255|255|
ALT |NUL|NUL|NUL|NUL|NUL|NUL|   |NUL|SOH|NUL|EOT|   |NUL|NUL|255|255|
SYM |   |   |   |   |   |   | ( |   |   |   |   | 3 |   |   |   |   |
```
← ─────────────── View Manager State ─────────────── →

```
BYTE|184|185|186|187|188|189|190|191|192|193|194|195|196|197|198|199|
HEX | 00| 00| 02| 00| F8| 39| 00| 00| 00| 00| 01| 00| 00| 00| 00| 00|
DEC |  0|  0|  2|  0|248| 57|  0|  0|  0|  0|  1|  0|  0|  0|  0|  0|
ASC | ^@| ^@| ^B| ^@|248|   | ^@| ^@| ^@| ^@| ^A| ^@| ^@| ^@| ^@| ^@|
ALT |NUL|NUL|STX|NUL|248|   |NUL|NUL|NUL|NUL|SOH|NUL|NUL|NUL|NUL|NUL|
SYM |   |   |   |   |   | 9 |   |   |   |   |   |   |   |   |   |   |
```
← ─────────────── View Manager State ─────────────── →

```
BYTE|200|201|202|203|204|205|206|207|208|209|210|211|212|213|214|215|
HEX | 00| 00| FF| FF| 02| 00| 00| 00| 00| 00| 00| 00| FF| FF| 03| 00|
DEC |  0|  0|255|255|  2|  0|  0|  0|  0|  0|  0|  0|255|255|  3|  0|
ASC | ^@| ^@|255|255| ^B| ^@| ^@| ^@| ^@| ^@| ^@| ^@|255|255| ^C| ^@|
ALT |NUL|NUL|255|255|STX|NUL|NUL|NUL|NUL|NUL|NUL|NUL|255|255|ETX|NUL|
SYM |   |   |   |   |   |   |   |   |   |   |   |   |   |   |   |   |
```
← ─────────────── View Manager State ─────────────── |

```
BYTE|216|217|218|219|220|221|222|223|224|225|226|227|228|229|230|231|
HEX | 08| 00| 00| 00| 15| 00| 80| 02| BF| 00| 16| 00| 00| 00| 00| 00|
DEC |  8|  0|  0|  0| 21|  0|128|  2|191|  0| 22|  0|  0|  0|  0|  0|
ASC | ^H| ^@| ^@| ^@| ^U| ^@|128| ^B|191| ^@| ^V| ^@| ^@| ^@| ^@| ^@|
ALT | BS|NUL|NUL|NUL|NAK|NUL|128|STX|191|NUL|SYN|NUL|NUL|NUL|NUL|NUL|
SYM |   |   |   |   |   |   |   |   |   |   |   |   |   |   |   |   |
```
| ← ────── View Manager Scaling ────── → | ← ── Form View ── → |

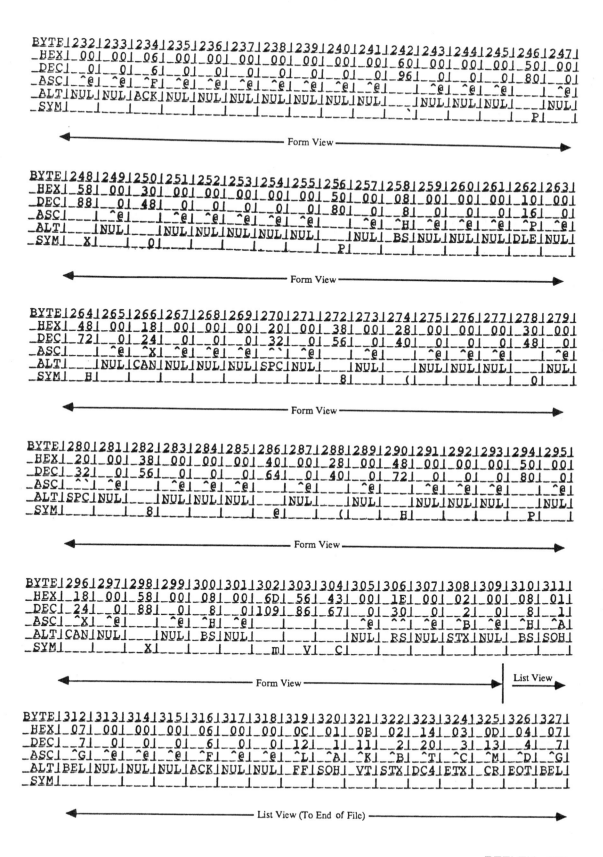

Form View

Form View

Form View

Form View

Form View — List View

List View (To End of File)

```
BYTE|328|329|330|331|332|333|334|335|336|337|338|339|340|341|342|343|
_HEX| 05| 0A| FF| 08| 00| 00| 00| 00| 00| 00| 00| 00| 00| 00| 00| 00|
_DEC|  5| 10|255|  8|  0|  0|  0|  0|  0|  0|  0|  0|  0|  0|  0|  0|
_ASC| ^E| ^J|255| ^H| ^@| ^@| ^@| ^@| ^@| ^@| ^@| ^@| ^@| ^@| ^@| ^@|
_ALT|ENQ| LF|255| BS|NUL|NUL|NUL|NUL|NUL|NUL|NUL|NUL|NUL|NUL|NUL|NUL|
_SYM|___|___|___|___|___|___|___|___|___|___|___|___|___|___|___|___|


BYTE|344|345|346|347|348|349|350|351|352|353|354|355|356|357|358|359|
_HEX| 00| 00| 00| 00| 00| 00| 00| 00| 00| 00| 00| 00| 00| 00| 00| 00|
_DEC|  0|  0|  0|  0|  0|  0|  0|  0|  0|  0|  0|  0|  0|  0|  0|  0|
_ASC| ^@| ^@| ^@| ^@| ^@| ^@| ^@| ^@| ^@| ^@| ^@| ^@| ^@| ^@| ^@| ^@|
_ALT|NUL|NUL|NUL|NUL|NUL|NUL|NUL|NUL|NUL|NUL|NUL|NUL|NUL|NUL|NUL|NUL|
_SYM|___|___|___|___|___|___|___|___|___|___|___|___|___|___|___|___|


BYTE|360|361|362|363|364|365|366|367|368|369|370|371|372|373|374|375|
_HEX| 00| 00| 00| 00| 00| 00| 00| 00| 00| 00| 00| 00| 00| 00| 00| 00|
_DEC|  0|  0|  0|  0|  0|  0|  0|  0|  0|  0|  0|  0|  0|  0|  0|  0|
_ASC| ^@| ^@| ^@| ^@| ^@| ^@| ^@| ^@| ^@| ^@| ^@| ^@| ^@| ^@| ^@| ^@|
_ALT|NUL|NUL|NUL|NUL|NUL|NUL|NUL|NUL|NUL|NUL|NUL|NUL|NUL|NUL|NUL|NUL|
_SYM|___|___|___|___|___|___|___|___|___|___|___|___|___|___|___|___|


BYTE|376|377|378|379|380|381|382|383|384|385|386|387|388|389|390|391|
_HEX| 00| 00| 00| 00| 00| 00| 00| 00| 00| 00| 00| 00| 00| 00| 00| 00|
_DEC|  0|  0|  0|  0|  0|  0|  0|  0|  0|  0|  0|  0|  0|  0|  0|  0|
_ASC| ^@| ^@| ^@| ^@| ^@| ^@| ^@| ^@| ^@| ^@| ^@| ^@| ^@| ^@| ^@| ^@|
_ALT|NUL|NUL|NUL|NUL|NUL|NUL|NUL|NUL|NUL|NUL|NUL|NUL|NUL|NUL|NUL|NUL|
_SYM|___|___|___|___|___|___|___|___|___|___|___|___|___|___|___|___|


BYTE|392|393|394|395|396|397|398|399|400|401|402|403|404|405|406|407|
_HEX| 00| 00| 00| 00| 00| 00| 00| 00| 00| 00| 00| 00| 00| 00| 00| 00|
_DEC|  0|  0|  0|  0|  0|  0|  0|  0|  0|  0|  0|  0|  0|  0|  0|  0|
_ASC| ^@| ^@| ^@| ^@| ^@| ^@| ^@| ^@| ^@| ^@| ^@| ^@| ^@| ^@| ^@| ^@|
_ALT|NUL|NUL|NUL|NUL|NUL|NUL|NUL|NUL|NUL|NUL|NUL|NUL|NUL|NUL|NUL|NUL|
_SYM|___|___|___|___|___|___|___|___|___|___|___|___|___|___|___|___|


BYTE|408|409|410|411|412|413|414|415|416|417|418|419|420|421|422|423|
_HEX| 00| 00| 00| 00| 00| 00| 00| 00| 00| 00| 00| 00| 00| 00| 00| 00|
_DEC|  0|  0|  0|  0|  0|  0|  0|  0|  0|  0|  0|  0|  0|  0|  0|  0|
_ASC| ^@| ^@| ^@| ^@| ^@| ^@| ^@| ^@| ^@| ^@| ^@| ^@| ^@| ^@| ^@| ^@|
_ALT|NUL|NUL|NUL|NUL|NUL|NUL|NUL|NUL|NUL|NUL|NUL|NUL|NUL|NUL|NUL|NUL|
_SYM|___|___|___|___|___|___|___|___|___|___|___|___|___|___|___|___|
```

```
BYTE|424|425|426|427|428|429|430|431|432|433|434|435|436|437|438|439|
_HEX|_00|_00|_00|_00|_00|_00|_00|_00|_00|_00|_00|_00|_00|_00|_00|_00|
_DEC|__0|__0|__0|__0|__0|__0|__0|__0|__0|__0|__0|__0|__0|__0|__0|__0|
_ASC|_^@|_^@|_^@|_^@|_^@|_^@|_^@|_^@|_^@|_^@|_^@|_^@|_^@|_^@|_^@|_^@|
_ALT|NUL|NUL|NUL|NUL|NUL|NUL|NUL|NUL|NUL|NUL|NUL|NUL|NUL|NUL|NUL|NUL|
_SYM|___|___|___|___|___|___|___|___|___|___|___|___|___|___|___|___|


BYTE|440|441|442|443|444|445|446|447|448|449|450|451|452|453|454|455|
_HEX|_00|_00|_00|_00|_00|_00|_00|_00|_00|_00|_00|_00|_00|_00|_00|_00|
_DEC|__0|__0|__0|__0|__0|__0|__0|__0|__0|__0|__0|__0|__0|__0|__0|__0|
_ASC|_^@|_^@|_^@|_^@|_^@|_^@|_^@|_^@|_^@|_^@|_^@|_^@|_^@|_^@|_^@|_^@|
_ALT|NUL|NUL|NUL|NUL|NUL|NUL|NUL|NUL|NUL|NUL|NUL|NUL|NUL|NUL|NUL|
_SYM|___|___|___|___|___|___|___|___|___|___|___|___|___|___|___|


BYTE|456|457|458|459|460|461|462|463|464|465|466|467|468|469|470|471|
_HEX|_00|_00|_00|_00|_00|_00|_00|_00|_00|_00|_00|_00|_00|_00|_00|_00|
_DEC|__0|__0|__0|__0|__0|__0|__0|__0|__0|__0|__0|__0|__0|__0|__0|__0|
_ASC|_^@|_^@|_^@|_^@|_^@|_^@|_^@|_^@|_^@|_^@|_^@|_^@|_^@|_^@|_^@|_^@|
_ALT|NUL|NUL|NUL|NUL|NUL|NUL|NUL|NUL|NUL|NUL|NUL|NUL|NUL|NUL|NUL|
_SYM|___|___|___|___|___|___|___|___|___|___|___|___|___|___|___|


BYTE|472|473|474|475|476|477|478|479|480|481|482|483|484|485|486|487|
_HEX|_00|_00|_00|_00|_00|_00|_00|_00|_00|_00|_00|_00|_00|_00|_00|_00|
_DEC|__0|__0|__0|__0|__0|__0|__0|__0|__0|__0|__0|__0|__0|__0|__0|__0|
_ASC|_^@|_^@|_^@|_^@|_^@|_^@|_^@|_^@|_^@|_^@|_^@|_^@|_^@|_^@|_^@|_^@|
_ALT|NUL|NUL|NUL|NUL|NUL|NUL|NUL|NUL|NUL|NUL|NUL|NUL|NUL|NUL|NUL|
_SYM|___|___|___|___|___|___|___|___|___|___|___|___|___|___|___|


BYTE|488|489|490|491|492|493|494|495|496|497|498|499|500|501|502|503|
_HEX|_00|_00|_00|_00|_00|_00|_00|_00|_00|_00|_00|_00|_00|_00|_00|_00|
_DEC|__0|__0|__0|__0|__0|__0|__0|__0|__0|__0|__0|__0|__0|__0|__0|__0|
_ASC|_^@|_^@|_^@|_^@|_^@|_^@|_^@|_^@|_^@|_^@|_^@|_^@|_^@|_^@|_^@|_^@|
_ALT|NUL|NUL|NUL|NUL|NUL|NUL|NUL|NUL|NUL|NUL|NUL|NUL|NUL|NUL|NUL|
_SYM|___|___|___|___|___|___|___|___|___|___|___|___|___|___|___|


BYTE|504|505|506|507|508|509|510|511|512|513|514|515|516|517|518|519|
_HEX|_00|_00|_00|_00|_00|_00|_00|_00|_00|_00|_00|_00|_00|_00|_00|_00|
_DEC|__0|__0|__0|__0|__0|__0|__0|__0|__0|__0|__0|__0|__0|__0|__0|__0|
_ASC|_^@|_^@|_^@|_^@|_^@|_^@|_^@|_^@|_^@|_^@|_^@|_^@|_^@|_^@|_^@|_^@|
_ALT|NUL|NUL|NUL|NUL|NUL|NUL|NUL|NUL|NUL|NUL|NUL|NUL|NUL|NUL|NUL|
_SYM|___|___|___|___|___|___|___|___|___|___|___|___|___|___|___|
```

```
BYTE|520|521|522|523|524|525|526|527|528|529|530|531|532|533|534|535|
HEX | 00| 00| 00| 00| 00| 00| 00| 00| 00| 00| 00| 00| 00| 00| 00| 00|
DEC | 0| 0| 0| 0| 0| 0| 0| 0| 0| 0| 0| 0| 0| 0| 0| 0|
ASC | ^@| ^@| ^@| ^@| ^@| ^@| ^@| ^@| ^@| ^@| ^@| ^@| ^@| ^@| ^@| ^@|
ALT |NUL|NUL|NUL|NUL|NUL|NUL|NUL|NUL|NUL|NUL|NUL|NUL|NUL|NUL|NUL|NUL|
SYM |   |   |   |   |   |   |   |   |   |   |   |   |   |   |   |   |


BYTE|536|537|538|539|540|541|542|543|544|545|546|547|548|549|550|551|
HEX | 00| 00| 00| 00| 00| 00| 00| 00| 00| 00| 00| 00| 00| 00| 00| 00|
DEC | 0| 0| 0| 0| 0| 0| 0| 0| 0| 0| 0| 0| 0| 0| 0| 0| 0|
ASC | ^@| ^@| ^@| ^@| ^@| ^@| ^@| ^@| ^@| ^@| ^@| ^@| ^@| ^@| ^@| ^@|
ALT |NUL|NUL|NUL|NUL|NUL|NUL|NUL|NUL|NUL|NUL|NUL|NUL|NUL|NUL|NUL|NUL|
SYM |   |   |   |   |   |   |   |   |   |   |   |   |   |   |   |   |


BYTE|552|553|554|555|556|557|558|559|560|561|562|563|564|565|566|567|
HEX | 00| 00| 00| 00| 00| 00| 00| 00| 00| 00| 00| 00| 00| 00| 00| 00|
DEC | 0| 0| 0| 0| 0| 0| 0| 0| 0| 0| 0| 0| 0| 0| 0| 0| 0|
ASC | ^@| ^@| ^@| ^@| ^@| ^@| ^@| ^@| ^@| ^@| ^@| ^@| ^@| ^@| ^@| ^@|
ALT |NUL|NUL|NUL|NUL|NUL|NUL|NUL|NUL|NUL|NUL|NUL|NUL|NUL|NUL|NUL|NUL|
SYM |   |   |   |   |   |   |   |   |   |   |   |   |   |   |   |   |


BYTE|568|569|570|571|572|573|574|575|  0|  0|  0|  0|  0|  0|  0|  0|
HEX | 00| 00| 00| 00| 00| 00| 00| 00| XX| XX| XX| XX| XX| XX| XX| XX|
DEC | 0| 0| 0| 0| 0| 0| 0| 0| 0| 0| 0| 0| 0| 0| 0| 0|
ASC | ^@| ^@| ^@| ^@| ^@| ^@| ^@| ^@|XXX|XXX|XXX|XXX|XXX|XXX|XXX|XXX|
ALT |NUL|NUL|NUL|NUL|NUL|NUL|NUL|NUL|XXX|XXX|XXX|XXX|XXX|XXX|XXX|XXX|
SYM |   |   |   |   |   |   |   |   |   |   |   |   |   |   |   |   |


BYTE|575|  0|  0|  0|  0|  0|  0|  0|  0|  0|  0|  0|  0|  0|  0|  0|
HEX | 00| XX| XX| XX| XX| XX| XX| XX| XX| XX| XX| XX| XX| XX| XX| XX|
DEC | 0| 0| 0| 0| 0| 0| 0| 0| 0| 0| 0| 0| 0| 0| 0| 0|
ASC | ^@|XXX|XXX|XXX|XXX|XXX|XXX|XXX|XXX|XXX|XXX|XXX|XXX|XXX|XXX|XXX|
ALT |NUL|XXX|XXX|XXX|XXX|XXX|XXX|XXX|XXX|XXX|XXX|XXX|XXX|XXX|XXX|XXX|
SYM |   |   |   |   |   |   |   |   |   |   |   |   |   |   |   |   |


BYTE|  0|  0|  0|  0|  0|  0|  0|  0|  0|  0|  0|  0|  0|  0|  0|  0|
HEX | XX| XX| XX| XX| XX| XX| XX| XX| XX| XX| XX| XX| XX| XX| XX| XX|
DEC | 0| 0| 0| 0| 0| 0| 0| 0| 0| 0| 0| 0| 0| 0| 0| 0|
ASC |XXX|XXX|XXX|XXX|XXX|XXX|XXX|XXX|XXX|XXX|XXX|XXX|XXX|XXX|XXX|XXX|
ALT |XXX|XXX|XXX|XXX|XXX|XXX|XXX|XXX|XXX|XXX|XXX|XXX|XXX|XXX|XXX|XXX|
SYM |   |   |   |   |   |   |   |   |   |   |   |   |   |   |   |   |
```

```
BYTE|__0|__0|__0|__0|__0|__0|__0|__0|__0|__0|__0|__0|__0|__0|__0|__0|
_HEX|_XX|_XX|_XX|_XX|_XX|_XX|_XX|_XX|_XX|_XX|_XX|_XX|_XX|_XX|_XX|_XX|
_DEC|__0|__0|__0|__0|__0|__0|__0|__0|__0|__0|__0|__0|__0|__0|__0|__0|
_ASC|XXX|XXX|XXX|XXX|XXX|XXX|XXX|XXX|XXX|XXX|XXX|XXX|XXX|XXX|XXX|XXX|
_ALT|XXX|XXX|XXX|XXX|XXX|XXX|XXX|XXX|XXX|XXX|XXX|XXX|XXX|XXX|XXX|XXX|
_SYM|___|___|___|___|___|___|___|___|___|___|___|___|___|___|___|___|
```

Super Project Sample File

BYTE	0	1	2	3	4	5	6	7	8	9	10	11	12	13	14	15
HEX	AA	81	80	00	28	43	29	20	31	39	38	35	20	43	4F	4D
DEC	170	129	128	0	40	67	41	32	49	57	56	53	32	67	79	77
ASC	170	129	128	^@				^^						^^		
ALT	170	129	128	NUL			SPC					SPC				
SYM					(	C	)		1	9	8	5		C	O	M

File Holder Record Type | 128 Bytes | ◄─── Copyright Notice ───►

BYTE	16	17	18	19	20	21	22	23	24	25	26	27	28	29	30	31
HEX	50	55	54	45	52	20	41	53	53	4F	43	49	41	54	45	53
DEC	80	85	84	69	82	32	65	83	83	79	67	73	65	84	69	83
ASC						^^										
ALT						SPC										
SYM	P	U	T	E	R		A	S	S	O	C	I	A	T	E	S

◄───────────── Copyright ─────────────►

BYTE	32	33	34	35	36	37	38	39	40	41	42	43	44	45	46	47
HEX	20	20	20	20	30	35	2D	32	33	2D	38	37	20	31	37	3A
DEC	32	32	32	32	48	53	45	50	51	45	56	55	32	49	55	58
ASC	^^	^^	^^	^^									^^			
ALT	SPC	SPC	SPC	SPC									SPC			
SYM					0	5	-	2	3	-	8	7		1	7	:

2 Spaces | Creation Date | Space | Time of

BYTE	48	49	50	51	52	53	54	55	56	57	58	59	60	61	62	63
HEX	30	37	3A	33	39	3A	36	33	20	20	20	56	45	52	3A	20
DEC	48	55	58	51	57	58	54	51	32	32	32	86	69	82	58	32
ASC									^^	^^	^^					^^
ALT									SPC	SPC	SPC					SPC
SYM	0	7	:	3	9	:	6	3				V	E	R	:	

◄───── Creation ─────► | 3 Spaces | Version #

BYTE	64	65	66	67	68	69	70	71	72	73	74	75	76	77	78	79
HEX	32	2E	30	30	20	20	20	20	20	20	20	20	20	20	20	20
DEC	50	46	48	48	32	32	32	32	32	32	32	32	32	32	32	32
ASC					^^	^^	^^	^^	^^	^^	^^	^^	^^	^^	^^	^^
ALT					SPC	SPC	SPC	SPC	SPC	SPC	SPC	SPC	SPC	SPC	SPC	SPC
SYM	2	.	0	0												

◄─── Version ───► | ◄─────── 13 Spaces ───────►

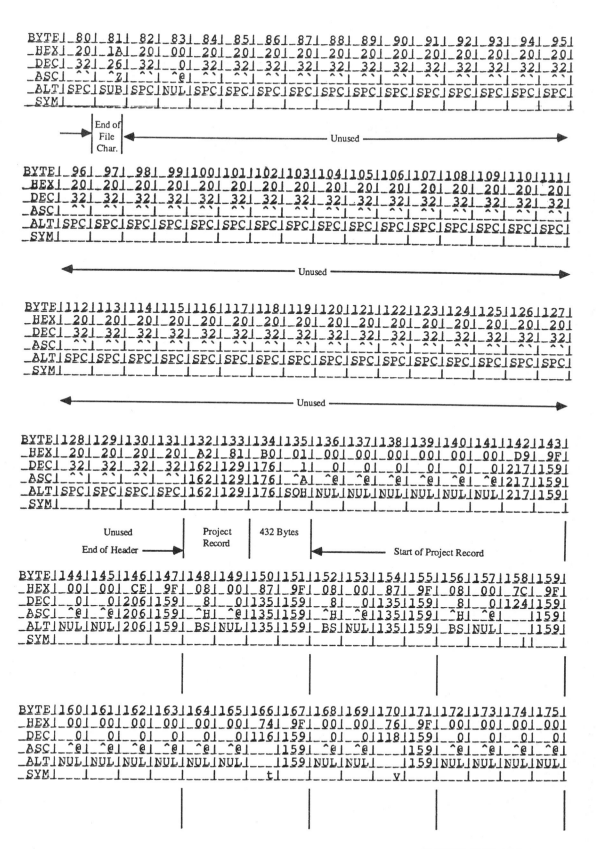

```
BYTE|176|177|178|179|180|181|182|183|184|185|186|187|188|189|190|191|
_HEX|_00|_00|_00|_00|_00|_00|_00|_00|_00|_00|_00|_00|_08|_00|_C7|_9F|
_DEC|_01|_01|_01|_01|_01|_01|_01|_01|_01|_01|_01|_01|_81|_01|199|159|
_ASC|_^@|_^@|_^@|_^@|_^@|_^@|_^@|_^@|_^@|_^@|_^@|_^@|_^H|_^@|199|159|
_ALT|NUL|NUL|NUL|NUL|NUL|NUL|NUL|NUL|NUL|NUL|NUL|NUL|_BS|NUL|199|159|
_SYM|___|___|___|___|___|___|___|___|___|___|___|___|___|___|___|___|
```

```
BYTE|192|193|194|195|196|197|198|199|200|201|202|203|204|205|206|207|
_HEX|_41|_40|_08|_00|_7C|_9F|_00|_00|_00|_00|_01|_00|_04|_00|_03|_00|
_DEC|_65|_64|_81|_01|124|159|_01|_01|_01|_01|_11|_01|_41|_01|_31|_01|
_ASC|___|___|_^H|_^@|___|159|_^@|_^@|_^@|_^@|_^A|_^@|_^D|_^@|_^C|_^@|
_ALT|___|___|_BS|NUL|___|159|NUL|NUL|NUL|NUL|SOH|NUL|EOT|NUL|ETX|NUL|
_SYM|_A|_@|___|___|_|_|___|___|___|___|___|___|___|___|___|___|___|
```

Project Flags	Undefined	Displace Starting Task	Displace Start Resource Assignment	Project ID#	Next Task ID # Avail.	Next Resource ID Avail.

```
BYTE|208|209|210|211|212|213|214|215|216|217|218|219|220|221|222|223|
_HEX|_04|_00|_03|_00|_0F|_00|_00|_00|_00|_00|_00|_00|_00|_00|_00|_00|
_DEC|_41|_01|_31|_01|151|_01|_01|_01|_01|_01|_01|_01|_01|_01|_01|_01|
_ASC|_^D|_^@|_^C|_^@|_^O|_^@|_^@|_^@|_^@|_^@|_^@|_^@|_^@|_^@|_^@|_^@|
_ALT|EOT|NUL|ETX|NUL|_SI|NUL|NUL|NUL|NUL|NUL|NUL|NUL|NUL|NUL|NUL|NUL|
_SYM|___|___|___|___|___|___|___|___|___|___|___|___|___|___|___|___|
```

# Tasks in Project	# Resources in Project	Critical Path Dur. (Days)	Critical Path Dur. (Hrs.)	Project Revision #	Undefined	◄— Project Total Var. Costs

```
BYTE|224|225|226|227|228|229|230|231|232|233|234|235|236|237|238|239|
_HEX|_00|_30|_B1|_40|_00|_00|_00|_00|_00|_00|_00|_00|_00|_00|_00|_00|
_DEC|_01|_48|177|_64|_01|_01|_01|_01|_01|_01|_01|_01|_01|_01|_01|_01|
_ASC|_^@|___|177|_64|_^@|_^@|_^@|_^@|_^@|_^@|_^@|_^@|_^@|_^@|_^@|_^@|
_ALT|NUL|___|177|_64|NUL|NUL|NUL|NUL|NUL|NUL|NUL|NUL|NUL|NUL|NUL|NUL|
_SYM|___|_0|___|_@|___|___|___|___|___|___|___|___|___|___|___|___|
```

Var. Costs —►◄—	Project Total Fixed Costs —►◄—	Project Total Actual

```
BYTE|240|241|242|243|244|245|246|247|248|249|250|251|252|253|254|255|
_HEX|_00|_00|_00|_00|_00|_00|_00|_00|_B0|_00|_00|_00|_28|_00|_00|_00|
_DEC|_01|_01|_01|_01|_01|_01|_01|_01|176|_01|_01|_01|_40|_01|_01|_01|
_ASC|_^@|_^@|_^@|_^@|_^@|_^@|_^@|_^@|176|_^@|_^@|_^@|_(_|_^@|_^@|_^@|
_ALT|NUL|NUL|NUL|NUL|NUL|NUL|NUL|NUL|176|NUL|NUL|NUL|___|NUL|NUL|NUL|
_SYM|___|___|___|___|___|___|___|___|___|___|___|___|_(_|___|___|___|
```

Costs —►	Project Total Actual Hours	Project Total Resource Assignment Hrs.	Project Total Assignment Overscheduled

```
BYTE|256|257|258|259|260|261|262|263|264|265|266|267|268|269|270|271|
_HEX|_EB|_33|_FF|_33|_00|_08|_EB|_33|_EB|_33|_45|_18|_07|_11|_00|_00|
_DEC|235|_51|255|_51|_01|_81|235|_51|235|_51|_69|_24|__7|_17|_01|_01|
_ASC|235|___|255|___|_^@|_^H|235|___|235|___|___|_^X|_^G|_^Q|_^@|_^@|
_ALT|235|___|255|___|NUL|_BS|235|___|235|___|___|CAN|BEL|DC1|NUL|NUL|
_SYM|___|_3|___|_3|___|___|___|_3|___|_3|_E|___|___|___|___|___|
```

Project Start Date	Project Finish Date	Start Hr.	Finish Hr.	Date Project Created	Date Last Written to Disk	Time Project was Last Written to Disk	Project Lock Combo

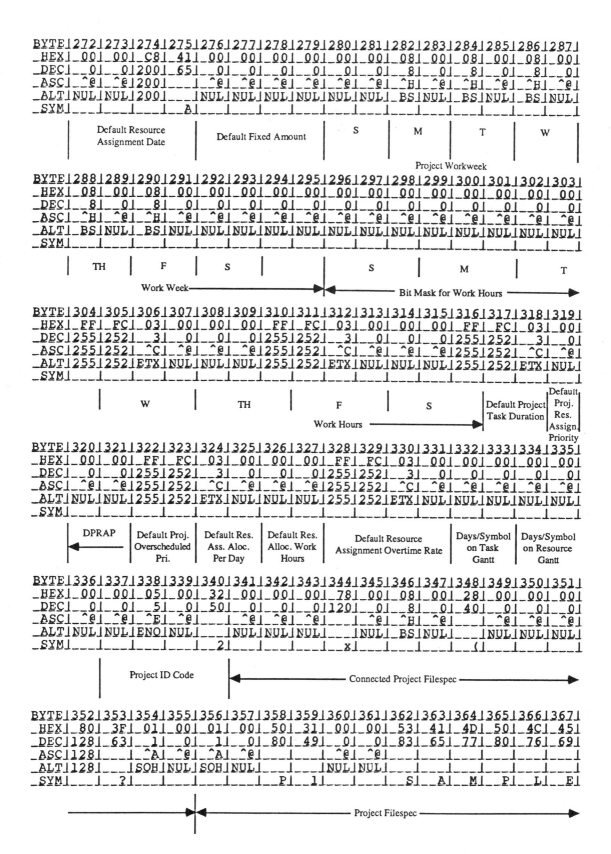

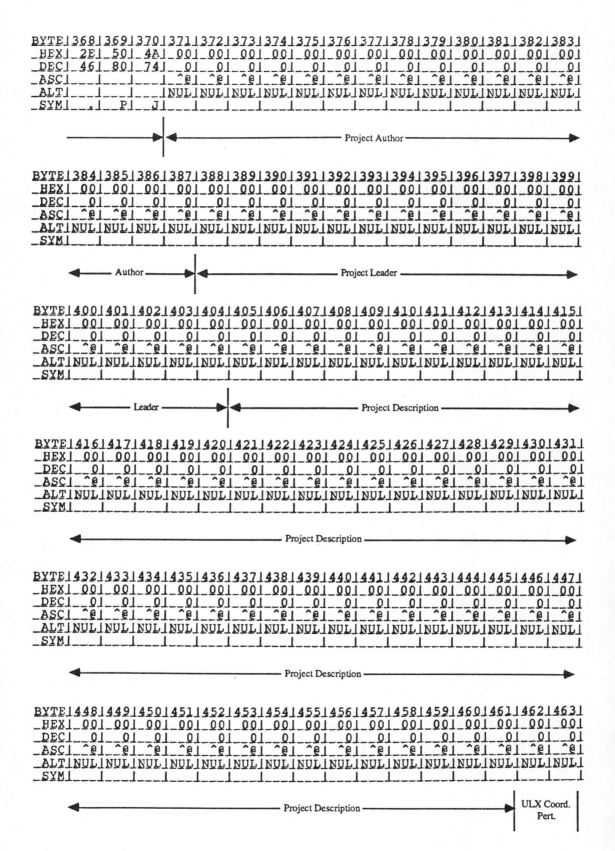

BYTE|368|369|370|371|372|373|374|375|376|377|378|379|380|381|382|383|
_HEX| 2E| 50| 4A| 00| 00| 00| 00| 00| 00| 00| 00| 00| 00| 00| 00| 00|
_DEC| 46| 80| 74| _0| _0| _0| _0| _0| _0| _0| _0| _0| _0| _0| _0| _0|
_ASC|___|___|___| ^@| ^@| ^@| ^@| ^@| ^@| ^@| ^@| ^@| ^@| ^@| ^@| ^@|
_ALT|___|___|___|NUL|NUL|NUL|NUL|NUL|NUL|NUL|NUL|NUL|NUL|NUL|NUL|NUL|
_SYM|___.| P| J|___|___|___|___|___|___|___|___|___|___|___|___|___|

|←————————————————►|◄———————————————————— Project Author —————————————————►|

BYTE|384|385|386|387|388|389|390|391|392|393|394|395|396|397|398|399|
_HEX| 00| 00| 00| 00| 00| 00| 00| 00| 00| 00| 00| 00| 00| 00| 00| 00|
_DEC| _0| _0| _0| _0| _0| _0| _0| _0| _0| _0| _0| _0| _0| _0| _0| _0|
_ASC| ^@| ^@| ^@| ^@| ^@| ^@| ^@| ^@| ^@| ^@| ^@| ^@| ^@| ^@| ^@| ^@|
_ALT|NUL|NUL|NUL|NUL|NUL|NUL|NUL|NUL|NUL|NUL|NUL|NUL|NUL|NUL|NUL|NUL|
_SYM|___|___|___|___|___|___|___|___|___|___|___|___|___|___|___|___|

|◄——— Author ———►|◄———————————————————— Project Leader —————————————————►|

BYTE|400|401|402|403|404|405|406|407|408|409|410|411|412|413|414|415|
_HEX| 00| 00| 00| 00| 00| 00| 00| 00| 00| 00| 00| 00| 00| 00| 00| 00|
_DEC| _0| _0| _0| _0| _0| _0| _0| _0| _0| _0| _0| _0| _0| _0| _0| _0|
_ASC| ^@| ^@| ^@| ^@| ^@| ^@| ^@| ^@| ^@| ^@| ^@| ^@| ^@| ^@| ^@| ^@|
_ALT|NUL|NUL|NUL|NUL|NUL|NUL|NUL|NUL|NUL|NUL|NUL|NUL|NUL|NUL|NUL|NUL|
_SYM|___|___|___|___|___|___|___|___|___|___|___|___|___|___|___|___|

|◄——— Leader ———►|◄———————————————————— Project Description —————————————►|

BYTE|416|417|418|419|420|421|422|423|424|425|426|427|428|429|430|431|
_HEX| 00| 00| 00| 00| 00| 00| 00| 00| 00| 00| 00| 00| 00| 00| 00| 00|
_DEC| _0| _0| _0| _0| _0| _0| _0| _0| _0| _0| _0| _0| _0| _0| _0| _0|
_ASC| ^@| ^@| ^@| ^@| ^@| ^@| ^@| ^@| ^@| ^@| ^@| ^@| ^@| ^@| ^@| ^@|
_ALT|NUL|NUL|NUL|NUL|NUL|NUL|NUL|NUL|NUL|NUL|NUL|NUL|NUL|NUL|NUL|NUL|
_SYM|___|___|___|___|___|___|___|___|___|___|___|___|___|___|___|___|

|◄———————————————————— Project Description —————————————————►|

BYTE|432|433|434|435|436|437|438|439|440|441|442|443|444|445|446|447|
_HEX| 00| 00| 00| 00| 00| 00| 00| 00| 00| 00| 00| 00| 00| 00| 00| 00|
_DEC| _0| _0| _0| _0| _0| _0| _0| _0| _0| _0| _0| _0| _0| _0| _0| _0|
_ASC| ^@| ^@| ^@| ^@| ^@| ^@| ^@| ^@| ^@| ^@| ^@| ^@| ^@| ^@| ^@| ^@|
_ALT|NUL|NUL|NUL|NUL|NUL|NUL|NUL|NUL|NUL|NUL|NUL|NUL|NUL|NUL|NUL|NUL|
_SYM|___|___|___|___|___|___|___|___|___|___|___|___|___|___|___|___|

|◄———————————————————— Project Description —————————————————►|

BYTE|448|449|450|451|452|453|454|455|456|457|458|459|460|461|462|463|
_HEX| 00| 00| 00| 00| 00| 00| 00| 00| 00| 00| 00| 00| 00| 00| 00| 00|
_DEC| _0| _0| _0| _0| _0| _0| _0| _0| _0| _0| _0| _0| _0| _0| _0| _0|
_ASC| ^@| ^@| ^@| ^@| ^@| ^@| ^@| ^@| ^@| ^@| ^@| ^@| ^@| ^@| ^@| ^@|
_ALT|NUL|NUL|NUL|NUL|NUL|NUL|NUL|NUL|NUL|NUL|NUL|NUL|NUL|NUL|NUL|NUL|
_SYM|___|___|†__|___|___|___|___|___|___|___|___|___|___|___|___|___|

|◄———————————————————— Project Description —————————————————►|ULX Coord.|
| | Pert. |

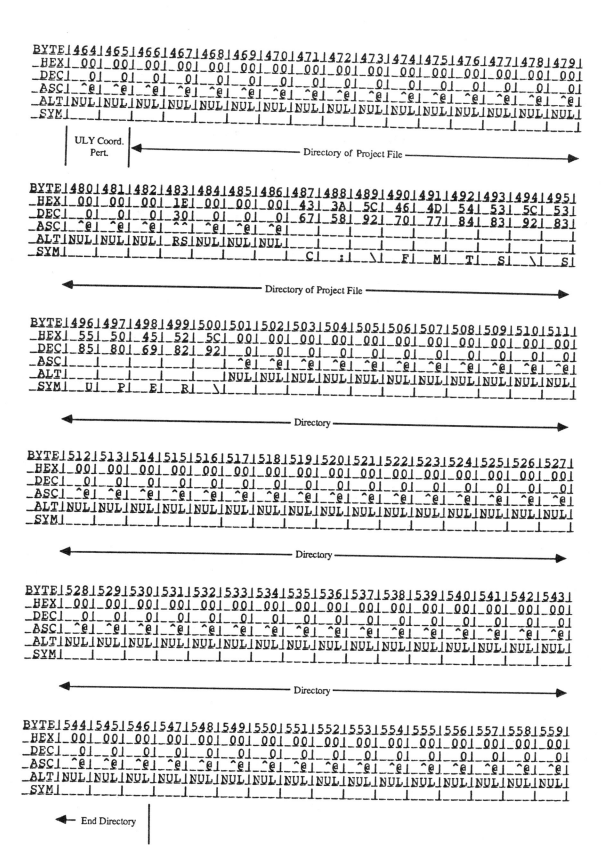

BYTE 560–575

BYTE	560	561	562	563	564	565	566	567	568	569	570	571	572	573	574	575
HEX	00	00	00	00	00	00	00	00	A4	81	BE	00	08	00	BB	9F
DEC	01	01	01	01	01	01	01	01	164	129	190	01	08	01	187	159
ASC	^@	^@	^@	^@	^@	^@	^@	^@	164	129	190	^@	^H	^@	187	159
ALT	NUL	NUL	NUL	NUL	NUL	NUL	NUL	NUL	164	129	190	NUL	BS	NUL	187	159
SYM																

| End of Project Record | | | | | | | | Task Record ID | | 190 Bytes | | U | | U | |

BYTE 576–591

BYTE	576	577	578	579	580	581	582	583	584	585	586	587	588	589	590	591
HEX	00	00	00	00	00	00	00	00	00	00	00	00	08	00	93	9F
DEC	01	01	01	01	01	01	01	01	01	01	01	01	08	01	147	159
ASC	^@	^@	^@	^@	^@	^@	^@	^@	^@	^@	^@	^@	^H	^@	147	159
ALT	NUL	NUL	NUL	NUL	NUL	NUL	NUL	NUL	NUL	NUL	NUL	NUL	BS	NUL	147	159
SYM																

| U | | U | | U | | U | | U | | U | | U | | U | |

BYTE 592–607

BYTE	592	593	594	595	596	597	598	599	600	601	602	603	604	605	606	607
HEX	08	00	C7	9F	00	00	E5	9F	00	00	00	00	04	00	F1	33
DEC	08	01	199	159	01	01	229	159	01	01	01	01	04	01	241	51
ASC	^H	^@	199	159	^@	^@	229	159	^@	^@	^@	^@	^D	^@	241	
ALT	BS	NUL	199	159	NUL	NUL	229	159	NUL	NUL	NUL	NUL	EOT	NUL	241	
SYM																3

| U | | U | | U | | U | | U | | U | | Task Flags | | U | |

BYTE 608–623

BYTE	608	609	610	611	612	613	614	615	616	617	618	619	620	621	622	623
HEX	0A	00	27	00	01	00	08	00	00	00	EB	33	ED	33	F1	33
DEC	10	01	39	01	11	01	08	01	01	01	235	51	237	51	241	51
ASC	^J	^@	'	^@	^A	^@	^H	^@	^@	^@	235		237		241	
ALT	LF	NUL	'	NUL	SOH	NUL	BS	NUL	NUL	NUL	235		237		241	
SYM				'								3		3		3

| Y Coordinate Pert. BX Ctr. | | X Coordinate Pert. BY Ctr. | | Task ID Displayed | | U | | 1st Hook to Show on Task Details | | Task Early Start Date | | Task Late Start Date | | Task Early Finish Date | |

BYTE 624–639

BYTE	624	625	626	627	628	629	630	631	632	633	634	635	636	637	638	639
HEX	F1	33	00	00	00	00	00	00	00	00	ED	33	F1	33	00	00
DEC	241	51	01	01	01	01	01	01	01	01	237	51	241	51	01	01
ASC	241		^@	^@	^@	^@	^@	^@	^@	^@	237		241		^@	^@
ALT	241		NUL	NUL	NUL	NUL	NUL	NUL	NUL	NUL	237		241		NUL	NUL
SYM		3										3		3		

| Task Late Finish Date | | Must Start Date | | Must Finish Date | | Actual Start Date | | Actual Finish Date | | Scheduled Start Date | | Scheduled Finish Date | | Planned Start Date | |

BYTE 640–655

BYTE	640	641	642	643	644	645	646	647	648	649	650	651	652	653	654	655
HEX	00	00	00	00	08	08	00	00	00	00	00	08	00	00	05	00
DEC	01	01	01	01	08	08	01	01	01	01	01	08	01	01	05	01
ASC	^@	^@	^@	^@	^H	^H	^@	^@	^@	^@	^@	^H	^@	^@	^E	^@
ALT	NUL	NUL	NUL	NUL	BS	BS	NUL	NUL	NUL	NUL	NUL	BS	NUL	NUL	ENQ	NUL
SYM																

| Planned Finish Date | | Early Start Hr. | Late Start Hr. | Early Finish Hr. | Late Finish Hr. | Must Start Hr. | Must Finish Hr. | Actual Start Hr. | Actual Finish Hr. | Sched. Start Hr. | Sched. Finish Hr. | Plan Start Hr. | Plan Finish Hr. | Duration | |

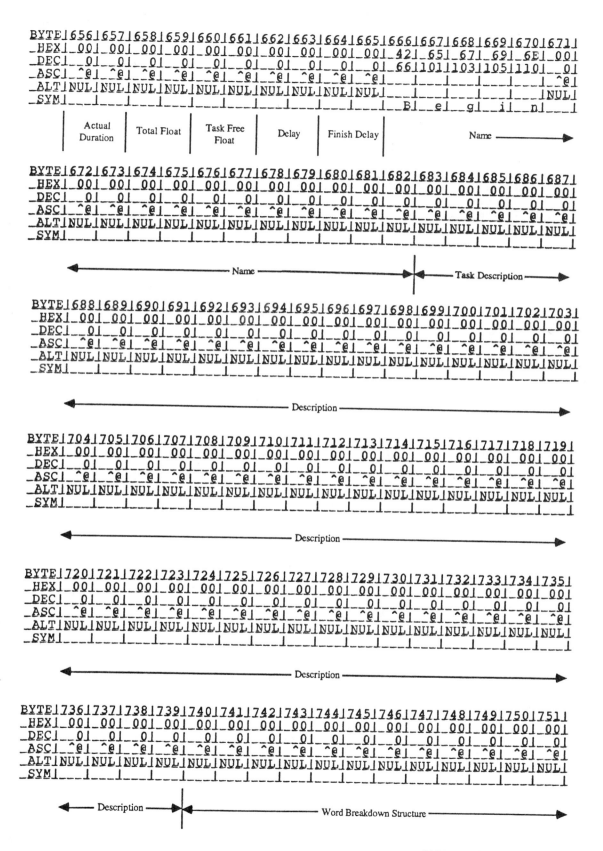

```
BYTE|752|753|754|755|756|757|758|759|760|761|762|763|764|765|766|767|
HEX| 00| 00| 00| 00| 00| 00| 00| 00| 00| 00| A4| 81| BE| 00| 00| 00|
DEC|  0|  0|  0|  0|  0|  0|  0|  0|  0|  0|164|129|190|  0|  0|  0|
ASC| ^@| ^@| ^@| ^@| ^@| ^@| ^@| ^@| ^@| ^@|164|129|190| ^@| ^@| ^@|
ALT|NUL|NUL|NUL|NUL|NUL|NUL|NUL|NUL|NUL|NUL|164|129|190|NUL|NUL|NUL|
SYM|   |   |   |   |   |   |   |   |   |   |   |   |   |   |   |   |
```

```
◄── Word Breakdown Structure ──►  |   U   |   U   |   U   | Task Rec. |    190    |
                                                              ID          Bytes
```

```
BYTE|768|769|770|771|772|773|774|775|776|777|778|779|780|781|782|783|
HEX| 9C| 9F| 00| 00| D9| 9F| 00| 00| 00| 00| 00| 00| A8| 9F| 00| 00|
DEC|156|159|  0|  0|217|159|  0|  0|  0|  0|  0|  0|168|159|  0|  0|
ASC|156|159| ^@| ^@|217|159| ^@| ^@| ^@| ^@| ^@| ^@|168|159| ^@| ^@|
ALT|156|159|NUL|NUL|217|159|NUL|NUL|NUL|NUL|NUL|NUL|168|159|NUL|NUL|
SYM|   |   |   |   |   |   |   |   |   |   |   |   |   |   |   |   |
```

```
BYTE|784|785|786|787|788|789|790|791|792|793|794|795|796|797|798|799|
HEX| 00| 00| 00| 00| AA| 9F| 00| 00| E5| 9F| 00| 00| 00| 00| 04| 00|
DEC|  0|  0|  0|  0|170|159|  0|  0|229|159|  0|  0|  0|  0|  4|  0|
ASC| ^@| ^@| ^@| ^@|170|159| ^@| ^@|229|159| ^@| ^@| ^@| ^@| ^D| ^@|
ALT|NUL|NUL|NUL|NUL|170|159|NUL|NUL|229|159|NUL|NUL|NUL|NUL|EOT|NUL|
SYM|   |   |   |   |   |   |   |   |   |   |   |   |   |   |   |   |
```

```
BYTE|800|801|802|803|804|805|806|807|808|809|810|811|812|813|814|815|
HEX| FF| 33| 0A| 00| 3F| 00| 02| 00| 08| 00| 00| 00| F1| 33| F4| 33|
DEC|255| 51| 10|  0| 63|  0|  2|  0|  8|  0|  0|  0|241| 51|244| 51|
ASC|255|   | ^J| ^@|   | ^@| ^B| ^@| ^H| ^@| ^@| ^@|241|   |244|   |
ALT|255|   | LF|NUL|   |NUL|STX|NUL| BS|NUL|NUL|NUL|241|   |244|   |
SYM|   |  3|   |   |  ?|   |   |   |   |   |   |   |   |  3|   |  3|
```

```
BYTE|816|817|818|819|820|821|822|823|824|825|826|827|828|829|830|831|
HEX| FF| 33| FF| 33| 00| 00| 00| 00| 00| 00| 00| 00| F4| 33| FF| 33|
DEC|255| 51|255| 51|  0|  0|  0|  0|  0|  0|  0|  0|244| 51|255| 51|
ASC|255|   |255|   | ^@| ^@| ^@| ^@| ^@| ^@| ^@| ^@|244|   |255|   |
ALT|255|   |255|   |NUL|NUL|NUL|NUL|NUL|NUL|NUL|NUL|244|   |255|   |
SYM|   |  3|   |  3|   |   |   |   |   |   |   |   |   |  3|   |  3|
```

```
BYTE|832|833|834|835|836|837|838|839|840|841|842|843|844|845|846|847|
HEX| 00| 00| 00| 00| 08| 00| 08| 08| 00| 00| 00| 00| 00| 08| 00| 00|
DEC|  0|  0|  0|  0|  8|  0|  8|  8|  0|  0|  0|  0|  0|  8|  0|  0|
ASC| ^@| ^@| ^@| ^@| ^H| ^@| ^H| ^H| ^@| ^@| ^@| ^@| ^@| ^H| ^@| ^@|
ALT|NUL|NUL|NUL|NUL| BS|NUL| ES| BS|NUL|NUL|NUL|NUL|NUL| BS|NUL|NUL|
SYM|   |   |   |   |   |   |   |   |   |   |   |   |   |   |   |   |
```

```
BYTE|848|849|850|851|852|853|854|855|856|857|858|859|860|861|862|863|
 HEX| 0A| 00| 00| 00| 00| 00| 00| 00| 00| 00| 00| 00| 54| 61| 73| 6B|
 DEC| 10|  0|  0|  0|  0|  0|  0|  0|  0|  0|  0|  0| 84| 97|115|107|
 ASC| ^J| ^@| ^@| ^@| ^@| ^@| ^@| ^@| ^@| ^@| ^@| ^@|   |   |   |   |
 ALT| LF|NUL|NUL|NUL|NUL|NUL|NUL|NUL|NUL|NUL|NUL|NUL|   |   |   |   |
 SYM|   |   |   |   |   |   |   |   |   |   |   |   |  T|  a|  s|  k|


BYTE|864|865|866|867|868|869|870|871|872|873|874|875|876|877|878|879|
 HEX| 2D| 32| 00| 00| 00| 00| 00| 00| 00| 00| 00| 00| 00| 00| 00| 00|
 DEC| 45| 50|  0|  0|  0|  0|  0|  0|  0|  0|  0|  0|  0|  0|  0|  0|
 ASC|   |   | ^@| ^@| ^@| ^@| ^@| ^@| ^@| ^@| ^@| ^@| ^@| ^@| ^@| ^@|
 ALT|   |   |NUL|NUL|NUL|NUL|NUL|NUL|NUL|NUL|NUL|NUL|NUL|NUL|NUL|NUL|
 SYM|  -|  2|   |   |   |   |   |   |   |   |   |   |   |   |   |   |


BYTE|880|881|882|883|884|885|886|887|888|889|890|891|892|893|894|895|
 HEX| 00| 00| 00| 00| 00| 00| 00| 00| 00| 00| 00| 00| 00| 00| 00| 00|
 DEC|  0|  0|  0|  0|  0|  0|  0|  0|  0|  0|  0|  0|  0|  0|  0|  0|
 ASC| ^@| ^@| ^@| ^@| ^@| ^@| ^@| ^@| ^@| ^@| ^@| ^@| ^@| ^@| ^@| ^@|
 ALT|NUL|NUL|NUL|NUL|NUL|NUL|NUL|NUL|NUL|NUL|NUL|NUL|NUL|NUL|NUL|NUL|
 SYM|   |   |   |   |   |   |   |   |   |   |   |   |   |   |   |   |


BYTE|896|897|898|899|900|901|902|903|904|905|906|907|908|909|910|911|
 HEX| 00| 00| 00| 00| 00| 00| 00| 00| 00| 00| 00| 00| 00| 00| 00| 00|
 DEC|  0|  0|  0|  0|  0|  0|  0|  0|  0|  0|  0|  0|  0|  0|  0|  0|
 ASC| ^@| ^@| ^@| ^@| ^@| ^@| ^@| ^@| ^@| ^@| ^@| ^@| ^@| ^@| ^@| ^@|
 ALT|NUL|NUL|NUL|NUL|NUL|NUL|NUL|NUL|NUL|NUL|NUL|NUL|NUL|NUL|NUL|NUL|
 SYM|   |   |   |   |   |   |   |   |   |   |   |   |   |   |   |   |


BYTE|912|913|914|915|916|917|918|919|920|921|922|923|924|925|926|927|
 HEX| 00| 00| 00| 00| 00| 00| 00| 00| 00| 00| 00| 00| 00| 00| 00| 00|
 DEC|  0|  0|  0|  0|  0|  0|  0|  0|  0|  0|  0|  0|  0|  0|  0|  0|
 ASC| ^@| ^@| ^@| ^@| ^@| ^@| ^@| ^@| ^@| ^@| ^@| ^@| ^@| ^@| ^@| ^@|
 ALT|NUL|NUL|NUL|NUL|NUL|NUL|NUL|NUL|NUL|NUL|NUL|NUL|NUL|NUL|NUL|NUL|
 SYM|   |   |   |   |   |   |   |   |   |   |   |   |   |   |   |   |


BYTE|928|929|930|931|932|933|934|935|936|937|938|939|940|941|942|943|
 HEX| 00| 00| 00| 00| 00| 00| 00| 00| 00| 00| 00| 00| 00| 00| 00| 00|
 DEC|  0|  0|  0|  0|  0|  0|  0|  0|  0|  0|  0|  0|  0|  0|  0|  0|
 ASC| ^@| ^@| ^@| ^@| ^@| ^@| ^@| ^@| ^@| ^@| ^@| ^@| ^@| ^@| ^@| ^@|
 ALT|NUL|NUL|NUL|NUL|NUL|NUL|NUL|NUL|NUL|NUL|NUL|NUL|NUL|NUL|NUL|NUL|
 SYM|   |   |   |   |   |   |   |   |   |   |   |   |   |   |   |   |
```

```
BYTE|944|945|946|947|948|949|950|951|952|953|954|955|956|957|958|959|
_HEX|_001_001_001_001_001_001_001_001_001_001_001_001_A4|_81|_BE|_001
_DEC|_01|_01|_01|_01|_01|_01|_01|_01|_01|_01|_01|_01|164|129|190|_01|
_ASC|_^@|_^@|_^@|_^@|_^@|_^@|_^@|_^@|_^@|_^@|_^@|_^@|164|129|190|_^@|
_ALT|NUL|NUL|NUL|NUL|NUL|NUL|NUL|NUL|NUL|NUL|NUL|NUL|164|129|190|NUL|
_SYM|___|___|___|___|___|___|___|___|___|___|___|___|___|___|___|___|
```

Task Record ID	190 Bytes

```
BYTE|960|961|962|963|964|965|966|967|968|969|970|971|972|973|974|975|
_HEX|_08|_00|_87|_9F|_08|_00|_BB|_9F|_00|_00|_00|_00|_08|_00|_93|_9F|
_DEC|_81|_01|135|159|_81|_01|187|159|_01|_01|_01|_01|_81|_01|147|159|
_ASC|_^H|_^@|135|159|_^H|_^@|187|159|_^@|_^@|_^@|_^@|_^H|_^@|147|159|
_ALT|_BS|NUL|135|159|_BS|NUL|187|159|NUL|NUL|NUL|NUL|_BS|NUL|147|159|
_SYM|___|___|___|___|___|___|___|___|___|___|___|___|___|___|___|___|
```

```
BYTE|976|977|978|979|980|981|982|983|984|985|986|987|988|989|990|991|
_HEX|_00|_00|_74|_9F|_08|_00|_95|_9F|_00|_00|_E5|_9F|_00|_00|_00|_00|
_DEC|_01|_01|116|159|_81|_01|149|159|_01|_01|229|159|_01|_01|_01|_01|
_ASC|_^@|_^@|___|159|_^H|_^@|149|159|_^@|_^@|229|159|_^@|_^@|_^@|_^@|
_ALT|NUL|NUL|___|159|_BS|NUL|149|159|NUL|NUL|229|159|NUL|NUL|NUL|NUL|
_SYM|___|___|_t_|___|___|___|___|___|___|___|___|___|___|___|___|___|
```

```
BYTE|992|993|994|995|996|997|998|999|__0|_1|_2|_3|_4|_5|_6|_7|
_HEX|_00|_00|_FB|_33|_11|_00|_3F|_00|_03|_00|_00|_00|_00|_00|_F1|_33|
_DEC|_01|_01|251|_51|_17|_01|_63|_01|__3|_01|_01|_01|_01|_01|241|_51|
_ASC|_^@|_^@|251|___|___|_^O|_^@|___|_^@|_^C|_^@|_^@|_^@|_^@|_^@|241|___|
_ALT|NUL|NUL|251|___|_DC1|NUL|___|NUL|ETX|NUL|NUL|NUL|NUL|NUL|241|___|
_SYM|___|___|___|_3|___|_!_|___|_?|___|___|___|___|___|___|___|_3|
```

```
BYTE|__8|_9|10|11|12|13|14|15|16|17|18|19|20|21|22|23|
_HEX|_F7|_33|_F8|_33|_FD|_33|_00|_00|_00|_00|_00|_00|_00|_00|_F4|_33|
_DEC|247|_51|248|_51|253|_51|_01|_01|_01|_01|_01|_01|_01|_01|244|_51|
_ASC|247|___|248|___|253|___|_^@|_^@|_^@|_^@|_^@|_^@|_^@|_^@|244|___|
_ALT|247|___|248|___|253|___|NUL|NUL|NUL|NUL|NUL|NUL|NUL|NUL|244|___|
_SYM|___|_3|___|_3|___|_3|___|___|___|___|___|___|___|___|___|_3|
```

```
BYTE|_24|25|26|27|28|29|30|31|32|33|34|35|36|37|38|39|
_HEX|_F8|_33|_00|_00|_00|_00|_08|_00|_08|_08|_00|_00|_00|_00|_00|_08|
_DEC|248|_51|_01|_01|_01|_01|_81|_01|_81|_81|_01|_01|_01|_01|_01|_81|
_ASC|248|___|_^@|_^@|_^@|_^@|_^H|_^@|_^H|_^H|_^@|_^@|_^@|_^@|_^@|_^H|
_ALT|248|___|NUL|NUL|NUL|NUL|_BS|NUL|_BS|_BS|NUL|NUL|NUL|NUL|NUL|_BS|
_SYM|___|_3|___|___|___|___|___|___|___|___|___|___|___|___|___|___|
```

BYTE	40	41	42	43	44	45	46	47	48	49	50	51	52	53	54	55
HEX	00	00	05	00	00	00	03	00	00	00	00	00	00	00	54	61
DEC	0	0	5	0	0	0	3	0	0	0	0	0	0	0	84	97
ASC	^@	^@	^E	^@	^@	^@	^C	^@	^@	^@	^@	^@	^@	^@		
ALT	NUL	NUL	ENQ	NUL	NUL	NUL	ETX	NUL	NUL	NUL	NUL	NUL	NUL	NUL		
SYM															T	a

BYTE	56	57	58	59	60	61	62	63	64	65	66	67	68	69	70	71
HEX	73	6B	2D	33	00	00	00	00	00	00	00	00	00	00	00	00
DEC	115	107	45	51	0	0	0	0	0	0	0	0	0	0	0	0
ASC					^@	^@	^@	^@	^@	^@	^@	^@	^@	^@	^@	^@
ALT					NUL	NUL	NUL	NUL	NUL	NUL	NUL	NUL	NUL	NUL	NUL	NUL
SYM	s	k	-	3												

BYTE	72	73	74	75	76	77	78	79	80	81	82	83	84	85	86	87
HEX	00	00	00	00	00	00	00	00	00	00	00	00	00	00	00	00
DEC	0	0	0	0	0	0	0	0	0	0	0	0	0	0	0	0
ASC	^@	^@	^@	^@	^@	^@	^@	^@	^@	^@	^@	^@	^@	^@	^@	^@
ALT	NUL	NUL	NUL	NUL	NUL	NUL	NUL	NUL	NUL	NUL	NUL	NUL	NUL	NUL	NUL	NUL
SYM																

BYTE	88	89	90	91	92	93	94	95	96	97	98	99	100	101	102	103
HEX	00	00	00	00	00	00	00	00	00	00	00	00	00	00	00	00
DEC	0	0	0	0	0	0	0	0	0	0	0	0	0	0	0	0
ASC	^@	^@	^@	^@	^@	^@	^@	^@	^@	^@	^@	^@	^@	^@	^@	^@
ALT	NUL	NUL	NUL	NUL	NUL	NUL	NUL	NUL	NUL	NUL	NUL	NUL	NUL	NUL	NUL	NUL
SYM																

BYTE	104	105	106	107	108	109	110	111	112	113	114	115	116	117	118	119
HEX	00	00	00	00	00	00	00	00	00	00	00	00	00	00	00	00
DEC	0	0	0	0	0	0	0	0	0	0	0	0	0	0	0	0
ASC	^@	^@	^@	^@	^@	^@	^@	^@	^@	^@	^@	^@	^@	^@	^@	^@
ALT	NUL	NUL	NUL	NUL	NUL	NUL	NUL	NUL	NUL	NUL	NUL	NUL	NUL	NUL	NUL	NUL
SYM																

BYTE	120	121	122	123	124	125	126	127	128	129	130	131	132	133	134	135
HEX	00	00	00	00	00	00	00	00	00	00	00	00	00	00	00	00
DEC	0	0	0	0	0	0	0	0	0	0	0	0	0	0	0	0
ASC	^@	^@	^@	^@	^@	^@	^@	^@	^@	^@	^@	^@	^@	^@	^@	^@
ALT	NUL	NUL	NUL	NUL	NUL	NUL	NUL	NUL	NUL	NUL	NUL	NUL	NUL	NUL	NUL	NUL
SYM																

```
BYTE|136|137|138|139|140|141|142|143|144|145|146|147|148|149|150|151|
_HEX|_00|_00|_00|_00|_00|_00|_00|_00|_00|_00|_00|_00|_00|_00|_A4|_81|
_DEC|__0|__0|__0|__0|__0|__0|__0|__0|__0|__0|__0|__0|__0|__0|164|129|
_ASC|_^@|_^@|_^@|_^@|_^@|_^@|_^@|_^@|_^@|_^@|_^@|_^@|_^@|_^@|164|129|
_ALT|NUL|NUL|NUL|NUL|NUL|NUL|NUL|NUL|NUL|NUL|NUL|NUL|NUL|NUL|164|129|
_SYM|___|___|___|___|___|___|___|___|___|___|___|___|___|___|___|___|
```

```
                                                              | Task
                                                              | Record ID
```

```
BYTE|152|153|154|155|156|157|158|159|160|161|162|163|164|165|166|167|
_HEX|_BE|_00|_00|_00|_00|_00|_00|_00|_9C|_9F|_00|_00|_00|_00|_00|_00|
_DEC|190|__0|__0|__0|__0|__0|__0|__0|156|159|__0|__0|__0|__0|__0|__0|
_ASC|190|_^@|_^@|_^@|_^@|_^@|_^@|_^@|156|159|_^@|_^@|_^@|_^@|_^@|_^@|
_ALT|190|NUL|NUL|NUL|NUL|NUL|NUL|NUL|156|159|NUL|NUL|NUL|NUL|NUL|NUL|
_SYM|___|___|___|___|___|___|___|___|___|___|___|___|___|___|___|___|
```

```
     | 190 Bytes |
```

```
BYTE|168|169|170|171|172|173|174|175|176|177|178|179|180|181|182|183|
_HEX|_74|_9F|_00|_00|_00|_00|_00|_00|_76|_9F|_00|_00|_E5|_9F|_00|_00|
_DEC|116|159|__0|__0|__0|__0|__0|__0|118|159|__0|__0|229|159|__0|__0|
_ASC|___|159|_^@|_^@|_^@|_^@|_^@|_^@|___|159|_^@|_^@|229|159|_^@|_^@|
_ALT|___|159|NUL|NUL|NUL|NUL|NUL|NUL|___|159|NUL|NUL|229|159|NUL|NUL|
_SYM|__t|___|___|___|___|___|___|___|___|___|___|__v|___|___|___|___|
```

```
BYTE|184|185|186|187|188|189|190|191|192|193|194|195|196|197|198|199|
_HEX|_00|_00|_00|_80|_FF|_33|_0C|_00|_5D|_00|_04|_00|_08|_00|_00|_00|
_DEC|__0|__0|__0|128|255|_51|_12|__0|_93|__0|__4|__0|__8|__0|__0|__0|
_ASC|_^@|_^@|_^@|128|255|___|_^L|_^@|___|_^@|_^D|_^@|_^H|_^@|_^@|_^@|
_ALT|NUL|NUL|NUL|128|255|___|_FF|NUL|___|NUL|EOT|NUL|_BS|NUL|NUL|NUL|
_SYM|___|___|___|___|___|__3|___|___|__1|___|___|___|___|___|___|___|
```

```
BYTE|200|201|202|203|204|205|206|207|208|209|210|211|212|213|214|215|
_HEX|_F8|_33|_FE|_33|_FC|_33|_FF|_33|_00|_00|_00|_00|_00|_00|_00|_00|
_DEC|248|_51|254|_51|252|_51|255|_51|__0|__0|__0|__0|__0|__0|__0|__0|
_ASC|248|___|254|___|252|___|255|___|_^@|_^@|_^@|_^@|_^@|_^@|_^@|_^@|
_ALT|248|___|254|___|252|___|255|___|NUL|NUL|NUL|NUL|NUL|NUL|NUL|NUL|
_SYM|___|__3|___|__3|___|__3|___|__3|___|___|___|___|___|___|___|___|
```

```
BYTE|216|217|218|219|220|221|222|223|224|225|226|227|228|229|230|231|
_HEX|_FB|_33|_FC|_33|_00|_00|_00|_00|_08|_00|_08|_08|_00|_00|_00|_00|
_DEC|251|_51|252|_51|__0|__0|__0|__0|__8|__0|__8|__8|__0|__0|__0|__0|
_ASC|251|___|252|___|_^@|_^@|_^@|_^@|_^H|_^@|_^H|_^H|_^@|_^@|_^@|_^@|
_ALT|251|___|252|___|NUL|NUL|NUL|NUL|_BS|NUL|_BS|_BS|NUL|NUL|NUL|NUL|
_SYM|___|__3|___|__3|___|___|___|___|___|___|___|___|___|___|___|___|
```

BYTE	232	233	234	235	236	237	238	239	240	241	242	243	244	245	246	247
HEX	00	08	00	00	10	00	00	00	18	00	18	00	00	00	00	00
DEC	0	8	0	0	16	0	0	0	24	0	24	0	0	0	0	0
ASC	^@	^H	^@	^@	^P	^@	^@	^@	^X	^@	^X	^@	^@	^@	^@	^@
ALT	NUL	BS	NUL	NUL	DLE	NUL	NUL	NUL	CAN	NUL	CAN	NUL	NUL	NUL	NUL	NUL
SYM																

BYTE	248	249	250	251	252	253	254	255	256	257	258	259	260	261	262	263
HEX	54	61	73	6B	2D	34	00	00	00	00	00	00	00	00	00	00
DEC	84	97	115	107	45	52	0	0	0	0	0	0	0	0	0	0
ASC							^@	^@	^@	^@	^@	^@	^@	^@	^@	^@
ALT							NUL	NUL	NUL	NUL	NUL	NUL	NUL	NUL	NUL	NUL
SYM	T	a	s	k	-	4										

BYTE	264	265	266	267	268	269	270	271	272	273	274	275	276	277	278	279
HEX	00	00	00	00	00	00	00	00	00	00	00	00	00	00	00	00
DEC	0	0	0	0	0	0	0	0	0	0	0	0	0	0	0	0
ASC	^@	^@	^@	^@	^@	^@	^@	^@	^@	^@	^@	^@	^@	^@	^@	^@
ALT	NUL	NUL	NUL	NUL	NUL	NUL	NUL	NUL	NUL	NUL	NUL	NUL	NUL	NUL	NUL	NUL
SYM																

BYTE	280	281	282	283	284	285	286	287	288	289	290	291	292	293	294	295
HEX	00	00	00	00	00	00	00	00	00	00	00	00	00	00	00	00
DEC	0	0	0	0	0	0	0	0	0	0	0	0	0	0	0	0
ASC	^@	^@	^@	^@	^@	^@	^@	^@	^@	^@	^@	^@	^@	^@	^@	^@
ALT	NUL	NUL	NUL	NUL	NUL	NUL	NUL	NUL	NUL	NUL	NUL	NUL	NUL	NUL	NUL	NUL
SYM																

BYTE	296	297	298	299	300	301	302	303	304	305	306	307	308	309	310	311
HEX	00	00	00	00	00	00	00	00	00	00	00	00	00	00	00	00
DEC	0	0	0	0	0	0	0	0	0	0	0	0	0	0	0	0
ASC	^@	^@	^@	^@	^@	^@	^@	^@	^@	^@	^@	^@	^@	^@	^@	^@
ALT	NUL	NUL	NUL	NUL	NUL	NUL	NUL	NUL	NUL	NUL	NUL	NUL	NUL	NUL	NUL	NUL
SYM																

BYTE	312	313	314	315	316	317	318	319	320	321	322	323	324	325	326	327
HEX	00	00	00	00	00	00	00	00	00	00	00	00	00	00	00	00
DEC	0	0	0	0	0	0	0	0	0	0	0	0	0	0	0	0
ASC	^@	^@	^@	^@	^@	^@	^@	^@	^@	^@	^@	^@	^@	^@	^@	^@
ALT	NUL	NUL	NUL	NUL	NUL	NUL	NUL	NUL	NUL	NUL	NUL	NUL	NUL	NUL	NUL	NUL
SYM																

BYTE	328	329	330	331	332	333	334	335	336	337	338	339	340	341	342	343
HEX	00	00	00	00	00	00	00	00	00	00	00	00	00	00	00	00
DEC	0	0	0	0	0	0	0	0	0	0	0	0	0	0	0	0
ASC	^@	^@	^@	^@	^@	^@	^@	^@	^@	^@	^@	^@	^@	^@	^@	^@
ALT	NUL	NUL	NUL	NUL	NUL	NUL	NUL	NUL	NUL	NUL	NUL	NUL	NUL	NUL	NUL	NUL
SYM																

BYTE	344	345	346	347	348	349	350	351	352	353	354	355	356	357	358	359
HEX	A6	81	AA	00	08	00	B0	9F	00	00	00	00	08	00	C7	9F
DEC	166	129	170	0	8	0	176	159	0	0	0	0	8	0	199	159
ASC	166	129	170	^@	^H	^@	176	159	^@	^@	^@	^@	^H	^@	199	159
ALT	166	129	170	NUL	BS	NUL	176	159	NUL	NUL	NUL	NUL	BS	NUL	199	159
SYM																

Resource Record ID	170 Bytes	U		U		U	

BYTE	360	361	362	363	364	365	366	367	368	369	370	371	372	373	374	375
HEX	00	00	00	00	00	00	00	00	00	00	E5	9F	00	00	00	00
DEC	0	0	0	0	0	0	0	0	0	0	229	159	0	0	0	0
ASC	^@	^@	^@	^@	^@	^@	^@	^@	^@	^@	229	159	^@	^@	^@	^@
ALT	NUL	NUL	NUL	NUL	NUL	NUL	NUL	NUL	NUL	NUL	229	159	NUL	NUL	NUL	NUL
SYM																

U				U				U				U			

BYTE	376	377	378	379	380	381	382	383	384	385	386	387	388	389	390	391
HEX	00	00	00	00	00	00	00	00	00	00	00	00	01	00	00	00
DEC	0	0	0	0	0	0	0	0	0	0	0	0	1	0	0	0
ASC	^@	^@	^@	^@	^@	^@	^@	^@	^@	^@	^@	^@	^A	^@	^@	^@
ALT	NUL	NUL	NUL	NUL	NUL	NUL	NUL	NUL	NUL	NUL	NUL	NUL	SOH	NUL	NUL	NUL
SYM																

U				U				Resource Flags	First Hook to Show	Internal Resource #	S

BYTE	392	393	394	395	396	397	398	399	400	401	402	403	404	405	406	407
HEX	08	00	08	00	08	00	08	00	08	00	00	00	00	00	32	00
DEC	8	0	8	0	8	0	8	0	8	0	0	0	0	0	50	0
ASC	^H	^@	^H	^@	^H	^@	^H	^@	^H	^@	^@	^@	^@	^@		^@
ALT	BS	NUL	BS	NUL	BS	NUL	BS	NUL	BS	NUL	NUL	NUL	NUL	NUL		NUL
SYM															2	

M		T		W		TH		F		S		8th Day		Default Res. Assign. Pri.	

BYTE	408	409	410	411	412	413	414	415	416	417	418	419	420	421	422	423
HEX	00	00	00	00	01	00	00	00	00	00	00	00	00	00	78	00
DEC	0	0	0	0	1	0	0	0	0	0	0	0	0	0	120	0
ASC	^@	^@	^@	^@	^A	^@	^@	^@	^@	^@	^@	^@	^@	^@		^@
ALT	NUL	NUL	NUL	NUL	SOH	NUL	NUL	NUL	NUL	NUL	NUL	NUL	NUL	NUL		NUL
SYM															x	

U		Cost Accrual Method		# Resource Units		# Hours Resource is Overscheduled			# Calendar Overtime Hours			Default Res. Alloc. Type	

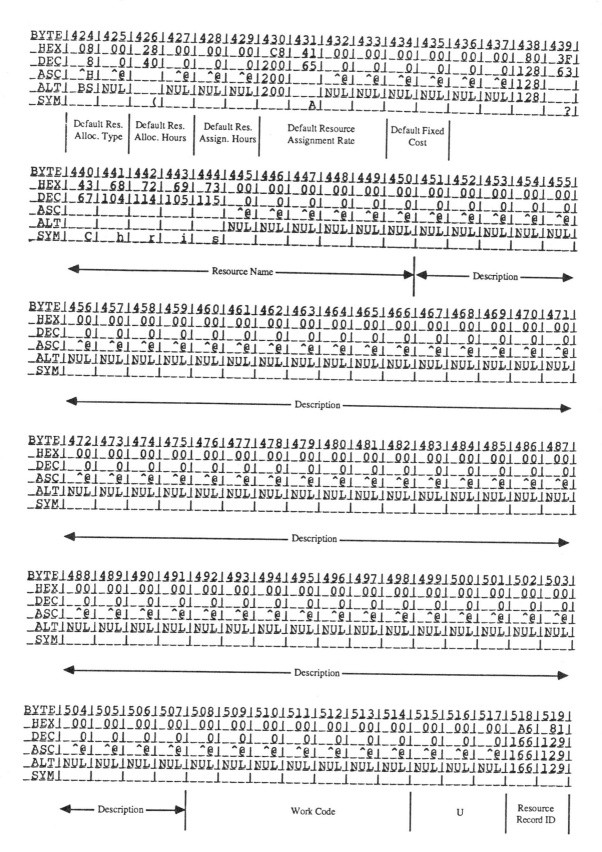

BYTE	424	425	426	427	428	429	430	431	432	433	434	435	436	437	438	439
HEX	08	00	28	00	00	00	C8	41	00	00	00	00	00	00	80	3F
DEC	81	01	40	01	01	01	200	65	01	01	01	01	01	01	80	63
ASC	^H	^@	(	^@	^@	^@	200		^@	^@	^@	^@	^@	^@	128	63
ALT	BS	NUL		NUL	NUL	NUL	200		NUL	NUL	NUL	NUL	NUL	NUL	128	
SYM			(					A								?

Default Res. Alloc. Type	Default Res. Alloc. Hours	Default Res. Assign. Hours	Default Resource Assignment Rate	Default Fixed Cost

BYTE	440	441	442	443	444	445	446	447	448	449	450	451	452	453	454	455
HEX	43	68	72	69	73	00	00	00	00	00	00	00	00	00	00	00
DEC	67	104	114	105	115	01	01	01	01	01	01	01	01	01	01	01
ASC						^@	^@	^@	^@	^@	^@	^@	^@	^@	^@	^@
ALT						NUL	NUL	NUL	NUL	NUL	NUL	NUL	NUL	NUL	NUL	NUL
SYM	C	h	r	i	s											

← ——————————— Resource Name ——————————— → ← ————— Description ————— →

BYTE	456	457	458	459	460	461	462	463	464	465	466	467	468	469	470	471
HEX	00	00	00	00	00	00	00	00	00	00	00	00	00	00	00	00
DEC	01	01	01	01	01	01	01	01	01	01	01	01	01	01	01	01
ASC	^@	^@	^@	^@	^@	^@	^@	^@	^@	^@	^@	^@	^@	^@	^@	^@
ALT	NUL	NUL	NUL	NUL	NUL	NUL	NUL	NUL	NUL	NUL	NUL	NUL	NUL	NUL	NUL	
SYM																

← ———————————————— Description ———————————————— →

BYTE	472	473	474	475	476	477	478	479	480	481	482	483	484	485	486	487
HEX	00	00	00	00	00	00	00	00	00	00	00	00	00	00	00	00
DEC	01	01	01	01	01	01	01	01	01	01	01	01	01	01	01	01
ASC	^@	^@	^@	^@	^@	^@	^@	^@	^@	^@	^@	^@	^@	^@	^@	^@
ALT	NUL	NUL	NUL	NUL	NUL	NUL	NUL	NUL	NUL	NUL	NUL	NUL	NUL	NUL	NUL	
SYM																

← ———————————————— Description ———————————————— →

BYTE	488	489	490	491	492	493	494	495	496	497	498	499	500	501	502	503
HEX	00	00	00	00	00	00	00	00	00	00	00	00	00	00	00	00
DEC	01	01	01	01	01	01	01	01	01	01	01	01	01	01	01	01
ASC	^@	^@	^@	^@	^@	^@	^@	^@	^@	^@	^@	^@	^@	^@	^@	^@
ALT	NUL	NUL	NUL	NUL	NUL	NUL	NUL	NUL	NUL	NUL	NUL	NUL	NUL	NUL	NUL	
SYM																

← ———————————————— Description ———————————————— →

BYTE	504	505	506	507	508	509	510	511	512	513	514	515	516	517	518	519
HEX	00	00	00	00	00	00	00	00	00	00	00	00	00	00	A6	81
DEC	01	01	01	01	01	01	01	01	01	01	01	01	01	01	166	129
ASC	^@	^@	^@	^@	^@	^@	^@	^@	^@	^@	^@	^@	^@	^@	166	129
ALT	NUL	NUL	NUL	NUL	NUL	NUL	NUL	NUL	NUL	NUL	NUL	NUL	NUL	NUL	166	129
SYM																

← Description →	Work Code	U	Resource Record ID

```
BYTE|520|521|522|523|524|525|526|527|528|529|530|531|532|533|534|535|
 HEX| AA| 00| 08| 00| 7C| 9F| 00| 00| CE| 9F| 08| 00| 95| 9F| 00| 00|
 DEC|170| 0| 8| 0|124|159| 0| 0|206|159| 8| 0|149|159| 0| 0|
 ASC|170| ^@| ^H| ^@| |159| ^@| ^@|206|159| ^H| ^@|149|159| ^@| ^@|
 ALT|170|NUL| BS|NUL| |159|NUL|NUL|206|159| BS|NUL|149|159|NUL|NUL|
 SYM|   |   |   |   |   |   |  |   |   |   |   |   |   |   |   |   |
```

```
|
| 170 Bytes |
|
```

```
BYTE|536|537|538|539|540|541|542|543|544|545|546|547|548|549|550|551|
 HEX| 00| 00| 00| 00| 00| 00| 00| 00| E5| 9F| 00| 00| 00| 00| 00| 00|
 DEC| 0| 0| 0| 0| 0| 0| 0| 0|229|159| 0| 0| 0| 0| 0| 0|
 ASC| ^@| ^@| ^@| ^@| ^@| ^@| ^@| ^@|229|159| ^@| ^@| ^@| ^@| ^@| ^@|
 ALT|NUL|NUL|NUL|NUL|NUL|NUL|NUL|NUL|229|159|NUL|NUL|NUL|NUL|NUL|NUL|
 SYM|   |   |   |   |   |   |   |   |   |   |   |   |   |   |   |   |
```

```
BYTE|552|553|554|555|556|557|558|559|560|561|562|563|564|565|566|567|
 HEX| 00| 00| 00| 00| 00| 00| 00| 00| 00| 00| 02| 00| 00| 00| 08| 00|
 DEC| 0| 0| 0| 0| 0| 0| 0| 0| 0| 0| 2| 0| 0| 0| 8| 0|
 ASC| ^@| ^@| ^@| ^@| ^@| ^@| ^@| ^@| ^@| ^@| ^B| ^@| ^@| ^@| ^H| ^@|
 ALT|NUL|NUL|NUL|NUL|NUL|NUL|NUL|NUL|NUL|NUL|STX|NUL|NUL|NUL| BS|NUL|
 SYM|   |   |   |   |   |   |   |   |   |   |   |   |   |   |   |   |
```

```
BYTE|568|569|570|571|572|573|574|575|576|577|578|579|580|581|582|583|
 HEX| 08| 00| 08| 00| 08| 00| 08| 00| 00| 00| 00| 00| 32| 00| 00| 00|
 DEC| 8| 0| 8| 0| 8| 0| 8| 0| 0| 0| 0| 0| 50| 0| 0| 0|
 ASC| ^H| ^@| ^H| ^@| ^H| ^@| ^H| ^@| ^@| ^@| ^@| ^@| |  ^@| ^@| ^@|
 ALT| BS|NUL| BS|NUL| BS|NUL| BS|NUL|NUL|NUL|NUL|NUL| |  NUL|NUL|NUL|
 SYM|   |   |   |   |   |   |   |   |   |   |   |   | 2|   |   |   |
```

```
BYTE|584|585|586|587|588|589|590|591|592|593|594|595|596|597|598|599|
 HEX| 00| 00| 01| 00| 00| 00| 00| 00| 00| 00| 00| 00| 78| 00| 08| 00|
 DEC| 0| 0| 1| 0| 0| 0| 0| 0| 0| 0| 0| 0|120| 0| 8| 0|
 ASC| ^@| ^@| ^A| ^@| ^@| ^@| ^@| ^@| ^@| ^@| ^@| ^@| |  ^@| ^H| ^@|
 ALT|NUL|NUL|SOH|NUL|NUL|NUL|NUL|NUL|NUL|NUL|NUL|NUL| |  NUL| BS|NUL|
 SYM|   |   |   |   |   |   |   |   |   |   |   |   | x|   |   |   |
```

```
BYTE|600|601|602|603|604|605|606|607|608|609|610|611|612|613|614|615|
 HEX| 28| 00| 00| 00| C8| 41| 00| 00| 00| 00| 00| 00| 80| 3F| 4D| 61|
 DEC| 40| 0| 0| 0|200| 65| 0| 0| 0| 0| 0| 0|128| 63| 77| 97|
 ASC| |  ^@| ^@| ^@|200| |  ^@| ^@| ^@| ^@| ^@| ^@|128| |  |  |
 ALT| |  NUL|NUL|NUL|200| |  NUL|NUL|NUL|NUL|NUL|NUL|128| |  |  |
 SYM| (|   |   |   |   | A|   |   |   |   |   |   |   | ?| M| a|
```

BYTE	616	617	618	619	620	621	622	623	624	625	626	627	628	629	630	631
HEX	72	6B	00	32	00	00	00	00	00	00	00	00	00	00	00	00
DEC	114	107	0	50	0	0	0	0	0	0	0	0	0	0	0	0
ASC			^@		^@	^@	^@	^@	^@	^@	^@	^@	^@	^@	^@	^@
ALT			NUL		NUL	NUL	NUL	NUL	NUL	NUL	NUL	NUL	NUL	NUL	NUL	NUL
SYM	r	k		2												

BYTE	632	633	634	635	636	637	638	639	640	641	642	643	644	645	646	647
HEX	00	00	00	00	00	00	00	00	00	00	00	00	00	00	00	00
DEC	0	0	0	0	0	0	0	0	0	0	0	0	0	0	0	0
ASC	^@	^@	^@	^@	^@	^@	^@	^@	^@	^@	^@	^@	^@	^@	^@	^@
ALT	NUL	NUL	NUL	NUL	NUL	NUL	NUL	NUL	NUL	NUL	NUL	NUL	NUL	NUL	NUL	
SYM																

BYTE	648	649	650	651	652	653	654	655	656	657	658	659	660	661	662	663
HEX	00	00	00	00	00	00	00	00	00	00	00	00	00	00	00	00
DEC	0	0	0	0	0	0	0	0	0	0	0	0	0	0	0	0
ASC	^@	^@	^@	^@	^@	^@	^@	^@	^@	^@	^@	^@	^@	^@	^@	^@
ALT	NUL	NUL	NUL	NUL	NUL	NUL	NUL	NUL	NUL	NUL	NUL	NUL	NUL	NUL	NUL	
SYM																

BYTE	664	665	666	667	668	669	670	671	672	673	674	675	676	677	678	679
HEX	00	00	00	00	00	00	00	00	00	00	00	00	00	00	00	00
DEC	0	0	0	0	0	0	0	0	0	0	0	0	0	0	0	0
ASC	^@	^@	^@	^@	^@	^@	^@	^@	^@	^@	^@	^@	^@	^@	^@	^@
ALT	NUL	NUL	NUL	NUL	NUL	NUL	NUL	NUL	NUL	NUL	NUL	NUL	NUL	NUL	NUL	
SYM																

BYTE	680	681	682	683	684	685	686	687	688	689	690	691	692	693	694	695
HEX	00	00	00	00	00	00	00	00	00	00	00	00	A6	81	AA	00
DEC	0	0	0	0	0	0	0	0	0	0	0	0	166	129	170	0
ASC	^@	^@	^@	^@	^@	^@	^@	^@	^@	^@	^@	^@	166	129	170	^@
ALT	NUL	NUL	NUL	NUL	NUL	NUL	NUL	NUL	NUL	NUL	NUL	NUL	166	129	170	NUL
SYM																

	Resource Record ID	170 Bytes

BYTE	696	697	698	699	700	701	702	703	704	705	706	707	708	709	710	711
HEX	00	00	00	00	08	00	B0	9F	00	00	76	9F	00	00	00	00
DEC	0	0	0	0	8	0	176	159	0	0	118	159	0	0	0	0
ASC	^@	^@	^@	^@	^H	^@	176	159	^@	^@		159	^@	^@	^@	^@
ALT	NUL	NUL	NUL	NUL	BS	NUL	176	159	NUL	NUL		159	NUL	NUL	NUL	NUL
SYM												v				

```
BYTE|712|713|714|715|716|717|718|719|720|721|722|723|724|725|726|727|
HEX| 00| 00| 00| 00| 00| 00| E5| 9F| 00| 00| 00| 00| 00| 00| 00| 00|
DEC| 0| 0| 0| 0| 0| 0|229|159| 0| 0| 0| 0| 0| 0| 0| 0|
ASC| ^@| ^@| ^@| ^@| ^@| ^@|229|159| ^@| ^@| ^@| ^@| ^@| ^@| ^@| ^@|
ALT|NUL|NUL|NUL|NUL|NUL|NUL|229|159|NUL|NUL|NUL|NUL|NUL|NUL|NUL|NUL|
SYM|   |   |   |   |   |   |   |   |   |   |   |   |   |   |   |   |


BYTE|728|729|730|731|732|733|734|735|736|737|738|739|740|741|742|743|
HEX| 00| 00| 00| 00| 00| 00| 00| 00| 03| 00| 00| 00| 08| 00| 08| 00|
DEC| 0| 0| 0| 0| 0| 0| 0| 0| 3| 0| 0| 0| 8| 0| 8| 0|
ASC| ^@| ^@| ^@| ^@| ^@| ^@| ^@| ^@| ^C| ^@| ^@| ^@| ^H| ^@| ^H| ^@|
ALT|NUL|NUL|NUL|NUL|NUL|NUL|NUL|NUL|ETX|NUL|NUL|NUL| BS|NUL| BS|NUL|
SYM|   |   |   |   |   |   |   |   |   |   |   |   |   |   |   |   |


BYTE|744|745|746|747|748|749|750|751|752|753|754|755|756|757|758|759|
HEX| 08| 00| 08| 00| 08| 00| 00| 00| 00| 00| 32| 00| 00| 00| 00| 00|
DEC| 8| 0| 8| 0| 8| 0| 0| 0| 0| 0| 50| 0| 0| 0| 0| 0|
ASC| ^H| ^@| ^H| ^@| ^H| ^@| ^@| ^@| ^@| ^@| 2| ^@| ^@| ^@| ^@| ^@|
ALT| BS|NUL| BS|NUL| BS|NUL|NUL|NUL|NUL|NUL|   |NUL|NUL|NUL|NUL|NUL|
SYM|   |   |   |   |   |   |   |   |   |   | 2|   |   |   |   |   |


BYTE|760|761|762|763|764|765|766|767|768|769|770|771|772|773|774|775|
HEX| 01| 00| 00| 00| 00| 00| 00| 00| 00| 00| 78| 00| 08| 00| 28| 00|
DEC| 1| 0| 0| 0| 0| 0| 0| 0| 0| 0|120| 0| 8| 0| 40| 0|
ASC| ^A| ^@| ^@| ^@| ^@| ^@| ^@| ^@| ^@| ^@| x| ^@| ^H| ^@| (| ^@|
ALT|SOH|NUL|NUL|NUL|NUL|NUL|NUL|NUL|NUL|NUL|   |NUL| BS|NUL|   |NUL|
SYM|   |   |   |   |   |   |   |   |   |   | x|   |   |   | (|   |


BYTE|776|777|778|779|780|781|782|783|784|785|786|787|788|789|790|791|
HEX| 00| 00| C8| 41| 00| 00| 00| 00| 00| 00| 80| 3F| 54| 6F| 6D| 00|
DEC| 0| 0|200| 65| 0| 0| 0| 0| 0| 0|128| 63| 84|111|109| 0|
ASC| ^@| ^@|200|   | ^@| ^@| ^@| ^@| ^@| ^@|128|   |   |   |   | ^@|
ALT|NUL|NUL|200|   |NUL|NUL|NUL|NUL|NUL|NUL|128|   |   |   |   |NUL|
SYM|   |   |   | A|   |   |   |   |   |   |   | ?| T| o| m|   |


BYTE|792|793|794|795|796|797|798|799|800|801|802|803|804|805|806|807|
HEX| 2D| 33| 00| 00| 00| 00| 00| 00| 00| 00| 00| 00| 00| 00| 00| 00|
DEC| 45| 51| 0| 0| 0| 0| 0| 0| 0| 0| 0| 0| 0| 0| 0| 0|
ASC|   |   | ^@| ^@| ^@| ^@| ^@| ^@| ^@| ^@| ^@| ^@| ^@| ^@| ^@| ^@|
ALT|   |   |NUL|NUL|NUL|NUL|NUL|NUL|NUL|NUL|NUL|NUL|NUL|NUL|NUL|NUL|
SYM| -| 3|   |   |   |   |   |   |   |   |   |   |   |   |   |   |
```

```
BYTE|808|809|810|811|812|813|814|815|816|817|818|819|820|821|822|823|
HEX | 00| 00| 00| 00| 00| 00| 00| 00| 00| 00| 00| 00| 00| 00| 00| 00|
DEC |  0|  0|  0|  0|  0|  0|  0|  0|  0|  0|  0|  0|  0|  0|  0|  0|
ASC | ^@| ^@| ^@| ^@| ^@| ^@| ^@| ^@| ^@| ^@| ^@| ^@| ^@| ^@| ^@| ^@|
ALT |NUL|NUL|NUL|NUL|NUL|NUL|NUL|NUL|NUL|NUL|NUL|NUL|NUL|NUL|NUL|NUL|
SYM |   |   |   |   |   |   |   |   |   |   |   |   |   |   |   |   |


BYTE|824|825|826|827|828|829|830|831|832|833|834|835|836|837|838|839|
HEX | 00| 00| 00| 00| 00| 00| 00| 00| 00| 00| 00| 00| 00| 00| 00| 00|
DEC |  0|  0|  0|  0|  0|  0|  0|  0|  0|  0|  0|  0|  0|  0|  0|  0|
ASC | ^@| ^@| ^@| ^@| ^@| ^@| ^@| ^@| ^@| ^@| ^@| ^@| ^@| ^@| ^@| ^@|
ALT |NUL|NUL|NUL|NUL|NUL|NUL|NUL|NUL|NUL|NUL|NUL|NUL|NUL|NUL|NUL|NUL|
SYM |   |   |   |   |   |   |   |   |   |   |   |   |   |   |   |   |


BYTE|840|841|842|843|844|845|846|847|848|849|850|851|852|853|854|855|
HEX | 00| 00| 00| 00| 00| 00| 00| 00| 00| 00| 00| 00| 00| 00| 00| 00|
DEC |  0|  0|  0|  0|  0|  0|  0|  0|  0|  0|  0|  0|  0|  0|  0|  0|
ASC | ^@| ^@| ^@| ^@| ^@| ^@| ^@| ^@| ^@| ^@| ^@| ^@| ^@| ^@| ^@| ^@|
ALT |NUL|NUL|NUL|NUL|NUL|NUL|NUL|NUL|NUL|NUL|NUL|NUL|NUL|NUL|NUL|NUL|
SYM |   |   |   |   |   |   |   |   |   |   |   |   |   |   |   |   |


BYTE|856|857|858|859|860|861|862|863|864|865|866|867|868|869|870|871|
HEX | 00| 00| 00| 00| 00| 00| 00| 00| 00| 00| 00| A8| 81| 68| 00| 04| 00|
DEC |  0|  0|  0|  0|  0|  0|  0|  0|  0|  0|168|129|104|  0|  4|  0|
ASC | ^@| ^@| ^@| ^@| ^@| ^@| ^@| ^@| ^@| ^@|168|129|104|  0|  4|  0|
ALT |NUL|NUL|NUL|NUL|NUL|NUL|NUL|NUL|NUL|NUL|168|129|   | ^@| ^D| ^@|
SYM |   |   |   |   |   |   |   |   |   |   |168|129|   |NUL|EOT|NUL|
```

	Resource Assignment Record	104 Bytes	Resource Assignment Task ID

```
BYTE|872|873|874|875|876|877|878|879|880|881|882|883|884|885|886|887|
HEX | 03| 00| 08| 00| 95| 9F| 00| 00| 00| 00| 00| 00| 00| 00| 08| 00|
DEC | 31|  0|  8|  0|149|159|  0|  0|  0|  0|  0|  0|  0|  0|  8|  0|
ASC | ^C| ^@| ^H| ^@|149|159| ^@| ^@| ^@| ^@| ^@| ^@| ^@| ^@| ^H| ^@|
ALT |ETX|NUL| BS|NUL|149|159|NUL|NUL|NUL|NUL|NUL|NUL|NUL|NUL| BS|NUL|
SYM |   |   |   |   |   |   |   |   |   |   |   |   |   |   |   |   |
```

Resource Assignment Resource ID	U	U	U	U

```
BYTE|888|889|890|891|892|893|894|895|896|897|898|899|900|901|902|903|
HEX | 7C| 9F| 08| 00| 87| 9F| 00| 00| E5| 9F| 00| 00| 00| 00| 00| 00|
DEC |124|159|  8|  0|135|159|  0|  0|229|159|  0|  0|  0|  0|  0|  0|
ASC |   |159| ^H| ^@|135|159| ^@| ^@|229|159| ^@| ^@| ^@| ^@| ^@| ^@|
ALT |   |159| BS|NUL|135|159|NUL|NUL|229|159|NUL|NUL|NUL|NUL|NUL|NUL|
SYM |   |159|   |   |   |   |   |   |   |   |   |   |   |   |   |   |
```

U	U	U	U	U

BYTE	904	905	906	907	908	909	910	911	912	913	914	915	916	917	918	919
HEX	00	00	00	00	00	00	02	00	FB	33	FC	33	FE	33	FF	33
DEC	0	0	0	0	0	0	2	0	251	51	252	51	254	51	255	51
ASC	^@	^@	^@	^@	^@	^@	^B	^@	251		252		254		255	
ALT	NUL	NUL	NUL	NUL	NUL	NUL	STX	NUL	251		252		254		255	
SYM										3		3		3		3

U	U	Resource Assignment Flags	Scheduled Start Date	Scheduled Finish Date	Late Start Date	Late Finish Date

BYTE	920	921	922	923	924	925	926	927	928	929	930	931	932	933	934	935
HEX	00	08	00	08	00	00	00	00	32	00	10	00	00	00	00	00
DEC	0	8	0	8	0	0	0	0	50	0	16	0	0	0	0	0
ASC	^@	^H	^@	^H	^@	^@	^@	^@			^P	^@	^@	^@	^@	^@
ALT	NUL	BS	NUL	BS	NUL	NUL	NUL	NUL		NUL	DLE	NUL	NUL	NUL	NUL	NUL
SYM									2							

Sched Ot. Hr.	Sched Fin. Hr.	Late Start Hour	Late Fin. Hour	Resource Assignment Total Float	Delay From Task Sched. Start	Priority	Hours to Work on This Task	Oversched. Hrs to Work on This Task	Actual Hrs. Worked on This Task

BYTE	936	937	938	939	940	941	942	943	944	945	946	947	948	949	950	951
HEX	78	00	08	00	00	00	00	00	00	00	C8	41	00	00	00	00
DEC	120	0	8	0	0	0	0	0	0	0	200	65	0	0	0	0
ASC		^@	^H	^@	^@	^@	^@	^@	^@	^@	200		^@	^@	^@	^@
ALT		NUL	BS	NUL	NUL	NUL	NUL	NUL	NUL	NUL	200		NUL	NUL	NUL	NUL
SYM	x											A				

Resource Assignment Allocation Type	Allocation Hours	Actual Cost	Assignment Rate	Assignment Fixed Cost →

BYTE	952	953	954	955	956	957	958	959	960	961	962	963	964	965	966	967
HEX	01	00	00	00	20	03	20	03	20	03	20	03	00	00	00	00
DEC	1	0	0	0	32	3	32	3	32	3	32	3	0	0	0	0
ASC	^A	^@	^@	^@	^	^C	^	^C	^	^C	^	^C	^@	^@	^@	^@
ALT	SOH	NUL	NUL	NUL	SPC	ETX	SPC	ETX	SPC	ETX	SPC	ETX	NUL	NUL	NUL	NUL
SYM																

← A.F.C.	# Units of Resource Assigned	U	Allocation of First Day of Res. Assign.	Allocation of Last Day of Res. Assign.	U	U	Res. Assign. Finish Delay

BYTE	968	969	970	971	972	973	974	975	976	977	978	979	980	981	982	983
HEX	00	00	FB	33	00	00	A8	81	68	00	03	00	02	00	00	00
DEC	0	0	251	51	0	0	168	129	104	0	3	0	2	0	0	0
ASC	^@	^@	251		^@	^@	168	129		^@	^C	^@	^B	^@	^@	^@
ALT	NUL	NUL	251		NUL	NUL	168	129		NUL	ETX	NUL	STX	NUL	NUL	NUL
SYM				3					h							

U	Resource Assignment Record	104 Bytes

BYTE	984	985	986	987	988	989	990	991	992	993	994	995	996	997	998	999
HEX	AA	9F	00	00	AA	9F	00	00	00	00	08	00	B0	9F	00	00
DEC	170	159	0	0	170	159	0	0	0	0	8	0	176	159	0	0
ASC	170	159	^@	^@	170	159	^@	^@	^@	^@	^H	^@	176	159	^@	^@
ALT	170	159	NUL	NUL	170	159	NUL	NUL	NUL	NUL	BS	NUL	176	159	NUL	NUL
SYM																

BYTE	0	1	2	3	4	5	6	7	8	9	10	11	12	13	14	15
HEX	9C	9F	00	00	E5	9F	00	00	00	00	00	00	00	00	00	00
DEC	156	159	0	0	229	159	0	0	0	0	0	0	0	0	0	0
ASC	156	159	^@	^@	229	159	^@	^@	^@	^@	^@	^@	^@	^@	^@	^@
ALT	156	159	NUL	NUL	229	159	NUL	NUL	NUL	NUL	NUL	NUL	NUL	NUL	NUL	NUL
SYM																

BYTE	16	17	18	19	20	21	22	23	24	25	26	27	28	29	30	31
HEX	76	9F	02	00	F4	33	F8	33	F7	33	FD	33	00	08	00	08
DEC	118	159	2	0	244	51	248	51	247	51	253	51	0	8	0	8
ASC		159	^B	^@	244		248		247		253		^@	^H	^@	^H
ALT		159	STX	NUL	244		248		247		253		NUL	BS	NUL	BS
SYM	v					3		3		3		3				

BYTE	32	33	34	35	36	37	38	39	40	41	42	43	44	45	46	47
HEX	00	00	00	00	32	00	28	00	28	00	00	00	78	00	08	00
DEC	0	0	0	0	50	0	40	0	40	0	0	0	120	0	8	0
ASC	^@	^@	^@	^@		^@		^@		^@	^@	^@		^@	^H	^@
ALT	NUL	NUL	NUL	NUL		NUL		NUL		NUL	NUL	NUL		NUL	BS	NUL
SYM					2		(		(				x			

BYTE	48	49	50	51	52	53	54	55	56	57	58	59	60	61	62	63
HEX	00	00	00	00	00	00	C8	41	00	00	00	00	01	00	A0	0F
DEC	0	0	0	0	0	0	200	65	0	0	0	0	1	0	160	15
ASC	^@	^@	^@	^@	^@	^@	200		^@	^@	^@	^@	^A	^@	160	15
ALT	NUL	NUL	NUL	NUL	NUL	NUL	200		NUL	NUL	NUL	NUL	SOH	NUL	160	SI
SYM								A								

BYTE	64	65	66	67	68	69	70	71	72	73	74	75	76	77	78	79
HEX	20	03	20	03	20	03	20	03	00	00	00	00	00	00	F4	33
DEC	32	3	32	3	32	3	32	3	0	0	0	0	0	0	244	51
ASC	^^	^C	^^	^C	^^	^C	^^	^C	^@	^@	^@	^@	^@	^@	244	
ALT	SPC	ETX	SPC	ETX	SPC	ETX	SPC	ETX	NUL	NUL	NUL	NUL	NUL	NUL	244	
SYM																3

BYTE	80	81	82	83	84	85	86	87	88	89	90	91	92	93	94	95
HEX	00	00	A8	81	68	00	02	00	02	00	08	00	C7	9F	00	00
DEC	0	0	168	129	104	0	2	0	2	0	8	0	199	159	0	0
ASC	^@	^@	168	129		^@	^B	^@	^B	^@	^H	^@	199	159	^@	^@
ALT	NUL	NUL	168	129		NUL	STX	NUL	STX	NUL	BS	NUL	199	159	NUL	NUL
SYM					h											

Resource Assignment Record | 104 Bytes

BYTE	96	97	98	99	100	101	102	103	104	105	106	107	108	109	110	111
HEX	00	00	00	00	00	00	08	00	B0	9F	08	00	BB	9F	00	00
DEC	0	0	0	0	0	0	8	0	176	159	8	0	187	159	0	0
ASC	^@	^@	^@	^@	^@	^@	^H	^@	176	159	^H	^@	187	159	^@	^@
ALT	NUL	NUL	NUL	NUL	NUL	NUL	BS	NUL	176	159	BS	NUL	187	159	NUL	NUL
SYM																

BYTE	112	113	114	115	116	117	118	119	120	121	122	123	124	125	126	127
HEX	E5	9F	00	00	00	00	00	00	00	00	08	00	95	9F	02	00
DEC	229	159	0	0	0	0	0	0	0	0	8	0	149	159	2	0
ASC	229	159	^@	^@	^@	^@	^@	^@	^@	^@	^H	^@	149	159	^B	^@
ALT	229	159	NUL	NUL	NUL	NUL	NUL	NUL	NUL	NUL	BS	NUL	149	159	STX	NUL
SYM																

BYTE	128	129	130	131	132	133	134	135	136	137	138	139	140	141	142	143
HEX	F4	33	FF	33	F4	33	FF	33	00	08	00	08	00	00	00	00
DEC	244	51	255	51	244	51	255	51	0	8	0	8	0	0	0	0
ASC	244		255		244		255		^@	^H	^@	^H	^@	^@	^@	^@
ALT	244		255		244		255		NUL	BS	NUL	BS	NUL	NUL	NUL	NUL
SYM		3		3		3		3								

BYTE	144	145	146	147	148	149	150	151	152	153	154	155	156	157	158	159
HEX	32	00	50	00	00	00	00	00	78	00	08	00	00	00	00	00
DEC	50	0	80	0	0	0	0	0	120	0	8	0	0	0	0	0
ASC		^@		^@	^@	^@	^@	^@		^@	^H	^@	^@	^@	^@	^@
ALT		NUL		NUL	NUL	NUL	NUL	NUL		NUL	BS	NUL	NUL	NUL	NUL	NUL
SYM	2		P						x							

BYTE	160	161	162	163	164	165	166	167	168	169	170	171	172	173	174	175
HEX	00	00	C8	41	00	00	00	00	01	00	00	00	20	03	20	03
DEC	0	0	200	65	0	0	0	0	1	0	0	0	32	3	32	3
ASC	^@	^@	200		^@	^@	^@	^@	^A	^@	^@	^@	^^	^C	^^	^C
ALT	NUL	NUL	200		NUL	NUL	NUL	NUL	SOH	NUL	NUL	NUL	SPC	ETX	SPC	ETX
SYM				A												

BYTE	176	177	178	179	180	181	182	183	184	185	186	187	188	189	190	191
HEX	20	03	20	03	00	00	00	00	00	00	F4	33	00	00	A8	81
DEC	32	3	32	3	0	0	0	0	0	0	244	51	0	0	168	129
ASC	^^	^C	^^	^C	^@	^@	^@	^@	^@	^@	244		^@	^@	168	129
ALT	SPC	ETX	SPC	ETX	NUL	NUL	NUL	NUL	NUL	NUL	244		NUL	NUL	168	129
SYM												3				

Resource
Assignment
Record

BYTE	192	193	194	195	196	197	198	199	200	201	202	203	204	205	206	207
HEX	68	00	01	00	01	00	00	00	00	00	00	00	00	00	00	00
DEC	104	0	1	0	1	0	0	0	0	0	0	0	0	0	0	0
ASC		^@	^A	^@	^A	^@	^@	^@	^@	^@	^@	^@	^@	^@	^@	^@
ALT		NUL	SOH	NUL	SOH	NUL	NUL	NUL	NUL	NUL	NUL	NUL	NUL	NUL	NUL	NUL
SYM	b															

104 Bytes

BYTE	208	209	210	211	212	213	214	215	216	217	218	219	220	221	222	223
HEX	00	00	00	00	CE	9F	00	00	D9	9F	00	00	E5	9F	00	00
DEC	0	0	0	0	206	159	0	0	217	159	0	0	229	159	0	0
ASC	^@	^@	^@	^@	206	159	^@	^@	217	159	^@	^@	229	159	0	0
ALT	NUL	NUL	NUL	NUL	206	159	NUL	NUL	217	159	NUL	NUL	229	159	^@	^@
SYM															NUL	NUL

BYTE	224	225	226	227	228	229	230	231	232	233	234	235	236	237	238	239
HEX	00	00	00	00	00	00	00	00	AA	9F	02	00	ED	33	F1	33
DEC	0	0	0	0	0	0	0	0	170	159	2	0	237	51	241	51
ASC	^@	^@	^@	^@	^@	^@	^@	^@	170	159	^B	^@	237		241	
ALT	NUL	NUL	NUL	NUL	NUL	NUL	NUL	NUL	170	159	STX	NUL	237		241	
SYM														3		3

BYTE	240	241	242	243	244	245	246	247	248	249	250	251	252	253	254	255
HEX	ED	33	F1	33	00	08	00	08	00	00	00	00	32	00	28	00
DEC	237	51	241	51	0	8	0	8	0	0	0	0	50	0	40	0
ASC	237		241		^@	^H	^@	^H	^@	^@	^@	^@	50	0	40	0
ALT	237		241		NUL	BS	NUL	BS	NUL	NUL	NUL	NUL		NUL		NUL
SYM		3		3										2		(

BYTE	256	257	258	259	260	261	262	263	264	265	266	267	268	269	270	271
HEX	00	00	00	00	78	00	08	00	00	00	00	00	00	00	C8	41
DEC	0	0	0	0	120	0	8	0	0	0	0	0	0	0	200	65
ASC	^@	^@	^@	^@		^@	^H	^@	^@	^@	^@	^@	^@	^@	200	
ALT	NUL	NUL	NUL	NUL		NUL	BS	NUL	NUL	NUL	NUL	NUL	NUL	NUL	200	
SYM					x											A

BYTE	272	273	274	275	276	277	278	279	280	281	282	283	284	285	286	287
HEX	00	00	00	00	01	00	00	00	20	03	20	03	20	03	20	03
DEC	0	0	0	0	1	0	0	0	32	3	32	3	32	3	32	3
ASC	^@	^@	^@	^@	^A	^@	^@	^@	^^	^C	^^	^C	^^	^C	^^	^C
ALT	NUL	NUL	NUL	NUL	SOH	NUL	NUL	NUL	SPC	ETX	SPC	ETX	SPC	ETX	SPC	ETX
SYM																

Block (bytes 288–303):

BYTE	288	289	290	291	292	293	294	295	296	297	298	299	300	301	302	303
HEX	00	00	00	00	00	00	ED	33	00	00	A1	81	22	00	03	00
DEC	0	0	0	0	0	0	237	51	0	0	161	129	34	0	3	0
ASC	^@	^@	^@	^@	^@	^@	237		^@	^@	161	129		^@	^C	^@
ALT	NUL	NUL	NUL	NUL	NUL	NUL	237		NUL	NUL	161	129		NUL	ETX	NUL
SYM								3					"			

Labels: Link Record ID | 34 Bytes | Link From Task ID #

Block (bytes 304–319):

BYTE	304	305	306	307	308	309	310	311	312	313	314	315	316	317	318	319
HEX	04	00	08	00	93	9F	00	00	00	00	00	00	00	00	00	00
DEC	4	0	8	0	147	159	0	0	0	0	0	0	0	0	0	0
ASC	^D	^@	^H	^@	147	159	^@	^@	^@	^@	^@	^@	^@	^@	^@	^@
ALT	EOT	NUL	BS	NUL	147	159	NUL	NUL	NUL	NUL	NUL	NUL	NUL	NUL	NUL	NUL
SYM																

Labels: Link to Task ID # | U | U | U | U

Block (bytes 320–335):

BYTE	320	321	322	323	324	325	326	327	328	329	330	331	332	333	334	335
HEX	9C	9F	08	00	87	9F	00	00	E5	9F	00	00	00	00	00	00
DEC	156	159	8	0	135	159	0	0	229	159	0	0	0	0	0	0
ASC	156	159	^H	^@	135	159	^@	^@	229	159	^@	^@	^@	^@	^@	^@
ALT	156	159	BS	NUL	135	159	NUL	NUL	229	159	NUL	NUL	NUL	NUL	NUL	NUL
SYM																

Labels: U | U | U | Link Flags | Link Lead Lag Duration | Link Type

Block (bytes 336–351):

BYTE	336	337	338	339	340	341	342	343	344	345	346	347	348	349	350	351
HEX	A1	81	22	00	01	00	03	00	00	00	A8	9F	00	00	00	00
DEC	161	129	34	0	1	0	3	0	0	0	168	159	0	0	0	0
ASC	161	129		^@	^A	^@	^C	^@	^@	^@	168	159	^@	^@	^@	^@
ALT	161	129		NUL	SOH	NUL	ETX	NUL	NUL	NUL	168	159	NUL	NUL	NUL	NUL
SYM			"													

Labels: Link Record ID | 34 Bytes

Block (bytes 352–367):

BYTE	352	353	354	355	356	357	358	359	360	361	362	363	364	365	366	367
HEX	00	00	A8	9F	00	00	D9	9F	00	00	9C	9F	00	00	E5	9F
DEC	0	0	168	159	0	0	217	159	0	0	156	159	0	0	229	159
ASC	^@	^@	168	159	^@	^@	217	159	^@	^@	156	159	^@	^@	229	159
ALT	NUL	NUL	168	159	NUL	NUL	217	159	NUL	NUL	156	159	NUL	NUL	229	159
SYM																

Block (bytes 368–383):

BYTE	368	369	370	371	372	373	374	375	376	377	378	379	380	381	382	383
HEX	00	00	00	00	00	00	A1	81	22	00	01	00	02	00	00	00
DEC	0	0	0	0	0	0	161	129	34	0	1	0	2	0	0	0
ASC	^@	^@	^@	^@	^@	^@	161	129		^@	^A	^@	^B	^@	^@	^@
ALT	NUL	NUL	NUL	NUL	NUL	NUL	161	129		NUL	SOH	NUL	STX	NUL	NUL	NUL
SYM									"							

Labels: Link Record ID | 34 Bytes

```
BYTE|384|385|386|387|388|389|390|391|392|393|394|395|396|397|398|399|
_HEX|_00|_00|_00|_00|_00|_00|_00|_00|_00|_00|_00|_00|_D9|_9F|_08|_00|
_DEC|__0|__0|__0|__0|__0|__0|__0|__0|__0|__0|__0|__0|217|159|__8|__0|
_ASC|_^@|_^@|_^@|_^@|_^@|_^@|_^@|_^@|_^@|_^@|_^@|_^@|217|159|__8|__0|
_ALT|NUL|NUL|NUL|NUL|NUL|NUL|NUL|NUL|NUL|NUL|NUL|NUL|217|159|_^H|_^@|
_SYM|___|___|___|___|___|___|___|___|___|___|___|___|217|159|_BS|NUL|


BYTE|400|401|402|403|404|405|406|407|408|409|410|411|__0|__0|__0|__0|
_HEX|_BB|_9F|_00|_00|_E5|_9F|_02|_00|_00|_00|_00|_00|_XX|_XX|_XX|_XX|
_DEC|187|159|__0|__0|229|159|__2|__0|__0|__0|__0|__0|_XX|_XX|_XX|_XX|
_ASC|187|159|_^@|_^@|229|159|_^B|_^@|_^@|_^@|_^@|_^@|XXX|XXX|XXX|XXX|
_ALT|187|159|NUL|NUL|229|159|STX|NUL|NUL|NUL|NUL|NUL|XXX|XXX|XXX|XXX|
_SYM|187|159|___|___|229|159|___|___|___|___|___|___|XXX|XXX|XXX|XXX|
```

SuperCalc4 Sample File

```
BYTE|  0|  1|  2|  3|  4|  5|  6|  7|  8|  9| 10| 11| 12| 13| 14| 15|
HEX | 53| 75| 70| 65| 72| 43| 61| 6C| 63| 20| 76| 65| 72| 2E| 20| 20|
DEC | 83|117|112|101|114| 67| 97|108| 99| 32|118|101|114| 46| 32| 32|
ASC |   |   |   |   |   |   |   |   |   |^` |   |   |   |   |   |   |
ALT |   |   |   |   |   |   |   |   |SPC|   |   |   |   |   |SPC|SPC|
SYM | S | u | p | e | r | C | a | l | c |   | v | e | r | . |   |   |
```
◄─────────────────────── Supercalc Name ───────────────────────►

```
BYTE| 16| 17| 18| 19| 20| 21| 22| 23| 24| 25| 26| 27| 28| 29| 30| 31|
HEX | 31| 2E| 31| 30| 0D| 0A| 00| 00| 00| 00| 00| 00| 00| 00| 00| 00|
DEC | 49| 46| 49| 48| 13| 10|  0|  0|  0|  0|  0|  0|  0|  0|  0|  0|
ASC |   |   |   |   |^M |^J |^@ |^@ |^@ |^@ |^@ |^@ |^@ |^@ |^@ |^@ |
ALT |   |   |   |   |CR |LF |NUL|NUL|NUL|NUL|NUL|NUL|NUL|NUL|NUL|NUL|
SYM | 1 | . | 1 | 0 |   |   |   |   |   |   |   |   |   |   |   |   |
```
| Version & Level | New Line | ◄──────── Worksheet Title ────────►

```
BYTE| 32| 33| 34| 35| 36| 37| 38| 39| 40| 41| 42| 43| 44| 45| 46| 47|
HEX | 00| 00| 00| 00| 00| 00| 00| 00| 00| 00| 00| 00| 00| 00| 00| 00|
DEC |  0|  0|  0|  0|  0|  0|  0|  0|  0|  0|  0|  0|  0|  0|  0|  0|
ASC |^@ |^@ |^@ |^@ |^@ |^@ |^@ |^@ |^@ |^@ |^@ |^@ |^@ |^@ |^@ |^@ |
ALT |NUL|NUL|NUL|NUL|NUL|NUL|NUL|NUL|NUL|NUL|NUL|NUL|NUL|NUL|NUL|NUL|
SYM |   |   |   |   |   |   |   |   |   |   |   |   |   |   |   |   |
```
◄─────────────────────── Worksheet Title ───────────────────────►

```
BYTE| 48| 49| 50| 51| 52| 53| 54| 55| 56| 57| 58| 59| 60| 61| 62| 63|
HEX | 00| 00| 00| 00| 00| 00| 00| 00| 00| 00| 00| 00| 00| 00| 00| 00|
DEC |  0|  0|  0|  0|  0|  0|  0|  0|  0|  0|  0|  0|  0|  0|  0|  0|
ASC |^@ |^@ |^@ |^@ |^@ |^@ |^@ |^@ |^@ |^@ |^@ |^@ |^@ |^@ |^@ |^@ |
ALT |NUL|NUL|NUL|NUL|NUL|NUL|NUL|NUL|NUL|NUL|NUL|NUL|NUL|NUL|NUL|NUL|
SYM |   |   |   |   |   |   |   |   |   |   |   |   |   |   |   |   |
```
◄─────────────────────── Worksheet Title ───────────────────────►

```
BYTE| 64| 65| 66| 67| 68| 69| 70| 71| 72| 73| 74| 75| 76| 77| 78| 79|
HEX | 00| 00| 00| 00| 00| 00| 00| 00| 00| 00| 00| 00| 00| 00| 00| 00|
DEC |  0|  0|  0|  0|  0|  0|  0|  0|  0|  0|  0|  0|  0|  0|  0|  0|
ASC |^@ |^@ |^@ |^@ |^@ |^@ |^@ |^@ |^@ |^@ |^@ |^@ |^@ |^@ |^@ |^@ |
ALT |NUL|NUL|NUL|NUL|NUL|NUL|NUL|NUL|NUL|NUL|NUL|NUL|NUL|NUL|NUL|NUL|
SYM |   |   |   |   |   |   |   |   |   |   |   |   |   |   |   |   |
```
◄─────────────────────── Worksheet Title ───────────────────────►

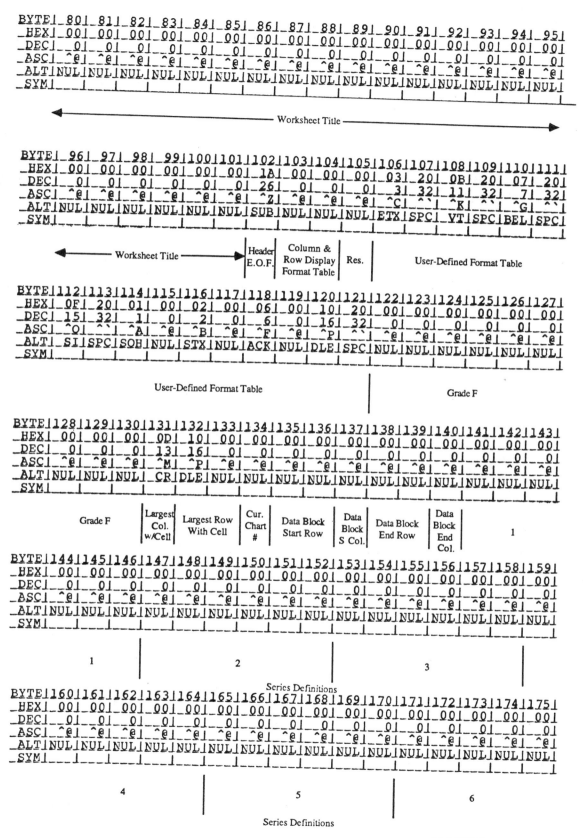

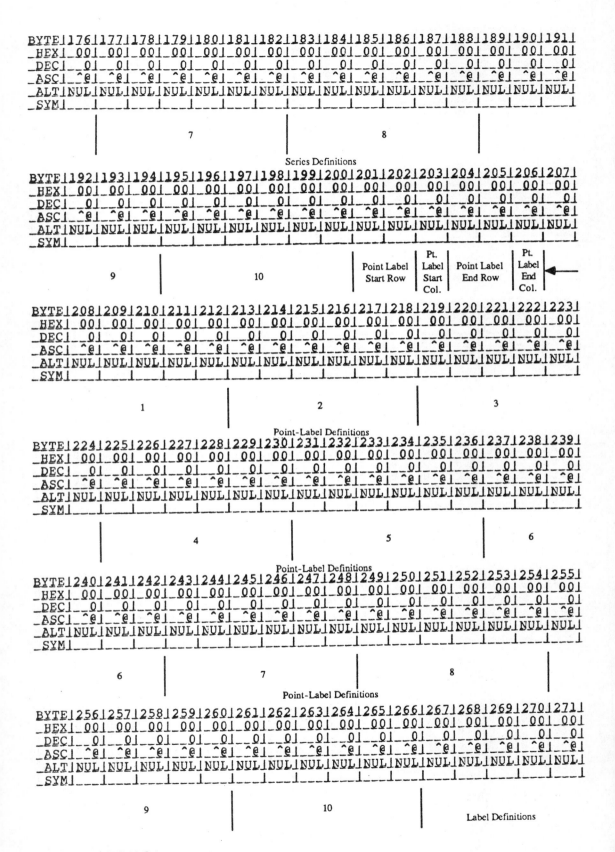

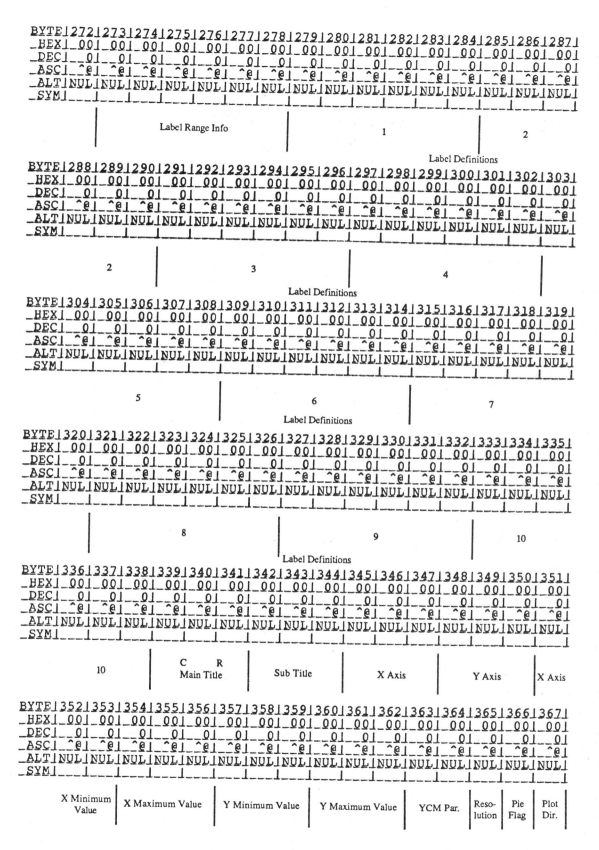

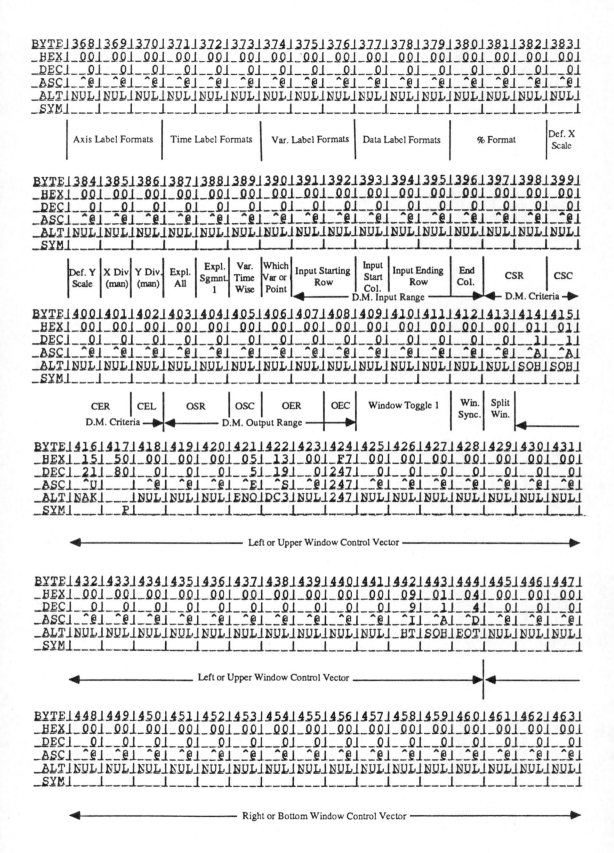

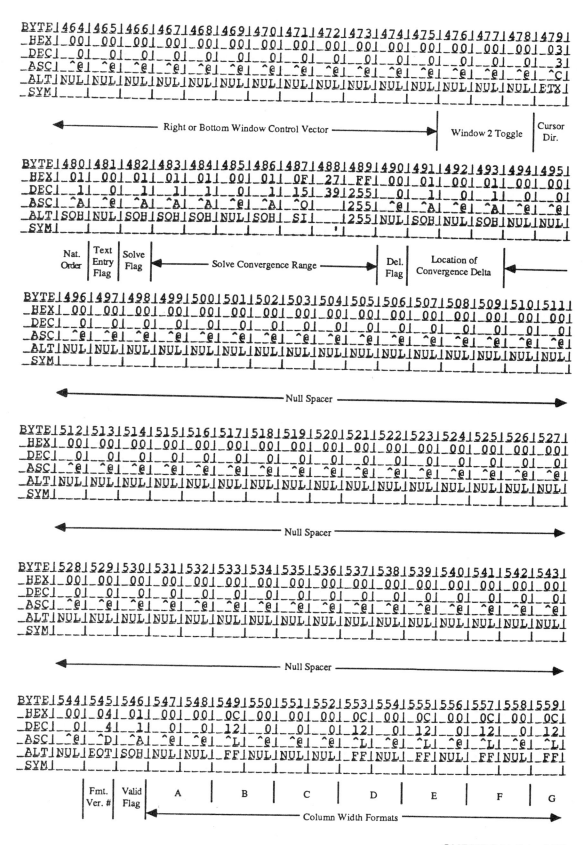

BYTE|464|465|466|467|468|469|470|471|472|473|474|475|476|477|478|479|
HEX|_00|_00|_00|_00|_00|_00|_00|_00|_00|_00|_00|_00|_00|_00|_00|_03|
DEC|__0|__0|__0|__0|__0|__0|__0|__0|__0|__0|__0|__0|__0|__0|__0|__3|
ASC|_^@|_^@|_^@|_^@|_^@|_^@|_^@|_^@|_^@|_^@|_^@|_^@|_^@|_^@|_^@|__3|
ALT|NUL|NUL|NUL|NUL|NUL|NUL|NUL|NUL|NUL|NUL|NUL|NUL|NUL|NUL|NUL|^C|
SYM|___|___|___|___|___|___|___|___|___|___|___|___|___|___|___|ETX|

◄─────────── Right or Bottom Window Control Vector ───────────►│ Window 2 Toggle │ Cursor Dir.

BYTE|480|481|482|483|484|485|486|487|488|489|490|491|492|493|494|495|
HEX|_01|_00|_01|_01|_01|_00|_01|_0F|_27|_FF|_00|_01|_00|_01|_00|_00|
DEC|__1|__0|__1|__1|__1|__0|__1|_15|_39|255|__0|__1|__0|__1|__0|__0|
ASC|_^A|_^@|_^A|_^A|_^A|_^@|_^A|_^O|__'|255|_^@|_^A|_^@|_^A|_^@|_^@|
ALT|SOH|NUL|SOH|SOH|SOH|NUL|SOH|SI_|__'|255|NUL|SOH|NUL|SOH|NUL|NUL|
SYM|___|___|___|___|___|___|___|___|_'_|___|___|___|___|___|___|___|

Nat. Order │ Text Entry Flag │ Solve Flag │◄───── Solve Convergence Range ─────►│ Del. Flag │ Location of Convergence Delta ◄───

BYTE|496|497|498|499|500|501|502|503|504|505|506|507|508|509|510|511|
HEX|_00|_00|_00|_00|_00|_00|_00|_00|_00|_00|_00|_00|_00|_00|_00|_00|
DEC|__0|__0|__0|__0|__0|__0|__0|__0|__0|__0|__0|__0|__0|__0|__0|__0|
ASC|_^@|_^@|_^@|_^@|_^@|_^@|_^@|_^@|_^@|_^@|_^@|_^@|_^@|_^@|_^@|_^@|
ALT|NUL|NUL|NUL|NUL|NUL|NUL|NUL|NUL|NUL|NUL|NUL|NUL|NUL|NUL|NUL|NUL|
SYM|___|___|___|___|___|___|___|___|___|___|___|___|___|___|___|___|

◄───────────────────── Null Spacer ─────────────────────►

BYTE|512|513|514|515|516|517|518|519|520|521|522|523|524|525|526|527|
HEX|_00|_00|_00|_00|_00|_00|_00|_00|_00|_00|_00|_00|_00|_00|_00|_00|
DEC|__0|__0|__0|__0|__0|__0|__0|__0|__0|__0|__0|__0|__0|__0|__0|__0|
ASC|_^@|_^@|_^@|_^@|_^@|_^@|_^@|_^@|_^@|_^@|_^@|_^@|_^@|_^@|_^@|_^@|
ALT|NUL|NUL|NUL|NUL|NUL|NUL|NUL|NUL|NUL|NUL|NUL|NUL|NUL|NUL|NUL|NUL|
SYM|___|___|___|___|___|___|___|___|___|___|___|___|___|___|___|___|

◄───────────────────── Null Spacer ─────────────────────►

BYTE|528|529|530|531|532|533|534|535|536|537|538|539|540|541|542|543|
HEX|_00|_00|_00|_00|_00|_00|_00|_00|_00|_00|_00|_00|_00|_00|_00|_00|
DEC|__0|__0|__0|__0|__0|__0|__0|__0|__0|__0|__0|__0|__0|__0|__0|__0|
ASC|_^@|_^@|_^@|_^@|_^@|_^@|_^@|_^@|_^@|_^@|_^@|_^@|_^@|_^@|_^@|_^@|
ALT|NUL|NUL|NUL|NUL|NUL|NUL|NUL|NUL|NUL|NUL|NUL|NUL|NUL|NUL|NUL|NUL|
SYM|___|___|___|___|___|___|___|___|___|___|___|___|___|___|___|___|

◄───────────────────── Null Spacer ─────────────────────►

BYTE|544|545|546|547|548|549|550|551|552|553|554|555|556|557|558|559|
HEX|_00|_04|_01|_00|_00|_0C|_00|_00|_00|_0C|_00|_0C|_00|_0C|_00|_0C|
DEC|__0|__4|__1|__0|__0|_12|__0|__0|__0|_12|__0|_12|__0|_12|__0|_12|
ASC|_^@|_^D|_^A|_^@|_^@|_^L|_^@|_^@|_^@|_^L|_^@|_^L|_^@|_^L|_^@|_^L|
ALT|NUL|EOT|SOH|NUL|NUL|_FF|NUL|NUL|NUL|_FF|NUL|_FF|NUL|_FF|NUL|_FF|
SYM|___|___|___|___|___|___|___|___|___|___|___|___|___|___|___|___|

Fmt. Ver. # │ Valid Flag │ A │ B │ C │ D │ E │ F │ G

◄──────────────── Column Width Formats ────────────────►

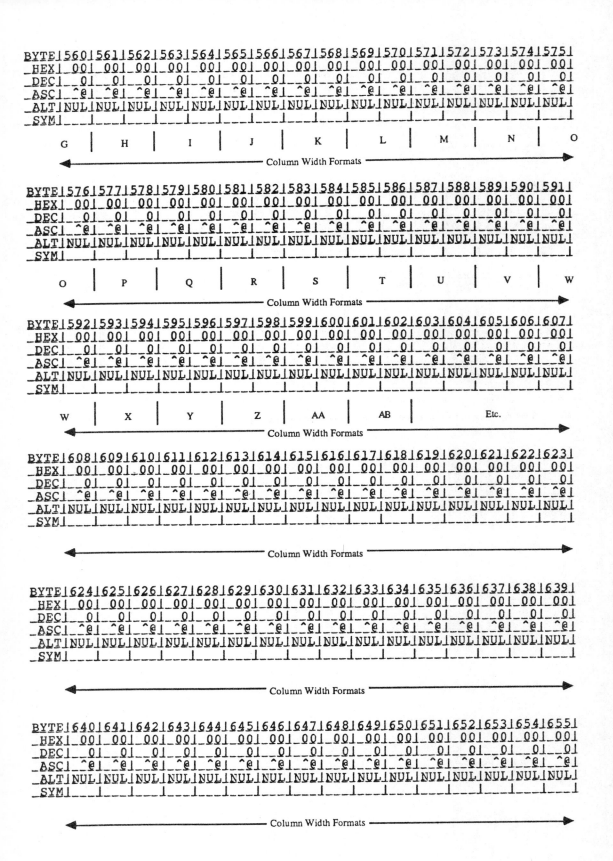

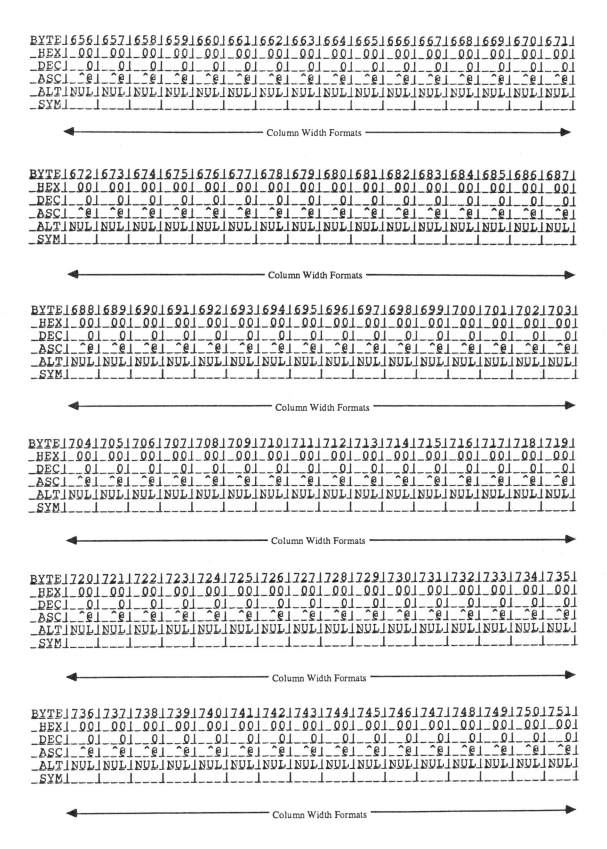

BYTE|656|657|658|659|660|661|662|663|664|665|666|667|668|669|670|671|
_HEX|_00|_00|_00|_00|_00|_00|_00|_00|_00|_00|_00|_00|_00|_00|_00|_00|
_DEC|_01|_01|_01|_01|_01|_01|_01|_01|_01|_01|_01|_01|_01|_01|_01|_01|
ASC|^@|_^@|_^@|_^@|_^@|_^@|_^@|_^@|_^@|_^@|_^@|_^@|_^@|_^@|_^@|_^@|
_ALT|NUL|NUL|NUL|NUL|NUL|NUL|NUL|NUL|NUL|NUL|NUL|NUL|NUL|NUL|NUL|NUL|
_SYM|___|___|___|___|___|___|___|___|___|___|___|___|___|___|___|___|

◄─────────────── Column Width Formats ───────────────►

BYTE|672|673|674|675|676|677|678|679|680|681|682|683|684|685|686|687|
_HEX|_00|_00|_00|_00|_00|_00|_00|_00|_00|_00|_00|_00|_00|_00|_00|_00|
_DEC|_01|_01|_01|_01|_01|_01|_01|_01|_01|_01|_01|_01|_01|_01|_01|_01|
ASC|^@|_^@|_^@|_^@|_^@|_^@|_^@|_^@|_^@|_^@|_^@|_^@|_^@|_^@|_^@|_^@|
_ALT|NUL|NUL|NUL|NUL|NUL|NUL|NUL|NUL|NUL|NUL|NUL|NUL|NUL|NUL|NUL|NUL|
_SYM|___|___|___|___|___|___|___|___|___|___|___|___|___|___|___|___|

◄─────────────── Column Width Formats ───────────────►

BYTE|688|689|690|691|692|693|694|695|696|697|698|699|700|701|702|703|
_HEX|_00|_00|_00|_00|_00|_00|_00|_00|_00|_00|_00|_00|_00|_00|_00|_00|
_DEC|_01|_01|_01|_01|_01|_01|_01|_01|_01|_01|_01|_01|_01|_01|_01|_01|
ASC|^@|_^@|_^@|_^@|_^@|_^@|_^@|_^@|_^@|_^@|_^@|_^@|_^@|_^@|_^@|_^@|
_ALT|NUL|NUL|NUL|NUL|NUL|NUL|NUL|NUL|NUL|NUL|NUL|NUL|NUL|NUL|NUL|NUL|
_SYM|___|___|___|___|___|___|___|___|___|___|___|___|___|___|___|___|

◄─────────────── Column Width Formats ───────────────►

BYTE|704|705|706|707|708|709|710|711|712|713|714|715|716|717|718|719|
_HEX|_00|_00|_00|_00|_00|_00|_00|_00|_00|_00|_00|_00|_00|_00|_00|_00|
_DEC|_01|_01|_01|_01|_01|_01|_01|_01|_01|_01|_01|_01|_01|_01|_01|_01|
ASC|^@|_^@|_^@|_^@|_^@|_^@|_^@|_^@|_^@|_^@|_^@|_^@|_^@|_^@|_^@|_^@|
_ALT|NUL|NUL|NUL|NUL|NUL|NUL|NUL|NUL|NUL|NUL|NUL|NUL|NUL|NUL|NUL|NUL|
_SYM|___|___|___|___|___|___|___|___|___|___|___|___|___|___|___|___|

◄─────────────── Column Width Formats ───────────────►

BYTE|720|721|722|723|724|725|726|727|728|729|730|731|732|733|734|735|
_HEX|_00|_00|_00|_00|_00|_00|_00|_00|_00|_00|_00|_00|_00|_00|_00|_00|
_DEC|_01|_01|_01|_01|_01|_01|_01|_01|_01|_01|_01|_01|_01|_01|_01|_01|
ASC|^@|_^@|_^@|_^@|_^@|_^@|_^@|_^@|_^@|_^@|_^@|_^@|_^@|_^@|_^@|_^@|
_ALT|NUL|NUL|NUL|NUL|NUL|NUL|NUL|NUL|NUL|NUL|NUL|NUL|NUL|NUL|NUL|NUL|
_SYM|___|___|___|___|___|___|___|___|___|___|___|___|___|___|___|___|

◄─────────────── Column Width Formats ───────────────►

BYTE|736|737|738|739|740|741|742|743|744|745|746|747|748|749|750|751|
_HEX|_00|_00|_00|_00|_00|_00|_00|_00|_00|_00|_00|_00|_00|_00|_00|_00|
_DEC|_01|_01|_01|_01|_01|_01|_01|_01|_01|_01|_01|_01|_01|_01|_01|_01|
ASC|^@|_^@|_^@|_^@|_^@|_^@|_^@|_^@|_^@|_^@|_^@|_^@|_^@|_^@|_^@|_^@|
_ALT|NUL|NUL|NUL|NUL|NUL|NUL|NUL|NUL|NUL|NUL|NUL|NUL|NUL|NUL|NUL|NUL|
_SYM|___|___|___|___|___|___|___|___|___|___|___|___|___|___|___|___|

◄─────────────── Column Width Formats ───────────────►

SUPERCALC4 **289**

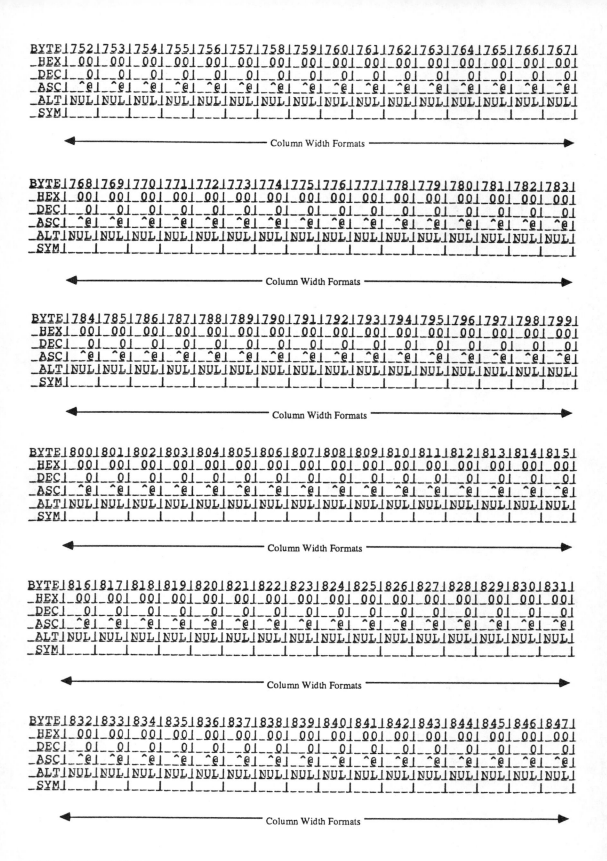

```
BYTE|752|753|754|755|756|757|758|759|760|761|762|763|764|765|766|767|
_HEX|_00|_00|_00|_00|_00|_00|_00|_00|_00|_00|_00|_00|_00|_00|_00|_00|
_DEC|__0|__0|__0|__0|__0|__0|__0|__0|__0|__0|__0|__0|__0|__0|__0|__0|
_ASC|_^@|_^@|_^@|_^@|_^@|_^@|_^@|_^@|_^@|_^@|_^@|_^@|_^@|_^@|_^@|_^@|
_ALT|NUL|NUL|NUL|NUL|NUL|NUL|NUL|NUL|NUL|NUL|NUL|NUL|NUL|NUL|NUL|NUL|
_SYM|___|___|___|___|___|___|___|___|___|___|___|___|___|___|___|___|
```

◄─────────────── Column Width Formats ───────────────►

```
BYTE|768|769|770|771|772|773|774|775|776|777|778|779|780|781|782|783|
_HEX|_00|_00|_00|_00|_00|_00|_00|_00|_00|_00|_00|_00|_00|_00|_00|_00|
_DEC|__0|__0|__0|__0|__0|__0|__0|__0|__0|__0|__0|__0|__0|__0|__0|__0|
_ASC|_^@|_^@|_^@|_^@|_^@|_^@|_^@|_^@|_^@|_^@|_^@|_^@|_^@|_^@|_^@|_^@|
_ALT|NUL|NUL|NUL|NUL|NUL|NUL|NUL|NUL|NUL|NUL|NUL|NUL|NUL|NUL|NUL|NUL|
_SYM|___|___|___|___|___|___|___|___|___|___|___|___|___|___|___|___|
```

◄─────────────── Column Width Formats ───────────────►

```
BYTE|784|785|786|787|788|789|790|791|792|793|794|795|796|797|798|799|
_HEX|_00|_00|_00|_00|_00|_00|_00|_00|_00|_00|_00|_00|_00|_00|_00|_00|
_DEC|__0|__0|__0|__0|__0|__0|__0|__0|__0|__0|__0|__0|__0|__0|__0|__0|
_ASC|_^@|_^@|_^@|_^@|_^@|_^@|_^@|_^@|_^@|_^@|_^@|_^@|_^@|_^@|_^@|_^@|
_ALT|NUL|NUL|NUL|NUL|NUL|NUL|NUL|NUL|NUL|NUL|NUL|NUL|NUL|NUL|NUL|NUL|
_SYM|___|___|___|___|___|___|___|___|___|___|___|___|___|___|___|___|
```

◄─────────────── Column Width Formats ───────────────►

```
BYTE|800|801|802|803|804|805|806|807|808|809|810|811|812|813|814|815|
_HEX|_00|_00|_00|_00|_00|_00|_00|_00|_00|_00|_00|_00|_00|_00|_00|_00|
_DEC|__0|__0|__0|__0|__0|__0|__0|__0|__0|__0|__0|__0|__0|__0|__0|__0|
_ASC|_^@|_^@|_^@|_^@|_^@|_^@|_^@|_^@|_^@|_^@|_^@|_^@|_^@|_^@|_^@|_^@|
_ALT|NUL|NUL|NUL|NUL|NUL|NUL|NUL|NUL|NUL|NUL|NUL|NUL|NUL|NUL|NUL|NUL|
_SYM|___|___|___|___|___|___|___|___|___|___|___|___|___|___|___|___|
```

◄─────────────── Column Width Formats ───────────────►

```
BYTE|816|817|818|819|820|821|822|823|824|825|826|827|828|829|830|831|
_HEX|_00|_00|_00|_00|_00|_00|_00|_00|_00|_00|_00|_00|_00|_00|_00|_00|
_DEC|__0|__0|__0|__0|__0|__0|__0|__0|__0|__0|__0|__0|__0|__0|__0|__0|
_ASC|_^@|_^@|_^@|_^@|_^@|_^@|_^@|_^@|_^@|_^@|_^@|_^@|_^@|_^@|_^@|_^@|
_ALT|NUL|NUL|NUL|NUL|NUL|NUL|NUL|NUL|NUL|NUL|NUL|NUL|NUL|NUL|NUL|NUL|
_SYM|___|___|___|___|___|___|___|___|___|___|___|___|___|___|___|___|
```

◄─────────────── Column Width Formats ───────────────►

```
BYTE|832|833|834|835|836|837|838|839|840|841|842|843|844|845|846|847|
_HEX|_00|_00|_00|_00|_00|_00|_00|_00|_00|_00|_00|_00|_00|_00|_00|_00|
_DEC|__0|__0|__0|__0|__0|__0|__0|__0|__0|__0|__0|__0|__0|__0|__0|__0|
_ASC|_^@|_^@|_^@|_^@|_^@|_^@|_^@|_^@|_^@|_^@|_^@|_^@|_^@|_^@|_^@|_^@|
_ALT|NUL|NUL|NUL|NUL|NUL|NUL|NUL|NUL|NUL|NUL|NUL|NUL|NUL|NUL|NUL|NUL|
_SYM|___|___|___|___|___|___|___|___|___|___|___|___|___|___|___|___|
```

◄─────────────── Column Width Formats ───────────────►

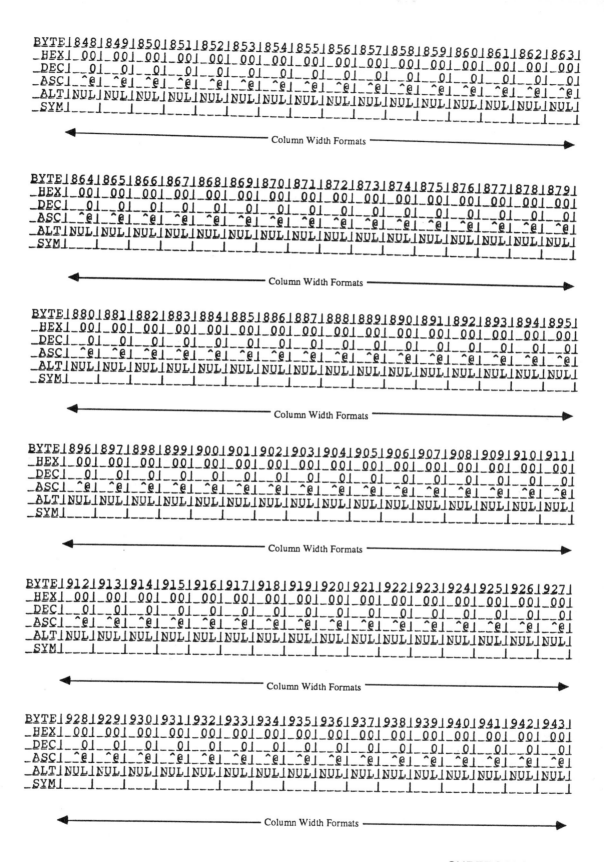

```
BYTE|944|945|946|947|948|949|950|951|952|953|954|955|956|957|958|959|
_HEX|_00|_00|_00|_00|_00|_00|_00|_00|_00|_00|_00|_00|_00|_00|_00|_00|
_DEC|_01|_01|_01|_01|_01|_01|_01|_01|_01|_01|_01|_01|_01|_01|_01|_01|
_ASC|_^@|_^@|_^@|_^@|_^@|_^@|_^@|_^@|_^@|_^@|_^@|_^@|_^@|_^@|_^@|_^@|
_ALT|NUL|NUL|NUL|NUL|NUL|NUL|NUL|NUL|NUL|NUL|NUL|NUL|NUL|NUL|NUL|NUL|
_SYM|___|___|___|___|___|___|___|___|___|___|___|___|___|___|___|___|
```

◄——————————— Column Width Formats ———————————►

```
BYTE|960|961|962|963|964|965|966|967|968|969|970|971|972|973|974|975|
_HEX|_00|_00|_00|_00|_00|_00|_00|_00|_00|_00|_00|_00|_00|_00|_00|_00|
_DEC|_01|_01|_01|_01|_01|_01|_01|_01|_01|_01|_01|_01|_01|_01|_01|_01|
_ASC|_^@|_^@|_^@|_^@|_^@|_^@|_^@|_^@|_^@|_^@|_^@|_^@|_^@|_^@|_^@|_^@|
_ALT|NUL|NUL|NUL|NUL|NUL|NUL|NUL|NUL|NUL|NUL|NUL|NUL|NUL|NUL|NUL|NUL|
_SYM|___|___|___|___|___|___|___|___|___|___|___|___|___|___|___|___|
```

◄——————————— Column Width Formats ———————————►

```
BYTE|976|977|978|979|980|981|982|983|984|985|986|987|988|989|990|991|
_HEX|_00|_00|_00|_00|_00|_00|_00|_00|_00|_00|_00|_00|_00|_00|_00|_00|
_DEC|_01|_01|_01|_01|_01|_01|_01|_01|_01|_01|_01|_01|_01|_01|_01|_01|
_ASC|_^@|_^@|_^@|_^@|_^@|_^@|_^@|_^@|_^@|_^@|_^@|_^@|_^@|_^@|_^@|_^@|
_ALT|NUL|NUL|NUL|NUL|NUL|NUL|NUL|NUL|NUL|NUL|NUL|NUL|NUL|NUL|NUL|NUL|
_SYM|___|___|___|___|___|___|___|___|___|___|___|___|___|___|___|___|
```

◄——————————— Column Width Formats ———————————►

```
BYTE|992|993|994|995|996|997|998|999|__0|__1|__2|__3|__4|__5|__6|__7|
_HEX|_00|_00|_00|_00|_00|_00|_00|_00|_00|_00|_00|_00|_00|_00|_00|_00|
_DEC|_01|_01|_01|_01|_01|_01|_01|_01|_01|_01|_01|_01|_01|_01|_01|_01|
_ASC|_^@|_^@|_^@|_^@|_^@|_^@|_^@|_^@|_^@|_^@|_^@|_^@|_^@|_^@|_^@|_^@|
_ALT|NUL|NUL|NUL|NUL|NUL|NUL|NUL|NUL|NUL|NUL|NUL|NUL|NUL|NUL|NUL|NUL|
_SYM|___|___|___|___|___|___|___|___|___|___|___|___|___|___|___|___|
```

◄——————————— Column Width Formats ———————————►

```
BYTE|__8|__9|_10|_11|_12|_13|_14|_15|_16|_17|_18|_19|_20|_21|_22|_23|
_HEX|_00|_00|_00|_00|_00|_00|_00|_00|_00|_00|_00|_00|_00|_00|_00|_00|
_DEC|_01|_01|_01|_01|_01|_01|_01|_01|_01|_01|_01|_01|_01|_01|_01|_01|
_ASC|_^@|_^@|_^@|_^@|_^@|_^@|_^@|_^@|_^@|_^@|_^@|_^@|_^@|_^@|_^@|_^@|
_ALT|NUL|NUL|NUL|NUL|NUL|NUL|NUL|NUL|NUL|NUL|NUL|NUL|NUL|NUL|NUL|NUL|
_SYM|___|___|___|___|___|___|___|___|___|___|___|___|___|___|___|___|
```

◄——————————— Column Width Formats ———————————►

```
BYTE|_24|_25|_26|_27|_28|_29|_30|_31|_32|_33|_34|_35|_36|_37|_38|_39|
_HEX|_00|_00|_00|_00|_00|_00|_00|_00|_00|_00|_00|_00|_00|_00|_00|_00|
_DEC|_01|_01|_01|_01|_01|_01|_01|_01|_01|_01|_01|_01|_01|_01|_01|_01|
_ASC|_^@|_^@|_^@|_^@|_^@|_^@|_^@|_^@|_^@|_^@|_^@|_^@|_^@|_^@|_^@|_^@|
_ALT|NUL|NUL|NUL|NUL|NUL|NUL|NUL|NUL|NUL|NUL|NUL|NUL|NUL|NUL|NUL|NUL|
_SYM|___|___|___|___|___|___|___|___|___|___|___|___|___|___|___|___|
```

◄——————————— Column Width Formats ———————————►

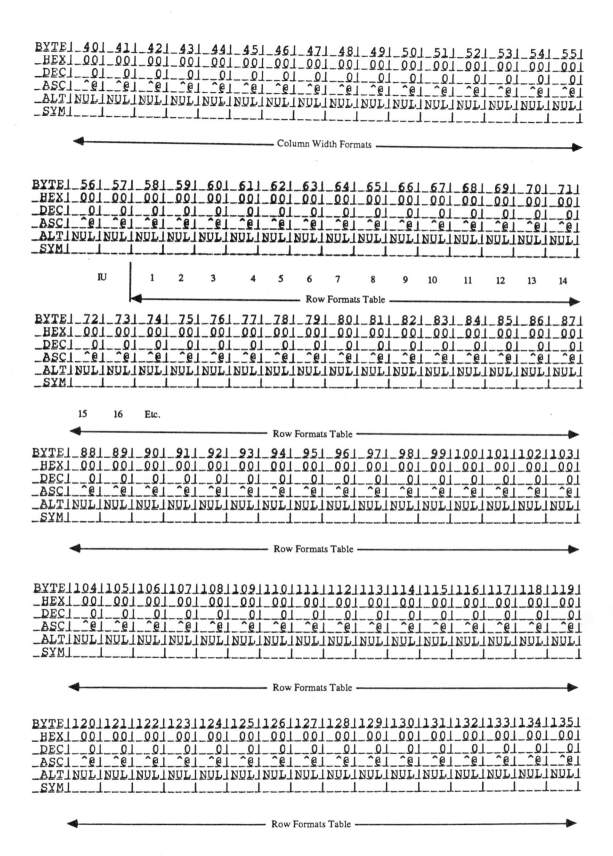

```
BYTE|136|137|138|139|140|141|142|143|144|145|146|147|148|149|150|151|
_HEX|_00|_00|_00|_00|_00|_00|_00|_00|_00|_00|_00|_00|_00|_00|_00|_00|
_DEC|__0|__0|__0|__0|__0|__0|__0|__0|__0|__0|__0|__0|__0|__0|__0|__0|
_ASC|_^@|_^@|_^@|_^@|_^@|_^@|_^@|_^@|_^@|_^@|_^@|_^@|_^@|_^@|_^@|_^@|
_ALT|NUL|NUL|NUL|NUL|NUL|NUL|NUL|NUL|NUL|NUL|NUL|NUL|NUL|NUL|NUL|NUL|
_SYM|___|___|___|___|___|___|___|___|___|___|___|___|___|___|___|___|
```

◄──────────────── Row Formats Table ────────────────►

```
BYTE|152|153|154|155|156|157|158|159|160|161|162|163|164|165|166|167|
_HEX|_00|_00|_00|_00|_00|_00|_00|_00|_00|_00|_00|_00|_00|_00|_00|_00|
_DEC|__0|__0|__0|__0|__0|__0|__0|__0|__0|__0|__0|__0|__0|__0|__0|__0|
_ASC|_^@|_^@|_^@|_^@|_^@|_^@|_^@|_^@|_^@|_^@|_^@|_^@|_^@|_^@|_^@|_^@|
_ALT|NUL|NUL|NUL|NUL|NUL|NUL|NUL|NUL|NUL|NUL|NUL|NUL|NUL|NUL|NUL|NUL|
_SYM|___|___|___|___|___|___|___|___|___|___|___|___|___|___|___|___|
```

◄──────────────── Row Formats Table ────────────────►

```
BYTE|168|169|170|171|172|173|174|175|176|177|178|179|180|181|182|183|
_HEX|_00|_00|_00|_00|_00|_00|_00|_00|_00|_00|_00|_00|_00|_00|_00|_00|
_DEC|__0|__0|__0|__0|__0|__0|__0|__0|__0|__0|__0|__0|__0|__0|__0|__0|
_ASC|_^@|_^@|_^@|_^@|_^@|_^@|_^@|_^@|_^@|_^@|_^@|_^@|_^@|_^@|_^@|_^@|
_ALT|NUL|NUL|NUL|NUL|NUL|NUL|NUL|NUL|NUL|NUL|NUL|NUL|NUL|NUL|NUL|NUL|
_SYM|___|___|___|___|___|___|___|___|___|___|___|___|___|___|___|___|
```

◄──────────────── Row Formats Table ────────────────►

```
BYTE|184|185|186|187|188|189|190|191|192|193|194|195|196|197|198|199|
_HEX|_00|_00|_00|_00|_00|_00|_00|_00|_00|_00|_00|_00|_00|_00|_00|_00|
_DEC|__0|__0|__0|__0|__0|__0|__0|__0|__0|__0|__0|__0|__0|__0|__0|__0|
_ASC|_^@|_^@|_^@|_^@|_^@|_^@|_^@|_^@|_^@|_^@|_^@|_^@|_^@|_^@|_^@|_^@|
_ALT|NUL|NUL|NUL|NUL|NUL|NUL|NUL|NUL|NUL|NUL|NUL|NUL|NUL|NUL|NUL|NUL|
_SYM|___|___|___|___|___|___|___|___|___|___|___|___|___|___|___|___|
```

◄──────────────── Row Formats Table ────────────────►

```
BYTE|200|201|202|203|204|205|206|207|208|209|210|211|212|213|214|215|
_HEX|_00|_00|_00|_00|_00|_00|_00|_00|_00|_00|_00|_00|_00|_00|_00|_00|
_DEC|__0|__0|__0|__0|__0|__0|__0|__0|__0|__0|__0|__0|__0|__0|__0|__0|
_ASC|_^@|_^@|_^@|_^@|_^@|_^@|_^@|_^@|_^@|_^@|_^@|_^@|_^@|_^@|_^@|_^@|
_ALT|NUL|NUL|NUL|NUL|NUL|NUL|NUL|NUL|NUL|NUL|NUL|NUL|NUL|NUL|NUL|NUL|
_SYM|___|___|___|___|___|___|___|___|___|___|___|___|___|___|___|___|
```

◄──────────────── Row Formats Table ────────────────►

```
BYTE|216|217|218|219|220|221|222|223|224|225|226|227|228|229|230|231|
_HEX|_00|_00|_00|_00|_00|_00|_00|_00|_00|_00|_00|_00|_00|_00|_00|_00|
_DEC|__0|__0|__0|__0|__0|__0|__0|__0|__0|__0|__0|__0|__0|__0|__0|__0|
_ASC|_^@|_^@|_^@|_^@|_^@|_^@|_^@|_^@|_^@|_^@|_^@|_^@|_^@|_^@|_^@|_^@|
_ALT|NUL|NUL|NUL|NUL|NUL|NUL|NUL|NUL|NUL|NUL|NUL|NUL|NUL|NUL|NUL|NUL|
_SYM|___|___|___|___|___|___|___|___|___|___|___|___|___|___|___|___|
```

◄──────────────── Row Formats Table ────────────────►

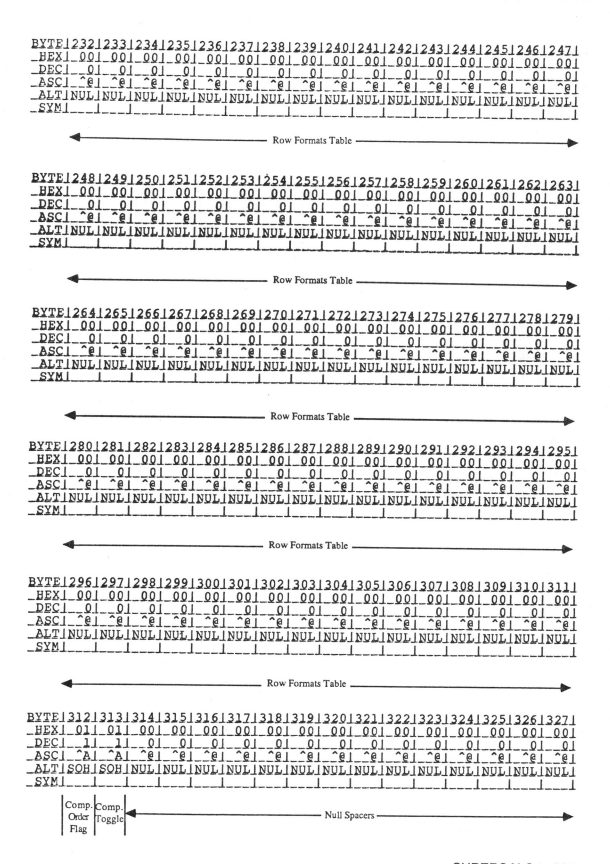

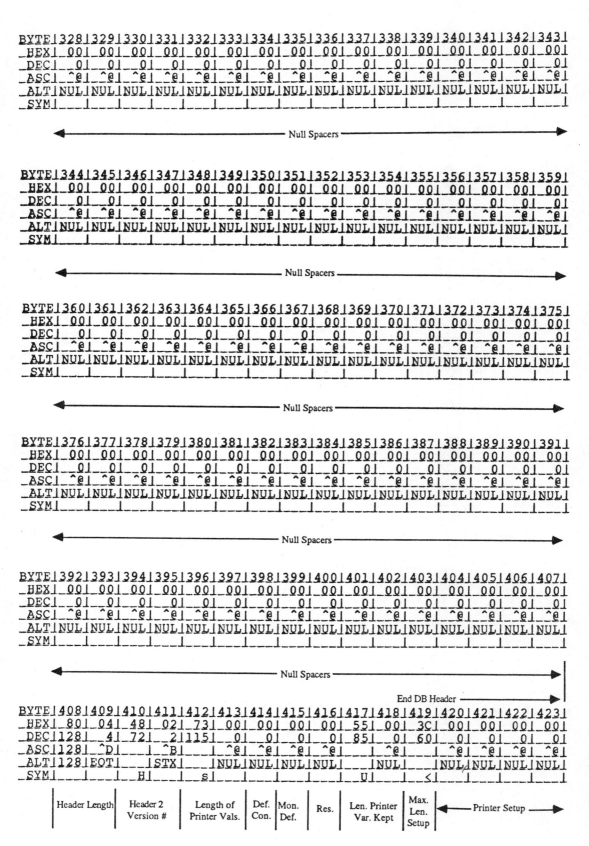

BYTE	424	425	426	427	428	429	430	431	432	433	434	435	436	437	438	439
HEX	00	00	00	00	00	00	00	00	00	00	00	00	00	00	00	00
DEC	0	0	0	0	0	0	0	0	0	0	0	0	0	0	0	0
ASC	^@	^@	^@	^@	^@	^@	^@	^@	^@	^@	^@	^@	^@	^@	^@	^@
ALT	NUL	NUL	NUL	NUL	NUL	NUL	NUL	NUL	NUL	NUL	NUL	NUL	NUL	NUL	NUL	NUL
SYM																

←────────────── Printer Setup String ──────────────→

BYTE	440	441	442	443	444	445	446	447	448	449	450	451	452	453	454	455
HEX	00	00	00	00	00	00	00	00	00	00	00	00	00	00	00	00
DEC	0	0	0	0	0	0	0	0	0	0	0	0	0	0	0	0
ASC	^@	^@	^@	^@	^@	^@	^@	^@	^@	^@	^@	^@	^@	^@	^@	^@
ALT	NUL	NUL	NUL	NUL	NUL	NUL	NUL	NUL	NUL	NUL	NUL	NUL	NUL	NUL	NUL	NUL
SYM																

←────────────── Printer Setup String ──────────────→

BYTE	456	457	458	459	460	461	462	463	464	465	466	467	468	469	470	471
HEX	00	00	00	00	00	00	00	00	00	00	00	00	00	00	00	00
DEC	0	0	0	0	0	0	0	0	0	0	0	0	0	0	0	0
ASC	^@	^@	^@	^@	^@	^@	^@	^@	^@	^@	^@	^@	^@	^@	^@	^@
ALT	NUL	NUL	NUL	NUL	NUL	NUL	NUL	NUL	NUL	NUL	NUL	NUL	NUL	NUL	NUL	NUL
SYM																

←────────────── Printer Setup String ──────────────→

BYTE	472	473	474	475	476	477	478	479	480	481	482	483	484	485	486	487
HEX	00	00	00	00	00	00	00	00	00	7C	00	04	01	42	00	50
DEC	0	0	0	0	0	0	0	0	0	124	0	4	1	66	0	80
ASC	^@	^@	^@	^@	^@	^@	^@	^@	^@	|	^@	^D	^A		^@	
ALT	NUL	NUL	NUL	NUL	NUL	NUL	NUL	NUL	NUL		NUL	EOT	SOH		NUL	
SYM														B		P

								End of String	Border Char.	Toggle Border	Printer Mode	Paper Wait Flag	Page Len.	Res.	Page Width
Setup String →															

BYTE	488	489	490	491	492	493	494	495	496	497	498	499	500	501	502	503
HEX	00	02	00	02	00	04	00	01	00	01	00	00	00	00	00	00
DEC	0	2	0	2	0	4	0	1	0	1	0	0	0	0	0	0
ASC	^@	^B	^@	^B	^@	^D	^@	^A	^@	^A	^@	^@	^@	^@	^@	^@
ALT	NUL	STX	NUL	STX	NUL	EOT	NUL	SOH	NUL	SOH	NUL	NUL	NUL	NUL	NUL	NUL
SYM																

Res.	Top Margin		Bottom Margin		Left Margin		Out OPX	Out UNF	# Copies	Reserved				# Headers Active	# Footers Active

BYTE	504	505	506	507	508	509	510	511	512	513	514	515	516	517	518	519
HEX	00	00	FF	FF	FF	FF	FF	FF	00	FF	FF	FF	FF	FF	FF	00
DEC	0	0	255	255	255	255	255	255	0	255	255	255	255	255	255	0
ASC	^@	^@	255	255	255	255	255	255	^@	255	255	255	255	255	255	^@
ALT	NUL	NUL	255	255	255	255	255	255	NUL	255	255	255	255	255	255	NUL
SYM																

Title Flags	Res.	Print Range							Horizontal Title Range Output						

```
BYTE|520|521|522|523|524|525|526|527|528|529|530|531|532|533|534|535|
HEX| FF| FF| FF| FF| FF| FF| 00| 0B| 00| 00| 00| 00| 00| 00| 00| 00|
DEC|255|255|255|255|255|255|  0| 11|  0|  0|  0|  0|  0|  0|  0|  0|
ASC|255|255|255|255|255|255| ^@| ^K| ^@| ^@| ^@| ^@| ^@| ^@| ^@| ^@|
ALT|255|255|255|255|255|255|NUL| VT|NUL|NUL|NUL|NUL|NUL|NUL|NUL|NUL|
SYM|   |   |   |   |   |   |   |   |   |   |   |   |   |   |   |   |
    |                               |              |         |             |
    |        Vertical Title Range    |  Length of   |  R  |  C  |  R  |  C  |
    |                               | Other Values |             |         |
    |                               |  in Header   | Learn Range |  End of |
    |                               |              |             | Learn Range |


BYTE|536|537|538|539|540|541|542|543|544|545|546|547|548|549|550|551|
HEX| 01| 01| 03| 02| 00| 00| 00| 00| 00| 00| 00| 00| 00| 00| 00| 00|
DEC|  1|  1|  3|  2|  0|  0|  0|  0|  0|  0|  0|  0|  0|  0|  0|  0|
ASC| ^A| ^A| ^C| ^B| ^@| ^@| ^@| ^@| ^@| ^@| ^@| ^@| ^@| ^@| ^@| ^@|
ALT|SOH|SOH|ETX|STX|NUL|NUL|NUL|NUL|NUL|NUL|NUL|NUL|NUL|NUL|NUL|NUL|
SYM|   |   |   |   |   |   |   |   |   |   |   |   |   |   |   |   |
    |Global|    |
    |Label | Res.|
    |Flag  |    |


BYTE|552|553|554|555|556|557|558|559|560|561|562|563|564|565|566|567|
HEX| 00| 00| 00| 00| 00| 00| 00| 00| 00| 00| 00| 00| 00| 00| 00| 00|
DEC|  0|  0|  0|  0|  0|  0|  0|  0|  0|  0|  0|  0|  0|  0|  0|  0|
ASC| ^@| ^@| ^@| ^@| ^@| ^@| ^@| ^@| ^@| ^@| ^@| ^@| ^@| ^@| ^@| ^@|
ALT|NUL|NUL|NUL|NUL|NUL|NUL|NUL|NUL|NUL|NUL|NUL|NUL|NUL|NUL|NUL|NUL|
SYM|   |   |   |   |   |   |   |   |   |   |   |   |   |   |   |   |


BYTE|568|569|570|571|572|573|574|575|576|577|578|579|580|581|582|583|
HEX| 00| 00| 00| 00| 00| 00| 00| 00| 00| 00| 00| 00| 00| 00| 00| 00|
DEC|  0|  0|  0|  0|  0|  0|  0|  0|  0|  0|  0|  0|  0|  0|  0|  0|
ASC| ^@| ^@| ^@| ^@| ^@| ^@| ^@| ^@| ^@| ^@| ^@| ^@| ^@| ^@| ^@| ^@|
ALT|NUL|NUL|NUL|NUL|NUL|NUL|NUL|NUL|NUL|NUL|NUL|NUL|NUL|NUL|NUL|NUL|
SYM|   |   |   |   |   |   |   |   |   |   |   |   |   |   |   |   |


BYTE|584|585|586|587|588|589|590|591|592|593|594|595|596|597|598|599|
HEX| 00| 00| 00| 00| 00| 00| 00| 00| 00| 00| 00| 00| 00| 00| 00| 00|
DEC|  0|  0|  0|  0|  0|  0|  0|  0|  0|  0|  0|  0|  0|  0|  0|  0|
ASC| ^@| ^@| ^@| ^@| ^@| ^@| ^@| ^@| ^@| ^@| ^@| ^@| ^@| ^@| ^@| ^@|
ALT|NUL|NUL|NUL|NUL|NUL|NUL|NUL|NUL|NUL|NUL|NUL|NUL|NUL|NUL|NUL|NUL|
SYM|   |   |   |   |   |   |   |   |   |   |   |   |   |   |   |   |


BYTE|600|601|602|603|604|605|606|607|608|609|610|611|612|613|614|615|
HEX| 00| 00| 00| 00| 00| 00| 00| 00| 00| 00| 00| 00| 00| 00| 00| 00|
DEC|  0|  0|  0|  0|  0|  0|  0|  0|  0|  0|  0|  0|  0|  0|  0|  0|
ASC| ^@| ^@| ^@| ^@| ^@| ^@| ^@| ^@| ^@| ^@| ^@| ^@| ^@| ^@| ^@| ^@|
ALT|NUL|NUL|NUL|NUL|NUL|NUL|NUL|NUL|NUL|NUL|NUL|NUL|NUL|NUL|NUL|NUL|
SYM|   |   |   |   |   |   |   |   |   |   |   |   |   |   |   |   |
```

```
BYTE|616|617|618|619|620|621|622|623|624|625|626|627|628|629|630|631|
_HEX| 00| 00| 00| 00| 00| 00| 00| 00| 00| 00| 00| 00| 00| 00| 00| 00|
_DEC|  0|  0|  0|  0|  0|  0|  0|  0|  0|  0|  0|  0|  0|  0|  0|  0|
_ASC| ^@| ^@| ^@| ^@| ^@| ^@| ^@| ^@| ^@| ^@| ^@| ^@| ^@| ^@| ^@| ^@|
_ALT|NUL|NUL|NUL|NUL|NUL|NUL|NUL|NUL|NUL|NUL|NUL|NUL|NUL|NUL|NUL|NUL|
_SYM|___|___|___|___|___|___|___|___|___|___|___|___|___|___|___|___|


BYTE|632|633|634|635|636|637|638|639|640|641|642|643|644|645|646|647|
_HEX| 00| 00| 00| 00| 00| 00| 00| 00| 00| 00| 00| 00| 00| 00| 00| 00|
_DEC|  0|  0|  0|  0|  0|  0|  0|  0|  0|  0|  0|  0|  0|  0|  0|  0|
_ASC| ^@| ^@| ^@| ^@| ^@| ^@| ^@| ^@| ^@| ^@| ^@| ^@| ^@| ^@| ^@| ^@|
_ALT|NUL|NUL|NUL|NUL|NUL|NUL|NUL|NUL|NUL|NUL|NUL|NUL|NUL|NUL|NUL|NUL|
_SYM|___|___|___|___|___|___|___|___|___|___|___|___|___|___|___|___|


BYTE|648|649|650|651|652|653|654|655|656|657|658|659|660|661|662|663|
_HEX| 00| 00| 00| 00| 00| 00| 00| 00| 00| 00| 00| 00| 00| 00| 00| 00|
_DEC|  0|  0|  0|  0|  0|  0|  0|  0|  0|  0|  0|  0|  0|  0|  0|  0|
_ASC| ^@| ^@| ^@| ^@| ^@| ^@| ^@| ^@| ^@| ^@| ^@| ^@| ^@| ^@| ^@| ^@|
_ALT|NUL|NUL|NUL|NUL|NUL|NUL|NUL|NUL|NUL|NUL|NUL|NUL|NUL|NUL|NUL|NUL|
_SYM|___|___|___|___|___|___|___|___|___|___|___|___|___|___|___|___|


BYTE|664|665|666|667|668|669|670|671|672|673|674|675|676|677|678|679|
_HEX| 00| 00| 00| 00| 00| 00| 00| 00| 00| 00| 00| 00| 00| 00| 00| 00|
_DEC|  0|  0|  0|  0|  0|  0|  0|  0|  0|  0|  0|  0|  0|  0|  0|  0|
_ASC| ^@| ^@| ^@| ^@| ^@| ^@| ^@| ^@| ^@| ^@| ^@| ^@| ^@| ^@| ^@| ^@|
_ALT|NUL|NUL|NUL|NUL|NUL|NUL|NUL|NUL|NUL|NUL|NUL|NUL|NUL|NUL|NUL|NUL|
_SYM|___|___|___|___|___|___|___|___|___|___|___|___|___|___|___|___|


BYTE|680|681|682|683|684|685|686|687|688|689|690|691|692|693|694|695|
_HEX| 00| 00| 00| 00| 00| 00| 00| 00| 00| 00| 00| 00| 00| 00| 00| 00|
_DEC|  0|  0|  0|  0|  0|  0|  0|  0|  0|  0|  0|  0|  0|  0|  0|  0|
_ASC| ^@| ^@| ^@| ^@| ^@| ^@| ^@| ^@| ^@| ^@| ^@| ^@| ^@| ^@| ^@| ^@|
_ALT|NUL|NUL|NUL|NUL|NUL|NUL|NUL|NUL|NUL|NUL|NUL|NUL|NUL|NUL|NUL|NUL|
_SYM|___|___|___|___|___|___|___|___|___|___|___|___|___|___|___|___|


BYTE|696|697|698|699|700|701|702|703|704|705|706|707|708|709|710|711|
_HEX| 00| 00| 00| 00| 00| 00| 00| 00| 00| 00| 00| 00| 00| 00| 00| 00|
_DEC|  0|  0|  0|  0|  0|  0|  0|  0|  0|  0|  0|  0|  0|  0|  0|  0|
_ASC| ^@| ^@| ^@| ^@| ^@| ^@| ^@| ^@| ^@| ^@| ^@| ^@| ^@| ^@| ^@| ^@|
_ALT|NUL|NUL|NUL|NUL|NUL|NUL|NUL|NUL|NUL|NUL|NUL|NUL|NUL|NUL|NUL|NUL|
_SYM|___|___|___|___|___|___|___|___|___|___|___|___|___|___|___|___|
```

BYTE	712	713	714	715	716	717	718	719	720	721	722	723	724	725	726	727
HEX	00	00	00	00	00	00	00	00	00	00	00	00	00	00	00	00
DEC	0	0	0	0	0	0	0	0	0	0	0	0	0	0	0	0
ASC	^@	^@	^@	^@	^@	^@	^@	^@	^@	^@	^@	^@	^@	^@	^@	^@
ALT	NUL	NUL	NUL	NUL	NUL	NUL	NUL	NUL	NUL	NUL	NUL	NUL	NUL	NUL	NUL	NUL
SYM																

BYTE	728	729	730	731	732	733	734	735	736	737	738	739	740	741	742	743
HEX	00	00	00	00	00	00	00	00	00	00	00	00	00	00	00	00
DEC	0	0	0	0	0	0	0	0	0	0	0	0	0	0	0	0
ASC	^@	^@	^@	^@	^@	^@	^@	^@	^@	^@	^@	^@	^@	^@	^@	^@
ALT	NUL	NUL	NUL	NUL	NUL	NUL	NUL	NUL	NUL	NUL	NUL	NUL	NUL	NUL	NUL	NUL
SYM																

BYTE	744	745	746	747	748	749	750	751	752	753	754	755	756	757	758	759
HEX	00	00	00	00	00	00	00	00	00	00	00	00	00	00	00	00
DEC	0	0	0	0	0	0	0	0	0	0	0	0	0	0	0	0
ASC	^@	^@	^@	^@	^@	^@	^@	^@	^@	^@	^@	^@	^@	^@	^@	^@
ALT	NUL	NUL	NUL	NUL	NUL	NUL	NUL	NUL	NUL	NUL	NUL	NUL	NUL	NUL	NUL	NUL
SYM																

BYTE	760	761	762	763	764	765	766	767	768	769	770	771	772	773	774	775
HEX	00	00	00	00	00	00	00	00	00	00	00	00	00	00	00	00
DEC	0	0	0	0	0	0	0	0	0	0	0	0	0	0	0	0
ASC	^@	^@	^@	^@	^@	^@	^@	^@	^@	^@	^@	^@	^@	^@	^@	^@
ALT	NUL	NUL	NUL	NUL	NUL	NUL	NUL	NUL	NUL	NUL	NUL	NUL	NUL	NUL	NUL	NUL
SYM																

BYTE	776	777	778	779	780	781	782	783	784	785	786	787	788	789	790	791
HEX	00	00	00	00	00	00	00	00	00	00	00	00	00	00	00	00
DEC	0	0	0	0	0	0	0	0	0	0	0	0	0	0	0	0
ASC	^@	^@	^@	^@	^@	^@	^@	^@	^@	^@	^@	^@	^@	^@	^@	^@
ALT	NUL	NUL	NUL	NUL	NUL	NUL	NUL	NUL	NUL	NUL	NUL	NUL	NUL	NUL	NUL	NUL
SYM																

BYTE	792	793	794	795	796	797	798	799	800	801	802	803	804	805	806	807
HEX	00	00	00	00	00	00	00	00	00	00	00	00	00	00	00	00
DEC	0	0	0	0	0	0	0	0	0	0	0	0	0	0	0	0
ASC	^@	^@	^@	^@	^@	^@	^@	^@	^@	^@	^@	^@	^@	^@	^@	^@
ALT	NUL	NUL	NUL	NUL	NUL	NUL	NUL	NUL	NUL	NUL	NUL	NUL	NUL	NUL	NUL	NUL
SYM																

BYTE	808	809	810	811	812	813	814	815	816	817	818	819	820	821	822	823
HEX	00	00	00	00	00	00	00	00	00	00	00	00	00	00	00	00
DEC	0	0	0	0	0	0	0	0	0	0	0	0	0	0	0	0
ASC	^@	^@	^@	^@	^@	^@	^@	^@	^@	^@	^@	^@	^@	^@	^@	^@
ALT	NUL	NUL	NUL	NUL	NUL	NUL	NUL	NUL	NUL	NUL	NUL	NUL	NUL	NUL	NUL	NUL
SYM																

BYTE	824	825	826	827	828	829	830	831	832	833	834	835	836	837	838	839
HEX	00	00	00	00	00	00	00	00	00	00	00	00	00	00	00	00
DEC	0	0	0	0	0	0	0	0	0	0	0	0	0	0	0	0
ASC	^@	^@	^@	^@	^@	^@	^@	^@	^@	^@	^@	^@	^@	^@	^@	^@
ALT	NUL	NUL	NUL	NUL	NUL	NUL	NUL	NUL	NUL	NUL	NUL	NUL	NUL	NUL	NUL
SYM																

BYTE	840	841	842	843	844	845	846	847	848	849	850	851	852	853	854	855
HEX	00	00	00	00	00	00	00	00	00	00	00	00	00	00	00	00
DEC	0	0	0	0	0	0	0	0	0	0	0	0	0	0	0	0
ASC	^@	^@	^@	^@	^@	^@	^@	^@	^@	^@	^@	^@	^@	^@	^@	^@
ALT	NUL	NUL	NUL	NUL	NUL	NUL	NUL	NUL	NUL	NUL	NUL	NUL	NUL	NUL	NUL
SYM																

BYTE	856	857	858	859	860	861	862	863	864	865	866	867	868	869	870	871
HEX	00	00	00	00	00	00	00	00	00	00	00	00	00	00	00	00
DEC	0	0	0	0	0	0	0	0	0	0	0	0	0	0	0	0
ASC	^@	^@	^@	^@	^@	^@	^@	^@	^@	^@	^@	^@	^@	^@	^@	^@
ALT	NUL	NUL	NUL	NUL	NUL	NUL	NUL	NUL	NUL	NUL	NUL	NUL	NUL	NUL	NUL
SYM																

BYTE	872	873	874	875	876	877	878	879	880	881	882	883	884	885	886	887
HEX	00	00	00	00	00	00	00	00	00	00	00	00	00	00	00	00
DEC	0	0	0	0	0	0	0	0	0	0	0	0	0	0	0	0
ASC	^@	^@	^@	^@	^@	^@	^@	^@	^@	^@	^@	^@	^@	^@	^@	^@
ALT	NUL	NUL	NUL	NUL	NUL	NUL	NUL	NUL	NUL	NUL	NUL	NUL	NUL	NUL	NUL
SYM																

BYTE	888	889	890	891	892	893	894	895	896	897	898	899	900	901	902	903
HEX	00	00	00	00	00	00	00	00	00	00	00	00	00	00	00	00
DEC	0	0	0	0	0	0	0	0	0	0	0	0	0	0	0	0
ASC	^@	^@	^@	^@	^@	^@	^@	^@	^@	^@	^@	^@	^@	^@	^@	^@
ALT	NUL	NUL	NUL	NUL	NUL	NUL	NUL	NUL	NUL	NUL	NUL	NUL	NUL	NUL	NUL
SYM																

```
BYTE|904|905|906|907|908|909|910|911|912|913|914|915|916|917|918|919|
_HEX|_00|_00|_00|_00|_00|_00|_00|_00|_00|_00|_00|_00|_00|_00|_00|_00|
_DEC|__0|__0|__0|__0|__0|__0|__0|__0|__0|__0|__0|__0|__0|__0|__0|__0|
_ASC|_^@|_^@|_^@|_^@|_^@|_^@|_^@|_^@|_^@|_^@|_^@|_^@|_^@|_^@|_^@|_^@|
_ALT|NUL|NUL|NUL|NUL|NUL|NUL|NUL|NUL|NUL|NUL|NUL|NUL|NUL|NUL|NUL|NUL|
_SYM|___|___|___|___|___|___|___|___|___|___|___|___|___|___|___|___|


BYTE|920|921|922|923|924|925|926|927|928|929|930|931|932|933|934|935|
_HEX|_00|_00|_00|_00|_00|_00|_00|_00|_00|_00|_00|_00|_00|_00|_00|_00|
_DEC|__0|__0|__0|__0|__0|__0|__0|__0|__0|__0|__0|__0|__0|__0|__0|__0|
_ASC|_^@|_^@|_^@|_^@|_^@|_^@|_^@|_^@|_^@|_^@|_^@|_^@|_^@|_^@|_^@|_^@|
_ALT|NUL|NUL|NUL|NUL|NUL|NUL|NUL|NUL|NUL|NUL|NUL|NUL|NUL|NUL|NUL|
_SYM|___|___|___|___|___|___|___|___|___|___|___|___|___|___|___|


BYTE|936|937|938|939|940|941|942|943|944|945|946|947|948|949|950|951|
_HEX|_00|_00|_00|_00|_00|_00|_00|_00|_00|_00|_00|_00|_00|_00|_00|_00|
_DEC|__0|__0|__0|__0|__0|__0|__0|__0|__0|__0|__0|__0|__0|__0|__0|__0|
_ASC|_^@|_^@|_^@|_^@|_^@|_^@|_^@|_^@|_^@|_^@|_^@|_^@|_^@|_^@|_^@|_^@|
_ALT|NUL|NUL|NUL|NUL|NUL|NUL|NUL|NUL|NUL|NUL|NUL|NUL|NUL|NUL|NUL|
_SYM|___|___|___|___|___|___|___|___|___|___|___|___|___|___|___|


BYTE|952|953|954|955|956|957|958|959|960|961|962|963|964|965|966|967|
_HEX|_00|_00|_00|_00|_00|_00|_00|_00|_00|_00|_00|_00|_00|_00|_00|_00|
_DEC|__0|__0|__0|__0|__0|__0|__0|__0|__0|__0|__0|__0|__0|__0|__0|__0|
_ASC|_^@|_^@|_^@|_^@|_^@|_^@|_^@|_^@|_^@|_^@|_^@|_^@|_^@|_^@|_^@|_^@|
_ALT|NUL|NUL|NUL|NUL|NUL|NUL|NUL|NUL|NUL|NUL|NUL|NUL|NUL|NUL|NUL|
_SYM|___|___|___|___|___|___|___|___|___|___|___|___|___|___|___|


BYTE|968|969|970|971|972|973|974|975|976|977|978|979|980|981|982|983|
_HEX|_00|_00|_00|_00|_00|_00|_00|_00|_00|_00|_00|_00|_00|_00|_00|_00|
_DEC|__0|__0|__0|__0|__0|__0|__0|__0|__0|__0|__0|__0|__0|__0|__0|__0|
_ASC|_^@|_^@|_^@|_^@|_^@|_^@|_^@|_^@|_^@|_^@|_^@|_^@|_^@|_^@|_^@|_^@|
_ALT|NUL|NUL|NUL|NUL|NUL|NUL|NUL|NUL|NUL|NUL|NUL|NUL|NUL|NUL|NUL|
_SYM|___|___|___|___|___|___|___|___|___|___|___|___|___|___|___|


BYTE|984|985|986|987|988|989|990|991|992|993|994|995|996|997|998|999|
_HEX|_00|_00|_00|_00|_00|_00|_00|_00|_00|_00|_00|_00|_00|_00|_00|_00|
_DEC|__0|__0|__0|__0|__0|__0|__0|__0|__0|__0|__0|__0|__0|__0|__0|__0|
_ASC|_^@|_^@|_^@|_^@|_^@|_^@|_^@|_^@|_^@|_^@|_^@|_^@|_^@|_^@|_^@|_^@|
_ALT|NUL|NUL|NUL|NUL|NUL|NUL|NUL|NUL|NUL|NUL|NUL|NUL|NUL|NUL|NUL|
_SYM|___|___|___|___|___|___|___|___|___|___|___|___|___|___|___|
```

```
BYTE|__0|__1|__2|__3|__4|__5|__6|__7|__8|__9|_10|_11|_12|_13|_14|_15|
_HEX|_00|_00|_00|_00|_00|_00|_00|_00|_00|_00|_00|_00|_00|_00|_00|_00|
_DEC|__0|__0|__0|__0|__0|__0|__0|__0|__0|__0|__0|__0|__0|__0|__0|__0|
_ASC|_^@|_^@|_^@|_^@|_^@|_^@|_^@|_^@|_^@|_^@|_^@|_^@|_^@|_^@|_^@|_^@|
_ALT|NUL|NUL|NUL|NUL|NUL|NUL|NUL|NUL|NUL|NUL|NUL|NUL|NUL|NUL|NUL|NUL|
_SYM|___|___|___|___|___|___|___|___|___|___|___|___|___|___|___|___|


BYTE|_16|_17|_18|_19|_20|_21|_22|_23|_24|_25|_26|_27|_28|_29|_30|_31|
_HEX|_00|_00|_00|_00|_00|_00|_00|_00|_00|_00|_00|_00|_00|_00|_00|_00|
_DEC|__0|__0|__0|__0|__0|__0|__0|__0|__0|__0|__0|__0|__0|__0|__0|__0|
_ASC|_^@|_^@|_^@|_^@|_^@|_^@|_^@|_^@|_^@|_^@|_^@|_^@|_^@|_^@|_^@|_^@|
_ALT|NUL|NUL|NUL|NUL|NUL|NUL|NUL|NUL|NUL|NUL|NUL|NUL|NUL|NUL|NUL|NUL|
_SYM|___|___|___|___|___|___|___|___|___|___|___|___|___|___|___|___|


BYTE|_32|_33|_34|_35|_36|_37|_38|_39|_40|_41|_42|_43|_44|_45|_46|_47|
_HEX|_00|_00|_00|_00|_00|_00|_00|_00|_00|_00|_00|_00|_00|_00|_00|_00|
_DEC|__0|__0|__0|__0|__0|__0|__0|__0|__0|__0|__0|__0|__0|__0|__0|__0|
_ASC|_^@|_^@|_^@|_^@|_^@|_^@|_^@|_^@|_^@|_^@|_^@|_^@|_^@|_^@|_^@|_^@|
_ALT|NUL|NUL|NUL|NUL|NUL|NUL|NUL|NUL|NUL|NUL|NUL|NUL|NUL|NUL|NUL|NUL|
_SYM|___|___|___|___|___|___|___|___|___|___|___|___|___|___|___|___|


BYTE|_48|_49|_50|_51|_52|_53|_54|_55|_56|_57|_58|_59|_60|_61|_62|_63|
_HEX|_00|_00|_00|_24|_00|_AB|_00|_00|_20|_42|_4D|_2F|_42|_44|_2F|_59|
_DEC|__0|__0|__0|_36|__0|171|__0|__0|_32|_66|_77|_47|_66|_68|_47|_89|
_ASC|_^@|_^@|_^@|___|_^@|171|_^@|_^@|_^`|___|___|___|___|___|___|___|
_ALT|NUL|NUL|NUL|___|NUL|171|NUL|NUL|SPC|___|___|___|___|___|___|___|
_SYM|___|___|___|_$_|___|___|___|___|___|_B_|_M_|_/_|_B_|_D_|_/_|_Y_|


BYTE|_64|_65|_66|_67|_68|_69|_70|_71|_72|_73|_74|_75|_76|_77|_78|_79|
_HEX|_59|_59|_59|_00|_00|_00|_00|_00|_00|_00|_00|_00|_00|_44|_44|_2D|
_DEC|_89|_89|_89|__0|__0|__0|__0|__0|__0|__0|__0|__0|__0|_68|_68|_45|
_ASC|___|___|___|_^@|_^@|_^@|_^@|_^@|_^@|_^@|_^@|_^@|_^@|___|___|___|
_ALT|___|___|___|NUL|NUL|NUL|NUL|NUL|NUL|NUL|NUL|NUL|NUL|___|___|___|
_SYM|_Y_|_Y_|_Y_|___|___|___|___|___|___|___|___|___|___|_D_|_D_|_-_|


BYTE|_80|_81|_82|_83|_84|_85|_86|_87|_88|_89|_90|_91|_92|_93|_94|_95|
_HEX|_4D|_4D|_4D|_2D|_59|_59|_00|_00|_00|_00|_00|_00|_00|_00|_00|_00|
_DEC|_77|_77|_77|_45|_89|_89|__0|__0|__0|__0|__0|__0|__0|__0|__0|__0|
_ASC|___|___|___|___|___|___|_^@|_^@|_^@|_^@|_^@|_^@|_^@|_^@|_^@|_^@|
_ALT|___|___|___|___|___|___|NUL|NUL|NUL|NUL|NUL|NUL|NUL|NUL|NUL|NUL|
_SYM|_M_|_M_|_M_|_-_|_Y_|_Y_|___|___|___|___|___|___|___|___|___|___|
```

```
BYTE| 96| 97| 98| 99|100|101|102|103|104|105|106|107|108|109|110|111|
HEX| 00| 00| 44| 44| 2D| 4D| 4D| 4D| 00| 00| 00| 00| 00| 00| 00| 00|
DEC|  0|  0| 68| 68| 45| 77| 77| 77|  0|  0|  0|  0|  0|  0|  0|  0|
ASC| ^@| ^@|   |   |   |   |   |   | ^@| ^@| ^@| ^@| ^@| ^@| ^@| ^@|
ALT|NUL|NUL|   |   |   |   |   |   |NUL|NUL|NUL|NUL|NUL|NUL|NUL|NUL|
SYM|   |   |  D|  D| -|  M|  M|  M|   |   |   |   |   |   |   |   |
```

```
BYTE|112|113|114|115|116|117|118|119|120|121|122|123|124|125|126|127|
HEX| 00| 00| 00| 00| 00| 00| 00| 4D| 4D| 4D| 2D| 59| 59| 00| 00| 00|
DEC|  0|  0|  0|  0|  0|  0|  0| 77| 77| 77| 45| 89| 89|  0|  0|  0|
ASC| ^@| ^@| ^@| ^@| ^@| ^@| ^@|   |   |   |   |   |   | ^@| ^@| ^@|
ALT|NUL|NUL|NUL|NUL|NUL|NUL|NUL|   |   |   |   |   |   |NUL|NUL|NUL|
SYM|   |   |   |   |   |   |   |  M|  M|  M| -|  Y|  Y|   |   |   |
```

```
BYTE|128|129|130|131|132|133|134|135|136|137|138|139|140|141|142|143|
HEX| 00| 00| 00| 00| 00| 00| 00| 00| 00| 00| 00| 00| 4D| 4D| 2F| 44|
DEC|  0|  0|  0|  0|  0|  0|  0|  0|  0|  0|  0|  0| 77| 77| 47| 68|
ASC| ^@| ^@| ^@| ^@| ^@| ^@| ^@| ^@| ^@| ^@| ^@| ^@|   |   |   |   |
ALT|NUL|NUL|NUL|NUL|NUL|NUL|NUL|NUL|NUL|NUL|NUL|NUL|   |   |   |   |
SYM|   |   |   |   |   |   |   |   |   |   |   |   |  M|  M|  /|  D|
```

```
BYTE|144|145|146|147|148|149|150|151|152|153|154|155|156|157|158|159|
HEX| 44| 2F| 59| 59| 00| 00| 00| 00| 00| 00| 00| 00| 00| 00| 00| 00|
DEC| 68| 47| 89| 89|  0|  0|  0|  0|  0|  0|  0|  0|  0|  0|  0|  0|
ASC|   |   |   |   | ^@| ^@| ^@| ^@| ^@| ^@| ^@| ^@| ^@| ^@| ^@| ^@|
ALT|   |   |   |   |NUL|NUL|NUL|NUL|NUL|NUL|NUL|NUL|NUL|NUL|NUL|
SYM|  D|  /|  Y|  Y|   |   |   |   |   |   |   |   |   |   |   |   |
```

```
BYTE|160|161|162|163|164|165|166|167|168|169|170|171|172|173|174|175|
HEX| 00| 4D| 4D| 2F| 44| 44| 00| 00| 00| 00| 00| 00| 00| 00| 00| 00|
DEC|  0| 77| 77| 47| 68| 68|  0|  0|  0|  0|  0|  0|  0|  0|  0|  0|
ASC| ^@|   |   |   |   |   | ^@| ^@| ^@| ^@| ^@| ^@| ^@| ^@| ^@| ^@|
ALT|NUL|   |   |   |   |   |NUL|NUL|NUL|NUL|NUL|NUL|NUL|NUL|NUL|NUL|
SYM|   |  M|  M|  /|  D|  D|   |   |   |   |   |   |   |   |   |   |
```

```
BYTE|176|177|178|179|180|181|182|183|184|185|186|187|188|189|190|191|
HEX| 00| 00| 00| 00| 00| 00| 59| 59| 2D| 4D| 4D| 2D| 44| 44| 00| 00|
DEC|  0|  0|  0|  0|  0|  0| 89| 89| 45| 77| 77| 45| 68| 68|  0|  0|
ASC| ^@| ^@| ^@| ^@| ^@| ^@|   |   |   |   |   |   |   |   | ^@| ^@|
ALT|NUL|NUL|NUL|NUL|NUL|NUL|   |   |   |   |   |   |   |   |NUL|NUL|
SYM|   |   |   |   |   |   |  Y|  Y| -|  M|  M| -|  D|  D|   |   |
```

```
BYTE|192|193|194|195|196|197|198|199|200|201|202|203|204|205|206|207|
HEX | 00| 00| 00| 00| 00| 00| 00| 00| 00| 00| 00| 44| 44| 2E| 4D| 4D|
DEC | 0 | 0 | 0 | 0 | 0 | 0 | 0 | 0 | 0 | 0 | 0 | 68| 68| 46| 77| 77|
ASC | ^@| ^@| ^@| ^@| ^@| ^@| ^@| ^@| ^@| ^@| ^@|   |   |   |   |   |
ALT |NUL|NUL|NUL|NUL|NUL|NUL|NUL|NUL|NUL|NUL|NUL|   |   |   |   |   |
SYM |   |   |   |   |   |   |   |   |   |   |   | D | D | . | M | M |


BYTE|208|209|210|211|212|213|214|215|216|217|218|219|220|221|222|223|
HEX | 2E| 59| 59| 00| 00| 00| 00| 00| 00| 00| 00| 00| 00| 00| 00| 00|
DEC | 46| 89| 89| 0 | 0 | 0 | 0 | 0 | 0 | 0 | 0 | 0 | 0 | 0 | 0 | 0 |
ASC |   |   |   | ^@| ^@| ^@| ^@| ^@| ^@| ^@| ^@| ^@| ^@| ^@| ^@| ^@|
ALT |   |   |   |NUL|NUL|NUL|NUL|NUL|NUL|NUL|NUL|NUL|NUL|NUL|NUL|NUL|
SYM | . | Y | Y |   |   |   |   |   |   |   |   |   |   |   |   |   |


BYTE|224|225|226|227|228|229|230|231|232|233|234|235|236|237|238|239|
HEX | 13| 01| 00| 03| 20| 0B| 20| 07| 20| 0F| 20| 01| 00| 02| 00| 06|
DEC | 19| 1 | 0 | 3 | 32| 11| 32| 7 | 32| 15| 32| 1 | 0 | 2 | 0 | 6 |
ASC | ^S| ^A| ^@| ^C| ^^| ^K| ^^| ^G| ^^| ^O| ^^| ^A| ^@| ^B| ^@| ^F|
ALT |DC3|SOH|NUL|ETX|SPC| VT|SPC|BEL|SPC| SI|SPC|SOH|NUL|STX|NUL|ACK|
SYM |   |   |   |   |   |   |   |   |   |   |   |   |   |   |   |   |


BYTE|240|241|242|243|244|245|246|247|248|249|250|251|252|253|254|255|
HEX | 00| 10| 20| FF| 00| 00| 00| 00| 00| 00| 00| 00| 00| 00| 00| 00|
DEC | 0 | 16| 32|255| 0 | 0 | 0 | 0 | 0 | 0 | 0 | 0 | 0 | 0 | 0 | 0 |
ASC | ^@| ^P| ^^|255| ^@| ^@| ^@| ^@| ^@| ^@| ^@| ^@| ^@| ^@| ^@| ^@|
ALT |NUL|DLE|SPC|255|NUL|NUL|NUL|NUL|NUL|NUL|NUL|NUL|NUL|NUL|NUL|NUL|
SYM |   |   |   |   |   |   |   |   |   |   |   |   |   |   |   |   |


BYTE|256|257|258|259|260|261|262|263|264|265|266|267|268|269|270|271|
HEX | 00| 00| 00| FF| 00| 00| 00| 00| 00| 00| 00| 00| 00| 00| 00| 00|
DEC | 0 | 0 | 0 |255| 0 | 0 | 0 | 0 | 0 | 0 | 0 | 0 | 0 | 0 | 0 | 0 |
ASC | ^@| ^@| ^@|255| ^@| ^@| ^@| ^@| ^@| ^@| ^@| ^@| ^@| ^@| ^@| ^@|
ALT |NUL|NUL|NUL|255|NUL|NUL|NUL|NUL|NUL|NUL|NUL|NUL|NUL|NUL|NUL|NUL|
SYM |   |   |   |   |   |   |   |   |   |   |   |   |   |   |   |   |


BYTE|272|273|274|275|276|277|278|279|280|281|282|283|284|285|286|287|
HEX | 00| 00| 00| FF| 00| 00| 00| 00| 00| 00| 00| 00| 00| 00| 00| 00|
DEC | 0 | 0 | 0 |255| 0 | 0 | 0 | 0 | 0 | 0 | 0 | 0 | 0 | 0 | 0 | 0 |
ASC | ^@| ^@| ^@|255| ^@| ^@| ^@| ^@| ^@| ^@| ^@| ^@| ^@| ^@| ^@| ^@|
ALT |NUL|NUL|NUL|255|NUL|NUL|NUL|NUL|NUL|NUL|NUL|NUL|NUL|NUL|NUL|NUL|
SYM |   |   |   |   |   |   |   |   |   |   |   |   |   |   |   |   |
```

```
BYTE|288|289|290|291|292|293|294|295|296|297|298|299|300|301|302|303|
HEX | 00| 00| 00| FF| 00| 00| 00| 00| 00| 00| 00| 00| 00| 00| 00| 00|
DEC |  0|  0|  0|255|  0|  0|  0|  0|  0|  0|  0|  0|  0|  0|  0|  0|
ASC | ^@| ^@| ^@|255| ^@| ^@| ^@| ^@| ^@| ^@| ^@| ^@| ^@| ^@| ^@| ^@|
ALT |NUL|NUL|NUL|255|NUL|NUL|NUL|NUL|NUL|NUL|NUL|NUL|NUL|NUL|NUL|NUL|
SYM |   |   |   |   |   |   |   |   |   |   |   |   |   |   |   |   |


BYTE|304|305|306|307|308|309|310|311|312|313|314|315|316|317|318|319|
HEX | 00| 00| 00| FF| 00| 00| 00| 00| 00| 00| 00| 00| 00| 00| 00| 00|
DEC |  0|  0|  0|255|  0|  0|  0|  0|  0|  0|  0|  0|  0|  0|  0|  0|
ASC | ^@| ^@| ^@|255| ^@| ^@| ^@| ^@| ^@| ^@| ^@| ^@| ^@| ^@| ^@| ^@|
ALT |NUL|NUL|NUL|255|NUL|NUL|NUL|NUL|NUL|NUL|NUL|NUL|NUL|NUL|NUL|NUL|
SYM |   |   |   |   |   |   |   |   |   |   |   |   |   |   |   |   |


BYTE|320|321|322|323|324|325|326|327|328|329|330|331|332|333|334|335|
HEX | 00| 00| 00| FF| 00| 00| 00| 00| 00| 00| 00| 00| 00| 00| 00| 00|
DEC |  0|  0|  0|255|  0|  0|  0|  0|  0|  0|  0|  0|  0|  0|  0|  0|
ASC | ^@| ^@| ^@|255| ^@| ^@| ^@| ^@| ^@| ^@| ^@| ^@| ^@| ^@| ^@| ^@|
ALT |NUL|NUL|NUL|255|NUL|NUL|NUL|NUL|NUL|NUL|NUL|NUL|NUL|NUL|NUL|NUL|
SYM |   |   |   |   |   |   |   |   |   |   |   |   |   |   |   |   |


BYTE|336|337|338|339|340|341|342|343|344|345|346|347|348|349|350|351|
HEX | 00| 00| 00| FF| 00| 00| 00| 00| 00| 00| 00| 00| 00| 00| 00| 00|
DEC |  0|  0|  0|255|  0|  0|  0|  0|  0|  0|  0|  0|  0|  0|  0|  0|
ASC | ^@| ^@| ^@|255| ^@| ^@| ^@| ^@| ^@| ^@| ^@| ^@| ^@| ^@| ^@| ^@|
ALT |NUL|NUL|NUL|255|NUL|NUL|NUL|NUL|NUL|NUL|NUL|NUL|NUL|NUL|NUL|NUL|
SYM |   |   |   |   |   |   |   |   |   |   |   |   |   |   |   |   |


BYTE|352|353|354|355|356|357|358|359|360|361|362|363|364|365|366|367|
HEX | 00| 00| 00| FF| 00| 00| 00| 00| 00| 00| 00| 00| 00| 00| 00| 00|
DEC |  0|  0|  0|255|  0|  0|  0|  0|  0|  0|  0|  0|  0|  0|  0|  0|
ASC | ^@| ^@| ^@|255| ^@| ^@| ^@| ^@| ^@| ^@| ^@| ^@| ^@| ^@| ^@| ^@|
ALT |NUL|NUL|NUL|255|NUL|NUL|NUL|NUL|NUL|NUL|NUL|NUL|NUL|NUL|NUL|NUL|
SYM |   |   |   |   |   |   |   |   |   |   |   |   |   |   |   |   |


BYTE|368|369|370|371|372|373|374|375|376|377|378|379|380|381|382|383|
HEX | 00| 00| 00| FF| 00| 00| 00| 00| 00| 00| 00| 00| 00| 00| 00| 00|
DEC |  0|  0|  0|255|  0|  0|  0|  0|  0|  0|  0|  0|  0|  0|  0|  0|
ASC | ^@| ^@| ^@|255| ^@| ^@| ^@| ^@| ^@| ^@| ^@| ^@| ^@| ^@| ^@| ^@|
ALT |NUL|NUL|NUL|255|NUL|NUL|NUL|NUL|NUL|NUL|NUL|NUL|NUL|NUL|NUL|NUL|
SYM |   |   |   |   |   |   |   |   |   |   |   |   |   |   |   |   |
```

```
BYTE|384|385|386|387|388|389|390|391|392|393|394|395|396|397|398|399|
_HEX|_00|_00|_00|_FF|_00|_00|_00|_00|_00|_00|_00|_00|_00|_00|_00|_00|
_DEC|_01|_01|_01|255|_01|_01|_01|_01|_01|_01|_01|_01|_01|_01|_01|_01|
_ASC|_^@|_^@|_^@|255|_^@|_^@|_^@|_^@|_^@|_^@|_^@|_^@|_^@|_^@|_^@|_^@|
_ALT|NUL|NUL|NUL|255|NUL|NUL|NUL|NUL|NUL|NUL|NUL|NUL|NUL|NUL|NUL|NUL|
_SYM|___|___|___|___|___|___|___|___|___|___|___|___|___|___|___|___|


BYTE|400|401|402|403|404|405|406|407|408|409|410|411|412|413|414|415|
_HEX|_00|_00|_00|_00|_00|_00|_00|_00|_00|_00|_00|_00|_00|_00|_00|_00|
_DEC|_01|_01|_01|_01|_01|_01|_01|_01|_01|_01|_01|_01|_01|_01|_01|_01|
_ASC|_^@|_^@|_^@|_^@|_^@|_^@|_^@|_^@|_^@|_^@|_^@|_^@|_^@|_^@|_^@|_^@|
_ALT|NUL|NUL|NUL|NUL|NUL|NUL|NUL|NUL|NUL|NUL|NUL|NUL|NUL|NUL|NUL|
_SYM|___|___|___|___|___|___|___|___|___|___|___|___|___|___|___|


BYTE|416|417|418|419|420|421|422|423|424|425|426|427|428|429|430|431|
_HEX|_00|_00|_00|_00|_00|_00|_00|_00|_00|_00|_00|_00|_00|_00|_00|_00|
_DEC|_01|_01|_01|_01|_01|_01|_01|_01|_01|_01|_01|_01|_01|_01|_01|_01|
_ASC|_^@|_^@|_^@|_^@|_^@|_^@|_^@|_^@|_^@|_^@|_^@|_^@|_^@|_^@|_^@|_^@|
_ALT|NUL|NUL|NUL|NUL|NUL|NUL|NUL|NUL|NUL|NUL|NUL|NUL|NUL|NUL|NUL|
_SYM|___|___|___|___|___|___|___|___|___|___|___|___|___|___|___|


BYTE|432|433|434|435|436|437|438|439|440|441|442|443|444|445|446|447|
_HEX|_00|_00|_00|_00|_00|_00|_00|_00|_00|_00|_00|_00|_00|_00|_00|_00|
_DEC|_01|_01|_01|_01|_01|_01|_01|_01|_01|_01|_01|_01|_01|_01|_01|_01|
_ASC|_^@|_^@|_^@|_^@|_^@|_^@|_^@|_^@|_^@|_^@|_^@|_^@|_^@|_^@|_^@|_^@|
_ALT|NUL|NUL|NUL|NUL|NUL|NUL|NUL|NUL|NUL|NUL|NUL|NUL|NUL|NUL|NUL|
_SYM|___|___|___|___|___|___|___|___|___|___|___|___|___|___|___|


BYTE|448|449|450|451|452|453|454|455|456|457|458|459|460|461|462|463|
_HEX|_00|_00|_00|_00|_00|_00|_00|_00|_00|_00|_00|_00|_00|_00|_00|_00|
_DEC|_01|_01|_01|_01|_01|_01|_01|_01|_01|_01|_01|_01|_01|_01|_01|_01|
_ASC|_^@|_^@|_^@|_^@|_^@|_^@|_^@|_^@|_^@|_^@|_^@|_^@|_^@|_^@|_^@|_^@|
_ALT|NUL|NUL|NUL|NUL|NUL|NUL|NUL|NUL|NUL|NUL|NUL|NUL|NUL|NUL|NUL|
_SYM|___|___|___|___|___|___|___|___|___|___|___|___|___|___|___|


BYTE|464|465|466|467|468|469|470|471|472|473|474|475|476|477|478|479|
_HEX|_00|_00|_00|_00|_00|_00|_00|_00|_00|_00|_00|_00|_00|_00|_00|_00|
_DEC|_01|_01|_01|_01|_01|_01|_01|_01|_01|_01|_01|_01|_01|_01|_01|_01|
_ASC|_^@|_^@|_^@|_^@|_^@|_^@|_^@|_^@|_^@|_^@|_^@|_^@|_^@|_^@|_^@|_^@|
_ALT|NUL|NUL|NUL|NUL|NUL|NUL|NUL|NUL|NUL|NUL|NUL|NUL|NUL|NUL|NUL|NUL|
_SYM|___|___|___|___|___|___|___|___|___|___|___|___|___|___|___|___|
```

```
BYTE|480|481|482|483|484|485|486|487|488|489|490|491|492|493|494|495|
HEX | 00| 00| 00| 00| 00| 00| 00| 00| 00| 00| 00| 00| 00| 00| 00| 00|
DEC | 0| 0| 0| 0| 0| 0| 0| 0| 0| 0| 0| 0| 0| 0| 0| 0|
ASC | ^@| ^@| ^@| ^@| ^@| ^@| ^@| ^@| ^@| ^@| ^@| ^@| ^@| ^@| ^@| ^@|
ALT |NUL|NUL|NUL|NUL|NUL|NUL|NUL|NUL|NUL|NUL|NUL|NUL|NUL|NUL|NUL|NUL|
SYM |   |   |   |   |   |   |   |   |   |   |   |   |   |   |   |   |


BYTE|496|497|498|499|500|501|502|503|504|505|506|507|508|509|510|511|
HEX | 00| 00| 00| 00| 00| 00| 00| 00| 00| 00| 00| 00| 00| 00| 00| 00|
DEC | 0| 0| 0| 0| 0| 0| 0| 0| 0| 0| 0| 0| 0| 0| 0| 0|
ASC | ^@| ^@| ^@| ^@| ^@| ^@| ^@| ^@| ^@| ^@| ^@| ^@| ^@| ^@| ^@| ^@|
ALT |NUL|NUL|NUL|NUL|NUL|NUL|NUL|NUL|NUL|NUL|NUL|NUL|NUL|NUL|NUL|NUL|
SYM |   |   |   |   |   |   |   |   |   |   |   |   |   |   |   |   |


BYTE|512|513|514|515|516|517|518|519|520|521|522|523|524|525|526|527|
HEX | 00| 00| 00| 00| 00| 00| 00| 00| 00| 00| 00| 00| 00| 00| 00| 00|
DEC | 0| 0| 0| 0| 0| 0| 0| 0| 0| 0| 0| 0| 0| 0| 0| 0|
ASC | ^@| ^@| ^@| ^@| ^@| ^@| ^@| ^@| ^@| ^@| ^@| ^@| ^@| ^@| ^@| ^@|
ALT |NUL|NUL|NUL|NUL|NUL|NUL|NUL|NUL|NUL|NUL|NUL|NUL|NUL|NUL|NUL|NUL|
SYM |   |   |   |   |   |   |   |   |   |   |   |   |   |   |   |   |


BYTE|528|529|530|531|532|533|534|535|536|537|538|539|540|541|542|543|
HEX | 00| 00| 00| 00| 00| 00| 00| 00| 00| 00| 00| 00| 00| 00| 00| 00|
DEC | 0| 0| 0| 0| 0| 0| 0| 0| 0| 0| 0| 0| 0| 0| 0| 0|
ASC | ^@| ^@| ^@| ^@| ^@| ^@| ^@| ^@| ^@| ^@| ^@| ^@| ^@| ^@| ^@| ^@|
ALT |NUL|NUL|NUL|NUL|NUL|NUL|NUL|NUL|NUL|NUL|NUL|NUL|NUL|NUL|NUL|NUL|
SYM |   |   |   |   |   |   |   |   |   |   |   |   |   |   |   |   |


BYTE|544|545|546|547|548|549|550|551|552|553|554|555|556|557|558|559|
HEX | 00| 00| 00| 00| 00| 00| 00| 00| 00| 00| 00| 00| 00| 00| 00| 00|
DEC | 0| 0| 0| 0| 0| 0| 0| 0| 0| 0| 0| 0| 0| 0| 0| 0|
ASC | ^@| ^@| ^@| ^@| ^@| ^@| ^@| ^@| ^@| ^@| ^@| ^@| ^@| ^@| ^@| ^@|
ALT |NUL|NUL|NUL|NUL|NUL|NUL|NUL|NUL|NUL|NUL|NUL|NUL|NUL|NUL|NUL|NUL|
SYM |   |   |   |   |   |   |   |   |   |   |   |   |   |   |   |   |

                                                         End of Header ———▶

BYTE|560|561|562|563|564|565|566|567|568|569|570|571|572|573|574|575|
HEX | 03| 00| 00| 00| 00| 03| 22| 50| 61| 79| 6D| 65| 6E| 74| 20| 41|
DEC | 3| 0| 0| 0| 0| 3| 34| 80| 97|121|109|101|110|116| 32| 65|
ASC | ^C| ^@| ^@| ^@| ^@| ^C|   |   |   |   |   |   |   |   | ^`|   |
ALT |ETX|NUL|NUL|NUL|NUL|ETX|   |   |   |   |   |   |   |   |SPC|   |
SYM |   |   |   |   |   |   | " | P | a | y | m | e | n | t |   | A |
```

	Col.	Row	Format	Cell Contents

BYTE	576	577	578	579	580	581	582	583	584	585	586	587	588	589	590	591
HEX	6E	61	6C	79	73	69	73	20	57	6F	72	6B	73	68	65	65
DEC	110	97	108	121	115	105	115	32	87	111	114	107	115	104	101	101
ASC								^`								
ALT								SPC								
SYM	n	a	l	y	s	i	s		W	o	r	k	s	h	e	e

BYTE	592	593	594	595	596	597	598	599	600	601	602	603	604	605	606	607
HEX	74	00	00	03	00	01	00	00	02	22	3D	3D	3D	3D	3D	3D
DEC	116	0	0	3	0	1	0	0	2	34	61	61	61	61	61	61
ASC		^@	^@	^C	^@	^A	^@	^@	^B							
ALT		NUL	NUL	ETX	NUL	SOH	NUL	NUL	STX							
SYM	t									"	=	=	=	=	=	=

BYTE	608	609	610	611	612	613	614	615	616	617	618	619	620	621	622	623
HEX	3D	3D	3D	3D	3D	3D	00	00	33	00	20	57	6F	72	04	00
DEC	61	61	61	61	61	61	0	0	51	0	32	87	111	114	4	0
ASC							^@	^@		^@	^`				^D	^@
ALT							NUL	NUL		NUL	SPC				EOT	NUL
SYM	=	=	=	=	=	=			3			W	o	r		

BYTE	624	625	626	627	628	629	630	631	632	633	634	635	636	637	638	639
HEX	01	00	00	02	22	3D	3D	3D	3D	3D	3D	3D	3D	3D	3D	3D
DEC	1	0	0	2	34	61	61	61	61	61	61	61	61	61	61	61
ASC	^A	^@	^@	^B												
ALT	SOH	NUL	NUL	STX												
SYM					"	=	=	=	=	=	=	=	=	=	=	=

BYTE	640	641	642	643	644	645	646	647	648	649	650	651	652	653	654	655
HEX	3D	3D	3D	00	00	20	57	6F	72	00	00	02	00	00	01	22
DEC	61	61	61	0	0	32	87	111	114	0	0	2	0	0	1	34
ASC				^@	^@	^`				^@	^@	^B	^@	^@	^A	
ALT				NUL	NUL	SPC				NUL	NUL	STX	NUL	NUL	SOH	
SYM	=	=	=				W	o	r							"

BYTE	656	657	658	659	660	661	662	663	664	665	666	667	668	669	670	671
HEX	4C	6F	61	6E	20	41	6D	74	00	6E	61	6C	01	00	02	40
DEC	76	111	97	110	32	65	109	116	0	110	97	108	1	0	2	64
ASC					^`				^@				^A	^@	^B	
ALT					SPC				NUL				SOH	NUL	STX	
SYM	L	o	a	n		A	m	t		n	a	l				@

BYTE	672	673	674	675	676	677	678	679	680	681	682	683	684	685	686	687
HEX	01	02	00	00	00	00	00	C0	B2	40	00	00	34	38	30	30
DEC	1	2	0	0	0	0	0	192	178	64	0	0	52	56	48	48
ASC	^A	^B	^@	^@	^@	^@	^@	192	178		^@	^@				
ALT	SOH	STX	NUL	NUL	NUL	NUL	NUL	192	178		NUL	NUL				
SYM										@			4	8	0	0

BYTE	688	689	690	691	692	693	694	695	696	697	698	699	700	701	702	703
HEX	00	46	31	36	00	00	29	00	00	03	00	00	01	22	49	6E
DEC	0	70	49	54	0	0	41	0	0	3	0	0	1	34	73	110
ASC	^@				^@	^@		^@	^@	^C	^@	^@	^A			
ALT	NUL				NUL	NUL		NUL	NUL	ETX	NUL	NUL	SOH			
SYM		F	1	6			)							"	I	n

BYTE	704	705	706	707	708	709	710	711	712	713	714	715	716	717	718	719
HEX	74	65	72	65	73	74	00	34	38	30	01	00	03	40	00	02
DEC	116	101	114	101	115	116	0	52	56	48	1	0	3	64	0	2
ASC							^@				^A	^@	^C		^@	^B
ALT							NUL				SOH	NUL	ETX		NUL	STX
SYM	t	e	r	e	s	t		4	8	0				@		

BYTE	720	721	722	723	724	725	726	727	728	729	730	731	732	733	734	735
HEX	AE	47	E1	7A	14	AE	C7	3F	00	00	2E	31	38	35	00	46
DEC	174	71	225	122	20	174	199	63	0	0	46	49	56	53	0	70
ASC	174		225		^T	174	199		^@	^@					^@	
ALT	174		225		DC4	174	199		NUL	NUL					NUL	
SYM		G		z				?			.	1	8	5		F

BYTE	736	737	738	739	740	741	742	743	744	745	746	747	748	749	750	751
HEX	31	36	00	00	29	00	00	04	00	00	01	22	4D	6F	20	50
DEC	49	54	0	0	41	0	0	4	0	0	1	34	77	111	32	80
ASC			^@	^@		^@	^@	^D	^@	^@	^A				^^	
ALT			NUL	NUL		NUL	NUL	EOT	NUL	NUL	SOH				SPC	
SYM	1	6			)							"	M	o		P

BYTE	752	753	754	755	756	757	758	759	760	761	762	763	764	765	766	767
HEX	6D	74	00	00	00	60	31	38	01	00	04	40	01	02	8F	C2
DEC	109	116	0	0	0	96	49	56	1	0	4	64	1	2	143	194
ASC			^@	^@	^@				^A	^@	^D		^A	^B	143	194
ALT			NUL	NUL	NUL				SOH	NUL	EOT		SOH	STX	143	194
SYM	m	t				`	1	8					@			

BYTE	768	769	770	771	772	773	774	775	776	777	778	779	780	781	782	783
HEX	F5	28	5C	D7	65	40	00	00	31	37	34	2E	37	33	00	36
DEC	245	40	92	215	101	64	0	0	49	55	52	46	55	51	0	54
ASC	245			215			^@	^@							^@	
ALT	245			215			NUL	NUL							NUL	
SYM		(	\		e	@			1	7	4	.	7	3		6

BYTE	784	785	786	787	788	789	790	791	792	793	794	795	796	797	798	799
HEX	00	00	29	00	00	05	00	00	01	22	50	65	72	69	6F	64
DEC	0	0	41	0	0	5	0	0	1	34	80	101	114	105	111	100
ASC	^@	^@		^@	^@	^E	^@	^@	^A							
ALT	NUL	NUL		NUL	NUL	ENQ	NUL	NUL	SOH							
SYM			)							"	P	e	r	i	o	d

BYTE	800	801	802	803	804	805	806	807	808	809	810	811	812	813	814	815
HEX	73	00	00	31	37	34	01	00	05	40	00	01	00	00	00	00
DEC	115	0	0	49	55	52	1	0	5	64	0	1	0	0	0	0
ASC		^@	^@				^A	^@	^E		^@	^A	^@	^@	^@	^@
ALT		NUL	NUL				SOH	NUL	ENQ		NUL	SOH	NUL	NUL	NUL	NUL
SYM	s			1	7	4				@						

BYTE	816	817	818	819	820	821	822	823	824	825	826	827	828	829	830	831
HEX	00	00	42	40	00	00	33	36	00	00	00	07	00	00	02	22
DEC	0	0	66	64	0	0	51	54	0	0	0	7	0	0	2	34
ASC	^@	^@			^@	^@			^@	^@	^@	^G	^@	^@	^B	
ALT	NUL	NUL			NUL	NUL			NUL	NUL	NUL	BEL	NUL	NUL	STX	
SYM			B	@			3	6								"

BYTE	832	833	834	835	836	837	838	839	840	841	842	843	844	845	846	847
HEX	2D	2D	2D	2D	2D	2D	2D	2D	2D	2D	2D	2D	2D	00	33	00
DEC	45	45	45	45	45	45	45	45	45	45	45	45	45	0	51	0
ASC														^@		^@
ALT														NUL		NUL
SYM	-	-	-	-	-	-	-	-	-	-	-	-	-		3	

BYTE	848	849	850	851	852	853	854	855	856	857	858	859	860	861	862	863
HEX	20	57	6F	72	01	00	07	00	00	02	22	2D	2D	2D	2D	2D
DEC	32	87	111	114	1	0	7	0	0	2	34	45	45	45	45	45
ASC	^^				^A	^@	^G	^@	^@	^B						
ALT	SPC				SOH	NUL	BEL	NUL	NUL	STX						
SYM		W	o	r							"	-	-	-	-	-

```
BYTE|864|865|866|867|868|869|870|871|872|873|874|875|876|877|878|879|
HEX | 2D| 2D| 2D| 2D| 2D| 2D| 2D| 2D| 00| 33| 00| 20| 57| 6F| 72| 02|
DEC | 45| 45| 45| 45| 45| 45| 45| 45|  0| 51|  0| 32| 87|111|114|  2|
ASC |   |   |   |   |   |   |   |   | ^@|   | ^@| ^^|   |   |   | ^B|
ALT |   |   |   |   |   |   |   |   |NUL|   |NUL|SPC|   |   |   |STX|
SYM | - | - | - | - | - | - | - | - |   | 3 |   |   | W | o | r |   |


BYTE|880|881|882|883|884|885|886|887|888|889|890|891|892|893|894|895|
HEX | 00| 07| 00| 00| 02| 22| 2D| 2D| 2D| 2D| 2D| 2D| 2D| 2D| 2D| 2D|
DEC |  0|  7|  0|  0|  2| 34| 45| 45| 45| 45| 45| 45| 45| 45| 45| 45|
ASC | ^@| ^G| ^@| ^@| ^B|   |   |   |   |   |   |   |   |   |   |   |
ALT |NUL|BEL|NUL|NUL|STX|   |   |   |   |   |   |   |   |   |   |   |
SYM |   |   |   |   |   | " | - | - | - | - | - | - | - | - | - | - |


BYTE|896|897|898|899|900|901|902|903|904|905|906|907|908|909|910|911|
HEX | 2D| 2D| 2D| 00| 33| 00| 20| 57| 6F| 72| 03| 00| 07| 00| 00| 02|
DEC | 45| 45| 45|  0| 51|  0| 32| 87|111|114|  3|  0|  7|  0|  0|  2|
ASC |   |   |   | ^@|   | ^@| ^^|   |   |   | ^C| ^@| ^G| ^@| ^@| ^B|
ALT |   |   |   |NUL|   |NUL|SPC|   |   |   |ETX|NUL|BEL|NUL|NUL|STX|
SYM | - | - | - |   | 3 |   |   | W | o | r |   |   |   |   |   |   |


BYTE|912|913|914|915|916|917|918|919|920|921|922|923|924|925|926|927|
HEX | 22| 2D| 2D| 2D| 2D| 2D| 2D| 2D| 2D| 2D| 2D| 2D| 2D| 2D| 00| 33|
DEC | 34| 45| 45| 45| 45| 45| 45| 45| 45| 45| 45| 45| 45| 45|  0| 51|
ASC |   |   |   |   |   |   |   |   |   |   |   |   |   |   | ^@|   |
ALT |   |   |   |   |   |   |   |   |   |   |   |   |   |   |NUL|   |
SYM | " | - | - | - | - | - | - | - | - | - | - | - | - | - |   | 3 |


BYTE|928|929|930|931|932|933|934|935|936|937|938|939|940|941|942|943|
HEX | 00| 20| 57| 6F| 72| 04| 00| 07| 00| 00| 02| 22| 2D| 2D| 2D| 2D|
DEC |  0| 32| 87|111|114|  4|  0|  7|  0|  0|  2| 34| 45| 45| 45| 45|
ASC | ^@| ^^|   |   |   | ^D| ^@| ^G| ^@| ^@| ^B|   |   |   |   |   |
ALT |NUL|SPC|   |   |   |EOT|NUL|BEL|NUL|NUL|STX|   |   |   |   |   |
SYM |   |   | W | o | r |   |   |   |   |   |   | " | - | - | - | - |


BYTE|944|945|946|947|948|949|950|951|952|953|954|955|956|957|958|959|
HEX | 2D| 2D| 2D| 2D| 2D| 2D| 2D| 2D| 2D| 00| 33| 00| 20| 57| 6F| 72|
DEC | 45| 45| 45| 45| 45| 45| 45| 45| 45|  0| 51|  0| 32| 87|111|114|
ASC |   |   |   |   |   |   |   |   |   | ^@|   | ^@| ^^|   |   |   |
ALT |   |   |   |   |   |   |   |   |   |NUL|   |NUL|SPC|   |   |   |
SYM | - | - | - | - | - | - | - | - | - |   | 3 |   |   | W | o | r |
```

```
BYTE|960|961|962|963|964|965|966|967|968|969|970|971|972|973|974|975|
HEX | 05| 00| 07| 00| 00| 02| 22| 2D| 2D| 2D| 2D| 2D| 2D| 2D| 2D| 2D|
DEC |  5|  0|  7|  0|  0|  2| 34| 45| 45| 45| 45| 45| 45| 45| 45| 45|
ASC | ^E| ^@| ^G| ^@| ^@| ^B|   |   |   |   |   |   |   |   |   |   |
ALT |ENQ|NUL|BEL|NUL|NUL|STX|   |   |   |   |   |   |   |   |   |   |
SYM |   |   |   |   |   |   |  "|  -|  -|  -|  -|  -|  -|  -|  -|  -|


BYTE|976|977|978|979|980|981|982|983|984|985|986|987|988|989|990|991|
HEX | 2D| 2D| 2D| 2D| 00| 33| 00| 20| 57| 6F| 72| 06| 00| 07| 00| 00|
DEC | 45| 45| 45| 45|  0| 51|  0| 32| 87|111|114|  6|  0|  7|  0|  0|
ASC |   |   |   | ^@|   | ^@| ^`|   |   |   | ^F| ^@| ^G| ^@| ^@|
ALT |   |   |   |NUL|   |NUL|SPC|   |   |   |ACK|NUL|BEL|NUL|NUL|
SYM |  -|  -|  -|  -|   |  3|   |   |  W|  o|  r|   |   |   |   |   |


BYTE|992|993|994|995|996|997|998|999|  0|  1|  2|  3|  4|  5|  6|  7|
HEX | 02| 22| 2D| 2D| 2D| 2D| 2D| 2D| 2D| 2D| 2D| 2D| 2D| 2D| 2D| 00|
DEC |  2| 34| 45| 45| 45| 45| 45| 45| 45| 45| 45| 45| 45| 45| 45|  0|
ASC | ^B|   |   |   |   |   |   |   |   |   |   |   |   |   |   | ^@|
ALT |STX|   |   |   |   |   |   |   |   |   |   |   |   |   |   |NUL|
SYM |   |  "|  -|  -|  -|  -|  -|  -|  -|  -|  -|  -|  -|  -|  -|   |


BYTE|  8|  9| 10| 11| 12| 13| 14| 15| 16| 17| 18| 19| 20| 21| 22| 23|
HEX | 33| 00| 20| 57| 6F| 72| 07| 00| 07| 00| 00| 02| 22| 2D| 2D| 2D|
DEC | 51|  0| 32| 87|111|114|  7|  0|  7|  0|  0|  2| 34| 45| 45| 45|
ASC |   | ^@| ^`|   |   |   | ^G| ^@| ^G| ^@| ^@| ^B|   |   |   |   |
ALT |   |NUL|SPC|   |   |   |BEL|NUL|BEL|NUL|NUL|STX|   |   |   |   |
SYM |  3|   |   |  W|  o|  r|   |   |   |   |   |   |  "|  -|  -|  -|


BYTE| 24| 25| 26| 27| 28| 29| 30| 31| 32| 33| 34| 35| 36| 37| 38| 39|
HEX | 2D| 2D| 2D| 2D| 2D| 2D| 2D| 2D| 2D| 00| 33| 00| 20| 57| 6F|
DEC | 45| 45| 45| 45| 45| 45| 45| 45| 45|  0| 51|  0| 32| 87|111|
ASC |   |   |   |   |   |   |   |   |   | ^@|   | ^@| ^`|   |   |
ALT |   |   |   |   |   |   |   |   |   |NUL|   |NUL|SPC|   |   |
SYM |  -|  -|  -|  -|  -|  -|  -|  -|  -|   |  3|   |   |  W|  o|


BYTE| 40| 41| 42| 43| 44| 45| 46| 47| 48| 49| 50| 51| 52| 53| 54| 55|
HEX | 72| 08| 00| 07| 00| 00| 02| 22| 2D| 2D| 2D| 2D| 2D| 2D| 2D| 2D|
DEC |114|  8|  0|  7|  0|  0|  2| 34| 45| 45| 45| 45| 45| 45| 45| 45|
ASC |   | ^H| ^@| ^G| ^@| ^@| ^B|   |   |   |   |   |   |   |   |   |
ALT |   | BS|NUL|BEL|NUL|NUL|STX|   |   |   |   |   |   |   |   |   |
SYM |  r|   |   |   |   |   |   |  "|  -|  -|  -|  -|  -|  -|  -|  -|
```

BYTE	56	57	58	59	60	61	62	63	64	65	66	67	68	69	70	71
HEX	2D	2D	2D	2D	2D	00	33	00	20	57	6F	72	09	00	07	00
DEC	45	45	45	45	45	0	51	0	32	87	111	114	9	0	7	0
ASC						^@		^@	^`				^I	^@	^G	^@
ALT						NUL		NUL	SPC				HT	NUL	BEL	NUL
SYM	-	-	-	-	-		3			W	o	r				

BYTE	72	73	74	75	76	77	78	79	80	81	82	83	84	85	86	87
HEX	00	02	22	2D	2D	2D	2D	2D	2D	2D	2D	2D	2D	2D	2D	2D
DEC	0	2	34	45	45	45	45	45	45	45	45	45	45	45	45	45
ASC	^@	^B														
ALT	NUL	STX														
SYM			"	-	-	-	-	-	-	-	-	-	-	-	-	-

BYTE	88	89	90	91	92	93	94	95	96	97	98	99	100	101	102	103
HEX	00	33	00	20	57	6F	72	0A	00	07	00	00	02	22	2D	2D
DEC	0	51	0	32	87	111	114	10	0	7	0	0	2	34	45	45
ASC	^@		^@	^`				^J	^@	^G	^@	^@	^B			
ALT	NUL		NUL	SPC				LF	NUL	BEL	NUL	NUL	STX			
SYM		3			W	o	r							"	-	-

BYTE	104	105	106	107	108	109	110	111	112	113	114	115	116	117	118	119
HEX	2D	2D	2D	2D	2D	2D	2D	2D	2D	2D	2D	00	33	00	20	57
DEC	45	45	45	45	45	45	45	45	45	45	45	0	51	0	32	87
ASC												^@		^@	^`	
ALT												NUL		NUL	SPC	
SYM	-	-	-	-	-	-	-	-	-	-	-		3			W

BYTE	120	121	122	123	124	125	126	127	128	129	130	131	132	133	134	135
HEX	6F	72	0B	00	07	00	00	02	22	2D	2D	2D	2D	2D	2D	2D
DEC	111	114	11	0	7	0	0	2	34	45	45	45	45	45	45	45
ASC			^K	^@	^G	^@	^@	^B								
ALT			VT	NUL	BEL	NUL	NUL	STX								
SYM	o	r							"	-	-	-	-	-	-	-

BYTE	136	137	138	139	140	141	142	143	144	145	146	147	148	149	150	151
HEX	2D	2D	2D	2D	2D	2D	00	33	00	20	57	6F	72	0C	00	07
DEC	45	45	45	45	45	45	0	51	0	32	87	111	114	12	0	7
ASC							^@		^@	^`				^L	^@	^G
ALT							NUL		NUL	SPC				FF	NUL	BEL
SYM	-	-	-	-	-	-		3			W	o	r			

BYTE	152	153	154	155	156	157	158	159	160	161	162	163	164	165	166	167
HEX	00	00	02	22	2D	2D	2D	2D	2D	2D	2D	2D	2D	2D	2D	2D
DEC	0	0	2	34	45	45	45	45	45	45	45	45	45	45	45	45
ASC	^@	^@	^B													
ALT	NUL	NUL	STX													
SYM			"	-	-	-	-	-	-	-	-	-	-	-	-	-

BYTE	168	169	170	171	172	173	174	175	176	177	178	179	180	181	182	183
HEX	2D	00	33	00	20	57	6F	72	00	00	08	00	50	01	22	50
DEC	45	0	51	0	32	87	111	114	0	0	8	0	80	1	34	80
ASC		^@		^@	^^				^@	^@	^H	^@		^A		
ALT		NUL		NUL	SPC				NUL	NUL	BS	NUL		SOH		
SYM	-		3			W	o	r					P		"	P

BYTE	184	185	186	187	188	189	190	191	192	193	194	195	196	197	198	199
HEX	6D	74	20	4E	6F	00	2D	2D	2D	2D	2D	01	00	08	00	18
DEC	109	116	32	78	111	0	45	45	45	45	45	1	0	8	0	24
ASC			^^			^@						^A	^@	^H	^@	^X
ALT			SPC			NUL						SOH	NUL	BS	NUL	CAN
SYM	m	t		N	o		-	-	-	-	-					

BYTE	200	201	202	203	204	205	206	207	208	209	210	211	212	213	214	215
HEX	01	22	49	6E	74	20	50	64	00	2D	2D	2D	2D	2D	02	00
DEC	1	34	73	110	116	32	80	100	0	45	45	45	45	45	2	0
ASC	^A					^^			^@						^B	^@
ALT	SOH					SPC			NUL						STX	NUL
SYM		"	I	n	t		P	d		-	-	-	-	-		

BYTE	216	217	218	219	220	221	222	223	224	225	226	227	228	229	230	231
HEX	08	00	00	01	22	50	72	63	20	50	64	00	2D	2D	2D	2D
DEC	8	0	0	1	34	80	114	99	32	80	100	0	45	45	45	45
ASC	^H	^@	^@	^A					^^			^@				
ALT	BS	NUL	NUL	SOH					SPC			NUL				
SYM					"	P	r	c		P	d		-	-	-	-

BYTE	232	233	234	235	236	237	238	239	240	241	242	243	244	245	246	247
HEX	2D	03	00	08	00	00	01	22	52	65	6D	61	69	6E	20	42
DEC	45	3	0	8	0	0	1	34	82	101	109	97	105	110	32	66
ASC		^C	^@	^H	^@	^@	^A								^^	
ALT		ETX	NUL	BS	NUL	NUL	SOH								SPC	
SYM	-							"	R	e	m	a	i	n		B

	248	249	250	251	252	253	254	255	256	257	258	259	260	261	262	263
HEX	61	6C	00	2D	04	00	08	00	00	01	22	49	6E	74	20	74
DEC	97	108	0	45	4	0	8	0	0	1	34	73	110	116	32	116
ASC			^@		^D	^@	^H	^@	^@	^A					^^	
ALT			NUL		EOT	NUL	BS	NUL	NUL	SOH					SPC	
SYM	a	l		-							"	I	n	t		t

	264	265	266	267	268	269	270	271	272	273	274	275	276	277	278	279
HEX	6F	20	44	61	74	65	00	05	00	08	00	00	01	22	50	52
DEC	111	32	68	97	116	101	0	5	0	8	0	0	1	34	80	82
ASC		^^					^@	^E	^@	^H	^@	^@	^A			
ALT		SPC					NUL	ENQ	NUL	BS	NUL	NUL	SOH			
SYM	o		D	a	t	e								"	P	R

	280	281	282	283	284	285	286	287	288	289	290	291	292	293	294	295
HEX	43	20	74	6F	20	44	61	74	65	00	06	00	08	00	00	02
DEC	67	32	116	111	32	68	97	116	101	0	6	0	8	0	0	2
ASC		^^			^^					^@	^F	^@	^H	^@	^@	^B
ALT		SPC			SPC					NUL	ACK	NUL	BS	NUL	NUL	STX
SYM	C		t	o		D	a	t	e							

	296	297	298	299	300	301	302	303	304	305	306	307	308	309	310	311
HEX	22	50	61	69	64	20	74	6F	20	44	61	74	65	00	00	33
DEC	34	80	97	105	100	32	116	111	32	68	97	116	101	0	0	51
ASC						^^			^^					^@	^@	
ALT						SPC			SPC					NUL	NUL	
SYM	"	P	a	i	d		t	o		D	a	t	e			3

	312	313	314	315	316	317	318	319	320	321	322	323	324	325	326	327
HEX	00	20	57	6F	72	00	00	09	00	00	02	22	2D	2D	2D	2D
DEC	0	32	87	111	114	0	0	9	0	0	2	34	45	45	45	45
ASC	^@	^^				^@	^@	^I	^@	^@	^B					
ALT	NUL	SPC				NUL	NUL	HT	NUL	NUL	STX					
SYM			W	o	r							"	-	-	-	-

	328	329	330	331	332	333	334	335	336	337	338	339	340	341	342	343
HEX	2D	2D	2D	2D	2D	2D	2D	2D	2D	00	33	00	20	57	6F	72
DEC	45	45	45	45	45	45	45	45	45	0	51	0	32	87	111	114
ASC										^@		^@	^^			
ALT										NUL		NUL	SPC			
SYM	-	-	-	-	-	-	-	-	-		3			W	o	r

```
BYTE|344|345|346|347|348|349|350|351|352|353|354|355|356|357|358|359|
_HEX|_01|_00|_09|_00|_00|_02|_22|_2D|_2D|_2D|_2D|_2D|_2D|_2D|_2D|_2D|
_DEC|__1|__0|__9|__0|__0|__2|_34|_45|_45|_45|_45|_45|_45|_45|_45|_45|
_ASC|_^A|_^@|_^I|_^@|_^@|_^B|___|___|___|___|___|___|___|___|___|___|
_ALT|SOH|NUL|_HT|NUL|NUL|STX|___|___|___|___|___|___|___|_*_|___|___|
_SYM|___|___|___|___|___|___|_"_|_-_|_-_|_-_|_-_|_-_|_-_|_-_|_-_|_-_|


BYTE|360|361|362|363|364|365|366|367|368|369|370|371|372|373|374|375|
_HEX|_2D|_2D|_2D|_2D|_00|_33|_00|_20|_57|_6F|_72|_02|_00|_09|_00|_00|
_DEC|_45|_45|_45|_45|__0|_51|__0|_32|_87|111|114|__2|__0|__9|__0|__0|
_ASC|___|___|___|___|_^@|___|_^@|_^`|___|___|___|_^B|_^@|_^I|_^@|_^@|
_ALT|___|___|___|___|NUL|___|NUL|SPC|___|___|___|STX|NUL|_HT|NUL|NUL|
_SYM|_-_|_-_|_-_|_-_|___|_3_|___|___|_W_|_o_|_r_|___|___|___|___|___|


BYTE|376|377|378|379|380|381|382|383|384|385|386|387|388|389|390|391|
_HEX|_02|_22|_2D|_2D|_2D|_2D|_2D|_2D|_2D|_2D|_2D|_2D|_2D|_2D|_2D|_00|
_DEC|__2|_34|_45|_45|_45|_45|_45|_45|_45|_45|_45|_45|_45|_45|_45|__0|
_ASC|_^B|___|___|___|___|___|___|___|___|___|___|___|___|___|___|_^@|
_ALT|STX|___|___|___|___|___|___|___|___|___|___|___|___|___|___|NUL|
_SYM|___|_"_|_-_|_-_|_-_|_-_|_-_|_-_|_-_|_-_|_-_|_-_|_-_|_-_|_-_|___|


BYTE|392|393|394|395|396|397|398|399|400|401|402|403|404|405|406|407|
_HEX|_33|_00|_20|_57|_6F|_72|_03|_00|_09|_00|_00|_02|_22|_2D|_2D|_2D|
_DEC|_51|__0|_32|_87|111|114|__3|__0|__9|__0|__0|__2|_34|_45|_45|_45|
_ASC|___|_^@|_^`|___|___|___|_^C|_^@|_^I|_^@|_^@|_^B|___|___|___|___|
_ALT|___|NUL|SPC|___|___|___|ETX|NUL|_HT|NUL|NUL|STX|___|___|___|___|
_SYM|_3_|___|___|_W_|_o_|_r_|___|___|___|___|___|___|_"_|_-_|_-_|_-_|


BYTE|408|409|410|411|412|413|414|415|416|417|418|419|420|421|422|423|
_HEX|_2D|_2D|_2D|_2D|_2D|_2D|_2D|_2D|_2D|_2D|_00|_33|_00|_20|_57|_6F|
_DEC|_45|_45|_45|_45|_45|_45|_45|_45|_45|_45|__0|_51|__0|_32|_87|111|
_ASC|___|___|___|___|___|___|___|___|___|___|_^@|___|_^@|_^`|___|___|
_ALT|___|___|___|___|___|___|___|___|___|___|NUL|___|NUL|SPC|___|___|
_SYM|_-_|_-_|_-_|_-_|_-_|_-_|_-_|_-_|_-_|_-_|___|_3_|___|___|_W_|_o_|


BYTE|424|425|426|427|428|429|430|431|432|433|434|435|436|437|438|439|
_HEX|_72|_04|_00|_09|_00|_00|_02|_22|_2D|_2D|_2D|_2D|_2D|_2D|_2D|_2D|
_DEC|114|__4|__0|__9|__0|__0|__2|_34|_45|_45|_45|_45|_45|_45|_45|_45|
_ASC|___|_^D|_^@|_^I|_^@|_^@|_^B|___|___|___|___|___|___|___|___|___|
_ALT|___|EOT|NUL|_HT|NUL|NUL|STX|___|___|___|___|___|___|___|___|___|
_SYM|_r_|___|___|___|___|___|___|_"_|_-_|_-_|_-_|_-_|_-_|_-_|_-_|_-_|
```

BYTE	440	441	442	443	444	445	446	447	448	449	450	451	452	453	454	455
HEX	2D	2D	2D	2D	2D	00	33	00	20	57	6F	72	05	00	09	00
DEC	45	45	45	45	45	0	51	0	32	87	111	114	5	0	9	0
ASC						^@		^@	^`				^E	^@	^I	^@
ALT						NUL		NUL	SPC				ENQ	NUL	HT	NUL
SYM	-	-	-	-	-		3			W	o	r				

BYTE	456	457	458	459	460	461	462	463	464	465	466	467	468	469	470	471
HEX	00	02	22	2D	2D	2D	2D	2D	2D	2D	2D	2D	2D	2D	2D	2D
DEC	0	2	34	45	45	45	45	45	45	45	45	45	45	45	45	45
ASC	^@	^B														
ALT	NUL	STX														
SYM			"	-	-	-	-	-	-	-	-	-	-	-	-	-

BYTE	472	473	474	475	476	477	478	479	480	481	482	483	484	485	486	487
HEX	00	33	00	20	57	6F	72	06	00	09	00	00	02	22	2D	2D
DEC	0	51	0	32	87	111	114	6	0	9	0	0	2	34	45	45
ASC	^@		^@	^`				^F	^@	^I	^@	^@	^B			
ALT	NUL		NUL	SPC				ACK	NUL	HT	NUL	NUL	STX			
SYM		3			W	o	r							"	-	-

BYTE	488	489	490	491	492	493	494	495	496	497	498	499	500	501	502	503
HEX	2D	2D	2D	2D	2D	2D	2D	2D	2D	2D	2D	00	33	00	20	57
DEC	45	45	45	45	45	45	45	45	45	45	45	0	51	0	32	87
ASC												^@		^@	^`	
ALT												NUL		NUL	SPC	
SYM	-	-	-	-	-	-	-	-	-	-	-		3			W

BYTE	504	505	506	507	508	509	510	511	512	513	514	515	516	517	518	519
HEX	6F	72	07	00	09	00	00	02	22	2D	2D	2D	2D	2D	2D	2D
DEC	111	114	7	0	9	0	0	2	34	45	45	45	45	45	45	45
ASC			^G	^@	^I	^@	^@	^B								
ALT			BEL	NUL	HT	NUL	NUL	STX								
SYM	o	r							"	-	-	-	-	-	-	-

BYTE	520	521	522	523	524	525	526	527	528	529	530	531	532	533	534	535
HEX	2D	2D	2D	2D	2D	2D	00	33	00	20	57	6F	72	08	00	09
DEC	45	45	45	45	45	45	0	51	0	32	87	111	114	8	0	9
ASC							^@		^@	^`				^H	^@	^I
ALT							NUL		NUL	SPC				BS	NUL	HT
SYM	-	-	-	-	-	-		3			W	o	r			

```
BYTE|536|537|538|539|540|541|542|543|544|545|546|547|548|549|550|551|
_HEX| 00| 00| 02| 22| 2D| 2D| 2D| 2D| 2D| 2D| 2D| 2D| 2D| 2D| 2D| 2D|
_DEC|  0|  0|  2| 34| 45| 45| 45| 45| 45| 45| 45| 45| 45| 45| 45| 45|
_ASC| ^@| ^@| ^B|   |   |   |   |   |   |   |   |   |   |   |   |   |
_ALT|NUL|NUL|STX|   |   |   |   |   |   |   |   |   |   |   |   |   |
_SYM|   |   |   |  "|  -|  -|  -|  -|  -|  -|  -|  -|  -|  -|  -|  -|


BYTE|552|553|554|555|556|557|558|559|560|561|562|563|564|565|566|567|
_HEX| 2D| 00| 33| 00| 20| 57| 6F| 72| 00| 00| 0A| 40| 00| 01| 00| 00|
_DEC| 45|  0| 51|  0| 32| 87|111|114|  0|  0| 10| 64|  0|  1|  0|  0|
_ASC|   | ^@|   | ^@| ^`|   |   |   | ^@| ^@| ^J|   | ^@| ^A| ^@| ^@|
_ALT|   |NUL|   |NUL|SPC|   |   |   |NUL|NUL| LF|   |NUL|SOH|NUL|NUL|
_SYM|  -|   |  3|   |   |  W|  o|  r|   |   |   |  @|   |   |   |   |


BYTE|568|569|570|571|572|573|574|575|576|577|578|579|580|581|582|583|
_HEX| 00| 00| 00| 00| F0| 3F| 00| 00| 31| 00| 00| 01| 00| 0A| 80| 01|
_DEC|  0|  0|  0|  0|240| 63|  0|  0| 49|  0|  0|  1|  0| 10|128|  1|
_ASC| ^@| ^@| ^@| ^@|240|   | ^@| ^@|   | ^@| ^@| ^A| ^@| ^J|128| ^A|
_ALT|NUL|NUL|NUL|NUL|240|   |NUL|NUL|   |NUL|NUL|SOH|NUL| LF|128|SOH|
_SYM|   |   |   |   |   |  ?|   |   |  1|   |   |   |   |   |   |   |


BYTE|584|585|586|587|588|589|590|591|592|593|594|595|596|597|598|599|
_HEX| 03| 00| 00| 00| 00| 00| 80| 52| 40| 00| 00| 2B| 28| 42| 33| 2A|
_DEC|  3|  0|  0|  0|  0|  0|128| 82| 64|  0|  0| 43| 40| 66| 51| 42|
_ASC| ^C| ^@| ^@| ^@| ^@| ^@|128|   |   | ^@| ^@|   |   |   |   |   |
_ALT|ETX|NUL|NUL|NUL|NUL|NUL|128|   |   |NUL|NUL|   |   |   |   |   |
_SYM|   |   |   |   |   |   |   |  R|  @|   |   |  +|  (|  B|  3|  *|


BYTE|600|601|602|603|604|605|606|607|608|609|610|611|612|613|614|615|
_HEX| 42| 34| 29| 2F| 31| 32| 00| 31| 32| 00| 20| 20| 20| 20| 02| 00|
_DEC| 66| 52| 41| 47| 49| 50|  0| 49| 50|  0| 32| 32| 32| 32|  2|  0|
_ASC|   |   |   |   |   |   | ^@|   |   | ^@| ^`| ^`| ^`| ^`| ^B| ^@|
_ALT|   |   |   |   |   |   |NUL|   |   |NUL|SPC|SPC|SPC|SPC|STX|NUL|
_SYM|  B|  4|  )|  /|  1|  2|   |  1|  2|   |   |   |   |   |   |   |


BYTE|616|617|618|619|620|621|622|623|624|625|626|627|628|629|630|631|
_HEX| 0A| 80| 01| 02| 1E| 85| EB| 51| B8| 2E| 59| 40| 00| 00| 2B| 42|
_DEC| 10|128|  1|  2| 30|133|235| 81|184| 46| 89| 64|  0|  0| 43| 66|
_ASC| ^J|128| ^A| ^B| ^^|133|235|   |184|   |   |   | ^@| ^@|   |   |
_ALT| LF|128|SOH|STX| RS|133|235|   |184|   |   |   |NUL|NUL|   |   |
_SYM|   |   |   |   |   |   |   |  Q|   |  .|  Y|  @|   |   |  +|  B|
```

```
BYTE|632|633|634|635|636|637|638|639|640|641|642|643|644|645|646|647|
_HEX| 35| 2D| 42| 31| 31| 00| 2F| 31| 32| 03| 00| 0A| 80| 01| 02| EC|
_DEC| 53| 45| 66| 49| 49|  0| 47| 49| 50|  3|  0| 10|128|  1|  2|236|
_ASC|___|___|___|___| ^@|___|___|___| ^C| ^@| ^J|128| ^A| ^B|236|
_ALT|___|___|___|___|NUL|___|___|___|ETX|NUL| LF|128|SOH|STX|236|
_SYM|  5|  -|  B|  1|  1|___| /|  1|  2|___|___|___|___|___|___|___|


BYTE|648|649|650|651|652|653|654|655|656|657|658|659|660|661|662|663|
_HEX| 51| B8| 1E| 45| 5B| B2| 40| 00| 00| 2B| 42| 33| 2D| 43| 31| 31|
_DEC| 81|184| 30| 69| 91|178| 64|  0|  0| 43| 66| 51| 45| 67| 49| 49|
_ASC|___|184| ^^|___|___|178|___|___| ^@| ^@|___|___|___|___|___|___|
_ALT|___|184| RS|___|___|178|___|___|NUL|NUL|___|___|___|___|___|___|
_SYM|  0|___|___|  E|  1|___|  @|___|___|  +|  B|  3|  -|  C|  1|  1|


BYTE|664|665|666|667|668|669|670|671|672|673|674|675|676|677|678|679|
_HEX| 00| 2F| 31| 32| 04| 00| 0A| 80| 01| 02| 00| 00| 00| 00| 00| 80|
_DEC|  0| 47| 49| 50|  4|  0| 10|128|  1|  2|  0|  0|  0|  0|  0|128|
_ASC| ^@|___|___|___| ^D| ^@| ^J|128| ^A| ^B| ^@| ^@| ^@| ^@| ^@|128|
_ALT|NUL|___|___|___|EOT|NUL| LF|128|SOH|STX|NUL|NUL|NUL|NUL|NUL|128|
_SYM|___|  /|  1|  2|___|___|___|___|___|___|___|___|___|___|___|___|


BYTE|680|681|682|683|684|685|686|687|688|689|690|691|692|693|694|695|
_HEX| 52| 40| 00| 00| 2B| 42| 31| 31| 00| 31| 31| 00| 2F| 31| 32| 05|
_DEC| 82| 64|  0|  0| 43| 66| 49| 49|  0| 49| 49|  0| 47| 49| 50|  5|
_ASC|___|___| ^@| ^@|___|___|___|___| ^@|___|___| ^@|___|___|___| ^E|
_ALT|___|___|NUL|NUL|___|___|___|NUL|___|___|NUL|___|___|___|___|ENO|
_SYM|  R|  @|___|___|  +|  B|  1|  1|___|  1|  1|___|  /|  1|  2|___|


BYTE|696|697|698|699|700|701|702|703|704|705|706|707|708|709|710|711|
_HEX| 00| 0A| 80| 01| 02| 1E| 85| EB| 51| B8| 2E| 59| 40| 00| 00| 2B|
_DEC|  0| 10|128|  1|  2| 30|133|235| 81|184| 46| 89| 64|  0|  0| 43|
_ASC| ^@| ^J|128| ^A| ^B| ^^|133|235|___|184|___|___|___| ^@| ^@|___|
_ALT|NUL| LF|128|SOH|STX| RS|133|235|___|184|___|___|___|NUL|NUL|___|
_SYM|___|___|___|___|___|___|___|___|  0|___|  .|  Y|  @|___|___|  +|


BYTE|712|713|714|715|716|717|718|719|720|721|722|723|724|725|726|727|
_HEX| 43| 31| 31| 00| 31| 31| 00| 2F| 31| 32| 06| 00| 0A| 80| 01| 02|
_DEC| 67| 49| 49|  0| 49| 49|  0| 47| 49| 50|  6|  0| 10|128|  1|  2|
_ASC|___|___|___| ^@|___|___| ^@|___|___|___| ^F| ^@| ^J|128| ^A| ^B|
_ALT|___|___|___|NUL|___|___|NUL|___|___|___|ACK|NUL| LF|128|SOH|STX|
_SYM|  C|  1|  1|___|  1|  1|___|  /|  1|  2|___|___|___|___|___|___|
```

BYTE	728	729	730	731	732	733	734	735	736	737	738	739	740	741	742	743
HEX	8F	C2	F5	28	5C	D7	65	40	00	00	2B	45	31	31	2B	46
DEC	143	194	245	40	92	215	101	64	0	0	43	69	49	49	43	70
ASC	143	194	245			215			^@	^@						
ALT	143	194	245			215			NUL	NUL						
SYM				(	\		e	@			+	E	1	1	+	F

BYTE	744	745	746	747	748	749	750	751	752	753	754	755	756	757	758	759
HEX	31	31	00	31	32	00	00	0B	40	00	01	00	00	00	00	00
DEC	49	49	0	49	50	0	0	11	64	0	1	0	0	0	0	0
ASC			^@			^@	^@	^K		^@	^A	^@	^@	^@	^@	^@
ALT			NUL			NUL	NUL	VT		NUL	SOH	NUL	NUL	NUL	NUL	NUL
SYM	1	1		1	2				@							

BYTE	760	761	762	763	764	765	766	767	768	769	770	771	772	773	774	775
HEX	00	00	40	00	00	32	00	31	01	00	0B	80	01	03	9A	E3
DEC	0	0	64	0	0	50	0	49	1	0	11	128	1	3	154	227
ASC	^@	^@		^@	^@		^@		^A	^@	^K	128	^A	^C	154	227
ALT	NUL	NUL		NUL	NUL		NUL		SOH	NUL	VT	128	SOH	ETX	154	227
SYM			@			2		1								

BYTE	776	777	778	779	780	781	782	783	784	785	786	787	788	789	790	791
HEX	EF	F1	9C	1C	52	40	00	00	2B	28	44	31	31	2A	24	42
DEC	239	241	156	28	82	64	0	0	43	40	68	49	49	42	36	66
ASC	239	241	156	^\			^@	^@								
ALT	239	241	156	FS			NUL	NUL								
SYM					R	@			+	(	D	1	1	*	$	B

BYTE	792	793	794	795	796	797	798	799	800	801	802	803	804	805	806	807
HEX	24	34	29	2F	31	32	00	20	20	20	20	02	00	0B	80	01
DEC	36	52	41	47	49	50	0	32	32	32	32	2	0	11	128	1
ASC							^@	^`	^`	^`	^`	^B	^@	^K	128	^A
ALT							NUL	SPC	SPC	SPC	SPC	STX	NUL	VT	128	SOH
SYM	$	4	)	/	1	2										

BYTE	808	809	810	811	812	813	814	815	816	817	818	819	820	821	822	823
HEX	02	84	A1	FB	5F	1B	92	59	40	00	00	2B	24	42	24	35
DEC	2	132	161	251	95	27	146	89	64	0	0	43	36	66	36	53
ASC	^B	132	161	251		^[	146			^@	^@					
ALT	STX	132	161	251		ESC	146			NUL	NUL					
SYM								Y	@			+	$	B	$	5

BYTE	824	825	826	827	828	829	830	831	832	833	834	835	836	837	838	839
HEX	2D	42	31	32	00	29	03	00	0B	80	01	02	66	63	38	B1
DEC	45	66	49	50	0	41	3	0	11	128	1	2	102	99	56	177
ASC					^@		^C	^@	^K	128	^A	^B				177
ALT					NUL		ETX	NUL	VT	128	SOH	STX				177
SYM	-	B	1	2		)							f	c	8	

BYTE	840	841	842	843	844	845	846	847	848	849	850	851	852	853	854	855
HEX	FC	F4	B1	40	00	00	2B	44	31	31	2D	43	31	32	00	00
DEC	252	244	177	64	0	0	43	68	49	49	45	67	49	50	0	0
ASC	252	244	177		^@	^@									^@	^@
ALT	252	244	177		NUL	NUL									NUL	NUL
SYM				@			+	D	1	1	-	C	1	2		

BYTE	856	857	858	859	860	861	862	863	864	865	866	867	868	869	870	871
HEX	29	04	00	0B	80	01	02	CD	F1	F7	78	4E	4E	62	40	00
DEC	41	4	0	11	128	1	2	205	241	247	120	78	78	98	64	0
ASC		^D	^@	^K	128	^A	^B	205	241	247						^@
ALT		EOT	NUL	VT	128	SOH	STX	205	241	247						NUL
SYM	)										x	N	N	b	@	

BYTE	872	873	874	875	876	877	878	879	880	881	882	883	884	885	886	887
HEX	00	2B	45	31	31	2B	42	31	32	00	00	29	05	00	0B	80
DEC	0	43	69	49	49	43	66	49	50	0	0	41	5	0	11	128
ASC	^@									^@	^@		^E	^@	^K	128
ALT	NUL									NUL	NUL		ENQ	NUL	VT	128
SYM		+	E	1	1	+	B	1	2			)				

BYTE	888	889	890	891	892	893	894	895	896	897	898	899	900	901	902	903
HEX	01	02	51	93	F3	D8	69	60	69	40	00	00	2B	46	31	31
DEC	1	2	81	147	243	216	105	96	105	64	0	0	43	70	49	49
ASC	^A	^B		147	243	216					^@	^@				
ALT	SOH	STX		147	243	216					NUL	NUL				
SYM			Q				i	`	i	@			+	F	1	1

BYTE	904	905	906	907	908	909	910	911	912	913	914	915	916	917	918	919
HEX	2B	43	31	32	00	00	29	06	00	0B	80	01	02	8F	C2	F5
DEC	43	67	49	50	0	0	41	6	0	11	128	1	2	143	194	245
ASC					^@	^@		^F	^@	^K	128	^A	^B	143	194	245
ALT					NUL	NUL		ACK	NUL	VT	128	SOH	STX	143	194	245
SYM	+	C	1	2			)									

BYTE	920	921	922	923	924	925	926	927	928	929	930	931	932	933	934	935
HEX	28	5C	D7	75	40	00	00	2B	45	31	32	2B	46	31	32	00
DEC	40	92	215	117	64	0	0	43	69	49	50	43	70	49	50	0
ASC			215			^@	^@									^@
ALT			215			NUL	NUL									NUL
SYM	(	\		u	@			+	E	1	2	+	F	1	2	

BYTE	936	937	938	939	940	941	942	943	944	945	946	947	948	949	950	951
HEX	00	29	00	00	0C	40	00	01	00	00	00	00	00	00	08	40
DEC	0	41	0	0	12	64	0	1	0	0	0	0	0	0	8	64
ASC	^@		^@	^@	^L		^@	^A	^@	^@	^@	^@	^@	^@	^H	
ALT	NUL		NUL	NUL	FF		NUL	SOH	NUL	NUL	NUL	NUL	NUL	NUL	BS	
SYM		)				@										@

BYTE	952	953	954	955	956	957	958	959	960	961	962	963	964	965	966	967
HEX	00	00	33	00	31	01	00	0C	80	01	03	53	09	9E	A4	B1
DEC	0	0	51	0	49	1	0	12	128	1	3	83	9	158	164	177
ASC	^@	^@		^@		^A	^@	^L	128	^A	^C		^I	158	164	177
ALT	NUL	NUL		NUL		SOH	NUL	FF	128	SOH	ETX		HT	158	164	177
SYM			3		1							S				

BYTE	968	969	970	971	972	973	974	975	976	977	978	979	980	981	982	983
HEX	B7	51	40	00	00	2B	28	44	31	32	2A	24	42	24	34	29
DEC	183	81	64	0	0	43	40	68	49	50	42	36	66	36	52	41
ASC	183			^@	^@											
ALT	183			NUL	NUL											
SYM		Q	@			+	(	D	1	2	*	$	B	$	4	)

BYTE	984	985	986	987	988	989	990	991	992	993	994	995	996	997	998	999
HEX	2F	31	32	00	20	20	20	20	02	00	0C	80	01	02	CB	7B
DEC	47	49	50	0	32	32	32	32	2	0	12	128	1	2	203	123
ASC				^@	^^	^^	^^	^^	^B	^@	^L	128	^A	^B	203	
ALT				NUL	SPC	SPC	SPC	SPC	STX	NUL	FF	128	SOH	STX	203	
SYM	/	1	2													{

BYTE	0	1	2	3	4	5	6	7	8	9	10	11	12	13	14	15
HEX	4D	AD	06	F7	59	40	00	00	2B	24	42	24	35	2D	42	31
DEC	77	173	6	247	89	64	0	0	43	36	66	36	53	45	66	49
ASC		173	^F	247			^@	^@								
ALT		173	ACK	247			NUL	NUL								
SYM	M				Y	@			+	$	B	$	5	-	B	1

BYTE	16	17	18	19	20	21	22	23	24	25	26	27	28	29	30	31
HEX	33	00	29	03	00	0C	80	01	02	77	2D	83	96	20	8D	B1
DEC	51	0	41	3	0	12	128	1	2	119	45	131	150	32	141	177
ASC		^@		^C	^@	^L	128	^A	^B			131	150	^^	141	177
ALT		NUL		ETX	NUL	FF	128	SOH	STX			131	150	SPC	141	177
SYM	3		)							w	-					

BYTE	32	33	34	35	36	37	38	39	40	41	42	43	44	45	46	47
HEX	40	00	00	2B	44	31	32	2D	43	31	33	00	00	29	04	00
DEC	64	0	0	43	68	49	50	45	67	49	51	0	0	41	4	0
ASC		^@	^@									^@	^@		^D	^@
ALT		NUL	NUL									NUL	NUL		EOT	NUL
SYM	@			+	D	1	2	-	C	1	3			)		

BYTE	48	49	50	51	52	53	54	55	56	57	58	59	60	61	62	63
HEX	0C	80	01	02	77	F6	46	4B	27	2A	6B	40	00	00	2B	45
DEC	12	128	1	2	119	246	70	75	39	42	107	64	0	0	43	69
ASC	^L	128	^A	^B		246								^@	^@	
ALT	FF	128	SOH	STX		246								NUL	NUL	
SYM					w		F	K	'	*	k	@			+	E

BYTE	64	65	66	67	68	69	70	71	72	73	74	75	76	77	78	79
HEX	31	32	2B	42	31	33	00	00	29	05	00	0C	80	01	02	9B
DEC	49	50	43	66	49	51	0	0	41	5	0	12	128	1	2	155
ASC							^@	^@		^E	^@	^L	128	^A	^B	155
ALT							NUL	NUL		ENQ	NUL	FF	128	SOH	STX	155
SYM	1	2	+	B	1	3										

BYTE	80	81	82	83	84	85	86	87	88	89	90	91	92	93	94	95
HEX	28	CD	97	F6	2D	73	40	00	00	2B	46	31	32	2B	43	31
DEC	40	205	151	246	45	115	64	0	0	43	70	49	50	43	67	49
ASC		205	151	246				^@	^@							
ALT		205	151	246				NUL	NUL							
SYM	(				-	s	@			+	F	1	2	+	C	1

BYTE	96	97	98	99	100	101	102	103	104	105	106	107	108	109	110	111
HEX	33	00	00	29	06	00	0C	80	01	02	EB	51	B8	1E	85	61
DEC	51	0	0	41	6	0	12	128	1	2	235	81	184	30	133	97
ASC		^@	^@		^F	^@	^L	128	^A	^B	235		184	^^	133	97
ALT		NUL	NUL		ACK	NUL	FF	128	SOH	STX	235		184	RS	133	
SYM	3			)								Q				a

BYTE	112	113	114	115	116	117	118	119	120	121	122	123	124	125	126	127
HEX	80	40	00	00	2B	45	31	33	2B	46	31	33	00	00	29	00
DEC	128	64	0	0	43	69	49	51	43	70	49	51	0	0	29	0
ASC	128		^@	^@									^@	^@		^@
ALT	128		NUL	NUL									NUL	NUL		NUL
SYM		@			+	E	1	3	+	F	1	3			)	

BYTE	128	129	130	131	132	133	134	135	136	137	138	139	140	141	142	143
HEX	00	0D	40	00	01	00	00	00	00	00	00	10	40	00	00	34
DEC	0	13	64	0	1	0	0	0	0	0	0	16	64	0	0	52
ASC	^@	^M		^@	^A	^@	^@	^@	^@	^@	^@	^P		^@	^@	
ALT	NUL	CR		NUL	SOH	NUL	NUL	NUL	NUL	NUL	NUL	DLE		NUL	NUL	
SYM			@											@		4

BYTE	144	145	146	147	148	149	150	151	152	153	154	155	156	157	158	159
HEX	00	31	01	00	0D	80	01	03	2D	E5	F8	0B	38	51	51	40
DEC	0	49	1	0	13	128	1	3	45	229	248	11	56	81	81	64
ASC	^@		^A	^@	^M	128	^A	^C		229	248	^K				
ALT	NUL		SOH	NUL	CR	128	SOH	ETX		229	248	VT				
SYM		1							-				8	0	0	@

BYTE	160	161	162	163	164	165	166	167	168	169	170	171	172	173	174	175
HEX	00	00	2B	28	44	31	33	2A	24	42	24	34	29	2F	31	32
DEC	0	0	43	40	68	49	51	42	36	66	36	52	41	47	49	50
ASC	^@	^@														
ALT	NUL	NUL														
SYM			+	(	D	1	3	*	$	B	$	4	)	/	1	2

BYTE	176	177	178	179	180	181	182	183	184	185	186	187	188	189	190	191
HEX	00	20	20	20	20	02	00	0D	80	01	02	F1	9F	F2	45	80
DEC	0	32	32	32	32	2	0	13	128	1	2	241	159	242	69	128
ASC	^@	^^	^^	^^	^^	^B	^@	^M	128	^A	^B	241	159	242		128
ALT	NUL	SPC	SPC	SPC	SPC	STX	NUL	CR	128	SOH	STX	241	159	242		128
SYM															E	

BYTE	192	193	194	195	196	197	198	199	200	201	202	203	204	205	206	207
HEX	5D	5A	40	00	00	2B	24	42	24	35	2D	42	31	34	00	29
DEC	93	90	64	0	0	43	36	66	36	53	45	66	49	52	0	41
ASC				^@	^@										^@	
ALT				NUL	NUL										NUL	
SYM	1	Z	@			+	$	B	$	5	-	B	1	4		)

BYTE	208	209	210	211	212	213	214	215	216	217	218	219	220	221	222	223
HEX	03	00	0D	80	01	02	F7	62	6B	95	AA	23	B1	40	00	00
DEC	3	0	13	128	1	2	247	98	107	149	170	35	177	64	0	0
ASC	^C	^@	^M	128	^A	^B	247			149	170		177		^@	^@
ALT	ETX	NUL	CR	128	SOH	STX	247			149	170		177		NUL	NUL
SYM								b	k			#		@		

BYTE	224	225	226	227	228	229	230	231	232	233	234	235	236	237	238	239
HEX	2B	44	31	33	2D	43	31	34	00	00	29	04	00	0D	80	01
DEC	43	68	49	51	45	67	49	52	0	0	41	4	0	13	128	1
ASC									^@	^@		^D	^@	^M	128	^A
ALT									NUL	NUL		EOT	NUL	CR	128	SOH
SYM	+	D	1	3	-	C	1	4			)					

BYTE	240	241	242	243	244	245	246	247	248	249	250	251	252	253	254	255
HEX	02	87	B4	A1	A8	61	E9	71	40	00	00	2B	45	31	33	2B
DEC	2	135	180	161	168	97	233	113	64	0	0	43	69	49	51	43
ASC	^B	135	180	161	168		233			^@	^@					
ALT	STX	135	180	161	168		233			NUL	NUL					
SYM						a		q	@			+	E	1	3	+

BYTE	256	257	258	259	260	261	262	263	264	265	266	267	268	269	270	271
HEX	42	31	34	00	00	29	05	00	0D	80	01	02	97	D0	49	A9
DEC	66	49	52	0	0	41	5	0	13	128	1	2	151	208	73	169
ASC				^@	^@		^E	^@	^M	128	^A	^B	151	208		169
ALT				NUL	NUL		ENQ	NUL	CR	128	SOH	STX	151	208		169
SYM	B	1	4			)									I	

BYTE	272	273	274	275	276	277	278	279	280	281	282	283	284	285	286	287
HEX	56	C5	79	40	00	00	2B	46	31	33	2B	43	31	34	00	00
DEC	86	197	121	64	0	0	43	70	49	51	43	67	49	52	0	0
ASC		197			^@	^@									^@	^@
ALT		197			NUL	NUL									NUL	NUL
SYM	V		y	@			+	F	1	3	+	C	1	4		

BYTE	288	289	290	291	292	293	294	295	296	297	298	299	300	301	302	303
HEX	29	06	00	0D	80	01	02	8F	C2	F5	28	5C	D7	85	40	00
DEC	41	6	0	13	128	1	2	143	194	245	40	92	215	133	64	0
ASC		^F	^@	^M	128	^A	^B	143	194	245			215	133		^@
ALT		ACK	NUL	CR	128	SOH	STX	143	194	245			215	133		NUL
SYM	)										(	\			@	

```
BYTE|304|305|306|307|308|309|310|311|312|313|314|315|316|317|318|319|
HEX | 00| 2B| 45| 31| 34| 2B| 46| 31| 34| 00| 00| 29| 00| 00| 0E| 40|
DEC |  0| 43| 69| 49| 52| 43| 70| 49| 52|  0|  0| 41|  0|  0| 14| 64|
ASC | ^@|   |   |   |   |   |   |   |   | ^@| ^@|   | ^@| ^@| ^N|   |
ALT |NUL|   |   |   |   |   |   |   |   |NUL|NUL|   |NUL|NUL| SO|   |
SYM |   |  +|  E|  1|  4|  +|  F|  1|  4|   |   |  )|   |   |   |  @|


BYTE|320|321|322|323|324|325|326|327|328|329|330|331|332|333|334|335|
HEX | 00| 01| 00| 00| 00| 00| 00| 00| 14| 40| 00| 00| 35| 00| 31| 01|
DEC |  0|  1|  0|  0|  0|  0|  0|  0| 20| 64|  0|  0| 53|  0| 49|  1|
ASC | ^@| ^A| ^@| ^@| ^@| ^@| ^@| ^@| ^T|   | ^@| ^@|   | ^@|   | ^A|
ALT |NUL|SOH|NUL|NUL|NUL|NUL|NUL|NUL|DC4|   |NUL|NUL|   |NUL|   |SOH|
SYM |   |   |   |   |   |   |   |   |   |  @|   |   |  5|   |  1|   |


BYTE|336|337|338|339|340|341|342|343|344|345|346|347|348|349|350|351|
HEX | 00| 0E| 80| 01| 03| 45| 35| 11| 04| 2A| E9| 50| 40| 00| 00| 2B|
DEC |  0| 14|128|  1|  3| 69| 53| 17|  4| 42|233| 80| 64|  0|  0| 43|
ASC | ^@| ^N|128| ^A| ^C|   |   | ^Q| ^D|   |233|   |   | ^@| ^@|   |
ALT |NUL| SO|128|SOH|ETX|   |   |DC1|EOT|   |233|   |   |NUL|NUL|   |
SYM |   |   |   |   |   |  E|  5|   |   |  *|   |  P|  @|   |   |  +|


BYTE|352|353|354|355|356|357|358|359|360|361|362|363|364|365|366|367|
HEX | 28| 44| 31| 34| 2A| 24| 42| 24| 34| 29| 2F| 31| 32| 00| 20| 20|
DEC | 40| 68| 49| 52| 42| 36| 66| 36| 52| 41| 47| 49| 50|  0| 32| 32|
ASC |   |   |   |   |   |   |   |   |   |   |   |   |   | ^@|   |   |
ALT |   |   |   |   |   |   |   |   |   |   |   |   |   |NUL|SPC|SPC|
SYM |  (|  D|  1|  4|  *|  $|  B|  $|  4|  )|  /|  1|  2|   |   |   |


BYTE|368|369|370|371|372|373|374|375|376|377|378|379|380|381|382|383|
HEX | 20| 20| 02| 00| 0E| 80| 01| 02| D9| 4F| DA| 4D| 8E| C5| 5A| 40|
DEC | 32| 32|  2|  0| 14|128|  1|  2|217| 79|218| 77|142|197| 90| 64|
ASC |   |   | ^B| ^@| ^N|128| ^A| ^B|217|   |218|   |142|197|   |   |
ALT |SPC|SPC|STX|NUL| SO|128|SOH|STX|217|   |218|   |142|197|   |   |
SYM |   |   |   |   |   |   |   |   |   |  O|   |  M|   |   |  Z|  @|


BYTE|384|385|386|387|388|389|390|391|392|393|394|395|396|397|398|399|
HEX | 00| 00| 2B| 24| 42| 24| 35| 2D| 42| 31| 35| 00| 29| 03| 00| 0E|
DEC |  0|  0| 43| 36| 66| 36| 53| 45| 66| 49| 53|  0| 41|  3|  0| 14|
ASC | ^@| ^@|   |   |   |   |   |   |   |   |   | ^@|   | ^C| ^@| ^N|
ALT |NUL|NUL|   |   |   |   |   |   |   |   |   |NUL|   |ETX|NUL| SO|
SYM |   |   |  +|  $|  B|  $|  5|  -|  B|  1|  5|   |  )|   |   |   |
```

BYTE	400	401	402	403	404	405	406	407	408	409	410	411	412	413	414	415
HEX	80	01	02	B8	F9	33	5C	94	B8	B0	40	00	00	2B	44	31
DEC	128	1	2	184	249	51	92	148	184	176	64	0	0	43	68	49
ASC	128	^A	^B	184	249		148	184	176		^@	^@				
ALT	128	SOH	STX	184	249		148	184	176		NUL	NUL				
SYM						3	\				@			+	D	1

BYTE	416	417	418	419	420	421	422	423	424	425	426	427	428	429	430	431
HEX	34	2D	43	31	35	00	00	29	04	00	0E	80	01	02	D8	01
DEC	52	45	67	49	53	0	0	41	4	0	14	128	1	2	216	1
ASC						^@	^@		^D	^@	^N	128	^A	^B	216	^A
ALT						NUL	NUL		EOT	NUL	SO	128	SOH	STX	216	SOH
SYM	4	-	C	1	5			)								

BYTE	432	433	434	435	436	437	438	439	440	441	442	443	444	445	446	447
HEX	A6	29	AC	23	76	40	00	00	2B	45	31	34	2B	42	31	35
DEC	166	41	172	35	118	64	0	0	43	69	49	52	43	66	49	53
ASC	166		172			^@	^@									
ALT	166		172			NUL	NUL									
SYM		)		‡	v	@			+	E	1	4	+	B	1	5

BYTE	448	449	450	451	452	453	454	455	456	457	458	459	460	461	462	463
HEX	00	00	29	05	00	0E	80	01	02	47	32	60	1E	5D	3B	80
DEC	0	0	41	5	0	14	128	1	2	71	50	96	30	93	59	128
ASC	^@	^@		^E	^@	^N	128	^A	^B				^^			128
ALT	NUL	NUL		ENQ	NUL	SO	128	SOH	STX				RS			128
SYM			)							G	2	`		]	;	

BYTE	464	465	466	467	468	469	470	471	472	473	474	475	476	477	478	479
HEX	40	00	00	2B	46	31	34	2B	43	31	35	00	00	29	06	00
DEC	64	0	0	43	70	49	52	43	67	49	53	0	0	41	6	0
ASC		^@	^@									^@	^@		^F	^@
ALT		NUL	NUL									NUL	NUL		ACK	NUL
SYM	@			+	F	1	4	+	C	1	5			)		

BYTE	480	481	482	483	484	485	486	487	488	489	490	491	492	493	494	495
HEX	0E	80	01	02	33	33	33	33	33	4D	8B	40	00	00	2B	45
DEC	14	128	1	2	51	51	51	51	51	77	139	64	0	0	43	69
ASC	^N	128	^A	^B							139		^@	^@		
ALT	SO	128	SOH	STX							139		NUL	NUL		
SYM					3	3	3	3	3	M		@			+	E

```
BYTE|496|497|498|499|500|501|502|503|504|505|506|507|508|509|510|511|
_HEX| 31| 35| 2B| 46| 31| 35| 00| 00| 29| 00| 00| 0F| 40| 00| 01| 00|
_DEC| 49| 53| 43| 70| 49| 53| _0| _0| 41| _0| _0| 15| 64| _0| _1| _0|
_ASC|___|___|___|___|___|___| ^@| ^@|___| ^@| ^@| ^O|___| ^@| ^A| ^@|
_ALT|___|___|___|___|___|___|NUL|NUL|___|NUL|NUL| SI|___|NUL|SOH|NUL|
_SYM|__1|__5|__+|__F|__1|__5|___|___|__)|___|___|___|__@|___|___|___|


BYTE|512|513|514|515|516|517|518|519|520|521|522|523|524|525|526|527|
_HEX| 00| 00| 00| 00| 00| 18| 40| 00| 00| 36| 00| 31| 01| 00| 0F| 80|
_DEC| _0| _0| _0| _0| _0| 24| 64| _0| _0| 54| _0| 49| _1| _0| 15|128|
_ASC| ^@| ^@| ^@| ^@| ^@| ^X|___| ^@| ^@|___| ^@|___| ^A| ^@| ^O|128|
_ALT|NUL|NUL|NUL|NUL|NUL|CAN|___|NUL|NUL|___|NUL|___|SOH|NUL| SI|128|
_SYM|___|___|___|___|___|___|__@|___|___|__6|___|__1|___|___|___|___|


BYTE|528|529|530|531|532|533|534|535|536|537|538|539|540|541|542|543|
_HEX| 01| 03| D7| D0| BB| 50| 81| 7F| 50| 40| 00| 00| 2B| 28| 44| 31|
_DEC| _1| _3|215|208|187| 80|129|127| 80| 64| _0| _0| 43| 40| 68| 49|
_ASC| ^A| ^C|215|208|187|___|129| ^?|___|___| ^@| ^@| 43| 40| 68| 49|
_ALT|SOH|ETX|215|208|187|___|129|DEL|___|___|NUL|NUL|___|___|___|___|
_SYM|___|___|___|___|___|__P|___|___|__P|__@|___|___|__+|__(|__D|__1|


BYTE|544|545|546|547|548|549|550|551|552|553|554|555|556|557|558|559|
_HEX| 35| 2A| 24| 42| 24| 34| 29| 2F| 31| 32| 00| 20| 20| 20| 20| 02|
_DEC| 53| 42| 36| 66| 36| 52| 41| 47| 49| 50| _0| 32| 32| 32| 32| _2|
_ASC|___|___|___|___|___|___|___|___|___|___| ^@| ^^| ^^| ^^| ^^| ^B|
_ALT|___|___|___|___|___|___|___|___|___|___|NUL|SPC|SPC|SPC|SPC|STX|
_SYM|__5|__*|__$|__B|__$|__4|__)|__/|__1|__2|___|___|___|___|___|___|


BYTE|560|561|562|563|564|565|566|567|568|569|570|571|572|573|574|575|
_HEX| 00| 0F| 80| 01| 02| 47| B4| 2F| 01| 37| 2F| 5B| 40| 00| 00| 2B|
_DEC| _0| 15|128| _1| _2| 71|180| 47| _1| 55| 47| 91| 64| _0| _0| 43|
_ASC| ^@| ^O|128| ^A| ^B|___|180|___| ^A|___| 55| 91| 64| _0| _0| 43|
_ALT|NUL| SI|128|SOH|STX|___|180|___|SOH|___|___|___|___|NUL|NUL|___|
_SYM|___|___|___|___|___|__G|___|__/|___|__7|__/|__[|__@|___|___|__+|


BYTE|576|577|578|579|580|581|582|583|584|585|586|587|588|589|590|591|
_HEX| 24| 42| 24| 35| 2D| 42| 31| 36| 00| 29| 03| 00| 0F| 80| 01| 02|
_DEC| 36| 66| 36| 53| 45| 66| 49| 54| _0| 41| _3| _0| 15|128| _1| _2|
_ASC|___|___|___|___|___|___|___|___| ^@|___| ^C| ^@| ^O|128| ^A| ^B|
_ALT|___|___|___|___|___|___|___|___|NUL|___|ETX|NUL| SI|128|SOH|STX|
_SYM|__$|__B|__$|__5|__-|__B|__1|__6|___|__)|___|___|___|___|___|___|
```

BYTE	592	593	594	595	596	597	598	599	600	601	602	603	604	605	606	607
HEX	E7	3A	2F	80	D7	4B	B0	40	00	00	2B	44	31	35	2D	43
DEC	231	58	47	128	215	75	176	64	0	0	43	68	49	53	45	67
ASC	231			128	215		176			^@	^@					
ALT	231			128	215		176			NUL	NUL					
SYM		:	/			K		@			+	D	1	5	-	C

BYTE	608	609	610	611	612	613	614	615	616	617	618	619	620	621	622	623
HEX	31	36	00	00	29	04	00	0F	80	01	02	0E	F6	D4	7D	8C
DEC	49	54	0	0	41	4	0	15	128	1	2	14	246	212	125	140
ASC			^@	^@		^D	^@	^O	128	^A	^B	^N	246	212		140
ALT			NUL	NUL		EOT	NUL	SI	128	SOH	STX	SO	246	212		140
SYM	1	6			)											

BYTE	624	625	626	627	628	629	630	631	632	633	634	635	636	637	638	639
HEX	43	7A	40	00	00	2B	45	31	35	2B	42	31	36	00	00	29
DEC	67	122	64	0	0	43	69	49	53	43	66	49	54	0	0	41
ASC				^@	^@									^@	^@	
ALT				NUL	NUL									NUL	NUL	
SYM	C	z	@			+	E	1	5	+	B	1	6			)

BYTE	640	641	642	643	644	645	646	647	648	649	650	651	652	653	654	655
HEX	05	00	0F	80	01	02	D0	28	86	FE	43	A1	83	40	00	00
DEC	5	0	15	128	1	2	208	40	134	254	67	161	131	64	0	0
ASC	^E	^@	^O	128	^A	^B	208		134	254		161	131		^@	^@
ALT	ENQ	NUL	SI	128	SOH	STX	208		134	254		161	131		NUL	NUL
SYM									(			C			@	

BYTE	656	657	658	659	660	661	662	663	664	665	666	667	668	669	670	671
HEX	2B	46	31	35	2B	43	31	36	00	00	29	06	00	0F	80	01
DEC	43	70	49	53	43	67	49	54	0	0	41	6	0	15	128	1
ASC									^@	^@		^F	^@	^O	128	^A
ALT									NUL	NUL		ACK	NUL	SI	128	SOH
SYM	+	F	1	5	+	C	1	6			)					

BYTE	672	673	674	675	676	677	678	679	680	681	682	683	684	685	686	687
HEX	02	EC	51	B8	1E	85	61	90	40	00	00	2B	45	31	36	2B
DEC	2	236	81	184	30	133	97	144	64	0	0	43	69	49	54	43
ASC	^B	236		184	^^	133		144			^@	^@				
ALT	STX	236		184	RS	133		144		NUL	NUL					
SYM			O			a		@			+	E	1	6	+

```
BYTE|688|689|690|691|692|693|694|695|696|697|698|699|700|701|702|703|
_HEX| 46| 31| 36| 00| 00| 29| 1A| 1A| 1A| 1A| 1A| 1A| 1A| 1A| 1A| 1A|
_DEC| 70| 49| 54|  0|  0| 41| 26| 26| 26| 26| 26| 26| 26| 26| 26| 26|
_ASC|___|___|___| ^@| ^@|___| ^Z| ^Z| ^Z| ^Z| ^Z| ^Z| ^Z| ^Z| ^Z| ^Z|
_ALT|___|___|___|NUL|NUL|___|SUB|SUB|SUB|SUB|SUB|SUB|SUB|SUB|SUB|SUB|
_SYM|  F|  1|  6|___|___|  )|___|___|___|___|___|___|___|___|___|___|


BYTE|704|705|706|707|708|709|710|711|712|713|714|715|716|717|718|719|
_HEX| 1A| 1A| 1A| 1A| 1A| 1A| 1A| 1A| 1A| 1A| 1A| 1A| 1A| 1A| 1A| 1A|
_DEC| 26| 26| 26| 26| 26| 26| 26| 26| 26| 26| 26| 26| 26| 26| 26| 26|
_ASC| ^Z| ^Z| ^Z| ^Z| ^Z| ^Z| ^Z| ^Z| ^Z| ^Z| ^Z| ^Z| ^Z| ^Z| ^Z| ^Z|
_ALT|SUB|SUB|SUB|SUB|SUB|SUB|SUB|SUB|SUB|SUB|SUB|SUB|SUB|SUB|SUB|SUB|
_SYM|___|___|___|___|___|___|___|___|___|___|___|___|___|___|___|___|


BYTE|720|721|722|723|724|725|726|727|728|729|730|731|732|733|734|735|
_HEX| 1A| 1A| 1A| 1A| 1A| 1A| 1A| 1A| 1A| 1A| 1A| 1A| 1A| 1A| 1A| 1A|
_DEC| 26| 26| 26| 26| 26| 26| 26| 26| 26| 26| 26| 26| 26| 26| 26| 26|
_ASC| ^Z| ^Z| ^Z| ^Z| ^Z| ^Z| ^Z| ^Z| ^Z| ^Z| ^Z| ^Z| ^Z| ^Z| ^Z| ^Z|
_ALT|SUB|SUB|SUB|SUB|SUB|SUB|SUB|SUB|SUB|SUB|SUB|SUB|SUB|SUB|SUB|SUB|
_SYM|___|___|___|___|___|___|___|___|___|___|___|___|___|___|___|___|


BYTE|  0|  0|  0|  0|  0|  0|  0|  0|  0|  0|  0|  0|  0|  0|  0|  0|
_HEX| XX| XX| XX| XX| XX| XX| XX| XX| XX| XX| XX| XX| XX| XX| XX| XX|
_DEC|  0|  0|  0|  0|  0|  0|  0|  0|  0|  0|  0|  0|  0|  0|  0|  0|
_ASC|XXX|XXX|XXX|XXX|XXX|XXX|XXX|XXX|XXX|XXX|XXX|XXX|XXX|XXX|XXX|XXX|
_ALT|XXX|XXX|XXX|XXX|XXX|XXX|XXX|XXX|XXX|XXX|XXX|XXX|XXX|XXX|XXX|XXX|
_SYM|___|___|___|___|___|___|___|___|___|___|___|___|___|___|___|___|
```

Volkswriter 3 Sample File

BYTE	0	1	2	3	4	5	6	7	8	9	10	11	12	13	14	15
HEX	2E	2E	4C	41	59	4F	55	54	20	33	20	20	0D	0A	20	20
DEC	46	46	76	65	89	79	85	84	32	51	32	32	13	10	32	32
ASC													^M	^J		
ALT									SPC		SPC	SPC	CR	LF	SPC	SPC
SYM	.	.	L	A	Y	O	U	T		3						

Layout for This Document   New Line

BYTE	16	17	18	19	20	21	22	23	24	25	26	27	28	29	30	31
HEX	20	20	20	20	20	20	20	20	20	20	20	20	20	20	20	20
DEC	32	32	32	32	32	32	32	32	32	32	32	32	32	32	32	32
ASC																
ALT	SPC	SPC	SPC	SPC	SPC	SPC	SPC	SPC	SPC	SPC	SPC	SPC	SPC	SPC	SPC	SPC
SYM																

BYTE	32	33	34	35	36	37	38	39	40	41	42	43	44	45	46	47
HEX	20	20	20	10	12	54	68	65	20	47	65	74	74	79	73	62
DEC	32	32	32	16	18	84	104	101	32	71	101	116	116	121	115	98
ASC				^P	^R											
ALT	SPC	SPC	SPC	DLE	DC2				SPC							
SYM						T	h	e		G	e	t	t	y	s	b

Begin Block | Bold

BYTE	48	49	50	51	52	53	54	55	56	57	58	59	60	61	62	63
HEX	75	72	67	20	41	64	64	72	65	73	73	12	11	07	14	0D
DEC	117	114	103	32	65	100	100	114	101	115	115	18	17	7	20	13
ASC												^R	^Q	^G	^T	^M
ALT				SPC								DC2	DC1	BEL	DC4	CR
SYM	u	r	g		A	d	d	r	e	s	s					

Bold Off | End Block | Center | End Paragraph | New Line

BYTE	64	65	66	67	68	69	70	71	72	73	74	75	76	77	78	79
HEX	0A	0D	0A	46	6F	75	72	73	63	6F	72	65	20	61	6E	64
DEC	10	13	10	70	111	117	114	115	99	111	114	101	32	97	110	100
ASC	^J	^M	^J													
ALT	LF	CR	LF										SPC			
SYM				F	o	u	r	s	c	o	r	e		a	n	d

New Line

BYTE	80	81	82	83	84	85	86	87	88	89	90	91	92	93	94	95
HEX	20	73	65	76	65	6E	20	79	65	61	72	73	20	61	67	6F
DEC	32	115	101	118	101	110	32	121	101	97	114	115	32	97	103	111
ASC	^^						^^									
ALT	SPC						SPC						SPC			
SYM		s	e	v	e	n		y	e	a	r	s		a	g	o

BYTE	96	97	98	99	100	101	102	103	104	105	106	107	108	109	110	111
HEX	20	6F	75	72	20	66	61	74	68	65	72	73	20	62	72	6F
DEC	32	111	117	114	32	102	97	116	104	101	114	115	32	98	114	111
ASC	^^				^^								^^			
ALT	SPC				SPC								SPC			
SYM		o	u	r		f	a	t	h	e	r	s		b	r	o

BYTE	112	113	114	115	116	117	118	119	120	121	122	123	124	125	126	127
HEX	75	67	68	74	20	66	6F	72	74	68	20	6F	6E	20	74	68
DEC	117	103	104	116	32	102	111	114	116	104	32	111	110	32	116	104
ASC					^^						^^			^^		
ALT					SPC						SPC			SPC		
SYM	u	g	h	t		f	o	r	t	h		o	n		t	h

BYTE	128	129	130	131	132	133	134	135	136	137	138	139	140	141	142	143
HEX	69	73	0D	0A	63	6F	6E	74	69	6E	65	6E	74	2C	20	61
DEC	105	115	13	10	99	111	110	116	105	110	101	110	116	44	32	97
ASC			^M	^J										^^		
ALT			CR	LF											SPC	
SYM	i	s			c	o	n	t	i	n	e	n	t	,		a

BYTE	144	145	146	147	148	149	150	151	152	153	154	155	156	157	158	159
HEX	20	6E	65	77	20	6E	61	74	69	6F	6E	2C	20	63	6F	6E
DEC	32	110	101	119	32	110	97	116	105	111	110	44	32	99	111	110
ASC	^^				^^							^^				
ALT	SPC				SPC							SPC				
SYM		n	e	w		n	a	t	i	o	n	,		c	o	n

BYTE	160	161	162	163	164	165	166	167	168	169	170	171	172	173	174	175
HEX	63	65	69	76	65	64	20	69	6E	20	1F	4C	69	62	65	72
DEC	99	101	105	118	101	100	32	105	110	32	31	76	105	98	101	114
ASC							^^		^^	^						
ALT							SPC		SPC	US						
SYM	c	e	i	v	e	d		i	n			L	i	b	e	r

```
BYTE|176|177|178|179|180|181|182|183|184|185|186|187|188|189|190|191|
_HEX| 74| 79| 1F| 2C| 20| 61| 6E| 64| 20| 64| 65| 64| 69| 63| 61| 74|
_DEC|116|121| 31| 44| 32| 97|110|100| 32|100|101|100|105| 99| 97|116|
_ASC|   |   | ^_|   | ^`|   |   |   | ^`|   |   |   |   |   |   |   |
_ALT|   |   |US |   |SPC|   |   |   |SPC|   |   |   |   |   |   |   |
_SYM| t|  y|   |  ,|   |  a|  n|  d|   |  d|  e|  d|  i|  c|  a|  t|
```

```
BYTE|192|193|194|195|196|197|198|199|200|201|202|203|204|205|206|207|
_HEX| 65| 64| 20| 74| 6F| 0D| 0A| 74| 68| 65| 20| 70| 72| 6F| 70| 6F|
_DEC|101|100| 32|116|111| 13| 10|116|104|101| 32|112|114|111|112|111|
_ASC|   |   | ^`|   |   | ^M| ^J|   |   |   | ^`|   |   |   |   |   |
_ALT|   |   |SPC|   |   |CR |LF |   |   |   |SPC|   |   |   |   |   |
_SYM|  e|  d|   |  t|  o|   |   |  t|  b|  e|   |  p|  r|  o|  p|  o|
```

```
BYTE|208|209|210|211|212|213|214|215|216|217|218|219|220|221|222|223|
_HEX| 73| 69| 74| 69| 6F| 6E| 20| 74| 68| 61| 74| 20| 61| 6C| 6C| 20|
_DEC|115|105|116|105|111|110| 32|116|104| 97|116| 32| 97|108|108| 32|
_ASC|   |   |   |   |   |   | ^`|   |   |   |   | ^`|   |   |   | ^`|
_ALT|   |   |   |   |   |   |SPC|   |   |   |   |SPC|   |   |   |SPC|
_SYM|  s|  i|  t|  i|  o|  n|   |  t|  b|  a|  t|   |  a|  l|  l|   |
```

```
BYTE|224|225|226|227|228|229|230|231|232|233|234|235|236|237|238|239|
_HEX| 6D| 65| 6E| 20| 61| 72| 65| 20| 63| 72| 65| 61| 74| 65| 64| 20|
_DEC|109|101|110| 32| 97|114|101| 32| 99|114|101| 97|116|101|100| 32|
_ASC|   |   |   | ^`|   |   |   | ^`|   |   |   |   |   |   |   | ^`|
_ALT|   |   |   |SPC|   |   |   |SPC|   |   |   |   |   |   |   |SPC|
_SYM|  m|  e|  n|   |  a|  r|  e|   |  c|  r|  e|  a|  t|  e|  d|   |
```

```
BYTE|240|241|242|243|244|245|246|247|248|249|250|251|252|253|254|255|
_HEX| 65| 71| 75| 61| 6C| 2E| 14| 0D| 0A| 14| 0D| 0A| 4E| 6F| 77| 20|
_DEC|101|113|117| 97|108| 46| 20| 13| 10| 20| 13| 10| 78|111|119| 32|
_ASC|   |   |   |   |   |   | ^T| ^M| ^J| ^T| ^M| ^J|   |   |   | ^`|
_ALT|   |   |   |   |   |   |DC4|CR |LF |DC4|CR |LF |   |   |   |SPC|
_SYM|  e|  q|  u|  a|  l|  .|   |   |   |   |   |   |  N|  o|  w|   |
```

```
BYTE|256|257|258|259|260|261|262|263|264|265|266|267|268|269|270|271|
_HEX| 77| 65| 20| 61| 72| 65| 20| 65| 6E| 67| 61| 67| 65| 64| 20| 69|
_DEC|119|101| 32| 97|114|101| 32|101|110|103| 97|103|101|100| 32|105|
_ASC|   |   | ^`|   |   |   | ^`|   |   |   |   |   |   |   | ^`|   |
_ALT|   |   |SPC|   |   |   |SPC|   |   |   |   |   |   |   |SPC|   |
_SYM|  w|  e|   |  a|  r|  e|   |  e|  n|  g|  a|  g|  e|  d|   |  i|
```

```
BYTE|272|273|274|275|276|277|278|279|280|281|282|283|284|285|286|287|
HEX | 6E| 20| 61| 20| 67| 72| 65| 61| 74| 20| 63| 69| 76| 69| 6C| 20|
DEC |110| 32| 97| 32|103|114|101| 97|116| 32| 99|105|118|105|108| 32|
ASC |   | ^^|   | ^^|   |   |   |   |   | ^^|   |   |   |   |   | ^^|
ALT |   |SPC|   |SPC|   |   |   |   |   |SPC|   |   |   |   |   |SPC|
SYM | n |   | a |   | g | r | e | a | t |   | c | i | v | i | l |   |
```

```
BYTE|288|289|290|291|292|293|294|295|296|297|298|299|300|301|302|303|
HEX | 77| 61| 72| 2C| 20| 74| 65| 73| 74| 69| 6E| 67| 20| 77| 68| 65|
DEC |119| 97|114| 44| 32|116|101|115|116|105|110|103| 32|119|104|101|
ASC |   |   |   |   | ^^|   |   |   |   |   |   |   | ^^|   |   |   |
ALT |   |   |   |   |SPC|   |   |   |   |   |   |   |SPC|   |   |   |
SYM | w | a | r | , |   | t | e | s | t | i | n | g |   | w | h | e |
```

```
BYTE|304|305|306|307|308|309|310|311|312|313|314|315|316|317|318|319|
HEX | 74| 68| 65| 72| 20| 74| 68| 61| 74| 0D| 0A| 6E| 61| 74| 69| 6F|
DEC |116|104|101|114| 32|116|104| 97|116| 13| 10|110| 97|116|105|111|
ASC |   |   |   |   | ^^|   |   |   |   | ^M| ^J|   |   |   |   |   |
ALT |   |   |   |   |SPC|   |   |   |   | CR| LF|   |   |   |   |   |
SYM | t | h | e | r |   | t | h | a | t |   |   | n | a | t | i | o |
```

```
BYTE|320|321|322|323|324|325|326|327|328|329|330|331|332|333|334|335|
HEX | 6E| 20| 6F| 72| 20| 61| 6E| 79| 20| 6E| 61| 74| 69| 6F| 6E| 20|
DEC |110| 32|111|114| 32| 97|110|121| 32|110| 97|116|105|111|110| 32|
ASC |   | ^^|   |   | ^^|   |   |   | ^^|   |   |   |   |   |   | ^^|
ALT |   |SPC|   |   |SPC|   |   |   |SPC|   |   |   |   |   |   |SPC|
SYM | n |   | o | r |   | a | n | y |   | n | a | t | i | o | n |   |
```

```
BYTE|336|337|338|339|340|341|342|343|344|345|346|347|348|349|350|351|
HEX | 73| 6F| 20| 63| 6F| 6E| 63| 65| 69| 76| 65| 64| 20| 61| 6E| 64|
DEC |115|111| 32| 99|111|110| 99|101|105|118|101|100| 32| 97|110|100|
ASC |   |   | ^^|   |   |   |   |   |   |   |   |   | ^^|   |   |   |
ALT |   |   |SPC|   |   |   |   |   |   |   |   |   |SPC|   |   |   |
SYM | s | o |   | c | o | n | c | e | i | v | e | d |   | a | n | d |
```

```
BYTE|352|353|354|355|356|357|358|359|360|361|362|363|364|365|366|367|
HEX | 20| 73| 6F| 20| 64| 65| 64| 69| 63| 61| 74| 65| 64| 20| 63| 61|
DEC | 32|115|111| 32|100|101|100|105| 99| 97|116|101|100| 32| 99| 97|
ASC | ^^|   |   | ^^|   |   |   |   |   |   |   |   |   | ^^|   |   |
ALT |SPC|   |   |SPC|   |   |   |   |   |   |   |   |   |SPC|   |   |
SYM |   | s | o |   | d | e | d | i | c | a | t | e | d |   | c | a |
```

BYTE	368	369	370	371	372	373	374	375	376	377	378	379	380	381	382	383
HEX	6E	20	6C	6F	6E	67	0D	0A	65	6E	64	75	72	65	2E	20
DEC	110	32	108	111	110	103	13	10	101	110	100	117	114	101	46	32
ASC		^`					^M	^J								^`
ALT		SPC					CR	LF								SPC
SYM	n		l	o	n	g			e	n	d	u	r	e	.	

BYTE	384	385	386	387	388	389	390	391	392	393	394	395	396	397	398	399
HEX	20	57	65	20	61	72	65	20	6D	65	74	20	6F	6E	20	61
DEC	32	87	101	32	97	114	101	32	109	101	116	32	111	110	32	97
ASC	^`			^`				^`								^`
ALT	SPC			SPC				SPC				SPC			SPC	
SYM		W	e		a	r	e		m	e	t		o	n		a

BYTE	400	401	402	403	404	405	406	407	408	409	410	411	412	413	414	415
HEX	20	67	72	65	61	74	20	62	61	74	74	6C	65	66	69	65
DEC	32	103	114	101	97	116	32	98	97	116	116	108	101	102	105	101
ASC	^`							^`								
ALT	SPC						SPC									
SYM		g	r	e	a	t		b	a	t	t	l	e	f	i	e

BYTE	416	417	418	419	420	421	422	423	424	425	426	427	428	429	430	431
HEX	6C	64	20	6F	66	20	74	68	61	74	20	77	61	72	2E	20
DEC	108	100	32	111	102	32	116	104	97	116	32	119	97	114	46	32
ASC			^`		^`						^`					^`
ALT			SPC		SPC						SPC					SPC
SYM	l	d		o	f		t	h	a	t		w	a	r	.	

BYTE	432	433	434	435	436	437	438	439	440	441	442	443	444	445	446	447
HEX	20	57	65	20	68	61	76	65	0D	0A	63	6F	6D	65	20	74
DEC	32	87	101	32	104	97	118	101	13	10	99	111	109	101	32	116
ASC	^`			^`					^M	^J						^`
ALT	SPC			SPC					CR	LF					SPC	
SYM		W	e		b	a	v	e			c	o	m	e		t

BYTE	448	449	450	451	452	453	454	455	456	457	458	459	460	461	462	463
HEX	6F	20	64	65	64	69	63	61	74	65	20	61	20	70	6F	72
DEC	111	32	100	101	100	105	99	97	116	101	32	97	32	112	111	114
ASC		^`									^`		^`			
ALT		SPC									SPC		SPC			
SYM	o		d	e	d	i	c	a	t	e		a		p	o	r

BYTE	464	465	466	467	468	469	470	471	472	473	474	475	476	477	478	479
HEX	74	69	6F	6E	20	6F	66	20	74	68	61	74	20	66	69	65
DEC	116	105	111	110	32	111	102	32	116	104	97	116	32	102	105	101
ASC					^`			^`					^`			
ALT					SPC			SPC					SPC			
SYM	t	i	o	n		o	f		t	h	a	t		f	i	e

BYTE	480	481	482	483	484	485	486	487	488	489	490	491	492	493	494	495
HEX	6C	64	2C	20	61	73	20	61	20	66	69	6E	61	6C	20	72
DEC	108	100	44	32	97	115	32	97	32	102	105	110	97	108	32	114
ASC				^`			^`		^`						^`	
ALT				SPC			SPC		SPC						SPC	
SYM	l	d	,		a	s		a		f	i	n	a	l		r

BYTE	496	497	498	499	500	501	502	503	504	505	506	507	508	509	510	511
HEX	65	73	74	69	6E	67	0D	0A	70	6C	61	63	65	20	66	6F
DEC	101	115	116	105	110	103	13	10	112	108	97	99	101	32	102	111
ASC							^M	^J						^`		
ALT							CR	LF						SPC		
SYM	e	s	t	i	n	g			p	l	a	c	e		f	o

BYTE	512	513	514	515	516	517	518	519	520	521	522	523	524	525	526	527
HEX	72	20	74	68	6F	73	65	20	77	68	6F	20	68	65	72	65
DEC	114	32	116	104	111	115	101	32	119	104	111	32	104	101	114	101
ASC		^`						^`				^`				
ALT		SPC						SPC				SPC				
SYM	r		t	h	o	s	e		w	h	o		h	e	r	e

BYTE	528	529	530	531	532	533	534	535	536	537	538	539	540	541	542	543
HEX	20	67	61	76	65	20	74	68	65	69	72	20	6C	69	76	65
DEC	32	103	97	118	101	32	116	104	101	105	114	32	108	105	118	101
ASC	^`					^`						^`				
ALT	SPC					SPC						SPC				
SYM		g	a	v	e		t	h	e	i	r		l	i	v	e

BYTE	544	545	546	547	548	549	550	551	552	553	554	555	556	557	558	559
HEX	73	20	74	68	61	74	20	74	68	61	74	20	6E	61	74	69
DEC	115	32	116	104	97	116	32	116	104	97	116	32	110	97	116	105
ASC		^`					^`					^`				
ALT		SPC					SPC					SPC				
SYM	s		t	h	a	t		t	h	a	t		n	a	t	i

BYTE	560	561	562	563	564	565	566	567	568	569	570	571	572	573	574	575
HEX	6F	6E	20	6D	69	67	68	74	0D	0A	6C	69	76	65	2E	20
DEC	111	110	32	109	105	103	104	116	13	10	108	105	118	101	46	32
ASC			^^						^M	^J						^^
ALT			SPC						CR	LF						SPC
SYM	o	n		m	i	g	h	t			l	i	v	e	.	

BYTE	576	577	578	579	580	581	582	583	584	585	586	587	588	589	590	591
HEX	20	49	74	20	69	73	20	61	6C	74	6F	67	65	74	68	65
DEC	32	73	116	32	105	115	32	97	108	116	111	103	101	116	104	101
ASC	^^			^^			^^									
ALT	SPC			SPC			SPC									
SYM		I	t		i	s		a	l	t	o	g	e	t	h	e

BYTE	592	593	594	595	596	597	598	599	600	601	602	603	604	605	606	607
HEX	72	20	66	69	74	74	69	6E	67	20	61	6E	64	20	70	72
DEC	114	32	102	105	116	116	105	110	103	32	97	110	100	32	112	114
ASC		^^								^^				^^		
ALT		SPC								SPC				SPC		
SYM	r		f	i	t	t	i	n	g		a	n	d		p	r

BYTE	608	609	610	611	612	613	614	615	616	617	618	619	620	621	622	623
HEX	6F	70	65	72	20	74	68	61	74	20	77	65	20	64	6F	20
DEC	111	112	101	114	32	116	104	97	116	32	119	101	32	100	111	32
ASC					^^					^^		^^		^^		^^
ALT					SPC					SPC		SPC		SPC		SPC
SYM	o	p	e	r		t	h	a	t		w	e		d	o	

BYTE	624	625	626	627	628	629	630	631	632	633	634	635	636	637	638	639
HEX	74	68	69	73	2E	14	0D	0A	1A	1A	4C	41	59	4F	55	54
DEC	116	104	105	115	46	20	13	10	26	26	76	65	89	79	85	84
ASC						^T	^M	^J	^Z	^Z						
ALT						DC4	CR	LF	SUB	SUB						
SYM	t	h	i	s	.						L	A	Y	O	U	T

End of Par.	New Line	2 Control-2's

BYTE	640	641	642	643	644	645	646	647	648	649	650	651	652	653	654	655
HEX	20	30	30	30	0D	0A	1A	1A	1A	1A	1A	1A	1A	1A	1A	1A
DEC	32	48	48	48	13	10	26	26	26	26	26	26	26	26	26	26
ASC	^^				^M	^J	^Z	^Z	^Z	^Z	^Z	^Z	^Z	^Z	^Z	^Z
ALT	SPC				CR	LF	SUB	SUB	SUB	SUB	SUB	SUB	SUB	SUB	SUB	SUB
SYM		0	0	0												

New Line	Enough Control-2's to Pad to End of Sector

```
BYTE|656|657|658|659|660|661|662|663|664|665|666|667|668|669|670|671|
_HEX|_1A|_1A|_1A|_1A|_1A|_1A|_1A|_1A|_1A|_1A|_1A|_1A|_1A|_1A|_1A|_1A|
_DEC|_26|_26|_26|_26|_26|_26|_26|_26|_26|_26|_26|_26|_26|_26|_26|_26|
_ASC|_^Z|_^Z|_^Z|_^Z|_^Z|_^Z|_^Z|_^Z|_^Z|_^Z|_^Z|_^Z|_^Z|_^Z|_^Z|_^Z|
_ALT|SUB|SUB|SUB|SUB|SUB|SUB|SUB|SUB|SUB|SUB|SUB|SUB|SUB|SUB|SUB|SUB|
_SYM|___|___|___|___|___|___|___|___|___|___|___|___|___|___|___|___|


BYTE|672|673|674|675|676|677|678|679|680|681|682|683|684|685|686|687|
_HEX|_1A|_1A|_1A|_1A|_1A|_1A|_1A|_1A|_1A|_1A|_1A|_1A|_1A|_1A|_1A|_1A|
_DEC|_26|_26|_26|_26|_26|_26|_26|_26|_26|_26|_26|_26|_26|_26|_26|_26|
_ASC|_^Z|_^Z|_^Z|_^Z|_^Z|_^Z|_^Z|_^Z|_^Z|_^Z|_^Z|_^Z|_^Z|_^Z|_^Z|_^Z|
_ALT|SUB|SUB|SUB|SUB|SUB|SUB|SUB|SUB|SUB|SUB|SUB|SUB|SUB|SUB|SUB|SUB|
_SYM|___|___|___|___|___|___|___|___|___|___|___|___|___|___|___|___|


BYTE|688|689|690|691|692|693|694|695|696|697|698|699|700|701|702|703|
_HEX|_1A|_1A|_1A|_1A|_1A|_1A|_1A|_1A|_1A|_1A|_1A|_1A|_1A|_1A|_1A|_1A|
_DEC|_26|_26|_26|_26|_26|_26|_26|_26|_26|_26|_26|_26|_26|_26|_26|_26|
_ASC|_^Z|_^Z|_^Z|_^Z|_^Z|_^Z|_^Z|_^Z|_^Z|_^Z|_^Z|_^Z|_^Z|_^Z|_^Z|_^Z|
_ALT|SUB|SUB|SUB|SUB|SUB|SUB|SUB|SUB|SUB|SUB|SUB|SUB|SUB|SUB|SUB|SUB|
_SYM|___|___|___|___|___|___|___|___|___|___|___|___|___|___|___|___|


BYTE|704|705|706|707|708|709|710|711|712|713|714|715|716|717|718|719|
_HEX|_1A|_1A|_1A|_1A|_1A|_1A|_1A|_1A|_1A|_1A|_1A|_1A|_1A|_1A|_1A|_1A|
_DEC|_26|_26|_26|_26|_26|_26|_26|_26|_26|_26|_26|_26|_26|_26|_26|_26|
_ASC|_^Z|_^Z|_^Z|_^Z|_^Z|_^Z|_^Z|_^Z|_^Z|_^Z|_^Z|_^Z|_^Z|_^Z|_^Z|_^Z|
_ALT|SUB|SUB|SUB|SUB|SUB|SUB|SUB|SUB|SUB|SUB|SUB|SUB|SUB|SUB|SUB|SUB|
_SYM|___|___|___|___|___|___|___|___|___|___|___|___|___|___|___|___|


BYTE|720|721|722|723|724|725|726|727|728|729|730|731|732|733|734|735|
_HEX|_1A|_1A|_1A|_1A|_1A|_1A|_1A|_1A|_1A|_1A|_1A|_1A|_1A|_1A|_1A|_1A|
_DEC|_26|_26|_26|_26|_26|_26|_26|_26|_26|_26|_26|_26|_26|_26|_26|_26|
_ASC|_^Z|_^Z|_^Z|_^Z|_^Z|_^Z|_^Z|_^Z|_^Z|_^Z|_^Z|_^Z|_^Z|_^Z|_^Z|_^Z|
_ALT|SUB|SUB|SUB|SUB|SUB|SUB|SUB|SUB|SUB|SUB|SUB|SUB|SUB|SUB|SUB|SUB|
_SYM|___|___|___|___|___|___|___|___|___|___|___|___|___|___|___|___|


BYTE|736|737|738|739|740|741|742|743|744|745|746|747|748|749|750|751|
_HEX|_1A|_1A|_1A|_1A|_1A|_1A|_1A|_1A|_1A|_1A|_1A|_1A|_1A|_1A|_1A|_1A|
_DEC|_26|_26|_26|_26|_26|_26|_26|_26|_26|_26|_26|_26|_26|_26|_26|_26|
_ASC|_^Z|_^Z|_^Z|_^Z|_^Z|_^Z|_^Z|_^Z|_^Z|_^Z|_^Z|_^Z|_^Z|_^Z|_^Z|_^Z|
_ALT|SUB|SUB|SUB|SUB|SUB|SUB|SUB|SUB|SUB|SUB|SUB|SUB|SUB|SUB|SUB|SUB|
_SYM|___|___|___|___|___|___|___|___|___|___|___|___|___|___|___|___|
```

```
BYTE|752|753|754|755|756|757|758|759|760|761|762|763|764|765|766|767|
HEX | 1A| 1A| 1A| 1A| 1A| 1A| 1A| 1A| 1A| 1A| 1A| 1A| 1A| 1A| 1A| 1A|
DEC | 26| 26| 26| 26| 26| 26| 26| 26| 26| 26| 26| 26| 26| 26| 26| 26|
ASC | ^Z| ^Z| ^Z| ^Z| ^Z| ^Z| ^Z| ^Z| ^Z| ^Z| ^Z| ^Z| ^Z| ^Z| ^Z| ^Z|
ALT |SUB|SUB|SUB|SUB|SUB|SUB|SUB|SUB|SUB|SUB|SUB|SUB|SUB|SUB|SUB|SUB|
SYM |   |   |   |   |   |   |   |   |   |   |   |   |   |   |   |   |
```

```
BYTE|768|769|770|771|772|773|774|775|776|777|778|779|780|781|782|783|
HEX | AA| 03| 02| 03| 01| 00| 01| 00| 08| 42| 06| 00| 0A| 00| 00| 01|
DEC |170|  3|  2|  3|  1|  0|  1|  0|  8| 66|  6|  0| 10|  0|  0|  1|
ASC |170| ^C| ^B| ^C| ^A| ^@| ^A| ^@| ^H|   | ^F| ^@| ^J| ^@| ^@| ^A|
ALT |170|ETX|STX|ETX|SOH|NUL|SOH|NUL| BS|   |ACK|NUL| LF|NUL|NUL|SOH|
SYM |   |   |   |   |   |   |   |   |   | B |   |   |   |   |   |   |
```

Length of Record	Version #	# Layouts	Avail.	Reserved	Printer Code	LPP	LPI	Extra Space	CHR	Reserved	L Border

```
BYTE|784|785|786|787|788|789|790|791|792|793|794|795|796|797|798|799|
HEX | 00| 00| 00| 00| 00| 00| 01| 00| 01| 00| 01| 06| 3C| 00| 00| 03|
DEC |  0|  0|  0|  0|  0|  0|  1|  0|  1|  0|  1|  6| 60|  0|  0|  3|
ASC | ^@| ^@| ^@| ^@| ^@| ^@| ^A| ^@| ^A| ^@| ^A| ^F|   | ^@| ^@| ^C|
ALT |NUL|NUL|NUL|NUL|NUL|NUL|SOH|NUL|SOH|NUL|SOH|ACK|   |NUL|NUL|ETX|
SYM |   |   |   |   |   |   |   |   |   |   |   |   | < |   |   |   |
```

Reserved	Pagi-nate	Printer Reset Flag	Reform	Res.	Forms	Next Page	Reserved

```
BYTE|800|801|802|803|804|805|806|807|808|809|810|811|812|813|814|815|
HEX | 03| 00| 3F| 00| 00| 00| 41| 00| 00| 00| FA| 00| 5C| 2D| 2D| 2D|
DEC |  3|  0| 63|  0|  0|  0| 65|  0|  0|  0|250|  0| 92| 45| 45| 45|
ASC | ^C| ^@|   | ^@| ^@| ^@|   | ^@| ^@| ^@|250| ^@|   |   |   |   |
ALT |ETX|NUL|   |NUL|NUL|NUL|   |NUL|NUL|NUL|250|NUL|   |   |   |   |
SYM |   |   | ? |   |   |   | A |   |   |   |   |   | \ | - | - | - |
```

Reserved	Justify	Prop SPC	Reserved	Margin Line Len.	◄─── Ruler ───►

```
BYTE|816|817|818|819|820|821|822|823|824|825|826|827|828|829|830|831|
HEX | 23| 2D| 2D| 2D| 2D| 2B| 2D| 2D| 2D| 2D| 2B| 2D| 2D| 2D| 2D| 2D|
DEC | 35| 45| 45| 45| 45| 43| 45| 45| 45| 45| 43| 45| 45| 45| 45| 45|
ASC |   |   |   |   |   |   |   |   |   |   |   |   |   |   |   |   |
ALT |   |   |   |   |   |   |   |   |   |   |   |   |   |   |   |   |
SYM | # | - | - | - | - | + | - | - | - | - | + | - | - | - | - | - |
```

◄─────────────────────── Ruler ───────────────────────►

```
BYTE|832|833|834|835|836|837|838|839|840|841|842|843|844|845|846|847|
HEX | 2D| 2D| 2D| 2D| 2D| 2D| 2D| 2D| 2D| 2D| 2D| 2B| 2D| 2D| 2D| 2D|
DEC | 45| 45| 45| 45| 45| 45| 45| 45| 45| 45| 45| 43| 45| 45| 45| 45|
ASC |   |   |   |   |   |   |   |   |   |   |   |   |   |   |   |   |
ALT |   |   |   |   |   |   |   |   |   |   |   |   |   |   |   |   |
SYM | - | - | - | - | - | - | - | - | - | - | - | + | - | - | - | - |
```

◄─────────────────────── Ruler ───────────────────────►

```
BYTE|848|849|850|851|852|853|854|855|856|857|858|859|860|861|862|863|
 HEX| 2D| 2D| 2D| 2D| 2D| 2D| 2D| 2D| 2D| 2D| 2D| 2D| 2D| 2D| 2D| 2D|
 DEC| 45| 45| 45| 45| 45| 45| 45| 45| 45| 45| 45| 45| 45| 45| 45| 45|
 ASC|   |   |   |   |   |   |   |   |   |   |   |   |   |   |   |   |
 ALT|   |   |   |   |   |   |   |   |   |   |   |   |   |   |   |   |
 SYM| - | - | - | - | - | - | - | - | - | - | - | - | - | - | - | - |
```

<--------------------------------- Ruler --------------------------------->

```
BYTE|864|865|866|867|868|869|870|871|872|873|874|875|876|877|878|879|
 HEX| 2B| 2D| 2D| 2D| 2D| 2D| 2D| 2D| 2D| 2D| 40| 2D| 2F| 2D| 2D| 2D|
 DEC| 43| 45| 45| 45| 45| 45| 45| 45| 45| 45| 64| 45| 47| 45| 45| 45|
 ASC|   |   |   |   |   |   |   |   |   |   |   |   |   |   |   |   |
 ALT|   |   |   |   |   |   |   |   |   |   |   |   |   |   |   |   |
 SYM| + | - | - | - | - | - | - | - | - | - | @ | - | / | - | - | - |
```

```
BYTE|880|881|882|883|884|885|886|887|888|889|890|891|892|893|894|895|
 HEX| 2D| 2D| 2D| 2D| 2D| 2D| 2B| 2D| 2D| 2D| 2D| 2D| 2D| 2D| 2D| 2D|
 DEC| 45| 45| 45| 45| 45| 45| 43| 45| 45| 45| 45| 45| 45| 45| 45| 45|
 ASC|   |   |   |   |   |   |   |   |   |   |   |   |   |   |   |   |
 ALT|   |   |   |   |   |   |   |   |   |   |   |   |   |   |   |   |
 SYM| - | - | - | - | - | - | + | - | - | - | - | - | - | - | - | - |
```

```
BYTE|896|897|898|899|900|901|902|903|904|905|906|907|908|909|910|911|
 HEX| 2B| 2D| 2D| 2D| 2D| 2D| 2D| 2D| 2D| 2D| 2B| 2D| 2D| 2D| 2D| 2D|
 DEC| 43| 45| 45| 45| 45| 45| 45| 45| 45| 45| 43| 45| 45| 45| 45| 45|
 ASC|   |   |   |   |   |   |   |   |   |   |   |   |   |   |   |   |
 ALT|   |   |   |   |   |   |   |   |   |   |   |   |   |   |   |   |
 SYM| + | - | - | - | - | - | - | - | - | - | + | - | - | - | - | - |
```

```
BYTE|912|913|914|915|916|917|918|919|920|921|922|923|924|925|926|927|
 HEX| 2D| 2D| 2D| 2D| 2B| 2D| 2D| 2D| 2D| 2D| 2D| 2D| 2D| 2D| 2B| 2D|
 DEC| 45| 45| 45| 45| 43| 45| 45| 45| 45| 45| 45| 45| 45| 45| 43| 45|
 ASC|   |   |   |   |   |   |   |   |   |   |   |   |   |   |   |   |
 ALT|   |   |   |   |   |   |   |   |   |   |   |   |   |   |   |   |
 SYM| - | - | - | - | + | - | - | - | - | - | - | - | - | - | + | - |
```

```
BYTE|928|929|930|931|932|933|934|935|936|937|938|939|940|941|942|943|
 HEX| 2D| 2D| 2D| 2D| 2D| 2D| 2D| 2D| 2B| 2D| 2D| 2D| 2D| 2D| 2D| 2D|
 DEC| 45| 45| 45| 45| 45| 45| 45| 45| 43| 45| 45| 45| 45| 45| 45| 45|
 ASC|   |   |   |   |   |   |   |   |   |   |   |   |   |   |   |   |
 ALT|   |   |   |   |   |   |   |   |   |   |   |   |   |   |   |   |
 SYM| - | - | - | - | - | - | - | - | + | - | - | - | - | - | - | - |
```

BYTE	944	945	946	947	948	949	950	951	952	953	954	955	956	957	958	959
HEX	2D	2D	2B	2D	2D	2D	2D	2D	2D	2D	2D	2D	2B	2D	2D	2D
DEC	45	45	43	45	45	45	45	45	45	45	45	45	43	45	45	45
ASC																
ALT																
SYM	-	-	+	-	-	-	-	-	-	-	-	-	+	-	-	-

BYTE	960	961	962	963	964	965	966	967	968	969	970	971	972	973	974	975
HEX	2D	2D	2D	2D	2D	2D	2B	2D	2D	2D	2D	2D	2D	2D	2D	2D
DEC	45	45	45	45	45	45	43	45	45	45	45	45	45	45	45	45
ASC																
ALT																
SYM	-	-	-	-	-	-	+	-	-	-	-	-	-	-	-	-

BYTE	976	977	978	979	980	981	982	983	984	985	986	987	988	989	990	991
HEX	2B	2D	2D	2D	2D	2D	2D	2D	2D	2D	2B	2D	2D	2D	2D	2D
DEC	43	45	45	45	45	45	45	45	45	45	43	45	45	45	45	45
ASC																
ALT																
SYM	+	-	-	-	-	-	-	-	-	-	+	-	-	-	-	-

BYTE	992	993	994	995	996	997	998	999	0	1	2	3	4	5	6	7
HEX	2D	2D	2D	2D	2B	2D	2D	2D	2D	2D	2D	2D	2D	2D	2B	2D
DEC	45	45	45	45	43	45	45	45	45	45	45	45	45	45	43	45
ASC																
ALT																
SYM	-	-	-	-	+	-	-	-	-	-	-	-	-	-	+	-

BYTE	8	9	10	11	12	13	14	15	16	17	18	19	20	21	22	23
HEX	2D	2D	2D	2D	2D	2D	2D	2D	2B	2D	2D	2D	2D	2D	2D	2D
DEC	45	45	45	45	45	45	45	45	43	45	45	45	45	45	45	45
ASC																
ALT																
SYM	-	-	-	-	-	-	-	-	+	-	-	-	-	-	-	-

BYTE	24	25	26	27	28	29	30	31	32	33	34	35	36	37	38	39
HEX	2D	2D	2B	2D	2D	2D	2D	2D	2D	2D	2D	2D	2B	2D	2D	2D
DEC	45	45	43	45	45	45	45	45	45	45	45	45	43	45	45	45
ASC																
ALT																
SYM	-	-	+	-	-	-	-	-	-	-	-	-	+	-	-	-

```
BYTE| 40| 41| 42| 43| 44| 45| 46| 47| 48| 49| 50| 51| 52| 53| 54| 55|
HEX | 2D| 2D| 2D| 2D| 2D| 2D| 2B| 2D| 2D| 2D| 2D| 2D| 2D| 2D| 2D| 2D|
DEC | 45| 45| 45| 45| 45| 45| 43| 45| 45| 45| 45| 45| 45| 45| 45| 45|
ASC |   |   |   |   |   |   |   |   |   |   |   |   |   |   |   |   |
ALT |   |   |   |   |   |   |   |   |   |   |   |   |   |   |   |   |
SYM | - | - | - | - | - | - | + | - | - | - | - | - | - | - | - | - |


BYTE| 56| 57| 58| 59| 60| 61| 62| 63| 64| 65| 66| 67| 68| 69| 70| 71|
HEX | 2B| 2D| 2D| 2D| 2D| 02| 06| 01| 00| 00| 00| 00| 00| 00| 00| 00|
DEC | 43| 45| 45| 45| 45|  2|  6|  1|  0|  0|  0|  0|  0|  0|  0|  0|
ASC |   |   |   |   |   | ^B| ^F| ^A| ^@| ^@| ^@| ^@| ^@| ^@| ^@| ^@|
ALT |   |   |   |   |   |STX|ACK|SOH|NUL|NUL|NUL|NUL|NUL|NUL|NUL|NUL|
SYM | + | - | - | - | - |   |   |   |   |   |   |   |   |   |   |   |
```

| 1st P. Top Mar. | Even P. Border Mar. | ←——————— Reserved ———————→ |

```
BYTE| 72| 73| 74| 75| 76| 77| 78| 79| 80| 81| 82| 83| 84| 85| 86| 87|
HEX | 00| 00| 00| 00| 00| 00| 00| 00| 00| 00| 00| 00| 01| 00| 00| 00|
DEC |  0|  0|  0|  0|  0|  0|  0|  0|  0|  0|  0|  0|  1|  0|  0|  0|
ASC | ^@| ^@| ^@| ^@| ^@| ^@| ^@| ^@| ^@| ^@| ^@| ^@| ^A| ^@| ^@| ^@|
ALT |NUL|NUL|NUL|NUL|NUL|NUL|NUL|NUL|NUL|NUL|NUL|NUL|SOH|NUL|NUL|NUL|
SYM |   |   |   |   |   |   |   |   |   |   |   |   |   |   |   |   |
```

| ←——————— Reserved ———————→ | Avail. | ← Reserved → |

```
BYTE| 88| 89| 90| 91| 92| 93| 94| 95| 96| 97| 98| 99|100|101|102|103|
HEX | 08| 42| 06| 01| 0A| 00| 00| 01| 00| 00| 00| 00| 00| 00| 01| 00|
DEC |  8| 66|  6|  1| 10|  0|  0|  1|  0|  0|  0|  0|  0|  0|  1|  0|
ASC | ^H|   | ^F| ^A| ^J| ^@| ^@| ^A| ^@| ^@| ^@| ^@| ^@| ^@| ^A| ^@|
ALT | BS|   |ACK|SOH| LF|NUL|NUL|SOH|NUL|NUL|NUL|NUL|NUL|NUL|SOH|NUL|
SYM |   | B |   |   |   |   |   |   |   |   |   |   |   |   |   |   |


BYTE|104|105|106|107|108|109|110|111|112|113|114|115|116|117|118|119|
HEX | 01| 00| 01| 06| 3C| 00| 00| 03| 03| 00| 3F| 00| 00| 00| 41| 00|
DEC |  1|  0|  1|  6| 60|  0|  0|  3|  3|  0| 63|  0|  0|  0| 65|  0|
ASC | ^A| ^@| ^A| ^F|   | ^@| ^@| ^C| ^C| ^@|   | ^@| ^@| ^@|   | ^@|
ALT |SOH|NUL|SOH|ACK|   |NUL|NUL|ETX|ETX|NUL|   |NUL|NUL|NUL|   |NUL|
SYM |   |   |   |   | < |   |   |   |   |   | ? |   |   |   | A |   |


BYTE|120|121|122|123|124|125|126|127|128|129|130|131|132|133|134|135|
HEX | 00| 00| FA| 00| 2D| 2D| 2D| 2D| 2D| 2D| 2D| 2D| 2D| 5C| 2D| 2D|
DEC |  0|  0|250|  0| 45| 45| 45| 45| 45| 45| 45| 45| 45| 92| 45| 45|
ASC | ^@| ^@|250| ^@|   |   |   |   |   |   |   |   |   | 92|   |   |
ALT |NUL|NUL|250|NUL|   |   |   |   |   |   |   |   |   |   |   |   |
SYM |   |   |   |   | - | - | - | - | - | - | - | - | - | \ | - | - |
```

BYTE	136	137	138	139	140	141	142	143	144	145	146	147	148	149	150	151
HEX	2D	2D	2B	2D	2D	2D	2D	2D	2D	2D	2D	2D	2D	2D	2D	2D
DEC	45	45	43	45	45	45	45	45	45	45	45	45	45	45	45	45
ASC																
ALT																
SYM	-	-	+	-	-	-	-	-	-	-	-	-	-	-	-	-

BYTE	152	153	154	155	156	157	158	159	160	161	162	163	164	165	166	167
HEX	2D	2D	2D	2B	2D	2D	2D	2D	2D	2D	2D	2D	2D	2D	2D	2D
DEC	45	45	45	43	45	45	45	45	45	45	45	45	45	45	45	45
ASC																
ALT																
SYM	-	-	-	+	-	-	-	-	-	-	-	-	-	-	-	-

BYTE	168	169	170	171	172	173	174	175	176	177	178	179	180	181	182	183
HEX	2D	2D	2D	2D	2D	2D	2D	2D	2B	2D	2D	2D	2D	2D	2D	40
DEC	45	45	45	45	45	45	45	45	43	45	45	45	45	45	45	64
ASC																
ALT																
SYM	-	-	-	-	-	-	-	-	+	-	-	-	-	-	-	@

BYTE	184	185	186	187	188	189	190	191	192	193	194	195	196	197	198	199
HEX	2D	2F	2D	2D	2D	2D	2D	2D	2D	2D	2D	2D	2D	2D	2B	2D
DEC	45	47	45	45	45	45	45	45	45	45	45	45	45	45	43	45
ASC																
ALT																
SYM	-	/	-	-	-	-	-	-	-	-	-	-	-	-	+	-

BYTE	200	201	202	203	204	205	206	207	208	209	210	211	212	213	214	215
HEX	2D	2D	2D	2D	2D	2D	2D	2D	2B	2D	2D	2D	2D	2D	2D	2D
DEC	45	45	45	45	45	45	45	45	43	45	45	45	45	45	45	45
ASC																
ALT																
SYM	-	-	-	-	-	-	-	-	+	-	-	-	-	-	-	-

BYTE	216	217	218	219	220	221	222	223	224	225	226	227	228	229	230	231
HEX	2D	2D	2B	2D	2D	2D	2D	2D	2D	2D	2D	2D	2B	2D	2D	2D
DEC	45	45	43	45	45	45	45	45	45	45	45	45	43	45	45	45
ASC																
ALT																
SYM	-	-	+	-	-	-	-	-	-	-	-	-	+	-	-	-

BYTE	232	233	234	235	236	237	238	239	240	241	242	243	244	245	246	247
HEX	2D	2D	2D	2D	2D	2D	2B	2D	2D	2D	2D	2D	2D	2D	2D	2D
DEC	45	45	45	45	45	45	43	45	45	45	45	45	45	45	45	45
ASC																
ALT																
SYM	-	-	-	-	-	-	+	-	-	-	-	-	-	-	-	-

BYTE	248	249	250	251	252	253	254	255	256	257	258	259	260	261	262	263
HEX	2B	2D	2D	2D	2D	2D	2D	2D	2D	2D	2B	2D	2D	2D	2D	2D
DEC	43	45	45	45	45	45	45	45	45	45	43	45	45	45	45	45
ASC																
ALT																
SYM	+	-	-	-	-	-	-	-	-	-	+	-	-	-	-	-

BYTE	264	265	266	267	268	269	270	271	272	273	274	275	276	277	278	279
HEX	2D	2D	2D	2D	2B	2D	2D	2D	2D	2D	2D	2D	2D	2D	2B	2D
DEC	45	45	45	45	43	45	45	45	45	45	45	45	45	45	43	45
ASC																
ALT																
SYM	-	-	-	-	+	-	-	-	-	-	-	-	-	-	+	-

BYTE	280	281	282	283	284	285	286	287	288	289	290	291	292	293	294	295
HEX	2D	2D	2D	2D	2D	2D	2D	2D	2B	2D	2D	2D	2D	2D	2D	2D
DEC	45	45	45	45	45	45	45	45	43	45	45	45	45	45	45	45
ASC																
ALT																
SYM	-	-	-	-	-	-	-	-	+	-	-	-	-	-	-	-

BYTE	296	297	298	299	300	301	302	303	304	305	306	307	308	309	310	311
HEX	2D	2D	2B	2D	2D	2D	2D	2D	2D	2D	2D	2D	2B	2D	2D	2D
DEC	45	45	43	45	45	45	45	45	45	45	45	45	43	45	45	45
ASC																
ALT																
SYM	-	-	+	-	-	-	-	-	-	-	-	-	+	-	-	-

BYTE	312	313	314	315	316	317	318	319	320	321	322	323	324	325	326	327
HEX	2D	2D	2D	2D	2D	2D	2B	2D	2D	2D	2D	2D	2D	2D	2D	2D
DEC	45	45	45	45	45	45	43	45	45	45	45	45	45	45	45	45
ASC																
ALT																
SYM	-	-	-	-	-	-	+	-	-	-	-	-	-	-	-	-

BYTE	328	329	330	331	332	333	334	335	336	337	338	339	340	341	342	343
HEX	2B	2D	2D	2D	2D	2D	2D	2D	2D	2D	2B	2D	2D	2D	2D	2D
DEC	43	45	45	45	45	45	45	45	45	45	43	45	45	45	45	45
ASC																
ALT																
SYM	+	-	-	-	-	-	-	-	-	-	+	-	-	-	-	-

BYTE	344	345	346	347	348	349	350	351	352	353	354	355	356	357	358	359
HEX	2D	2D	2D	2D	2B	2D	2D	2D	2D	2D	2D	2D	2D	2D	2B	2D
DEC	45	45	45	45	43	45	45	45	45	45	45	45	45	45	43	45
ASC																
ALT																
SYM	-	-	-	-	+	-	-	-	-	-	-	-	-	-	+	-

BYTE	360	361	362	363	364	365	366	367	368	369	370	371	372	373	374	375
HEX	2D	2D	2D	2D	2D	2D	2D	2D	2B	2D	2D	2D	2D	02	06	01
DEC	45	45	45	45	45	45	45	45	43	45	45	45	45	2	6	1
ASC														^B	^F	^A
ALT														STX	ACK	SOH
SYM	-	-	-	-	-	-	-	-	+	-	-	-	-			

End of Ruler ➜

BYTE	376	377	378	379	380	381	382	383	384	385	386	387	388	389	390	391
HEX	00	00	00	00	00	00	00	00	00	00	00	00	00	00	00	00
DEC	0	0	0	0	0	0	0	0	0	0	0	0	0	0	0	0
ASC	^@	^@	^@	^@	^@	^@	^@	^@	^@	^@	^@	^@	^@	^@	^@	^@
ALT	NUL	NUL	NUL	NUL	NUL	NUL	NUL	NUL	NUL	NUL	NUL	NUL	NUL	NUL	NUL	NUL
SYM																

BYTE	392	393	394	395	396	397	398	399	400	401	402	403	404	405	406	407
HEX	00	00	00	00	01	1A	01	00	08	42	06	00	0A	00	00	01
DEC	0	0	0	0	1	26	1	0	8	66	6	0	10	0	0	1
ASC	^@	^@	^@	^@	^A	^Z	^A	^@	^H		^F	^@	^J	^@	^@	^A
ALT	NUL	NUL	NUL	NUL	SOH	SUB	SOH	NUL	BS		ACK	NUL	LF	NUL	NUL	SOH
SYM										B						

BYTE	408	409	410	411	412	413	414	415	416	417	418	419	420	421	422	423
HEX	00	00	00	00	00	00	01	00	01	00	01	06	3C	00	00	03
DEC	0	0	0	0	0	0	1	0	1	0	1	6	60	0	0	3
ASC	^@	^@	^@	^@	^@	^@	^A	^@	^A	^@	^A	^F		^@	^@	^C
ALT	NUL	NUL	NUL	NUL	NUL	NUL	SOH	NUL	SOH	NUL	SOH	ACK		NUL	NUL	ETX
SYM													<			

BYTE	424	425	426	427	428	429	430	431	432	433	434	435	436	437	438	439
HEX	03	00	3F	00	00	00	41	00	00	00	FA	00	5C	2D	2D	2D
DEC	3	0	63	0	0	0	65	0	0	0	250	0	92	45	45	45
ASC	^C	^@		^@	^@	^@		^@	^@	^@	250	^@				
ALT	ETX	NUL		NUL	NUL	NUL		NUL	NUL	NUL	250	NUL				
SYM			?				A						\	-	-	-

BYTE	440	441	442	443	444	445	446	447	448	449	450	451	452	453	454	455
HEX	2D	2D	2D	2D	2D	2B	2D	2D	2D	2D	2B	2D	2D	2D	2D	2D
DEC	45	45	45	45	45	43	45	45	45	45	43	45	45	45	45	45
ASC																
ALT																
SYM	-	-	-	-	-	+	-	-	-	-	+	-	-	-	-	-

BYTE	456	457	458	459	460	461	462	463	464	465	466	467	468	469	470	471
HEX	2D	2D	2D	2D	2D	2D	2D	2D	2D	2D	2D	2B	2D	2D	2D	2D
DEC	45	45	45	45	45	45	45	45	45	45	45	43	45	45	45	45
ASC																
ALT																
SYM	-	-	-	-	-	-	-	-	-	-	-	+	-	-	-	-

BYTE	472	473	474	475	476	477	478	479	480	481	482	483	484	485	486	487
HEX	2D	2D	2D	2D	2D	2D	2D	2D	2D	2D	2D	2D	2D	2D	2D	2D
DEC	45	45	45	45	45	45	45	45	45	45	45	45	45	45	45	45
ASC																
ALT																
SYM	-	-	-	-	-	-	-	-	-	-	-	-	-	-	-	-

BYTE	488	489	490	491	492	493	494	495	496	497	498	499	500	501	502	503
HEX	2B	2D	2D	2D	2D	2D	2D	2D	2D	2D	40	2D	2F	2D	2D	2D
DEC	43	45	45	45	45	45	45	45	45	45	64	45	47	45	45	45
ASC																
ALT																
SYM	+	-	-	-	-	-	-	-	-	-	@	-	/	-	-	-

BYTE	504	505	506	507	508	509	510	511	512	513	514	515	516	517	518	519
HEX	2D	2D	2D	2D	2D	2D	2B	2D	2D	2D	2D	2D	2D	2D	2D	2D
DEC	45	45	45	45	45	45	43	45	45	45	45	45	45	45	45	45
ASC																
ALT																
SYM	-	-	-	-	-	-	+	-	-	-	-	-	-	-	-	-

BYTE	520	521	522	523	524	525	526	527	528	529	530	531	532	533	534	535
HEX	2B	2D	2D	2D	2D	2D	2D	2D	2D	2D	2B	2D	2D	2D	2D	2D
DEC	43	45	45	45	45	45	45	45	45	45	43	45	45	45	45	45
ASC																
ALT																
SYM	+	-	-	-	-	-	-	-	-	-	+	-	-	-	-	-

BYTE	536	537	538	539	540	541	542	543	544	545	546	547	548	549	550	551
HEX	2D	2D	2D	2D	2B	2D	2D	2D	2D	2D	2D	2D	2D	2D	2B	2D
DEC	45	45	45	45	43	45	45	45	45	45	45	45	45	45	43	45
ASC																
ALT																
SYM	-	-	-	-	+	-	-	-	-	-	-	-	-	-	+	-

BYTE	552	553	554	555	556	557	558	559	560	561	562	563	564	565	566	567
HEX	2D	2D	2D	2D	2D	2D	2D	2D	2B	2D	2D	2D	2D	2D	2D	2D
DEC	45	45	45	45	45	45	45	45	43	45	45	45	45	45	45	45
ASC																
ALT																
SYM	-	-	-	-	-	-	-	-	+	-	-	-	-	-	-	-

BYTE	568	569	570	571	572	573	574	575	576	577	578	579	580	581	582	583
HEX	2D	2D	2B	2D	2D	2D	2D	2D	2D	2D	2D	2D	2B	2D	2D	2D
DEC	45	45	43	45	45	45	45	45	45	45	45	45	43	45	45	45
ASC																
ALT																
SYM	-	-	+	-	-	-	-	-	-	-	-	-	+	-	-	-

BYTE	584	585	586	587	588	589	590	591	592	593	594	595	596	597	598	599
HEX	2D	2D	2D	2D	2D	2D	2B	2D	2D	2D	2D	2D	2D	2D	2D	2D
DEC	45	45	45	45	45	45	43	45	45	45	45	45	45	45	45	45
ASC																
ALT																
SYM	-	-	-	-	-	-	+	-	-	-	-	-	-	-	-	-

BYTE	600	601	602	603	604	605	606	607	608	609	610	611	612	613	614	615
HEX	2B	2D	2D	2D	2D	2D	2D	2D	2D	2D	2B	2D	2D	2D	2D	2D
DEC	43	45	45	45	45	45	45	45	45	45	43	45	45	45	45	45
ASC																
ALT																
SYM	+	-	-	-	-	-	-	-	-	-	+	-	-	-	-	-

BYTE	616	617	618	619	620	621	622	623	624	625	626	627	628	629	630	631
HEX	2D	2D	2D	2D	2B	2D	2D	2D	2D	2D	2D	2D	2D	2D	2B	2D
DEC	45	45	45	45	43	45	45	45	45	45	45	45	45	45	43	45
ASC																
ALT																
SYM	-	-	-	-	+	-	-	-	-	-	-	-	-	-	+	-

BYTE	632	633	634	635	636	637	638	639	640	641	642	643	644	645	646	647
HEX	2D	2D	2D	2D	2D	2D	2D	2D	2B	2D	2D	2D	2D	2D	2D	2D
DEC	45	45	45	45	45	45	45	45	43	45	45	45	45	45	45	45
ASC																
ALT																
SYM	-	-	-	-	-	-	-	-	+	-	-	-	-	-	-	-

BYTE	648	649	650	651	652	653	654	655	656	657	658	659	660	661	662	663
HEX	2D	2D	2B	2D	2D	2D	2D	2D	2D	2D	2D	2D	2B	2D	2D	2D
DEC	45	45	43	45	45	45	45	45	45	45	45	45	43	45	45	45
ASC																
ALT																
SYM	-	-	+	-	-	-	-	-	-	-	-	-	+	-	-	-

BYTE	664	665	666	667	668	669	670	671	672	673	674	675	676	677	678	679
HEX	2D	2D	2D	2D	2D	2D	2B	2D	2D	2D	2D	2D	2D	2D	2D	2D
DEC	45	45	45	45	45	45	43	45	45	45	45	45	45	45	45	45
ASC																
ALT																
SYM	-	-	-	-	-	-	+	-	-	-	-	-	-	-	-	-

BYTE	680	681	682	683	684	685	686	687	688	689	690	691	692	693	694	695
HEX	2B	2D	2D	2D	2D	02	06	01	00	00	00	00	00	00	00	00
DEC	43	45	45	45	45	2	6	1	0	0	0	0	0	0	0	0
ASC						^B	^F	^A	^@	^@	^@	^@	^@	^@	^@	^@
ALT						STX	ACK	SOH	NUL	NUL	NUL	NUL	NUL	NUL	NUL	NUL
SYM	+	-	-	-	-											

BYTE	696	697	698	699	700	701	702	703	704	705	706	707	708	709	710	711
HEX	00	00	00	00	00	00	00	00	00	00	00	00	00	00	00	00
DEC	0	0	0	0	0	0	0	0	0	0	0	0	0	0	0	0
ASC	^@	^@	^@	^@	^@	^@	^@	^@	^@	^@	^@	^@	^@	^@	^@	^@
ALT	NUL	NUL	NUL	NUL	NUL	NUL	NUL	NUL	NUL	NUL	NUL	NUL	NUL	NUL	NUL	NUL
SYM																

```
BYTE|712|713|714|715|716|717|718|719|720|721|722|723|724|725|726|727|
HEX | 08| 42| 00| 00| 0A| 00| 00| 01| 00| 00| 00| 00| 00| 00| 01| 00|
DEC |  8| 66|  0|  0| 10|  0|  0|  1|  0|  0|  0|  0|  0|  0|  1|  0|
ASC | ^H|   | ^@| ^@| ^J| ^@| ^@| ^A| ^@| ^@| ^@| ^@| ^@| ^@| ^A| ^@|
ALT | BS|   |NUL|NUL| LF|NUL|NUL|SOH|NUL|NUL|NUL|NUL|NUL|NUL|SOH|NUL|
SYM |   |  B|   |   |   |   |   |   |   |   |   |   |   |   |   |   |


BYTE|728|729|730|731|732|733|734|735|736|737|738|739|740|741|742|743|
HEX | 00| 00| 01| 06| 3C| 00| 00| 00| 00| 00| 00| 00| 00| 00| 00| 00|
DEC |  0|  0|  1|  6| 60|  0|  0|  0|  0|  0|  0|  0|  0|  0|  0|  0|
ASC | ^@| ^@| ^A| ^F|   | ^@| ^@| ^@| ^@| ^@| ^@| ^@| ^@| ^@| ^@| ^@|
ALT |NUL|NUL|SOH|ACK|   |NUL|NUL|NUL|NUL|NUL|NUL|NUL|NUL|NUL|NUL|NUL|
SYM |   |   |   |   |  <|   |   |   |   |   |   |   |   |   |   |   |


BYTE|744|745|746|747|748|749|750|751|752|753|754|755|756|757|758|759|
HEX | 00| 00| 00| 00| 00| 00| 00| 00| 00| 00| 00| 00| 00| 00| 00| 00|
DEC |  0|  0|  0|  0|  0|  0|  0|  0|  0|  0|  0|  0|  0|  0|  0|  0|
ASC | ^@| ^@| ^@| ^@| ^@| ^@| ^@| ^@| ^@| ^@| ^@| ^@| ^@| ^@| ^@| ^@|
ALT |NUL|NUL|NUL|NUL|NUL|NUL|NUL|NUL|NUL|NUL|NUL|NUL|NUL|NUL|NUL|
SYM |   |   |   |   |   |   |   |   |   |   |   |   |   |   |   |   |


BYTE|760|761|762|763|764|765|766|767|768|769|770|771|772|773|774|775|
HEX | 00| 00| 00| 00| 00| 00| 00| 00| 00| 00| 00| 00| 00| 00| 00| 00|
DEC |  0|  0|  0|  0|  0|  0|  0|  0|  0|  0|  0|  0|  0|  0|  0|  0|
ASC | ^@| ^@| ^@| ^@| ^@| ^@| ^@| ^@| ^@| ^@| ^@| ^@| ^@| ^@| ^@| ^@|
ALT |NUL|NUL|NUL|NUL|NUL|NUL|NUL|NUL|NUL|NUL|NUL|NUL|NUL|NUL|NUL|
SYM |   |   |   |   |   |   |   |   |   |   |   |   |   |   |   |   |


BYTE|776|777|778|779|780|781|782|783|784|785|786|787|788|789|790|791|
HEX | 00| 00| 00| 00| 00| 00| 00| 00| 00| 00| 00| 00| 00| 00| 00| 00|
DEC |  0|  0|  0|  0|  0|  0|  0|  0|  0|  0|  0|  0|  0|  0|  0|  0|
ASC | ^@| ^@| ^@| ^@| ^@| ^@| ^@| ^@| ^@| ^@| ^@| ^@| ^@| ^@| ^@| ^@|
ALT |NUL|NUL|NUL|NUL|NUL|NUL|NUL|NUL|NUL|NUL|NUL|NUL|NUL|NUL|NUL|
SYM |   |   |   |   |   |   |   |   |   |   |   |   |   |   |   |   |


BYTE|792|793|794|795|796|797|798|799|800|801|802|803|804|805|806|807|
HEX | 00| 00| 1A| 1A| 1A| 1A| 1A| 1A| 1A| 1A| 1A| 1A| 1A| 1A| 1A| 1A|
DEC |  0|  0| 26| 26| 26| 26| 26| 26| 26| 26| 26| 26| 26| 26| 26| 26|
ASC | ^@| ^@| ^Z| ^Z| ^Z| ^Z| ^Z| ^Z| ^Z| ^Z| ^Z| ^Z| ^Z| ^Z| ^Z| ^Z|
ALT |NUL|NUL|SUB|SUB|SUB|SUB|SUB|SUB|SUB|SUB|SUB|SUB|SUB|SUB|SUB|SUB|
SYM |   |   |   |   |   |   |   |   |   |   |   |   |   |   |   |   |
```

```
BYTE|808|809|810|811|812|813|814|815|816|817|818|819|820|821|822|823|
_HEX|_1A|_1A|_1A|_1A|_1A|_1A|_1A|_1A|_1A|_1A|_1A|_1A|_1A|_1A|_1A|_1A|
_DEC|_26|_26|_26|_26|_26|_26|_26|_26|_26|_26|_26|_26|_26|_26|_26|_26|
_ASC|_^Z|_^Z|_^Z|_^Z|_^Z|_^Z|_^Z|_^Z|_^Z|_^Z|_^Z|_^Z|_^Z|_^Z|_^Z|_^Z|
_ALT|SUB|SUB|SUB|SUB|SUB|SUB|SUB|SUB|SUB|SUB|SUB|SUB|SUB|SUB|SUB|SUB|
_SYM|___|___|___|___|___|___|___|___|___|___|___|___|___|___|___|___|


BYTE|824|825|826|827|828|829|830|831|832|833|834|835|836|837|838|839|
_HEX|_1A|_1A|_1A|_1A|_1A|_1A|_1A|_1A|_1A|_1A|_1A|_1A|_1A|_1A|_1A|_1A|
_DEC|_26|_26|_26|_26|_26|_26|_26|_26|_26|_26|_26|_26|_26|_26|_26|_26|
_ASC|_^Z|_^Z|_^Z|_^Z|_^Z|_^Z|_^Z|_^Z|_^Z|_^Z|_^Z|_^Z|_^Z|_^Z|_^Z|_^Z|
_ALT|SUB|SUB|SUB|SUB|SUB|SUB|SUB|SUB|SUB|SUB|SUB|SUB|SUB|SUB|SUB|SUB|
_SYM|___|___|___|___|___|___|___|___|___|___|___|___|___|___|___|___|


BYTE|840|841|842|843|844|845|846|847|848|849|850|851|852|853|854|855|
_HEX|_1A|_1A|_1A|_1A|_1A|_1A|_1A|_1A|_1A|_1A|_1A|_1A|_1A|_1A|_1A|_1A|
_DEC|_26|_26|_26|_26|_26|_26|_26|_26|_26|_26|_26|_26|_26|_26|_26|_26|
_ASC|_^Z|_^Z|_^Z|_^Z|_^Z|_^Z|_^Z|_^Z|_^Z|_^Z|_^Z|_^Z|_^Z|_^Z|_^Z|_^Z|
_ALT|SUB|SUB|SUB|SUB|SUB|SUB|SUB|SUB|SUB|SUB|SUB|SUB|SUB|SUB|SUB|SUB|
_SYM|___|___|___|___|___|___|___|___|___|___|___|___|___|___|___|___|


BYTE|856|857|858|859|860|861|862|863|864|865|866|867|868|869|870|871|
_HEX|_1A|_1A|_1A|_1A|_1A|_1A|_1A|_1A|_1A|_1A|_1A|_1A|_1A|_1A|_1A|_1A|
_DEC|_26|_26|_26|_26|_26|_26|_26|_26|_26|_26|_26|_26|_26|_26|_26|_26|
_ASC|_^Z|_^Z|_^Z|_^Z|_^Z|_^Z|_^Z|_^Z|_^Z|_^Z|_^Z|_^Z|_^Z|_^Z|_^Z|_^Z|
_ALT|SUB|SUB|SUB|SUB|SUB|SUB|SUB|SUB|SUB|SUB|SUB|SUB|SUB|SUB|SUB|SUB|
_SYM|___|___|___|___|___|___|___|___|___|___|___|___|___|___|___|___|


BYTE|872|873|874|875|876|877|878|879|880|881|882|883|884|885|886|887|
_HEX|_1A|_1A|_1A|_1A|_1A|_1A|_1A|_1A|_1A|_1A|_1A|_1A|_1A|_1A|_1A|_1A|
_DEC|_26|_26|_26|_26|_26|_26|_26|_26|_26|_26|_26|_26|_26|_26|_26|_26|
_ASC|_^Z|_^Z|_^Z|_^Z|_^Z|_^Z|_^Z|_^Z|_^Z|_^Z|_^Z|_^Z|_^Z|_^Z|_^Z|_^Z|
_ALT|SUB|SUB|SUB|SUB|SUB|SUB|SUB|SUB|SUB|SUB|SUB|SUB|SUB|SUB|SUB|SUB|
_SYM|___|___|___|___|___|___|___|___|___|___|___|___|___|___|___|___|


BYTE|888|889|890|891|892|893|894|895|896|897|898|899|900|901|902|903|
_HEX|_1A|_1A|_1A|_1A|_1A|_1A|_1A|_1A|_1A|_1A|_1A|_1A|_1A|_1A|_1A|_1A|
_DEC|_26|_26|_26|_26|_26|_26|_26|_26|_26|_26|_26|_26|_26|_26|_26|_26|
_ASC|_^Z|_^Z|_^Z|_^Z|_^Z|_^Z|_^Z|_^Z|_^Z|_^Z|_^Z|_^Z|_^Z|_^Z|_^Z|_^Z|
_ALT|SUB|SUB|SUB|SUB|SUB|SUB|SUB|SUB|SUB|SUB|SUB|SUB|SUB|SUB|SUB|SUB|
_SYM|___|___|___|___|___|___|___|___|___|___|___|___|___|___|___|___|
```

BYTE	904	905	906	907	908	909	910	911	912	913	914	915	916	917	918	919
HEX	1A	1A	1A	1A	1A	1A	1A	1A	1A	1A	1A	1A	1A	1A	1A	1A
DEC	26	26	26	26	26	26	26	26	26	26	26	26	26	26	26	26
ASC	^Z	^Z	^Z	^Z	^Z	^Z	^Z	^Z	^Z	^Z	^Z	^Z	^Z	^Z	^Z	^Z
ALT	SUB	SUB	SUB	SUB	SUB	SUB	SUB	SUB	SUB	SUB	SUB	SUB	SUB	SUB	SUB	SUB
SYM																

WordPerfect Sample File

```
BYTE|  0|  1|  2|  3|  4|  5|  6|  7|  8|  9| 10| 11| 12| 13| 14| 15|
_HEX| C3| 00| 2A| 1F| C3| 9D| 54| 68| 65| 20| 47| 65| 74| 74| 79| 73|
_DEC|195|  0| 42| 31|195|157| 84|104|101| 32| 71|101|116|116|121|115|
_ASC|195|  ^@|   |  ^_ |195|157|   |   |   |  ^`|   |   |   |   |   |   |
_ALT|195|NUL|   | US|195|157|   |   |   |SPC|   |   |   |   |   |   |
_SYM|   |   |  *|   |   |   |  T|  h|  e|   |  G|  e|  t|  t|  y|  s|
```

Center Text	Betw. Marg.	Center Col. 42	Start w/ Col. 31	Center Text	Bold On

```
BYTE| 16| 17| 18| 19| 20| 21| 22| 23| 24| 25| 26| 27| 28| 29| 30| 31|
_HEX| 62| 75| 72| 67| 20| 41| 64| 64| 72| 65| 73| 73| 9C| 83| 0A| 0A|
_DEC| 98|117|114|103| 32| 65|100|100|114|101|115|115|156|131| 10| 10|
_ASC|   |   |   |  ^` |   |   |   |   |   |   |   |   |   |   |   |   |
_ALT|   |   |   |SPC|   |   |   |   |   |   |   |   |156|131|  ^J|  ^J|
_SYM|  b|  u|  r|  g|   |  A|  d|  d|  r|  e|  s|  s|   |   |   |   |
```

												Bold Off	End Ctr. Text	LF	LF

```
BYTE| 32| 33| 34| 35| 36| 37| 38| 39| 40| 41| 42| 43| 44| 45| 46| 47|
_HEX| 46| 6F| 75| 72| 73| 63| 6F| 72| 65| 20| 61| 6E| 64| 20| 73| 65|
_DEC| 70|111|117|114|115| 99|111|114|101| 32| 97|110|100| 32|115|101|
_ASC|   |   |   |   |   |   |   |   |   |  ^` |   |   |   |  ^` |   |   |
_ALT|   |   |   |   |   |   |   |   |   |SPC|   |   |   |SPC|   |   |
_SYM|  F|  o|  u|  r|  s|  c|  o|  r|  e|   |  a|  n|  d|   |  s|  e|
```

```
BYTE| 48| 49| 50| 51| 52| 53| 54| 55| 56| 57| 58| 59| 60| 61| 62| 63|
_HEX| 76| 65| 6E| 20| 79| 65| 61| 72| 73| 20| 61| 67| 6F| 20| 6F| 75|
_DEC|118|101|110| 32|121|101| 97|114|115| 32| 97|103|111| 32|111|117|
_ASC|   |   |   |  ^` |   |   |   |   |   |  ^` |   |   |   |  ^` |   |   |
_ALT|   |   |   |SPC|   |   |   |   |   |SPC|   |   |   |SPC|   |   |
_SYM|  v|  e|  n|   |  y|  e|  a|  r|  s|   |  a|  g|  o|   |  o|  u|
```

```
BYTE| 64| 65| 66| 67| 68| 69| 70| 71| 72| 73| 74| 75| 76| 77| 78| 79|
_HEX| 72| 20| 66| 61| 74| 68| 65| 72| 73| 20| 62| 72| 6F| 75| 67| 68|
_DEC|114| 32|102| 97|116|104|101|114|115| 32| 98|114|111|117|103|104|
_ASC|   |  ^` |   |   |   |   |   |   |   |  ^` |   |   |   |   |   |   |
_ALT|   |SPC|   |   |   |   |   |   |   |SPC|   |   |   |   |   |   |
_SYM|  r|   |  f|  a|  t|  h|  e|  r|  s|   |  b|  r|  o|  u|  g|  h|
```

```
BYTE|  80|  81|  82|  83|  84|  85|  86|  87|  88|  89|  90|  91|  92|  93|  94|  95|
 HEX|  74|  20|  66|  6F|  72|  74|  68|  20|  6F|  6E|  20|  74|  68|  69|  73|  0D|
 DEC| 116|  32| 102| 111| 114| 116| 104|  32| 111| 110|  32| 116| 104| 105| 115|  13|
 ASC|    |  ^`|    |    |    |    |    |  ^`|    |    |  ^`|    |    |    |    |  ^M|
 ALT|    | SPC|    |    |    |    |    | SPC|    |    | SPC|    |    |    |    |  CR|
 SYM|   t|    |   f|   o|   r|   t|   b|    |   o|   n|    |   t|   b|   i|   s|    |
```

```
BYTE|  96|  97|  98|  99| 100| 101| 102| 103| 104| 105| 106| 107| 108| 109| 110| 111|
 HEX|  63|  6F|  6E|  74|  69|  6E|  65|  6E|  74|  2C|  20|  61|  20|  6E|  65|  77|
 DEC|  99| 111| 110| 116| 105| 110| 101| 110| 116|  44|  32|  97|  32| 110| 101| 119|
 ASC|    |    |    |    |    |    |    |    |    |    |  ^`|    |  ^`|    |    |    |
 ALT|    |    |    |    |    |    |    |    |    |    | SPC|    | SPC|    |    |    |
 SYM|   c|   o|   n|   t|   i|   n|   e|   n|   t|   ,|    |   a|    |   n|   e|   w|
```

```
BYTE| 112| 113| 114| 115| 116| 117| 118| 119| 120| 121| 122| 123| 124| 125| 126| 127|
 HEX|  20|  6E|  61|  74|  69|  6F|  6E|  2C|  20|  63|  6F|  6E|  63|  65|  69|  76|
 DEC|  32| 110|  97| 116| 105| 111| 110|  44|  32|  99| 111| 110|  99| 101| 105| 118|
 ASC|  ^`|    |    |    |    |    |    |    |  ^`|    |    |    |    |    |    |    |
 ALT| SPC|    |    |    |    |    |    |    | SPC|    |    |    |    |    |    |    |
 SYM|    |   n|   a|   t|   i|   o|   n|   ,|    |   c|   o|   n|   c|   e|   i|   v|
```

```
BYTE| 128| 129| 130| 131| 132| 133| 134| 135| 136| 137| 138| 139| 140| 141| 142| 143|
 HEX|  65|  64|  20|  69|  6E|  20|  94|  4C|  69|  62|  65|  72|  74|  79|  95|  2C|
 DEC| 101| 100|  32| 105| 110|  32| 148|  76| 105|  98| 101| 114| 116| 121| 149|  44|
 ASC|    |    |  ^`|    |    |  ^`| 148|    |    |    |    |    |    |    | 149|    |
 ALT|    |    | SPC|    |    | SPC| 148|    |    |    |    |    |    |    | 149|    |
 SYM|   e|   d|    |   i|   n|    |    |   L|   i|   b|   e|   r|   t|   y|    |   ,|
```

```
                        |                                         |
                        | UL                                      | UL
                        | On                                      | Off
                        |                                         |
```

```
BYTE| 144| 145| 146| 147| 148| 149| 150| 151| 152| 153| 154| 155| 156| 157| 158| 159|
 HEX|  20|  61|  6E|  64|  20|  64|  65|  64|  69|  63|  61|  74|  65|  64|  20|  74|
 DEC|  32|  97| 110| 100|  32| 100| 101| 100| 105|  99|  97| 116| 101| 100|  32| 116|
 ASC|  ^`|    |    |    |  ^`|    |    |    |    |    |    |    |    |    |  ^`|    |
 ALT| SPC|    |    |    | SPC|    |    |    |    |    |    |    |    |    | SPC|    |
 SYM|    |   a|   n|   d|    |   d|   e|   d|   i|   c|   a|   t|   e|   d|    |   t|
```

```
BYTE| 160| 161| 162| 163| 164| 165| 166| 167| 168| 169| 170| 171| 172| 173| 174| 175|
 HEX|  6F|  0D|  74|  68|  65|  20|  70|  72|  6F|  70|  6F|  73|  69|  74|  69|  6F|
 DEC| 111|  13| 116| 104| 101|  32| 112| 114| 111| 112| 111| 115| 105| 116| 105| 111|
 ASC|    |  ^M|    |    |    |  ^`|    |    |    |    |    |    |    |    |    |    |
 ALT|    |  CR|    |    |    | SPC|    |    |    |    |    |    |    |    |    |    |
 SYM|   o|    |   t|   b|   e|    |   p|   r|   o|   p|   o|   s|   i|   t|   i|   o|
```

BYTE	176	177	178	179	180	181	182	183	184	185	186	187	188	189	190	191
HEX	6E	20	74	68	61	74	20	61	6C	6C	20	6D	65	6E	20	61
DEC	110	32	116	104	97	116	32	97	108	108	32	109	101	110	32	97
ASC		^`					^`								^`	
ALT		SPC					SPC				SPC				SPC	
SYM	n		t	b	a	t		a	l	l		m	e	n		a

BYTE	192	193	194	195	196	197	198	199	200	201	202	203	204	205	206	207
HEX	72	65	20	63	72	65	61	74	65	64	20	65	71	75	61	6C
DEC	114	101	32	99	114	101	97	116	101	100	32	101	113	117	97	108
ASC			^`								^`					
ALT			SPC								SPC					
SYM	r	e		c	r	e	a	t	e	d		e	q	u	a	l

BYTE	208	209	210	211	212	213	214	215	216	217	218	219	220	221	222	223
HEX	2E	0A	0A	4E	6F	77	20	77	65	20	61	72	65	20	65	6E
DEC	46	10	10	78	111	119	32	119	101	32	97	114	101	32	101	110
ASC		^J	^J				^`			^`				^`		
ALT		LF	LF				SPC			SPC				SPC		
SYM	.			N	o	w		w	e		a	r	e		e	n

BYTE	224	225	226	227	228	229	230	231	232	233	234	235	236	237	238	239
HEX	67	61	67	65	64	20	69	6E	20	61	20	67	72	65	61	74
DEC	103	97	103	101	100	32	105	110	32	97	32	103	114	101	97	116
ASC						^`			^`		^`					
ALT						SPC			SPC		SPC					
SYM	g	a	g	e	d		i	n		a		g	r	e	a	t

BYTE	240	241	242	243	244	245	246	247	248	249	250	251	252	253	254	255
HEX	20	63	69	76	69	6C	20	77	61	72	2C	20	74	65	73	74
DEC	32	99	105	118	105	108	32	119	97	114	44	32	116	101	115	116
ASC	^`						^`					^`				
ALT	SPC						SPC					SPC				
SYM		c	i	v	i	l		w	a	r	,		t	e	s	t

BYTE	256	257	258	259	260	261	262	263	264	265	266	267	268	269	270	271
HEX	69	6E	67	20	77	68	65	74	68	65	72	20	74	68	61	74
DEC	105	110	103	32	119	104	101	116	104	101	114	32	116	104	97	116
ASC				^`								^`				
ALT				SPC								SPC				
SYM	i	n	g		w	h	e	t	h	e	r		t	h	a	t

BYTE	272	273	274	275	276	277	278	279	280	281	282	283	284	285	286	287
HEX	0D	6E	61	74	69	6F	6E	20	6F	72	20	61	6E	79	20	6E
DEC	13	110	97	116	105	111	110	32	111	114	32	97	110	121	32	110
ASC	^M							^`			^`				^`	
ALT	CR							SPC			SPC				SPC	
SYM		n	a	t	i	o	n		o	r		a	n	y		n

BYTE	288	289	290	291	292	293	294	295	296	297	298	299	300	301	302	303
HEX	61	74	69	6F	6E	20	73	6F	20	63	6F	6E	63	65	69	76
DEC	97	116	105	111	110	32	115	111	32	99	111	110	99	101	105	118
ASC						^`			^`							
ALT						SPC			SPC							
SYM	a	t	i	o	n		s	o		c	o	n	c	e	i	v

BYTE	304	305	306	307	308	309	310	311	312	313	314	315	316	317	318	319
HEX	65	64	20	61	6E	64	20	73	6F	20	64	65	64	69	63	61
DEC	101	100	32	97	110	100	32	115	111	32	100	101	100	105	99	97
ASC			^`				^`			^`						
ALT			SPC				SPC			SPC						
SYM	e	d		a	n	d		s	o		d	e	d	i	c	a

BYTE	320	321	322	323	324	325	326	327	328	329	330	331	332	333	334	335
HEX	74	65	64	20	63	61	6E	20	6C	6F	6E	67	0D	65	6E	64
DEC	116	101	100	32	99	97	110	32	108	111	110	103	13	101	110	100
ASC				^`				^`					^M			
ALT				SPC				SPC					CR			
SYM	t	e	d		c	a	n		l	o	n	g		e	n	d

BYTE	336	337	338	339	340	341	342	343	344	345	346	347	348	349	350	351
HEX	75	72	65	2E	20	20	57	65	20	61	72	65	20	6D	65	74
DEC	117	114	101	46	32	32	87	101	32	97	114	101	32	109	101	116
ASC					^`	^`			^`				^`			
ALT					SPC	SPC			SPC				SPC			
SYM	u	r	e	.			W	e		a	r	e		m	e	t

BYTE	352	353	354	355	356	357	358	359	360	361	362	363	364	365	366	367
HEX	20	6F	6E	20	61	20	67	72	65	61	74	20	62	61	74	74
DEC	32	111	110	32	97	32	103	114	101	97	116	32	98	97	116	116
ASC	^`			^`		^`						^`				
ALT	SPC			SPC		SPC						SPC				
SYM		o	n		a		g	r	e	a	t		b	a	t	t

BYTE	368	369	370	371	372	373	374	375	376	377	378	379	380	381	382	383
HEX	6C	65	66	69	65	6C	64	20	6F	66	20	74	68	61	74	20
DEC	108	101	102	105	101	108	100	32	111	102	32	116	104	97	116	32
ASC										^`			^`			^`
ALT										SPC			SPC			SPC
SYM	l	e	f	i	e	l	d		o	f		t	h	a	t	

BYTE	384	385	386	387	388	389	390	391	392	393	394	395	396	397	398	399
HEX	77	61	72	2E	20	20	57	65	20	68	61	76	65	0D	63	6F
DEC	119	97	114	46	32	32	87	101	32	104	97	118	101	13	99	111
ASC					^`	^`			^`					^M		
ALT					SPC	SPC			SPC					CR		
SYM	w	a	r	.			W	e		h	a	v	e		c	o

BYTE	400	401	402	403	404	405	406	407	408	409	410	411	412	413	414	415
HEX	6D	65	20	74	6F	20	64	65	64	69	63	61	74	65	20	61
DEC	109	101	32	116	111	32	100	101	100	105	99	97	116	101	32	97
ASC			^`			^`									^`	
ALT			SPC			SPC									SPC	
SYM	m	e		t	o		d	e	d	i	c	a	t	e		a

BYTE	416	417	418	419	420	421	422	423	424	425	426	427	428	429	430	431
HEX	20	70	6F	72	74	69	6F	6E	20	6F	66	20	74	68	61	74
DEC	32	112	111	114	116	105	111	110	32	111	102	32	116	104	97	116
ASC	^`							^`			^`					
ALT	SPC							SPC			SPC					
SYM		p	o	r	t	i	o	n		o	f		t	h	a	t

BYTE	432	433	434	435	436	437	438	439	440	441	442	443	444	445	446	447
HEX	20	66	69	65	6C	64	2C	20	61	73	20	61	20	66	69	6E
DEC	32	102	105	101	108	100	44	32	97	115	32	97	32	102	105	110
ASC	^`							^`			^`		^`			
ALT	SPC							SPC			SPC		SPC			
SYM		f	i	e	l	d	,		a	s		a		f	i	n

BYTE	448	449	450	451	452	453	454	455	456	457	458	459	460	461	462	463
HEX	61	6C	20	72	65	73	74	69	6E	67	0D	70	6C	61	63	65
DEC	97	108	32	114	101	115	116	105	110	103	13	112	108	97	99	101
ASC			^`								^M					
ALT			SPC								CR					
SYM	a	l		r	e	s	t	i	n	g		p	l	a	c	e

```
BYTE|464|465|466|467|468|469|470|471|472|473|474|475|476|477|478|479|
HEX | 20| 66| 6F| 72| 20| 74| 68| 6F| 73| 65| 20| 77| 68| 6F| 20| 68|
DEC | 32|102|111|114| 32|116|104|111|115|101| 32|119|104|111| 32|104|
ASC | ^`|   |   |   | ^`|   |   |   |   |   | ^`|   |   |   | ^`|   |
ALT |SPC|   |   |   |SPC|   |   |   |   |   |SPC|   |   |   |SPC|   |
SYM |   | f| o| r|   | t| h| o| s| e|   | w| h| o|   | h|
```

```
BYTE|480|481|482|483|484|485|486|487|488|489|490|491|492|493|494|495|
HEX | 65| 72| 65| 20| 67| 61| 76| 65| 20| 74| 68| 65| 69| 72| 20| 6C|
DEC |101|114|101| 32|103| 97|118|101| 32|116|104|101|105|114| 32|108|
ASC |   |   |   | ^`|   |   |   |   | ^`|   |   |   |   |   | ^`|   |
ALT |   |   |   |SPC|   |   |   |   |SPC|   |   |   |   |   |SPC|   |
SYM | e| r| e|   | g| a| v| e|   | t| h| e| i| r|   | l|
```

```
BYTE|496|497|498|499|500|501|502|503|504|505|506|507|508|509|510|511|
HEX | 69| 76| 65| 73| 20| 74| 68| 61| 74| 20| 74| 68| 61| 74| 20| 6E|
DEC |105|118|101|115| 32|116|104| 97|116| 32|116|104| 97|116| 32|110|
ASC |   |   |   |   | ^`|   |   |   |   | ^`|   |   |   |   | ^`|   |
ALT |   |   |   |   |SPC|   |   |   |   |SPC|   |   |   |   |SPC|   |
SYM | i| v| e| s|   | t| h| a| t|   | t| h| a| t|   | n|
```

```
BYTE|512|513|514|515|516|517|518|519|520|521|522|523|524|525|526|527|
HEX | 61| 74| 69| 6F| 6E| 20| 6D| 69| 67| 68| 74| 0D| 6C| 69| 76| 65|
DEC | 97|116|105|111|110| 32|109|105|103|104|116| 13|108|105|118|101|
ASC |   |   |   |   |   | ^`|   |   |   |   |   | ^M|   |   |   |   |
ALT |   |   |   |   |   |SPC|   |   |   |   |   | CR|   |   |   |   |
SYM | a| t| i| o| n|   | m| i| g| h| t|   | l| i| v| e|
```

```
BYTE|528|529|530|531|532|533|534|535|536|537|538|539|540|541|542|543|
HEX | 2E| 20| 20| 49| 74| 20| 69| 73| 20| 61| 6C| 74| 6F| 67| 65| 74|
DEC | 46| 32| 32| 73|116| 32|105|115| 32| 97|108|116|111|103|101|116|
ASC |   | ^`| ^`|   |   | ^`|   |   | ^`|   |   |   |   |   |   |   |
ALT |   |SPC|SPC|   |   |SPC|   |   |SPC|   |   |   |   |   |   |   |
SYM | .|   |   | I| t|   | i| s|   | a| l| t| o| g| e| t|
```

```
BYTE|544|545|546|547|548|549|550|551|552|553|554|555|556|557|558|559|
HEX | 68| 65| 72| 20| 66| 69| 74| 74| 69| 6E| 67| 20| 61| 6E| 64| 20|
DEC |104|101|114| 32|102|105|116|116|105|110|103| 32| 97|110|100| 32|
ASC |   |   |   | ^`|   |   |   |   |   |   |   | ^`|   |   |   | ^`|
ALT |   |   |   |SPC|   |   |   |   |   |   |   |SPC|   |   |   |SPC|
SYM | h| e| r|   | f| i| t| t| i| n| g|   | a| n| d|   |
```

BYTE	560	561	562	563	564	565	566	567	568	569	570	571	572	573	574	575
HEX	70	72	6F	70	65	72	20	74	68	61	74	20	77	65	20	64
DEC	112	114	111	112	101	114	32	116	104	97	116	32	119	101	32	100
ASC											^`			^`		
ALT							SPC					SPC			SPC	
SYM	p	r	o	p	e	r		t	b	a	t		w	e		d

BYTE	576	577	578	579	580	581	582	0	0	0	0	0	0	0	0	0
HEX	6F	20	74	68	69	73	2E	XX	XX	XX	XX	XX	XX	XX	XX	XX
DEC	111	32	116	104	105	115	46	0	0	0	0	0	0	0	0	0
ASC		^`						XXX	XXX	XXX	XXX	XXX	XXX	XXX	XXX	XXX
ALT		SPC						XXX	XXX	XXX	XXX	XXX	XXX	XXX	XXX	XXX
SYM	o		t	b	i	s	.									

FilePrint
Utility Source Code

This program will print out the contents of a PC-DOS text file in the same format that this Reference Guide uses here. It is written in Turbo Pascal.

FilePrint asks for a file name, reads it, and prints the file. As written, it does no checking or error trapping. FilePrint is also limited in the size of the file it can print for two reasons: the byte numbers are integers, and there is about a 1:30 expansion ratio between the size of the file as it appears on disk, and the number of bytes FilePrint causes it to take up in memory. A 5000-byte file on disk can expand to over 150,000 characters in memory.

```
Program FilePrint (Input, Output);
{$U+}
{FilePrint Copyright 1985, 1986, 1987 by Jeff Walden.          }
{All Rights Reserved, including those                          }
{ of international copyright.                                   }

Const
  Maxarraysize        =    47;
  NumberRecsPerLine   =    15;  {48 bytes displayed per screen}
  CtrlCodes           =    33;
  EOM                 =    '';

Type
  Flag          = Boolean;
  Character     = String[1];
  CellString    = String[3];
  RowName       = String[4];
  PathName      = String[64];
  BigString     = String[64];

  BytePTR       = ^DiskContents;
  DiskContents  = Record
                    ByteNum   : Integer;
                    Value     : Byte;
                    Prior     : BytePTR;
                    Next      : BytePTR;
                  End;

  DisplayRec    = Record
                    ByteNum          : Integer;
                    Value            : Byte;
                    TwoValHexChar    : CellString;
                    DecimalVal       : Integer;
                    ASCII_Contents   : CellString;
                    ALT_Display      : CellString;
                    Symbol           : CellString;
                  End;

  CTRLMnemonics = Record
                    Index : Integer;
                    Code  : CellString;
                  End;
  Var {Global Variables}
     Display_Val_Array : Array [0..MaxArraySize] of DisplayRec;
     Control_Codes     : Array [0..CtrlCodes] of CTRLMnemonics;
     ActiveFile        : PathName;
     DiskFile          : File of Byte;
     Filehead          : BytePTR;
     Filetail          : BytePTR;
     Filepointer       : BytePTR;
     Newbyte           : BytePTR;
     Heaptop           : ^Integer;
     i                 : Integer;
```

(continued)

```
Procedure Read_Disk(Currentfile : Pathname);
  Var
    i, j, n      : Integer;
    x            : Integer;
    C            : Byte;
  Begin
    Mark(Heaptop);
    Filehead := NIL;
    i := 0;
    Assign(DiskFile, CurrentFile);
    Reset(DiskFile);
    While NOT EOF(DiskFile) Do
      Begin
        Gotoxy(1,1);
        Seek(DiskFile, i);
        Read(DiskFile, C);
        New(Newbyte);
        Newbyte^.Bytenum := i;
        Newbyte^.Value   := C;
        If Filehead = NIL Then
          Begin
            Filehead := Newbyte;
            Filehead^.Prior := NIL;
          End
        Else
          Begin
            Filetail^.Next := Newbyte;
            Newbyte^.Prior := Filetail;
          End;
        Filetail := Newbyte;
        Filetail^.Next := Nil;
        i := i + 1;
      End;         {While NOT EOF}
    Close(DiskFile);
    Write('File now closed - printing will begin.');
    Filepointer := Filehead;
  End;   {Read_Disk}

Procedure Load_File;
  Begin
    Release(Heaptop);
    Write('Enter Filename: ');
    Read(Activefile);
    Read_Disk(Activefile);
  End;

Procedure INIT;
  Var
    i : Integer;
  Begin
    ClrScr;
    Mark(Heaptop);
    For i := 0 to 32 Do
```

(continued)

```
     Begin
       With Control_Codes[i] Do
         Begin
            Index := i;
         End; {With Control_Codes[i] Do}
     End;      {For i := 0 to 32 Do}


   Control_Codes[33].Index := 127;


   Control_Codes[0].Code    := 'NUL';
   Control_Codes[1].Code    := 'SOH';
   Control_Codes[2].Code    := 'STX';
   Control_Codes[3].Code    := 'ETX';
   Control_Codes[4].Code    := 'EOT';
   Control_Codes[5].Code    := 'ENQ';
   Control_Codes[6].Code    := 'ACK';
   Control_Codes[7].Code    := 'BEL';
   Control_Codes[8].Code    := ' BS';
   Control_Codes[9].Code    := ' HT';
   Control_Codes[10].Code   := ' LF';
   Control_Codes[11].Code   := ' VT';
   Control_Codes[12].Code   := ' FF';
   Control_Codes[13].Code   := ' CR';
   Control_Codes[14].Code   := ' SO';
   Control_Codes[15].Code   := ' SI';
   Control_Codes[16].Code   := 'DLE';
   Control_Codes[17].Code   := 'DC1';
   Control_Codes[18].Code   := 'DC2';
   Control_Codes[19].Code   := 'DC3';
   Control_Codes[20].Code   := 'DC4';
   Control_Codes[21].Code   := 'NAK';
   Control_Codes[22].Code   := 'SYN';
   Control_Codes[23].Code   := 'ETB';
   Control_Codes[24].Code   := 'CAN';
   Control_Codes[25].Code   := ' EM';
   Control_Codes[26].Code   := 'SUB';
   Control_Codes[27].Code   := 'ESC';
   Control_Codes[28].Code   := ' FS';
   Control_Codes[29].Code   := ' GS';
   Control_Codes[30].Code   := ' RS';
   Control_Codes[31].Code   := ' US';
   Control_Codes[32].Code   := 'SPC';
   Control_Codes[33].Code   := 'DEL';

   End;            {Procedure INIT}

Procedure Produce_Display_Val_Array;
  Var
    Lclpointer : BytePTR;
    i : Integer;
    ASCII_Contents : CellString;
    ALT_Display    : CellString;
```

(continued)

```
Procedure HexIn_CharOut (HexIn : Byte;
                         Var Charout : CellString);
  Begin  {HexIn_CharOut}
    Case Hexin of
      0..9 : Str(HexIn:1,CharOut);
        10 : CharOut := 'A';
        11 : CharOut := 'B';
        12 : CharOut := 'C';
        13 : CharOut := 'D';
        14 : CharOut := 'E';
        15 : CharOut := 'F';
      Else   CharOut := 'X';
    End; {Case HexIn of}
  End;   {HexIn_CharOut}
Procedure Two_Char_Hex_Convert (Hex_Contents : Byte;
                    Var Hex_As_String : CellString);
  Var
    i, j    : Byte;
    TempStr : CellString;
  Begin  {Two_Char_Hex_Convert}
    Hex_As_String := '';
    i := Hex_Contents;
    j := Hex_Contents;
    i := i DIV 16;
    j := j MOD 16;
    HexIn_CharOut (i,Hex_As_String);
    HexIn_CharOut (j,TempStr);
    Hex_As_String := (Hex_As_String + TempStr);
  End;   {Two_Char_Hex_Convert}

Procedure Handle_Control_Codes (Hex_Contents       : Byte;
                     Var ASCII_Contents : CellString;
                     Var ALT_Display    : CellString);
  Const
    Offset = 64;
  Begin  {Handle_Control_Codes}
    ASCII_Contents := ('^' + (Chr(Hex_Contents + Offset)));
    Case Hex_Contents of
      0..32 : ALT_Display :=
                      Control_Codes[Hex_Contents].code;
        127 : ALT_Display := Control_Codes[33].code;
      Else    ALT_Display := '!!!!';
    End; {Case Hex_Contents of}
  End;   {Handle_Control_Codes}

Procedure Handle_Printing_Chars (Hex_Contents       : Byte;
                      Var ASCII_Contents : CellString;
                      Var ALT_Display    : CellString);
  Begin  {Handle_Printing_Chars}
    ASCII_Contents := ('  ' + (Chr(Hex_Contents)));
    ALT_Display := ASCII_Contents;
  End;   {Handle_Printing_Chars}
```

(continued)

```
Procedure Handle_HiBit_Chars (Hex_Contents      : Byte;
                     Var ASCII_Contents : CellString;
                     Var ALT_Display    : CellString);
  Begin   {Handle_HiBit_Chars}
    Str(Hex_Contents:3,ASCII_Contents);
    ALT_Display := ASCII_Contents;
  End;   {Handle_HiBit_Chars}
  Begin   {Produce_Display_Val_Array}
    LclPointer := Filepointer;
    ASCII_Contents := '';
    ALT_Display    := '';
      For i := 0 to MaxArraySize Do
          With Display_Val_Array[i] Do
            If Lclpointer <> NIL Then
              Begin
                ByteNum     := Lclpointer^.ByteNum MOD 1000;
                Value       := Lclpointer^.Value;
                DecimalVal  := Value;
                Two_Char_Hex_Convert (Value,TwoValHexChar);
                Case Value of
                    0..32,127 : Begin
                                  Handle_Control_Codes (Value,
                                    ASCII_Contents, ALT_Display);
                                  Symbol := '';{ALT_Display;}
                                End;
                     33..126 : Begin
                                  Handle_Printing_Chars (Value,
                                    ASCII_Contents, ALT_Display);
                                  Symbol := Chr(Value);
                                End;
                    128..255 : Begin
                                  Handle_HiBit_Chars (Value,
                                    ASCII_Contents, ALT_Display);
                                  Symbol := Chr(Value);
                                End;
                         Else  Begin
                                  ASCII_Contents := '!!!!';
                                  ALT_Display    := '!!!!';
                                  Symbol := '!';
                                End; {Else}
                End; {Case}
                Lclpointer := Lclpointer^.Next;
              End
            Else
              Begin
                Bytenum := 0;
                Value   := 0;
                TwoValhexChar :='XX';
                DecimalVal := 0;
                ASCII_Contents := 'XXX';
                ALT_Display := 'XXX';
                Symbol := '';
              End;
  End;      {Produce_Display_Val_Array}                    (continued)
```

```
Procedure Printer_Dump;

   Const
     Pagewidth = 80;
     Printlen  = 55;
     VTABlen   =  3;
     FF = #12;
     CR = #13;
     LF = #10;

   Var
     PCount, i : Integer;
     CurrPTR : BytePTR;
     Rowcount: Integer;

   Procedure VerticalTab;
     Var
       i : Integer;
     Begin
       For i := 1 to VTABlen Do
         Writeln(LST);
     End;

   Procedure Underline;
     Const
       LLen = 70;
     Var
       i : Integer;
     Begin
       Write(LST,CR);
       For i := 0 to LLen Do
         Write(LST,'_');
     End;

   Procedure Dump_Array;
     Var
       i, k, j : Integer;
     Begin
       k := NumberRecsPerLine+1;
       For i := 0 to 2 Do
         Begin
           Write(LST,'BYTE|');
           For j := 0 to NumberRecsPerLine Do
             Write(LST,Display_Val_Array[(i*k)+j].ByteNum:3,'|');
           Underline;
           Writeln(LST);

           Write(LST,' HEX|');
           For j := 0 to NumberRecsPerLine Do
Write(LST,Display_Val_Array[(i*k)+j].TwoValHexChar:3,'|');
           Underline;
           Writeln(LST);
```

(continued)

```
          Write(LST,' DEC|');
          For j := 0 to NumberRecsPerLine Do
            Write(LST,Display_Val_Array[(i*k)+j].DecimalVal:3,'|');
          Underline;
          Writeln(LST);

          Write(LST,' ASC|');
          For j := 0 to NumberRecsPerLine Do
            Write(LST,Display_Val_Array[(i*k)+j].ASCII_Contents:3,'|');
          Underline;
          Writeln(LST);

          Write(LST,' ALT|');
          For j := 0 to NumberRecsPerLine Do
            Write(LST,Display_Val_Array[(i*k)+j].ALT_Display:3,'|');
          Underline;
          Writeln(LST);

          Write(LST,' SYM|');
          For j := 0 to NumberRecsPerLine Do
            If (Display_Val_Array[(i*k)+j].DecimalVal > 127) Then
              Write(LST,'   |')
            Else
              Write(LST,Display_Val_Array[(i*k)+j].Symbol:3,'|');
          Underline;
          Writeln(LST);

          VerticalTab;

        End;


    End;

Begin {Printer_Dump}
  CurrPTR := Filepointer;
  Filepointer := Filehead;
  Rowcount := 0;
  PCount   := 1;
  While (Filepointer^.Next <> NIL) Do
    Begin
      Produce_Display_Val_Array;
      VerticalTab;
      Write(LST,Activefile,' Page#',PCount);
      VerticalTab;
      Dump_Array;
      PCount := PCount + 1;
      For i := 0 to MaxArraySize Do
        If (Filepointer^.Next <> NIL) Then
          Filepointer := Filepointer^.Next
        Else
          Filepointer := Filetail;
      Produce_Display_Val_Array;
      Dump_Array;
```

(continued)

```
        For i := 0 to MaxarraySize Do
            If (Filepointer^.Next <> NIL) Then
                Filepointer := Filepointer^.Next
            Else
                Filepointer := Filetail;
            Write(LST,FF);
        End;
    Filepointer := CurrPTR;
  End;   {Printer_Dump}



Begin
    INIT;
    Load_File;
    Produce_Display_VAl_Array;
    Printer_Dump;
    Release(heaptop);
    Writeln('Thank you for using FilePrint(tm).');
  End.
```